THE INTIMATE COUPLE

THE INTIMATE
COUPLE

Jon Carlson & Len Sperry, Editors

Foreword by Harry J. Aponte

BRUNNER/MAZEL
· Taylor & Francis Group ·

USA	Publishing Office:	BRUNNER/MAZEL *A member of the Taylor & Francis Group* 325 Chestnut Street Philadelphia, PA 19106 Tel: (215) 625-8900 Fax: (215) 625-2940
	Distribution Center:	BRUNNER/MAZEL *A member of the Taylor & Francis Group* 47 Runway Road Levittown, PA 19057 Tel: (215) 269-0400 Fax: (215) 269-0363
UK		BRUNNER/MAZEL *A member of the Taylor & Francis Group* 1 Gunpowder Square London EC4A 3DE Tel: +44 171 583 0490 Fax: +44 171 583 0581

THE INTIMATE COUPLE

1 2 3 4 5 6 7 8 9 0

Printed by Edwards Brothers, Ann Arbor, MI, 1998.

Cover design by Michelle Fleitz.

A CIP catalog record for this book is available from the British Library.
⊗ The paper in this publication meets the requirements of the ANSI Standard Z39.48-1984 (Permanence of Paper).

Library of Congress Cataloging-in-Publication Data

The intimate couple/Jon Carlson & Len Sperry, editors; forward by Harry J. Aponte.
    p. cm.
    Includes bibiliographical references and index.
    ISBN 0-87630-880-9
    1. Marital psychotherapy. 2. Intimacy (Psychology) 3. Man-woman relationships. I. Carson, Jon. II. Sperry, Len.
RC488.5.I5845 1998   98-29774
616.89'156--dc21   CIP

Dedication
Candace Ward Howell
(1952–1997)

Table 4
Assessment of Intimacy I
Observation of Intimate Interactions

Behavior: Strengths
Openness, freedom, and spontaneity of expression.
Congruence between verbal and nonverbal communication.
Clarity and specificity of expression.
A minimum of interruptions.
Listening partner can reflect and restate effectively.
Expressions of concern, compassion, appreciation, empathy.
A varied and rich feeling vocabulary.

Behavior: Targets for Intervention
Walking on eggshells.
Words that say one thing while face or voice say another.
Vague overgeneralizations.
Partners seem to be waiting for the other to finish so they can have their own say.
Listening partner gives advice, criticizes, or dismisses.
Absence of positive affect or support.
No direct acknowledgement of feelings.

Affect: Strengths
Nonverbal demonstrations of affection (e.g., affectionate touches)
Verbal expressions of caring
Nonverbal posture: forward lean, maintains gaze, smile, turns toward partner.
Partners express positive affect in response to therapist's queries.

Affect: Targets for Intervention
Stony unresponsiveness
Unresponsive, dismissive, or critical.
Nonverbal posture: leans back, turns away from partner, averts gaze, expression of contempt, impatience, embarrassment.
One or both partners express anxiety, embarrassment, shame, or contempt.

Cognition: Strengths
Assumption that intimacy, support, nurturance, understanding are needs felt by all human beings.
Expectation that my partner is trustworthy and will handle my confidences with care.
Assumption that whether I confide or listen to confidence, I am giving something important to my partner.
Expectation that my partner can understand and appreciate me.
Assumption that I can make myself understood.

Cognition: Targets of Intervention
Sex-role stereotypes: "Real men" don't disclose, express feelings, need to talk things out. These needs are a sign of weakness or dependency.

Expectation that my partner specifically will betray my confidences.

Assumption that listening or confiding means I owe something that I cannot deliver.
Expectation that my partner cannot understand or appreciate me.

Behavior: Strengths
Partners treat the problem as one that they share. Each acknowledges his/her part in the problem.
Partners can define the problem and label their emotions clearly.

Partners can stick to their agenda.

Partners can acknowledge one another's needs and wants.

Behavior: Targets for Intervention
Partners blame one another and fail to see their own contribution to the problem.
Partners' definition of the problem and their expressions of their wants and needs are vague.
Partners get sidetracked during their discussion and fail to return to the problem at hand.
Partners push their own agenda, cross-complain, disqualify and discount one another or withdraw, and fail to listen to or acknowledge their partner's agenda. Partners "debate the truth" or otherwise get sidetracked and lose their focus.

Affect: Strengths
Partners respond to each other's negative affect with humor, support, or other positive behavior.
Partners' nonverbal affective expressions convey respect and concern.

Partners accept the full range of their own emotions.

Affect: Targets for Intervention
Partners reciprocate negative affect which then escalates as they continue their discussion.
Partners' nonverbal affective expressions convey contempt and dismissal. One partner expresses frustration through criticism and demands while the other is withdrawn in angry "stony silence."
Partners hide vulnerabilities and attack when threatened.

Cognition: Strengths
Partners assume that everyone has needs for privacy and separateness.
Partners assume that some of their reactions to each other are generalizations from other times and other relationships.
Each partner assumes that the other will periodically behave in thoughtless or inconsiderate ways.

Cognition: Targets for Intervention
Partners interpret bids for separateness as rejection or lack of love.
Partners attribute their emotional reactivity solely to the other's behavior.
Each partner expects the other to behave perfectly, and attributes "slips" to malevolent intent on the part of the other.

Contents

SECTION ONE: OVERVIEW

SECTION TWO: METHODS OF CREATING INTIMACY

SECTION THREE: INTIMATE CHALLENGES

Contributors

Harlene Anderson, Ph.D., is founder of and a faculty member at the Houston Galveston Institute (Texas) and the Taos Institute (New Mexico). She is the author of *Conversation, Language and Possibilities: A Postmodern Approach to Therapy* (New York: Basic Books), and coeditor of the *Journal of Systemic Therapies*. She received a Lifetime Achievement Award from the Texas Association for Marriage and Family Therapy in 1998.

Ellyn Bader, Ph.D., is codirector of The Couples Institute in Menlo Park, CA. She coauthored *In Quest of the Mythical Mate: A Developmental Approach to Couples Therapy* (New York: Brunner/Mazel). She conducts workshops and seminars and was awarded the Clark Vincent Award for an outstanding literary contribution from the California Association of Marriage and Family Therapists.

Dennis A. Bagarozzi, Ph.D., is a licensed psychologist and licensed marriage and family therapist. He is a fellow and approved supervisor in AAMFT and a fellow in family psychology in the American Psychological Association. He is director of Human Resources Consultants, a private clinical/consulting firm with offices in Atlanta and Athens, GA. Dr. Bagarozzi has authored or coauthored six textbooks and has written more than 70 articles and book chapters. He is on the editorial boards of numerous journals and is the editor of the Family Measurement Techniques section of *The American Journal of Family Therapy*.

Insoo Kim Berg, M.S.W., is director of the Brief Family Therapy Center in Milwaukee, WI. She has authored many articles and books showing the application of solution-focused brief therapy.

Jan T. Brown, M.S., is a licensed marriage and family therapist in private practice in Austin, TX. She is a couples workshop presenter, consultant, speaker, and an experienced presenter at state and national conferences.

Jon Carlson, Psy.D., Ed.D., is a professor of psychology and counseling at Governors State University in Illinois and psychologist at the Lake Geneva Wellness Clinic in Wisconsin. He is a past president of the International Association of Marriage and Family Counselors and editor of *The Family Journal: Counseling and Therapy for Couples and Families*. He holds a diplomate in family psychology (ABPP) and marital and family therapy (ABFamP). He has authored 25 books and 120 articles.

Diana Carleton, Ed.D., is on the faculty of the Houston Galveston Institute and Our Lady of the Lake University in Houston as program director for the M.S. in psychology. She has nearly 20 years experience in teaching, training, and supervision in marriage and family therapy. She is a regular presenter at numerous state and national conferences.

Michael L. Dimitroff, Ph.D., is a professor of psychology and counseling at Governors State University and on the staff of St. Anthony Medical Center in Crown Point, IN, as well as Charter Hospital in Hobart, IN. He has published papers on the spiritually-disordered couple as well as in the field of personality disorders and has participated in the research, revision, and validation project of the Millon Clinical Multiaxial Inventory-III and Millon Adolescent Clinical Inventory. He owns and supervises Christian Counseling in Dyer, IN.

Carlos Durana, Ph.D., M.Ac., works in a private practice in Reston, VA, with individuals, couples, and groups. He specializes in the area of behavioral medicine, integrating a variety of theoretical approaches and methods for the treatment of psychophysical and psychological problems. He has published numerous articles in leading family therapy journals.

Arthur Freeman, Ed.D., ABPP, is Professor and chair of the Department of Psychology at The Philadelphia College of Osteopathic Medicine and director of the doctoral program of clinical psychology. He is the past president of the

Association for Advancement of Behavior Therapy. Dr. Freeman has earned diplomates in both clinical and behavioral psychology from the American Board of Professional Psychology. He has published 17 books and more than 50 chapters, journal articles and reviews. His work has been translated from English into nine other languages.

Bernard G. Guerney, Jr, Ph.D., ABPP, is director of the National Institute of Relationship Enhancement, Bethesda, MD. Dr. Guerney has produced several books including *Relationship Enhancement (RE): Skill Training Programs for Therapy, Problems Prevention, and Enrichment* (San Francisco: Jossey Bass) which Douglas Sprenkle, Ph.D., has called, "seminal and potentially revolutionary." Dr. Guerney has won major awards from national organizations for originating the RE approach. Nationally and abroad, he oversees the training, supervision, and certification of RE program leaders and therapists, and conducts RE therapy demonstrations and workshops.

Gay Hendricks, Ph.D., and **Kathlyn Hendricks**, Ph.D., have been partners in work and life since 1980. Between them, they have published over 20 books and made several hundred professional presentations. The books include the best selling, *Conscious Loving* (Bantam, 1990), *At the Speed of Life* (Bantam, 1992), and *The Conscious Heart* (Bantam, 1997). They direct the Hendricks Institute in Santa Barbara, CA.

Mark A. Karpel, Ph.D., is a clinical psychologist in private practice in western Massachusetts, specializing in couple and sex therapy. He is a visiting lecturer on psychology in the Department of Psychiatry, Harvard Medical School. He is also a fellow and approved supervisor for the American Association of Marriage and Family Therapy and a fellow of the Massachusetts Psychological Association. He is the author of *Evaluating Couples: A Handbook for Practitioners* (Evanston, IL: Norton) and the editor of *Family Resources: The Hidden Partner in Family Therapy* (New York: Guilford).

Luciano L'Abate, Ph.D., ABPP is a professor emeritus of psychology at Georgia State University. Dr. L'Abate has authored more than 200 papers and chapters and 28 books and has two books in press. He has received major awards from professional associations and the Outstanding Citizen Award from the state of Georgia in 1984.

Pat Love, Ed.D., is a licensed marriage and family therapist in Austin, TX. She has published several professional articles and has authored three books including *Hot Monogamy* (New York: Dutton).

Michael P. Maniacci, Psy.D., is a clinical psychologist in private practice and a core faculty member and clinical supervisor at the Adler School of Professional

Psychology in Chicago. He has published numerous professional articles and chapters.

David R. Matteson, Ph.D., is a professor of psychology and counseling at Governors State University. He maintains a small private practice in the area. He is active in the profeminist men's movement and in AIDS prevention work. He has written numerous book chapters and articles and authored and coauthored two books *Adolescence Today: Sex Roles and the Search for Identity* (Homewood, IL: Dorsey-Irwin) and *Ego Identity: A Handbook for Psychosocial Research* (New York: Springer-Verlag).

Augustus Y. Napier, Ph.D., currently lives in Brevard, NC, where he works as a supervisor and consultant. He also leads workshops in the United States and Canada. Formerly director of the Family Workshop in Atlanta, he is clinical associate professor of psychiatry and behavioral sciences in the Department of Psychiatry at Emory University. He is the author, with Carl Whitaker, M.D., of the best-selling *The Family Crucible* and of *The Fragile Bond*.

Bill O'Hanlon, M.S., and **Steffanie O'Hanlon**, M.S.W., reside in Santa Fe, NM. Bill is an internationally renowned workshop presenter and author while Steffanie is an author and therapist. Bill has authored several books including *In Search of Solutions* and *Rewriting Love Stories*. Steffanie has edited the text *Evolving Possibilities* and coauthored *Brief Couples Therapy Homework Assignments*.

Peter T. Pearson, Ph.D., is codirector of The Couples Institute and consulting associate professor at Stanford University. He is the coauthor of *In Quest of the Mythical Mate: A Developmental Approach to Couples Therapy* (Brunner/Mazel) and is frequently a speaker at national and international conferences.

Dorothy E. Peven, M.S.W., is a licensed clinical social worker in private practice in the Chicago metropolitan area and professor at the Adler School of Professional Psychology, Chicago. She has served as vice president of the North American Society of Adlerian Psychology and authored major papers in Adlerian psychotherapy and psychopathology.

Karen J. Prager, Ph.D., is a professor of psychology at the University of Texas at Dallas and adjunct professor of clinical psychology at the University of Texas Southwestern Medical Center. She maintains a private psychological practice with a specialization in couples therapy and has conducted couple training workshops for professional and graduate students. She has written many articles and is author of *The Psychology of Intimacy* (New York: Guilford).

David E. Scharff, M.D., is the codirector of the International Institute of Object Relations Therapy and is clinical professor of psychiatry at Georgetown and the Uniformed Services University of the Health Sciences. Dr. Scharff writes on the application of object relations theory to many modalities of therapy and teaches widely in the United States and abroad. He is the author of many books in the field and is coauthor (with Jill Savege Scharff) of *Object Relations Individual Therapy*, *Objects Relations Couple Therapy* and *Object Relations Family Therapy*, all published by Jason Aronson in Northvale, NJ.

Richard C. Schwartz, Ph.D., is on the faculty of The Family Institute at Northwestern University. He is known as the developer of the Internal Family Systems model and has authored *Internal Family Systems Therapy* (New York: Guilford). Dr. Schwartz is a popular workshop presenter and author of many other books and articles.

Bernard H. Shulman, M.D., is life fellow of the American Psychiatric Association and formerly clinical professor of psychiatry at both Northwestern University School of Medicine and the Stritch Medical School at Loyola University. He is the past president of the North American Society of Individual Psychology and of the International Association of Individual Psychology. He is the coauthor of several books, including *How to Survive Your Aging Parents*.

Steven Slavik, M.A., is a therapist and author in Victoria, British Columbia. He has written several articles and coedited the book *Techniques in Adlerian Psychology* (Philadelphia: Taylor & Francis). He currently serves as the editor of the *Canadian Journal of Individual Psychology*.

Maryhelen Snyder, Ph.D., is the clinical director of the New Mexico Relationship Enhancement Institute. She is an adjunct faculty at the University of New Mexico Department of Psychology and the UNM Medical School Psychiatry Department. She is editor of the book, *Ethical Issues in Feminist Therapy* (New York: Haworth Press) and the author of numerous articles and book chapters in the field of relationships and relational psychotherapy.

Len Sperry, M.D., Ph.D., is vice chair and professor of psychiatry and behavioral medicine at the Medical College of Wisconsin. In addition, he is director of its Division of Organizational Psychiatry and Corporate Health, and executive director of the Foley Center for Aging and Development. Dr. Sperry is board certified in psychiatry, preventive medicine, and clinical psychology, and is a fellow of the Division of Family Psychology of the American Psychological Association. He has published 25 professional books including *Martial Therapy: Integrating Theory and Technique* and more than 200 chapters and journal articles and he is also associate editor for research for *The Family Journal*. He is a member of the American Family Therapy Academy and of the Coalition of Family Diagnosis.

Susan Swim, M.A., is on the faculty of the Houston Galveston Institute. She has a history of teaching in marriage and family training programs and in consulting and training. She has published articles in several books and journals.

Robert E. Wubbolding, Ed.D., is the director of the Center for Reality Therapy and professor of counseling at Xavier University. Dr. Wubbolding has taught reality therapy in North America, Asia, Europe, and the Middle East. He has authored many publications including *Using Reality Therapy* (New York: Harper Collins), *Understanding Reality Therapy* (New York: Harper Collins), and *Employee Motivation: What to Do When What You Say Isn't Working* (Knoxville: SPC Press).

Foreword to *The Intimate Couple*

Through a prism of varied perspectives, *The Intimate Couple* invites us to examine the personal closeness that we call intimacy. It looks at sexual, emotional, and even spiritual intimacy. Carlson and Sperry recognize the diversity of perspectives that our society brings to this universal human experience of personal intimacy. They wisely do not attempt to reconcile the contradictions and complexity with a single unifying concept of intimacy. Moreover, many of the book's contributors include love in their idea of intimacy, thereby deepening what it means to be intimate into the mystique of love.

In today's world of transient relationships and unattached people, to talk about intimacy and love is to step into the realm of confusing and contradictory definitions and philosophies. Although the most universally-recognized human need and spiritual ideal is to love and be loved, there is no universal consensus about the meaning and place of love in our lives. This book exemplifies some of these differences, and the reader, as I do, will quarrel with some of the book's clinical and moral views about the nature of love. That is the world we live in and the difficulty facing all therapists—the radical differences in values in our society. In particular, attempting to focus on such a fundamental issue as personal intimacy is like grappling with the weather in the era of *el niño* and *la niña*.

As complex and controversial as would be a definition of intimacy, clinicians, especially family therapists, are called to work with the connection between people in the personal relationship. While living without a common understanding of the term, the realm of family therapists, in particular, is intimacy. Our work with couples calls for identifying, measuring, evaluating, repairing, and fostering intimacy. Therapists must also judge whether to impede and discourage intimacy where it is harmful and inappropriate.

Clinicians are like meteorologists trying to understand the caprices of nature, in this case our human emotions. However, like engineers trying to harness the forces of nature, clinicians attempt to work with people's personal relationships. Even if we could predict and measure the wind and the tides, could we really contain and tame them? Intimacy with love is a mysterious sphere at the heart of the human relationship. In intimacy, soul speaks to soul. Who can explain why lovers fall in love? Who can plumb the depths of the love in a life-long marriage? Love in all its forms and ardor is more than a therapist can comprehend. It does not have a single shape. It is as mysterious and complex as the human heart.

Like water in vases of varied shapes and colors, intimacy assumes the form of the people, their relationships, and their lives. As water leaking from a defective or cracked vase, intimacy often makes itself evident to therapists when it is unattained or betrayed in the relationships of the people who come to us. It comes hidden in their grief and complaints. In working to solve a problem, we often find ourselves trying to nurture and further their relationships in ways that are healthy and right.

As clinicians, we need help in identifying what is intimacy and its big cousin, love. In a world where people are intensely debating the rules of love, and the when and how of commitment, we need to know when intimacy is healthy rather than harmful and morally right rather than wrong in relationships. The very nature of couples work begs that we grasp what makes up intimacy. Our effort with couples calls for standards by which to judge the strength and legitimacy of intimacy. These are no mean challenges in today's culturally and politically fractured society.

We also need to develop the methods and skills for helping people with their pain, anxieties, and hopes about intimacy. Somehow, we need to find ways to predict and catch the wind and tides so that we can help and not hurt those people who come to us looking for personal closeness. Fortunately, even in the face of all the ambiguity and debate, we do not have to definitively describe intimacy in order to recognize it. We are clinicians, but we are also ordinary people with ordinary emotions. We too know intimacy and love in our personal lives more or less successfully. Moreover, as we wrestle with our respective notions of how to work with intimacy, we look to learn from one another's similarities and differences in our therapeutic models and personal life experiences. We learn not just from books. We learn from life, striving to fit our theories and techniques to real life experience, our own and our clients'.

Finally, we come to the place where we meet out clients, and they too have their own notions about intimacy and love. The art of our work is in the relationship between clinician and client. In the real human connection of therapy, clinician and client negotiate their philosophies and notions about intimacy even as they attempt to agree on a path for change and improvement in the client's life. Within the professional boundaries of therapy, there develops a kind of personal intimacy shared by clinician and client through which they create a healing experience. Therapists get a glimpse at how clients relate at home and utilize their connection with clients to support and encourage them. The clinician-client relationship is the heart of the shared effort called therapy.

As therapists, we are speaking to intimacy and, consequently, also to love. As scientists, we are daring to address nature, a reality that is not just a subject of our work, but also something we live. As people who, by our very nature, live within a moral framework, we are treating of love that is not just emotion, but also moral choice. In writing about love and intimacy, we are considering as rich and complex a subject as there is. My hope is that Carlson and Sperry's noble effort to gather this distinguished collection of thinkers about, and doers of, therapy will spur us, the readers, to consider more deeply our own views about intimacy and love.

Harry J. Aponte

Preface

The reader looking for the definitive one-line description of intimacy is sure to be disappointed. There seem to be as many definitions of intimacy as there are individuals writing about intimacy. Following are some representative examples. From the *Random House Dictionary* we read that intimacy is a "close, familiar and usually affectionate or loving personal relationship with another person." Robert Beavers, a psychiatrist and family therapy researcher, defines intimacy as "the joy of being known and accepted by another who is loved. There is no intimacy except where there is equal overt power" (Beavers, 1985, p. 52). Luciano L'Abate, a clinical psychologist and family researcher and therapist, describes intimacy as: "sharing of joys, hurts, and fears of being hurt" (L'Abate, 1997, p. 36). Augustus Napier, a writer, clinician and trainer of family therapists, indicates that intimacy is "a non-hierarchial, caring, honest, mutual, more-or-less simultaneous sharing of unprotectedness or vulnerability between two emotionally 'differentiated' individuals" (Napier, 1996, p. 468).

In short, intimacy is a lot like pornography. We know what it is when we see it, but being able to clearly articulate its meaning and its boundaries from other related concepts or constructs is quite challenging. There is no concensus on either its definition or clinical applications. A review of two dozen texts on martial and family therapy reveals that intimacy is more likely to be discussed in a few sentences scattered across a number of chapters than to be presented systematically in a separate chapter. It should not be surprising then that many of these texts do not even have a listing for intimacy in their indexes. In fact, there are very few professional and trade books in print that address the topic of intimacy. Furthermore, having intimacy in the title is no guarantee that the book will address the topic of intimacy directly or in detail. Presumably, the imprecision about the meaning and parameters of this term also accounts for the limited research literature on this topic to date. Since marital and family therapy is still a relatively new branch of the behavioral science, it just may be that an informed elaboration of this topic is premature at this time. Based on the status of current publications, this conclusion seems warranted.

AN OVERVIEW OF THE BOOK

Despite their differences in theoretical orientation and clinical experience, all the authors of chapters in this book agree with the following premise: individuals have needs for both belonging and autonomy, and the challenge of balancing these two needs is the basic challenge in intimate relationships. The chapters address this challenge both theoretically and clinically. The book is divided into three sections.

Section One is entitled "Overview." It articulates the construct of intimacy within a number of contexts. Karen Preger details a five-layered context for thinking about intimacy, ranging from the immediate to the sociocultural. Len Sperry describes intimacy in terms of three styles and several levels. Insoo Berg, Len Sperry and Jon Carlson converse about the cultural dimensions of intimacy and some very practical clinical implications of these differences. Pat Love and Jan Brown describe their program for engendering and reengendering passion in couples' relationships. Dennis Bagarozzi reports on the Marital Intimacy Needs Questionnaire that he developed as a clinical aid with couples in therapy. Mark Karpel describes seven strategies for assessing intimacy in the clinical context. These range from self-report to formal assessment instruments. Karpel emphasizes the importance of multidimensional assessment of intimacy and illustrates this process with a compelling case study.

Section Two is entitled "Methods of Creating Intimacy." Karen Preger begins this section with a description of her intimacy-oriented couples therapy. This cognitive-behavioral approach cognitively addresses fears of intimacy stemming from earlier negative experiences in relationships, and then behaviorally addresses the attendant communication skill defects. Arthur Freeman also describes a cognitive-behavioral approach to intimacy problems that draws on Adlerian theory and interventions. David Scarff provides a very readable introduction to an object relations approach to intimacy and sexual problems.

Harlene Anderson and colleagues then describe their unique postmodern collaborative approach to intimacy problems. Following that Bob Wubbolding describes the application of reality therapy to problems in intimate relationships. Next, Steffanie and Bill O'Hanlon present their solution-oriented approach to the intimacy issue. Richard Schwartz then illustrates the internal family systems model, a family systems approach to intimacy problems. The next two chapters, the first by Dorothy Peven and Bernie Schulman, and the second by Steve Slavik and the editors of this book, describe and illustrate the Adlerian couples therapy approach to intimacy. Augustus Napier articulates, with a compelling case study, the symbolic experiential approach to intimacy. Lou L'Abate and Margaret S. Baggett then provide an alternative modality for working with intimacy issues. They describe distance approaches to intimacy problems as an alternative to the traditional face-to-face therapy that most clinicians provide. Carlos Durana follows this with a discussion of the application of his integrated psychoeducational approach. This approach, which utilizes the Practical Application of Intimate Relationship Skills (PAIRS) program, is a comprehensive intervention that can be a complete therapy approach or an adjunctive intervention. Maryhelen Snyder and Bernard Guerney then demonstrate the value of the Relationship Enhancement couple therapy approach to intimacy problems. This is followed by Ellyn Bader and Peter Pearson's presentation of their developmental object-relations approach to intimacy issues. The section concludes with Gay and Kathy Hendricks' unique body-centered approach to intimacy.

Section Three, entitled "Intimate Challenges," contains three chapters that address issues of considerable importance for clinicians in practice today. The first chapter by Michael Dimitroff looks at the matter of spirituality and its relationship to intimacy. The second by David Matteson addresses the unique and sensitive issues involving intimacy in bisexual couples. Finally, Mike Maniacci addresses intimacy issues in a couples format when one or both partners in a relationship present with severe psychiatric disorders.

Jon Carlson
Len Sperry

SECTION ONE

Overview

CHAPTER 1

Introduction: A Context for Thinking About Intimacy

Jon Carlson
Len Sperry

Before proceeding, it may be useful to specify a context for thinking about the notion of intimacy. Such a context should provide the reader with some conceptual boundaries regarding intimacy. These boundaries include mature intimacy vs. immature intimacy, love vs. intimacy, intimacy vs. passion vs. commitment, and boundaries vs. power vs. intimacy.

MATURE INTIMACY VS. IMMATURE INTIMACY

The first obvious boundary is that of mature vs. immature intimacy. Husband-wife relationships are capable of mature intimacy whereas mother-child relationships are not capable of mature intimacy. Obviously, a couple's relationship can be characterized by immature intimacy, despite their capacity to relate maturely, whereas immature intimacy is the only capacity for mother-child relationships. In this regard, the dictionary definition given earlier does not distinguish between mature and immature intimacy. On the other hand,

Beavers (1985) and Napier (1996) assume this distinction by specifying that the individuals have equal overt power or are emotionally differentiated persons. L'Abate (1997) implies such equality. Whitaker and Ryan (1989) add that intimacy develops in tandem with self-autonomy, and that autonomy increases as a function of intimacy.

LOVE VS. INTIMACY

A second boundary involves the distinction of love and intimacy. L'Abate and Talmadge (1987) describe love as a development process consisting of three elements: behavioral, cognitive and emotional. The behavioral element consists of the capacity to be caring and to accept care. The cognitive element consists of the capacity to see good in another and the capacity for forgiveness. The emotional element is, of course, intimacy. Intimacy consists of the capacity to be dependent on the other as well as the capacity to express, withstand, understand, and resolve the conflict and hostility that occur in intimate relationships. In other words, intimacy, according to these researchers, is only one element of love.

INTIMACY VS. PASSION
VS. COMMITMENT

A third boundary involves the relationship of intimacy to passion and commitment. Sternberg (1986, 1988) describes what he calls the "triangle of love." It consists of three components: commitment, passion, and intimacy. For Sternberg intimacy encompasses the affects and feeling states of closeness, connectedness, and bondedness. Passion is described as encompassing the drive leading to physical attraction, romance, and sexual consummation of the relationship. Commitment differs from passion and intimacy, in that it involves short-term and long-term decisions. The short-term decision is to love the other individual, while the long-term decision is to maintain that love. Developmentally, intimacy, passion and commitment change in degree or level during the course of an on-going relationship (Sternberg, 1986). Passion becomes increasingly intense early in the relationship in conjunction with a rapid rise in intimacy. Commitment, however, develops much more slowly and steadily. As the relationship continues to develop, commitment rises to match the level of intimacy while the level of passion often decreases significantly.

Accordingly, when a couple complains that their "love has cooled" or "the romance is gone," what they are really speaking about is a change in the level of passion in their relationship. When passion decreases but the levels of intimacy and commitment remain adequate, the relationship is not in jeopardy, but rather one element of it has changed.

INTIMACY VS. POWER VS. BOUNDARIES

A fourth boundary involves the relationship of intimacy to power and boundaries. Berman and Leif (1975) were the first to differentiate power and boundary dimensions from intimacy. The intimacy dimension involves self-disclosure, friendship, caring and appreciation of individual uniqueness. It involves negotiating both the emotional and physical distances between partners, so as to balance the need for autonomy with the need for belonging. Boundary issues in couples' relationships center on membership and structure: membership in terms of who is involved in the couples' system and to what degree, and structure in terms of the extent to which partners are part of, but at the same time apart from, the couple subsystem. Boundary also refers to the degree of intrusiveness that will be accepted in the relationship. For the married couple, commitment to their marriage is the core boundary issue, along with related commitment to jobs, friends, extended family, and outside interests. Power issues include responsibility, discipline, control, role negotiation, and decision making. Couple relationships continually involve both overt and covert efforts to influence decisions and behaviors of the partners. Power issues are tied to money, privileges, and rewards. They are also more subtly manifest in struggles for control of the relationship, including one-upmanship efforts and escalation of conflict. The power dimension "predicts" who will pursue and who will distance in the relationship. In marital conflict it "determines" who tells whom what to do in specific situations. The power dimension greatly impacts both boundaries and the level and nature of intimacy.

Optimal couple functioning and self-differentiation results when boundary and power issues are reasonably resolved so that the partners can relate in a healthy and intimate manner (Doherty & Colangelo, 1984).

In short, the construct of intimacy is similar to but can be differentiated from related constructs such as love, passion, power, boundaries, autonomy, closeness and commitment. Now that the reader has some contextual basis for thinking about intimacy in couple relationships we move to an overview of the chapters in this book.

Concluding Note

As important as intimacy is in our personal and professional lives, intimacy as a theoretical and clinical construct still remains an illusive phenomenon. This state of affairs has challenged us in our roles as clinicians and educators. We want to provide the best possible clinical milieu for the couples with whom we work in therapy and in couples workshops, and we want to provide our trainees with the most current, cutting-edge theory and research available. For this reason we have assembled a group of expert clinicians, theorists, and researchers and challenged them to move the field of couple and marital therapy into its prime. We expected them to present cutting-edge developments in the clinical, theoretical and research domains of intimacy.

Authors who prepare a book for publication are challenged to specify the compelling reasons why the proposed book should be published. We easily made the case that there was no single compendium that adequately addressed theoretical and practical considerations relative to intimacy. We were also certain that we could enlist the cooperation of the experts to make a much needed contribution to the field. We had no illusions that this project would result in either the final definition of the term or the definitive treatment of choice. We did, however, expect to provide the reader with the most current insights and provocative discussions of the theory and practice of the multi-faceted topic of intimacy. The next stage in the development of knowledge in this area will be achieving consensus on an operational definition and clinical parameters. It is our hope that this book will stimulate that development.

REFERENCES

L'Abate, L. & Talmadege, W. (1987). Love, intimacy, and sex. In G. Weeks & L. Hof (Eds.), *Integrating sex and marital therapy: A clinical guide*, pp. 23–34. New York: Brunner/Mazel.

L'Abate, L. (1997). *The self in the family: A classification of personality, criminality, and psychopathology*. New York: Wiley.

Beavers, R. (1985). *Successful marriage: A family systems approach to couples therapy*. New York: Norton.

Berman, E., & Leif, H. (1975). Marital therapy from psychiatric perspective: An overview. *American Journal of Psychiatry, 132*, 583–591.

Doherty, W. & Colangelo, N. (1984). The family FIRO model: A modest proposal for organizing family treatment. *Journal of Marital and Family Therapy, 10*, 19–29.

Napier, A. (1996). Of men and intimacy: A contextual approach. In L. Vandecreek, S. Knapp, & T. Jackson, (Eds.), *Innovations in clinical practice: A source book*. (pp. 467–480). Sarasota, FL: Professional Resources Press.

Sternberg, R. (1986). A triangular theory of love. *Psychological Reviews, 93* (2), 119–135.

Sternberg, R. (1987). *The triangle of love: Intimacy, passion, commitment*. New York: Basic Books.

Whitaker, C. & Ryan, M. (1989). *Midnight musings of a family therapist*. New York: Norton.

CHAPTER 2

The Multilayered Context
of Intimacy

Karen J. Prager

It might seem that nothing is more private and exclusively dyadic than intimacy. Intimate contact flourishes and provides its most exhilarating moments during those times that the dyad can shut themselves away from the demands, interferences, and distractions of the world. Yet for all its personal, private character, intimacy, like any other aspect of couple relationships, occurs within a multifaceted context that will shape, for good or ill, the partners' experience of intimacy with one another. Consider the following effort by John and Marsha to have some time for intimate conversation:

John and Marsha lived busy lives trying to make ends meet on a small budget and raise four children in a small suburban home. When they decided they wanted to get away together one Saturday evening, they had to ask John's parents to stay with their children as a favor, since they could not afford a baby sitter. Because John's relationship with his parents is strained, the parents agreed only reluctantly, and John guessed from his previous experience with them that he would have to pay for the favor with effusive expressions of gratitude and accompanying feelings of guilt and anger. John and Marsha did not feel free to leave his parents in their small house with four children for long, so they tried to think of a way to enjoy some rare private time in a three-hour period. They carefully selected a new restaurant in town where the lights were low and the dining room wasn't too crowded. When they got there, however, they were interrupted repeatedly by a waiter asking them, "Is there anything else I can do for you?" They also had to speak loudly because of the poor acoustics in the room. As if these distractions were not enough, John and Marsha had relationship problems to contend with. John was opposed to too much open talk

7

because he believed that showing vulnerability to his wife violated his responsibilities as a breadwinner, which in his mind included being calm and in control of himself for his wife and children's sake. Marsha found this reticence frustrating and was willing to push hard to get John to share more of his thoughts and feelings with her. Marsha, however, had her own unconscious attachment to the strong and confident role John played for her, and she tended to discourage him inadvertently if he did drop some of his defenses. John, subconsciously picking up on Marsha's ambivalence, was all too willing to shut down. In addition, he was not in a good frame of mind this particular evening because he was dreading having to contend with his parents. As a result of all of these factors, each felt frustrated with their conversation, and wondered whether the effort was worth it.

Perhaps most couples do not have as many factors impinging on their intimate time as John and Marsha do. Nevertheless, many therapists working with distressed couples have tried to help couples find time for a bit of intimacy and have heard stories that were not too different from this one. John and Marsha's story illustrates the many contextual factors that can affect couple intimacy. The contextual factors illustrated in the example can determine whether a couple engages in any kind of intimate interaction at all, and what their experience will be like when they do. They may also determine whether experiences of intimacy leave a residue of good will that can help the partners tolerate, with a generous spirit, the less rewarding times in their relationship.

PURPOSE OF THE CHAPTER

The purpose of this chapter is to place intimacy in couple relationships within a multilayered context that determines (a) how frequently a couple will engage in intimate interaction, (b) what the nature of that intimate interaction will be, and (c) whether one or both partners is likely to initiate intimate contact, and how each partner will respond to the other's initiatives. To accomplish this purpose requires three steps. First, it is necessary to articulate a working definition of intimacy. This chapter will treat the intimate interaction as the basic unit of intimacy. Second, it is important to map out the mutually embedded contexts that affect intimacy. Through this mapping, I plan to illustrate how the various contexts can separately and simultaneously affect the frequency, quality, and impact of intimacy. Third, factors within each contextual level will be discussed in light of what we know from research on their impact and of what we can surmise from clinical experience might be useful ways to intervene.

A MULTITIERED DEFINITION
OF INTIMACY

Elsewhere, I have defined intimacy as a kind of interaction that has experiential (cognitive and affective) components and sequelae (Prager, 1995). Intimate interactions have immediate, short-term effects on individuals and (if applicable) their relationship, and, when repeated frequently, exert a cumulative effect on the more abiding perceptions and feelings partners have about themselves, one another, and their relationship. It is these more abiding effects that form the building blocks of intimate relationships.

To distinguish intimate interactions from other kinds of couple interactions, I define intimate behaviors as those in which partners share something meaningful, personal, and private with each other, whether verbally or nonverbally. Intimate experiences are positive thoughts, feelings, and perceptions about the partner, oneself, and the relationship. Open and clear communication that results in negative feelings about oneself or the other (or no feelings at all) is not intimate behavior by this definition. While many interactions may contain one or more of the elements of intimate interaction, these are not intimate interactions unless the components are combined.

Intimate interactions affect the individual partners and their relationship. Because intimacy contributes to the fulfillment of needs, it exerts positive effects on the individual partner's well-being. The positive experiences of intimate contact enhance the functioning of the relationship. The perception that one is fully known and understood on the one hand, and loved, respected, and cared for on the other is a crucial part of feeling loved (Fromm, 1956; Jourard, 1971; Rogers, 1951). One must believe that the partner understands and knows one's true self before the partner's expressions of love and caring are meaningful (Kohut, 1980). Further, when one loves, one often wants to know the other as fully and completely as the other can be known, and wants to be in a position to continue learning about the other over time.

Intimacy, when repeated over time, has long-term emotional and cognitive consequences for the individuals and their relationship. The repetition of intimate experiences across time and occasions transforms momentary positive feelings into enduring attitudes and expectations about the partner. We call these enduring attitudes and expectations (the sequelae of intimate interactions) by names such as love, caring, trust, and respect. Intimate interactions offer partners an unparalleled opportunity to know one another deeply and authentically, in a way that others may not, and to love and care for all that they know of one another. This combination of knowing another fully while still accepting and loving that person may fulfill needs for intimacy and thereby explain the uniquely beneficial and rewarding effect of intimate interactions on the people who engage in them and on their relationships (Ojeda & Prager, 1997).

OVERVIEW OF INTIMACY IN CONTEXT

While there is only one definition of an intimate interaction in this chapter, this definition encompasses many forms of intimacy, and it is likely that each couple will develop a style of intimate relating that is uniquely their own. The uniqueness of each couple's style of intimate relating is due in part to the configuration of contextual factors that nurture and impinge upon the couple's relationship.

Figure 1 displays a five-level scheme for classifying contextual factors that affect or are affected by intimacy. This scheme is based on an earlier model developed by Adams and Blieszner (1994) whose purpose was to provide a framework for the integration of both psychological and sociological variables

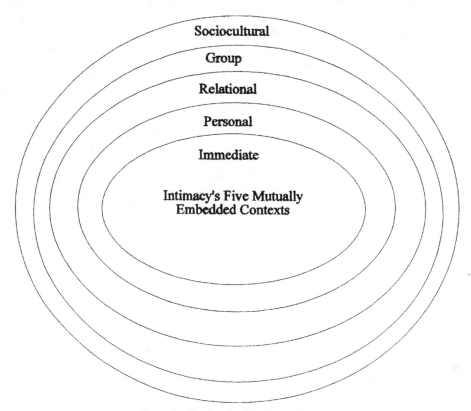

Figure 1   Five Levels of Intimacy Context.

into a theory of relationships. In the present scheme, the innermost circle depicts the immediate contextual level, which refers to those factors that are closest in time and space to the interaction itself. The immediate context refers to situational variables such as the physical surroundings within which partners attempt to engage in intimate interaction (Is there a television turned on and are children about? vs. Can they control interruptions, noise and distractions?). It also refers to the immediate circumstances that have brought the partners together to engage in a potentially intimate interaction.

At the personal level are factors specific to the individual partners. Every couple relationship is composed of two unique individuals with their own genetic heritages and personal life histories. This combination of inherited traits and life experience makes each person unique, and determines what each brings into the relationship and how each reacts to the other.

The relational context includes characteristics of the couple's relationship, such as how the partners met, how their relationship developed, the partners' level of commitment to their relationship, and how they interact in noninti-mate situations. It also includes other relational pressures on the couple, such as dampening effects of dysfunctional problem-solving efforts on the partners' desire for intimate contact.

The group context refers to other groups that the couple is affiliated with, by necessity or by choice, that affect the couple's relationship and hence the quality of their interactions. Two groups are most salient here: (a) the couple's network of extended family and friends, and (b) the organizations with which the couple is affiliated—primarily the workplace, but also children's school(s), churches, volunteer organizations, and so forth. Other important groups (e.g., Alcoholics Anonymous) with which one or both partners are affiliated may also be included in the group context.

Finally, the sociocultural level encompasses the norms of identity groups, societies, and cultures of which the couple are a part. To the extent that sociocultural norms are internalized by the partners and used as blueprints for planning their lives, they will have a substantial though often invisible impact on the way each partner behaves in intimate situations and the way each experiences intimacy within the relationship.

Some contextual factors can be meaningfully conceptualized at more than one level. In particular, gender can be understood as a situational, personal, relational, group, and sociocultural variable. Further, the effects of gender on intimacy are especially prone to interact with the effects of other contextual factors. An in-depth discussion of gender will illustrate processes by which contextual factors exert interacting influences on intimacy while simultane-ously exposing the inadequacy of overly simplistic notions of gender.

Contextual factors can affect the functioning of an intimate relationship in three ways. They may directly affect the partners' opportunities to engage in satisfying intimate exchanges. For example, the specific situations that partners find themselves in (immediate context), their personal characteristics (personal context), and the nature of their relationship (relational context), each or in combination, may ease or obstruct couple intimacy. Consider a husband who experiences fear of his own vulnerability every time he is intimate with his wife. To reduce his fearful feelings when they become too intense, he withdraws from her and becomes cold and unresponsive. This sequence of behavior is so aversive to both of them that eventually their intimate interactions drastically decrease in frequency.

Second, contextual factors may modify the partners' experiences of intimacy within their interactions. The extent to which "intimate behaviors" (i.e., verbal disclosure, sexual initiatives, affectionate touches, and so forth) are experienced as intimate by one or both partners will depend upon the context in which they occur. For example, for one couple who engaged in frequent, acrimonious quarrels, the initiation of affectionate touch by either partner lost its power to induce feelings of intimacy. The built-up resentments overwhelmed any positive feelings that an intimate gesture could provide.

Finally, contextual factors can modify the importance partners place on intimate relating relative to other aspects of their relationship. How crucial is it to each partner's happiness in the relationship that intimate interactions occur frequently? This will depend upon the context within which interactions occur and the context within which the partners build and maintain their relationship. The presence of children, for example, might strongly influence the importance partners place on intimacy versus other dimensions of their relationship. When partners share responsibility for caring for young children, each person's relationship satisfaction may depend more on the other's willingness to fulfill his or her share of the child-care duties than on any intimate behaviors initiated by either.

This chapter has the following aims:

1   identify specific factors that fall into each of the five mutually embedded levels of context listed in Figure 1,

2   discuss ways that these factors are likely to affect intimate relating,

3   describe ways that these different levels of context interact with one another, using gender as a case in point, and

4   suggest ways to intervene at each contextual level.

THE IMMEDIATE CONTEXT

The immediate or situational context refers to factors that exist within the place and time frame of the interaction itself. Situational contextual factors include the nature of the occasion, the physical setting, the mood of one or both partners, and the sex of the partners. Some immediate contextual factors likely to affect intimacy are discussed next.

The physical setting of an intimate interaction is important because the experience of intimacy is likely enhanced by privacy, quiet, and a minimum of interruptions, whether we are talking about verbal or physical/sexual intimacy. The presence of children in the immediate vicinity is a common intimacy inhibitor. Young children have many needs that require immediate attention and that, therefore, can interrupt couples who are trying to grab some quiet time together. Older children may stay up as late as the adults do, thus leaving the adults little time to be alone. Further, adults may reasonably feel inhibited about their sexual activity while living with sexually knowledgeable adolescents.

Physical proximity can enhance people's opportunities for intimate exchange while physical distance may make intimacy more difficult. Since traveling for business is a way of life for many Americans, it is not unusual for partners to be physically together for only part of the week. Frequent business travel puts substantial pressure on the couple to make the most of the time that they do have. Unfortunately, partners often have different agendas for that time: while one may be eager to have sexual contact, the other may be most invested in getting the spouse to lend a hand with domestic responsibilities. The strain of having to condense their time together into a few days or a weekend can increase the likelihood that the couple will quarrel, each feeling that the other's demands are more than she or he can accommodate. However, physical distances may also sustain relationships because, for some couples, intermittent intimacy is optimum.

The mood of one or both partners can affect the quality of intimate interactions. People who are depressed, for example, can interpret relatively benign initiatives by another as critical or provocative of conflict (Hoehn-Hyde, Schlottmann, & Rush, 1982; Kowalik & Gotlib, 1987). Partners may tend to seek intimate contact at different times during the day or week, and confront time-specific resistance from one another. For example, one partner may prefer to take time for intimate talk when the partners arrive home from their work day while the other may prefer quiet, alone time to unwind from the stress of work. Often, simply postponing conversation for half an hour can result in better moods and therefore more rewarding interaction.

The couple's purpose for talking can affect how they experience one another's intimate behavior. The troubled couples in my practice report that when they do sit down to talk with one another, it is usually an effort to resolve hurt feelings that resulted from nonproductive, emotionally destructive conflict. While partners may, early in their relationship, find that this "post-argument repair work" engenders experiences of intimacy, this effect may diminish with time as they realize that the patterns of destructive interaction have not abated and the post-argument repair work has only short-term effects.

Research indicates that the sex of the partners is systematically associated with some aspects of intimacy. Gay male couples on average become sexually intimate more quickly and engage in sexual activity more frequently than heterosexual couples, while lesbian partners typically engage in less frequent sexual activity than their heterosexual counterparts (Blumstein & Schwartz, 1983). Gay male couples may also maintain a higher frequency of sexual activity for a longer period in their relationship than either heterosexual or lesbian couples do (Kurdek, 1994).

Women tend to engage in more verbally intimate behavior with friends and relationship partners than men do. Other evidence suggests that both men and women will disclose more fully to a female partner than to a male (Dindia & Allen, 1992), although it is unclear whether this finding applies to couple relationships. Verbal intimacy may be a stronger determiner of relationship satisfaction among lesbian couples than among their gay or heterosexual counterparts (Peplau, Cochran, Rook, & Padesky, 1978).

One of the difficulties with research on sex differences is that it explains little or nothing about why gender-related behavioral patterns occur. At the immediate level, gender refers to nothing more than sex-category: the label given to a person based on his or her physical, anatomical attributes. As a result, one must turn to other gendered contextual factors to find an explanation for sex differences at the immediate level. Contextual factors are "gendered" when they disproportionately affect or characterize one sex over the other. Most gendered contextual factors have little to do with sex and its associated anatomical and physiological aspects; they therefore reflect the different sociocultural- and group-level milieus within which women and men operate. It is to these other contextual influences that we now turn.

THE PERSONAL CONTEXT

The personal context refers to the individual partners' personalities, attitudes and beliefs about couple relationships in general and about intimacy in particular. It also refers to their emotional reactions to intimacy (Do they welcome opportunities for intimate contact? Are they impatient with it? Do they fear the consequences of intimacy?) and to their beliefs about it (Can one be intimate and still be "self-reliant?" Does intimacy leave me vulnerable to exploitation?). Individual characteristics may emerge through the influence of a person's genetic heritage, through their life experience, or, most likely, through the interactive effects of the two. The personal context should be a familiar one to most therapists who treat couples, since most of us are trained to consider first individuals and their dynamics, and only later learn to expand our focus to relationships.

Much of what scholars know about personality's effects on intimate relating can be drawn from studies of self-disclosing behavior. These studies ask people to report how much they remember having disclosed to various relationship partners and then correlate their self-disclosure scores with other self-reported personality traits. This body of work has shown that the following personality traits are directly and inversely related to people's tendencies to self-disclose: introversion (Jourard, 1971), neuroticism (anxiety and negativism) (Jourard, 1971), conventionality (Kent, 1975), external locus of control (Prager, 1986), and trait anxiety (Prager, 1986). Positively related to people's tendencies to self-disclose are sensation-seeking (Franken, Gibson, & Mohan, 1990), self-esteem (Cramer, 1990), a secure attachment style (Mikulincer & Nachshon, 1991), and empathy (Todd & Shapira, 1974). Relationships between general adjustment and tendencies to self-disclose are positive (see review by Archer, 1979). When self-disclosure is assessed through observational methods, it is rarer for researchers to find significant associations with personality (Cozby, 1973). An exception to this pattern is people's self-monitoring tendencies, which have consistently been related to both self-report and observed self-disclosure.

There are two types of self-monitoring tendencies that are related to self-disclosure. Davis and Franzoi (1987) called the first type *private self-consciousness*, a tendency to attend to and monitor the more private, covert aspects of oneself. They found that private self-consciousness was consistently related to self-disclosure within important close relationships such as friendship or couple relationships. Davis and Franzoi explained this finding by arguing that the increased awareness of one's inner life that comes with an inward focus of attention gives privately self-conscious people access to a richer and more clearly delineated self to share with others. Further, according to Davis and Franzoi, privately self-conscious people may be fostering intimacy simply by talking about what is interesting to them—in their case, their own inner worlds.

A second type of self-monitoring is *public self-monitoring* which describes people's tendencies to monitor their social behavior and to adjust it to fit with the appropriateness norms of various social situations. Snyder and Simpson (1984) found that publicly self-conscious people were more likely than others to disclose, but not necessarily in close relationships. Rather, public self-monitors reciprocate self-disclosures while getting acquainted with another person because this behavior is appropriate and desirable. Publicly self-monitoring individuals have also been observed changing dating partners early in a relationship (Snyder & Simpson, 1984), which suggests that their ability to be socially appropriate and engaging when getting acquainted is not necessarily related to a genuine interest in establishing and maintaining an intimate relationship.

People's needs, motives, and goals, particularly with regard to intimacy, seem to have an effect on how people approach intimacy. Individuals can vary in the overall strength of their need or desire for intimacy. Research evidence documenting individual differences in need strengths extends back over several decades (see review by McClelland, 1985). McAdams (1988) has documented differences in intimacy need strength that predict a variety of interpersonal behaviors (e.g., see Craig, Koestner, & Zuroff, 1994; McAdams, Healy &

Krause, 1984). Partners may also differ in the processes by which they prefer to meet their intimacy needs. Some people strongly prefer verbal intimacies, while others feel most intimate when they share quiet time or enjoyable activities. Finally, people may seek intimate interactions for different reasons. By definition, all intimate interactions should fulfill our needs to be understood and accepted, but they can also offer other provisions: guidance and advice, opportunities for catharsis or self-clarification, and an affirmation of a close relationship (Derlega & Grzelak, 1979). Particularly for women, intimate interactions may be an important source of support and inspiration for pursuing more agentic needs, such as those for achievement and recognition (Ojeda & Prager, 1997).

An individual's experience of intimacy may also vary as a function of his or her capacity for intimacy. A capacity for intimacy is a set of skills that, when used appropriately, maximizes both partners' intimate experiences. The capacity for intimacy likely includes a capacity for empathy and perspective-taking, and skills for communicating empathically. Perspective-taking is a cognitive ability to take the perspective of the other person and look at the world through the lenses of his or her experience. Empathy is affective and involves warmth, caring, and concern for the experiences of others, especially a capacity to feel what others would likely feel in a given situation (Eisenberg, Murphy, & Shepard, 1997). It may be difficult for those who lack empathy to experience intimacy as pleasurable and need-fulfilling. An absence of empathy may be reflected in a preoccupation with the self in the face of others' distress (or joy): an inward focus on one's own reactions to the other's experience, and an awkward inability to say the right thing. It seems that those who have difficulty with empathy believe that they should feel caring and concern but are unable to access those feelings (Eisenberg, et al., 1997). Self-focused concern may be associated with desires to escape the interaction; thus, a lack of empathy could result in a person avoiding intimate interactions that may demand the demonstration of empathic concern.

Basic listening skills are also important contributors to intimate experiences. Basic listening skills involve the ability to attend, paraphrase, reflect the other's feelings, and give feedback in a constructive manner. They also involve an ability to hear and retain the message of another person without defensiveness or planning what one will say next. Many people are not aware that how they listen shuts down communication.

An individual's developmental stage can influence his or her experience of intimacy. It can affect the person's preferred mode of meeting intimacy needs, and can affect the emphasis the person places on meeting intimacy needs relative to other important psychological needs. Although empirical evidence is scarce, there is reason to believe that young adults, mid-life adults, and older adults have different intimacy-related concerns and preoccupations, and that intimacy is not an equally salient concern at all stages of adulthood. Because the markers of development do not closely correspond to specific ages in adulthood, it is sometimes easy to forget that adults, like children, will have different vulnerabilities and strengths to bring to their intimate relationships at each stage of their lives (see Prager, 1995, for a review).

Young adulthood, more than any other stage in life, seems to be a time when people are preoccupied with intimacy: with finding a partner and sharing intimate contact with that partner (Erikson, 1963). Young adulthood (and the early stages of couple relationships) are times of relatively frequent sexual (Kurdek, 1994) and affectionate (Huston, McHale, & Crouter, 1986) contact. Relative to mid-life and older adults, young adults are emotionally expressive and reactive in their communication (Sillars, Weisberg, Burgraf & Zietlow, 1990). The capacity to make a commitment to the person with whom one is emotionally and sexually intimate is a prominent challenge for many young adults (Cantor, Acker, & Cook-Flannagan, 1992). The transition to parenthood, an event that is likely to occur during young adulthood, challenges young adults to shift their most prominent preoccupation from their own life as a couple to being good parents and raising a healthy child. This shift in focus exceeds the developmental readiness of many young parents and under the best of circumstances can contribute to difficulties with intimacy.

The birth of children aggravates what appears to be an extremely common decline in satisfaction and intimacy over time in couple relationships (Harriman, 1983; Ryder, 1973). A decline in relationship intimacy may not create a crisis for the couple, however. Adults who are in what Erikson (1963) called the "generativity stage" do not seem to be especially preoccupied with intimacy although they are often aware that their intimacy needs are not being fully satisfied. They may accept unfulfilled intimacy needs with relative composure because of the greater importance that they are placing on making a difference in the larger world, either through parenting, mentoring, volunteerism, or creative activity (Whitbourne, 1986).

Older adults may experience a renewed interest and enjoyment in intimate contact, particularly once their children are launched and their responsibilities at work are reduced. Many older adults are able to maintain frequent (i.e., weekly) sexual contact (Kaplan, 1990) and share a high degree of enjoyable companionship (Condie, 1989). Sillars et al. (1990) found that older adults were less emotionally expressive and seemed to put less of a premium on intimate talk than their younger counterparts. Whether this is a cohort effect or will repeat itself as young cohorts reach their later years has yet to be determined.

Gendered orientations or styles, at the personal level, have been proposed as explanations for the sex differences that are found at the situational level in intimate behavior and motivations. Masculine and feminine social styles refer to a combination of innate and learned traits that encompass the kinds of interpersonal goals and values a person holds and the skills that she or he cultivates in order to meet those goals. Psychological masculinity, from this perspective, is an approach to interaction that values assertiveness and competitiveness and the promotion of the self, while psychological femininity is an approach to interaction that values cooperation and downplays the self in the interest of fostering relationship (e.g., see Maccoby, 1990).

Extensive literature has attempted to relate couple functioning to the presence or absence of feminine and masculine sex-typed personality traits in the partners. In some studies, both women and men who describe their partners as androgynous, or as possessing both feminine and masculine sex-typed traits, rate their relationships as more satisfying (Gano-Phillips, 1996; Siavela & Lamke, 1992). Other studies, however, show that feminine characteristics alone seem to be sufficient for sustaining a satisfying relationship (e.g., Antill, 1983; Bradbury, Campbell, & Fincham, 1995). Husbands' masculine sex-typed characteristics may affect wives' changes in satisfaction over time, with desirable masculine sex-typed characteristics predicting positive changes and negative masculine characteristics predicting negative changes in satisfaction (Bradbury, et al., 1995).

Gendered personality traits may shape people's goals for interactions which, in turn, may explain gendered patterns of self-disclosure. Research by Prager, Fuller, and Gonzalez (1989) found that people's purposes for self-disclosing varied systematically by sex, and that those purposes accounted, in part, for the level of personal facts and expressed emotion in self-disclosure. Women more than men may expect their intimate interactions with their partners to contribute to the fulfillment of a wide variety of needs (Prager & Buhrmester, in press). While men's expectations for fulfillment seem to be restricted to those gratifications traditionally associated with intimacy—needs for nurturance, love and affection, sexual gratification, and acceptance—women's expectations seem to extend to other needs as well. In our study, women, more than men, expected their intimate interactions with their partners to bolster confidence in their ability to pursue achievement goals successfully.

A third personal-context variable that may help explain gender differences in intimate behavior are mean differences in women's and men's intimacy preferences. There is evidence, for example, that women may have stricter and narrower standards than men for what constitutes intimate interaction. Women and girls make clearer distinctions between intimate and nonintimate friendships (Prager, 1995). For women, a friend who is not a confidante is not an intimate friend, although she may be a sparkling companion with whom to share common interests. In contrast, men are more likely to claim that people with whom they share interests and activities are as intimate to them as are those with whom they can exchange confidences. Further, men see shared activities as opportunities for intimacy in a way that women typically do not. For women, if there is not face-to-face disclosing interaction, then little in the way of intimacy has occurred.

Similarly, women and men may, on average, stress different kinds of intimate experiences. Men are more likely to favor sexual intimacy over verbal intimacy while women are more likely to favor verbal intimacy (Engel & Saracino, 1986). Perhaps as a result, women initiate verbal intimacy contact more frequently than their male partners while men more frequently initiate sexual contact (Blumstein & Schwartz, 1983; Markman & Kraft, 1989). Women may weigh the quality of intimate contact in a relationship more heavily when deciding whether to commit to it and whether they are satisfied with it (Caldwell & Peplau, 1982). Women and men do not seem to define intimacy differently, however. Both see self-disclosure to an attentive listener as the sina qua non of intimacy (Monsour, 1992).

THE RELATIONAL CONTEXT

The relational context includes characteristics of the relationship, whether result from the partners' histories or from the couple's unique set of interaction norms. Intimacy's relational context affects whether and how often partners will seek out and enjoy intimate contact with one another.

Perhaps nothing impinges more upon couple intimacy than the partners' definition of the relationship itself. Partners may disagree about what kind of relationship they have, and they may express different levels of commitment to its quality and its continuance. If partners do not agree on whether their relationship is headed toward marriage or other long-term commitment, intimate contact can become increasingly strained as one or both begin to protect themselves from increasing vulnerability to their partner.

Once partners agree that they are invested in their relationship, frequent intimate contact between them can foster trust, positive sentiment, and companionship. While there is little research on the long-term consequences of intimate relating for relationships, it is reasonable to presume that ongoing intimate experiences give people reason to trust one another. Through shared experiences of intimacy, partners learn that they can reveal personal, private, and vulnerable aspects of themselves without the other person intentionally using their confidences for hurtful or harmful purposes. Further, because intimate experiences are positive, (i.e., encompass positive feelings about oneself and the other), the repetition of such feelings over time should engender persistent feelings of warmth, caring and love toward the other person. This kind of overriding positive sentiment towards the partner may allow couples to maintain their good will in the face of conflict or other frustrating interactions. Finally, it is likely that people who enjoy intimate relating will seek each other out for companionship. Sharing enjoyable, companionable time together creates opportunities for intimate moments even as it builds upon the positive sentiment that previous intimate encounters have created. Trust, positive sentiment, and companionship, then, are the byproducts of intimate relating that simultaneously foster and enhance couple intimacy.

   The preservation of intimacy between relationship partners depends on
these same qualities not being eroded by other relationship processes. Dysfunctional conflict and problem-solving processes are particularly likely to
erode the positive characteristics of relationships and reduce intimate contact.
Other kinds of incompatibilities, even in the absence of dysfunctional conflict,
may also affect intimacy. For example, sometimes it happens that people with
widely diverging interests and leisure pursuits form relationships only to find
that they have little in common and do not enjoy much companionship. These
couples may find it difficult to make time for intimate experiences because of
the amount of separateness in their relationship (Dickson, 1995).
   Intimacy itself can be a potent source of conflict. Since one of the main
rewards people seek in their relationships is intimate contact, people can be
disappointed to find that incompatibilities between themselves and their partners frustrate their efforts to fulfill their needs. Since all relationship partners
will have different intimacy needs to some extent, it is important to understand
how differences can become major battle grounds that contribute to relationship dysfunction and distress. Intimacy-related distress has two sources: first,
partner incompatibility (i.e., problems stemming from intimacy's individual
context), and second, dysfunctional intimacy regulation processes (i.e., the
couple is unable to move together and apart without disrupting their bond).
   The compatibility of partners' intimacy needs and styles likely contributes to
relationship satisfaction and to the amount of effort the pair must exert to
make the relationship a gratifying one for both. Partners can come into a
relationship with different tastes relative to the amount, intensity, and type of
intimate contact they prefer. Further, different kinds of intimate contact (e.g.,
verbal intimacy, sexual contact) can be laden with meaning for one or both
partners ("If she rejects my sexual initiatives, she is rejecting me totally." "If
he won't share his feelings with me, then I can never really know him.").
Intimacy incompatibilities can thereby generate intense emotions and cause
partners to expend considerable effort just to fulfill their needs. Possibly, the
harder the couple has to work to reconcile their incompatibilities, the more
vulnerable they are to developing intimacy-related dysfunctional problem-
solving styles. The paradox of dysfunctional interaction patterns is that the
couple's efforts to resolve their difficulties actually cause them to polarize
further (see Prager, 1998, Chap. 8 this volume, for a more detailed discussion
of dysfunctional intimacy-related conflict).
   Gender, at the relational level, refers to gendered patterns of interaction, in
which partners (whether lesbian, heterosexual or gay) can occupy positions and
take on responsibilities that correspond to stereotypic husband and wife roles.
For example, the traditional wife role involves paying close attention to the
quality of life in the home and to the family's emotional well-being. In the
process of fulfilling her role, a wife may find herself seeking more closeness
from her husband than he desires for himself. Research by Heavy, Layne, &
Christensen (1993) indicates that wives are more likely to be in the role of

pursuing intimate contact while husbands are more likely to be in the role of resisting demands for intimacy. This gender-related pattern is predictive of relationship distress and may both reflect and exacerbate the couple's difficulties with intimacy.

The gendered division of labor associated with traditional marriage is also an aspect of the gendered relational context. There is evidence that as long as the division of labor is satisfactory to the partners involved, it makes little difference how traditional that division is. However, once children are born, many couples fall into a gendered division of labor that is contrary to the wife's wishes (Belsky, Lang, & Rovine, 1985). When this occurs, it has a negative effect on the wife's marital satisfaction, although its effects on the husband are less clear.

THE GROUP CONTEXT

The group context refers to the couple's social network: extended family, friendships, religious communities, children's schools, neighborhoods, and workplaces. The social network can have direct or indirect effects on the couple's relationship as a whole and on their intimate relating in particular.

Social networks can enhance couple intimacy when they provide social support. Researchers (e.g., Cutrona, Suhr, & MacFarlane, 1990) have identified several types of social support. Instrumental support provides the couple with concrete assistance with problems, and may come in the form of babysitting networks, help with household chores when one or both partners is ill, or carpooling of children to school. Exchanges of instrumental support between the partners and the other people in their network can contribute to a sense of belonging, which is another important type of social support. A third kind of support is advice and guidance or informational support, which provides the partners with suggestions about how to manage the challenges of their lives including the relationship itself. Advice may contribute to the relationship's functioning, or it may interfere if advice comes from friends or family members who themselves are troubled and convey their despair and hopelessness about relationships to the partner in need of support.

A fourth type of support is emotional support, which refers to conversation that is usually intimate and has as its purpose comfort, consolation, and analysis of a person's feelings about a problem. It refers to active listening, expressions of affection, and positive feedback (e.g., "I'm proud of you."). Emotional support from others may help the couple by taking some of the pressure off of the partners to fulfill each other's every intimacy need.

In my own observations of distressed couples, I am struck by how many of the couples are socially isolated, with neither partner having close friends who might meet some of their needs for intimacy and companionship. Because North Americans commonly devote what time and energy they have for relationships to their immediate family members, other relationships may suffer.

Also problematic for the couple relationship are friendships or extended family that interfere with the couple relationship. Parents who disapprove of and criticize their son's or daughter's choice of partner can undermine the joy their offspring derives from the relationship. In addition, some friendships are threatening to the couple relationship. A coupled partner who wants to maintain "drinking buddies" whose shared interest was always to forge romantic liaisons through parties and bar-hopping may feel pressured to maintain the old single role when in their company—a stance likely to be unnerving for the other partner. Friendships with old girlfriends or boyfriends may also undermine the relationship in this way if they require that the individual not be coupled in order to continue their relationship as they had before.

THE SOCIOCULTURAL CONTEXT

The sociocultural context refers to norms and ideals that are implicitly and explicitly agreed upon by large numbers of people within a particular cultural group or subgroup. Norms affect daily intimate relating because they implicitly serve as maps that guide couples' expectations and hopes for their relationship.

Norms governing intimate interaction within American subgroups may either support or undermine couple intimacy. A norm that has permeated many different sectors of American society is the one that places high value on intimacy in couple relationships. Many young Americans expect to marry their best friends and to be able to confide in their spouses. They expect to enjoy their spouses' company, to find them pleasant and entertaining companions. Not so long ago, spouses were expected to fulfill traditional gender-typed roles; other kinds of intimacy or companionship were bonuses but were not necessarily the foundation of the relationship.

Which sociocultural norms most affect a couple's relationship may vary as a function of the couple's cohort. A cohort refers to a group of people who were all born at the same time within a given culture. Cohorts live through the same historical events at the same age. Thus, the cohort now celebrating 40th and 50th anniversaries lived through the Great Depression when they were first getting married, were often separated during their early married years because of World War II, and may believe that they should be satisfied with less intimacy and companionship than would younger cohorts, who grew up during a time of economic growth and plenty (Dickson, 1995).

Subgroup norms may affect the preferred form of intimate expression for a given couple. Groups who trace their lineages to Mediterranean cultures or to

Eastern Europe may be more comfortable with boisterous expressions of emotion than those who hail from Anglicized countries such as Canada, England, or Australia. People with Far Eastern ancestry are also likely to value restrained expressions of emotion, and may consider it rude or unseemly to allow their emotions to show in their faces. African Americans value openness and expressiveness while New Englanders may treasure tact and restraint (Thiederman, 1991).

Cultural characterizations cover a wide range of variation among the individuals who compose these subcultures. Individual values will vary as a function of acculturation: the longer a person's ancestors have resided in the United States, the more likely it is that their values will resemble those of most Americans. Subcultural communication norms may profoundly affect the kind of intimacy that the partners wish to experience within their relationships.

INTERACTIONS AMONG CONTEXTS

Sometimes contextual factors interact so that the presence of one contextual factor moderates the influence of another; that is, one context determines whether another will exert any influence, or how much influence it will exert (Baron & Kenny, 1986). It is also possible for one contextual factor to mediate the effects of another, in which it affects intimacy indirectly, through its effects on a second contextual factor that directly affects intimacy (Baron & Kenny, 1986). This section will explore some examples of moderating and mediating effects among contextual factors that affect couple intimacy.

Gender exemplifies the moderating and mediating effects of contextual factors on one another. Gender is meaningfully conceptualized as a variable operating at each contextual level, and its influence on intimacy depends on the presence, absence, or intensity of other contextual factors (Prager, 1995). Interactions between gender and other contextual factors determine whether partners will engage in intimate contact, how they will experience intimate contact, and how intimate contact will shape their relationship. Gender is a complicated set of forces that is as likely to modify the effects of other variables as it is to exert direct effects itself.

The first example of interacting contextual factors involves the partners' definition of their relationship (in the relational context) and gender (i.e., sex-category, in the immediate context). The partners' definition of the relationship interacts with sex so that sex differences in self-disclosure intimacy are only visible when partners are in a nonromantic relationship. Within nonromantic relationships (i.e., relationships between acquaintances or friends), one can make rough predictions about how intimately two people will talk to one another based on whether the pair consist of two women, two men, or a man and a woman. Outside of the context of a romantic relationship, both women and men tend to bring up more personal, private topics and to elaborate on them more fully when they are in conversation with a woman (Tscann, 1988). However, when the partners are in a couple (or romantic) relationship, the impact of partner sex is reduced, often to the point where it no longer seems to exert an effect on intimate talk or its importance to relationship functioning. Men report that their female romantic partners are their most intimate confidantes while women report that they disclose as much to their male relationship partners as to their close female friends (e.g., Rubin, 1983). In other words, within couple relationships, sex differences in self-disclosure intimacy are minimized.

The second example involves sex-typed personality traits and psychological androgyny (in the personal context) moderating the effects of sex-category on intimate disclosure. Research has shown that sex differences in self-disclosure can be accounted for, in part, by the sex-typed personality traits of the people involved (e.g., Siavela & Lamke, 1992). Androgynous and feminine sex-typed individuals tend to disclose more intimately to others, regardless of their sex-category (e.g., Antill, 1983; Sayers & Baucom, 1991). Thus, when women and men have similar personality traits, they are likely to engage in similar intimate behaviors.

The next set of examples shows how sociocultural gender norms may account for the effects of other gender-related contextual factors on intimacy. In U.S. society, behaviors that are considered desirable for men are agentic (Bakan, 1966). Agency refers to values and behaviors that encourage nurturance and enhancement of self, including the unencumbered pursuit of personal achievement goals, self-development, enlightened self-interest, recognition and notoriety, and the protection of personal rights and liberties. In contrast, behaviors that are considered most desirable for women are communal. Communion refers to values and behaviors that involve one in cooperative contact with others, that elevate the good of the community over the good of the self, and include self-sacrifice, nurturance, a willingness to help, and generosity. These cultural norms for desirable feminine and masculine behavior may foster the development of sex-typed personality traits. Sex-typed personality traits are known to be distributed disproportionately between women and men (so that women incorporate more feminine-typed traits and men incorporate more masculine-typed traits) (Spence & Helmreich, 1978). This distribution of traits may ensue when people strive to conform to sociocultural norms of ideal behavior for their sex. Sociocultural norms may thereby affect individual personality and self-concept which in turn affect intimate behavior and experience. Their impact on gendered intimacy behavior is therefore indirect.

The next example will demonstrate how gendered personality characteristics (i.e., gender schematicity) moderate the relationship between gendered sociocultural norms (i.e., associations between "masculinity" and self-reliance, and between "femininity" and needs for intimacy) and intimate relational processes. First, I will describe how a self-fulfilling prophecy process (in the relational context) may account for the frequency of norm-consistent gendered behavior in couple relationships. Next, I will describe how gender schematicity can determine what kinds of self-fulfilling prophecy processes a person will seek to incorporate into his or her relationship. Finally, I will describe how gender schematicity moderates the effects of gendered sociocultural norms on couple intimacy by determining mate choice.

Social psychologists have described a self-fulfilling prophecy process by which sociocultural gender norms become incorporated into the self as gender-typed personality traits (e.g., Geis, 1993). According to these theorists, a self-fulfilling prophecy process occurs when Person A's expectations about Person B's personality are conveyed to Person A and Person A, being influenced by the communication of those expectations, behaves just as Person B expected him or her to behave. This theory is based on the assumption that people's expectations are signaled to others via subtle yet powerful nonverbal and verbal cues during our day-to-day interactions with them. Reflected on the faces of their interaction partners, then, people see and are largely able to read the signs of pleasure, surprise, consternation, warmth, or irritation that they elicit as they interact. These signalled expectations affect behavior most when people are interacting with someone who is important to them. Under these conditions, the reactions of the other serve as powerful reinforcers (or punishers) of social behavior, increasing the likelihood that each will repeat (or not) their previous behavior. Self-fulfilling prophecy processes are known to provide reinforcement for behavior that is consistent with sociocultural gender norms (Geis, 1993).

People do not only react to others' signals, but actively seek out situations and people with whom they can be assured of reinforcement for behaviors they desire to perform. People who wish to conform to traditional sociocultural norms for their gender will therefore seek out people whose behavior tends to elicit and reinforce their own sex-typed behavior (e.g., a woman who behaves as though she were helpless is likely to elicit resourceful problem-solving behaviors from her partner). By choosing such a relationship partner, a person whose self-concept encompasses traditional sociocultural definitions of gender ensures, consciously or not, that she or he will not have to face challenges to that self-concept within the couple relationship.

Self-fulfilling prophecy processes, and people's efforts to choose relationship partners who reinforce their most cherished self-concepts, may explain the persistence and frequency of some common gender-related relational conflicts about intimacy. In the pursuer-distancer pattern, one partner, the pursuer, tries to engage a withdrawn or distant partner in intimate contact while the other, the distancer, withdraws in order to avoid feeling overwhelmed by the first partner's demands (Napier, 1978). The gendered nature of this pattern may reflect sociocultural norms that privilege communal behavior for women and denigrate it for men. Because of these sociocultural norms, many women may feel more "feminine" or "womanly" when they are pursuing intimate contact while men may similarly feel more "masculine" or "manly" when resisting or minimizing their need for intimate contact. As a result, despite how painful the pursuer-distancer pattern is, and despite its destructive impact on intimacy, couple therapists may see more intimacy-hungry women and distancing men than they would expect to see by chance alone because the secondary gain of this pattern is the reinforcement of behaviors that enhance sex-role identity.

As if the combined influence of the sociocultural, personal, and relational contexts were not complex enough in this example, it is likely that another person-level variable has a significant moderating effect on this pattern. An individual's gender schematicity may mitigate the reward value of a sex-typed gender identity. Gender schematicity describes variations in the extent to which "gender becomes a basic identifying feature of the self... [and] is chronically used in thinking about and describing and evaluating the self" (Cross & Markus, 1993, p. 76). For gender-schematic individuals, gender is an intensely salient aspect of the self-concept.

Perhaps gender-schematic people are more likely to seek out mates whose behavior reinforces their gender-typed behavior. Gender-schematic individuals should feel most attracted to and most comfortable interacting with people whose typical behavior elicits and reinforces their gender-typed behavior. The following example will illustrate this process:

> Carolyn complains that her husband George is uncommunicative, distant, and inexpressive of his affection for her. She complains that he spends most of his free time taking care of their finances, repairing things around the house, and tending to the yard. While she appreciates his efforts in these areas, she perceives that spending time with her is at the bottom of his list of priorities, and she yearns for more intimate contact with George. Yet, the more she tries to engage him in intimate activity—whether talking, sex, affection, or shared leisure activities—the more withdrawn and inexpressive he becomes. She feels lonely, yet acknowledges that he feels pressured and unappreciated. However, when asked why she chose George over another young man she was dating at the time, she answers, "George seemed so independent. With George, I never had to worry about spending time with my girlfriends or with other pursuits that didn't involve him because he was happy being alone. He never put pressure or demands on me. His independence made him seem secure and self-confident. The other man I was dating didn't seem as independent as George. Although he was more affectionate and expressive, I worried about how much he needed me. I didn't want to have to be the 'strong one' in the relationship."

Carolyn's attraction to George, despite the less-than-ideal relationship she was bound to have with him, may be accounted for in part by her high gender schematicity. Because Carolyn desires to maintain a normatively feminine self-concept, she is unlikely to stick with potential partners who fail to reinforce her view of herself as a traditional woman who is loving, open, affectionate and expressive of her feelings. Choosing a mate who seems to prefer less intimate contact than she does is the "best" way Carolyn has to continuously confirm this gender-typed self-concept. In a relationship with that mate, the role of initiating and pursuing intimate contact would fall to Carolyn because she prefers more intimate contact than her mate does. Each time Carolyn seeks intimate contact with George, she witnesses herself behaving according to the feminine-sex-typed traits she hopes characterize her (Guisinger & Blatt, 1994). If she were to become involved with a partner whose needs for intimacy were greater than hers, she would have to engage in limit-setting to avoid feeling overwhelmed by her partner's demands. This behavior might force her to revise her concept of herself as open, loving and giving.

This discussion of gender has demonstrated the multileveled nature of gender as a contextual factor and how its influence on intimacy in relationships is modified by the presence of other contextual factors. At the sociocultural level, norms for gendered behavior provide a blueprint for ideal selves and relationships. However, the impact of these sociocultural norms on selves and relationships is moderated by personal-level variables, particularly the individual's gender schematicity. Further, intimacy-related relationship processes (e.g., the pursuer-distancer pattern), are themselves more likely to emerge in the presence of certain sociocultural norms and individual personality characteristics. The likelihood that partners will engage in mutually satisfying intimate contact and the salience of that intimate contact for each partner within the relationship is a function of these multiple, interacting contextual variables impinging on the partners and their relationship.

CONCLUSIONS

This chapter has mapped out the multilayered context within which intimacy must be sustained or wither away. The multiple layers of context, in the current formulation, are: (1) the immediate context, the immediate time-and-space environment in which intimate interactions take place; (2) the personal context, the personality characteristics of the individuals involved; (3) the relational context, the nature of the partners' relationship, including the other kinds of interactions that the couple engages in day to day; (4) the group context, the other important relationships that make up the couple's extended network of friends, family, colleagues, and children; and (5) the sociocultural context, the norms for intimate relating, gender, family, and marriage that shape partners' expectations and ideals about relationships. Each of these contexts shapes, and is shaped by, the couple's intimate encounters. In addition to their direct effects on intimate relating, contextual factors also exert an indirect influence through their impact on each other.

Once we map the contextual factors that enhance or impede intimate contact, our perspective on relationships is broadened and our flexibility to intervene effectively as clinicians is increased. A contextual perspective may help therapist and client alike see clearly that no behavior is always effective and that certain contextual factors will render any behavior ineffective. Each contextual level offers opportunities for intervention, although the kind of intervention relevant to each differs. When problems with the immediate context inhibit couples' enjoyment of intimacy or limit their opportunities for intimate contact, the therapist can be helpful in bringing these factors to the couples' attention and, if necessary, engaging with them in a rational problem-solving process regarding how to reduce the negative impact of these factors. When couples realize they can make a difference in their relationship by changing apparently simple situational factors (such as the time of day when they set time aside for each other), they may feel more optimistic about taking on more challenging behavior changes to repair other aspects of their relationship.

One couple for example, complained that they were experiencing sexual inhibitions like never before, and rarely engaged in sexual activity. Careful probing by their therapist revealed that their bed backed up to a wall that separated their bedroom from their adolescent twin daughters' bedroom! Every time they made love, the bed made the wall vibrate noisily. Although the couple protested because they did not think that this problem "should" affect their sexual activity, a rearrangement of the family's home made a dramatic improvement in this couple's sexual intimacy.

When individual partner's personality characteristics inhibit intimate relating, the therapist has several alternatives. The first is to encourage the partners to accept their differences (i.e., to cease efforts to mold one another) and, through acceptance, help the couple find ways to meet both partners' needs for intimacy and separateness. As mentioned earlier, it is common for one partner in a couple to desire more intimate contact and to feel lonely more readily than the other. The therapist can help these couples accept their differences by pointing out what a remarkable coincidence it would be if they both had exactly the same preferences. This intervention often has the advantage of depersonalizing the dilemma: the less desirous partner is thereby not seen as personally rejecting the other, and the more desirous partner is not seen as insatiable or as a perpetual malcontent. The depersonalizing of the dilemma reduces the intensity of partners' emotional responses to it and opens the door for a rational problem-solving process.

The second alternative is to encourage behavior change in one or both partners. For example, we know that public self-monitors may disclose early in a relationship but may lose interest in disclosure once the relationship is established. Moreover, publicly self-monitoring partners may be mystified by their partner's distress with their lack of openness, because they are not intentionally withholding. Rather, the situation requiring their self-monitoring is long past and the reasons for self-disclosure have changed. Since the publicly self-monitoring individual has intimate communication skills, she or he might be motivated to use those skills more frequently once she or he understands their continued importance to the relationship.

The third alternative is individual therapy for one or both partners. Some personal-level factors may be resistant to intervention within conjoint couple therapy, such as deep-seated fears of intimacy and accompanying avoidance behaviors (see Prager, 1998, Chap. 8 this volume). Individual therapy may help individual partners reduce their intimacy-related anxiety through desensitization, cognitive restructuring, and role-play practice of new behaviors.

Therapists working with couples' intimacy dilemmas are likely to encounter couples who have other relational-level problems as well. My experience suggests that couples who lack intimacy are often inhibited about openly expressing their views in other situations. Problems with intimacy are often accompanied by fears of conflict and emotional intensity. In their efforts to avoid fighting—hurting or angering one another—some couples suppress the free-flowing expression of self that is part of what fuels intimacy. Therapists may therefore wish to supplement work on intimacy-related communication with work on other kinds of communication processes.

Group-context complaints among couples seeking therapy are common. Opposite-sex friendships that arouse suspicion for heterosexual relationship partners, extended family members and in-laws who seem rejecting or difficult to get along with, workplaces that demand too many hours and too much devotion from their employees: any of these can cause problems for couples. Couples are often quite aware of the detrimental effects of these group-level factors on their intimate contact with one another. On the one hand, partners risk alienating each other when they argue about the behavior of people or institutions toward which their partners feel a strong sense of loyalty or affection. On the other hand, anger and suspicion can be justified since other people and institutions sometimes intend to drive a wedge between the partners. Problems with the network may disguise or symbolize other problems in the couples' relationship, and occasionally these problems involve intimacy.

Finally, sociocultural norms exert profound effects on couple intimacy, but are often outside of the couple's awareness. Sociocultural norms are pervasive in their effects, but invisible unless pointed out, held up for scrutiny, or otherwise challenged. Therapists can provide significant assistance simply by making these pressures and expectations explicit and helping partners to understand whether, when, and how they came to adopt these norms as their own. Through this process partners can question the value of conformity to norms when that conformity does not fulfill their needs or enhance their relationship. Since gender-related norms are especially salient, particularly in the realm of intimate contact, it is important that the therapist expose clients to the full range of their effects. Therapists who equate sex category (male vs. female) with certain traits, preferences, role responsibilities, and other "es-

sences," as though sex-category were inevitably linked to them may unneces-
sarily restrict a couple's range of choices. Even more important, therapists
should avoid prescribing socioculturally normative behavior simply because it
is normative, and rather should encourage couples, to the extent that they are
able, to accept and appreciate one another as individuals.

An awareness of the multiple, interacting contexts that shape couples'
experiences with intimacy provides therapists with a broadened repertoire of
interventions for helping couples to maintain the kind of intimate contact they
desire. Intimacy provides many benefits to individuals and their relationships
but can break down in the face of the many contextual factors that intrude
upon it. By helping couples to become aware of and to manage these interferences and to maintain intimate contact as frequently they desire, therapists
provide the couples they work with a valuable service.

REFERENCES

Adams, R. G. & Blieszner, R. (1994). An integrative conceptual framework for friendship research. *Journal of Social and Personal Relationships, 11,* 163–184.

Antill, J. K. (1983). Sex-role complementarity versus similarity in married couples. *Journal of Personality and Social Psychology, 45,* 145–155.

Archer, R. L. (1979). Role of personality and the social situation. In G. J. Chelune (Ed.), *Self-Disclosure: Origins, Patterns, and Implicatons of Openness in Interpersonal Relationships* (pp. 28–58). San Francisco: Jossey-Bass.

Bakan, D. (1966). *The Duality of Human Existence.* Chicago: Rand McNally.

Baron, R. M. & Kenny, D. A. (1986). The moderator-mediator variable distinction in social psychological research: Conceptual, strategic and statistical considerations. *Journal of Personality and Social Psychology, 51,* 1173–1182.

Belsky, J., Lang, M. E. & Rovine, M. (1985). Stability and change in marriage across the transition to parenthood: A second study. *Journal of Marriage and the Family, 47,* 855–865.

Blumstein, P. & Schwartz, P. (1983). *American Couples: Money, Work, Sex.* New York: Morrow.

Bradbury, T. N., Campbell, S. M. & Fincham, F. D. (1995). Longitudinal and behavioral analysis of masculinity and femininity in marriage. *Journal of Personality and Social Psychology, 68,* 328–341.

Caldwell, M. A. & Peplau, L. A. (1982). Sex differences in same-sex friendship. *Sex Roles, 8,* 721–732.

Cantor, N., Acker, M. & Cook-Flannagan, C. (1992). Conflict and preoccupation in the intimacy life task. *Journal of Personality and Social Psychology, 63,* 644–655.

Condie, S. J. (1989). Older married couples. In S. J. Bahr & E. T. Peterson (Eds.), *Aging and the Family* (pp. 143–158). Lexington, MA: Heath.

Cozby, P. C. (1973). Self-disclosure: A literature review. *Psychological Bulletin, 79,* 73–91.

Craig, J. A., Koestner, R. & Zuroff, D.C. (1994). Implicit and self-attributed intimacy motivation. *Journal of Social and Personal Relationships, 11,* 491–507.

Cramer, D. (1990). Disclosure of personal problems, self-esteem, and the facilitativeness of friends and lovers. *British Journal of Guidance and Counseling, 18,* 186–196.

Cross, S. E. & Markus, H. R. (1993). Gender in thought, belief, and action: A social-cognitive approach. In A. E. Beall & R. J. Sternberg (Eds.), *The Psychology of Gender* (pp. 55–98). New York: Guilford.

Cutrona, C. E., Suhr, J. A., MacFarlane, R. (1990). Interpersonal transactions and the psychological sense of support. In S. Duck (Ed.), *Personal Relationships and Social Support* (pp. 30–45). London: Sage.

Davis, M. H. & Franzoi, S. L. (1987). Private self-consciousness and self-disclosure. In V. J. Derlega & J. H. Berg (Eds.), *Self-disclosure: Theory, Research and Therapy* (pp. 59–79). New York: Plenum.

Derlega, V. J. & Grzelak, J. (1979). Appropriateness of self-disclosure. In G. J. Chelune (Eds.), *Self-disclosure: Origins, patterns, and implications of openess in interpersonal relationships* (pp. 151–176). San Francisco: Jossey-Bass.

Dickson, F. (1995). The best is yet to be: Research on long-lasting marriages. In S. Duck (Ed.), *Understudied Relationships* (pp. 22–50). Thousand Oaks, CA: Sage.

Dindia, K. & Allan, M. (1992). Sex differences in self-disclosure: A meta analysis. *Psychological Bulletin, 112*, 106–124.

Eisenberg, N., Murphy, B. C. & Shepard, S. (1997). The development of empathic accuracy. In W. Ices (Ed.), *Empathic Acuracy* (pp. 73–116). New York: Guilford.

Engel, J. W. & Saracino, M. (1986). Love preferences and ideals: A comparison of homosexual, bisexual, and heterosexual groups. *Contemporary Family Therapy, 8*, 775–780.

Erikson, E. H. (1963). *Childhood and Society.* New York: Norton.

Franken, R. E., Gibson, K. J. & Mohan, P. (1990). Sensation-seeking and disclosure to close and casual friends. *Personality and Individual Differences, 11*, 829–832.

Fromm, E. (1956). *The Art of Loving.* New York: Harper & Row.

Gano-Phillips, S. (November, 1996). *His and her marriages: Sex role ideals, skills, and behaviors.* Paper presented at the annual meeting, Association for the Advancement of Behavior Therapy, New York, NY.

Geis, F. L. (1993). Self-fulfilling prophecies: A social-psychological view of gender. In A. E. Beall & R. J. Sternberg (Eds.), *The Psychology of Gender* (pp. 9–54). New York: Guilford.

Guisinger, S. & Blatt, S. J. (1994). Individuality and relatedness: Evolution of a fundamental dialectic. *American Psychologist, 49*, 104–111.

Harriman, L. C. (1983). Personal and marital changes accompanying parenthood. *Family Relations, 32*, 387–394.

Heavy, C. L., Layne, C. & Christensen, A. (1993). Gender and conflict structure in marital interaction: A replication and extension. *Journal of Consulting and Clinical Psychology, 61*, 16–27.

Hoen-Hyde, D., Schlottmann, R. S. & Rush, A. J. (1982). Perception of social interactions in depressed psychiatric patients. *Journal of Consulting and Clinical Psychology, 50*, 209–212.

Huston, T. L., McHale, S. M., & Crouter, A. C. (1986). When the honeymoon's over: Changes in the marriage relationship over the first year. In R. Gilmour & S. Duck (Eds.), *The Emerging Field of Personal Relationships* (pp. 53–90). New York: Academic Press.

Jourard, S. M. (1971). *The Transparent Self.* New York: Van Nostrand.

Kaplan, H. S. (1990). Sex, intimacy, and the aging process. *Journal of the American Academy of Psychoanalysis, 18*, 185–205.

Kent, J. H. K. (1975). Relation of personality, expectancy, and situational variables to self-disclosing behavior. *Journal of Consulting and Clinical Psychology, 43*, 120–121.

Kohut, H. (1980). *Advances in Self Psychology.* New York: International Universities Press.

Kowalik, D. L. & Gotlib, I. H. (1987). Depression and marital interaction: Concordance between intent and perception of communication. *Journal of Abnormal Psychology, 96*, 127–134.

Kurdek, L. A. (1994). The nature and correlates of relationship quality in gay, lesbian, and heterosexual cohabiting couples: A test of the individual difference, interdependence, and discrepancy models. In B. Greene & G.M. Herek (Eds.), *Lesbian and Gay Psychology* (pp. 133–155). Thousand Oaks, CA: Sage.

Maccoby, E. E. (1990). Gender and relationships. *American Psychologist, 45*, 513–520.

Markman, H. J. & Kraft, S. A. (1989). Men and women in marriage: Dealing with gender differences in marital therapy. *Behavior Therapist, 12*, 51–56.

McAdams, D. P. (1988). Personal needs and personal relationships. In S. W. Duck (Ed.), *Handbook of Personal Relationships* (pp. 7–22). New York: Wiley.

McAdams, D. P., Healy, S. & Krause, S. (1984). Social motives and patterns of friendship. *Journal of Personality and Social Psychology, 47*, 828–838.

McClelland, D. C. (1985). *Human Motivation.* Glenview, IL: Scott, Foresman.

Mikulincer, M., & Nachshon, O. (1991). Attachment styles and patterns of self-disclosure. *Journal of Personality and Social Psychology, 61*, 321–331.

Monsour, M. (1992). Meanings of intimacy in cross- and same-sex friendships. *Journal of Social and Personal Relationships, 9*, 277–296.

Napier, A. Y. (1978). The rejection-intrustion pattern: A central family dynamic. *Journal of Marital and Family Therapy, 4*, 5–12.

Ojeda, J. & Prager, K. J. (June, 1997). *Intimacy, mutual understanding, and need fulfillment in couple relationships.* Paper presented at the annual meeting, International Network for Personal Relationships, Oxford, Ohio.

Peplau, L. A., Cochran, S., Rook, K., Padesky, C. (1978). Loving women: Attachment and autonomy in lesbian relationships. *Journal of Social Issues, 34*, 7–27.

Prager, K. J. (1986). Intimacy status: Its relationship to locus of control, self-disclosure and anxiety. *Personality and Social Psychology Bulletin, 12*, 91–109.

Prager, K. J. (1995). *The Psychology of Intimacy.* New York: Guilford.

Prager, K. J. (1999). The intimacy dilemma: A guide for couple therapists. In J. Carlson & L. Sperry (Eds.), *The Intimate Couple*, pp. 109–157. Philadelphia: Taylor & Francis.

Prager, K. J. & Buhrmester, D. (in press). Intimacy and need fulfillment in couple relationships. *Journal of Social and Personal Relationships.*

Prager, K. J., Fuller, D. O. & Gonzalez, A. S. (1989). The function of self-disclosure in social interaction. *Journal of Social Behavior and Personality, 4*, 563–580.

Rogers, C. R. (1951). *Client-Centered Therapy.* Boston: Houghton Mifflin.

Rubin, L. (1983). *Intimate Strangers: Men and Women Together.* New York: Harper & Row.

Ryder, R. G. (1973). Longitudinal data relating marriage satisfaction and having a child. *Journal of Marriage and the Family, 35*, 604–606.

Sayers, S. L. & Baucom, D. H. (1991). The role of femininity and masculinity in distressed couples' communication. *Journal of Personality and Social Psychology, 61*, 641–647.

Siavelia, R. L. & Lamke, L. K. (1992). Instrumentalness and expressiveness: Predictors of heterosexual relationship satisfaction. *Sex Roles, 26*, 149–159.

Sillars, A. L., Weisberg, J., Burgraf, C. S. & Zietlow, P. H. (1990). Communication and understanding revisited: Married couples' understanding and recall of conversations. *Communication Research, 17*, 500–522.

Snyder, M. & Simpson, J.A. (1984). Self-monitoring and dating relationships. *Journal of Personality and Social Psychology, 47*, 1281–1291.

Spence, J. T. & Helmreich, R. L. (1978). *Masculinity and Femininity: Their Psychological Dimensions, Correlates, and Antecedents.* Austin, TX: The University of Texas Press.

Thiederman, S. (1991). *Bridging Cultural Barriers for Corporate Success.* New York: Lexington Books.

Todd, J. L. & Shapira, A. (1974). U.S. and British self-disclosure, anxiety, empathy and attitudes to psychotherapy. *Journal of Cross-Cultural Psychology, 5*, 364–369.

Tscann, J. M. (1988). Self-disclosure in adult friendship: Gender and marital status differences. *Journal of Social and Personal Relationships, 5*, 65–81.

Whitbourne, S. K. (1986). *The Me I Know: A Study of Adult Identity.* New York: Springer–Verlag.

CHAPTER 3

Levels and Styles
of Intimacy

Len Sperry, M.D., Ph.D.

Couples therapy textbooks and training programs typically engender the belief that most, if not all, couples have the capacity for intimacy and that one of the purposes of couples therapy is to increase this capacity. Similarly, it is generally assumed that real intimacy precludes sustained discord and disagreement. Ideally, the intimate couple is the couple that has learned to demonstrate care and concern through being available, utilizing reflective listening, particularly "I messages", and quickly resolving disagreements. However, neither the experience of seasoned clinicians nor recent laboratory research on normal and clinical couples confirms these beliefs about the capacity for intimacy (level), and the ideal style of intimate relationships. This chapter will briefly address both dimensions of levels and styles of intimacy. It will review models and research findings on intimate couple behaviors that are relevant for clinical practice.

LEVELS OF INTIMACY

Both clinical observation and research suggest that intimacy is not a skill that most individuals and couples exhibit or possess the capacity to consistently experience. This is not to suggest that intimacy is an all-or-nothing phenomenon, wherein certain individuals can rather consistently experience it, while other individuals never experience it. There is also a group of individuals who are capable of occasionally experiencing it, say in times of crisis such as funerals or following a serious accident. Rather, it appears that there are discrete levels of relational functioning that have been noted in individuals and couples. It is postulated that intimacy can be sustained at higher levels of relational functioning only. Following are descriptions of three different conceptualizations of levels of relational functioning.

The Spiral of Intimacy Model

L'Abate (1986, 1997) has proposed and begun testing a developmental model of interpersonal competence which highlights intimacy and its determinants. He has operationally defined intimacy as the sharing of joys, hurts, and fears of being hurt. This operationalization of intimacy as sharing hurts is a promising development in intimacy research. A self-report instrument called the Sharing of Hurt Scale (Stevens & L'Abate, 1989) is the basis of this line of research. To date the instrument has been validated against the Spanier Dyadic Adjustment Scale, Navran's Primary Communication Inventory, and the Marital Issues Questionnaire (L'Abate, 1997).

L'Abate (1997) relates the ability to love with the attribution of importance and the ability to share joys, hurts, or fears of being hurt. The result is committed, close, and prolonged relationships. According to recent research (Stevens & L'Abate, 1989; Cusinato & L'Abate, 1994) intimacy is not particularly common in relationships. Estimates are that no more than 15 percent of the total committed or married population experience it without a struggle, while only another 25 percent experience it occasionally such as at funerals, marriages, or sickness and accidents. Furthermore, this research indicates that relationships that are unable to share love or attribute importance to one another are likely to become dysfunctional.

Three prerequisites for intimacy are equality, commitment, and reciprocity and mutuality in relationship. From these flow six processes that produce what L'Abate (1997) calls the "spiral of intimacy": communication of personal values, respect for personal feelings, acceptance of personal limitations, affirmation, sharing of hurts and fears of being hurt, and forgiveness of errors. Once love is defined as attributing importance to oneself and to another, intimacy becomes part of the sharing and self-disclosure of both pleasurable and painful experiences. Accordingly, L'Abate (1997) contends that the process of intimacy formation cannot be separated from one's attribution to self and other. The sharing of hurts represents the ability to be separate and together simultaneously. It requires the strength to join another in sharing hurt, while being separate enough to be available to the other without the demand for perfection, solutions or performance. L'Abate (1997) contends that crying together is the ultimate demonstration of sharing hurts. Unconditional love is demonstrated by the ability to be available, which is operationalized as the ability to be available to share hurts or cry together. Because many dysfunctional individuals do not possess sufficient resources to share hurts, they are unable to model this level of sharing with their children and other family members.

In short, L'Abate (1997) proposes a two-level model of intimacy: non-intimacy and intimacy. The intimacy level includes six related sub-levels: communication ⇒ respect ⇒ acceptance ⇒ affirmation ⇒ sharing of hurts ⇒ forgiveness of errors.

Levels of Relational Functioning

Weltner (1992) describes four levels of relational functioning in couples based on clinical observation. For level one, the main issue involves the couple's capacity to provide basic nurturance and protection. Therefore, the basic treatment strategy is to mobilize available outside support to assist the single parent or the strongest member of the family who is facing severe stress or illness, including alcoholism. In level two, issues of authority and limits are prominent for the couple and family. Expectations may be unclear or unmet. The basic strategy is to clarify expectations and power issues by means of such techniques as written contracts, formation of coalitions, and behavioral reinforcements. Level three families and couples are more complicated. They have a structure and a style that appears to be functional, yet issues regarding boundaries are prominent. Resistance to change is another hallmark of this type of family or couple. The basic strategy is to create sufficient inner space for a spouse or specific family member, and to protect that spouse, family member, or subsystem from over involvement. Therapeutic techniques at this level include rebuilding alliances, paradox, and developing generational boundaries. Issues for level four couples and families are usually focused on intimacy and inner conflict. Whereas families and couples at levels one to three are immersed in day-to-day survival issues, level four couples are able to consider self-actualizing concerns. Insight is a basic therapeutic strategy, and techniques include marital and family enrichment, gestalt and experiential marital therapies, or even individual psychodynamically-oriented psychotherapy.

Levels of Relational Discord

Guerin, Fay, Burden, and Kautto (1987) describe couples in terms of four levels of relational discord based on clinical observation. The first level involves couples who demonstrate preclinical or minimal degree of marital conflict. Often this conflict has lasted for less than six months, and most often the couples are newlyweds. These couples readily respond to information focusing on how marriages work and do not work, and are able to apply this information to positively change their relationship for the better. Interventions at this level involve a range of psychoeducational methods to facilitate communication, negotiation and problem solving that foster intimacy.

Level two consists of couples who are experiencing significant marital conflicts lasting for greater than six months. Although their communication patterns remain open and adequate, criticism and projection have increased. When the therapist dissects the conflictual marital process, however, both spouses can generally move to a self-focus within six to eight sessions. Then the intensity of the conflict can be substantially reduced. Therapy in level two provides a structure for the couple which lowers emotional arousal and anxiety and helps the spouses reestablish self-focus.

Level three couples present with severe marital conflict. Often this conflict is greater than six months duration, and projection is intense. Anxiety and emotional arousal are high, as well as the intensity and polarization of surrounding triangles. Communication is typically closed, conflict is marked, and intimacy is unlikely. The degree of criticism is high and blaming is common. Therapy at this level is primarily focused on controlling the couple's reactivity, their tendency to react to each other emotionally without thinking. Even when a positive result is obtained through therapy, a recycling of conflicts inevitably occurs within the ensuing six to eight months. Guerin et al. (1987) notes that such recycling is a common phenomena at all levels of marital conflict, but particularly at this stage. When this recycling continues to occur, both spouses have probably lost most of their resilience and tend to be unresponsive to further treatment.

Finally, couples at level four are characterized by extremes in all the criteria that Guerin et al. (1987) uses for an evaluation of marital conflict. Communication is closed, information exchange is poor, criticism and blaming are very high, and self disclosure is basically absent in the relationship. Accordingly, intimacy in this relationship is nearly impossible. Relationship time and activity together are either minimal or nonexistent. In the vast majority of cases, attempts to keep the marriage from dissolution appear doomed. The goal becomes the successful disengagement from the relationship. Essentially, mediation is the treatment of choice.

Levels of Marital Stability

Gottman (1993; 1994a; 1994b) has described two levels of marital stability which have been derived from his unique laboratory research program. Based

Table 1   Theories of Intimacy by Levels of Intimacy

	L'Abate	Guerin	Gottman	Weltner
Intimacy	Forgiving errors Sharing hurts Affirmation	Stage 1	Stable marriage	Level 4
	Acceptance Respect Communicate values	Stage 2		
Pre-intimacy	Less dysfunctional couple	Stage 3		Level 3
			Unstable marriage	Level 2
	More dysfunctional couple	Stage 4		Level 1

on what he calls a behavioral exchange–balance theory of marriage, Gottman posits that there are essentially two types of marriage with regard to the exchange of intimacy-related behaviors: stable and unstable. Stable marriages have one of three relational styles—which are described in the subsequent section—but the relationship is likely to continue. On the other hand, unstable marriages have one of two relational styles and are predictive of marital dissolution (i.e., separation or divorce). By definition, couples in stable marriages are more likely to exhibit and experience intimacy than couples in unstable marriages.

Table 1 compares these four models specifying differing levels of intimacy.

STYLES OF INTIMACY

Gottman (1993; 1994b) has carefully studied over 2,000 couples and concludes that a lasting and satisfying intimate relationship depends primarily on the couple's ability to resolve the conflicts that are inevitable in any relationship. His research on couples systems reveals five different styles of conflict resolution or problem solving. They are: Validating, Volatile, Conflict-Avoiding, Hostile, and Hostile-Detached. These styles articulate the two levels of intimacy or relationship stability described in the preceding section.

Validating couples are characterized by their capacity to compromise, to work out problems calmly, and to accept their partner's unique differences. On the other hand, **volatile** couples can and do engage in intense disputes. They may also be defensive and act critically toward one another. Nevertheless, they seem to enjoy their intensity, which is followed by renewal, and conflict strengthens their sense of individuality. **Conflict-avoiding** couples merely leave their disagreements alone, minimize them, and use solitary activities to handle or relieve tensions. Despite this distancing style, these couples are relatively happy and satisfied with their relationship. These three styles are characteristic of stable relationship patterns. On the other hand, **hostile** couples and **hostile-detached** couples are considered to have unstable relationship patterns. Both tend to exhibit specific negative affects and use less effective problem-solving behaviors than the stable couples. Somewhat surprisingly, hostile-detached couples were found to be more negative and less positive than hostile couples. Hostile-detached husbands tended to show more disgust and less interest in their partner, while hostile-detached wives exhibited more verbal contempt, more disgust, and less interest in their partner than their counterparts in hostile relationships.

Gottman (1994b) points out that while clinicians tend to idealize and favor the validating style, the volatile and conflict-avoiding styles are also stable and satisfying relationship styles. Since the validating style is more compatible with a Rogerian or client-centered view of psychotherapy, many assume that validating style should be the ideal on which treatment goals and interventions are directed. The implications of this bias not only for clinical practice, but for research projects, textbooks, and training programs is immense.

Gottman (1994b) views couples relationships from a behavioral exchange–balance theory perspective. He has operationalized effective relational functioning of the couple system in terms of the ratio of positive feelings and interactions to negative feelings and interactions. Using a variety of measures—laughter, touching, facial expression, physiological measures, and frequency of fights— Gottman (1994b) found that a ratio of five or more positive interactions to one negative predicts marital stability, while a lesser ratio predicts marital dissolution, separation or divorce. In fact, this ratio can predict relational success with 94 percent accuracy.

Gottman (1994a) has also identified what he calls the "Four Horsemen," the warning signs that the relationship is failing and the couple is becoming increasingly preoccupied by negativity. **Criticism:** This means attack ad hominem, personalizing, blame, character attack. While expressing differences is healthy, blame and attack—listing multiple complaints which are never resolved, accusations of infidelity, over generalizations, "always" and "never" statements—are destructive. **Contempt:** This involves perception of the partner as devalued, as well as the desire to hurt, demean, or insult the partner. As a result, feelings of closeness and the capacity to compliment and support the other are lost in a flurry of sneering, eye-rolling, and name-calling. **Defensiveness:** This involves feeling hurt, victimized, and responding to deflect blows by refusing any responsibility for change. It means making excuses for actions rather than trying to modify them and attributing generalized negative beliefs and attitudes to the partner. **Stonewalling:** By emotionally withdrawing from their partner in the face of conflict or demand, relational distress actually

Table 2 Styles of Intimacy by Levels of Stability

	Styles of Intimacy		
Stable marriage	Validators	Volatiles	Avoiders
Unstable marriage	Hostile	Hostile-detached	

increases. While these four negative affects are prominent in unstable relationships, they can also be seen in stable ones as well.

Table 2 summarizes the five relational styles as they relate to two levels of intimacy or relational stability.

CONCLUDING NOTE

The current knowledge base on the topic of intimacy is quite limited. Nevertheless, recent theory and research are likely to revise some basic beliefs that both clinicians and the general public have about intimacy. First, in clinical language, intimacy is a much more circumscribed construct than that of popular parlance. A corollary is that sustained periods of intimacy are not likely to be present in most couple's relationships. Second, it seems useful to specify intimacy in terms of levels and styles. The four views of intimate relational functioning described in this chapter are merely the opening scene of a much larger production. Finally, Gottman's research on what can be thought of as "styles of intimacy" clearly suggest that the current bias of marital and family therapists, researchers, writers, and training programs toward the validating style is short-sighted and certainly not client-centered for couples who are not predisposed to that style.

REFERENCES

Cusinato, M. & L'Abate, L. (1994). A spiral model of intimacy. In S. Johnson & L. Greenberg (Eds.), *The heart of the matter: Perspectives on emotion in marital therapy* (pp. 108–123). New York: Brunner/Mazel.

Guerin, P., Fay, L., Burden, S., & Kautto, J. (1987). *The evaluation and treatment of marital conflict: A four stage approach.* New York: Basic Books.

Gottman, J. (1993). The roles of conflict engagement, escalation, and avoidance in marital interaction: A longitudinal view of five types of couples. *Journal of Consulting and Clinical Psychology, 61,* 1, 6–15.

Gottman, J. (1994a). An agenda for marital therapy. In S. Johnson & L. Greenberg (Eds.), *The heart of the matter: Perspectives on emotion in marital therapy* (pp. 256–293). New York: Brunner/Mazel.

Gottman, J. (1994b). *Why marriages succeed or fail.* New York: Simon & Schuster.

L'Abate, L. (1986). *Systematic family therapy.* New York: Brunner/Mazel.

L'Abate, L. (1997). *The self in the family: A classification of personality, criminality and psychopathology.* New York: Wiley.

Stevens. F. & L'Abate, L. (1989). Validity and reliability of a theory-derived measure of intimacy. *American Journal of Family Therapy, 17,* 359–368.

Weltner, J. (1992). Matchmaking: Therapist, client, and therapy. *Topics in Family Psychology and Counseling,* 1, 3, 37–52.

CHAPTER 4

Intimacy and Culture: A Solution-Focused Perspective

An Interview with Insoo Kim Berg, Len Sperry, and Jon Carlson

There is a commonly held belief among mental health professionals that intimacy has a single meaning and a preferred manifestation. When working in couples therapy with individuals, most therapists have as a value the goal for the couple to be reflecting each other's feelings and to be very respectful and reasonably rational. This preference is based on the clinical lore that mutual reflection of feelings is a surefire marker of couple intimacy. Unfortunately, such clinical lore does not match research data indicating there are different styles of intimacy (Gottman, 1994), or that trying to force couples to take on one particular kind might be very good for a certain part of the population, but not for others. In a larger sense, the notion of culture would make those style differences even more obvious. There is also some concern among clinicians about what intimacy should be like in the dominant American culture. And the meaning of intimacy becomes even more of a challenge then when clinicians are working with individuals from other cultures, particularly those who are not Western or mainline middle-class. Family therapists like Insoo Kim Berg, who were raised in a different culture and emigrated to the United States for professional training, provide clinicians with a unique view of the cultural component of intimacy.

INTIMACY AND CULTURE

Discussions about intimacy and culture can be quite abstract unless they are grounded in clinical case material or the topic is considerably focused, such as male views of intimacy or female notion about gender differences. Not surprisingly, gender difference and cultural difference are two related concerns that can constantly surface in the therapy process.

Berg: One of the first cultural differences that I faced when I came to the United States to train in family therapy was the use of closeness as a form of adolescent discipline. Parents of teenagers would complain about how they have to discipline their teens when they broke certain rules, such as not keeping their curfew, for which the parents would respond by grounding their adolescent. I had never heard of grounding, and when I would ask them about grounding they would look at me strangely and respond that removing a privilege such as the use of the telephone, so they couldn't talk with their friends, or not allowing them to leave the house was what grounding was about. I said, "You mean you punish them by making them stay with their family?" And I thought, "That's a strange form of discipline. Just because you break a rule, you're forced to be close with your family." Now, my concept of a family closeness is very different. I was brought up to believe that being with one's family was a privilege rather than a punishment.

I was really confused about this notion, yet I kept hearing about parents grounding the kids. My earliest memory of my professional training was this obvious cultural difference about the meaning and use of intimacy or closeness.

Carlson: What does intimacy mean to a Korean?

Berg: The term intimacy probably doesn't exist in Korean culture or language. The closest related concept is friendship between two adult male friends. This kind of friendship implies that both learn together, go through life together, and spend time with each other. In American culture intimacy typically implies a unique relationship between an adult male and female rather than same sex friendship. In places like Japan or Korea, when you walk down the street, it's quite common to see teenagers, teenage girls, teenage boys, children, walking down the street holding hands. It's very common. Two ladies who are friends will walk down the street together arm in arm. I don't think men do that, but it's implied. There's lot of poetry, a lot of literature around friendship between two men, because that's usually written by men. So we have more descriptions of that kind of friendship than [of friendship] between male and female.

Sperry: How does a long-term committed relationship like marriage differ from this?

Berg: A long-term committed relationship like marriage is similar but somewhat different from these friendships. Generally speaking, in oriental cultures marriage is taken for granted. It is understood that both partners will spend their whole life together. Healthy long-term relationships are very respectful. Respect develops well before intimacy or closeness. Respect means holding one's partner in very high esteem. It also means trust. It's the kind of trust that means we are in this relationship for the duration. Of course, it's supported by extended families. An intimate relationship is a partnership within the context of extended family. So the investment is not just between two people... because everybody is invested in this relationship working. The whole larger unit is invested in this partnership working.

Sperry: During my last two years of medical school, I lived in an apartment in Chicago near the medical center. A number of the nursing personnel and administrators who worked at the hospital, and happened to be Korean, also lived in this apartment complex. So, there was a Korean family that lived below us and one who lived above us. Based on my observation, it seemed that Korean family life was characterized by closeness, and that male/female relationships were marked by the kind of closeness that is referred to as togetherness. In fact, my first book on marriage was called *The Together Experience*, and I was criticized for using the word togetherness for describing a high functioning level of intimacy in American culture. Presumably, togetherness was a 1930's and 1940's word, but no longer fit relationships in American culture in the 1970's. But it very much seemed to fit the experience of the Korean couples in our apartment complex. When the Korean parents would go out, they would go out arm and arm, and their children would never be too far away. They were latency age children, and they would take responsibility for each other and be very protective. Parenthetically, none of my own kid's bikes or belongings were ever messed with by outsiders because the Korean children in our building would make sure that nothing bad would happen around there. In short, this sense of togetherness seemed to be more characteristic of a partnership and commonality and is rather different from the more individualistic view of close relationships wherein each partner values having his or her own space and considerably autonomy.

Carlson: What about sexual intimacy?

Berg: In Korean culture sex is an unspoken part of close relationships. Unlike American culture which is preoccupied about sex, Korean couples seldom discuss the topic with each other. Nobody gets concerned about sexual organs.

It is very normal to see kids with no diapers, no pants, they just run around with no bottoms. It's a lot easier if you don't have to pull the pants down to toilet, it's very natural. Families sleep in the same room, so I assume parents have sex in the same room with the kids, since they all sleep in the same room.

Carlson: What about the art and books on oriental lovemaking? Sex would seem to be a big part of life?

Berg: Interestingly, there is a considerable literature of erotic arts in China and in Japan. Erotic art, especially paintings, functioned as marriage manuals. They taught couples about sexual intercourse. In other words, art was an acceptable form of sex education. Because much of the population did not learn to read, erotic art was sanctioned. Until recently, only the upper class knew how to read. Education for the masses in the Orient—just as in the West—is a relatively recent phenomenon.

Sperry: Such erotic life looks so romantic.

Berg: Romance has not been part of Korean couples' experience. This contrasts with the western culture where romance is part of dating, and then later in marital therapy dating is often prescribed as a corrective romantic experience. In most oriental relationships, romance is not a feature of intimacy. Even now, many Korean marriages are arranged marriages. While highly educated Koreans might meet each other in college and start dating, dating is not common among the average high school students. They might go to a movie together or something similar, but dating relationships are rare because it is expected that such familiarity requires considerable family discernment. Their families must check out the other family's background to discern whether both families have a sufficiently similar kind of background to constitute a good match. This is decided by the adults in the family, not the young people. Someone else decides for you that this is good match, and you accept their decision. Even though much in Korean culture is changing, the notion of dating, choosing a partner, and companionate marriage is only slowly evolving.

Carlson: I'm still not sure I really understand what intimacy is for a Korean.

Berg: Another way of thinking about intimacy is cooperation. Harmony means you don't risk. You don't risk at all. So, in some ways it's really a closeness. This whole meaning in life is closeness, and the closeness being that you know the other person. You know what they like, and you provide what they like. They try to accommodate each other. They try to accommodate you and you try to accommodate them, and that's expected, that's assumed. It's sort of brought to their awareness when someone violates that. When individuals attempt to get out of their parameter, they're quickly brought back in. So, one is not really accountable to one's partner, but instead is accountable to the larger group or clan.

Sperry: If that's the case, there wouldn't seem to be much need for couples therapy.

Berg: It would seem that couple therapy would not be common in Korea, and neither would divorce. Nevertheless, there is currently a dramatic increase in the divorce rate, and this is very alarming to many Koreans. It means that couples either do not know how to or do not want to try to get along with each other within the parameters of their committed relationship.

Carlson: So you predict that marital therapy will be growing in Korea in the coming years?

Berg: Yes. But keep in mind that the purpose of the marital therapy in Korea is different than in America. When I return to Korea and give couples therapy workshops, I am reminded how much therapists focus on keeping marriages together. It's very openly stated that couples should remain together rather than divorce. Many religious groups offer and support counseling activities which have as their stated goal to keep families together. Even the government supports legislation which discourages divorce. In short, intimacy is harmony and togetherness and the goal of marital intervention is to bolster togetherness or reestablish it. When a relationship develops in such a cultural context, it presents unique challenges when couple therapy is conducted in a different cultural context.

Sperry: Could you illustrate this with a clinical example?

Berg: When a Korean-born couple comes for couples therapy in the United States the couple is likely to encounter a western-born therapist who has a different set of values. When I work with such a couple, they know, and I know, that divorce is not an option for a number of cultural reasons, including children and financial reasons. Even though they may hurl threats about divorce at each other, when it comes down to what they really want, they usually say divorce is not an option. This is even true for the professionally educated who have been acculturated to western norms and values. Typically, they will say they cannot divorce because they believe that divorce decreases the chances of their children having good marriages, and because divorce is a stigma; it damages their chances of ever getting into a good marital situation. Thus, divorce is not an option; it is seldom a choice they can make.

Carlson: You're implying that the outcome of couples therapy is basically to remain married.

Berg: This value and norm presents the dominant culture therapist with an interesting dilemma. Unless that's articulated as such, what the explicit goals of treatment are, it may well be that the dominant culture therapist will assume that divorce is, in fact, a viable option and proceeds on that assumption. Treatment might proceed with marital enrichment or skill-building activities in the early phases of treatment. These interventions are both prescription and diagnostic. If the couple cannot follow this prescription, it further confirms the therapist's belief that an amicable separation might be the way to go. In American training programs, the trainee would essentially say to such a couple: "What would that be like for you?" However, if the therapist is culturally sensitive, presumably this option is not presented to them. Nor will the couple be encouraged to "speak your mind," "stand up for yourself," and "assert yourself," which may be perfectly appropriate for couples with dominant cultural values, but not for this Korean couple. These prescriptions reflect the therapist's agenda, rather than the couple's needs.

Sperry: As when therapists essentially treat all couples the same?

Berg: The culturally-sensitive couple therapist's challenge is to work with the client's agenda. The culturally-different couple come wanting help and assume that the therapist is an authority and knows what they need. So if the therapist's agenda includes separation and divorce as a option when initial efforts to revitalize the relationship do not seem to be working, the prescription to separate is likely to create a major dilemma for the culturally-different couple.

Carlson: This would be very different for a couple from another culture.

Berg: Let's take a related situation with a couple from a different culture—for example a middle Eastern couple—where the male might be very content to hold to traditional values, particularly of control of the relationship and control of the spouse. As the woman wants to become more independent, that presents a very interesting challenge for the husband, and even the therapist. It is very easy for coalitions to form where the therapist might support one partner, for instance, the one who wants to emancipate, against the other partner. And, irrespective of the therapist's sensitivity to culture issues, this can be a most confusing and delicate situation. What do you do? Do you bring them together when one of them does not want that again? Do you try to change the other person, so that they both want more togetherness? Or do you do the opposite and get them so that they will become both more independent and interdependent? This is a complex and difficult clinical situation to navigate therapeutically.

Sperry: This would not be too dissimilar to working class couples.

Berg: This situation is somewhat similar to treating working-class couples. Even though these couples may be westerners, they constitute a subculture that is likely to be different from [that of] the typical couple therapist, particularly if the therapist has adopted the western therapeutic culture which tends to be decidedly middle class. They meet in high school, marry after they graduate, and then 10 years later they begin to recognize that they have grown apart. The husband may continue to subscribe to stereotypical male role behaviors and attitudes such as, "I hold the purse string, so I say what we buy," or "I'm go hunting with the guys, and I want you to stay home." The wife may feel increasingly trapped within these culturally loaded role expectations. Another situation involves middle Eastern couples where wives aspire to become medical doctors or enter another profession that was thought to be a male profession. These women think this is what they want. But yet, they're unsure if they are entitled to such a role as women, especially for women from their ethnic and cultural group. Because they are unsure, they are ambivalent which leads to strain in their marital relationships.

Carlson: You're implying that such issues pose challenges for today's therapists.

Berg: Because of the nature of training in marital and family therapy and because of the kind of people who are attracted [to] doing couples work in the United States, therapists can be expected to value companionate relationships and view this type of relationship as the ideal. Therefore, if the companionate relationship is the ideal, it is not unreasonable for therapists to think really healthy intimate relationships should be marked by closeness and respectfulness. That is more than mere togetherness because it is based on the premise of equality of power. In addition, there should be empathic communications— including the ability to identify and reflect feelings, as well as the capacity to quickly and easily transform anger and conflict. So, in a sense, couple therapy training and the predisposing values that clinicians tend to hold make cultural and sub-cultural issues very challenging. Not surprisingly, many couple therapists experience the tendency to want to try to fashion working-class couples into companionate relationships. They make the assumption that they want to become more like a middle-class couple in this upwardly mobile world. It is an assumption that is seldom scrutinized for many therapists.

Carlson: This was very confusing for me when I was doing couples therapy in Hawaii. In the islands it is common to work with several generations of the same Asian family. Each generation usually had very different ideas about what life was like and what was meaningful. The third generation wanted to find meaning totally outside of the family while the first generation focused on keeping the family together. This created some very interesting dynamics. When I lived in Hawaii, with all its cultural diversity, people really tended to minimize culture and believed in "one world, one people." In the 1970's, Hawaii was viewed as the great melting pot, and the unspoken expectation was for everyone to become acculturated to the dominant culture.

Berg: Returning to the case of the Asian couple who made some overtures of divorce, yet sought therapy, knowing divorce really isn't an option for them. The issue of intimacy becomes an important focus of treatment. What poses an even greater problem for these kinds of couples is that the male partner usually does not even show up. It is the woman who is usually dissatisfied rather than the male. The male's position is: "I am the husband. What's wrong with you? Why are you unhappy? You're supposed to adjust to me." When I first came to America, I discovered that a physics professor I had in Korea was now on the faculty at Marquette University. I was delighted to become reacquainted with him and to meet his wife. She was a successful medical doctor. They were a highly sophisticated and highly educated professional couple. To my surprise I learned that they had nine children: nine daughters. One day I asked the wife why she kept having children. She said, "Because we still don't have a son." I was shocked by this statement and the underlying belief about the importance of having at least one male child. It occurred to me that certain cultural attitudes and values do not change easily, even for couples who are otherwise very well acculturated to the dominant culture.

Sperry: In other words, gender roles are strongly influenced by culture.

Berg: If women like her presented for treatment to most therapists from the dominant culture and gave this history, but fully accepted this value about the primacy of male children, you can imagine what kind of havoc it would create in that couple's life.

Carlson: How would you treat this woman?

Berg: If someone with the value system of this Korean women would present for treatment with me, I would begin by recognizing that this belief and value was part of me, part of my culture or that culture is part of me. Yet I would focus all my energies on understanding the client's agenda because that is model that I have developed for myself. It is a model that is not a therapist driven model, but rather a client driven model. It's a model that makes sense to me in this multiethnic culture that we are living in, and that we will increasingly be living in. I believe this model is adaptable to whatever country I go to give workshops and seminars. My guess is the model works in so many cultures because it is client driven.

Carlson: How exactly do you operate within such client driven model?

Berg: I begin by asking the client what would be helpful for her. And she might say, help me get divorced, or help me learn to live with him. That is where I begin and focus my efforts. I try to stay within that unique client driven model. The client is a unique individual, irrespective of her or his ethnic and cultural heritage. I try not to focus on generalities about a culture as much as I focus on the uniqueness of the individual and his or her desire for change. Accordingly, I am very concerned about therapists who have been trained in a cross-cultural sensitivity that overemphasizes cultural differences. For example, textbooks and articles written for and by therapists tend to highlight differences supposedly unique to certain cultures. For instance, Asian-American families are supposedly education and achievement-oriented, or Hispanic husbands are this way, or middle Eastern wives are this way. There are serious shortcomings to emphasizing differences over similarities. Too much emphasis on difference, cultural differences, does not add to the cultural similarity or the similar human aspirations, human needs. We all have dreams about ourselves which are remarkably similar. So I think it's a matter of balancing. You're working within the differences, but you also have to highlight the similarities.

Carlson: If we can use that as a paradigm or maybe as a metaphor, then what it sounds like you're saying is that maybe what the commonalities are about intimacy are more about the respect, the togetherness, and probably less about romance. Or maybe different ideas about romance or different interpretations of what romance is.

Berg: The way that most people show intimacy in Korea can be illustrated with a metaphor. When you go to buy a piece of fish, you come to know that there are different cuts of a fish. Some are more tasty or nutritious or more valued. As a good Korean wife, I will want to serve my husband the best cut. That's probably no different than your wife doing the same thing with your steak. I think that's a sense of caring. You want to do or please what I know will please you. I think that's intimacy.

Sperry: So, intimacy is largely about doing thoughtful acts for one's partner.

Berg: We assume readers have a pretty good idea of the different models of marital therapy. In my opinion, these models are basically all the same. They teach communication, they teach conflict resolution, and they teach intimacy, which essentially means romance. Intimacy means holding hands or saying loving things. But when you give your partner the bigger piece or the better cut of a food, it's the way in which you do it and what you expect which is so important. You just want to do it because you want to do it.

Carlson: So how would you be intimate with Steve (De Shazer, her husband)?

Berg: As a way of being intimate with Steve, I think I might would express it by taking special care of his mother, because my way of paying respect to him is to pay respect to his mother, to his ancestors. For instance, on a special day that would honor his deceased grandfather, I might prepare a special food that we would take to his grandfather's grave site. That's my way of showing intimacy for him. Or, I might do something extra special for our children. Those are the kind of things. I'm not so sure that's all that different from American couples. You want to cook your husband's favorite meal because you just want to be nice to him, or because he was nice to you last week.

Sperry: How does one tell what is more intimate?

Berg: If you were to go take care of my mother's grave, in America that might be rated as a three or four on a scale of ten—where ten is the highest. While in Korea it would very likely be rated as an eight or nine. In America, being highly intimate would mean revealing more of yourself—which might mean your ideas, beliefs, feelings, or revealing more of your body. Or, it might mean revealing more of what you have to reveal, revealing feedback to me about me. In traditional Korean culture these would probably be considered as offensive. You have to get inside the Korean mindset to imagine what kind of havoc such manifestations of intimacy would create. There's a good example of this involving the Korean community in Los Angeles. There was a young woman in her early twenties who had committed suicide. The subsequent investigation uncovered the likely reason for the suicide. It seems that the woman's father had been sexually abusing her for a number of years. Like a good Korean daughter she did not report it. Yet, she had an American boyfriend who kept telling her that she must confront her father and report it to the authorities. So she did and her father admitted that he was guilty. Subsequently, he was prosecuted and sent to prison. As a result, her family and the Korean community alienated her so much that she could not bear it. Apparently, her solution was to end her life. By American standards she was doing the right thing, but she was still part of a Korean community in America. So she didn't know how to handle this, being excluded and being isolated from her own family, home, the church, everything. This case example has many implications for therapists in this culture working with that kind of family. This would be handled in a very quiet way, private way, rather than going public. He would have talked to this father privately and either talk about what the punishment should be, or what steps he needed to do to stop this. So this would be arranged privately. If this was in Korea, her grandfather, uncle, her brother, not her brother because he is of the same generation as she is, but somebody on higher level, more in terms of higher status, somebody with a higher status, would have a private talk with this father. In this culture, that's probably where the person would have learned it from, probably from a grandfather or an uncle or someone else. Is it possible that it's just OK that this goes on and the reason it's a problem is only because the girl brought it to the attention of someone?

Here is another example from my own family. I have a younger brother and I have older brother. Since my parents passed away, my older brother is like, sort of head of the clan. He makes sure that everybody is behaving and regularly checks up on them. When my younger brother hit his wife, it was not surprising that my older brother found out about it relatively quickly. Of course this abuse was not acceptable. So my older brother called in my younger brother, and he said this must end immediately. There was no yelling or screaming or anything, he calmly said this hitting was not to continue and it stopped. In many cultures the head of an extended family or clan has certain responsibilities. It's not just being respected. We all respect him because he is the oldest of all of us, but he also has the responsibility to make sure that everybody behaves properly. There's always somebody like that, and if you don't have somebody like that in your family or clan, that family is not...well...accepted in the neighborhood, and they become excluded. Exclusion is the biggest fear and the biggest punishment in Korean culture. If you are excluded from your family, you don't exist. You become a nonbeing.

Carlson: Things are culturally based, but today's problems and challenges have not existed before and there is no precedent.

Sperry: So, again we're implying that intimacy is culturally based, and, as the culture changes, the notion of what intimacy is is going to change, at least to some extent. That's the difference between intimacy in a traditional marriage and intimacy in companionate marriage. I still vividly recollect the cookbook my mother used that said in the title that the way to a man's heart is through his stomach. That sentiment well reflected the traditional American view of intimacy, which emphasized accommodating the partner's needs. Interestingly, that book had been out of print for several years, but is now back in print because of the nostalgia about traditional marriage, at least among a small minority of the population. For the most part, baby boomers were raised in traditional families, and they are the ones who are buying this reprinted cookbook. In the dominant western culture, intimacy seems to be stage dependent on the Baby Boom generation. The dominant culture is again configuring to reflect the values of this generation.

Berg: So, for some aging Baby Boomers intimacy becomes the way to a man's heart through cooking. About 20 years ago it was Alex Comfort advocating several positions that would supposedly lead to "the joy of sex."

Carlson: The media does pick up on these changing views of intimacy, even though they're often not labeled as such. I've observed that my younger kids are busy cooking for one another! So, Insoo, what is a solution-focused view of intimacy?

Berg: Basically, the solution-focused perspective is not therapy or ideology driven. Rather it is client driven. When couples come in and their initial complaints are that there is insufficient intimacy, I begin by saying, "So tell me what you'll be like when you are more intimate." They might say, "We hold hands, we have more sex, we whisper in our ears, or go away for the weekend without the kids." That's their own definition of intimacy rather than my definition of what intimacy ought to be like. My strategy is to work within their definition of intimacy.

Carlson: That's what you mean by client driven.

Berg: If someone's going to be client centered, therapy is going to be client driven. But most therapists don't. Most of us have never been trained to do that. While we've been trained to hold up the ideal, we're unlikely to apply this client centered ideal in actual practice. Rather, we simply assume that we know what intimacy is for a given couple, and what needs to be done to improve it. So, we take that role of being godlike and knowing what's best for couples. We become the expert of what's healthy behavior, and what is health producing.

Sperry: So through the use of scaling you're able to locate the couple's idea of what consitutes the adequacy of intimacy on a continuum. You're not simply asking questions that solve problems, rather your strategy is to design situations for achieving that measure of intimacy. And so, if a couple moves from a four to a five—which, if it is their endpoint for adequate intimacy—you aren't disappointed because they didn't aspire to a eight or nine.

Berg: No. I would say, "How satisfied are you, on a scale of one to 10?" Let's say they answer that five is their general level of intimacy. I keep that in mind, but say, "I want to ask you another set of numbers. This time, 10 means you're very satisfied with five. You can live with this, with five. And, one means you're not very happy with that. Where are you with that?" If she says 10, I say, "OK therapy's done." Let's assume she says she's a two with five. "Then we'll have to negotiate that. What would that be like?" And then you go to three.

Carlson: Many theorists, at least in practice, don't really deal with intimacy issues. They just remove the problems, and that's it. But through the use of your scaling questions the therapist can actually address it. The client answers in terms of their own scale, not my scale. I simply ask the client if they are content to live with this at five.

Berg: The Korean person might say, I want to have a very intimate relationship and give my husband that center cut of the mackerel. You don't say, "What in the heck does that mean?" Instead you might say, "Give him the fish head."

Sperry: Can you describe the solution focused theory of intimacy?

Berg: The solution focused view of intimacy currently doesn't have much in the way of theoretical premises. It may sound strange, but I think the most intimate thing I could do with you is to let you be who you are. That would mean I wouldn't intrude in your life. I would let you be who you are. Intimate is not a good word for that, because we have certain images associated with the word "intimacy," and I think that's what gets in the way.

Carlson: Here we are talking about intimacy as giving people the best cut of fish, and I'm thinking of my mother's cookbook, you know, the stomach. And now we're really talking about intimacy in another sense, and you brought it up about Alex Comfort, and it's more of a genital phenomenon. My guess is that everyone wants the same thing, that psychological sense of connection, whether you get it through fishheads or through sex or whatever.

Sperry: It might be instructive to describe a case where intimacy was developed in the course of treatment.

Berg: My videotape "Irreconcilable Differences," portrays a black professional couple who were highly conflicted. Her idea of intimacy is sitting down with him, having a glass of wine, talking at the end of the day, talking together, talking about what your day was like, and then maybe even ending up in bed. That's her idea of intimacy. This is how she would like it: he comes home, she puts the kids in bed early, and they have dinner together by candlelight. They have a glass of wine and talk, and maybe end up in bed. This is a common Western scenario for the way intimate couples ought to act. He can disagree with that. He points out that it was that way at one time. They don't say they want to be more intimate. Rather, they are describing what Westerners typically associate with being an intimate couple. He doesn't disagree with it, and says that would be nice. She pushes for this. She says, "I've gained weight since we've been married and had two kids, and I'm afraid that he doesn't find me attractive enough anymore. I worry that he stays out so long and works so much. I worry that he's going to go out and find something else." She says the kind of things that clients typically say in such situations. Yet, we never talked about intimacy directly. I never brought that up, because it's not a word they used. Rather, she says she wants him to help out more with the kids. She says she works 50 hours a week and comes home to housework, and that he never helps out. He asks why she doesn't hire somebody to do the dishes. So they have different solutions about her complaints. But eventually they come together and treatment ends after four or five sessions. In one regard, they were a very verbal couple, but they never talked directly about intimacy. But yet, they did. So he says, "That would be nice," in answer to her romantic candlelight evening.

Carlson: Is there any need to get anything more from him?

Berg: You might ask him if there was anything that his wife could do to make him come home. He might respond, "it would help if you'd stop nagging, if you'd stop checking on me. If you'd stop nagging, I would feel more like coming home. As soon as I walk in the door, you start screaming, and I can't stand it."

Sperry: Any final comments on intimacy?

Berg: The therapist's responsibility with regard to issues of intimacy is not a matter to be taken lightly. When it comes to intimacy, a couple may want to achieve a significant degree of satisfaction. Or they may prefer to have a platonic relationship which permits them to avoid what a therapist might see as issues of sexual fulfillment. Or they may just want to settle for what the therapist considers a rudimentary level of intimacy. This responsibility embodies a number of philosophical issues. So for a therapist who is trained and receives considerable gratification from doing intrapsychic work, it may seem almost fraudulent to deal only with surface issues—the issues which the couple brings up. That was a criticism of behavior therapy by the analysts, of doing superficial work which results in symptom substitution. Needless to say, this criticism has not been substantiated. We've tried to make the point that therapists who subscribe to the value of tailoring treatment to clients' needs and cultural values will also be sensitive to their desires and goals for treatment.

REFERENCES

Gottman, J. (1994). *Why marriages succeed or fail.* New York: Simon & Shuster.

CHAPTER 5

Creating Passion and Intimacy

Pat Love
Jan T. Brown

For the first time in history there is the expectation of finding both passion *and* security in one's primary love relationship. Couples want to find in their relationships a safe harbor to which they can retreat when they feel the world has dealt them a blow. A place where they can truly be just who they are, faults and all, and feel loved and accepted by their partner. It's in knowing that safety exists, that a sense of relaxed security is felt. But, as if that's not enough, they also want the same relationship or person to provide that juicy, delicious, exhilarating passion they see the movie stars regularly experience or read about in romance novels, or might have even experienced for themselves at the beginning of the relationship.

Couples who have committed, loving relationships, can find themselves in the therapist's office, wondering if they're missing out on something because the high feeling that passion brings is no longer there. They may say things like, "We love each other, but we're not 'in love' anymore." Then, there are the others (who also show up in the therapist's office), whose relationships are hot, steamy, romantic, exciting...then ultimately, chaotic, volatile, tenuous, crazy making. In most of these relationships, when the going gets tough, the tough get going to find yet another passionate relationship. They jump from one partner to another, not having a clue what to do when the high of passion starts to dwindle. These relationships can be watched from the sideline with a predictable outcome, yet there can still be a longing for the excitement and passion they have. A question often asked of the therapist is, "Is it possible to have that plus security?"

These high expectations are placed on the relationship, but little information is provided as to how this can be achieved. Most couples didn't grow up seeing their parents have a passionate and intimate relationship. But those parents probably didn't have expectations that they would either. Ward and June Cleaver seemed perfectly content with their secure, albeit unexciting relationship. But times have changed, and that sort of relationship is no longer satisfactory. The media inundates our society with sexual messages that create a longing for this idealized state. Most couples have found that it's possible to feel that passionate high at the beginning of a new relationship, but how to make it last still remains elusive. There are couples, however, who seem to be able to sustain that feeling. They are looked upon with envy, awe, or even suspicion.

Many, though, are totally confused. In their confusion, they may obsess—read every new relationship book, go to therapy, attend self-help seminars, or just decide to avoid the issue altogether and stay away from anything that even resembles passion or intimacy or both. They hear the word "relationship" and think "Pain". Their brain sends out an alert, and they go into a fight or flight survival mode. Fortunately, however, in the quest to understand this process of love, current research has provided us with a plenitude of new information. Information calms the fight or flight instinct. It reminds us that there is indeed order, even in the seemingly chaotic. The purpose of this chapter is to provide this new information in a way that makes sense, and makes the possibility of creating passion and intimacy a reality.

There are three biological stages of a love relationship: attraction, infatuation, and attachment. Attraction, the first stage, consists of a physical, a psychological, and a sociological component. In the physical component, it is known that people will be drawn to someone who is biologically different than they are. Nature has an investment in pairing them up with a mate that will ensure procreation. The more diverse a species is, the more likely that species is to survive over time. That is to say, that the person most different from them biologically, may actually hold the key to their survival. The latest research findings indicate that DNA plays a part in this stage. People are attracted to someone who may be similar to them, but in many other ways, different. It's through the difference, or diversity that they learn and grow. Many don't deal with diversity easily, may in fact resist it. In their resistance to change they may become very self-centered, which is one of the major blocks to creating passion and intimacy. Self-centeredness means there's only one way of thinking, or one reality, and it's mine. So, for example, if I'm outgoing and enjoy socializing, I think you should too. Or if, sexually, I get turned on easily, then I think you should be able to do the same. Or if it's easy for me to talk intimately, then it should be easy for you. And if you can't, then there's something wrong with you. When something is easy, we do it naturally. If it doesn't come naturally, as for example, the person who has difficulty talking intimately, it takes a lot of focus and concentration. The same applies for the person who is not easily aroused. That person can get aroused, yes, but it takes conscious, focused intention. When someone is into self-centered thinking, they don't understand that their partner's makeup is different, and that difference isn't wrong, or bad. The fantasy is that they'll find someone who is just like them. But the fact is, it's through diversity that they grow. In recent years many books have been written describing the differences in men and women. These books have been extremely popular because they help couples understand that they do think, feel, and behave differently for physiological reasons.

Pheremones (Fisher, 1992) are also a part of the physical element of attraction. A pheremone is a chemical substance animals excrete that elicits a specific response in another through the sense of smell. The smell, or essence of another can be an initial turn-on or turn-off. Pheremones travel through the air through the olfactory system to the brain. When we use the phrase, "There's just no chemistry," we are referring to pheremones. It's either there, and the attraction is felt; or it's not there, and there's no attraction.

Psychologically people are attracted to "familiar love" (Hendrix, 1985). They tend to be drawn to the familiar, or what they have experienced at some time in their lives. In studying the human brain, we find there is a reason for this. Experience goes through the amygdala, those two kernels in the brain that produce a hormonal wash that we experience as a rush. When experience comes through the amygdala to the neocortex, it's imprinted with emotion. This is where our emotion is stored. Familiar love has both an emotional and a hormonal response. To help get a sense of what one's familiar love was like, the following information can be useful: What was the early experience of love? How did it come embodied? What did it feel like? Think back with present information about what must have registered in the brain as the first experience of love. For example, as you were growing up, if your mother or father or both were overwhelmed, sad, hostile, depressed or preoccupied, today, when you meet someone who shares any of those characteristics, a buzzer goes off, and much to your dismay, you might experience a warm hormonal response or an exhilarating rush, and find yourself unexplainably attracted to that person. Your response to familiar love is as ingrained as it is to the person to whom you will be attracted.

People are drawn to familiar love, but they're also drawn to their opposite. The idea of complementarity plays a part in the attraction stage. What this means is that people are attracted to another person who has parts of themselves developed that they don't have, parts that might not have been allowed or acknowledged as they were growing up. For example, if a person wasn't allowed to be angry as a child and had to repress his or her anger, then as an adult, he or she will probably be drawn to an angry person. In fact, the more a person represses something (depression, sexuality, creativity), the more that person is attracted to it. It's as though they're looking for balance, or looking for indicators of those split-off parts of themselves. Harville Hendrix (1985), author of *Getting the Love You Want*, says that our relationship is the vehicle we use on the spiritual journey to reclaim our wholeness. We were born whole and healthy. In the socialization process, however, or perhaps because of the homes we grew up in, we had to give up parts of ourselves. The spiritual nature of relationships is that we attract into our lives the very person we need in order to gain an awareness to those heretofore lost, split-off parts. We're in each other's lives to learn lessons (Cashden, 1988).

After the attraction stage comes the infatuation stage. Unfortunately, in our society this is what is commonly referred to as love. When we say we're in love, we're really in infatuation. Other societies recognize this stage, but don't give it the value we do. Nature is invested in getting couples together sensually, sexually, and intimately for the purpose of procreation. So when a person is attracted to someone and nature thinks it's a good match, that person is rewarded with an adrenaline rush made up of dopamine, norepinephrine, and a big component of phenylethylamine (PEA) (Fisher, 1992). It's important to know that this is an altered state of consciousness. People will say and do things in this altered state that they wouldn't normally say and do. This experience lowers their defenses. However, it's in this stage that they get a glimpse of what they could be like in an undefended state. They say things like, "I've never been able to talk to anyone like this before," or "I've never felt so safe before." In this stage the likenesses between the partners are magnified, and the differences are not seen. They want to spend all their time together; their friends disappear. This is an attachment figure in the making. When people fall in love, to their subconscious their partner becomes the reasonable facsimile for anyone and everyone who ever loved or wounded you or both.

In the beginning, couples don't want to believe that this is a drug induced, passing phase. PEA is a stimulant that creates a euphoric state. Everything feels wonderful. It erradicates pain, so if someone is depressed or angry, in this stage those feelings are gone. PEA gives individuals positive outlook, raises their libidos, and, it's activated by their partners. This means the partner is the catalyst, so they seek proximity and want to be together. When in their partners' presence that wonderful delicious high is felt. Just daydreaming about the partner; the color of his eyes, or the smoothness of her skin, can bring on the feeling. Now the bad news about PEA. It's time limited and usually runs out in about three to six months, depending on how many times someone experienced it. The more times they've fallen in love, the shorter the illusion lasts. When it runs out, things begin to look and feel different. If they don't know this, and are not ready for it, it can come as quite a shock. If coupled individuals think that their partner is the one who caused this wonderful feeling, when the high begins to wear off, (as it should) they can begin to think that something is wrong with the other person or with their relationship. This infatuation stage is an addictive state. It sets up a craving that leaves a longing for more. Another characteristic of PEA is that it's enhanced by fear, risk, and danger. This is why secret relationships can be so confusing. The fear, risk, and danger involved can give the relationship a heightened sense of passion. The more risky or dangerous a relationship, the more passionate it may seem. When the risk and danger factors are taken out, as for example, if the betrayed spouse learns of the affair and dissolves the marriage, the passion often fizzles out in the affair relationship, and the same type of problems that were in the marriage appear.

Persons who grew up with a secure attachment to a parent will move naturally from the infatuation stage to the next stage, the attachment stage. Attachment and connection come naturally. What this means is that they can show love and receive love, they can touch and be touched, they're sexual and can show their sexual needs, they can collaborate, they can negotiate, they can delay gratification, they can soothe themselves, they can stimulate themselves, they can be altruistic, they can gaze and look, and can be gazed and looked upon, they can be comforted and give comfort. If they had good enough parenting, they will move naturally into doing attachment behaviors. These behaviors include touching, holding, gazing, comforting, validating, listening, responding, supporting, collaborating, and honoring. If they understand this and know how to do it, they'll get another chemical, hormonal bath at this time. They'll experience an endorphine response that produces a calm, safe, confident, comforted, and secure feeling. This is the key to long-lasting love.

But what of those who didn't experience secure attachment growing up? What if they didn't have parents attuned to their needs? Then like many, they get to this stage, feel at a loss, and freeze. If they don't know about stage three (attachment), all they know about is stage two (infatuation), they believe that the second stage is love. Remember, nature has an investment in getting couples together, but not necessarily staying together. And people only know what they've been taught. Some, for example, are comfortable showing and giving love, but, because they grew up not getting love, they're very uncomfortable receiving love. At their core, if they feel unlovable when they're in a relationship and their partner starts to love them, they won't trust the love and will suspect their partners' motives. Out of this suspicion, they may begin to test that love. If the first test is passed, the next test is more difficult, because to be loved by another is incongruent and somehow doesn't fit. So, what do people do if they don't attach naturally? They only know that they felt attached in stage two, infatuation, so they feel that must be love. The only thing known beyond stage two is work, raising kids, doing tasks, doing career, getting busy. So they keep moving or stay frozen.

John Bowlby (1969/1982), the developer of "attachment theory," says attachment itself is a human drive. That within all humans is an innate drive to connect with another, and that the satisfaction of this drive is paramount to one's survival. For years in our culture, the end to be strived for has been a state of autonomy, or individuation. This is the type of thinking that says you don't have an effect on me; I can do what I want to and it shouldn't effect you.

Our culture supports the idea that to need another is to be considered weak and dependent. The philosophy of attachment theory contradicts this. Bowlby says that one's attachment figure is directly connected to one's security. In childhood the attachment figure(s) is (are) the parent(s), and in adulthood that figure is the partner. When someone wants to be with her or his attachment figure, no one else will do. Different needs are met by an attachment relationship than by an affiliative or friendship relationship. Both are important and necessary for well-being. An attachment figure is one for whom there is no substitute, the person turned to in times of stress. This person prevents feelings of loneliness, provides a sense of security. Separations from one's attachment figure causes distress, and loss of this person causes one to not only to grieve, but also to mourn.

When a person does not have connection, either physically or emotionally with his or her attachment figure, Bowlby's findings teach us that there will be protest, despair, and detachment (Karen, 1994). In studying the behaviors of children separated from their parent for a period of time, he noticed that they would go through three distinct stages. First they would protest. They would cry, call for the parent, wait and watch constantly. If the parent did not return, next would come despair. They would grieve, withdraw, be despondent. Eventually the child would begin to look better; as if they were getting over the loss. They would begin to interact with others, or play with toys. What was happening here is that the child was in the detachment stage. When the parent did return, the child did not respond to loving behaviors. It was as if a wall of protection had been built.

The same three stages occur in our adult attachment relationships. It's important to recognize how they manifest in one's own behavior. In assisting a person to discover this the following information can be considered: What are you like when you do not have connection with your partner? What does your protest stage look like? You might get cranky, irritable, pick on your partner, or withdraw and get busy. If you still do not connect, you'll move to despair. You might start to think you'll never get your needs met, and begin to feel hopeless. (It's in this stage that many couples show up in the therapist's office). If you still do not connect, you may start to look better on the outside. You might call your friends, start a new project, or bury yourself in work. But on the inside a wall has gone up, and you feel detached. If connection can be established, you'll calm down, and again feel a sense of security. If a person can begin to identify her or his own particular style of doing each of these stages, then she or he can see them for what they really are—signals that connection with the partner is needed and not necessarily that this is the end of the relationship.

Mary Ainsworth, a student of John Bowlby's, conducted a study known as "The Strange Situation" (Ainsworth, Blehar, Waters, and Wall, 1978). She was able to identify three styles of attachment. An understanding of this study and the resulting identification of these styles is very important when it comes to sex, passion, intimacy, and security. The following is a description of the study done in the early 1960's. Ainsworth set up a room equipped with toys and a one-way mirror. A mother and her 12-month-old child were in the room. At one point, a "stranger" (a research assistant) was to enter and the mother was to leave for a period of no more that three minutes. The "reunion" behavior (i.e., how the child responded to the mother when she returned to the room after the short absence), was to be measured. The reunion behavior is what describes the attachment style. The group of children she labeled "securely attached" acted in similar ways. When the mother left, the child would cry; when she returned, the child would cry and move toward her. As the mother picked the child up, the crying might continue, but eventually the child would settle in and allow himself or herself to be consoled. The securely attached children were found to have had a loving caregiver attuned to their needs. The second group of children Ainsworth called the "anxious/ambivalently attached." These children also cried when mother left and again upon her return. They, too, would move toward her and appeared to want comforting. But when the mothers of these children would pick them up, they would continue to protest and not allow themselves to be comforted, wanting to be held, but at the same time protesting by pushing mother away. These children were found to have had very inconsistent parenting. The mother may have been preoccupied, overwhelmed, or anxious herself. She may have been loving at times and at other times neglectful or intrusive. The third classification was the "avoidantly attached" group. This child cried when mother left, but when she returned, the child barely noticed and appeared to be intently preoccupied with the toys. Instruments monitoring the child's heartbeat, however, showed a rapid increase indicating that the child indeed had noticed and inwardly reacted to mother's return, but instead of turning to her for comfort, was attempting to soothe himself or herself. The avoidantly attached children were found to have had cold, distant, rejecting, dismissive parenting.

Robert Karen (1994), in his book *Becoming Attached*, states that as people grow older they gradually make the transition from having that secure base relationship with our parent, to eventually having this responsibility rest fully on their mate. The three attachment styles also apply in adulthood. The securely attached adult is comfortable giving and receiving love, comfort, and affection. There's an open acknowledgement and discussion of problems within the relationship. Emotional intimacy comes naturally. Both partners are comfortable with their sexuality. In the situation of a separation between the two of them, there may be loneliness, anxiety even, but upon reunion, each partner allows herself or himself to be comforted. There's the feeling that they are each other's best and trusted friend. Each regards the other as reliable and responsive. Securely attached adults tend to have fewer divorces, and rarely show up in the therapist's office.

The anxious/ambivalently attached adult falls in love easily and tends to have relationships characterized by intensity and chaos. Typically the partner is seen as being unavailable, unreliable, and unresponsive These persons are usually overly emotionally invested in their partners. This is the man or woman who willingly gives up friends, hobbies, jobs, even children for the sake of the relationship. He or she fears the loss of the partner to the point of obsession. The adult, like the child, is anxious and angry but will not accept consolation from the partner. Forgiveness doesn't come easily. The inconsistent, ambivalent parenting received by this person, sets up a pattern that seems to be the trademark of this relationship style. Come close, go away; no, come close; no, go away. The ambivalence can effect not only the intimate relationship, but also all areas of one's life. If you go to law school, you should have gone to medical school; if you ordered ice cream, you should have ordered pie; if you get married, you should have stayed single. The focus is always on what you don't have, didn't do, should have done.

Avoidantly attached adults have a fear of closeness, intimacy and committment. They deny both their feelings and their needs. They're independent and prefer being alone. When separated from their partner, they deny the impact of the separation. They can be hostile or hypersensitive to rejection. It's hard to get close to this person. Behind that protective wall, however, the feeling is of loneliness and isolation. The avoidantly attached adult can minimize the importance of relationships and maximize the importance of career. Many are workaholics. They can be highly sexual, having taken all their emotional and physical needs and channeled them into that one area.

The anxious/ambivalent and the avoidant usually are attracted to each other. However, even if a person does not have an attachment style that allows for healthy relating, nature gives him or her a second chance. This opportunity comes from being sexual with the same partner over a period of time. When a person is sexual to the point of orgasm, the brain produces yet another hormone. This one is called oxytocin (Crenshaw, 1996). It triggers the orgasm, but it also produces a feeling of being bonded to one's partner. Oxytocin is referred to as the "snuggle hormone." It gives a person a feeling of safety and security, and promotes attachment behaviors. These are the same attachment behaviors that come naturally for those with a secure attachment style. Behaviors such as gazing, holding, touching, comforting, listening, and supporting. Oxytocin is also produced in the mother when she is nursing. This is to help her bond to her child. In the same way, it bonds a person to her or his partner. (In fact, if someone wants to break an attachment to another person, the first thing to do is stop having sex with him or her. Otherwise, even if that person knows it's the wrong relationship, he or she won't be able to end it because the feeling of attachment is so strong.) That feeling of safety and security while lying in your lover's arms following an intense session of lovemaking is oxytocin induced.

But what happens if a person has both an insecure attachment style and a low testosterone level (Love, 1994)? One's level of spontaneous sexual energy is correlated with hormonal makeup. A person's hormonal makeup is what he or she was born with. People with a high testosterone level have spontaneous thoughts of sex. They are aroused easily. They desire sex often. People with low levels of testosterone rarely even think of sex. They don't instantly "turn on." They can go without sex for long periods of time and not miss it. But a person can be a sensual and sexual individual regardless of hormonal makeup. All that is needed is a willingness, a desire to desire. Passion equals two sexual beings joined by intimacy. However, both sex and intimacy are the ingredients to a passionate relationship. In the typical relationship one partner will tend to have a higher sexual desire, and the other have a higher need for verbal intimacy. Furthermore, the one who tends to have the high desire for sex, also has a low desire for intimacy, and vice versa. Thus, the familiar power struggle: "If you'll be sexual with me, I can be intimate with you" vs. "If you'll be intimate with me, I can be sexual with you."

The following questions are relevant to the clinical setting and can be posed to the client in the following manner:

"Take a moment to answer the following questions True or False. Notice the questions that may be difficult for you to answer honestly."

T	F	Talking about sex is comfortable for me.
T	F	I feel fully informed about sex.
T	F	Verbal intimacy comes easily for me.
T	F	I am a confident lover.
T	F	I feel safe with our relationship.
T	F	I get the attention I need from my partner.
T	F	I am clear about my sexual needs.
T	F	My partner and I work out our differences easily.
T	F	My partner and I agree about sex.
T	F	I am aware of my changing sexual needs.
T	F	I can suggest changes to my partner with comfort.
T	F	I trust my partner without question.
T	F	I feel emotionally connected to my partner.
T	F	I get my nonsexual touching needs met by my partner.
T	F	I feel free from my past in relationship to sex.
T	F	My partner is sensitive to my needs.
T	F	Our love life is a priority for both of us.
T	F	I feel confident we can create the love we long for.
T	F	I am fully committed to working on this relationship.

Once the questions have been completed the therapist can process the experience by discussing any of the following questions: (1) What was your experience answering the questions, that is, thoughts, feelings, body sensations? (2) Did any insight or awareness occur as a result of answering these questions? (3) If you were to guess, how would your partner answer these questions? Are there differences? (4) What are the greatest differences in your answers? Is there a pattern? (5) If you were to make a behavior change moving closer to your partner's direction, what would that look like?

The act of moving in your partner's direction is a key to creating passion and intimacy, however it is important to give your partner what it is that she or he needs in order to feel loved. Giving in this manner can only come out of a state of fullness. When we feel loved by another, what overflows is the altruistic expression of giving. When you pay attention to who I truly am, and give me what I want and need, what wells up in me is an energy of love. And I, in turn, want to give you what it is that you truly want and need. This type of giving is totally different from the giving that comes from a state of depletion or emptiness. (If I'm feeling empty or unloved myself, but I give to you because I feel that's the only way I'll get what I want and need from you, I end up feeling angry and resentful and you know it.) It feels like manipulation (and it is). So where you start is by saying, "What can I give you that says I love you to you?" Most of us tend to give love the way we want to be loved. (I give you what I want. And then I'm confused that you're not appreciative.) That goes back to that self-centered thinking discussed earlier in the chapter. Remember, that's the thinking that says, "You should want what I want." Or, "I know even better than you what you should want." But if I truly want to be a lover, and have a loving relationship, I have to know what says "I love you" to my partner.

Getting what we want scares us to death. When someone has longed and yearned for something like love, touch, or attention, and finally gets it, it brings up feelings of anxiety and fear. There's a reason for this. The end of the longing is the beginning of the grief. It's called "reunion grief." When people are longing and yearning for love, they are holding at bay the grief of not having had the love they've needed. Therefore getting that love is terrifying and painful, full of angst and worth the price of feeling it. If they're not conscious and aware, they'll push it away. It's like the more someone loves them, the more frightened they are, and the more they push their partner away. They might do the "Come close/Go away" or might avoid their partner, depending upon their attachment style. The challenge of the conscious or mature person is to live through the terror of being loved and touched and held. Being known by, and connected to another, is the antidote to being anxiously or avoidantly attached or both. The antidote is to feel the terror and stay in relationship.

Intimacy is not just the prelude to passion, it's the precondition. Without the component of intimacy there will be no passion. To know and be known by another and live in connectedness is erotic. Libido literally means life energy. To combine this spirituality with the sexuality is an altered state. This type of love requires conscious, intentional, mature committment. It's difficult, frightening, painful and well worth the journey.

People often benefit from simple techniques with low psychological cost in an effort to improve their relationships. Knowing this, they might find it helpful to use the simple phrase "PLAY FAIR" to remind them of their committment to stay on this journey.

"F" stands for "Flirt." Be flirtatious with your partner; it's fun. It can be a touch, or a suggestive look. When flirting, a little goes a long way. It takes little time and gives great results.

The "A" stands for "Appreciate." Remember to show appreciation to your partner. The biggest complaint from men as a group, is that they do not feel appreciated for the things they do. However men and women both thrive in a context of appreciation.

"I" stands for "Intimacy." It's important to share your inner world with your partner. Knowing and being known by your partner creates an atmosphere of aliveness and energy, basic ingredients in passion.

"R" stands for "Risk." When given two choices, stretch and choose the riskier of the two. The tension created by risk can help keep passion and romance alive by giving us a jolt of that wonderful PEA.

REFERENCES

Ainsworth, M. D. C., Blehar, M. C., Waters, E., & Wall, S. (1978) *Patterns of Attachment: A psychological study of the strange situation*. Hillsdale, NJ: Erlbaum.

Bowlby, J. (1969/1982). *Attachment and loss: Vol. 1. Attachment*. New York: Basic Books.

Cashdan, S. (1988). *Objects relations therapy*. New York: W. W. Norton.

Crenshaw, T. L., (1996). *The alchemy of love and lust*. New York: G. P. Putnam's Sons.

Fisher, H. E. (1992). *Anatomy of love*. New York: W. W. Norton.

Hendrix, H., (1988). *Getting the love you want: A guide for couples*. New York: Henry Holt.

Karen, R. (1994). *Becoming attached*. New York: Warner Books.

Love, P. (1994). *Hot monogamy*. New York: Penguin Books.

CHAPTER 6

Marital Intimacy: Assessment and Clinical Considerations

Dennis A. Bagarozzi, Ph.D.

The *Random House Dictionary of the English Language* defines intimacy as a "close, familiar and usually affectionate or loving personal relationship with another person" which entails a "detailed knowledge or deep understanding" of the other as well as a proactive expression of one's thoughts, feeling, etc. which then serves as a "token of familiarity."

Intimacy is believed to be a vital, if not central and critical, aspect of committed relationships such as marriage. Some family researchers have treated intimacy as if it were a unidimensional construct (e.g., Alford, 1982; Braiker & Kelley, 1979; Guerney, 1977; Miller & Lefcourt, 1982; Orlofsky & Levitz-Jones, 1985; Walker & Thompson, 1983). Other researchers, recognizing the multidimensional nature of intimacy, have chosen to focus only on certain aspects of intimacy, for example, the behavioral (Berscheid, Snyder & Omoto, 1989; Ting-Toomey, 1983a, 1983b), the psychosocial (Tesch, 1985), and sexual (Derogatis, 1980; Hudson, 1982; Lo Piccolo & Steger, 1974). In 1981, Schaefer and Olson conducted an empirical study designed to assess seven different aspects or dimensions of intimacy previously identified by Olson (1975, 1977). These seven dimensions were (1) emotional, (2) social, (3) intellectual, (4) sexual, (5) recreational, (6) spiritual, and (7) aesthetic. A factor analytic study was then conducted by Schaefer and Olson (1981) who administered a 75-item questionnaire to 192 married couples. The items in this initial questionnaire addressed the seven prior categories of intimacy previously identified by Olson (1975, 1977). Five empirically derived factors were pro-duced. These included: emotional intimacy, social intimacy, sexual intimacy, intellectual intimacy and recreational intimacy. Schaefer and Olson (1981) then selected the 10 highest loading items, contained in each of the five factors, for inclusion in a 50-item Personal Assessment of Intimacy in Rela-tionships (PAIR) scale. The current version of PAIR is a 36-item scale which contains six items from each of the five subscales and a six-item conventional-ity subscale.

The PAIR is an easily administered and quickly scored instrument that provides the therapist with global ideal/perceived intimacy satisfaction com-parison scores for each spouse. Although the PAIR does take into account the multifaceted nature of intimacy, it does not deal with the full complexity of the construct. Several additional factors must be taken into consideration when assessing conjugal intimacy for clinical purposes. These are discussed below.

AGGREGATE NEED STRENGTH AND COMPONENT NEED STRENGTHS

The author conceptualizes the need for interpersonal intimacy as an extension of the more basic biologically based survival need for attachment (Bowlby, 1969). Interpersonal intimacy is seen as a developmentally more mature and advanced manifestation of this universal need for physical closeness and contact with another human being. However, the overall strength of this need for human connectedness differs for each individual, and the constituent components of this more general need also vary in strength from individual to individual. So, for example, two individuals with similar overall intimacy need strengths may differ drastically in the strengths of their component needs. When one considers these intraindividual differences, it is easy to understand how two spouses who have similar overall or aggregate intimacy need strengths may still be dissatisfied with the intimacy they experience in their marriage.

THE DYNAMICS OF INTIMACY: TRUST, RECEPTIVITY AND RECIPROCITY

Intimacy is a dynamic interactive process that evolves over time. Mutual trust is a sine qua non for its continued development. Therefore, if true intimacy is to flourish, each spouse must feel totally secure in sharing his or her inner most thoughts, feelings and self-disclosures with his or her partner without the fear of being judged, evaluated or ridiculed. In addition to knowing that one's spouse is open and receptive to whatever is shared, one must also feel that her or his mate is reciprocating similar depth levels of self-disclosure and self-revelation in order for intimacy to be maintained. It is this mutuality and reciprocity that allows the relationship to move forward into greater depths of intimacy and trust.

ASSESSMENT OF CONJUGAL INTIMACY: THE MARITAL INTIMACY NEEDS QUESTIONNAIRE

In order to determine whether one's conjugal intimacy needs are being met sufficiently, assessment should address four interrelated components of the construct: (1) the overall intimacy need strength of each spouse, (2) the strength of each component need for each spouse, (3) each spouse's satisfaction with his or her mate's openness, receptivity, responsiveness and ability to meet and satisfy the particular need in question, and (4) each spouse's satisfaction with her or his mate's ability to reciprocate similar depth levels of sharing, openness, self disclosure and personal exchange.

In order to help clients evaluate the degree to which their partners are actually meeting these intimacy needs, Bagarozzi (1990) developed the Marital Intimacy Needs Questionnaire. This clinical tool was designed to provide spouses with a concrete and meaningful way to discuss and explore intimacy in their marriage. Nine separate dimensions of intimacy are targeted: (1) emotional intimacy, (2) psychological intimacy, (3) intellectual intimacy, (4) sexual intimacy, (5) spiritual intimacy, (6) aesthetic intimacy, (7) social and recreational intimacy, (8) physical intimacy, and (9) temporal intimacy (i.e., the minimum amount of time that one would like to spend with his or her spouse, on a daily basis, in order to feel intimately connected).

For each dimension of intimacy, a definition is provided for the respondent. For example, emotional intimacy is defined as follows:

> Emotional intimacy is the need for communicating and sharing with your spouse/ partner all your feelings both positive (e.g., happiness, joy, elation, gladness, excitement), and negative (e.g., sadness, unhappiness, frustration, fear, anger, guilt, shame, loneliness, boredom, fatigue).

After reading each definition, the respondent is asked to answer a series of Likert-type questions about the particular dimension of intimacy under consideration. The questions designed to assess emotional intimacy are represented below:

a In general, how strong is your need to communicate and share your feelings with your spouse/partner? (Circle only one number).

Not A Strong Need At All								An Extremely Strong Need	
1	2	3	4	5	6	7	8	9	10

b How important is it for you that your spouse/partner be receptive to and listen to you whenever you share your feelings with him/her? (Circle only one number).

Not At All Important								Extremely Important	
1	2	3	4	5	6	7	8	9	10

c To what extent is your spouse/partner able to meet and satisfy your need for emotional intimacy? (Circle only one number).

Not At All Able To Satisfy This Need								Totally Satisfies This Need	
1	2	3	4	5	6	7	8	9	10

d How important is it for you and your satisfaction with your spouse/partner that he/she communicate and share with you his/her positive and negative feelings? (Circle only one number).

Not At All Important								Extremely Important	
1	2	3	4	5	6	7	8	9	10

e To what extent is your spouse/partner able to meet and satisfy your expectations for sharing and communicating his/her feelings to you? (Circle only one number).

Not At All Able To Satisfy My Expectations								Totally Satisfies My Expectations	
1	2	3	4	5	6	7	8	9	10

For the dimensions of emotional, psychological, intellectual, sexual, spiritual and aesthetic intimacy, the respondent receives three scores: (a) need strength, (b) satisfaction with one's spouse's or partner's receptivity to one's intimate self-disclosures and expressions of feelings, and (c) satisfaction with one's spouse's or partner's ability to reciprocate acceptable levels of intimate exchange and self-disclosure. Each respondent receives only two scores for the remaining dimensions of social and recreational intimacy and physical (nonsexual) intimacy. These scores are for need strength and receptivity satisfaction. A summary score for all eight need strengths (i.e., each separate dimension), is used for arriving at a spouse's or respondent's overall intimacy need strength. The last two questions of the Marital Intimacy Needs Questionnaire deal with the issue of time. Each spouse or partner is asked to evaluate whether the amount of time currently spent with his or her partner is considered to be sufficient for achieving the intimacy desired in the marriage. The final question asks the respondent to consider what she or he believes to be the minimum amount of time, on a daily basis, that she or he would like to share with her or his partner in order to feel intimately connected and satisfied with the relationship.

CLINICAL USES OF THE MARITAL INTIMACY NEEDS QUESTIONNAIRE

The Marital Intimacy Needs Questionnaire is one of several assessment tools and devices that can be used to develop a clinically relevant marital/family systems diagnostic profile that therapists can use to set achievable treatment goals and plan appropriate intervention strategies (Bagarozzi, 1985; L'Abate & Bagarozzi, 1993). The information gathered through the Marital Intimacy Needs Questionnaire can be shared with couples and used by the therapist to bring about cognitive modifications in how spouses perceive each other, to reframe spouses' behaviors, to defuse negative attributions and reverse perception of malintention, and to edit dysfunctional themes in a couple's conjugal mythology (Bagarozzi & Anderson, 1989). For example, when a therapist shares test results with spouses who have widely different needs for intimacy, each spouse is confronted with a graphic statistical representation of the strengths of his and her needs for interpersonal intimacy. When spouses are able to compare, contrast and discuss their similarities and differences, they are much more receptive to viewing these differences for what they truly are; differences, and not good or bad character traits, pathological desires for closeness or distance and so forth.

Similarly, when the therapist presents these differences in need strengths as reflective of a larger and more pervasive personality style (e.g., introversion or extraversion) that can be expected to remain stable throughout the life cycle, some couples who have been engaged in long-term struggles over closeness and separateness may finally find it possible to accept their differences and call a halt to their attempts to change their spouses.

It has been this writer's experience to find that the simple act of responding to the Marital Intimacy Needs Questionnaire can have profound effects upon individuals. For example, some clients (frequently men) are surprised to learn that intimacy is multifaceted and that sexual intimacy is only one aspect of a much larger need for interpersonal closeness. After completing the Marital Intimacy Needs Questionnaire and discussing the results with their spouses, some men who have sought counseling to deal with sexual difficulties in their marriage may begin to understand that, for their wives, sexual interest, sexual satisfaction and sexual fulfillment can only take place within the context of a broader intimate relationship.

In the following section, I will describe how the Marital Intimacy Needs Questionnaire can be used as a diagnostic aid in work with distressed relationship systems. It is important to keep in mind that the Marital Intimacy Needs Questionnaire is only one of a variety of instruments that are routinely used as part of a more comprehensive marital/family assessment and evaluation procedure that is conducted with couples and families who seek help with relationship problems (Bagarozzi, 1985, 1995, 1996; Bagarozzi & Anderson, 1989; L'Abate & Bagarozzi, 1993). Time and space considerations prohibit a detailed discussion of the full assessment process and the instruments, measures, procedures, etc. used to develop a marital/family diagnostic profile. However, the reader should remember that a spouse's satisfaction with the amount and levels of intimacy that he or she experiences in marriage will influence, to a large degree, how that spouse responds to all other instruments and procedures administered during the diagnostic process.

MR. AND MRS. WALTER

Mr. and Mrs. Walter had been married for seven and one-half years when they contacted me for their initial interview. What precipitated their call was Mrs. Walter's disclosure to her husband that she had been having an affair with another married man for the past 14 months. Mrs. Walter explained that overwhelming guilt and anxiety about her illicit relationship had forced her to tell her husband about her infidelity. In the privacy of her individual diagnostic session, Mrs. Walter said that although she had discontinued her sexual relationship with her lover, she still loved him and was not sure whether she would ever be able to find happiness and satisfaction with her husband, whom she "loved like a brother." Her reason for entering therapy was to explore whether she could recapture the passion, sexual desire and intimacy she once felt in her relationship with her husband. Mr. Walter, on the other hand, admitted to some strong prejudices about counseling. He was leery of therapists and skeptical about the counseling process although he had not had any prior experiences with therapists or therapy. A major factor contributing to his reluctance to seek professional help was his strong conviction that "people should be able to solve their own problems." Consulting a psychologist, for Mr. Walker, was tantamount to admitting personal failure.

Mr. Walter was clinically depressed. A major diagnostic consideration was to determine whether Mr. Walter's depression was a chronic condition that predated this current marital crisis.

Mr. Walter's personal history revealed a series of significant losses which began with the death of his older sister when he was 13. His sister, Angie, had had parental responsibilities for Mr. Walter from the time he was born, and it would be appropriate to say that she served as a maternal figure for him. After her death, he became attached to his second older sister, Laura, who took Angie's place to some degree. Both his mother and Laura doted on him after Angie's death, and Mr. Walter described himself as becoming a "mama's boy" at this time.

Shortly before Mr. Walter entered college, Laura married. Both Mr. Walter and his mother experienced this as another loss. When he left for college, his mother began to drink heavily. She expressed concern that her children would leave her alone in her old age. As her drinking got worse, she became estranged from her husband, but concern for their mothers's health kept all of her children, except Mr. Walter, close to home. Mr. Walter's two older brothers and Laura continued to work in the family business.

Mr. Walter's mother was not pleased when he announced his intention to marry Mrs. Walter rather than return home to work in the family business.

Mr. and Mrs. Walter had agreed to delay having children until Mrs. Walter received her master's degree and successfully launched her own career. After being married for almost two years, Mrs. Walter entered a two-year graduate program. This same year, Mr. Walter's father died. His father's death and his wife's return to school left Mr. Walter adrift. The only emotional support he received during this time came from his siblings. He became increasingly more involved with his family of origin while his wife pursued her studies. Pressures to return to his home state and to take part in the family business increased. This seemed to drive a wedge between Mr. Walter and his wife. Tension between the two increased.

During her individual diagnostic sessions, Mrs. Walter revealed that she felt alienated from her husband while she was in graduate school and had had a brief affair. She said she had always felt in competition with her husband's mother for Mr. Walter's affection and allegiance. Looking back on her relationship with Mr. Walter, Mrs. Walter said that she had never felt that he was "truly hers." Mrs. Walter's father had divorced her mother to marry a much younger woman when Mrs. Walter was 10 years old. Both she and her younger brother felt abandoned by him and her mother never overcame this loss. The theme of not fully "having" the man she loved was a central one in Mrs. Walter's personal mythology (Bagarozzi & Anderson, 1989), as was the theme of resolving never to suffer the same fate as her mother.

The interactive and complementary relationship between intraphysic dynamics and interpersonal homeostasis via symptom formation (Anderson & Bagarozzi, 1983, 1989; Bagarozzi, 1981; Bagarozzi & Anderson, 1982; 1989; Bagarozzi & Giddings, 1983) is illustrated clearly in this case. For Mrs. Walter, marrying her husband offered her an opportunity to rework, transferentially, several intrapersonal themes and conflicting identifications (e.g., active mastery of the trauma caused by her parents' divorce, identification with the abandoning father as a defense against being abandoned like her mother, and identification with the younger women for whom her father left her mother). Marital homeostasis was maintained, temporarily, through her first affair. However, the more time Mr. Walter spent with his family of origin, the more Mrs. Walter felt she was losing him. During her graduate education, involvement in her studies and a brief affair served to offset Mr. Walter's involvement with his family. However, when her husband's involvement with his family did not decrease after she began her career, the imbalance in their relationship grew more pronounced.

The intrapsychic conflicts associated with unresolved mourning and the system's stresses involving dual loyalties and intergenerational debt all found their symbolic expression in Mr. Walter's depression. In his relationship with his wife, Mr. Walter had been able to relive, transferentially, the pleasant experience he had enjoyed with his deceased sister. The periodic conflicts he had with his wife, during which she left home and threatened divorce, on the other hand, offered him an opportunity to relive the traumatic loss of his sister.

SALIENT ASSESSMENT FINDINGS

One of the assessment instruments, the Personal Authority in the Family Systems Questionnaire (Bray, Williamson & Malone, 1984) in addition to the Marital Intimacy Needs Questionnaire was particularly useful in helping Mr. and Mrs. Walter identify some of the salient intergenerational systemic issues that contributed to the development of their marital difficulties. How these two instruments were used to set treatment goals is discussed briefly in order to illustrate the relationship between assessment and treatment planning.

Table 1 shows the Marital Intimacy Needs comparison scores for Mr. and Mrs. Walter.

Table 1 reveals that there is a considerable difference in Total Needs Strength scores for Mr. and Mrs. Walter. Mr. Walter's Total Needs Strength score is 463. Mrs. Walter's Total Needs Strength score is 232. Total Needs Strength scores range from 10 to 800. In all my clinical work with couples, I have found that the average spread of scores for individuals r ues between 450–550. Therefore, Mr. Walter's score of 463 can be cons:.ieied to fall within the average range. Mrs. Walter's score of 232, however, places her at the low end in terms of her need for intimacy.

Prior to his knowledge of his wife's affair, Mr. Walter said that he perceived his wife to be meeting his needs for intimacy at satisfactory levels. After learning about her affair, however, he felt alienated from her. His Receptivity and Reciprocity Satisfaction scores, as shown in Table 1, reflect his evaluations

Table 1   Total Intimacy Needs Scores comparisons for Mr. and Mrs. Walter

Need		Husband	Wife
Emotional	Strength	35	35
	Receptivity Satisfaction	50%	100%
	Reciprocity Satisfaction	50%	100%
Psychological	Strength	72	48
	Receptivity Satisfaction	67%	100%
	Reciprocity Satisfaction	50%	100%
Intellectual	Strength	49	36
	Receptivity Satisfaction	100%	100%
	Reciprocity Satisfaction	100%	100%
Sexual	Strength	64	35
	Receptivity Satisfaction	38%	100%
	Reciprocity Satisfaction	25%	100%
Spiritual	Strength	49	20
	Receptivity Satisfaction	50%	100%
	Reciprocity Satisfaction	50%	100%
Aesthetic	Strength	49	18
	Receptivity Satisfaction	100%	100%
	Reciprocity Satisfaction	100%	100%
Social/	Strength	81	20
Recreational	Receptivity	60%	100%
Physical	Strength	64	20
	Receptivity	50%	100%
Total Need Strength		463	232

of these dimensions upon entering therapy one week after learning about his wife's infidelity.

Mrs. Walter, on the other hand, shows satisfaction scores which indicate that she is totally satisfied with the degree of intimacy she now shares with her husband. This was not the case prior to her affair. During that time in her marriage, she felt neglected and isolated. Her husband's job required that he spend much of the work week out of town. Frequently, on his trips out of town, he would visit his mother and siblings. She felt cut off from him, and although her overall need for intimacy was lower than her husband's, she still did not feel intimately connected to him in a meaningful and significant way. Even though she had discontinued all sexual involvement with her lover, she still turned to him to fulfill her other intimacy needs.

When Mr. and Mrs. Walter were presented with the finding from their Personal Authority in the Family Systems Questionnaires, the imbalance that existed in their marriage was illustrated graphically.

The Personal Authority in the Family Systems Questionnaire was developed to operationalize key concepts identified as important indicators of maturity and successful separation from one's family of origin by transgenerational therapists (e.g., Boszormenyi-Nagy & Spark, 1973; Bowen, 1978; Framo, 1981). Personal authority is viewed as a continuum with successful individuation at one end and intergenerational intimidation at the other. The instrument consists of eight factor-derived subscales. A score is computed for each subscale. Individual scores are then categorized. Three categories are used: low, medium, and high. The eight category groupings are self-explanatory. Mr. and Mrs. Walter's Personal Authority in the Family Systems Questionnaire subscale rankings are compared below:

Subscale Ranking	Husband	Wife
1. Spousal Intimacy	Low	Low
2. Spousal Fusion	Low	Low
3. Intergenerational Intimacy	High	Low
4. Intergenerational Fusion	High	Low
5. Nuclear Triangulation	High	Low
6. Intergenerational Triangulation	Medium	Low
7. Intergenerational Intimidation	High	Low
8. Personal Authority	Low	High

An examination of the Personal Authority in the Family Systems Questionnaire rankings for each subscale for Mr. and Mrs. Walter shows that Mrs. Walter has achieved a high degree of personal authority while her husband has not. It is appropriate to say that Mr. Walter is still firmly enmeshed in his family of origin while Mrs. Walter seems to have successfully separated from her parents and is not entangled in intergenerational fusion or caught in triangular relationship dynamics.

The Personal Authority in the Family Systems Questionnaire profiles of Mr. and Mrs. Walter are helpful in understanding how Mrs. Walter's affair served to balance out the system's disequilibrium created by Mr. Walter's involvement with his family of origin.

CLINICAL IMPLICATIONS

The case of Mr. and Mrs. Walter provides us with a good example for demonstrating how information gathered through systematic assessment can be used to set achievable treatment goals and guide clinical practice. In situations where an extramarital affair precipitates a couple's entrance into marital therapy, a structured separation (Toomen, 1972) is often helpful. This treatment strategy is particularly useful when the spouse who has had the affair is still ambivalent and uncertain about what course of action to follow. Structured separation is a time-limited approach designed to deal specifically with the immediate crisis in the marriage. The purpose of this clinical approach is to help the individual spouses gain an in-depth understanding of their relationship and the dynamic forces that brought them together. With increased understanding about themselves and the nature of their relationship, spouses can begin to make more informed, rational and less impulsive decisions about themselves, their partners and their marriage. A major assumption upon which this approach is based is that a meaningful relationship, once established, can never be lost. It can only be changed.

Mr. and Mrs. Walter were asked to make a three-month commitment to explore themselves and their marriage. As is customary, during this three-month period, Mr. and Mrs. Walter met with the therapist for individual and conjoint sessions. For the duration of the structured separation, they lived apart, having agreed not to consult an attorney or make any permanent financial or property arrangements. An important part of a structured separation agreement is for both spouses to contract to be together, outside the therapist's office, only if both are willing to have such contact. The duration of any meeting is determined by both spouses, and each spouse is free to terminate the contact whenever he or she desires to do so. Both Mr. and Mrs. Walter agreed to do this. Mr. and Mrs. Walter also were asked to consider whether sexual relations with other persons were acceptable during this three-month period. They agreed that sexual relations with others was unacceptable, and that sexual intercourse between them would only occur if both chose to engage in that behavior. Neither was to pressure the other for any type of sexual involvement. Mrs. Walter made it clear to her husband that during this three-month period she would continue to see her former lover. She said that this was essential in order for her to be able to make a more objective, rational and informed decision about her future, her marriage, and her life.

Living alone and apart from one's spouse is an essential aspect of a structured separation. Experiencing the separateness and the loneliness that is an inherent part of the process is extremely important for both spouses. These experiences were especially important for both Mr. and Mrs. Walter, who had never lived alone. Each lived with roommates in college until they moved in together a year prior to their marriage.

Individual sessions, during a structured separation, are used to achieve a number of goals. These are:

1   To help the spouse gain a better understanding of himself or herself.

2   To help the spouse gain an understanding of the unconscious motives and dynamic circumstances that might have contributed to choosing his or her partner.

3   To use the knowledge gained through these individual sessions to make a more informed and conscious decision about his or her spouse and the future of their relationship.

4   To begin the process of identifying and working through unresolved conflicts and issues from one's past and family of origin that might constitute impediments to true intimacy with one's spouse.

5   To experience, perhaps for the first time, a truly caring and professionally appropriate intimate relationship with the therapist that can serve as a model for developing a more meaningful, close and intimate relationship with one's spouse.

Marital sessions, during structured separations, are used to help couples develop greater intimacy in their marriage. Initially, the couple is taught to use functional communication skills (Bagarozzi & Anderson, 1989). Functional communication is a prerequisite for increasing marital intimacy. The nonjudgmental atmosphere that evolves as the couple learns how to communicate effectively makes it possible for the spouses to role-take, reverse perspectives, decenter and become more empathic in their relationship together. Empathic understanding increases acceptance of the other and facilitates the expression of one's true self. This meeting of selves in a trusting relationship constitutes true intimacy.

It is important to keep in mind that the Marital Intimacy Needs Questionnaire is simply a vehicle that a therapist can use to help spouses begin the process of becoming more intimate partners. The various dimensions identified in the Marital Intimacy Needs Questionnaire are used by the therapist to help spouses focus their discussion on the particular unmet intimacy need that concerns them. The therapist's role, during these discussions, is to help the spouses move toward ever increasing depth levels of self-knowledge, self-awareness and self-disclosure. With each new level of personal awareness and self-discovery, the spouses begin to experience themselves and each other as unique human beings. Although spouses might have seen each other physically naked thousands of time during the course of their marriage, the psychic nakedness that spouses experience with each other when they are truly intimate is something quite different. True intimacy creates a powerful connection between two people. It is exciting, exhilarating and, at the same time, frightening. It is through this type of transactional exchange that spouses can experience their personal strengths and their vulnerabilities. It is through such encounters that spouses can begin to experience their shared humanness.

Intimacy, by its very nature, is ephemeral. In any relationship, intimacy can only be sustained for short durations. Nevertheless, it is the nectar that nourishes a relationship between two individuals and sustains them through difficult times and the mundane realities of everday existence. Without intimacy, the most spouses can hope to achieve in their lives together is a sense of familiarity, security, comfort and predictability in a context of stable and cooperative togetherness. The attainment of stability, predictability and cooperation should not be seen as a relationship that is in some way inferior or "less than" a relationship with intimacy. Spouses who can work together as a collaborative team capable of raising secure and responsible children have achieved no small accomplishment. In my clinical work, I have found that many couples and families enter treatment with the goal of returning to just such a previously established homeostatic balance. Such an outcome would probably be sufficient for a couple to achieve desirable levels of marital satisfaction as measured by most commonly used instruments designed to assess marital satisfaction. Difficulties arise, at the outset of therapy, when spouses differ in the therapeutic outcomes they hope to achieve. This issue became increasingly clear as clinical work with Mr. and Mrs. Walter progressed.

Mr. Walter's goal for therapy was to return to the status quo that existed prior to his wife's affair. Although six of the eight dimensions of intimacy tapped by the Marital Intimacy Needs Questionnaire were identified by Mr. Walter as being problematic, and the amount of time spent with his wife was judged to be insufficient, Mr. Walter believed that marital satisfaction would be restored and intimacy would ensue if his wife simply would recommit to the marriage and agree to resume sexual relations with him. As far as he was concerned, he could not separate his commitment to his marriage vows from his commitment to his wife. They were one in the same. Similarly, Mr. Walter could not separate out sexual intimacy from most of the other dimensions of intimacy identified in the Marital Intimacy Needs Questionnaire. For him, if his sexual needs were met sufficiently, he would feel himself to be intimately related to his wife in most areas except, perhaps, in the area of social and recreational intimacy. Unfortunately, Mr. Walter would not use his individual sessions to explore his relationships with his mother and his siblings. His commitment to his family of origin was immutable, as was his commitment to marriage and his marriage vows. The structured separation time, for Mr.

Walter, was a three-month period that he had agreed to endure while his wife "made up her mind." In his individual sessions, Mr. Walter avoided exploring personal dynamics. He said there was "nothing to be gained" by delving into his marriage and the history of his relationship with his wife. This limited capacity for self-exploration and the lack of psychological insight also made it difficult for Mr. Walter to role-take and reverse perspectives in discussions with his wife.

During individual sessions with the therapist, Mrs. Walter began to develop some insight into the dynamics of her affairs. She was able to explore objectively her relationship with her husband and her attraction to her lover. As therapy progressed, it became clear that a major aspect of Mrs. Walter's attraction to her lover was his ability to listen to her, his capacity for empathy and his ability to validate her as a unique individual. She said that for the first time in her life, she had begun to feel enough trust to reveal her true self. Her attempts to reveal this newly found true self to her husband during marital sessions were unsuccessful. Each time Mrs. Walter began to share her feelings and thoughts about herself and her relationship with her husband, Mr. Walter became defensive. Her self-disclosure and attempts to have him respond to her in more than a superficial manner were met with silence. Psychological blocking, during these times, was evident, and Mr. Walter found it painful to talk. During one such episode, Mrs. Walter turned to the therapist and said that when her husband became silent she knew she had "gotten too close" and that it was time for her to "back off."

In a subsequent individual session, Mrs. Walter disclosed that her husband's defensiveness was a major stumbling block to intimacy in their relationship and an important factor in her decision to have an affair. When asked if she had responded honestly to the Marital Intimacy Needs Questionnaire she said that she had. However, she added that her answers would have been decidedly different if she had been asked to complete the Marital Intimacy Needs Questionnaire prior to having her affair. She explained that she was totally satisfied with the level of intimacy and involvement she now shared with her husband. At this point in the session, Mrs. Walter was asked if she would be willing to complete the Marital Intimacy Needs Questionnaire again, only this time, using her lover as the target of her responses. Mrs. Walter agreed. Comparison scores for her husband and her lover are shown in Table 2.

An examination of Table 2 shows that Mrs. Walter's total intimacy need strength score as measured by the Marital Intimacy Needs Questionnaire rose considerably (195) when the target person was her lover rather than her husband. Her total intimacy need strength score of 427, nevertheless, comes close to the average range of scores for this instrument. Mrs. Walter explained these findings by saying that her relationship with her lover had allowed her to access, express, experience and fulfill, for the first time in her life, the full range of feelings that had been dormant for years. Her husband, sadly, had been unable to awaken these feeling in her. With her lover, however, she felt

Table 2   A Comparison of Mrs. Walter's Scores For Her Husband and
Her Lover

Need		Husband	Lover
Emotional	Strength	*35*	*90*
	Receptivity Satisfaction	100%	100%
	Reciprocity Satisfaction	100%	100%
Psychological	Strength	*48*	*81*
	Receptivity Satisfaction	100%	100%
	Reciprocity Satisfaction	100%	100%
Intellectual	Strength	*36*	*36*
	Receptivity Satisfaction	100%	100%
	Reciprocity Satisfaction	100%	100%
Sexual	Strength	*35*	*90*
	Receptivity Satisfaction	100%	100%
	Reciprocity Satisfaction	100%	100%
Spirtual	Strength	*20*	*9*
	Receptivity Satisfaction	100%	100%
	Reciprocity Satisfaction	100%	100%
Aesthetic	Strength	*18*	*21*
	Receptivity Satisfaction	100%	100%
	Reciprocity Satisfaction	100%	100%
Social/ Recreational	Strength	*20*	*40*
	Receptivity	100%	50%
Physical	Strength	*20*	*64*
	Receptivity	100%	40%
Total Need Strength		*232*	*427*

alive, vibrant, passionate and sexual. With her husband, on the other hand, she felt constricted and asexual, but safe, secure and protected.

As the end of the structured separation period grew near, Mrs. Walter gradually began to sever ties with her lover. She found it increasingly more difficult to deal with her guilt—guilt for what she had done to her husband and guilt for breaking up her lover's family. Eventually, she decided to return to her husband and to recommit to her marriage.

DISCUSSION

In this chapter, the Marital Intimacy Needs Questionnaire was reviewed. Intimacy is conceptualized by the author as being a multidimensional construct consisting of eight separate components. The strength of each component is believed to vary from individual to individual and the aggregate strength of these component needs also is thought to vary from person to person. For this reason, two individuals having the same aggregate need strengths for intimacy still may find it difficult to develop a mutually satisfying intimate relationship if the strengths of their constituent needs differ greatly. In addition to these intraindividual differences in need strength, intimacy is seen as an interactive and reciprocal process that evolves along with the development of a committed relationship. One would expect, as a relationship grows and matures, for intimacy to deepen as self-awareness and self-disclosure increase, however, this may not always occur. A variety of factors, both external to the relationship itself and inherent in the personal make-ups of the individuals involved in the relationship, can cause the process to stagnate, reverse its course or dissolve completely. To illustrate the complex dynamics involved in this interactive and reciprocal process and to demonstrate how external forces and intrapersonal issues can influence its developmental progression, a case example was presented. In addition to its heuristic value, the case discussion also spotlights a number of theoretical and empirical questions that deserve some consideration. For example:

1   Are the eight constituent need components identified in the Marital Intimacy Needs Questionnaire statistically independent, and are there differences between the sexes in the ability to differentiate between and among these various need components?

2   If sex differences are found to exist, what implications do such differences have for the practice of marital/family therapy?

3   Is one's need for intimacy a fairly fixed and stable trait or does one's need for intimacy change over time or fluctuate, depending upon the stage of relationship development, one's interpersonal context and the identity of the target person?

For Mrs. Walter, it appears that the strength of her need for intimacy differed depending upon the identity of the target person, that is, Mr. Walter or her lover. However, Mrs. Walter's desire not to hurt or offend her husband further might have caused her to be dishonest when she completed the Marital Intimacy Needs Questionnaire. Therefore, it would be inappropriate to conclude that the strength of one's intimacy needs reflects an emotional state rather that a stable trait based solely upon one clinical observation. Nevertheless, this question is one that can be answered empirically.

As this chapter was being written, data collection, from a clinical sample, was nearing completion. At this time, therefore, the Marital Intimacy Needs Questionnaire should be considered an instrument in the process of development, the reliability and validity of which have yet to be demonstrated. However, as a clinical aid, the Marital Intimacy Needs Questionnaire can be a useful tool.

REFERENCES

Alford, R. D. (1982). Intimacy and disputing styles within kin and nonkin relationships. *Journal of Family Issues*, *3*, 361–374.

Anderson, S. A., & Bagarozzi, D. A. (1983). The use of family myths as an aid to strategic th⸌ ⸍apy. *Journal of Family Therapy*, *5*, 145–154.

Anderson, S. A., & Bagarozzi, D. A. (Eds.). (1989). Family myths: Psychotherapy implications. *Journal of Psychotherapy and the Family*, *3/4*.

Bagarozzi, D. A. (1981). The symbolic meaning of behavior exchanges in marital therapy. In A. S. Gurman (Ed.). *Questions and answers in the practice of family therapy.* (pp. 173–177) New York: Brunner/Mazel.

Bagarozzi, D. A. (1985). Dimensions of family evaluation. In L. L'Abate (Ed.). *Handbook of family psychology.* Homewood, IL: The Dorsey Press.

Bagarozzi, D. A. (1990). *Intimacy Needs Questionnaire.* Unpublished Instrument, Human Resources Consultants: Atlanta.

Bagarozzi, D. A. (1995). Evaluation, accountability and clinical expertise in managed mental health care: Basic consideration for the practice of family social work. *Journal of Family Social Work*, *1*, 101–116.

Bagarozzi, D. A. (1996). *The couple and family in managed care*: *Assessment, evaluation and treatment.* New York: Brunner/Mazel.

Bagarozzi, D. A. & Anderson, S. A. (1982). The evolution of family mythological systems: Considerations for meaning, clinical assessment, and treatment. *The Journal of Psychoanalytic Anthropology*, *5*, 71–90.

Bagarozzi, D. A. & Anderson, S. A. (1989). *Personal, marital and family myths*: *Theoretical formulations and clinical strategies.* New York; Norton.

Bagarozzi, D. A. & Giddings, C. W. (1983). The role of cognitive constructs and attributional processes in family therapy: Integrating intrapersonal, interpersonal and systems dynamics. In L. A. Wolberg, & M. L. Aronson (Eds.). *Group and family therapy 1983*: *An overview.* New York: Brunner/Mazel.

Berscheid, E., Snyder, M., & Omoto, A. M. (1989). Issues in studying close relationships. In C. Hendrick (Ed.). *Close relationships* (pp. 63–91). Newbury Park, CA: Sage.

Boszormenyi-Nagy, I., & Spark, G. M. (1973). *Invisible loyalties*: *Reciprocity in intergenerational family therapy.* New York: Harper & Row.

Bowen, M. (1978). *Family therapy in clinical practice.* Northvale, NJ: Jason Aronson.

Bowlby, J. (1969). *Attachment.* New York: Basic Books.

Braiker, H. B., & Kelley, H. H. (1979). Conflict in the development of close relationship. In R. L. Burgess & T. L. Huston (Eds.). *Social exchange in developing relationships* (pp. 135–168). New York: Academic Press.

Bray, J., Williamson, D., & Malone, P. (1984). Personal authority in the family system: Development of a questionnaire to measure personal authority in intergenerational family processes. *Journal of Marital and Family Therapy*, *10*, 167–178.

Derogatis, L. R. (1980). Psychological assessment of pychosexual functioning. *Psychiatric clinic of North America*, *3*, 113–131.

Framo, J. L. (1981). The integration of marital therapy with session with family of origin. In A. S. Gruman & D. P. Kniskern (Eds.). *Handbook of family therapy* (pp. 133–158). New York: Brunner/Mazel.

Gurney, B. G., Jr. (1977). *Relationship enhancement*: *Skill training programs for therapy, problem prevention and enrichment.* San Francisco: Jossey-Bass.

Hudson, W. W. (1982). A measurement package for clinical workers. *Journal of Applied Behavioral Science*, *17*, 229–238.

L'Abate, L., & Bagarozzi, D. A. (1993). *Sourcebook of marriage and family evaluation.* New York: Brunner/Mazel.

Lo Piccolo, J., & Steger, J. C. (1974). The Sexual Interaction Inventory: A new instrument for the assessment of sexual dysfunction. *Archives of Sexual Behavior, 3,* 585–595.

Miller, R. S., & Lefcourt, H. M. (1982). The assessment of social intimacy. *Journal of Personality Assessment, 46,* 514–518.

Olson, D. H. (1975). Intimacy and the aging family. *Realities of aging.* Minneapolis: University of Minnesota, Minneapolis.

Olson, D. H. (1977). *Quest for intimacy.* Unpublished manuscript, University of Minnesota, Minneapolis.

Orlofsky, J. L., & Levitz-Jones, E. M. (1985). Separation–individuation and intimacy capacity in college women. *Journal of Personality and Social Psychology, 49,* 156–169.

Schaefer, M. T., & Olson, D. H. (1981). Assessing intimacy: The Pair Inventory. *Journal of Marital and Family Therapy, 7,* 47–60.

Tesch, S. A. (1985). The Psychosocial Intimacy Questionnaire. Validation studies and an investigation of sex roles. *Journal of Personal Relations, 2,* 471–488.

Ting-Toomey, S. (1983a). An analysis of verbal communication patterns in high and low marital adjustments groups. *Human Communication Research, 9,* 306–319.

Ting-Toomey, S. (1983b). Coding conversation between intimates: A validation study of the Intimate Negotiation Coding System (INCS). *Communication Quarterly, 31,* 68–77.

Toomen, M. K. (1972). Structured separation with counseling: A therapeutic approach for couples in conflict. *Family Process, 11,* 299–310.

Walker, A. J., & Thompson, L. (1983). Intimacy and intergenerational aid and contact among mothers and daughters. *Journal of Marriage and the Family, 46,* 841–849.

CHAPTER 7

The Measurement of Sunlight: Assessing Intimacy in Couples Therapy

Mark A. Karpel, PhD

Sunlight cannot be reproduced, but must be represented by something else—by color.

Paul Cezanne

"Intimacy" stubbornly resists simple definition. Ephemeral and often elusive in daily life, it becomes even more so as the object of intellectual analysis. But if the concept of intimacy is blurry and indistinct, our longings for it are powerful, at times overwhelming. The pleasures of intimacy are so deeply satisfying, its failure so painful, its vissicitudes so central to the concerns of couples who seek therapy together, that it demands an effort to wrestle conceptually and clinically with its ambiguity.

What do clients tell us? One woman described intimacy as "sharing special moments; having him look at me; having a great connection and a fun sexual relationship, and caring for one another." Another woman said that intimacy meant "basic trust, physical intimacy, and a common world-view." For one husband, intimacy meant doing things together: "The two of us, ice-fishing together, and her happy to be there with me. That's heaven." Another man said, "Touching, gifts; thoughtful things; sex. Being friendly, not critical. Nothing dramatic really. Love, trust and caring." On the absence of intimacy, one woman said: "I felt like a plant that was never watered or fed."

We can think of intimacy as the subjective experience of a very personal and private connection to another person in which we feel known or understood and accepted. Intimacy is a feeling state and this accounts for some of its ambiguity. It can be achieved through a variety of interactive modalities. Couples can feel intimate through sexual contact; through conversation and self-disclosure; though intellectual or aesthetic interchange; through their "private language" of jokes, nicknames, and tacit references; or through the deep awareness of each other's idiosyncratic "ways." This variety of methods in the service of a core experience accounts for some of the slipperiness of attempts to define intimacy.

Intimacy involves a satisfying feeling of close connection with the other, a feeling of being "on the same wave-length," part of a "We" that, at least momentarily, shuts out the wider social world. If nothing else, intimacy is private. The individual feels known or understood and accepted by the partner. Intimacy is familiar and informal. The partners can "take liberties," say and do things with each other which they could not—and would not—say or do with acquaintances or strangers. Because the needs to touch and be touched are so central to emotional closeness and a sense of safety in humans, intimacy often has a physical dimension—physical closeness, touching, sex—which can be both soothing and exciting.

While the description above captures what most clients mean when they speak of intimacy, given human idiosyncracy and complexity, intimacy is itself predictably complex. Intimacy comes in different "flavors." It can be delirious and ecstatic, cozy and comfortable, raucous or quiet, or lusty. The experience of intimacy may or may not be mutual. One client remarked, "Although it seemed like we were in the same chorus, singing the same words and the same song, we weren't."

Intimacy can have a dark side. We can hate those with whom we are intimate (in fact, hatred may be the only form of intimacy available to some individuals whose tolerance for positive intimacy is limited). Intimacy can co-exist with exploitation. Survivors of incestuous abuse often struggle with the torturous tangle of feelings that exist for an abuser who undeniably exploits them, but may provide the only experience of intimacy available to them.

Intimacy can be difficult to tolerate, especially for those who have been deeply disappointed or injured in previous intimate relationships, whether in infancy, childhood or later life. In these cases, intimacy can feel threatening, dangerous, and overwhelming. Individuals come into couple relationships with differing capacities to tolerate intimacy and to respond empathically to the needs of the other. The gulf between longings for intimacy and the ability to tolerate it constitutes a central problem in many couple therapy cases.

ASSESSING INTIMACY

This chapter will focus on how couple therapists can assess intimacy in the clinical context. Evaluating couples involves more than assessing intimacy. Intimacy is only one dimension of couple relationships. Other areas of importance include: current life stresses, resources, patterns of fairness and trust, gender patterns, stages and transitions in the family life cycle, individual pathology (depression, OCD, dissociative disorders, substance abuse), definitions of the presenting problem, among others. (See Karpel (1994) for a comprehensive format for evaluating couples.) Having said this, how can couple therapists understand patterns of intimacy in a particular couple's relationship? We want to understand: (1) each partner's characteristic needs for intimacy (the kinds of intimate interactions which are satisfying for him or her), (2) each partner's ability to tolerate intimacy, (3) obstacles to intimacy in the relationship, and (4) whether there are satisfying forms of intimacy which already exist for both partners (What works?). Potential sources of information include: (1) self-report, (2) nonverbal information, (3) "tip-offs" in anecdotal reports, (4) specific probe questions, (5) information about the couple's sexual relationship, (6) individual sessions, and (7) assessment instruments.

SELF-REPORT

The simplest way to assess intimacy is to listen when the partners directly discuss their feelings about it. In some cases, the topic will come up immediately in the discussion of the presenting problem. One or both partners may say something like: "We've really grown apart," or "I feel like we're strangers," or even more directly, "There's not enough intimacy in this relationship." When clients raise the issue of intimacy themselves, ask them to describe what they mean by this. The goal is to understand what they need in order to feel satisfyingly close. What would it look like? What would the two of them be doing? What would be enough? However, given the difficulty of defining intimacy, try not to get bogged down at this point. If clinicians have difficulty defining intimacy, there's no reason for clients to have ready definitions at their fingertips.

If the clients indicate that there have been changes in intimacy ("We've become strangers." and "We're not close anymore."), inquire about when these changes seem to have occurred. This may guide you to possible precipitants which may contribute to a formulation. For example, did the couple become less intimate when an aged parent or a grown step-child moved into the home with them or when one of them developed a serious illness which has since become the center of their lives?

NONVERBAL INFORMATION

There are a number of nonverbal signals which may indicate intimacy or the lack thereof. I emphasize "may" because we cannot assume that we know how what we see feels to the individuals involved. If a woman no longer loves her partner, his arm around her shoulder during the session can feel proprietary and unwelcome. A couple whose relationship has become strained may touch each other constantly or smile rigidly in an effort to maintain the outward signs of intimacy when the inner experience of it has vanished.

Nevertheless, your observations of non-verbal behavior can complement other sources of information, contributing to your overall impression of a couple's intimacy. Not surprisingly given the relational roots of intimacy, important nonverbal clues to intimacy involve gaze and touch. Do they make eye contact at all or do they seem to avoid it strenuously or unconsciously? Do they touch at all? Do they seem comfortable with touching each other and with the ways in which the other touches them?

Are there moments when they appear to be on the same emotional wave-length—that is, "attuned" (Stern, 1985)—during the session? For example, do they smile at one another and are their smiles mutual or are they one-sided or out-of-synch? When discussing events which are sad or painful, do they seem to be sharing the pain or sadness? There is no reason to expect that this attunement be constant during the session but, for couples who experience some degree of intimacy, it will at least be episodic.

OTHER TIP-OFFS

Nonverbal behavior provides one set of tip-offs about a couple's level of intimacy but there are others. Do they share humor in any way during the session? Do they laugh at the same time about the same things? Humor is a powerful avenue for intimacy, especially because it is associated with vitality and positive feeling. The experience of what's funny is very close to the experience of what's fun. Do they have "in-jokes"—references which are cryptic or meaningless to outsiders but full of meaning for the two of them?

Do they have affectionate nick-names for one another? Do they have routine forms of physical contact, such as his kissing the bridge of her nose or their "spooning" (lying close together front-to-back) before they fall asleep at night? Can the therapist observe instances of tacit understanding, that is, certain phrases which only they understand and which refer to a shared experience or world-view? Together, these patterns constitute aspects of a private language which joins them together and sets them apart from the larger social world. The existence of a private language—or lack thereof—constitutes an important index of intimacy in a couple's relationship.

Finally, in the course of information-gathering, do they relate anecdotes or experiences which suggest intimacy? Examples: "When we first got married, before the kids, we used to lay in bed on Sunday mornings and talk for hours." "We both loved taking walks together." "She gives terrific backrubs." "My father's death was horrible, but John was with me every step of the way. I don't know what I would have done without him." Alternatively, does this history of satisfying attunement seem conspicuously absent?

PROBE QUESTIONS

Some couples introduce the topic of intimacy themselves; others may not do so unless the therapist inquires directly. Probe questions (Karpel and Strauss, 1983; Karpel, 1994) can be used with all couples clinically and are designed to surface information about specific aspects of a couple's relationship, helping the therapist to understand the relational context in which presenting problems are embedded.

Two probe questions which I have discussed previously (Karpel, 1994) are relevant to, although not strictly synonymous with, patterns of intimacy. A third, involving the couple's sexual relationship, will be discussed later in this chapter. You can ask the partners, "What are the best parts of this relationship?" Answers to this question indicate areas in which "something is going right," in which the partners feel that they are getting at least some of what they want. This may surface examples of what works for them in terms of intimacy. One couple, whose relationship was characterized by chronic conflict over the husband's drinking, surprised me with their answers to this question. The wife said, "I can talk to him more easily than to anyone else. Outside of this problem, I feel like we really understand each other." The husband added, "Humor—sex—and I feel like I can say anything to her." Their answers suggested a surprising degree of intimacy, in terms of trusting self-disclosure and feeling understood and accepted.

You can ask the partners for a rough gauge of overall satisfaction in the relationship. "If you think about when you are together, what percent of the time are you basically feeling good about what's going on between the two of you?" Make clear that "good" does not mean ecstatic or deliriously happy but simply good as opposed to sad, crummy, miserable, blah, etc. Answers to this question provide a rough measure of satisfaction with the overall relationship and, while satisfaction and intimacy are not identical, they are often related.

You can also inquire directly about intimacy. Introduce the subject with a general statement such as, "Most people feel a need to be emotionally and/or physically close, to some degree, with their spouse or partner." Following this, you can ask about specific patterns involving intimacy in their relationship. Questions involve each individual's understanding of their partner's and their own needs for intimacy, how each attempts to initiate intimacy, and how each typically responds to the other's initiations. Their answers to these questions will probably provide the most concise summary of intimacy patterns in the relationship.

Begin the inquiry by asking: "How do you think your partner most enjoys being close or intimate?" Asking first about the partner's needs for intimacy allows you to see how well they understand each other's needs. Following this, ask each to express directly how he or she most enjoys being close. Remember that highly discrepant answers (between what he thinks she wants and what she says she wants) may indicate an emotional and communicational chasm between the partners, but they do not reveal whether the discrepancy is due to one partner's lack of interest or understanding, the other's difficulty articulating his or her needs, or a combination of both. These questions may stimulate discussion ("That's so typical. He's been saying that for 14 years. That is not what I want!"). If so, this may be productive and you should allow it to continue. However, try to clear room for one partner to complete his or her answer before the other provides "corrections" or affirmation.

This same sequencing of questions can be used for inquiry into the initiation of intimacy. For example: "What does your partner do when he or she wants to feel close?" and "How do you typically respond?" Once again, the questions can be turned around: "What do you do when you want to feel close?" "How does your partner typically respond?" These questions may also generate useful discussion. It may be interesting for an individual to realize that his partner completely misunderstands his signals for closeness or that what he intends as an inviting overture is experienced by his partner as a turn-off.

The couple's answers to these questions—about preferences for intimacy, initiation and response—provide one of the best gauges of intimacy in a couple's relationship. Their ability—or lack thereof—to correctly identify how the other likes to be intimate provides a powerful measure of attunement and emotional understanding in the relationship. Their answers about typical responses to intimacy shed light on the degree to which they will feel accepted by each other.

When couples describe little intimacy in the present, asking whether they have ever experienced intimacy, or satisfying closeness, in the past—and, if so, when—may contribute to closeness by invoking the memory of it. Asking about the circumstances of those occasions may help the couple to identify the conditions which facilitate intimacy for them. Finally, when neither can remember ever having felt satisfying closeness together, the partners and the

therapist will probably more clearly understand the limitations in the relationship up to this point.

THE COUPLE'S SEXUAL RELATIONSHIP

Sexuality is a core aspect of intimacy for most couples. What does and doesn't
go on in bed may tell the therapist more about the vissicitudes of intimacy in a
couple's relationship than what they argue about at the dinner table. For this
reason, therapists should inquire directly about the couple's sexual relationship
unless there are strong indications that this will seriously threaten alliance-
building. By doing so, you deepen your understanding of intimacy in the
couple's relationship and you signal that you are comfortable with the subject.
Couples with sexual concerns who are not yet comfortable raising them may be
reassured by this and therefore more likely to raise their concerns at some
point.

     One useful way to pose the question (Karpel, 1994) involves asking: "How
has your sexual relationship changed over time?" The phrasing is as neutral as
possible and the emphasis on change softens what might otherwise be an
uncomfortably direct inquiry ("Tell me about your sex life."). Clients can—and
do—choose how general or detailed they wish to be in answering this question
which provides clues as to how specifically the therapist can inquire further.
One area of particular interest in a couple's physical relationship is kissing.
Kissing is an extremely intimate act, in some ways more intimate than intercourse. Some couples manage to have a regular sexual relationship but their
conflicts over kissing provide an eloquent commentary on their difficulties with
intimacy and attunement.

INDIVIDUAL SESSIONS

Some couple therapists routinely include at least one individual session with
each partner as part of the initial evaluation; others, citing concerns over
imbalanced siding, secrets and expenditure of time and money, do not. When
therapists do meet with the partners individually, these sessions can be used to
further assess patterns involving intimacy in the relationship. This may simply
involve revisiting probe questions concerning intimacy discussed earlier. If
these questions were not utilized in the initial couple session, they can be
included in the individual sessions. In addition, the therapist can sometimes get
a truer picture of the individual's actual feelings about his or her partner in the

individual sessions and, in doing so, identify obstacles to intimacy. For example, a wife who is afraid of hurting her husband's feelings may reveal that his refusal to wash before sex seriously interferes with her sexual desire. The therapist may be able to help the couple de-toxify these issues, thereby enhancing the possibility of more satisfying intimacy.

ASSESSMENT INSTRUMENTS

Admittedly, there is something rather unintimate about using paper-and-pencil instruments to assess intimacy. Nevertheless, there are a number of such instruments designed to assess aspects of a couple's relationship which relate to intimacy. Whether one feels comfortable with and finds it useful to use such instruments is a matter of personal conviction and therapeutic style. I should note that I do not; I prefer to assess intimacy via clinical interviews. However, some readers may want to learn more about this method of assessment. Instruments which may be helpful for clinicians who want to assess intimacy include: the Personal Assessment of Intimacy in Relationships (PAIR) inventory (Schaeffer and Olson, 1981); PREPARE-ENRICH (Olson, Fournier, & Druckman, 1986; Fowers & Olson, 1986, 1989, 1992; Larson & Olson, 1989); the Interpersonal Relationship Scale (Schein, 1971); the Locke-Wallace Marital Adjustment Test (Locke & Wallace, 1959); the Spanier Dyadic Adjustment Scale (Spanier, 1976); and the Marital Intimacy Questionnaire (Bagarozzi, 1990). Further information about these measures can also be found in L'Abate and Bagarozzi (1993) and O'Leary and Arias (1987).

Basic Considerations in Assessing Intimacy

There are several basic guidelines which apply to all aspects of assessing intimacy in couple relationships. First, remember that acceptable and unacceptable levels of intimacy must be defined by the clients, not the therapist. If couples who barely speak to one another do not report dissatisfaction with intimacy, then intimacy is not a problem (unless you can plausibly demonstrate that other problems they identify are directly related to this lack of closeness). Second, consider similarities and differences in both partners' characteristic needs for—and capacity to tolerate—intimacy. Like sexual scripts (Rosen & Leiblum, 1992; Money, 1986), the partners' needs for intimacy and preferences for certain forms of intimacy may or may not overlap. The Greek term used to describe a particular type of chronic pain on intercourse, "dyspareunia," literally means "badly matched in bed." Some couples may simply be badly matched for intimacy.

Finally, when intimacy is problematic for a couple, the therapist tries to understand the forces or patterns which may constitute obstacles to satisfying closeness. Are one person's unrealistic expectations concerning intimacy intimidating or overwhelming for the partner? Are there unrecognized ethnic or gender differences which frustrate their attempts at intimacy? Do one or both partners' fears associated with intimacy sabotage their efforts to be close? Are they simply so overwhelmed by current or chronic stressors in their lives that they lack the energy needed for intimacy? Is one partner seriously depressed? Has trust been damaged by destructive actions taken in the past and left unresolved since that time? Identifying obstacles such as these may suggest courses of treatment which can minimize or dilute them, enhancing the conditions which foster satisfying intimacy.

CASE EXAMPLE: SANDY AND PAUL

What follows are excerpts from the first three evaluative sessions with a couple. Transcribed dialogue alternates with bracketed comments which illustrate the assessment methods being utilized, explicate the therapist's thoughts and reactions to material presented, and summarize sections of dialogue for the sake of brevity.

Paul is a 29-year-old engineer; Sandy, a 26-year-old psychiatric nurse. Seven months before requesting couple therapy they became engaged. One month after that, Sandy became pregnant unexpectedly. A wedding date has been set nine months in the future. They have been living together for only four months after an on-again-off-again long-distance relationship of two years.

The primary problem they present involves Sandy's fears and ambivalence concerning marriage. Sometimes Sandy feels comfortable with the thought of marrying Paul; other times, she wants to live with him but not formally marry; and sometimes she feels convinced that the relationship is a mistake and wants to end it. She expresses frustration over Paul's reluctance to have "intellectual conversations" with her and is concerned with feeling less physical attraction and passion for him than she has felt in earlier relationships. She wonders whether it is marriage in general which accounts for her ambivalence or marriage to Paul.

They have repeated exchanges which lead to Sandy angrily insisting that she wants to end the relationship although she does not follow through on these threats. Sandy notes that she had been taking antidepressants for about a year but discontinued them when she found out that she was pregnant. Paul presents himself as unambivalent by comparison. He feels that he loves Sandy and wants to marry her. He does get fed up with the roller coaster of Sandy's ambivalence but expresses optimism that things will work out between them over time.

[During the opening minutes of the first session, both partners seem fairly comfortable and there is warm laughter between them. There is also friendly laughter over who will start, that is, respond to the opening question about why they are seeking treatment. This moment in the session which can be tense and conflictual for many couples appears not to be for them. So, nonverbal signals from the opening of the session suggest that comfort and warmth are at least sometimes possible for these partners. When discussing her fears and doubts concerning marriage, Sandy notes that the unplanned pregnancy has propelled them forward in the evolution of the relationship.]

Sandy: I thought I could handle it when it looked like I'd have a whole year to work through my feelings, and then it was like BAM! We're having a baby. ... I felt that I was cheated out of working on this relationship with Paul. ... I felt like I had work to do on the relationship and the commitment and intimacy of it and haven't been able to do that.

[This highlights the role of an unexpected event in creating stress for the couple and in increasing tension in the already conflicted area of commitment. This stressor comes on the heels of another—their engagement—one month earlier and is soon followed by their move-in together, creating a pile-up of stressors in a relatively short time. The normal stress associated with these events is amplified by Sandy's fears and doubts related to commitment. The subject of intimacy has now been raised via the couple's self-report. I ask Sandy to tell me more.]

Sandy: There is a pattern I see us playing out a lot, which is that when things start to go really good and we're talking about getting married and it feels like it's gonna work out, I freak out and we'll have a big fight. "Forget it. I'm calling everything off. I'm out of here. You're pushing me." You know, that whole "Get away from me. I can't do this." I get too scared. I have this fear fantasy that I've had for years of waking up some day being 40 years old in my house with a bunch of kids and getting in my car and driving to the store and never going home. Just waking up and feeling like I'm unhappy, I'm stuck in this relationship. I hate it. I hate my life. I'm out of here. And that's a big fear that I have, and I think just the "marriage" and "forever" part of that just means you're stuck and you're in it forever no matter what.

[Sandy's rejection of Paul is often triggered "when things start to go really good." This raises a question about whether Sandy has difficulty tolerating intimacy, a possible obstacle to intimacy in the relationship. She describes a fear of being trapped; I wonder about its origins.]

Th.: Do you have any hunches where you got this?

Sandy: Yeah, I was in a pretty unhealthy relationship. Well, it wasn't unhealthy until the last two years, but I was in it much longer than I should have been. But I didn't really have the strength to leave and just was real stuck. I knew I wasn't happy but couldn't leave.

Th.: So you learned that you can't necessarily trust your ability to get out, if you should get out.

Sandy: Right. And I eventually did get out but it was hellish. ... And it scares me to think that I would allow myself to do that. And so what's to say that it wouldn't happen again.

[Sandy traces her fears to an earlier adult relationship. Powerful feelings like these often have their origins in distressing experiences in earlier life but, for now, I accept Sandy's explanation. Later, I ask both partners about the best parts of the relationship, using a probe question to explore patterns which may be related to intimacy.]

Sandy: Right now? [nervous laughter] I can think of a lot more in the past! [more laughter]

Th.: Let's hear about those.

Sandy: We have a lot of fun together. We do activities. We go rafting. We jump out of airplanes together. We do very exciting things. We travel a lot. And we do nice things, like picnic and eat cheese and drink wine.

[It's unclear to me whether this is a description of the current state of the relationship or its past. They indicate that these activities are less common in the present.]

Sandy: So those are the things I like the best, the weekends when you can take time for each other and just stay home all day Saturday. And sit around naked and have sex all day, you know, those kinds of things.

[There is no way for a therapist to know whether certain activities feel intimate to both partners but the picture Sandy draws gives me the sense that this couple probably has experienced satisfying intimacy together in the past. However, it seems that this is more difficult currently. When asked about this, Sandy replies first.]

Sandy: I feel that a lot of the best parts that I liked are very minimal now. They may happen but ... [doesn't finish the sentence].

Th.: Do you have a sense of why that is?

Sandy: Yup. Mostly because he works a lot now. And I've been depressed and off my medication so that really put a damper on things. ... I've been really tired and unmotivated and real negative. My attitude sucks about everything.

[Sandy identifies two possible obstacles to intimacy: Paul's focus on work and her own depression. Next, I ask Paul about the best parts.]

Paul: The same things. I love to travel. I have a passion for eating, and she loves to go eat. I have a passion for wine and she loves to drink wine. ...And there was a strong sexual attraction to her. ...We do a lot less of those things now because I work so much and sometimes I find her attitude to be [shrugs, a nonverbal portrayal of indifference].

[Paul agrees on the activities included in the best parts of the relationship and reinforces Sandy's inclusion of sexuality in this context. He also agrees that these experiences are less common currently. Later, I use probe questions to inquire directly about intimacy, beginning by exploring how well Sandy understand Paul's needs for intimacy.]

Th.: One of the reasons that people get into couple relationships is because they like being close. Sandy, you used the word "intimacy" earlier. What are the ways that Paul likes to be intimate?

Sandy: Paul likes to do things with me. It could be anything, like going out to dinner or taking a trip. ...Just spending time with me, doing something enjoyable.

Th.: [to Paul] Do you see it the same way?

Paul: Yes. She's right on the head as far as what I like.

Th.: How does Sandy most like or want to be intimate?

Paul: When we do those things, it brings out a comfortable atmosphere to where she can get intimate also. She has to be comfortable to be intimate. She has a low threshold of stress. She's the kind of person that wants to lay around all day long and be intimate, whether it be sexually intimate or talk all day long.

Th.: [to Sandy] Do you feel he understands you correctly on this?

Sandy: Yeah,...a lot of it has to do with feeling comfortable, and I would prefer to stay at home and talk as opposed to being out somewhere doing something. ...I remember being on vacation and being able to really feel close to you. The times that I remember and like the best were times that we were in your apartment, and we were home.

[Sandy indicates that she has felt close to Paul and that, although she enjoys their outings, she most enjoys time spent together at home. Both partners understand how the other likes to be intimate; this constitutes a good sign. If they understand what the other needs, the odds are better that some of those needs can be met. The next set of questions explores patterns of initiating intimacy and typical responses.]

Th.: [to Paul] When Sandy wants to be close, how does she initiate it? How does she let you know? Does she signal you?

Paul: [thoughtful] I definitely pick it up, and I'm trying to think how. She gets needy and she attacks that portion of me that's very intimate and very loving, very quickly. I come from a very loving family, a very touching family. She hits that.

[I'm struck by the words "needy" and "attack." Do they indicate fears and discomfort with intimacy on Paul's part or are they nonmeaningful examples of Paul's sometimes elaborate style of speaking?]

Th.: You mean she'll come up and show you that she needs a hug or something like that?

Paul: Yeah, it's mostly physical. Body language.

Th.: And does that generally get a good response from you?

Paul: Yeah, but not all the time. I can be distracted. Often I'll also want to be with her but we all need our space, I guess.

[Paul acknowledges that he doesn't always respond positively to Sandy's overtures, indicating that he has some self-awareness and can accept some responsibility for problems. He identifies his distraction and "needing space" which may constitute obstacles to intimacy.]

Th.: [to Sandy] Does that fit your sense of what goes on pretty well?

Sandy: That's part of it. The other part is that I'll sit there and say, "Can we talk about this?" like I did last night, and you were just so overwhelmed with your day that you couldn't do it. And there have been other times when I tried to get him to talk with me and he hasn't been able to go there, which is a big concern of mine.

Th.: What do you mean?

Sandy: Because I feel that I don't know whether I want to be married to someone who can't share my passion for feeding my soul or mind. I feel like a lot of the time he's too busy or too concrete to really have a great discussion about religion with me.

[These exchanges deepen my understanding of patterns of intimacy in the relationship, especially the couple's difficulty feeling intimate currently and Sandy's experience of an important area in which Paul does not meet her intimacy needs—for discussions which "feed her soul." I find myself cringing internally at her casual reference to Paul as "concrete." I wonder if Sandy talks to him this way often and whether it pushes him away from her. I wonder whether it is intended to do just that. I ask whether Sandy feels that they had discussions like these in the past. She says yes but wonders if this was because she was still seeing her ex-boyfriend Eric, noting that she and Paul used to spend a lot of time talking about that relationship.]

Th.: [to Paul] What does that look like from your side?

Paul: I've always told her that she thinks too much. She says I'm too concrete, and I think she's too abstract.

Th.: So you wish she'd "give it a rest" more.

Paul: Yeah, but I've come to realize that that's the person she is and who she wants to be, because that's the profession she's chosen. I speak numbers; she speaks feelings. And meeting in the middle is hard.

[Paul confirms the difficulty they experience in talking together, one of Sandy's preferred modes of intimacy. He acknowledges his own differences and realizes that he has to accept Sandy's needs as a necessary part of who she is. He introduces the theme of "meeting in the middle." I wonder if Sandy devalues the forms of intimacy which Paul prefers and sees her own preference—indoors, talk—as "better." Will Paul need my help in validating the legitimacy of his needs? With the phrase "I speak numbers; she speaks feelings," he also succinctly describes stereotypic gender differences. I begin to look for "what works," areas in the current relationship where intimacy may be more easily achieved.]

Th.: Just one question about this. Is it less difficult when you're traveling—what you called "meeting in the middle?"

Paul: When we're traveling alone, it's easy to do. When we're traveling with mother and time schedules, it's very difficult. More difficult than if we were at home.

[Here's an oasis—traveling together (a common one for couples)—in which intimacy is easier to achieve. Next, I ask Sandy about patterns of initiation and response.]

Th.: I'd like to flip this question around. How does he let you know when he wants to be close? How does he signal?

Sandy: He doesn't signal. He blows up. ...I don't know how he does it, to be honest. I don't think he does it.

Th.: [to Paul] Let me check it from your side. What do you think?

Paul: I guess I do it much less pronounced. I'll feed her by being there.

Sandy: No, this is for *you* we're talking about, not for me.

Paul: So how do I tell you that I'm needing something? [long pause] I'll say, "Hey, let's go to dinner." Or when I come home she'll be on the couch. And

I'll jump on the couch and lay my head on her and try to slow down from the day and get into being with her.

Th.: And when you do those things, how does she generally respond?

Paul: I think she responds by becoming closer to me but it depends on the mood she's in when I get home.

[A significant discrepancy opens up in the discussion of Paul's initiating intimacy. Sandy gives several seemingly contradictory answers: Paul does not initiate closeness; he "blows up;" she doesn't know how he does it. Paul has to think for quite a while but then expresses his own sense that he does initiate closeness and in fairly direct ways. Their answers are confusing but this very confusion and the heat generated by this question suggests that this area is worth exploring further. Paul's reference to Sandy's mood again suggests that her depression may be an obstacle to intimacy. Later, I ask directly about the couple's sexual relationship.]

Th.: How has your sexual relationship changed in the time you've been together?

Sandy: [to Paul] Do you want to go there? [loud, nervous laughter]

Paul: It was very intense when we would see each other [long-distance] and go on vacations and it was almost to the point of needy.

[They go on to describe a significant change since that time, with sex being much less frequent. It is unclear whether this follows the engagement, the pregnancy or moving in together, but the changes are noticeable.]

Sandy: The big thing that I see is that there was a point where I was just physically not attracted. I have no desire, no passion, and I don't want to.

Th.: When was this?

Sandy: Not too long ago. Two months ago maybe.

Th.: So, since the pregnancy?

Sandy: Yup. Yeah, when I first got pregnant I was really horny all the time [laughs], but then I think I became unhappy with a lot of things and pushed him away and that got really hard for both of us.

Paul: [interrupts] There was a long period of time there, almost a month, that I physically couldn't have sex with her, just my body would not respond to her intimacy. I'd get an erection and then lose it almost immediately.

Th.: So something in there was saying "No," was uncomfortable.

Paul: Yeah, it's just the passion wasn't there, and I rely on that.

[Changes in the couple's sexual relationship directly parallel those in their experience of intimacy: strong during the long-distance phase of their relationship but tapering off since. Did the literal distance in the early part of their relationship protect both from a shared difficulty tolerating intimacy? Did the existence of a third party, Sandy's former boyfriend, serve a similar function? Or are these changes simply a normal response to the pile-up of stress they have experienced? Paul again uses the word "needy," this time even more strikingly. Their sexual relationship was "almost to the point of needy," as though this were some kind of extreme, even dangerous, state. Is this turn of phrase meaningful? Sandy describes the loss of sexual desire. Does this once again signal depression or difficulty tolerating intimacy or stress? Paul began to have difficulty with erections; he says "my body just would not respond to her intimacy." This confusing tangle of changes, multiple precipitants and competing formulations is characteristic of couple therapy, especially in its early stages. Part of the work of treatment is to try to clarify what has happened, and why, in an effort to improve things for both partners to whatever extent this is possible. Finally, at the end of the session, I ask both partners about their goals for treatment.]

Sandy: I want to have less fears about marrying this man, and I really want Paul to be able to talk with me, if not all the time, then just to know that he has the ability to do that when he's in the right space. I think that would relieve a lot of tension that I feel. Those are the two biggest things that I'm looking for.

Th.: Good. [to Paul] What about for you?

Paul: The same thing, the first thing she said, because it definitely lowers my self-esteem when she says, "No, I don't want to marry you. I don't want to be with you." And...

Sandy: [interrupting] I never say I don't want to *be* with you. I never said that.

Th.: [to Paul] But they mean the same for you.

Paul: Yeah, that's right. They mean the same thing. ... And while she's aiming for me to get to a certain point in communication, I'm aiming for a middle ground somewhere, so that I can get to that point too and trigger her and make her feel comfortable with the relationship, but at the same time get what I want out of the relationship too.

[Both partners echo their earlier discussion of intimacy in describing their goals for treatment. Sandy wants to know that Paul is willing and able to talk with her, "to feed my soul," as she said earlier. Paul says that he is willing to try but reminds Sandy about "a middle ground" in which both of their needs are met. Their goals for treatment are not in obvious conflict, another good prognostic sign.]

Following the initial couple session, I meet with both partners individually. I want to understand better the origins of Sandy's fears of being trapped in a relationship. I want to get a history of previous romantic relationships in order to better understand her "relational profile" (Karpel, 1994), the characteristic ways in which she attaches in a close emotional relationship. With Paul, I want to explore further his references to "neediness." The first individual session, simply by virtue of scheduling, is with Sandy.

Sandy reports that her father was easy-going and quiet and that she loved him a lot. Her mother, she says, was more complicated. Mother was "very reactive," inflexible and would punish with cold silence. She "never cut me a break;" negotiating with her never worked. What stands out, however, is Sandy's description of her relationship with her younger sister.]

Sandy: My younger sister was the problem child. You know, the whole thing: colicky, wetting the bed, trouble with peers, stayed back in school. There was a lot of negative attention on her. ...The relationship that I had with my younger sister was terrible. I hated her for a long time. When I was 14 or 15, I actually moved out of the house and lived with one of my best friends and her family for the summer, because I couldn't deal with my younger sister. My parents didn't intervene or help at all. ...She was just mean. She did things just to be mean to me. When I had braces, every time she would just punch me in the mouth because she knew that my lips would bleed. There was a lot of fistfighting. I understand now that I was the target for my sister's anger at the whole family, but then it was just terrible. I always felt that I asked my parents for help, and they didn't help.

[I'm struck by the intensity of this experience for Sandy, feeling trapped, helpless, at the mercy of her sister with no one helping her. I wonder if this has anything to do with her fears of being trapped in a bad marriage and needing to run away. As a teenager, she did have to run away, in that she actually left home to escape from this situation. When I ask her about the worst feeling she has ever had, she refers back to this experience with her sister. Later in the session, she describes her first romantic relationships.]

Sandy: I was 16 years old. He's the love of my life. We were together for two years. With him, I really felt that I could be myself. He was the first person where I could tell him I was upset and he would sit and listen and hug me and make me feel better. And I could tell him the bad things I'd done, and he didn't think I was bad person because of it. I could go out and party with him. I could stay home and watch TV with him.

[Sandy tells me that she wanted to marry this man and had no doubts about it. However, she then discloses that she cheated on him in college, which led to the breakup of the relationship.]

Sandy: I wrecked something beautiful.

[I notice Sandy's use of the present tense: he "is" the love of my life. When I ask about this, she confirms that she has never loved anyone as much as him. I also note that she had no doubts and fears about marrying him. This information may indicate that there is something important missing in the chemistry between Paul and herself and that, because of this, the relationship may not work out. However, certainty about marriage for a teenager may not be a useful gauge for the feelings of a 26-year-old woman. Sandy's feelings in this early relationship provide an excellent description of intimacy; they convey safety, comfort, acceptance, and enjoyable activity together. I am, therefore, struck to hear that Sandy sabotaged this relationship. This deepens my suspicion that she may find it difficult to tolerate intimacy. Next, we talk about the five-year relationship with Eric, which she found so difficult to end. She tells me that at first she was the distancer, as she is now with Paul.]

Sandy: But then he wasn't able to get close like I needed. He was just so cold and unemotional that I felt like if I reacted enough he would see that this was important to me. He would see that this is serious. I tried to say it a hundred different ways, but he didn't get it.

[I'm struck by Sandy's description of Eric's coldness and the effect which this seems to have had of making him even more compelling to her. I wonder if this echoes her feelings for her mother who also could be cold and withholding. Later, I ask how she understands her fears of being trapped in a relationship.]

Sandy: Because I'm afraid of being unhappy again.

Th.: Have you ever felt like this apart from Eric?

Sandy: Yeah, with my sister, that summer that I felt that I can't live in this house; I cannot stay here. . . . And I felt like I had been asking for help and asking for help: "This is what's wrong." And nobody helped; nobody did anything.

[Both of us are struck by how similar her present fears of being trapped with Paul are to her feelings of being trapped with her sister. I notice the same feeling of desperate pleading—"asking and asking for help . . . and nobody helped"—that she expressed earlier in relation to Eric, saying it "a hundred different ways, but he just didn't get it." This feeling-state may be a core element of Sandy's relational profile in which case we would expect it to be part of her experience with Paul as well. I ask Sandy how she understands why she sometimes "freaks out" when things are going well between Paul and herself.]

Sandy: I don't know. Maybe if I ever came around to saying, "Okay, I really want to get close to you. I really want to get married," he would say, "Oh, forget it." That could be it. I can't say. . . . Also I like my alone time. It makes me feel strong as a person; it keeps me feeding myself. With Eric, I really feel that I lost my self in that relationship. Paul is able to give me more space, and I'm able to take more space but there are times when I'm like "No no no no!" and he'll do it anyway. ... I say "No" a hundred times and I start to cry and I get that overwhelmed feeling 'cause you're not listening.

[Here, as expected, we can see Sandy's feeling-state of desperate-pleading-without-success in relation to Paul: "I say 'No' a hundred times and I start to cry and I get that overwhelmed feeling 'cause you're not listening." Sandy wonders whether she becomes upset when things are going well because she is afraid of being rejected. This hunch certainly fits the pattern well. If it is accurate, it identifies a major obstacle to intimacy but at this point Sandy is only guessing. It's too soon for any of us to feel confidant that we understand the factors which underlie this pattern. Finally, I ask Sandy to describe how she feels about Paul.]

Sandy: I care about him a lot. I like to be with him. I like to be around him. I think we get along really well. We work together pretty well as a team. ... Can I say that I love him and want to spend the rest of my life with him? I don't know if I can say that about anybody right now.

[I ask whether she feels she would be with Paul if she weren't pregnant.]

Sandy: I don't think it's just the baby keeping us together. I really don't. We got engaged before I got pregnant and both very clearly knew we wanted at some point to get married and try and make things work together.

Th.: You did?

Sandy: I very much don't want him to leave. I just don't want the commitment of forever.

[The session ends with Sandy expressing positive feelings for Paul and a moment later, in keeping with her ambivalence, worrying about not feeling intensely attracted to him physically. The individual session has helped to identify an "emotional allergy" (Karpel, 1994) of Sandy's as well as earlier relational experiences which may create obstacles to satisfying intimacy in this relationship. It has also provided a clearer picture of Sandy's positive feelings for Paul in the present.

  Next, I meet individually with Paul who describes a happy childhood in a very traditional family. He tells me that he did not enjoy dating and that he ended the two serious relationships he had before Sandy. He explains how he sees himself emotionally.]

Paul: I very much keep my emotions inside, to the point where I don't get disturbed by most things. It takes a lot for me to get upset. I soak in a lot. I take a lot of stress. I'm very, very optimistic.

[This is consistent with Paul's presentation in the first couple session, and it is fairly typical of male socialization. However, Sandy may misinterpret Paul's outward evenness as deafness, triggering her feeling of pleading without being heard. This may, in fact, be an important dynamic in the interchanges in which Sandy "freaks out." Identifying this pattern and educating both partners about it may be an important intervention in couple therapy. Later, Paul discusses his concerns about his relationship with Sandy.]

Paul: There's a difficulty between us in integration. Sandy is such a strong personality that I don't feel integrated with her, and she probably doesn't really feel integrated with me because...she's responding to me not being integrated with her.

[I ask if Paul is talking about feeling close.]

Paul: Yeah, feeling close. When our relationship started, we were very close, to the point where we talked two or three times a day. I feel that we were closer then than we are now. ...I don't feel that we're a couple.

Th.: Like a "We."

Paul: Right, and when I approach her with that, she says, "Well, you're not trying to do it either." I feel like it starts with her and comes to me, and I send a signal back so we're pushing further apart.

[Paul's description of the "difficulty in integration" in the relationship underscores the lack of intimacy currently. I'm especially struck by the bluntness of his saying, "I don't feel that we're a couple." Therapists sometimes get a truer picture of "how bad" things are or how upset the individual really is in the *individual session* than in the initial couple session. Paul comments that Sandy is "extremely truthful, brutally honest even" and goes on to describe the mixed signals he received early on in the relationship.]

Paul: She kept saying, "I don't want to be in a relationship," but she'd do things and send signals that she *did* want to be in a relationship with me. I think her depression was at its peak then. ...She would come to see me because she felt that it was a safe house for her. She was very comfortable in my house. When she would come down, she would never want to leave, kind of like, this is really where she would want to be.

[Paul's description of Sandy as "brutally honest" reminds me of my reaction earlier when she referred to him as "concrete." His description of patterns in the beginning of the relationship suggests an element of counterdependency on Sandy's part, avoiding being with Paul because she was so comfortable at his house. Later, Paul agrees that they have probably never felt as close as they did in the beginning of the relationship "when Eric was in the picture." He goes on to describe how reactive he is to Sandy's—or anyone else's—moods.]

Paul: I'm always waiting for something to happen. I'm a very reactional person, and I look for that in her. And that's what kept us together.

Th.: You mean that if you get something positive from her, you react to that, and if you get a "freak out," rejection, you react to that?

Paul: I react to that. And I've always been that way. ... Easily molded. So right now, when she gets in her lows, I get in my lows too. And when she gets in her highs, we're both high and everything is great.

[The more reactive Paul is to Sandy's mood shifts, the more extreme the effects of her ambivalence will be on the relationship. It may help both of them if Paul can learn to be more emotionally independent from Sandy's sometimes rapid emotional shifts. However, this will have to be done carefully so as not to precipitate her feelings of being ignored when she needs a response. Bowen's (1978) notion of maintaining self while remaining emotionally connected will probably be a useful guide in this case. Later, Paul compares his feelings for Sandy with her feelings for Eric early on.]

Paul: When we were dating, my love for her and her love for Eric were almost the same in that I needed her. It was a need-based love and she needed Eric. I don't feel that now. And that may be healthy that we got rid of that continual need. That's what she thinks love is, and she doesn't have that with me right now. ... but I see it as healthy. It was almost unhealthy for me because there was so much of a need for her. ... It was overpowering. It was very blind. It was puppeting.

Th.: Do you mean that it gave her too much control?

Paul: Yeah.

[Here is the clearest example yet of Paul's discomfort with the level of need he felt for Sandy early on. The language is powerful: "unhealthy," "overpowering," "blinding," and "puppeting." His way of expressing this is somewhat confusing. Does he mean it when he says that it's better that "she doesn't have that with me" or is this a rationalization? In either case, his discomfort with his own needs for attachment is apparent. Paul begins to seem more like Sandy than he did initially, that is, uncomfortable with and in reaction to his own needs for attachment.]

The sessions described above utilize several methods to assess intimacy, including: nonverbal cues, self-report, probe questions (including direct inquiry about intimacy), asking about the couple's sexual relationship, and individual sessions. These are used to explore each partner's characteristic needs for intimacy (and the degree of "fit" between them), their ability to tolerate intimacy, what works currently, and possible obstacles to intimacy.

Sandy and Paul seem to have experienced satisfying intimacy at one time, particularly in the early stages of their relationship, and can still do so under certain circumstances, for example, when they are away on vacation. However, the experience of intimacy has become more difficult for them over the past year. The reasons for this are unclear. Obstacles to intimacy may be relatively straightforward. It may be that Sandy and Paul are simply overwhelmed by an accumulation of stresses, particularly an unplanned pregnancy which amplifies Sandy's pre-existing fears of commitment to a long-term relationship. Sandy's depression and Paul's involvement with his work may be major factors.

Obstacles to intimacy may be less obvious and more complex. Both partners may have difficulty tolerating intimacy which is suggested by a number of factors uncovered during the evaluation. It may be that Sandy's lack of intense sexual attraction to and persistent uncertainty about Paul, especially when compared to her feelings for her first boyfriend, are signs of a lack of chemistry that will ultimately doom this relationship. It is too soon for any of us to know which of these scenarios—or others not yet identified—is closest to the truth.

Couple therapy will be an arena in which to explore these questions further by testing possibilities and resources. Can the dialogue which takes place in treatment foster discussions which "feed" Sandy's "soul" outside the office? Does Paul's "concreteness" activate Sandy's emotional allergy, a feeling of desperate-pleading-without-response? Will Paul be willing and can he learn to respond to Sandy when she feels this way in ways which are good enough for her? Is any response good enough when she feels this way? Does Sandy's bluntness drive Paul away from her and make him feel and appear weaker? Can Sandy moderate these expressions and will it make any difference? What more can we learn about whether and how Paul initiates intimacy? Can his needs and ways of initiating be validated and benefit both partners? Can the conditions which make intimacy more accessible on vacations be identified and imported into the couple's relationship at home? Ultimately, we hope to find out whether this couple can more easily experience satisfying intimacy together and, if so, whether this helps Sandy to overcome her doubts and fears about marriage to Paul.

SUMMARY

Frustration and despair over the inability to achieve satisfying intimacy are central to the concerns of many individuals and couples who request couple therapy. This chapter has suggested a variety of methods which therapists can use to try to understand the experience of intimacy in their clients' relationships. As therapists, we should be careful not to impose idealized, external criteria for intimacy. We should be as interested in "what works" already for the couple as we are in what doesn't work for them. Intimacy must be understood and assessed in context, that is, in the context of chronic and recent stresses, individuals' relational histories, individual psychopathology, and strengths or resources which exist in the couple's relationship (Karpel,

1986). The experience of intimacy can be both deeply gratifying and maddeningly elusive. In light of its elusiveness, trying to assess intimacy, like trying to define it, can feel like trying to measure sunlight. It's gratifications make it worth it, both for clients and for therapists.

REFERENCES

Bagarozzi, D. (1990). Spousal inventory of desired changes and relationship barriers. In J. Touliatos, B. Perlmutter, & M. Straus, (Eds.). *Handbook of family measurement techniques* (pp. 469–470). Newbury Park, CA: Sage.

Bowen, M. (1978). *Family therapy in clinical practice.* New York: Jason Aronson.

Fowers, B., & Olson, D. (1986). Predicting marital success with PREPARE: A predictive validity study. *Journal of Marital and Family Therapy, 12,* 403–413.

Fowers, B., & Olson, D. (1989). ENRICH marital inventory: A discriminant validity study. *Journal of Marital and Family Therapy, 15,* 65–79.

Fowers, B., & Olson, D. (1992). Four types of premarital couples: An empirical typology based on PREPARE. *Journal of Family Psychology, 6,* 10–12.

Karpel. M. (Ed.). (1986). *Family resources: The hidden partner in family therapy.* New York: Guilford.

Karpel, M. (1994). *Evaluating couples: A handbook for practitioners.* New York: Norton.

Karpel, M., & Strauss, E. (1983). *Family evaluation.* Needham Heights, MA: Allyn & Bacon.

L'Abate, L., & Bagarozzi, D. (1993). *Sourcebook of marriage and family evaluation.* New York: Brunner/Mazel.

Larson, A., & Olson, D. (1989). Predicting marital satisfaction using PREPARE: A replication study. *Journal of Marital and Family Therapy, 15,* 311–322.

Locke, H., & Wallace, K. (1959). Short marital-adjustment and prediction tests. Their reliability and validity. *Marriage and Family Living, 21,* 251–255.

Money, J. (1986). *Lovemaps: Clinical concepts of sexual/erotic health and pathology, paraphilia, and gender transposition in childhood, adolescence, and maturity.* New York: Irvington Publishers.

O'Leary, K., & Arias, L. (1987). Marital assessment in clinical practice. In K. O'Leary (Ed.), *Assessment of marital discord.* Hillsdale, NJ: Erlbaum.

Olson, D., Fournier, D., & Druckman, J. (1986). Revised Edition. *PREPARE/ENRICH Inventories: Counselor's Manual.* Minneapolis, MN: PREPARE/ENRICH, Inc.

Rosen, R., & Leiblum, S. (1992). *Erectile disorders: Assessment and treatment.* New York: Guilford.

Schaeffer, M., & Olson, D. (1981). Assessing intimacy: The PAIR inventory. *Journal of Marriage and the Family, 7,* 47–60.

Schein, S. (1971). *Training dating couples in empathic and open communication: An experimental evaluation of a potential mental health program.* Unpublished doctoral dissertation, Pennsylvania State University, University Park.

Spanier, G. (1976). Measuring dyadic adjustment: New scales for assessing the quality of marriage and similar dyads. *Journal of Marriage and the Family, 38,* 15–28.

Stern, D. (1985). *The interpersonal world of the infant: A view from psychoanalysis and developmental psychology.* New York: Basic.

SECTION TWO

Methods of
Creating Intimacy

CHAPTER 8

The Intimacy Dilemma: A Guide for Couples Therapists

Karen J. Prager, Ph.D.

Couples often encounter a dilemma when they relate intimately to one another. On the one hand, their intimate interactions are immensely rewarding. They reveal their private selves to one another, drop public roles, personas, and defenses, and share the parts of themselves that are ordinarily hidden and perhaps less socially desirable. Ideally, they receive one another's disclosures with nonjudgmental acceptance and continued interest, attraction, and caring, and validate one another by indicating that they too have had such thoughts, feelings, and experiences. Assuming that some or all of these ingredients are present, the couple has an intimate interaction, and the effect of that intimacy can range from mildly pleasant to exhilarating. On the other hand, these kinds of intimate exchanges bring with them intense emotional vulnerability. The partners expose themselves to the risk of hurt and betrayal. They become more attached to each other and, as a result, are more likely to experience emotional anguish if separated. Intimate interaction, then, increases the potential for both joy and sorrow in the relationship. I call this dual potential the *intimacy dilemma*.

Most people reach adulthood with a subliminal if not explicit awareness of the risks of intimacy. As a result, most people find their own idiosyncratic ways of protecting themselves from those risks. These methods of protection are rarely fully conscious or acknowledged and can be relatively benign. Partners pursue separate interests, or retreat quietly to separate parts of the house.

Self-protection may also involve subtle distancing behaviors, such as avoiding eye contact with the partner or withdrawing affection. Petty quarrels have a similar impact. Some self-protective behaviors are considerably more destructive to the relationship, however: having affairs, developing a critical, verbally denigrating stance toward the partner, working long hours away from home, and so forth.

Couples also frequently get into conflict about intimacy itself. They can find themselves locked into power struggles over how much time to spend together, how much to disclose to or to listen to one another, how often and under what circumstances to have sexual relations, and how much touching and affection to give and receive. Research evidence indicates that these kinds of intimacy tugs of war are associated with the most therapeutically recalcitrant couples, and that these kinds of interactions are characterized by rapidly escalating anger during conflict (e.g., Babcock & Jacobson, 1993).

It is important for therapists to understand intimacy and help couples negotiate the intimacy dilemma. Research indicates that intimate contact brings many benefits with it, not only for relationships but also for individual health and well-being (see review by Prager, 1995). Intimacy serves as a buffer against the pathogenic effects of stress while self-concealment is associated with poor health, particularly when the social network lacks intimate relationships. The ability to confide is an especially important component of couple relationships; without it, they provide no buffer against the effects of stress. Further, poorly functioning relationships are themselves associated with negative outcomes, particularly depression (e.g., Beach, Sandeen & O'Leary, 1990). Finally, intimate relationships are routinely rated as more satisfying and rewarding than nonintimate relationships (e.g., Antill & Cotton, 1987).

Therapists can assist couples in their efforts to navigate the waters of the intimacy dilemma although they cannot remove the risks that intimacy brings with it. Therapists can help couples find a rhythm which allows them to experience the joy and satisfaction of the intimate contact they desire, while at the same time allows them to withdraw from intimacy without undue guilt or a disruption of the bond between them.

Problems with intimacy can be some of the thorniest that the couple therapist faces. First, they present an assessment challenge. They may be at the forefront of a couple's presenting complaints, but are just as likely to be subliminal, hidden within a pattern of destructive conflict, distancing, or emotional abuse. Second, they are a treatment challenge. In order to reap the benefits of intimate relating, couples must often rebuild a trust that has been seriously eroded from years of destructive interaction. Partners may be justifiably resistant to interventions that increase their vulnerability when they have learned over the years that they cannot trust their partners to be sensitive and gentle. They may claim that they want nothing more than to stop the fighting and the pain that goes with it. Most couples want this and more, however. They want the many benefits that intimate contact provides.

In order to maximize their effectiveness as guides through the intimacy dilemma, couple therapists must have access to two things—a conceptual model for understanding intimacy issues in couple relationships, and a set of strategies and techniques for helping couples to effectively negotiate the intimacy dilemma. My purpose is to provide a conceptual model, and to review couple therapy techniques that will benefit couples who wrestle with this dilemma. Specifically the chapter proposes the following,

1   Couple therapists need a clear definition of intimacy. First, this chapter presents a conceptual model that defines intimacy and the individual and relational contexts within which intimate interactions take place.

2   There are normal intimacy dilemmas that all couples face. Next, I outline normal intimacy dilemmas involving individual differences in (a) people's needs for intimacy, (b) the processes by which people meet their intimacy needs, (c) the various psychological needs people hope their intimate interactions will fulfill, and (d) fears of the risks of intimacy.

3   Couples with relational difficulties are often coping with incompatible preferences for intimate relating. Third, I discuss three sources of intimacy incompatibility: (a) incompatibilities stemming from normal individual differences brought into the relationship, (b) incompatibilities stemming from one or both partners' individual problems with being intimate (perhaps stemming from their own developmental history), and (c) incompatibilities stemming from either or both partners' inability to constructively communicate about intimacy and solve problems related to it.

4   Couples' intimacy dilemmas can be assessed through self-report and observational techniques. Fourth, I will demonstrate how techniques familiar to cognitive-behavioral therapists can be used to assess a couple's intimacy-related compatibilities and conflict.

5   The treatment of intimacy-related dilemmas usually requires both acceptance and change-oriented treatment strategies. Lastly, couples often need assistance in setting obtainable goals and focusing on appropriate targets. I suggest ways of matching intervention approaches to specific therapeutic goals and targets.

A MULTITIERED DEFINITION
OF INTIMACY

Neither scholars nor clinicians have been able to agree upon what intimacy is. The psychological literature offers up a cornucopia of intimacy concepts and definitions, varying in scope from those referring only to microbehaviors within interactions (e.g., maintaining gaze, leaning forward while communicating) to those encompassing every aspect of a relationship (e.g., sexuality, emotional expression, shared recreation, etc.) (see Prager, 1995, for a detailed discussion). Lay populations hold overlapping but not identical conceptions that emphasize self-disclosure, intense emotional experiences, and self-transcendence (e.g., Register & Henley, 1992). I have defined intimacy as a kind of interaction that has experiential components and sequelae (Prager, 1995). Further, I define intimacy within its individual and relational context. Individual capacities and fears on the one hand, and relational communication processes on the other, affect how the intimacy process unfolds and how it affects the individual partners and their relationship.

Figure 1 illustrates a multitiered conception of intimacy. Within the upper tier are aspects of the intimacy process itself. The lower tier contains contextual factors that affect the intimacy process.

Intimate interactions   Intimate interaction has a behavioral, a cognitive, and an affective component. Its behavioral component is the act of sharing, verbally or nonverbally, something that is private and personal with another. The private and personal nature of what is shared affirms the specialness of the relationship and the other person. When one partner shares authentic and private aspects of him or herself, the other partner thereby has the opportunity to really know the partner who shares and to convey acceptance to him or her. The risk of sharing is that acceptance is not always the outcome of the sharing. Sharing therefore involves a willingness to trust on the part of the one who shares and, ultimately, a history of trustworthiness on the part of the other.

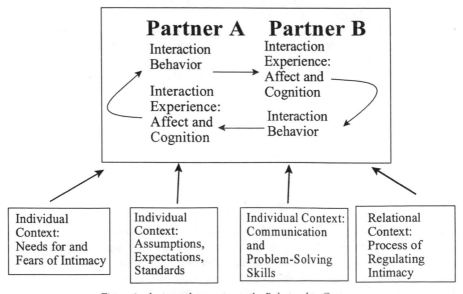

Figure 1   Intimate Interaction in Its Relationship Context.

The cognitive and affective components together make up the experiential component of intimacy. The cognitive component is the perception, within the interaction, that one is truly and fully understood by the partner. Equally satisfying is the perception that one truly and fully understands the other, that the other has let him or herself be fully known. There is evidence, that, particularly for women, one or both are necessary in order for the interaction to fulfill important psychological needs (Prager & Buhrmester, in press).

The affective component of intimacy consists of the positive feelings partners have about themselves and their partners during (or as a result of) the interaction. Warmth, closeness, empathy, laughter, pride in the other and so forth are an integral part of intimacy. Otherwise, the interaction may be open and blunt and may lead to mutual understanding, but it is not intimate (Derlega & Chaikin, 1975).

The context of intimacy   Intimate interactions do not exist in a vacuum, but affect and are affected by characteristics of the individual partners and of their relationship. There are individual and relational factors that affect the quality of intimate interactions and each partner's capacity for reaping their benefits. In order for intimate interactions to satisfy the needs of both partners, these contextual components must be intimacy-enhancing or, at least, intimacy-allowing.

The individual context refers to each partner's individual capacity for intimacy. Individual factors fall into three categories: behavioral, cognitive, and affective.

1   The term individual behavioral capacities refers to the communication skills that each partner is able to make use of in the context of the relationship. Of primary concern are (a) active listening and empathic expression, (b) the ability to articulate inner experience (e.g., see Davis & Franzoi, 1987), and (c) the ability to convey that one has heard, understood, and can accept the other's message.

2   Relevant individual cognitions are each partner's assumptions, expectations, and standards about intimate contact, and how those cognitions get expressed or acted upon within the relationship.

3   Individual affective characteristics include each partner's individual need for intimacy and related provisions and each partner's fears of intimacy.

The relational context refers to other characteristics of the partners' relationship that affect their opportunities for intimate contact. Theoretically, these could include any aspect of the relationship. In this chapter, I will focus on the intimacy regulation process (i.e., the set of behaviors and communication processes partners typically use to regulate intimate contact).

In sum, this definition includes behavioral, affective, and cognitive aspects of intimacy, and it defines individual and relational contextual variables that affect intimate interaction. Interventions can target the intimacy process itself or they can target individual or relational contextual factors that affect those interactions.

Normal Intimacy Dilemmas in
Couple Relationships

When two individuals decide to become a couple, they bring with them a host of individual differences in needs, preferences, and coping styles (McAdams, 1988). Variations in people's needs and preferences for intimate contact can be a source of intense frustration and distress. If partners fail to identify ways to meet their respective intimacy needs, they are likely to find themselves dissatisfied with their relationship. Since partners are more likely than not to have different needs and preferences, even the most satisfied and harmonious partners will eventually confront those differences and attempt to resolve them.

The need for intimacy encompasses two interwoven needs: a need for another person to fully know and understand us as we know and understand ourselves, and a need for that same person to also fully accept us as we are (also see Jourard, 1971, and Reis & Shaver, 1988). Intimacy needs can differ from one person to the next in several ways.

People have intimacy needs of varying strengths   Individuals vary in the strength of their needs, and these individual differences affect how they perceive and behave in different situations (e.g., McClelland, 1985). Henry Murray's typology of needs (1938) and his concept of a need as a stable individual disposition gave birth to a research tradition that reliably measures need strengths and has demonstrated their effectiveness for predicting behavior. McAdams (1984) measured intimacy motivation by coding stories people wrote in response to TAT stimuli for intimacy-related content. Intimacy-related content was defined as any theme related to relationships that involved positive affect and people engaged in two-way dialogues. The strength or pervasiveness of intimacy-related content was further scored through themes of psychological growth and coping, commitment or concern, time-space transcendence, union, harmony, surrender of control, escape to intimacy, and connection with the outside world. People whose stories contained these themes were more likely to self-disclose in group interaction, reported having more meaningful conversations during the week following the assessment, and described their relationships as more satisfying (Craig, Koestner, & Zuroff, 1994; McAdams, Healy & Krause, 1984).

People vary in how they meet their needs for intimacy Not unrelated to individual need strengths are the ways that people get their needs for intimacy met. As psychologists, we often think of intimacy in terms of intense interaction (e.g., Beach & Tesser, 1988). My own research has shown that people get their intimacy needs met in a variety of ways. My students and I recently interviewed 133 couples (266 individuals), and asked them to describe how they currently met their needs for intimacy and how their partners contributed to the fulfillment of those needs. Table 1 presents a synopsis of the results from

Table 1
"What Does Your Partner Do to Fulfill Your Intimacy Needs?"
Data From 133 Couples in a Suburban Sample[1]

I want my partner to:

Self-disclose to me.
"talk more about his feelings"
"to verbally...express her emotions and feelings"
"to be honest about her feelings"
"ask for what he needs"

Solicit self-disclosure from me.
"asking how it went with me for the day (showing interest)"
"asking probing questions...to help me identify my feelings"

Don't push me to self-disclose
"not pressure her"
"listen to what he says without pushing him to say more"
"he expects her to understand (accept) that he doesn't share his feelings because of the way he was brought up"

Talk to me about daily events
"talk with me more about daily occurrences"
"be available to talk"

Listen to me when I talk
"to listen and be interested and enthusiastic"
"listen and be supportive and encouraging"
"listen without judgement"
"be quiet when he's trying to tell me about his feelings instead of prematurely interpreting and vebalizing"

I want my partner to listen and:

Provide me with verbal consolation, support, and affirmation
"by providing verbal and physical comfort when telling something secret"
"by providing verbal acceptance when discussing private matters"
"by verbally reassuring her when she's feeling down about her divorce situation"

Show me she/he comprehends and is responsive to my feelings/needs
"just saying "I understand""
"recognizing; perceptive to moods and energy levels"
"provide recognition of his sharing of very private thoughts by some...response of deeper understanding" (to show that she listened)"
"to have my wife understand why I get upset and understand why I'm happy, sad, angry"

While keeping an open mind
"not be critical"
"listen without judgement"

Give me feedback/advice
"by listening to you and offering insight"
"to offer advice and feedback from personal experience"

Avoid offering solutions or interrupting
"asking about and listening to his needs without interruptions and distractions"
"by not trying to fix the problem, but just being there to listen to it"
"patient--waiting for her to be able to express her feelings"

I want my partner to:

Know what I need without my having to say.
"reading his mind--knowing when he does and doesn't want to be affectionate"
"know how I feel without me telling him and respond accordingly"

Spend time with me
"making time to be together for the two of them..."
"spend time with her; plan weekend activities and spend weekends together since they are so busy during the week"
"visit family and friends"

Initiate interactions with me
"wants her to continue to initiate intimacy and affectionate behaviors"
"take a more active role in initiating sexual activities"
"initiate conversations"
"be more pro-active; go get a babysitter, say we're going out"

Be physically affectionate with me
"touching, kissing..."
"reciprocate my hug, show emotions in the hug, hug me back"
"be there to hold her a lot"
"back rub and kissing"

Initiate, be responsive sexually
"more sex"
"to give her an orgasm"
"to be sexually available and willing"

Avoid pushing sexual contact/physical intimacy with me
"not so demanding with sex"
"understanding about...not wanting to be touched sometimes"

Acknowledge me in social situations
"when we're in a group, be with him and show that we're together"
"paying attention to her while with others"

Allow me to cultivate and enjoy outside relationships
"allow him time with his friends and not get upset about it (even if he spends more time with them than with her)"
"not getting jealous of the time, money, etc. she spends discussing her feelings with people other than me"

Make thoughtful gestures/gifts, be romantic
"notes for each other; give each other little gifts"
"to be more romantic"

Tangential Replies
"[he] expects when I am given advice to carry it out"

[1]Data compiled and categorized by Laura McCracken and Laurie Laughlin Davis

this study and reveals the variety of different categories of responses. Some of these categories are just what scholars and clinicians would have expected—self-disclosure, an attentive and accepting listener, affectionate and sexual contact. Other responses were more idiosyncratic (e.g, to avoid initiating sexual contact). It would be relatively easy for couples to find that they favor different ways of fulfilling their intimacy needs.

Different individuals seek to fulfill different needs through intimate interactions   While all intimate interactions should by definition fulfill our needs to be understood and accepted, they can also offer other provisions: guidance and advice, opportunities for catharsis or self-clarification, and an affirmation of a close relationship (Derlega & Grzelak, 1979). Preliminary findings from my own research indicate that reasons for seeking intimate contact vary from one individual to the next. I asked the same group of 133 couples to tell me how their partners contributed to the fulfillment of their achievement needs. The findings revealed that a substantial number of the participants listed some kind of intimate contact with the partner (e.g., listen, give me feedback, express pride in my accomplishments, express affection and respect) as contributing to the fulfillment of their achievement needs as well as of their intimacy needs.

People have different fears about intimacy   Research on nonclinical populations has shown that people can have fears about the risks of intimacy.[1] These risks are:

1   *Exposure*: We fear that important others will find out what is wrong with or shameful about us.
2   *Abandonment*: Once wrong or shameful things about us are exposed, we worry that the other may abandon us.
3   *Fear of our vulnerabilities being used against us*: We worry that our partners may gossip about our disclosures to others who will judge us negatively. Our partners may also use our vulnerabilities to denounce, criticize, or belittle us.
4   *Fear of loss of control*: Many people, especially men, believe they must be in control all the time. Being in control often translates into having no strong emotions except anger, so that one can always maintain a calm, unruffled exterior. It also can mean being able to dominate and control others.
5   *Fear of one's own destructive impulses*: People are afraid they will act irresponsibly because their emotions are so intense, so they keep them bottled up and hidden.
6   *Fear of being engulfed*: Engulfment occurs when a person cannot speak genuinely or reveal their own opinions, beliefs, values, or ideas without encountering anger or guilt induction from significant others. It also occurs

[1] This list is borrowed from Hatfield (1984).

when one cannot listen to another person's feelings or wants for fear of being obligated to sacrifice oneself completely to fulfill them.

Recognizing that intimacy carries a number of risks as well as benefits, Erik Erikson (1968) suggested that not only must everyone learn how to behave intimately, but each of us must also learn how to tolerate the anxiety that the risks of intimacy are bound to raise. Relationship partners, therefore, test each other's commitment to the relationship; they reveal themselves gradually to ensure that their partners are trustworthy; they develop ritualized ways of communicating with one another; they argue; they seek separateness as well as togetherness.

Relationship partners are bound to discover differences in one aspect of intimacy or another: the strength of their needs for intimacy; the strength of other needs that may compete with intimacy; their prefered ways of meeting intimacy needs; and their strategy for reducing the risks of intimacy. Individual differences between partners are normal and expected. Difficulties arise when these differences seem to create an unbreachable chasm or when couples are unable to resolve them.

Intimacy-Related Incompatibilities in Couple Relationships

Since all relationship partners will have different intimacy needs to some extent, it is important to understand how differences can become major battle grounds that contribute to relationship dysfunction and distress. Intimacy-related distress has two sources: partner incompatibility (i.e., problems stemming from intimacy's individual context) and dysfunctional intimacy regulation processes (i.e., the couple is unable to move together and apart without disrupting their bond).

The individual context: Personality and incompatibility   The compatibility of partners' intimacy needs and styles likely contributes to relationship satisfaction and to the amount of effort the pair must exert to make the relationship a gratifying one for both. Possibly, the harder the couple has to work to reconcile their incompatibilities, the more vulnerable they are to developing dysfunctional problem-solving styles with respect to intimacy.

Two types of individual differences can cause incompatibility: normal personality differences that are brought into the relationship and significant individual problems with intimacy. These individual differences may have their foundation in innate temperamental characteristics, or they may reflect the accumulated effects of prior experiences with intimate relationships or both. It is not uncommon for distressed couples to complain that their incompatibilities were apparent from the beginning, but that they stayed together anyway because they loved each other, or because they thought moving in together, marriage, having children, and so forth might attenuate their incompatibilities. For a variety of reasons, people who were incompatible from the beginning of their relationships can find themselves together and trying to work things out much later. Dysfunctional conflict can also create incompatibilities because of its polarizing effect on the partners. Incompatibilities stemming from the relational context will be discussed later.

Normal incompatibilities. Partners can bring one or several intimacy incompatibilities into their relationship. First, they can have incompatible intimacy need strengths. They may prefer intimacy at different intensities, different frequencies, and in different amounts. One partner may become intimacy-saturated before the other does. Laura may feel deprived of intimate contact with Lynn because Lynn seems to end their intimate conversations prematurely. Second, partners may have incompatible ways of fulfilling intimacy needs. For example, Maria may get her intimacy needs met through sexual activity, while Manuel fulfills his through talk. Third, partners may expect different kinds of rewards from their intimate interactions. Sally may seek intimate interactions for a variety of purposes (feelings of closeness, feedback and advice, an opportunity for catharsis, and so forth) while Saul only seeks intimacy when he desires to fulfill intimacy needs.

Three additional needs are worth considering as potential sources of incompatibility because they can appear to exist in opposition to intimacy. These are individuation, separateness, and privacy. Various scholars have viewed these needs as competing with, neutral to, or enhancing of intimacy need fulfillment (e.g., Bowlby, 1969; Kerr & Bowen, 1988). Dissatisfaction can arise if partners' efforts to fulfill these needs frustrate the intimacy needs of one or both partners.

It is not uncommon for partners to interpret each other's efforts to fulfill needs for individuation, separateness, or privacy as a personal rejection or a sign of failing love. It is therefore useful to clearly distinguish these needs from intimacy avoidance. Needs for individuation, separateness and privacy can be defined as follows:

1 The need for individuation is the need to maintain a subjective experience of distinctiveness and identity within a close relationship. Theoretically, this is the need to be true to oneself, the need to maintain a sense of personal integrity while still sustaining a loving attachment to another person. Behaviorally, individuation may be manifest in several ways in couple relationships. First, it encompasses the ability of each partner to express him or herself, and to tolerate the partner's expressions of personal beliefs, values, interests, goals, desires, wishes, and preferences without experiencing either as a betrayal of the relationship. Second, it is the ability of each partner to tolerate the other's

separate, independent work, hobbies, friendships, and other activities without belittling or undermining the partner or calling her or his loyalty and commitment to the relationship into question. Third, it is the ability of the partners to avoid emotionally intense, destructive conflict in the face of differences of opinion and desire. Fourth, it is the ability of each partner to retain meaningful decision-making power within the relationship. Violation of a person's needs for individuation may be experienced as psychological annihilation (Grotevant & Cooper, 1986).

2 The need for separateness is the need to be physically apart from another person (or to be completely alone). It seems to encompass a need to be free from the observing eye of another person, from interruptions and distractions, from noise, and from demands on one's attention. When we are needing separateness, the presence of someone that we love very much and would ordinarily enjoy being intimate with can be aversive.

3 The need for privacy is the need for control over the amount of information others have about us, and how much we divulge about ourselves. Privacy does not always require physical separateness; it does require control over access to the self. Violations of one's need for privacy are experienced as intrusive.

Compatibility of partners' needs for individuation, separation, and privacy may be as important to their relationship as compatibility of intimacy needs. We know little of how people go about meeting these needs; however, there is reason to believe that intimacy can both enhance and block their fulfillment. Possibly, one partner's preferred mode of fulfilling a need (e.g., involving the partner) can become a source of relationship discord if the other partner's preferred mode is different. Efforts to fulfill these needs outside of the context of interaction with the partner are not themselves symptoms of relationship distress or distancing; however, they can cause distress if they are interpreted as such (Moustakas, 1975). Couple therapists will need to make judgment calls, as distressed partners will sometimes mask desires to distance each other with claims that they are simply pursuing independent interests.

Psychological problems with intimacy. Besides experiencing incompatibilities in the normal ways they fulfill intimacy and related needs, individual partners may also have psychological problems with intimacy that create relational conflict. Partners' developmental histories in their families of origin, in their peer groups, or with previous relationship partners, may result in one or both maintaining dysfunctional patterns of thinking and feeling associated with intimate contact.

People who have chronic difficulties with intimacy may make unrealistic, distorted interpretations and evaluations of intimacy-related interactions and negotiations with their partners. These distorted thinking patterns can foster negative affect about the self, the partner, and the relationship, and set the stage for maladaptive relationship behaviors. Baucom and Epstein's (1990) five types of relationship cognitions can be used to chart faulty thinking patterns that can interfere with rewarding intimate contact. Examples of dysfunctional and functional assumptions, standards, perceptions, attributions, and expectancies can be viewed in Table 2.

Assumptions are beliefs about how relationships work, and about intimate contact in particular. These assumptions can be unrealistic, and can foster

Table 2
Contents of Intimacy-Related Cognitions: Some Examples[2]

Type of cognition	Unrealistic or Dysfunctional Examples	Realistic Alternatives: Examples
Assumptions: conceptions about why people do what they do, about interrelationships among people, and about what characteristics of people or objects go together.	a) When people love each other, they can't wait to be together. b) Men who confide their thoughts and feelings to their wives are weak and dependent.	a) Sometimes people who love each other like having some time apart. b) Masculinity and femininity are stereotypes that don't have to dictate how we run our relationships.
Standards: conceptions about how people and relationships should be.	a) Spouses should not need any privacy from each other; each should be like an open book to the other. b) A spouse should be available to me when I want to spend time together, and understanding and tolerant when I want to be alone.	a) Spouses who enjoy being open may nevertheless want some privacy (i.e., freedom from intrusion). b) Spouses can love and care about each other and still want different things at different times.
Perceptions: those aspects of information available in a situation that a person notices and that fits into categories that have meaning for him or her.	a) If I don't know where my partner is and what she is doing, I can't know whether she is being faithful to me. b) If I haven't noticed my partner doing nice things for me, that must mean he doesn't make the effort.	a) If I anticipate infidelity in every ambiguous situation, it is because I have difficulty trusting my partner. b) My partner may be doing nice things, even if I don't notice.
Attributions: thoughts about what causes events in the relationship, or about who is responsible for certain events.	a) My partner refuses to share his feelings with me in order to punish and reject me. b) My partner pursues me for intimate contact because she insists on being the center of my existence.	a) Perhaps my partner discloses less than I'd like because he has difficulty putting his feelings into words. b) Perhaps my partner seeks intimate contact with me because she finds it rewarding.
Expectancies: maps of the consequences of certain behaviors or events.	a) If I initiate sex with my partner tonight, she'll demand that I do so every night. b) If I open up and talk about my vulnerabilities, my partner will use them against me later.	a) Perhaps my partner only wants me to initiate sex part of the time. b) My father used to bring up my confidences to hurt me. My partner doesn't do that.

---

[2]The list of cognitions and their definitions in column 1 is from Baucom & Epstein (1990).

dissatisfaction and ineffective relationship behaviors. There are many opportunities, through movies, pulp fiction, and other media, to learn unrealistic assumptions about intimacy in long-term relationships. For example, one wife believed that the decreased intensity of her sexual attraction to her husband after four years of marriage was a sign that the marriage was failing. This belief was grounded in the assumption that successful relationships continue to be as exciting as they were during courtship. This assumption led her to avoid sexual contact with her husband, and blocked her from perceiving any constructive action she could take to make the sexual relationship more gratifying for herself. The assumption, together with the resulting behaviors, contributed to her feelings of dissatisfaction in the marriage.

Standards are beliefs about how marriages should be. Unrealistic standards may also contribute to dissatisfaction and ineffective behavior in relationships. The modern idealization of openness and self-expression in the United States, for example, may encourage people to set unrealistic standards for openness in their relationships. One very emotionally expressive man insisted that his shyer, less verbally facile partner change in order that their relationship might meet his standards for openess and intimacy. He believed that the only good relationships were those in which both partners were very open and expressive. He would often criticize and pressure his partner to communicate more openly, talk about his feelings, and so forth. These efforts to change the partner were causing resentment; the partner felt unappreciated and put down.

Perceptions or selective attention allow that partners do not always attend equally to all aspects of the relationship, and that what they do attend to will affect their relationship satisfaction. The person on the receiving end of the other's selectively negative recollections and perceptions can feel unappreciated, misunderstood, and unfairly accused. For example, partners may overlook many small acts of kindness and accomodation and focus instead on times when the other insists on having things his or her own way. In angry moments, one man only remembered other times in the relationship he had felt equally angry and frustrated with his wife. This selective memory caused him to conclude that the relationship was miserable and that he must get out as soon as possible. He communicated these feelings to his wife, and she responded with anger and fear of abandonment at his unfair perceptions.

Attributions refer to how partners explain each other's behavior to themselves. Research has shown that partners' efforts to assign responsibility and blame for negative relationship events can have detrimental effects on their feelings about the relationship and on their behavior towards each other (see review by Bradbury & Fincham, 1990). In intimacy-related matters, the most common dysfunctional attributions seem to center on a partner's efforts to spend time away from the partner or otherwise pursue separate friendships and interests. In these cases, negative attributions coincide with faulty assumptions about the need for the partners to be together and for their lives to intertwine at every moment. When efforts to individuate are interpreted as stemming from a lack of love, desires to escape from the partner, or deliberate efforts to deprive the partner of intimate contact, they can become the focus of conflict. Perhaps worse, when one partner capitulates to the other's demands, she or he can lose self-esteem, identity, and a sense of meaning and purpose.

Finally, *expectancies* refer to partners' beliefs about what is likely to occur in the future. They serve as maps of the consequences of certain behaviors or events. For example, a man may fear that if he expresses his vulnerabilities to his partner she will perceive him as less masculine and desirable. As a result of his expectation, he may inhibit his disclosures to her, thus compromising their opportunities to be intimate.

Faulty assumptions, unrealistic standards, selective attention, negative perceptions, blaming attributions, and negative expectations can each contribute to relationship dissatisfaction and increase the likelihood that partners' behavior will sabotage intimacy in their relationship. They are most likely to have a negative impact when they are accompanied by, or stem from, intense negative affect that has become associated with intimate contact or its possibility.

Dysfunctional thought processes both affect and are affected by intimacy-inhibiting affect. Anger, fear, disgust, shame, and guilt can be destructive when they become associated with partners' efforts to be intimate.

Figure 2 displays two layers of negative affect that can become associated with intimate contact. The top layer shows the emotions that are most accessible to awareness. The bottom layer shows emotions that may be masked by those in the top layer. Individuals who have severe or chronic problems with intimate contact may report feeling inappropriately angry, guilty, or disgusted with their partners. They seem less likely to report fear and shame, yet

Anger: Perception of other as intrusive, violating, demanding, or controlling.	Guilt: Perception of the self as not living up to one's own standards as a relationship partner.	Disgust: Intolerance or lack of empathy for others' "weaknesses."

Fear: Of rejection, belittlement, betrayal, coercion, loss of control, power.	Shame: Of one's own humanness, vulnerability.

Figure 2   Problematic Intimacy-Related Affect: Some Examples.

therapeutic work often reveals that these emotions are more difficult for people to tolerate. While any of these feelings can represent realistic responses to events in the relationship or the partner's behavior, I will address them here as though they are a result of individual partner difficulties with intimacy.

A person may respond with anger when opportunities for intimate contact arise if he or she experiences the other's initiatives as an intrusive or controlling. Assuming that these efforts are not especially controlling or intrusive, requests for affectionate or sexual contact, or queries about thoughts, feelings, concerns, events of the day, and so forth seem to be inappropriate stimuli for an angry response. Yet it is not uncommon to witness couples in which such efforts are more frequently than not rebuffed with anger. Nancy, for example, may or may not be able to identify her concerns about intrusiveness. Her emotional reactions stem from a history of childhood emotional (and perhaps sexual) abuse, during which she learned to associate closeness with shame. Angry emotions serve to mask and ward off the shame while at the same time discourage her partner from initiating intimate contact. Anger may also mask fears of losing control. Partners who fear their own vulnerability, perhaps because of earlier experiences of betrayal, may mask their fear with anger in order to avoid confronting it. If anger becomes a habitual response to intimacy, however, relationship dissatisfaction is likely to follow.

A partner who has chronic difficulties with intimacy may also respond with guilt when opportunities for intimate contact with the other arise. For example, when Jane believes she is not living up to her own model of a good relationship partner, she feels guity. Assuming that her standards are not overly perfectionistic, her guilt may be a response to her own lack of desire for intimate contact. When her partner makes requests or demands, Jane responds with self-deprecating thoughts and ensuing withdrawal. Rather than face the shame of her inability to experience the desires for closeness she believes she should have as a loving partner, she feels guilty about not living up to her standards and avoids situations in which she is likely to encounter requests for intimate contact. Her avoidance is frustrating to her partner, who is likely to respond to Jane's withdrawal by escalating her demands (Christensen & Shenk, 1991).

Finally, a person may feel disgust at what she or he perceives as the other partner's dependency or neediness. Because Abdul feels shame about his own needs, it is difficult or impossible for him to allow himself to feel empathy for his partner's needs. Therefore, he conveys an attitude of disgust toward her desires for sexual contact and open communication.

Some partners attempt to relieve their fears of abandonment and their needs for reassurance with intimate contact. Even when they find a partner who is glad to engage in intimate contact, the inevitable refusals that come from time to time can generate anxiety. In order to get the partner to comply and thereby to relieve that anxiety, these partners may behave in an increasingly coercive and demanding manner.

In sum, partners may bring longstanding problems with intimacy into their relationshps. Their faulty thinking patterns and negative affective reactions can wreak havoc on partners' efforts to enjoy intimate contact and maintain a positive attachment to one another. These individual problems may be associated with a DSM-IV Axis II diagnosis, and may only be ameliorated in couple therapy if they are not too severe.

The relational context: Dysfunctional conflict about intimacy   Dysfunctional interaction patterns make the partners appear to be more incompatible than they might otherwise seem by polarizing the partners until they seem to represent opposite ends of the intimacy continuum. There are two patterns of interaction that are associated with problems related to intimacy, the pursuer-distancer (or demand-withdraw) pattern, and the fight-to-distance pattern.

The pursuer-distancer pattern may create and exacerbate incompatibilities as much as it is a reaction to them. When partners bring different need strengths into the relationship with them, it may be easy to slip into a pattern in which the partner with stronger needs angrily demands to have his or her needs met, and is critical of the other when they are not, while the other partner seeks to avoid the demands (and criticism) through withdrawal and further distancing. This interaction pattern has been called by many different names: demand-withdraw, pursuer-distancer, engulfment-abandonment, closeness-distance, or affiliation-independence (Christensen & Shenk, 1991). It is a common pattern, it is destructive, and it frequently falls along gender lines.

In the fight-to-distance pattern, the partners engage in painful conflict that is sustained in part because it keeps them from becoming more intimate than either can tolerate without anxiety. The fighting of these conflict-habituated couples can become routinized, so that they automatically take on their different roles. While these routinized interactions may convince the partners that they want opposite things, they also allow them to maintain enough distance to reduce their anxiety about intimacy.

These dysfunctional communication patterns can focus on any content—how much time to spend together, how much to talk, how much and when to have sex, etc.—but the outcome tends to be the same. They polarize partners so that they seem opposite when their differences are only a matter of degree, and they protect the partners from getting too close for comfort. The problem is that these patterns generate as much negative affect as they avoid. Case 1 illustrates this destructive pattern.

In sum, intimacy needs come in many forms and there are many ways to get them met. Some forms represent normal variations in personality while others represent more dysfunctional approaches to intimacy. Still others are outgrowths of polarizing communication, which exacerbates differences. A good assessment is necessary for determining which combination of factors is operating in a particular relationship.

CASE 1
INTERVENTIONS ILLUSTRATED:
REFRAMING TO ENCOURAGE
ACCEPTANCE, AND BEHAVIORAL
CONTRACTING TO STRUCTURE
INTIMACY REGULATION

Rae Anne initiated couples counseling because she is angry, dissatisfied, and considering divorce, yet wants the marriage to work. Rae Anne is a 30-year-old woman with a history of bipolar disorder; her husband Larry (38) is an engineer who is bright and successful, but shows little affect and is extremely reserved. Larry is also rigid and not prone to compromise. The couple have been married eight years and have no children. Because her bipolar disorder prevents her from working full-time, Rae Anne is financially dependent on Larry.

Rae Anne complains that Larry comes home from work with scarcely a greeting and goes off to read the newspaper, play on his computer, or watch television for the remainder of the evening. She wants more contact with him—a hug and kiss when he gets home, and some conversation time. In order to increase their contact, she will follow him when he gets home from work and attempt to engage him in conversation. He frequently responds to these overtures with anger, and will withdraw further in stony silence in response to her efforts. Occasionally he refuses to emerge from his computer room even for dinner. Rae Anne then feels angry and rejected, and perceives that she is unloved. She reports that she is very lonely.

The couple is caught in a pursue-withdraw pattern. She seeks intimate contact, and he rejects her advances in favor of time alone.

Th: So what happens a lot when Larry comes home from work is Larry wants to disappear and just be alone and Rae Anne, who's been alone all day, wants to talk and have company.

[Therapist summarizes, shares her observations.]

Rae Anne: He'll go the whole evening without talking to me. Maybe he'll sit with me for 15 minutes or so at dinner. That's about it.

Larry: Well, maybe I would sit with you longer if you'd just give me some space for awhile...

Rae Anne: I give you space all the time, though. It doesn't seem to make any difference.

Larry: I don't call it space when you're in and out, talking to me, interrupting me when I just want to read the paper, talking about this, that, or the other. Everything you want me to do, right this minute...

Th: Okay, I'm getting the picture that you, Larry, really like the peace and quiet of coming home, that that's important to you as a way of winding down from your job, while you, Rae Anne, want contact with Larry, and no matter what you do, he just stays withdrawn. Like he wants so much peace and quiet you might never see him.

[Therapist validates each person's needs and perspective.]

Rae Anne: Right!

Th: Larry, let's you and I talk a minute about the way you handle stress and your love of peace and quiet. Have you always loved quiet like you do now, or does it seem you want more of it now that you're married to Rae Anne?

[Assessment issue: Are Larry's needs for separateness long-standing, or are they a result of his interactions with Rae Anne?]

Larry: I've always been a loner. I used to spend hours in my room. When I was a kid my favorite thing to do was to play with numbers, to figure things out. I've never been big on socializing.

Th: So you liked to play alone, in peace and quiet, even when you were a boy?

Larry: Our whole family's like that. None of us is a big talker. When we all came home after work or after school, we'd pretty much do our own thing.

Th: You know, it seems to me that a lot of people who go into engineering, at least that I've worked with, say that they are shy or introverted or like working alone.

[Therapist normalizes Larry's introversion, reframes it as a common personality trait.]

Larry: Yeah, I guess a lot of the people I work with are pretty similar to me. We still have to go to meetings, though—almost every day. But we get right to business because we're all under pressure from deadlines. There's not much socializing or joking around or anything like that.

Th: How was it when you first met Rae Anne [in college]? Were you as introverted then?

Larry: I guess I was, but I had to be a little bit outgoing to meet girls. Rae Anne was so outgoing she made it easy for me, I guess.

Th: So you knew Rae Anne was outgoing from the word go, it sounds like.

Larry: Yeah, I guess I did.

Th: Rae Anne, does Larry's description fit with your memory of how things went when you first met?

Rae Anne: Yes, I definitely did most of the talking. I interpreted his quietness as an inner strength at the time. He seemed really solid. I felt secure with him.

Th: Have you always been attracted to men who were quiet and reserved like Larry? Was there another relationship before Larry that was similar—or different?

[Therapist is reframing Rae Anne's problem with Larry as a source of attraction to encourage her acceptance.]

Rae Anne: Oh, yes, there was Bob. I dated him for a year before I met Larry. I just wasn't really that attracted to Bob, though. I much preferred Larry.

Th: What was Bob like? Was he reserved as well?

Rae Anne: Oh, no, Bob was so talkative. He always wanted to do things together, he was always calling me, and when he called he talked forever. I actually had trouble getting rid of him!

Th: But you didn't go for him?

Rae Anne: No, he was too much for me.

Th: Would it be fair to say that he was "in your face" all the time?

Rae Anne: That's exactly how it was.

Th: So you were much more attracted to Larry, who was quite reserved and who gave you plenty of space.

Rae Anne: Yes, I've always needed my space. I just can't stand it when someone is in my space.

Th: So, Rae Anne, if you were going to choose a husband all over again, I'll bet you would choose someone like Larry, no?

[Therapist encourages Rae Anne to consider the positive aspect of Larry's need for separateness.]

Rae Anne: Yes, I probably would.

Th: You know, Larry, it doesn't sound to me like Rae Anne really wants you to be very different than you are. [Therapist underscores Rae Anne's acceptance of Larry as he is.] It might be that she could be happy with changes that wouldn't be that dramatic.

Larry: Yeah, you may be right about that. It just doesn't seem that way when she nags me all the time.

Th: If Rae Anne were to give you a certain amount of space right after you came home from work, say an hour or so, do you think you'd be more open to spending time talking with her for awhile afterward? Maybe half an hour or an hour?

Rae Anne: I really don't need an hour. Half an hour would do!

Larry: I'd be willing to try that.

Th: Rae Anne, it sounds like that first hour after Larry gets home is crucial, and that you're not likely to get much out of him then. How would you feel about his having quiet time during that period if he promises to emerge and spend time after?

Rae Anne: That would be fine with me.

Th: I suggest that you test out this plan between now and our next session...

[The rest of the session involves helping the couple work out the terms of a behavior change contract in which Rae Anne agrees to refrain from interacting with Larry for an hour after he gets home, and he agrees in turn to give her his full attention during dinner (he agreed on an hour).

Assessment of Intimacy-Related Problems

Counter-indications for addressing intimacy issues   Before beginning my discussion of intimacy-related problems and their assessment, I present here four counter indications for addressing intimacy in couple therapy. Domestic violence, ongoing substance abuse, imminent separation or divorce, and the presence or revelation of an affair are all major crises in the life of a couple that destroy, or in some cases reflect, the shattered foundation of trust that prevents the couple from risking intimate contact. While a discussion of each of these severe marital problems is beyond the scope of this paper, Table 3 presents the clinical issues involved with each crisis and the necessary conditions for proceeding with couple therapy under each condition.

Ongoing domestic violence precludes the use of couple therapy. One violence-free year of living together should be a necessary minimum condition for conducting couple therapy. Even when this condition has been satisfied, the sequelae of the broken trust must not be underestimated. Trust will be long in rebuilding, and partners will need encouragement to be patient during that process. A good deal of intimacy, including sexual intimacy, may have to wait.

A substance abusing partner cannot effectively participate in couple therapy unless she or he has stopped using the substance. It is preferable if the recovering abuser is also in a treatment program to get assistance in staying off

Table 3
Counter-Indications for Addressing Intimacy Issues[3]

Crisis	Clinical Issues	Aim of Intervention
Domestic Violence **Battering **Sexual abuse/rape **Psychological or verbal abuse **Destruction of property or pets for purposes of intimidation	*Safety is the primary issue. *The abuser is fully responsible for his actions.	Complete cessation of violence. No reduction or partial relief from violence is acceptable. Couple therapy counterindicated if violence continues.
Substance Abuse **If either partner, upon commencing drinking, cannot predict the quantity of a substance consumed or the duration of the substance use, then a diagnosis of substance abuse is likely called for.	*Genuine intimacy is not possible with a substance abusing partner. *Couple with an alcoholic member: partner has not accommodated to the other's substance abuse. Drinking may be a response to other problems. *"Alcoholic couple": relationship is dominated by drinker's patterns of abuse; partner has accommodated by taking on more responsiblity.	Abstinence by the abuser. Ongoing support for abstinence through Alcoholics Anonymous or other substance abuse treatment. A (minimum) commitment to abstinence for the duration of couple therapy.
Imminent separation/divorce	*The fleeing partner's desperateness to avoid a painful or deadening trap; the bereft partner's desperate fear of upheaval and abandonment. *Working simultaneously on the negative, painful processes that brought the couple to the brink of divorce.	Contract with the partner(s) for a limited period of commitment in which some risk of intimacy can reasonably be taken.
Affairs	*Breach of contract/agreement *Lying to and disorienting the partner to keep the secret *The infidel is fully responsible for her/his affair. *Couple therapy should not be conducted in the presence of an ongoing, secret affair. *Intimacy is either impossible or severely curtailed in the absence of disclosure.	Once the affair is revealed: To create a calm, safe environment where the partners can understand the betrayal, and decide what to do next. To reassure each partner that they will survive the crisis, that their lives will continue, and that no course of action follows automatically from the revelation of an affair.

[3]These issues should be discussed and resolved before intimacy issues are addressed.

the substance, or is in a support group like Alcoholics Anonymous or both. Substance abuse can serve as an escape from the stresses and demands of an intimate relationship, and its cessation may cause fears and concerns about intimacy to come to the surface. As long as the recovering partner is substance-free, couples should be able to address these issues at their own pace (presuming no other counter-indications are present).

Imminent separation and divorce create a major crisis for a couple. Fears of abandonment are realized; the partners' attachment security is severely threatened. More often than not, partners talk of separation and divorce because they are desperately unhappy in the relationship, yet they seek therapy because they still have hope. Trust is damaged when separation and divorce are threatened. For this reason, the couple should, if possible, contract to stay with the relationship for a certain time period or for the duration of therapy. Once they have a contract, they are likely to need some time to rebuild trust before they risk more intimate contact.

Finally, few events shatter trust like a revealed, formerly secret affair. Couples who decide to remain together and rebuild the lost trust will often need to be cautioned to have patience and to give the trust time to rebuild before they risk new levels of intimate contact.

The basic couple assessment   Intimacy-related problems are best viewed in the context of the couple's other strengths and vulnerabilities. Problems with intimacy may be manifestations of other, more pervasive underlying themes (e.g., struggles for power and control) or they may themselves underlie various dysfunctional interaction patterns (e.g., withdrawal and avoidance). A thorough assessment of the couple will include the following five components:

1   The *presenting problem* is what brought the couple into treatment, and this is either what they are most urgently distressed about or what they are willing to talk about initially. Karpel (1994) reports that the most common presenting problems in couple therapy are (a) repetitive, unresolved conflict, (b) lost love, (c) conflict over intimacy, and (d) lack of intimacy. Whether couples initially complain of intimacy-related problems or not, however, any one of these may (or may not) suggest that intimacy is the problem that needs immediate attention.

Repetitive, unresolved conflict commonly centers on one or more themes: time together vs. time spent in independent pursuits; how money is spent; how often or under what circumstances to engage in sexual activity; how much affection is expressed between the partners; how much partners communicate openly and candidly with one another; how child-care and other responsibilities are assigned; personal habits (e.g., picking up after oneself or not); how decisions are made; how to handle conflict with in-laws; how to raise or discipline children; loss of romantic or loving feeling; feeling trapped, bored, neglected, or unfulfilled in the relationship; and the communication process itself (partners are critical of one another, attack one another, induce guilt, and so forth).

When intimacy is the issue, repetitive conflict may signal a fear of intimacy in one or both partners. Anger and arguments regulate intimate contact by making it undesirable. By staying in a state of conflict, partners avoid what is perhaps most threatening—the vulnerability of intimate contact.

When lost love is the primary complaint, one partner has often distanced her- or himself from the partner in one or more ways. Jeffrey is typical. He is not affectionate, not sexually involved, and not conversationally engaged with his partner Jeanette. Jeffrey reports that he can't help it when Jeanette asks for changes; he believes that his loss of affection is beyond his control. Unresolvable conflicts may cause a partner to distance, or the partner may never have been in love. Jeffrey believes he has been driven away by Jeanette's behavior, her unsatiable demands and her unrelenting criticism and abuse.

When intimacy-related conflict underlies complaints of lost love, it is often because the pursuing partner, having given up trying to engage the withdrawn partner, has no feelings of love left. Years of effort without fruit can result in despair and withdrawal on the part of the pursuer. While the withdrawn partner may sometimes rally to fill the gap, the couple may just as likely drift farther apart. Eventually, the lack of intimacy in the relationship causes one or the other to fall out of love.

When the presenting problem is conflict over intimacy, it is common to find a pattern of chronic and intense arguing about togetherness, sexual contact, communication, expressiveness, displays of affection, or support. Oftentimes, one partner has been labeled (perhaps by both) as the "bad" guy or gal who is identified as having problems with intimacy. This partner is usually the one who is resisting the other partner's efforts to establish intimate contact. For example, when Ed initiates intimate contact, Esther usually claims that she is busy with something else or otherwise has a good reason to postpone. She frequently feels ill. In these couples, tenderness, mutual comfort, expressions of love, and sexual contact are frequently constricted. Conspicuously missing in these relationships are occasions in which one person offers warmth, comfort, affection, or sexual overtures and the other accepts it.

Couples who complain of lack of intimacy may resemble Cuber and Haroff's (1965) devitalized couples. They lack intimacy or passion; neither takes the initiative. They live like roommates or brother and sister. One may be more dissatisfied than the other, but neither reports that the relationship is very satisfying.

2   An assessment of the *relationship history* can function as both a data-gathering mission and a therapeutic intervention. It is frequently helpful to ask the couple when and how they met, what attracted them to each other, what made each fall in love, and how they decided to get married (or live together). These questions can answer many important questions the therapist might have at the beginning of treatment. Has either partner's interests or lifestyle changed such that the relationship needs to change with him or her? Do partners relish memories of the past or regret them? Would they choose each other again? Are the partners fighting over the same issues that attracted them to each other in the first place (this is a common scenario)? A discussion of

these questions can be therapeutic when it reminds unhappy partners of a happier time, of why they wanted (and still want) to be together, and of the strengths that they may be overlooking in their relationship. Partners often leave a discussion of these issues feeling more optimistic about the future of the relationship.

3   *Direct observation of the couple's communication* is critical, as it is rare that couples are able to report accurately on all nuances of their communication. It is nearly always essential to observe (a) how the couple solves problems together, (b) whether either is able to listen empathically, (c) how they express themselves on an important or emotionally charged issue, and (d) how they express wants or preferences. In order to communicate effectively, couples must be able to express themselves clearly and specifically in such a way as to minimize defensiveness in the other, and listen and convey understanding. They also need to be able to verbally confront and resolve their problems while sticking to their agenda and avoiding emotional escalation.

4   Assess the couple's *current relationship functioning* in key areas outside of the presenting complaint. Find out whether they have strengths or weaknesses in the following areas: having fun together, sharing common interests, the sexual relationship, expressions of affection, decision-making, division of labor, child-rearing, solving problems, and so forth.

5   Check *individual strengths and vulnerabilities* by asking about the quality of parents' marriages, other dysfunction in the family of origin such as a history of emotional abuse, substance abuse, trauma and loss, instability, or mental illness. It is also important to learn about previous relationships and why they ended, affairs, employment status and satisfaction, other current close relationships (friends, family members, children), and individual histories of mental illness or substance abuse.

Assessing intimacy-related issues   The model depicted in Figure 1 can be used as a guide for the assessment of intimacy-related issues. Therapists must gauge the couple's ability to engage in intimate interaction, and must assess the individual and relational context within which these interactions take places. Partner incompatibilties, individual psychopathology, and dysfunctional problem-solving communication should all be assessed along with the partners' skills at communicating intimately.

The therapist can gain the most valuable information by combining direct observation of the couple's communication with a clinical interview. Therapists should view the couple engaged in intimate interaction, in problem-solving interaction, and while communicating their needs for intimacy and related provisions (individuation, separateness, and privacy). A check-list of behaviors to watch for when observing couples interact is displayed in Table 4; interview questions useful for assessing intimacy-related concerns are listed in Table 5.

Observational assessment of the couple's communication: intimate interactions. Since intimate interaction, by definition, involves the revelation of private, usually vulnerable aspects of oneself, it is instructive to observe partners

Table 4
Assessment of Intimacy I
Observation of Intimate Interactions

Behavior: Strengths
Openness, freedom, and spontaneity of expression.
Congruence between verbal and nonverbal communication.
Clarity and specificity of expression.
A minimum of interruptions.
Listening partner can reflect and restate effectively.
Expressions of concern, compassion, appreciation, empathy.
A varied and rich feeling vocabulary.

Behavior: Targets for Intervention
Walking on eggshells.
Words that say one thing while face or voice say another.
Vague overgeneralizations.
Partners seem to be waiting for the other to finish so they can have their own say.
Listening partner gives advice, criticizes, or dismisses.
Absence of positive affect or support.
No direct acknowledgement of feelings.

Affect: Strengths
Nonverbal demonstrations of affection (e.g., affectionate touches)
Verbal expressions of caring
Nonverbal posture: forward lean, maintains gaze, smile, turns toward partner.
Partners express positive affect in response to therapist's queries.

Affect: Targets for Intervention
Stony unresponsiveness
Unresponsive, dismissive, or critical.
Nonverbal posture: leans back, turns away from partner, averts gaze, expression of contempt, impatience, embarrassment.
One or both partners express anxiety, embarrassment, shame, or contempt.

Cognition: Strengths
Assumption that intimacy, support, nurturance, understanding are needs felt by all human beings.
Expectation that my partner is trustworthy and will handle my confidences with care.
Assumption that whether I confide or listen to confidence, I am giving something important to my partner.
Expectation that my partner can understand and appreciate me.
Assumption that I can make myself understood.

Cognition: Targets of Intervention
Sex-role stereotypes: "Real men" don't disclose, express feelings, need to talk things out. These needs are a sign of weakness or dependency.

Expectation that my partner specifically will betray my confidences.

Assumption that listening or confiding means I owe something that I cannot deliver.
Expectation that my partner cannot understand or appreciate me.

Behavior: Strengths
Partners treat the problem as one that they share. Each acknowledges his/her part in the problem.
Partners can define the problem and label their emotions clearly.

Partners can stick to their agenda.

Partners can acknowledge one another's needs and wants.

Behavior: Targets for Intervention
Partners blame one another and fail to see their own contribution to the problem.
Partners' definition of the problem and their expressions of their wants and needs are vague.
Partners get sidetracked during their discussion and fail to return to the problem at hand.
Partners push their own agenda, cross-complain, disqualify and discount one another or withdraw, and fail to listen to or acknowledge their partner's agenda. Partners "debate the truth" or otherwise get sidetracked and lose their focus.

Affect: Strengths
Partners respond to each other's negative affect with humor, support, or other positive behavior.
Partners' nonverbal affective expressions convey respect and concern.

Partners accept the full range of their own emotions.

Affect: Targets for Intervention
Partners reciprocate negative affect which then escalates as they continue their discussion.
Partners' nonverbal affective expressions convey contempt and dismissal. One partner expresses frustration through criticism and demands while the other is withdrawn in angry "stony silence."
Partners hide vulnerabilities and attack when threatened.

Cognition: Strengths
Partners assume that everyone has needs for privacy and separateness.
Partners assume that some of their reactions to each other are generalizations from other times and other relationships.
Each partner assumes that the other will periodically behave in thoughtless or inconsiderate ways.

Cognition: Targets for Intervention
Partners interpret bids for separateness as rejection or lack of love.
Partners attribute their emotional reactivity solely to the other's behavior.
Each partner expects the other to behave perfectly, and attributes "slips" to malevolent intent on the part of the other.

responding to one another's vulnerabilities as they are expressed. Johnson and Greenberg (1994) call the emotions of sadness, fear, pain and anxiety the "soft" emotions, because their expression tends to reveal vulnerabilities, minimize defensiveness, and promote intimate experience. Partners' responses to the expression of these feelings, when they are talking directly to each other (as opposed to talking through the therapist) should reveal each person's ability to express empathy and sensitivity and to communicate their understanding of their partner's message. The following topics can reveal problematic communication patterns in couples who are having difficulty with intimacy:

1   planning something pleasureable to do together.
2   listening and supporting the other as he or she expresses a concern or problem.
3   listening and supporting the other while she or he talks about something personal the partner may not have heard about before (e.g., how he or she feels about some aspect of their relationship, some experiences in his or her family of origin).

It can also be useful for the therapist to structure the interaction in order to observe the couple communicating under optimum conditions. This would allow the therapist to determine whether partners do not have good communication skills or whether they have them but are not able to make use of them within the context of their interactions. Examples of therapist structuring include (a) insisting that one partner listen quietly while the other speaks, (b) insisting that the listening partner repeat what she or he heard the other say, (c) stopping the speaking partner from attacking or blaming, and (d) instructing the speaking partner to use "I" language, to be specific, and to pause so the listener can respond. By observing how well the partners can respond to these instructions, the therapist can tell whether there is a gap between the partners' ability to communicate effectively and their performance of effective behavior.

The therapist can observe the couples' interactions to (a) assess behavior directly, (b) observe signs of unexpressed affect in facial expressions, gestures, and voice tone, and (c) make inferences about the partners' thinking patterns based on what they say and do. The list of intervention targets in Table 4 represents common dysfunctional behaviors, affective reactions, and thought processes. The ones listed are those that seem especially likely to have a negative impact on the couple's intimacy.

Strengths that are especially likely to enhance intimate relating are openness, spontaneity of expression, communicative congruence (i.e., nonverbal and verbal behavior give the same message), clarity (all present know what the speaker means), good listening skills (minimizes interruptions, reflects or restates, expresses concern, compassion, or appreciation for the partner's message in a believeable way), and a rich feeling vocabulary. Behavioral deficits that should be targeted for intervention include the following:

1   Guarded speech: partners are unable to express their private concerns, feelings, and so forth, thus shutting their partner out of their internal world. They may fail to express their needs and wants.

2 Incongruent communication: partners say one thing while their nonverbal behavior communicates a different message. In this case, the nonverbal message usually predominates.

3 Lack of listening skills: partners may lack these skills or may screen out each other's messages because they are threatening. They may fail to acknowledge each other's messages even when they hear them.

4 Lack of vocabulary for discussing feelings: Intimate communication requires some capacity for labeling and expressing emotion.

5 Unable to recognize feelings: Some individuals are unable to distinguish and therefore communicate about a variety of inner states. Others don't seem to experience a wide range of emotions.

Observation can also be used to gauge partners' emotional reactions to each other and to the therapy. Signs that partners are comfortable with the interaction include easy and automatic expressions of positive affect, demonstrations of warmth and fondness (through words or affectionate touches), and a relaxed posture. Partners' facial expressions, bodily posture, voice tone, and involuntary movements and gestures can also reveal negative emotional states. They may shrink away (nonverbally) from emotional intensity, or they may escalate it, matching negative statement with negative statement. They may also avoid intimate interaction or make attempts to reduce the emotional intensity of it by looking away, turning the head or body, and leaning backward away from the partner. Expression of the following negative emotional states may become apparent during attempts at intimate interaction:

1 Anxiety: Knowing another and being known and allowing one's vulnerabilities to be exposed create risks of betrayal, abandonment, and so forth. For example, George, who shared openly and freely, experienced anxiety with Gina who was more guarded and hidden, because her guardedness left him feeling more exposed.

2 Embarrassment/Shame: Example: Felicia felt embarrassed after disclosing because she believed that certain aspects of herself were unacceptable and somehow set her outside of the normal range of human experience.

3 Disgust, contempt: Example: Beatrice sometimes expressed contempt toward Bill because she would not accept the full range of his (or anyone else's) vulnerabilities.

Following the interaction, the therapist can use open-ended questions to explore any assumptions, perceptions, expectations, or attributions that accompanied the partners' verbal or affective expressions. Because automatic thoughts are often under specific stimulus control, they are most effectively accessed within the context of the interactions themselves. Identification of automatic thoughts through direct observation and inquiry may reveal information that cannot be gained from the interview or through paper-and-pencil inventories such as the Inventory of Relationship Beliefs (Eidelson & Epstein, 1982).

Observational assessment of the couple's communication: problem-solving interactions. Couples' styles of problem-solving about intimacy-related issues may be as important to observe as the intimate interactions themselves. Many couples have no difficulty participating effectively in intimate interactions once they get around to them, but couples' dysfunctional problem-solving efforts may essentially prevent them from doing so. If they cannot effectively resolve conflict about intimacy, the conflict can cause distress in and of itself, and it can leave a residue of frustration and anger that poisons further intimate interaction. Any and all of the following are likely to prevent effective problem-solving:

Dysfunctional Behavior

1 *Argumentativeness and blame.* Argumentativeness refers to a cluster of conflict-related behaviors that sabotage couples' efforts to define and resolve problems. First, couples debate the truth. They attempt to establish the validity, and thus the superiority, of their own views while refusing to validate the other's viewpoint and failing to discuss solutions. Second, couples try to determine fault rather than solving the problem. Finally, they put one another on the defensive when they assign blame, and do not see their own contribution to the problems.

2 *Lack of clarity in expression.* Partners express their needs and wants in vague terms, or are unable to label their emotions in a way that makes sense.

3 *Inability to stick to an agenda.* Partners may get sidetracked with irrelevancies during important discussions and fail to focus on solving their problems.

4 *Insensitive expression.* People may use words and phrases that are bound to put their partners on the defensive by insulting or demeaning the partner.

5 *Disqualifying or discounting.* Partners may "yes, but" one another, dismiss their positive efforts or qualities, or act like the other person never said anything and proceed with their own point.

6 *Cross-complaining.* Instead of listening to and acknowledging each other's concerns, partners compete with one another to come up with the concern of the day, in part to avoid having to deal with painful criticism from the other.

7 *Exaggerating or using absolutes:* Partners use words like always and never, right and wrong, and get into either-or debates.

8 *Polarization of content.* One person seems to want all the intimacy while the other either wants all the separateness or consistently rejects the first partner. Each expresses only one need and implicitly denies having the other need.

Dysfunctional Expression of Affect

Affect expression is dysfunctional when it escalates as communication continues and when it blocks listening and empathic responding. It is also dysfunctional when partners use their anger and frustration as excuses to attack and defend instead of in problem-solving.

Dysfunctional Thinking Patterns

People have cognitions about intimate communication or themselves as intimate communicators that contribute to their unwillingness and fear about intimate engagement. Commonly associated with intimacy are:

1 *Sex-role stereotypes.* Commonly seen in therapists' offices are those associated with masculinity (i.e., real men don't disclose, don't express feelings, don't need to talk, don't like that touchy-feeling stuff). Both women and men can hold these assumptions. Feminine stereotypes deny that women need independent pursuits, separateness, and individual identity. Partners may minimize their needs because they do not fit with prevailing stereotypes.

2 *Togetherness ideals.* Partners may believe that people who really love each other want to spend all their free time together. Efforts to make this a reality generate feelings of suffocation, irritation, and sabotage enjoyable intimate contact.

3 *Intimacy = love.* Partners may be less distressed by their lack of intimacy than by their assumption that less intimacy means less love. This is an example of "illusory correlation," which imposes an imaginary relationship between events or events and meanings.

4 *Scripts for events.* People may have overly rigid scripts about how certain events have to go (e.g., sexual encounters). The imposition of these scripts robs the couple of spontaneity and makes their interactions less rewarding or even punitive.

5 *Imposing self-schemas on others.* People presume that behaviors in the partner mean the same thing they would if they performed them themselves. For example, one wife complained about the extensive amount of time her husband spent playing tennis with the comment that, "If I was playing that much tennis, it would be because I was avoiding him and was unhappily married." This was not the case for her husband.

Assessing intimacy-related concerns via the clinical interview   Table 5 lists interview questions that can be useful for assessing the presence or nature of intimacy-related concerns. The interview is particularly useful for assessing the

Table 5
Assessment of Intimacy II
The Couple Interview

The Affective Context
Target Compatibility of Need Strengths

What kinds of things did you do to be close when you first met? Was it easy to be together and/or to find things you both enjoyed doing?

Did you ever have conflicts about how much time you would spend together? About how one or the other of you expressed love, caring or affection? About how much sexual contact you were having? About how much time you had alone together? About how much time one or the other of you spent working, studying, or pursuing hobbies that didn't involve the other?

Was there a particular time in your relationship when disagreements about any of these issues began? What else was going on at the time?

What kinds of feelings come up for you when you spend a lot of time with (or apart from) your partner? Do you ever find you get irritable or feel deprived? How do these times affect your feelings about your partner? About yourself? About other aspects of your relationship or family life?

How much closeness or intimacy do you generally prefer? Has this varied depending on your circumstances? Were there times when you wanted more or less closeness?

How much privacy (or separateness) do you generally prefer? Have you always had these preferences, or have they changed in recent years?

Have you ever felt that you were really alone in this relationship? How about in prior relationships? Can you remember a time in your life when you felt close to someone, cared for, and secure? When and with whom?

Have you ever felt that you gave your all and it still wasn't enough? Have there been prior relationships in which you couldn't seem to do enough for your partner? Have you felt inadequate in the face of others' demands at other times in your life? When and with whom?

Target Partners' Preferred Ways of Fulfilling Needs

Tell me about a time you remember in your relationship when you felt especially close to your partner.

Were you aware that this was such a special time for your partner?

What about that incident or time made it special?

What would you do now if you were interested in feeling close like that again?

Were you aware that this is what your partner does to feel close?

When, during your day to day lives, do you feel closest to your partner? When do you feel most distant?

Target Partners' Efforts to Regulate Intimacy and Separateness

What about times when you just need some space, time alone, or time pursuing independent activities? Have you experienced a time like this recently? What do you do when you want to have some time like this?

What does your partner do or say when she/he wants some space or for any other reason does not want to be close?

Are there times when you feel you *should* want to be close to your partner even though that's not what you want? How do you handle that?

How do you react to your partner's efforts to be closer to you?

How do you react to your partner's efforts to maintain distance?

Have you ever talked about how you establish closeness and distance? Have you agreed upon ways of communicating about this that work for you?

When are you most likely to have a big argument? Have you ever noticed that you tend to argue most either before a separation or after a time of intimacy?

partners' compatibility. Questions should address the following:

1   *Compatibility of partners' need strengths.* Therapists rarely have to ask to find out if couples want different amounts of contact and intimacy. This is usually distressful enough to be included in the partners' description of their

presenting problems. If not, this can be assessed straightforwardly through an exploration of the content areas listed in Table 5.

2 Sources of need strength incompatibilities: It is helpful to know whether partners brought their different need strengths with them to the relationship. If the problems were there from the beginning, yet the couple did not break up, then the presence of the problems may serve some unspoken function. For example, Kareem may fancy himself to be a very sexual person; his relationship with Bella, who is inhibited and mildly disgusted with sex, may be frustrating, but it pays off because it does not challenge his view of himself (he never has to say "no"). Alternatively, there may have been an identifiable time in the relationship when disagreements about sex began. In this case, it is helpful to know what else was going on at the time that may have preciptated their sexual problems. Finally, one or both partners may have changed over the course of the years of the relationship. Prager (1995) notes that people, in general, place differing emphases on intimate contact at different points in their lives.

3 *Compatibility of partners' goals for intimate interaction.* Apparent differences in intimacy need strengths may be due, in part, to one partner deriving a wider range of benefits from intimate contact than the other does. This may be especially true when one partner likes to spend more time in intimate conversation than the other, and one partner seeks more sexual contact than the other wants. Conversation and sexual activity can, for some individuals, fulfill a wide range of needs, not all of which are subsumed under needs for intimacy or needs for sexual fulfillment. These additional benefits may be illuminated by asking the partner to talk out loud to the other about the positive aspects of the desired activity for her or him. Common themes that may not emerge immediately include confirmation of one's attractiveness, reassurance of the partner's love and interest, and validation of one's own gender identity.

4 *Differing ways of getting intimacy needs met.* An additional source of incompatibility emerges when partners experience intimacy in response to different settings, behaviors, and so forth. It is therefore useful to find out when and under what circumstances each partner is likely to feel close to the other. Partners may be surprised to hear about the circumstances under which the other feels close or distant.

5 *Compatibility of needs potentially conflicting with intimacy.* It can be useful to ask each partner about the strength of their needs for separateness and privacy and how they experience those in the context of the relationship. Do they feel those needs are fulfilled? Do they ever experience the relationship or the partner as an intrusion? Under what circumstances does this occur? Can they contrast this with circumstances in which this is not the case? It can also be useful to ask one or both partners about how they meet individuation needs: that is, how does each fulfill needs to be his or her own person, to express his or her unique talents, abilities, beliefs, or values, or to make his or her unique contribution in the world.

6 *The regulation of intimacy within the relationship.* Questioning partners about how they regulate times of closeness and separateness can serve both an assessment and a treatment purpose. Simply through asking about this process, the therapist normalizes it, and suggests to couples that the problem is not having these differences but how the couple goes about coping with them.

Table 6
Goals of Intimacy-Oriented Couple Therapy

Affective:
    1. **Increasing each partner's acceptance of the other's individual differences.
    2. **Decreasing partner's fears about intimacy.

Cognitive:
    1. **Restructuring partners attitudes toward intimacy.
    2. **Restructuring partners' views of each other to facilitate understanding and acceptance of one another's more vulnerable aspects.

Behavioral:
    1. **Teaching partners skills for participating in and enjoying intimacy.
    2. **Teaching each partner to effectively regulate intimacy.
    3. **Teaching partners how to resolve intimacy-related problems.
    4. **Assisting each partner to more effectively express her/his "softer" side.

CONJOINT TREATMENT OF INTIMACY-RELATED PROBLEMS

I will present a cognitive-behavioral treatment of couples' intimacy-related concerns that is modeled after Christensen, Jacobson & Babcock's (1995) Integrative Behavioral Couple Therapy. This treatment program uses acceptance- and change-oriented therapeutic strategies to address relationship problems. Although behavioral, cognitive, and affective aspects of couples' functioning are closely intertwined, it is useful to think of them separately when setting goals for treatment. In brief, affective goals center on relieving fears of intimacy and increasing feelings of acceptance. Cognitive goals aim to restructure partners' attitudes towards intimacy and towards each other to facilitate acceptance and more effective relationship behavior. Finally, behavioral goals focus upon skill attainment, effective communication, and problem-solving (see Table 6).

Affective Goals of Intimacy-Oriented Couple Therapy

    1 Increase each partner's tolerance, acceptance, or even valuing of the other's individual differences in need strengths, preferences, and so forth. Johnson and Greenberg (1994) define acceptance as "a baseline attitude of consistent, genuine, noncritical interest, a tolerance" for all aspects of the partner. Acceptance also denotes an absence of any efforts to change the partner through reasoning, pleading, or coercion.

2 Ameliorate partners' fears and anxieties about intimacy, assuming that the fears are not based on previous experiences in the relationship. In the latter case, the goal is to help partners set a course for rebuilding trust.

Cognitive Goals of Intimacy-Oriented Couple Therapy

1 Restructure partners attitudes toward intimacy and separateness/privacy so as to minimize negative affect related to either. For example, when people view requests for intimate contact as intrusions upon their privacy or signs of unhealthy dependency, they are more likely to experience negative affect in response to these requests and to reject their parters' overtures. Cognitive restructuring can teach partners more realistic ideas about intimacy.

2 Restructure partners' views of each other to facilitate understanding and acceptance of one another's softer, more vulnerable aspects. Distressed couples commonly have difficulty seeing each other realistically. Rather, as Raush, Barry, Hertel, & Swain (1974) put it, they are likely to see every adversary they have ever faced embodied in their partner. This unrealistic perception may foster the negative attributions distressed partners commonly make about one another's motives (e.g., "she only does that because she knows it aggravates me"). Helping partners to restructure their views of one another can open the door to more benign attributions and, ultimately, to intimacy.

Behavioral Goals of Intimacy-Oriented Couple Therapy

1 Build skills for participating in and enjoying intimate interaction. Basic communication skills that provide validation and minimize defensiveness facilitate positive, intimate communication and encourage couples to take more risks with each other.

2 Build skills for effectively regulating intimacy. When one partner seeks separateness or privacy in the face of the other's explicit desire for intimate contact, the latter can feel rejected and devalued. Similarly, when one partner pursues intimate contact when the other needs separateness, the latter can feel smothered and intruded upon. An important goal in therapy is to validate both sets of needs and to help partners avoid personalizing one another's efforts to

meet needs for separateness. Partners can offset any negative impact by ensuring that the couple has time for intimacy (e.g., setting a later date for intimate contact when both will enjoy it).

3 Build skills for effectively discussing and resolving intimacy-related problems as they arise. Partners need good problem-solving skills when they face intimacy-related dilemmas. Confronting differences in needs for intimacy is an emotionally charged process. In part, this is because the couple relationship is often the most important source of intimate contact. There is a lot riding on the partners' willingness to contribute to the fulfillment of each other's intimacy needs. Further, it is easy for many relationship partners to interpret differences in intimacy needs as signs of waning love, faltering attraction, or failing interest on the part of the less intimacy-oriented partner. Systematic problem-solving processes can reduce the negative impact of differences on the relationship.

4 Assist each partner to be more effective in displaying her or his "softer" side. Johnson and Greenberg (1994) note that some self-expressions are more likely to elicit nurturance and cooperation from the partner while others are more likely to elicit defensiveness. Partners can become more skillful at expressing their needs and concerns in such a way as to maximize their partner's desire to cooperate and minimize defensiveness.

Therapeutic Strategies for Addressing Intimacy Dilemmas

Intimacy-oriented couple therapy addresses the familiar challenge couple therapists face when intervening with troubled relationships—to decide whether particular couple complaints are best addressed through acceptance- or change-oriented strategies. The first treatment challenge, then, is to match targets for change appropriately with interventions (see Table 7). While there are few empirical findings to suggest which set of strategies works best with which set of targets, my own clinical experience suggests the following:

1 Couples will benefit most from learning to accept (a) differences in their intimacy need strengths, (b) when, where, under what circumstances they prefer to get their intimacy needs met, (c) differences in how each uses intimate interactions (i.e., what kinds of gratifications intimate interactions provide), and (d) differences in their needs for separateness, privacy, and individuation. Recall that these are the kinds of differences that are often brought into relationships, and are likely to reflect personality characteristics that have grown out of early experiences with family, peer relationships, and prior romantic involvements.

2 Couples will benefit most from working to change (a) individual fears of intimacy that stem primarily from experiences prior to the current relationship,

Table 7
Targets of Acceptance- and Change-Oriented Strategies

Target: Individual Differences in Needs for Intimacy
Acceptance-oriented strategies for:
***Differences in partners' intimacy need strengths.
***Differences in how they prefer to get their intimacy needs met.
***Differences in how each use intimate interactions.

Change-oriented strategies for:
***Fears of intimacy stemming from individual learning histories.

Target: Assumptions, Expectations, Standards, Attributions
Change-oriented strategies for:
***Individual cognitions that inhibit enjoyment of intimacy.
***Dysfunctional attributions about the partner's participation (or failure to participate) in intimate contact.

Target: Communication and problem-solving skills
Change-oriented strategies for:
***Lack of communication skills.
***Minimizing the risks of intimacy.
***Destructive patterns of regulating intimacy that polarize the partners.

(b) unrealistic or distorted relationship cognitions, particularly if these inhibit their enjoyment of intimate contact, (c) distorted negative attributions about the partner's participation (or failure to participate) in intimate contact (i.e., inappropriate personalization of the partner's needs and actions), (d) lack of communication skills for engaging in intimate interactions, (e) destructive patterns of communication that shatter trust and thereby discourage intimate contact (e.g., active rejection of the other, belittlement, threats to abandon the relationship, efforts to control the partner), and (f) destructive patterns of regulating and negotiating intimacy that polarize the partners and thereby exaggerate their apparent incompatibilities.

THE COURSE OF TREATMENT

Since every couple is different, the following is only a rough outline of the course of treatment. It begins with classic behavioral marital therapy techniques that structure couples' efforts to bring positively reinforcing behaviors into the relationship (see Table 8). These techniques increase the partners'

Table 8
Therapeutic Strategies and Techniques
For Promoting Intimacy

Behavior Exchange: Partners increase the positively reinforcing behaviors they perform.

Cognitive Restructuring to Encourage Acceptance: The therapist models new ways of thinking about each partner and the relationship.

> **Specific techniques:**
> *Normalizing*. Through instruction and modeling, the therapist helps the partners to think of their differences as normal.
> *Validating*. The therapist presents each partner's perspective as reasonable and understandable given his/her life history and current situation.
> *Highlighting advantages*. The therapist encourages each partner to see the attractive side of the other's attributes.
> *Problems belong to the couple*. To diffuse the blame-and-defend cycle, the therapist reframes problems as belonging to the couple rather than the individuals.

Behavioral Contracting: Each partner agrees to change behavior for the benefit of the relationship. The "contract" specifies what each will do, when, and under what circumstances.

Communication and Problem-Solving Training: Teaches couples how to engage in problem-solving instead of arguments. Problem definition and problem solution phases are distinguished.

Intimacy enhancement: Teaches partners how to 1) be receptive and caring with each other's vulnerabilities, and 2) to express their "softer," more vulnerable side with the partner (rather than always expressing anger, withdrawing, being stoic, etc.).

hopefulness that the relationship can change for the better, and may rekindle some of the positive feelings that initially brought the partners together. This sets the stage for the acceptance strategies. Encouraging partners to desist from efforts to make one another "change their wicked ways" and to accept each other's quirks and proclivities, begins to create a climate in their relationship that reduces partners' defensiveness and makes it easier for them to embark on a journey of much-needed behavior change. Change-oriented strategies focused on behavior provide partners with alternative ways of interacting that promote cooperation and build a foundation of trust on which further explorations into intimacy must be based. Change-oriented strategies focused on effective intimacy build on earlier accomplishments of the couple, and encourage them to risk higher levels of vulnerability and to respond to each other with more sensitivity and acceptance when those risks are taken.

Behavior Exchange strives to change nonspecific negative affect in the relationship through increasing the positively reinforcing behaviors each partner performs. The optimum behavior exchange process involves identifying minimal cost behaviors that the giving partner can perform.[2] These are

---

[2] This technique is from Christensen, et al.'s Integrative Behavioral Couple Therapy, pp. 50–51.

behaviors that (a) are not controversial, (b) are low in cost, in that they do not require new skills, (c) increase positive rather than decrease negative behaviors, and (d) are positively reinforcing for the partner. Responsibility for deciding what might improve the relationship rests with the giver. The giver is then asked to do more of the identified behaviors during the course of a week. It is also reasonable for the partner to make direct requests, which the giver has said she or he is willing to fulfill. Christensen et al. (1995) say that allowing the giver "greater latitude in what is given and when" permits the giver a sense of choice (the giver chooses from a list in his or her own time framework) and allows the receiver to experience the gift as freely given and therefore more valued. Partners are then trained to notice and acknowledge the gift.

Cognitive restructuring to encourage acceptance. It is often advisable to begin treatment with acceptance-oriented strategies. As partners learn to accept one another, change becomes easier to tackle and therefore more likely. Restructuring indirectly targets intense, negative affective reactions by directly focusing on cognition. Cognitive restructuring encompasses several of the following specific techniques.

1 *Normalizing differences.* The therapist can help the couple to think of their differences as normal problems that most or all couples have to cope with. As partners change their assumptions and standards to reflect a more realistic picture of how much similarity they should expect from each other, the intensity of the affect they experience in response to these differences frequently dissipates.

2 *Validating each partner's views/experiences.* By modeling good listening skills and by exploring the developmental context of each partner's approach or perspective, the therapist can present each partner's experience or way of handling problems as reasonable and understandable given the situation. Perceiving the partner's perspective as reasonable (and then being willing to acknowledge it as such) is an important step toward increased acceptance between the partners. That is, partners are less likely to engage in coercive efforts to change one another if they understand and are even sympathetic with each other's point of view.

3 *Highlighting the attractive side of the partner's attributes.* It is a truism in couple therapy that the things that attract people to one another are the same things that become problems later on. When appropriate, the therapist can emphasize the qualities that attracted each to the other and can, through clever reframing, demonstrate how the things that are troubling them now are also the things that made the partner attractive during the initial stages of the relationship (see the case examples for reframing and restructuring in action).

4 *Defining their problems as relationship problems and defusing blame.* Because it is often difficult to perceive one's own contribution to a dysfunctional interaction pattern, partners tend to blame each other when the relationship is not harmonious. The therapist can help to foster cooperative mindsets in the couple by teaching them about reciprocal causality in couple interaction (I call it a "back-and-forth" pattern with the couples I work with).

This helps the couple think of the interaction pattern as the common problem that they must work together to solve. This cooperative mindset gives the therapist some leverage for teaching each how to take responsibility for changing her or his own contribution to the problematic pattern.

Behavioral Contracting is an excellent strategy to use once the partners have agreed to change their own behavior for the benefit of the relationship and the fulfillment of the other's needs. The optimal contract is specific to the problem at hand and spells out what each partner has agreed to do to make the relationship more rewarding for the other. Case Example 1 illustrates this technique.

Communication and Problem-Solving Therapy teaches couples skills for resolving conflicts. First, couples learn how to distinguish between arguments (a competitive struggle, with attack and defense) and problem solving (a collaborative process). Next, they learn to identify two stages in the problem-solving process: problem definition and problem solution. By ensuring that they move through both stages, couples avoid premature solutions and are more likely to maintain focus during problem solution (see Case 2). Some of the specific skills that couples learn through communication and problem-solving therapy are:

1   discuss one problem at a time;
2   present one's own and not one's partner's views;
3   attacks and other verbal abuse are not allowed;
4   begin one's statements with a paraphrase of the partner's point;
5   try to mention a positive along with the problem one wants to change;
6   be specific and descriptive when stating a problem, and avoid all-or-nothing language (e.g., right and wrong, always and never); avoid characterizing the person with trait-like adjectives; avoid therapizing/mind-reading;
7   express feelings about the problem while describing the problem;
8   acknowledge one's own role in the problem;
9   learn to acknowledge one's role and the other person's perspective without feeling trapped into a course of action;
10   agree on a succinct description of the problem before attempting to solve it;
11   avoid elaborating on the problem further once problem solving has begun;
12   begin problem solving with brainstorming, without criticizing any ideas;
13   discuss advantages and disadvantages of solutions suggested;

Communication skills are most effectively taught with the following process: (1) describe the skill specifically and behaviorally, (2) model the skill, (3) give reasons for using it, (4) give the partners an opportunity to rehearse it with a nonthreatening problem, and (5) give feedback and an opportunity to rehearse again while incorporating the feedback.

Once the couple has shown some mastery of the skills, select an upcoming (or recent) event in which these differences are likely to cause problems or have caused problems. Give them the opportunity to test the effectiveness of the new skills by practicing it in the session with this new situation. Encourage them to practice the skills during the week between sessions, and review this homework at the start of the next session. The review process can give the partners practice and in vivo experience with thinking about a common problem from a fresh perspective (i.e., as individual differences rather than opportunities to withhold from, deprive, criticize, or otherwise torment each other).

Intimacy enhancement teaches couples to be open and receptive to one another's vulnerabilities (see Case 3). As our data show, this process of self-disclosing, listening, accepting, and supporting is central to fulfilling needs for intimacy. Listening and acknowledgement skills are a prerequisite for beginning this work. Couples are encouraged in this work to go beyond listening and acknowledging and to express support and other positive sentiments towards their partners when they disclose. Intimacy enhancement includes the following:

1   *A focus on affect.* Emotional expression is a powerful part of intimate communication, because it conveys vulnerability, invites closeness, and, when congruent with nonverbal signs of emotion, communicates genuineness.
2   *Expressing positive feelings toward the partner.* The sine qua non of intimate expression is the verbal revelation of vulnerable aspects of the self; open and direct expression of one's appreciation, love, admiration, and devotion to one's partner is the sine qua non of verbal disclosure.
3   *Explicit sexual communication.* It is common for partners with intimacy-related difficulties to report that they do not express their desires and wants in bed. Giving couples exercises to do at home that encourage more sexual communication can create more opportunities for intimacy.
4   *Shared leisure.* Couples often fall in love while doing enjoyable things together. Shared leisure can provide time and space for intimate communication.

SUMMARY

While couples in therapy frequently struggle with intmacy-related issues, couple therapists have lacked clear, coherent models of the intimacy process to apply to clinical practice. Presented here is a multitiered conceptualization of intimate interactions and the individual and relational contextual factors that affect them.

Intimacy creates a dilemma for people. Intimate contact is both rewarding and emotionally risky. Further, people have different needs and tastes for intimate contact that must be negotiated within their intimate relationships. People yearn to get their intimacy needs met with their partners, and their conflicts about intimacy can be emotionally charged. As long as partners are not excessively incompatible coming into their relationship, effective problem-solving skills can result in intimate interactions that are rewarding for both partners. Couples who seek therapy, however, are likely to be stuck in nonproductive cycles of conflict about intimacy. This conflict is aggravated by escalating negative affect, distorted cognitions about intimacy, and ineffective, dysfunctional communication behavior.

Intimacy-oriented couples therapy is a cognitive-behavioral approach to treating couples' intimacy-related concerns. Through the use of familiar assessment and treatment strategies, therapists can help their clients to develop realistic assumptions and expectations about intimacy with their partners, to address fears about intimacy that stem from earlier negative experiences in relationships, and to draw on a repertoire of communication skills that allows the partners to enjoy rewarding intimate contact. The therapy aims to help partners with differing needs, fears, and expectations enjoy the intimacy that is right for them.

CASE II.
INTERVENTIONS ILLUSTRATED: REFRAMING CONFLICT AS INTIMACY REGULATION, AND COMMUNICATION SKILLS TRAINING

Barbara and Mitchell are both in their early 40s and have been married a little over two years. Barbara has grown children from her first marriage; Mitchell has no children. Barbara has sought couples therapy because she is very unhappy and is considering divorce. It is her third marriage, his second. After a glorious courtship, they have settled into a pattern of acrimonious arguments that escalate rapidly and resolve nothing. Arguments are followed by periods of silent withdrawal that sometimes last two or three days. The withdrawal is usually broken by Mitchell making an overture to Barbara, but the issues that caused the arguments are usually not raised again until the next argument. For a while, the periods between arguments were intimate, with the pair enjoying each other's company. Recently, however, the negative feelings from the arguing have overwhelmed Barbara's positive feelings about Mitchell. They rarely engage in sexual activity and, as Barbara puts it, she feels angry and disappointed with Mitchell most of the time.

Th: I'm getting a picture of a pattern in your relationship in which...Well, it seems that you two don't stay close or harmonious for very long before you have a big fight over something, and then you're each back in your corner, not speaking.

Barb.: I can't count on him to bring up the issues we need to discuss; so it's always me being the bad guy, and I get so frustrated. (To Mitchell) You would just sit there, you would go for days in silence if I didn't make sure we talked about things. You would let this drag out...

Mitch.: I just wish you'd talk more softly, I wish you'd stop yelling.

Barb.: I don't yell, but I do express myself. I have feelings, I want to express them. I don't know why you don't. Who would ever know what you're thinking! You're a sphinx. I just have no respect for you any more!

Th: Let me interrupt here. What I notice is the effect of these disruptions. They pull you apart. I might even say they give you a break from each other!

[Therapist reframes a bit dramatically here to stop their interaction from escalating. Therapist is proposing to the couple that arguments may be a way of regulating intimacy.]

[Couple is silent.]

Th: Think aloud with me. How *do* you go about taking a break from each other, from having to interact?

Mitch.: We get breaks automatically because we fight so much. We're so often not on speaking terms. It's the times that we're getting along that are unusual these days.

Th: Is this [kind of fighting] what it takes to get a break?

Mitch.: I'm not aware of wanting a break from Barbara. I want us to get along, honey, I do, but I don't know what to do or say when you get so angry.

Th: Mitchell, I wonder if Barbara sometimes needs a break from your closeness, but doesn't know how to get it, so she fights with you because she knows that works. She knows you'll withdraw from her and she'll get the space she needs. I say it this way on purpose, Barbara, because I believe that every partner in every relationship needs time for privacy, for aloneness, to be free not to interact. But in your family, there was no way to do that, am I right? So how could you have learned to do that?

[Therapist refers here to information gained in the assessment about Barbara's family of origin.]

Barb.: My family was always very expressive. It's true, we were always supposed to be together, to want to be together. Having your door closed was like an insult, an affront. All through high school I couldn't even close my door to get dressed. I used to hide behind the closet door! I hated that, though. I would never want that to be a part of my relationship with Mitchell.

Th: Could those experiences with your family be affecting your relationship with Mitchell now, despite your desire to avoid replicating them?

[Therapist is encouraging Barbara to reframe her assumptions about Mitchell's responsibility for their problems. The therapist is also checking the likely possibility that Barbara has a low tolerance for intimacy because of her negative experiences with "closeness" in her family of origin.]

Barb.: I do remember feeling guilty a lot back home, especially when I got into my teens and started wanting to have my own life. I fought the guilt, though; I just got angry. I was a real black sheep. My parents thought I was hopeless for a while there. We were always fighting. But I knew that underneath the fighting I felt guilty all the time.

Th: What about now? Do you ever feel guilty in your relationship with Mitchell?

Barb.: Sure I do, because I have to be the bad guy again. It's like when I was a kid—except in our case, Mitchell doesn't begrudge me my privacy or anything. But he never brings up any problems, so I always have to. And then it's like pulling teeth to get him to talk about anything. And because he hates my bringing things up so much, I have to weigh every issue and ask myself should I bring it up. I hold things back until I'm sure they're *really* bad before I bring them up because I know he hates it—and because I feel guilty, like maybe I am the troublemaker my parents thought I was.

Th: It seems that when you bring things up, it's a way to make sure you have contact, but it only works for a awhile. It ends up tearing you apart.

Mitch.: In my mind, we get along fine until something starts to bug her, and then she gets angry and "expresses herself" as you put it, Barbara, and pretty soon we're not speaking. Things don't bug me like they bug Barbara, though. It's true that I can let things slide more than she can.

Th: I want to go back to talking about how you get your space, your separateness, because I think this pattern you two are in is related to that issue.

Barb.: I would have to agree with Mitchell on this one. The issue of space just never comes up, because we have so much space as a result of our fighting.

Th: Between now and next week, I want each of you in your own way to entertain the idea that your arguments are—right now—the only way you have of getting privacy, separateness, space, whatever you want to call it. I wonder if your arguments, because they result in these times of no contact, don't give you an excuse to go do your own thing for awhile. Think about it, Barbara—they give you something in your relationship with Mitchell that you didn't have with your family. Space without feeling guilty.

Barb.: Well, I do feel guilty about the arguments and think that maybe I am too hard to please.

Th: Yes, you do feel some guilt, and I'd like us to work on creating a relationship that allows both of you to be together without having to feel guilty. But isn't this guilt different—it's not guilt about separateness, is it?

Barb.: That's true; I get so mad that not speaking seems perfectly justified and reasonable, at least for awhile.

Th: I want each of you to consider that your arguments are currently the only way to get space in your relationship. Neither you Barbara nor you Mitchell have a nonargumentative way of communicating a need for some separateness for yourself. So I don't want you to rush to change your pattern of arguing yet. What I would like to suggest is that together we develop an alternative means by which each of you can get some separateness within your relationship so that these arguments do not have to fulfill that purpose. Then, when we start working on your stopping the arguments, you will have a way of getting space already in place. It will make it easier for you to give up the fighting when the time comes because you won't need to use arguing for this purpose.

Th: Before we go, I'd like you to have a chance to practice a new way of getting separateness in your relationship that doesn't require fighting. This new way will involve one person directly communicating a need for separateness, time alone, whatever, and the other accepting that need. Later we'll work on ways of negotiating a little more, but let's start with this. Are you with me on this?

[Couple indicates they are ready.]

Th: Let's just spend a minute or two talking about what it feels like when you want some space. Barbara. Mitchell, are you both alright with my starting with Barbara on this? Barbara, you're more expressive so it seems logical to begin with you.

[Couple indicates ok.]

Th: Mitchell, I'd like you to just listen for a few minutes, then, because sometimes trying new things out in therapy can give relationship partners new perspectives on each other. In a few minutes, I'll work with you on some ways to receive Barbara's message. Okay? Now, Barbara, can you think about a time when you were really looking forward to peace and quiet, time alone, maybe an opportunity to do a favorite project uninterrupted?

[Therapist works with Barbara individually for a minute or two to help her get in touch with her own need for separateness.]

Th: What I'll do next is show you one way of communicating a need for time to yourself, no interruptions, and then give Barbara a chance to practice with Mitchell. Barbara, let me practice this with you first so you can get a feeling for what it would be like to be on the receiving end of this, alright?

[Therapist models an assertive, respectful request for some separate time.]

Th: What was it like to hear that message?

Barb.: It was okay—I felt respected. I liked it when you suggested we get together later. I knew you were planning on spending time with me that way.

Th: I'd like you to try communicating this to Mitchell now. Since you liked that part at the end, why don't you make a point of including it in your message to Mitchell. So sit and face Mitchell. Mitchell, please face Barbara. Now, Barbara, tell Mitchell that you would appreciate some alone, uninterrupted time and that you'd like a chance to spend time with him afterward—let's say at six o'clock, because it's a good idea to be specific. I'll stop you when you've conveyed your message or when you get stuck. We'll talk about how you like what you did and give you a chance to practice again at that point.

[Barbara practices expressing her needs for separateness to Mitchell. The therapist gives Mitchell some guidance about how to support her efforts through his response to her. Therapist helps Barbara express and understand any feelings she has about having needs for separateness and about communicating them openly.]

CASE III.
INTERVENTION ILLUSTRATED:
INTIMACY ENHANCEMENT TRAINING

Terry and Joe had separated about two weeks prior to their initial visit. This was a second marriage for both, and each had two grown children by their first marriages. Married not quite three years, the couple were very attracted to one another and had a passionate and satisfying sexual relationship. They shared many of the same interests and rarely quarreled while they were dating. Minor disagreements were treated with laughter and dismissal. After six months of some of the best times either had ever had, they decided to get married, and were wed and had moved in together two months later. Within a couple of months they began having nonproductive, long-winded conflicts that never seemed to resolve their problems. As the months went by, and the same issues continued to arise without resolution, these conflicts became more angry and intense.

The psychologist working with Terry and Joe noticed patterns of blame-and-defend in their problem-solving interactions that seemed to preclude their getting their problems defined and resolved. It seemed possible that teaching this couple some intimacy skills would enhance their problem-solving efforts.

Joe: It seems like no matter what I do it's never enough for you.

Terry: Like when do I do that. Give me an example.

Joe: Like when you're always nagging me about the laundry or the housework. Like you don't trust me to get to it.

Terry: When do you mean...when I asked you to do the laundry last week? I want you to know...

Joe: [interrupts] Yeah, I had been working my butt off all week.

Terry: I tried not to say anything! It was piling up, and it bothered me every time I walked in the door.

Joe: Didn't you know I'd get to it?

Terry: How am I supposed to know that, when so often you don't get to it until I say something?

Joe: You never notice when I do get to it. Like up until last week, I was doing it every weekend. But you know how hectic things got at work, what with that vendor holding up our supplies and me on the phone back and forth to them all week, and trying to placate our customers.

Terry: I think I was pretty understanding. It sat there for days without my saying anything! But you know how I hate to live in a pigsty.

Joe: See, that's what I mean! One week I don't get to the laundry, and it's a pigsty! And you have no faith.

Terry: If this happened once every six months or so, maybe I would! But it happens so often.

Joe: When did it happen before this? I've been doing it every week.

Terry: Just last month when you had that deal with your son.

Joe: But how many days was that really? One or two? See, no one can please you! I never feel like I'm doing enough!

Terry: And I'm always walking on eggshells around you, afraid to ask you to do anything because of the way you react!

Th: Let me ask you this: Is this going back and forth like you are right now—is this pretty typical for you, for you two to get stuck like this when you try to resolve problems?

[Therapist reframes their problem as a joint problem that prevents either of them from getting what they want.]

Terry: He's being a little nicer than usual because we're here with you. But yes, this is pretty typical.

Th: One thing that's coming across to me is that neither of you is getting much acknowledgement of your concerns. Joe, starting with you [Therapist implicitly communicates that she'll get to Terry], have you been aware of wanting to be acknowledged?

Joe: Yes. I don't feel like Terry really notices or appreciates the efforts I'm making, or how difficult things have been for me the past few years. It seems that I really make the effort, and then one little slip and I might as well have done nothing at all.

Th: How about you, Terry? Do you have some of the same feelings that Joe has—that your concerns are not being acknowledged?

Terry: Yes, it would be nice to think that you understood, realized, yes, acknowledged, that I make sacrifices, too, that I have been flexible about the house, and that I do wait to see if you'll do things on your own before I bring them up.

Th: I would really like to see each of you experience acknowledgement from the other during this session. Since we don't have time for both of you, is there someone willing to go first, to talk about some concerns or feelings that you have, so we can give the other the opportunity to do some acknowledging?

Joe: I'll go first.

Th: Alright, Terry, are you okay with you and I working together to help you to acknowledge Joe today?

Terry: Yes, I think it's very important that Joe get some acknowledgement today.

Th: Good start, Terry!

Th: Joe, please start by telling Terry what you were just saying, how difficult it is for you to make the changes she requests and still feel unappreciated. I'll work with Terry to help her to acknowledge those feelings. In order not to make things overly difficult for Terry, though, Joe, I'd like you to say what you're feeling without blaming or attacking Terry. Try just expressing what it feels like to be in your shoes these days.

Joe: [restates his concern]

Th: Terry, let's work together here a minute. Before you acknowledge Joe, I'd like you to tune into what you're feeling right now, having heard Joe's concern.

Terry: I feel bad for Joe, I know he's trying in his own way. But I'm also angry. I feel like I'm going to have to just accommodate more, that I'll just have to give up on what I want...

Th: You're onto something important here, Terry. A lot of people get that same idea—that if I acknowledge what my partner is going through, I'm going to be forced to capitulate to my partner's will somehow. I'll have to give up everything that I want if I allow his message in. Is that the thought that goes with your feeling right now?

Terry: Yes it is.

Th: I'd like you to try something new here, then. I'd like you to acknowledge Joe's concerns, but let me make clear right here to both you and Joe—acknowledgement is not the same as capitulating. We all need acknowledgement from each other, but deciding what to do is a whole other communication process, and acknowledging Joe does not at all mean that you have, therefore, given up on getting what you want. Will you now acknowledge Joe, now that I've made that clear?

Terry: Joe, I hear how much pain our arguments, our disagreements have caused you. I know you do try, and that you really believe that I don't notice or appreciate what you do. I know that must seem like I'm really against you sometimes, like I don't appreciate you. I want you to know that I do appreciate your efforts, though. I know that you're trying.

Th: Let's stop there. Joe, how did it feel to hear Terry's acknowledgement? Can you tell Terry how it felt to hear that?

Joe: I appreciate your appreciating me. I need to know that you notice the effort I put into our relationship.

Th: How about you, Terry? Let me add, too, that you're very good at this. I think you know how to do this.

Terry: It felt a little scarey to do it, like I'm giving up something. It's hard to get that idea out of my head. But I also feel good about saying that.

Th: Let me say this to both of you. These changes do not take place overnight. We'll spend next time working on acknowledgement again. For this week, though, I'd like each of you to think about separating acknowledgement from capitulating. I'd like each of you to keep a kind of journal, in which you write down times when you felt acknowledged or had the opportunity to acknowledge each other, even if you don't follow through on it. We'll use your notes next time to help each of you separate out acknowledging from giving in. I'd really like to see both of you get more acknowledgement in your relationship. It's something we all need.

[Therapist validates their needs for acknowledgement, structures their practice, gives homework.]

REFERENCES

Antill, J. K. & Cotton, S. (1987). Self-disclosure between husbands and wives: Its relationship to sex roles and marital happiness. *Australian Journal of Psychology, 39,* 11–24.

Babcock, J. C. & Jacobson, N. S. (1993). A program of research on behavioral marital therapy: Hot spots and smoldering embers in marital therapy research. *Journal of Social and Personal Relationships, 10,* 119–136.

Baucom, D. H. & Epstein, N. (1990). *Cognitive-behavioral marital therapy.* New York: Brunner/Mazel Publishers.

Beach, S. R. H., Sandeen, E. E., and O'Leary, K. D. (1990). *Depression in Marriage: A Model for Etiology and Treatment.* New York: Guilford Press.

Beach, S. R. H. & Tesser, A. (1988). Love in marriage: A cognitive account. In R. J. Sternberg & M. L. Barnes (Eds.), *The Psychology of Love* (pp. 330–358). New Haven, CT: Yale University Press.

Bowlby, J. (1969). *Attachment.* New York: Basic Books.

Bradbury, T. N. & Fincham, F. D. (1990). Attribution in marriage: Review and critique. *Psychological Bulletin, 107,* 3–33.

Christensen, A. & Shenk, C.L. (1991). Communication, conflict, and psychological distance in nondistressed, clinic, and divorcing couples. *Journal of Consulting and Clinical Psychology, 59,* 458–463.

Christensen, A., Jacobson, N.S., & Babcock, J.C. (1995). Integrative Behavioral Couple Therapy. In N.S. Jacobson & A.S. Gurman (Eds.), *Clinical Handbook of Couple Therapy* (pp. 31–64). New York: Guilford.

Craig, J. A., Koestner, R., and Zuroff, D. C. (1994). Implicit and self-attributed intimacy motivation. *Journal of Social and Personal Relationships, 11,* 491–507.

Cuber, J. & Haroff, P. (1965). *The significant Americans: A study of sexual behavior among the affluent.* New York: Appleton-Century-Crofts.

Davis, M. H. & Franzoi, S. L. (1987). Private self-consciousness and self-disclosure. In V.H. Derlega & J.H. Berg (Eds.), *Self-disclosure: Theory, research and therapy* (pp. 59–79). New York: Plenum.

Derlega, V. J. & Chaikin, A. (1975). *Sharing Intimacy.* Englewood Cliffs, NJ: Prentice Hall.

Derlega, V. J. & Grzelak, J. (1979). Appropriateness of self-disclosure. In G. J. Chelune (Ed.), *Self-Disclosure: Origins, Patterns, and Implications of Openness in Interpersonal Relationships* (pp. 151–176). San Francisco: Jossey-Bass.

Eidelson, R. J. & Epstein, N. (1982). Cognition and relationship maladjustment: Development of a measure of dysfunctional relationship beliefs. *Journal of Consulting and Clinical Psychology, 50,* 715–720.

Erikson, E. (1968). *Identity, Youth, and Crisis.* New York: Norton.

Grotevant, H.D. & Cooper, C.R. (1986). Individuation in family relationships: A perspective on individual differences in the development of identity and role-taking skill in adolescence. *Human Development, 29,* 82–100.

Hatfield, E. (1984). The dangers of intimacy. In V. J. Derlega (Ed.), *Communication, Intimacy, and Close Relationships* (pp. 207–220). Orlando, FL: Academic Press.

Johnson, S. M. & Greenberg, L. S. (1994). Emotion in intimate relationships: Theory and implications for therapy. In S.M. Johnson & L.S. Greenberg (Eds.), *The Heart of the Matter: Perspectives on Emotion in Martial Therapy* (pp. 3–26). New York: Brunner/Mazel Publishers.

Jourard, S. M. (1971). *The Transparent Self*. New York: Van Nostrand.

Karpel, M. A. (1994). *Evaluating Couples*. New York: Norton.

Kerr, M. E. & Bowen, M. (1988). *Family Evaluation: An Approach Based on Bowen Theory*. New York: Norton.

McAdams, D. P. (1984). Human motives and personal relationships. In V. J. Derlega (Ed.), *Communication, Intimacy and Close Relationships* (pp. 41–70). Orland, FL: Academic Press.

McAdams, D. P. (1988). *Power, Intimacy and the Life Story*. New York: Guilford Press.

McAdams, D. P., Healy, S., & Krauser, S. (1984). Social motives and patterns of friendship. *Journal of Personality and Social Psychology, 47*, 828–838.

McClelland, D. C. (1985). *Human Motivation*. Glenview, IL: Scott, Foresman.

Moustakas, C. E. (1975). *The Touch of Loneliness*. Englewood Cliffs, NJ: Prentice-Hall.

Murray, H. A. (1938). *Explorations in Personality*. New York: Oxford University Press.

Prager, K. J. (1995). *The Psychology of Intimacy*. New York: Guilford Press.

Prager, K. & Buhrmester, D. (in press). Intimacy and need fulfillment in couple relationships. *Journal of Social and Personal Relationships, 47*, 828–838.

Raush, H. L., Barry, W. A., Hertel, R. K. & Swain, M. A. (1974). *Communication, Conflict, and Marriage*. San Francisco: Jossey-Bass.

Register, L. M. & Henley, T. B. (1992). The phenomenology of intimacy. *Journal of Social and Personal Relationships, 9*, 467–482.

Reiss, H. T. & Shaver, P. (1988). Intimacy as interpersonal process. In S. Duck (Ed.), *Handbook of Personal Relationships: Theory, Research and Intervention*, (pp. 367–389). Chichester, UK: John Wiley & Sons.

CHAPTER 9

The Intimacy Styles Approach: A Cognitive-Behavioral Model for Understanding and Treating Problems of Intimacy

Arthur Freeman

I want someone to come home to.
I need someone to talk to.
I would like someone to tell my troubles to.

INTRODUCTION

Zorbaugh (1929) described life in Chicago before the Depression. Many men and women came to the "big city" from small towns in the Midwest, farms, and from the rural South. They came for many reasons: some to escape the problems of their homes, some to seek a golden future, and some to become lost in the sheer size of the city. Zorbaugh found that many couples lived together as married without the benefit of law or clergy, despite cohabitation being against the morals and religious scruples of the day. While there were financial advantages to cost sharing, this also could have been done with roommates or the renting of a furnished room. Within this part of the society, the need for contact, sharing, and communication outweighed all other considerations. It was, it seems, a desire for that elusive factor of intimacy that drove their behavior.

Intimate or *intimacy* are terms found widely in both professional and popular literature. Like the weather, intimacy is something that people often talk about, although doing something about it usually is quite a different story. It is at once a goal of relationships (We need to work toward being more intimate), and a challenge (What can we do to be more intimate?). It is both specific (We have to have greater sexual intimacy) and general (There is an overall lack of intimacy in our relationship). It can be part of a threat (Because of what you have said and done, there will be no more intimacy.), or an insult (You are so thick. You have no idea how to be intimate).

Intimacy is the avowed goal of most relationships, whether overtly or covertly stated. In fact, the term "intimate relationship" may be seen as redundant. After all, can one have a relationship that does not include some level or form of intimacy? Intimacy, or some synonym, is part of relationship literature, although it has not always been operationally defined, or, in some cases, defined at all. In the volume *Intimate Relationships, Marriage, and Family*, Coleman (1984) indexes the term "intimacy," but does not direct the reader to a page reference—rather to the cross-indexed terms, "relationships, cohabitation, courtship, encounters, and mate selection."

The ability to be intimate is the result of developing specific cognitive, affective, and behavioral skills. In the typical socialization process, these skills begin with the infant's earliest contact with caretakers. Constructs like Bowlby's attachment (1979, 1982, 1985) help us to understand how one acquires not only contact, but also contacting skills. Through the developmental process, the behavioral repertoire of attachment skills will, ideally, grow. Individuals will broaden and generalize their contact or attachment skills from the primary caretakers to include others, so that the toddler, child, adolescent, and adult increase their attachment population range, as well as their repertoire of contacting or intimate behaviors. Included in both the attachment and the motivation to build attachment skills are cognitive representations that have emotional sequelae, (i.e., "This person will be good to me and take care of me, therefore I feel good about being with them" or "This person does not meet my needs and leaves me wanting more contact/love/attention and I feel deprived and angry"). It is this repertoire of cognitive, behavioral, and affectively charged interaction skills that are the basic building blocks of intimacy and affect the ability and motivation to be intimate.

When individuals or couples contact a therapist about relationship-related problems, they often are asking for the therapy to be either remedial regarding their intimacy or corrective regarding their lack of intimacy. The therapist may see many different scenarios unfold in the evaluation of the couple. For example, it may be the case that whatever intimacy skills the couple have, or have used to maintain the relationship, are not adequate to the task. Or it may be that the couple always has had poor skills, or the skills that they have used in the past have been pushed aside by external stressors on the relationship. To understand the widespread interest in and importance of intimacy, one only has to walk to a newsstand or into a bookstore. One cannot pass a rack of monthly magazines without seeing intimacy, in its many forms, as a common "how to" topic in popular magazines.

Intimacy appears to be something most people want for themselves, something that they may be willing to work towards with a partner. When it is lacking in one's own life, there is envy of what they see to be the intimacy in the relationships of others. Given that it is a life goal for many, they remain unsure of what exactly intimacy is, where to find it, how to keep it, and how to develop it both intrapersonally and interpersonally. A popular country and western song laments that they are "looking for love in all the wrong places." Of course as therapists we might ask, "If you know what the wrong places and faces are, why can't you look in more appropriate places for more appropriate partners?"

One can search the literature and find entire chapters or books that have been written on the topic of intimacy, without ever indexing or operationally defining it. For example, Burns (1985) in *Intimate Connections*, Greenwald (1975) in *Creative Intimacy*, Guerney (1977) in *Relationship Enhancement*, and Gordon (1993) in *Passage to Intimacy* all offer programs to heal, direct, or increase intimacy without ever stopping to define the construct. Other books, chapters, or discussions on intimacy do offer definitions, but they are vague, amorphous, and global. This is problematic in that it is hard—or therapeutically impossible—to reach a goal that is vague, amorphous, and global either in life or, correctively, in therapy. An individual wishing to travel from New York to Los Angeles needs to set a route that is more detailed than traveling in a general westward direction. If one wants a general tour of the country, then a general direction may be just what the doctor ordered. However, if one wants to travel a specific route in the most scenic, most direct, least expensive, or easiest way, then a plan needs to be established and specific goals set.

A basic premise of the Cognitive Behavior Therapy (CBT) model is that vague goals invariably lead to vague therapy, which invariably leads to vague results. Therefore, it is incumbent upon the therapist and essential to the therapy that there is a clear, operationally-defined, collaboratively-set, and mutually agreed-upon goal to therapy. For individuals and couples seeking therapy to deal with problems of intimacy, it is basic to effective therapy that the patient(s) and therapist develop an operational definition for intimacy. The therapeutic goals need to be proximal, within or close to existing repertoire, workable, reasonable, and realistic. This would help individuals reach toward intimacy both within and without therapy.

Further, it is essential that we develop assessment tools and procedures for identifying and assessing the components of intimacy. The therapist needs to have a conceptual and developmental understanding of the factors that constitute intimacy and thereby the dysfunctions of intimacy. These factors would then be shared with the patients as an ingredient of the therapy. Based on that conceptualization, the therapist needs to work with the patient(s) to develop discrete strategies for change. Finally, we need to identify specific technical interventions that will achieve the clearly-stated goal of increasing intimacy.

DEFINING INTIMACY

The major difficulty that we see in understanding intimacy and in treating its problems is that most definitions make the fatal mistake of seeing intimacy as either unidimensional or as complex but still definable in a brief sentence. For example, we offer the following several definitions of intimacy. The common theme these share is that intimacy is seen as a reciprocal dyadic interaction between two equals. It often implies a sexual connotation and precludes having *non-sexual*, intimate relations with and within social or work groups, within families, or with children.

Intimacy is:

• "The joy of being known and accepted by another who is loved." Beavers (1985, p. 52).

• "Marked by a very close association, contact or familiarity; marked by a warm friendship; suggesting informal warmth or privacy; of a very personal or private nature" (Merriam-Webster, 1995).

• "Intimacy occurs when an individual achieves full self knowledge, and is fully in touch with his or her feelings and wishes" (Fisher & Stricker, 1982, p. xi).

• "A subjective state of closeness to another person that gratifies a wish for warmth and relatedness and provides an opportunity for expression of sexual and aggressive drives" (Campbell, 1989).

• "A person's ability to talk about who he really is, and say what he wants and needs to be heard by an intimate partner" (Scarf, 1986. p 49).

• "....the capacity to commit himself to concrete affiliations and partnerships and to develop the ethical strength to abide by such commitments even though they may call for significant sacrifices and compromises" (Erikson, 1963).

One of the most comprehensive definitions of intimacy is offered by Prager (1995). She proposes five functions of a working definition of intimacy.

1   the definition should be integrative and illuminate the linkages between extant theoretical perspectives,
2   the definition should "specify whether intimacy is an individual capacity, a property of interactions, or a characteristic of a relationship" (p. 13),
3   it should delineate between intimacy and the closely-related concepts of love, sexuality, closeness, and support.
4   the ultimate definition must be focused, rather than fuzzy, and broadly attainable, rather than esoteric,
5   the therapeutic/professional definition should be "reconcilable with (if not identical to) lay definitions" (p. 14).

The multidimensional nature of intimacy was described by Clinebell and Clinebell (1970) and Hof and Miller (1981). They have broadened the notion of intimacy from just sexual intimacy to include emotional, intellectual, aesthetic, communication, commitment, and creative intimacy. It is this multidimensional structure that underlies the present chapter.

This chapter's goal is to present a view of intimacy that conceptualizes it within a CBT framework. The chapter is divided into three parts. Part one focuses on the attributes of functional and dysfunctional relationships. Part two offers a cognitive behavioral definition and a formulation of intimacy as the Intimacy Styles Approach (ISA). Part three addresses the issues of assessment and therapy with couples having intimacy problems that are consistent with the basic ISA model.

ATTRIBUTES OF FUNCTIONAL AND DYSFUNCTIONAL RELATIONSHIPS

Problems of depression and/or anxiety frequently accompany intimacy dysfunction, as either causal or consequential to the problems in the relationship. What is different in the couple or family referral, as opposed to the typical individual referral, is that an individual may choose therapy after a brief time of discomfort or dysfunction (e.g., I've come for therapy because I've been terribly depressed for the last two weeks).

Couples, however, do not generally seek therapy at the onset or early stages of their difficulty (i.e., We have a wonderful relationship, but we're starting to experience some minor breakdown in our communication). The referral is more likely to come when the relationship is at risk for, or in significant danger of, collapse. Couples may seek therapy toward the bitter end of the difficulty. Referrals for relationship therapy often come from attorneys or by judicial direction; for many couples, therapy is seen as the court of last resort. Frequently, couples come for therapy after having said or done abusive, hurtful things to each other. If they have not already burned their bridges behind them, they have scattered the fuel, collected the kindling, and lit the fuses. At times, the interpersonal difficulties the couple experience are merely shadows of intrapersonal conflict. Either or both partners may experience depression, anxiety, phobia, or substance abuse. For example, a couple came for therapy after the husband had a lengthy battle with depression, which influenced his behavior and caused him to withdraw and to disengage from the relationship. After a certain point, his wife could not "stand it any longer." She then threatened to leave him unless he stopped being depressed. As can be imagined, the husband became even more depressed as result of the threat.

At other times, the interpersonal nature of the problem is paramount. One woman came for therapy reporting the following: "I found myself fantasizing violence against my husband. These are images and thoughts that I find abhorrent. I was at the Builder's Depot store, standing in front of a rack of axes, and we didn't have any firewood that needed to be cut."

There are distinct behaviors that delineate dysfunctional and functional relationships. The cognitive behavioral perspective looks at two broad areas: the cognitive processing of the partners and the demonstrated behavior. The cognitive elements have been broadly described and discussed (Beck, 1988; Baucom & Epstein, 1989; Cantor & Malley, 1991; Dattilio & Padesky, 1990; Derlega, 1984; Freeman & Oster, 1997; Ginsberg, 1997; and Waring, 1988). Klimek (1979) identified several qualities of relationships that had cognitive-affective valence, which then manifested in behavior. These included trust-mistrust, closeness-distance, openness-guardedness, and interdependence-avoidance of dependence/dependency reversals.

First, what is the behavioral focus for understanding intimacy? This examines the relative amount of positive and negative behavioral exchange between partners. Essentially, this measures the good and bad things that happen within the relationship between the individuals, and the relative balance between them. The greater the amount of negative exchange, the more dysfunctional the relationship. The greater the number of positive exchanges, the more functional—and, consequentially, the closer the relationship and greater the perception of intimacy.

Second, what is the degree to which the individuals have the skills for resolving conflict and for communicating appropriately? Often, the problems and difficulties are rooted in skill deficits that do not simply yield to high levels of interest or motivation. For many couples, their individual and joint problem-solving capacities may be adequate for low-stress circumstances and situations. However, when the heat is turned up and they find themselves confronted by external and internal stressors, they become scattered and seem unable to cope. It becomes a situation in which the spirit is willing but the skills are weak.

Third, what is the motivation to change? Why do people want to be different? Why do they want to do things differently than they have done them up to this point? Is the motivation to change intrinsic or extrinsic? Are they motivated to change, and will the level of motivation support the difficulty and stress of changing established cognitive, behavioral, and affective patterns? Will they be able to maintain their motivation over time?

Fourth, what is their individual and couples character style? This involves an exploration and schematic analysis of the individual's personal, cultural, religious, family, gender, and age-related schema. These must be explicated and understood by the individuals.

Fifth, what shared character style exists? What schema are shared, based in the individual's culture, religion, age, or family experience?

The essence of understanding relationships is to understand the cognitions that both reflect and drive the individual behavior. There are several types of cognitions that influence relationships, which can lead to significant problems or dysfunction. First, there are the assumptions that each partner makes about the nature of the world, the nature of self and other relationships, and the nature of self and partner. Second, there are the standards that each partner brings to the relationship, in terms of what they believe the behaviors and interactions should be. Third, there are the individual perceptions, specifically how they "see" and understand events. Fourth, there are attributions, which are the reasons that individuals give themselves for why events occur. And, finally, there are the expectancies that have to do with predicting what occurs.

THE MYTHS OF INTIMACY

Given that intimacy, certainly of a sexual variety, has been around since the beginning of time (or else we would not be around to write or read books on intimacy), it is interesting to explore some of the common myths regarding intimacy that we hear in therapy. The following list has been gathered from clinical practice with individuals and couples over the years, and from Bagarozzi and Anderson (1989).

1 Change is never possible.
This suggests that we are who and what we are, and modification is unlikely or impossible. It sets out a hopelessness to the therapeutic agenda.
2 Change is always possible.

While hope may spring eternal, this idea often sets the couple and the therapist up for failure. It presupposes that couples are motivated to change and have the skills to do so.

3   When individuals are in conflict, one partner is always to blame more than the other.

This comes from the "cheerleading" approach of family and friends. In their rush to support one of the members of the couple, they eagerly blame the partner. A more realistic approach can be stated as, "pathology in couples, like water, seeks it's own level." The couple have collaborated to bring the relationship to this brink of disaster.

4   Opposites attract.

This is more true for magnets than for people. It is likely that we are attracted to someone more like us than to someone less like us.

5   Couples must have the same sex drive and interest in sexual intimacy.

Sexual issues are among the most common cause of difficulty. Part of that difficulty stems from the erroneous notion stated above.

6   Relationships just seem to happen for lucky people.

This might be termed the Snow White effect. That is, if one lays perfectly still, perhaps near death, in a glass casket, and does nothing except look beautiful, a lost Prince will, purely by luck, happen upon her and fall deeply, permanently in love.

7   Couples must spend no time apart.

In today's highly mobile society, it would be unusual that the "Father Knows Best" couples model of a 9–5 job, five days per week, limited commuting, with the woman's job focused on the home still exists. Commuting, travel, work demands, and women more equally in the workforce all conspire to increase time apart.

8   Absolute honesty is essential.

The distinction must be made between absolute honesty and brutal honesty. Let us suppose that the question is asked, "Darling, am I the best lover you have ever been with?" One has to make a judgment as to what is the unspoken question, and what is the best answer. The seven-year-old asking, "Mommy, where did I come from?" may not require a discussion of the facts of life. He may be curious because a classmate was from Cleveland.

9   Mind-reading is the communication method of choice.

Couples who have lived together for a period of time often believe that they know what their partner or family member is thinking. This then gives them license to respond as if their perceptions are accurate.

10   Sexual interests or preferences should not have to be discussed.

This is a subset of #9. This is often framed as, "If you loved me, you would know without my having to tell you. If I have to say it, it loses something."

Baucom and Epstein (1989) identify several characteristics of successful relationships. First, the individuals have frequent, positive interactions. Second, these interactions are generally face-to-face. Third, these interactions occur across several behavioral and situational domains. Fourth, each individual has a substantial influence on the other's life. Fifth, there is anxiety in the absence of the partner. Sixth, there are attempts to restore proximity during the absence of a partner. Seventh, there is a reduction of anxiety upon the return of the partner. Eight, individuals develop a unique communication system. Ninth, there are mutual goals in behavior. Tenth, there is mutual self-disclosure.

ASSESSMENT

Couples come in for four common problems—situational, behavioral, cognitive, and affective. It is essential that, no matter where the therapy begins, each area is examined and that the therapy addresses all four areas.

The key to developing an appropriate treatment conceptualization involves the collection of data during a formal assessment. Assessment should include three parts, the first of which covers the history and general issues. The second part involves the use of the critical incident technique, and the final part includes the assessment of the intimacy styles.

There are two specific, general protocols that are necessary: a conjoint assessment of the couple and a personal assessment with each partner.

It is most helpful in the data-gathering process to set the first session up as a double session consultation with both partners. It is important that this is structured as a consultation, without any commitment to treat the couple. This commitment to treat is reserved, based on the information to be gathered in the assessment. Prior to meeting with the couple, the therapist is not in a position to agree to treat them. Ethically, a therapist should not take on a therapy case without knowing the problems, issues, and history. By setting up the initial session as a consultation, the therapist is able to gather data and make a determination of the most reasonable and beneficial recommendations and treatment plan, referral, or no treatment at all.

The initial part of the assessment involves meeting with the couple to gather information conjointly about what they see as the major areas of difficulty. The conjoint assessment offers the therapist a microcosmic look at the interaction, behavioral system, verbal ability, level of anger, ability to exercise control, strengths, and ability to relate to their partner and the therapist. For each of the areas of assessment, the therapist must maintain a high degree of control over the session. There will likely be an instant response to initiate a list of complaints and accusations against the other. The therapist must keep focusing on the importance of the data-gathering process. The therapist must allow each partner to speak and to make sure that fairness prevails and that there is an equal sharing of time. This "leveling" effect keeps the onus and blame away from either partner. This may, of course, mean that the therapist has to be active and directive and, if need be, stop one partner and turn to the other for their view. This precludes the monopolizing of time by a more verbal (or aggrieved) partner. To counter the likely negative focus, the first questions in the assessment address the positive nature and stronger, healthier aspects of the relationship. Prior to beginning the conjoint assessment, the therapist must inform the couple of the proposed sequence of events (conjoint interview followed by the individual interviews), that there is no final agreement to treat the couple prior to the final gathering of data, and that the result of the interviews will be a recommendation for a therapeutic direction. It is also imperative that the therapist inform the couple that the therapy room is "neutral" territory and that the therapist will limit and control the flow of the discussion for this initial contact. They are informed that each of them will be asked to answer the same question and that this is not a source of material for debate and controversy in the office. Each will be asked to tell their story, but the therapist cannot act as the arbiter of rightness or wrongness of a position, belief, or action. Setting out the parameters for the session and the rules of engagement sets up the assessment as a time of safety where both partners, and the therapist, can be safe from attack, both verbal and physical.

It is important to note that the very points of attraction in the relationship very often become points of conflict. The male who is seen initially as a "go getter" is now seen as "bossy." The woman who was originally seen as "lighthearted" is now seen as "dizzy" (Dattilio & Padesky, 1990).

The therapist must control the discussion, allowing equal time and firmly but gently cutting off extraneous discussion or angry interchanges.

The conjoint assessment will include the following questions.

How would each member describe their global satisfaction with the relationship?

- What are their specific satisfaction(s) with their partner?
- What were the initial attractions?
- What are the strengths of the relationship?
- They are asked to each summarize their relationship in terms of:

  a   verbal communication
  b   sex activity (between partners)
  c   emotional support of each other
  d   affection
  e   time together and time apart
  f   child management (if appropriate)
  g   conflict management and financial management
  h   trust
  i   household responsibilities

- What has prompted therapy at this point?

- What event or specific timing caused them to seek help?
- What are the specific presenting problems?
- What are the specific goals that the couple sets out for the therapy/change?
- What is the couple's view of the developmental history of the relationship—how it began and the various early stages, how it is developed, and how it has come to the present point?
- What are their patterns of communication?
- Are there behavioral excesses or deficits they can recognize in themselves or in their partner?
- What specific environmental stressors are they living with?

Having collected the conjoint information, it is now important to meet with each member of the dyad individually. While this presents some immediate problems in terms of the potential for collecting information and for finding out "secrets," it is important for the therapist to get not only a general sense of the interaction, but also of the specific issues that each member brings. Our goal is to discover a workable and reasonable treatment program that is data based. We need to collect that data.

We can offer the couple the choice of who would meet with the therapist first. Having made that decision, both individuals are assured by the therapist that what they say will be maintained in confidence, but it is emphasized that the therapist maintains the final decision as to whether he or she can help this dyad. Many of the same evaluation questions that were asked in the conjoint session are asked in the individual evaluation session. In the couple session, a partner may often voice the fact that he or she know there are communication difficulties, but would like to work them out. In the individual evaluation session, he or she may voice the fact that they have had a lover for several years and want to leave the relationship, but are concerned that, when they leave, their partner will be shattered and will fall apart into a million pieces. It is then their goal of therapy to leave the shards of their partner on the therapists' doorstep.

The personal assessment should include:

a personal history
b information about their family of origin
c their personal therapy goals
d their commitment to maintaining the relationship
e an evaluation of individual psychopathology
f history of previous treatment
g their expectations for treatment
h their sex history
i sexual preferences
j previous sexual behaviors and/or sexual abuse.

THE USE OF CRITICAL INCIDENT TECHNIQUE IN ASSESSMENT

One of the assessment tools that is very useful with couples is the critical incident technique. The critical incident question can be asked to both partners simultaneously in the conjoint interview or during the individual interview. The therapist asks each member for a single experience, event, or circumstance that, in their view, best describes the particular difficulty they are experiencing. This moves them away from the laundry list of complaints and asks for their most memorable or descriptive event. When asked conjointly, each member may choose a different experience. Each partner's critical incident is offered without comment (ideally) or editorializing (infrequently) by the partner.

For example, when asked for their critical incident, Sid and Miriam both agreed that the critical incident or event that best defined the difficulty they experienced had to do with an event that had occurred a month previous. Miriam introduced her critical incident by stating that she had great difficulty being on time. In virtually every situation, she found herself "running late." She was often late for work, social events, parties, concerts, or shows, which caused great conflict. She then started to offer an explanation for the lateness. She was asked by the therapist to omit the apology and move to a description of the critical incident.

The specific critical incident occurred when Sid's father was having a surprise 60th birthday party. Sid and Miriam had been invited by his older brother, who was planning the party. Unknown by Miriam, Sid was asked to be at his father's house, which was the party location, no later than 12:30 PM because they were going to bring father home from a shopping trip at 1:00 PM. Knowing that Miriam was often an hour late, Sid informed her that they must be at the party by 11:30 AM because his father would be there at 12:00 noon.

Miriam went on to describe that because of many problems (clothing, chipped nail, etc.), she was an hour late. Throughout the car ride to his father's house, Sid did what he would usually do, which was to express his upset and anger at the fact that they were going to be late and wouldn't be there until 12:30. She, in typical fashion, apologized and then got angry for his continued harping on the issue. When they arrived at father's house at 12:30, and she discovered that her father-in-law was not due until 1:00, she became furious and left the party. She accused her husband of being a liar and untrustworthy. This, she pointed out, was the major difficulty in the relationship, that he would lie to her and could not be trusted.

In describing the same critical incident, the husband described the situation in exactly the same terms and exactly the same way, but his conclusion was very different. To him, this critical incident demonstrated the fact that his wife was passive aggressive and could not be trusted, even for an event that had great meaning for him, his father, and his family.

After collecting the data, the therapist has to develop a conceptualization, decide on the strategies for treatment, and identify particular techniques for interventions. If, on the other hand, the therapist decides that they cannot work with the couple, they should be informed and the appropriate referral be made. Reasons for non-treatment might include: either or both of the members of the dyad are not motivated for therapy, either or both are involved in relationships that are or would remain in competition with the primary relationship, the problems that the couple pose are beyond the therapist's ability to work with, or limited time or finances preclude treatment at this point. The third part of the assessment, that with the earlier assessment will become the basis of the therapy, is the assessment of the individual intimacy styles.

THE INTIMACY STYLES APPROACH

The conceptual basis for the Intimacy Styles Approach (ISA) to relationship therapy includes the following basic premises:

1   Intimacy is a complex, multi-facet phenomenon.
2   Intimacy skills are reflected in spontaneous (automatic) thoughts and overt behaviors of individuals.
3   Intimacy skills are learned.
4   Intimacy skills are based on and reflect myriad schema.
5   From our earliest days, each individual builds a repertoire of intimacy skills.
6   The greater the repertoire, the easier it is to relate to a variety and range of people.
7   The connection between people reflects their shared styles.
8   A single shared style can hold a relationship together indefinitely.
9   The more shared styles, the stronger the relationship.
10   Intimacy skills must be explicated and can be modified.
11   A change in style, for whatever reason, can upset the homeostasis of a relationship.
12   Intimacy skills can be developed in the session and practiced for homework.

Intimacy styles are based on the familial, cultural, personal, gender, age-related, and religious schema we all develop. These schema direct every action and are the basic rules that govern everything that we do. Schema can be active and govern day-to-day behavior or dormant, only becoming active under stress. Further, schema can be compelling and difficult to ignore or non-compelling and rather easily surrendered. The intimacy styles are the behavioral manifestations of the schema.

Assessing Intimacy Style

Each of the styles represents an interaction between thoughts and actions, and is emotionally valent. Following Prager's (1995) formulation, what we shall call intimacy is comprised of many combinations and permutations of the following specific styles. The intimacy styles can be recorded on the Intimacy Styles Worksheet (Figure 1). Each partner is asked to evaluate where they perceive themselves to be on a 0–10 scale, to identify where they would, ideally like to be on that style, and to rank their partner.

After explaining the notion of intimacy styles, each partner evaluates their own and their partner's style profile and strength.

In column 1, they rate the strength of each style personally. In column 2, they indicate the increase or decrease they would like in that style for themselves. In column 3, they rate the strength of that style for their partner. In column 4, they indicate the increase or decrease they would like in that style for their partner.

Intimacy Styles

Lifestyle intimacy   Lifestyle may involve a place to live (e.g., an urban, suburban, or rural setting) or a particular place within that setting (e.g., someone choosing to live in New York City may live the elite lifestyle of Fifth Avenue, the artistic lifestyle of Greenwich Village, or the more academic lifestyle of Columbia University's Morningside Heights). The lifestyle will represent a way of expressing oneself. For example, a couple may choose a "hippy" lifestyle and live in a VW microbus. The lifestyle will be represented by the home, the clothing they wear, the schools that the children attend, and the car, so that some individuals will only drive a BMW or a Volvo.

For example, lifestyle was a point of conflict for Marsha and Alan. Alan had an image he wanted to achieve. He worked to make his life congruent with this image, much to the annoyance of Marsha, whose lifestyle image was much different. His was of a swinging, cool, urban lifestyle image. Hers was a home, family, PTA style.

Intimacy Styles Worksheet

Intimacy Style	Self		Partner	
	Strength of Style (0 – 10)	Goal Strength (0 – 10)	Strength of Style (0 – 10)	Goal Strength (0 – 10)
Lifestyle				
Third Party				
Affectionate				
Aggressive				
Historical				
Self-disclosing				
Professional				
Sexual				
Spiritual/Religious				
Humorous				
Intellectual				
Passive				
Competitive				
Avocational				
Geographic/Cultural				
Narcissistic				
Pathological				
Financial				
Convenient				
Gender				
Age				
Dependent				
Supportive				

Figure 1   Intimacy styles worksheet.

Third Party Intimacy   This involves a connection on a basis of a third party that may involve children, but may also involve a pet, family business, or even a house. The notion that a couple stay together for the children is the expression of this style. An individual who relates via third party intimacy may find that, when the last child leaves home, they have few points of relationship in common and may often seek separation and divorce at this point.

For example, Susan and Mitchell ran a family woman's clothing business originally inherited from her father. In the 35 years that they ran the business, they expanded it from one store to two stores in the downtown business part of their city. They each ran a store. They left for work together at 7:00 AM and worked until 6:00 PM Mitchell would drop Susan off at her store and go to his store.

When their children were younger and they only had one store, Susan would stay at home to get the children off to school and then come to the store. The children were now grown and out of the house.

They spoke on the phone a dozen times a day to inquire, "Do you have a style #433 blouse in white, size 12?" or some other business-related issue. They traveled to buying shows together and had common complaints about the sales help, the rising costs of merchandise, or the quality of goods coming into the store.

At about the time that they turned sixty, they were offered a very good price to sell the two stores. This was their chance to get out and retire, an opportunity that they took. They very quickly realized that, without the stores, they had very little to discuss and few issues and topics around which they could relate.

Affectionate Intimacy   This involves allowing another into personal space in a non-sexual way, and may involve verbal or physical action. Saying to a partner, "good morning, darling. I love you, you look very nice today," involves a positive exchange of three verbal affectionate elements. It may also involve simply a touch on the arm in passing.

For example, in the movie *Ghost*, Demi Moore's character complained that when she said, "I love you," to her husband, Patrick Swayze's character, his response was "ditto." What she wanted was the verbal affectionate response.

We may be affectionate with our children by hugging and kissing them, or "buddies" with the guys by back-slapping and bear-hugging them. In each case it is non-sexual, although it may be part of a broader sexual interaction. It should be viewed as separate.

Aggressive Intimacy   This involves individuals whose method of contact is aggressive. This often is culturally stylistic, as seen in the movies of Mel Brooks and Woody Allen. In his film *Annie Hall*, Woody Allen compares two family dinners; dinner at Annie's house by candlelight, soft music in the background, and discussions of art and music, and at Woody's house, built under the roller coaster at Coney Island, dinner involves loud exchanges with apparent rancor, but without anger.

For example, Elizabeth had great difficulty with Carmine's style. Often she would become frightened by the apparent angry exchanges he would have with his family, especially his father. Even though it seemed to her that they were close to blows, they always ended in hugs and warmth. She did not believe that this was the way love should be shown, and when he spoke loudly to her it was a source of upset. Carmine was upset because his expressions of love were unacceptable to Elizabeth.

Historical Intimacy   This applies to individuals that can relate on the basis of a shared history that may be generational or simply sharing an event. Individuals who remember the assassination of JFK will not only remember the event, but where they were and what they were doing. A discussion of those events will often immediately have the participants reminiscing. Participants in Woodstock will always have their brief moment together in the mud.

For example, Aaron had been married and divorced and then had remarried a woman twenty years his junior. His first wife was a contemporary and shared historical intimacy. Beth, his new wife, was not able to do so. Though she listened to his stories of times past, they were always just that—stories. She had no connection to the life and times he described. Aaron's frequent comment, which eventually angered Beth was, "She's so young that she thinks that the Big Bopper comes from Burger King."

For her part, Beth's history in terms of music and experience was as foreign to Aaron.

Self-disclosing Intimacy   This is the part of intimacy that is often seen to be the defining element of intimacy. Individuals are motivated and able to share their deepest thoughts, desires, concerns, likes, and dislikes with a special other without fear of anger, retribution, or ridicule.

For example, Morey, a product of the 1960's Human Potential Movement, having been a resident at Big Sur and been in groups led by Fritz Perls, self-disclosed to all in earshot. This was a source of great difficulty to his partner, Allen. Morey's openness was initially a point of contact and thought attractive by Allen. It now was wearing thin and was a source of conflict between them.

On the other hand, Myrna ended up badgering Roy to share his feelings. Roy had been brought up to hold his feelings in.

Professional Intimacy   Individuals may share a particular professional goal. It may be a broad professional goal, as in "healthcare," or more specific, as in Cardiology. An individual may have a friend in the office with whom they are very close from 9–5, but may make no attempt to see that person outside the office. Individuals who get together at a professional conference will often share a great feeling of togetherness that will last for the four days of the conference and will not be reactivated for a year.

For example, Marcia became upset and had difficulty understanding Dan's passing reference to his female secretary as his "office wife." In trying to explain that there was nothing sexual involved between Dan and the secretary, he explained that he spent eight hours a day with his secretary, more than he spent with any other woman in his life. His reference was to a professional intimacy commonly seen among colleagues and coworkers.

Sexual Intimacy   This involves the physical act of sex in all its variations. It may be part of a loving relationship or a physical act with nothing more meant or implied. Individuals may be transiently intimate on a first date that includes sexual expressions without a second date.

For example, when asked why she stayed with Hal, Helen said that Hal was the best lover she had ever been with. Even though he was sometimes abusive, "the making up was worth it." When Hal became depressed and had a low libidinal urge, Helen's attraction lessened and she was able to effect a separation.

Spiritual and Religious Intimacy   Religious leaders have often stressed that "the family that prays together stays together." While this may not always be true, it certainly is true that individuals who share a religious or spiritual goal have one more point of contact. If it involves getting up, dressing, and going to church and spending that hour together, it involves a sharing of rituals and beliefs. Family prayer hours or Bible classes serve as educational and religious activities that also bring family members into more frequent contact in this venue.

For example, Dorothy spent her junior year as an undergraduate in Paris, France. Raised Catholic, she had not gone to Mass since she was aged 13. For the year in France, she went to Mass every Sunday. It helped to assuage her loneliness by being with her co-religionists. The familiar ritual, Latin words, prayers, etc. were all points of contact with her family and home.

Humorous Intimacy   Individuals can share a similar sense of humor. This sharing may be gender based—men seem to enjoy The Three Stooges and that sort of slapstick and mayhem, whereas women generally see their antics as stupid and childish, something only men could enjoy. There is a "guy thing" over Curly or Moe, and that sharing is part of a gender-related humor connection. A couple will often have a shared sense of humor in terms of comedy broadly but, more specifically, they can share the content of the humor.

For example, when asked what was the best thing about Brad, Alice said, "his sense of humor." "There are times that he'll call me at work and share a pun or word play that he just made up. Sometimes I laugh so hard I think that I'll wet my pants."

Brad proceeded, unbidden, to demonstrate his word plays. The topic was bovine. For the two hour consultation session Brad stayed true to his theme, e.g., "That's no bull," "I have nothing to hide," "I have never let anyone buffalo me," "I will milk this for all its worth," and "We see to be on the horns of a dilemma." While the therapist had a strong negative countertransferential reaction, Alice laughed until there were tears streaming down her face.

Intellectual Intimacy   Individuals will share a level of intelligence, but moreover have a shared fund of knowledge. References made by one will be understood as a short hand by others. Couples may share information; intellectual issues; and pursuits in music, literature, languages, or mathematics.

These same shared issues are also found among colleagues and allied professionals. For example, if shared intellectual pursuits are important, one is more *likely* to find a partner with that attribute at a museum or concert, rather than at a sports bar.

Passive Intimacy   This involves what is termed parallel play in children. One can spend time in the company of another, but without necessarily interacting. A couple can go to the movies, watch television, or simply be driving together in a car without talking or physical contact, and have the experience of closeness, warmth, and a shared experience.

For example, one of the relationship positives identified by Harold and Cindy was their agreement to spend time every Sunday in bed with the Sunday papers. The paper came at 7:00 AM and from about 10:00 to noon their only verbal contact is, "Do you have the travel section" or "What is a seven letter word meaning...." At noon they had brunch. This is the quality time they had cut out of the week for themselves.

Competitive Intimacy   Individuals may share a strong competitive style that would demonstrate itself as a competition between partners, but also as a competition between the partners and any other partners. These are individuals you might see playing tennis against each other. The observer would think it was a world cup event. If one were to play doubles against them, one would see that it would be very difficult, as every ball even close to a line becomes a point of contention.

For example, Sean was very competitive while Mary was far less assertive. As is so often the case, Sean's assertiveness in college was what attracted Mary to him. He was, in her words, "a take-charge guy."

Sean was employed as a salesperson and was always in competition with other salespeople. His employer was constantly running contests to encourage sales. A critical incident shared by Mary was a game of Trivial Pursuit played by Mary and Sean and three other couples at a party.

She and Sean were in third place and, when they could not catch up, Sean became more and more irritated and verbal abused her and the others. When she missed an answer that Sean thought she should know he began calling her stupid and demanded that the game be terminated because his "own wife was sabotaging their chance to win." Her attempts to calm him down with the comment that "it was only a game," brought even more invective.

Avocational Intimacy   This involves the sharing of a hobby or avocational pursuit. Individuals may share interests in skiing, scuba diving, or travel, which will draw them together. If they were to share an interest in politics when election time comes around, the individuals would be out campaigning for a particular candidate or party, or collecting names on petitions.

For example, Mel and Bob belonged to a Thursday evening bowling league. The group would bowl as a team weekly, but would also meet for practice sessions at other times. After a league night, there was always beer and pizza. They had shirts with their team name on them and worked together to bring their partners and children into their sport. There was fellowship, camaraderie, and general good feelings amongst the members.

Geographical or Cultural Intimacy   Individuals may share either a particular place of origin or culture, or a present geographical site. Italians or Swedes may find themselves banding together and founding towns, clustering in neighborhoods, or forming their own churches and social clubs, based on national origin.

People from the northeast or the southwest may find an affinity and attraction with others from their geographical source. For example, in my teaching I travel throughout the United States. It is common to be asked, "Where are you from?" This refers not to my present domicile, but to my early origins in New York. If someone is also from New York, we might have a discussion about where in New York they were from, their high school, etc. The point of contact is that there was a period of time where we were raised within several miles of each other. Forty years later, it is our shared geographic experience.

Narcissistic Intimacy   Frequently, one's connection with one's partner is a reflection of narcissism. The partner may be seen as someone who will be seen by others as attractive, intelligent, desirable, sensuous, and connected to the partner in an unalterable way. If one believes, "I'm very special," then they may also believe, "since I am special, therefore my partner must also be very special." The parenthetic part of the idea, often unspoken, is that if my partner does not continue to enhance *my* image, then they must be abandoned for someone who will do so.

For example, Sally demanded that her husband start having hair implants at age 32, so that when he eventually went bald, there would be more than ample hair remaining. Since his hair started to naturally fall out in male pattern baldness at about this time, she was concerned that others would see him as aging, which would reflect badly on her. "After all," she stated, "I still wear the same size that I wore in high school. I exercise daily to keep my figure. It would look awful to be with someone who looks old and bald."

Pathological Intimacy The point of contact in this style is some point of pathology. It may be alcoholism, depression, gambling, overeating, drug use, or any other type of symptomatic behavior. The film *Days of Wine and Roses*, about a shared pathology of alcoholism, typifies this style. When both are drinking (or eating, drugging, gambling), there is little conflict. It is when one partner chooses a different course of action, such as sobriety, that this style is no longer shared, which then becomes a point of conflict.

The therapist must remember that any change in the homeostasis of the relationship system may bring about a deterioration of the system.

For example, Bud and Rosemary were both heavy smokers, each smoking one to one and a half packs of cigarettes each day. They had taken to smoking the same brand and there was always a carton or two in a kitchen cabinet. If Bud lit a cigarette and was smoking in the living room, Rosemary could take the cigarette and take a drag without censure or prohibition. Bud, of course, could do the same with Rosemary. When Rosemary decided to stop smoking, it was a loss of a shared style. In fact, Rosemary now forbid Bud to smoke in the house as it "smelled everything up."

Financial Intimacy   Individuals may stay together because it is a financially reasonable thing to do. Because of shared expenses and overhead, two people could live together for less money than either could living in a separate setting. Couples who are more roommates than a committed couple may do so because of tax implications, shared living, food or utility costs.

For example, Sue and Larry were separated and moving toward divorce but continued to share a house until the divorce, when Sue would be moving to another city. And Alex and Lauren were graduate students who chose to live together, in part, because they could qualify for couples housing on campus.

Convenient Intimacy   The point of contact for this style is convenience. In a committed relationship, one knows who they will be going to a special party with on Saturday night and who one will be sleeping with that night.

For example, Lenny stayed in a relationship with Esther because it was more convenient than looking for a new relationship. Although he did not find her as attractive as he once did, she lived nearby, was usually available, was familiar with his likes and dislikes, and was sexually available and interested. "Why go into the dating scene?" he said. "Its a zoo."

Gender Intimacy   This type of connection comes broadly under the heading of "us guys" or "us girls" and this involves a sharing of specific aspects of gender. If women talk about menstrual cramps, it is a problem that is specific to women and that men can understand only objectively. At best men can understand cramping as "it's kind of like ...."

Similarly, women can have difficulty understanding men's problems. For example, notions of "sisterhood" or the "sweat lodge" offer an opportunity to reconnect with gender-specific issues, problems, and joys. In fact, the loss of these gender connections has been hypothesized to be one cause of relationship difficulty, i.e., one cannot relate when one is not in touch with one's gender core.

Age Intimacy   This is a generational issue that has elements of historical intimacy. Individuals of a certain age share concerns of family, health, etc. You would see this in members of American Association of Retired Persons or a Golden Age or Seniors Club.

For example, Gert, 70 years old, was a widow. She was retired from a job at age 65 and now spent her days at a senior center with people who shared her lifestyle, problems, etc. These people were her friends and confidantes.

Dependent Intimacy   One individual may lean on the partner who plays the role of caretaker (supportive intimacy). Individuals can also be mutually-dependent, not co-dependent. They learn that individuals may lean on each other to be mutually supportive. Problems occur when one of the mutual-leaners is removed because of illness or death. It is at this point that the remaining leaner may topple.

For example, when Seymour died, Rose was set adrift. Rose and Seymour were mutually-dependent. He called her "Mother" and she referred to him as "Poppy." Through 50 years of marriage, they had helped each other along. Without his support and dependence, she was left feeling at a great loss and without an anchor in the world.

Supportive Intimacy   In this style, the individual takes the specific role as caretaker and supporter. These are the "strong" types that take the burdens of partners and children on their shoulders. It is when they sense that they are no longer needed that they become upset.

For example, Nora left college after her freshman year to marry David. After 20 years of marriage, David was a successful neurosurgeon. Their children were teenagers and did not need to be cared for. Nora had harbored a desire to return to school to get a teaching certificate and spoke to David about her interest. David's response was, "Why do you need to work? I make plenty of money." When she persisted, he became quite hostile, threatening to withhold tuition money and requiring her to reduce the household help, giving Nora more to do around the house. His need was to be in power, but also for her to be dependent on him.

Her persistent desire for empowerment, and personal efficacy, eventually led to divorce as David could not deal with an independent partner.

Treatment Goals Using the ISA:

1 Identify Intimacy styles
2 Identify desired changes to style
3 Develop style change interventions to include:
    a   Improve listening skills
    b   Improve self expression skills
    c   Build problem-solving skills
    d   Build conflict resolution skills
    e   Decrease negative behavioral exchanges
    f   Increase positive behavioral exchanges
4 Build de-escalation skills
5 Increase skills for cognitive restructuring

To set the scene for the therapy, several generic techniques will be used. These include:

1 Clarifying communication and communication patterns
2 Learning how to give feedback and how to deal with feedback
3 Assessing the value of change both individually and in the relationship
4 Understanding the implications of change
5 Examining options and alternatives of thought, action, and emotion
6 Using scaling and seeing change on a continuum rather than as all-or-nothing
7 Distribution of responsibility for change
8 Evaluating the advantages and disadvantages of changing
9 Turning adversity into advantage
10 Scheduling of change
11 Making small sequential steps

The treatment protocol will involve work both within the session as well as homework between sessions. It must be stressed to the couple that homework is essential because therapy cannot happen from only one hour a week in the consulting room. For them to meet their needs, therapy must proceed outside the consulting room and be practiced on a daily basis. The homework is the laboratory part of the therapy. The therapist can offer several reasons why the homework is important.

First, the homework is essential for effective treatment and offers continuity between sessions. Second, it will derive from the session material and will offer an extension of the therapy work. Third, the individuals can use the homework to build the necessary skills. Fourth, the homework must be very specific. Fifth, the results of the homework will be monitored at the next session, thereby assuring the patients that it is of value. Sixth, the homework will be set out as a no-fail experience, that is, used for data-gathering.

The ISA In-Session Exercises

The ISA exercise is described for the patients as an extensive evaluation exercise. Actually, it is part and parcel of the treatment.

The following materials must be available: a flip chart (black or white board or some other large writing surface), about twenty 3×5 index cards cut in half yielding 40 $2\frac{1}{2} \times 3$ inch cards, a flat surface for each partner to work on (desk or table top), and pens for each partner.

The procedure involves both partners being in the same room and working on the exercise individually. The instructions for the partners are as follows:

> This will help us to identify the strengths and areas for more intensive work, and also the interests that you have. What I will be asking you to do is to create the ideal partner. I am going to ask you to each come up with the characteristics or traits that you would like in an ideal partner. I would like you each to come up with a number of these attributes. Answer the question, What would I like in a partner. I am going to ask you to write each trait on a separate card. You will each build your own list so that there will be two sets of cards. Each of you will have your own set of cards. Who would like to start?

At this point, the therapist starts collecting traits and write each one on the board. Rather than have one individual list the traits they think most important, alternate each person listing one trait. For each trait listed, the therapist should write it on the board. Before the couple writes the trait on an index card, they must agree on the operational definition of what that trait means. For example, one partner might list "sensitivity." The couple must agree on an operational definition of sensitivity before the exercise continues.

If the couple has difficulty in discussing and coming up with a consensus meaning, the therapist can help them by offering information on better communication techniques. In this way the exercise helps the couple to do several things. First, they are working on a common problem. Second, they are doing problem-solving. Third, they are sharing ideas and coming up with definitions that heretofore were unspoken. Fourth, they are in a sharing mode. Fifth, they are involved in goal-oriented behavior that has a solution focus as its avowed goal. Sixth, they are speaking to one another.

The therapist intervenes only as necessary to steer the discussion and avoid intimidation, pressure, and insult. The exercise can last for several sessions, with the couple communicating throughout the session, without the all-to-common storytelling and accusation.

The list should not be more than 15 traits. Although there can be a multitude of traits possible, limit the couple to no more than 15. Ideally, 10 traits work best. When the list is complete, the individuals are given the following instructions by the therapist:

> I would now like you to arrange the cards in your set in an order, from the most important to the least important. The most important trait is number one and should be laid on the table (or desktop) at the top of the list. From there, all of the other traits are placed in descending order of importance. No two traits can share a placement. Now go to work, independently.

The therapist should give the partners ample time for their independent ordering of the traits. Once they are finished, the therapist gives the following instruction:

> Now that you have put the traits in an order, are you satisfied with the arrangement? If you are not satisfied, make any last changes. Once done, you cannot re-arrange them. Look at the traits in the order that you have placed them.

If there is a need to re-arrange, allow a few minutes. Once they are finished, ask that they do no more arrangement. Their lists are now "frozen."

> Let us assume that you were looking for a partner and you found someone with all of the traits that you have just listed, and they were available in the order that you have placed them, would you be satisfied? If so we can continue.

> Remove the least important trait at the bottom of the list. All of the other traits remain as arranged, but whatever trait was on the card that you removed is not available. Would that be acceptable? If it would be acceptable to give up that trait, we can continue. If that trait is too important to lose, replace it and consider the list frozen. Do nothing more until your partner is finished.

Keep removing the last remaining trait with the question, "Are you willing to give that trait up? If so, continue." If the individual wants that trait, it is replaced and they are frozen until the conclusion of the exercise.

When both partners are "frozen," the exercise is over. It is at this point that they are directed to look at the "bottom line" of what they want, and what they are willing to give up. The greater the list of what they want, in effect the more that they want, the smaller the probable pool of partners or the greater the demand on the present partner. The greater the number of shared traits and interests, the greater the connections that can be built between the couple.

If the exercise has served its purpose of working on mutual problem-solving and improving communication skills, the couple can now discuss their needs, interests, and prioritization of the expressed needs. By offering a structure to the therapy and focusing on skill-building, the partners can now work on resolving the issues that have caused the initial referral. Much of the work can now be done as homework.

One possible outcome of the ISA exercise is that the individuals may realize that their present partner does not meet their expressed needs. The question for the therapy is whether the expressed goal is realistic, is the partner motivated to change to be someone more closely approximating the desired ranking, or can the individual accept that their partner cannot and will not be able to change to become more closely identified with one's expressed needs.

Crises and Emergencies

If there are areas of concern that are of a more pressing or emergent nature, they can be dealt with as part of the agenda that is for the session. The session agenda could then include a review of the week and the homework, discussion of emergent issues, and the ISA work. The hardest job for the therapist will be to keep the couple focused and not get pushed into the "he said-she said" pattern.

SUMMARY

Intimacy is the glue that can keep a relationship strong and flexible. It is difficult to work with couples on problems of intimacy, in part because the definitions are often obscure, vague, or missing. This makes the treatment of couples with relationship problems difficult in that increased intimacy is a frequent goal of distressed couples.

Prager (1995) offers the most comprehensive definition of intimacy. She states that any definition of intimacy, to be integrative and illuminate the linkages between extant theoretical perspectives, must specify whether intimacy is an individual capacity, a property of interactions, or a characteristic of a relationship; must delineate between intimacy and the closely related concepts of love, sexuality, closeness, and support; and must offer a definition that is focused rather that fuzzy, broadly attainable rather that esoteric, and reconcilable with (if not identical to) lay definitions. It is within this definition that the ISA is offered as a model for the treatment of couples with interest in increasing intimacy.

Based on a broad cognitive-behavioral-communications approach, the ISA offers operational definitions for the component elements of what is termed intimacy, allowing for direct therapeutic intervention and skill building.

Identifying the component styles of intimacy as learned, well-practiced behavioral manifestations of interpersonal and intrapersonal schema, the ISA offers opportunity for assessment and building of requisite skills. The individuals can be helped, within a structured format, to identify their styles, rate the presence or absence of a style, choose a goal for themselves and for their partner, and then build the communications skills to reach those goals. The result will be better communication, improved problem-solving, and reduced conflict.

REFERENCES

Bagarozzi, D. A. & Anderson, S. A. (1989). *Personal, Marital, and Family Myths*. New York: W. W. Norton.

Baucom, D. & Epstein, N. (1989). *Cognitive Behavioral Marital Therapy*. New York: Brunner/Mazel.

Beavers, W. R. (1985). *Successful Marriage*. New York: W. W. Norton.

Beck, A. T. (1988). *Love is Never Enough*. New York: Harper & Row.

Bowlby, J. (1981). *Attachment and Loss (Vol. 1). Attachment* (2nd ed.) New York: Basic Books.

Bowlby, J. (1979). *The Making and Breaking of Affectional Bonds*. New York: Methuen.

Bowlby, J. (1981). *Attachment and Loss (Vol. 1). Attachment.* (2nd ed.) New York: Basic Books.

Bowlby, J. (1985). Childhood experience in cognitive disturbance. In M. J. Mahoney & A. Freeman. *Cognition and Psychotherapy*. New York: Plenum Publishing Co.

Burns, D. D. (1985). *Intimate Connections*. New York: William Morrow.

Campbell, R. J. (1989). *Psychiatric Dictionary*. (6th ed.) New York: Oxford University Press.

Cantor, N. & Malley J. (1991). Life tasks, personal needs, and close relationships. In G. J. O. Fletcher and F. F. Fincham (Eds.) *Cognition in Close Relationships*. Hillsdale, NJ: Lawrence Erlbaum.

Coleman, J. C. (1984). *Intimate Relationships, Marriage, and Family*. Indianapolis: Bobbs-Merrill.

Clinebell, H. & Clinebell, C. (1970). *The Intimate Marriage*. New York: Harper & Row.

Dattilio, F. M. & Padesky, C. A. (1990). *Cognitive Therapy with Couples*. Sarasota, FL: Professional Resource Exchange.

Derlega, V. J. (1984). Self disclosure and intimate relationshops. In V. J. Derlega (Ed.) *Communication, Intimacy, and Close Relationships* (pp 1–9). New York: Academic Press.

Erikson, E. (1963). *Childhood and Society*. New York: W. W. Norton.

Fisher, M. & Stricker, G. (Eds.) (1982). *Intimacy*. New York: Plenum.

Freeman, A. & Oster, C. (1997). Treatment of couples with relationship difficulty: A cognitive-behavioral perspective. In L. Sperry and J. Carlson. *The Disordered Couple*. Philadelphia: Brunner/Mazel.

Ginsburg, B. G. (1997). *Relationship Enhancement Family Therapy*. New York: John Wiley.

Gordon, L. H. (1993). *Passage to Intimacy*. New York: Simon & Shuster.

Greenwald, J. (1975). *Creative Intimacy*. New York: Jove.

Guerney, B. G. (1977). *Relationship Enhancement*. San Fransisco: Jossey-Bass.

Hof, L. & Miller, W. (1981). *Marriage Enrichment: Philosophy, Process and Program*. Bowie, MD: Prentice-Hall.

Klimek, D. (1979). *Beneath Mate Selection and Marriage*. New York: Van Nostrand Reinhold.

Merriam-Webster Dictionary (1995). Springfield, MA: Merriam-Webster.

Prager, K. J. (1995). *The Psychology of Intimacy*. New York: Guilford.

Scarf, M. (1986, November) Intimate partners: Patterns in love and marriage. *The Atlantic Monthly*, 45–93.

Zorbaugh, H. (1929). *Gold Coast and the Slum*. Chicago: University of Chicago Press.

CHAPTER 10

The Object Relations of
Sex and Intimacy

David E. Scharff, M.D.[1]

Sex and intimacy are fair-weather friends. When some couples experience a storm, intimacy may survive while the sex suffers; for others, the sex survives and the intimacy is eroded. Of course there are couples whose bond may strengthen in times of stress, but we tend not to see them clinically unless another family member becomes symptomatic. And then there are the many couples who find that their general level of intimacy deteriorates at the same time that sexuality becomes problematic.

Object relations theory holds that each of us has a fundamental need for relationships, and it is the vicissitudes of relationships—the need to be in them and yet to have our separate individuality within the context of relating—that give life its twists and turns. In my first clinical book, *The Sexual Relationship* (1982) I explored the developmental origins of sexuality in the growth of the individual, and the way sexual growth also reflected these fundamental needs to be in relationships, to be affirmed by another person, and yet to have one's own autonomy. In later books co-authored with Jill Savege Scharff (D. E. & J. S. Scharff, 1991; J. S. & D. E. Scharff, 1994), and in a number of other publications, I have explored the clinical approach to the developmental disorders of sexuality (1976, 1989a & b, 1990) and the treatment of sexual dysfunction (1978, 1988, 1992).

[1]David Scharff is Co-Director, International Institute of Object Relations Therapy, Bethesda, Maryland

I am grateful to the Family and Child Agency of Washington, DC and to the couple therapist for her collaboration in the case reported in this paper. *D.E.S.*

In this chapter, I want to explore the relationship between sex and intimacy through the vehicle of a case I saw for a single consultation interview. This couple, William and Janis, were unusually open and articulate. Although they had come for treatment because of sexual difficulty, they provided information during the interview which allowed me to understand a good deal about the link between their desire for intimacy and their sexual difficulty, the way their desire for intimacy made it hard for them to have a satisfactory sexual life.

As we progress with this couple through the interview, we will take time out to think about the development of intimacy and sexuality in this couple and, by extrapolation, in other couples. I saw this couple in consultation to a Mrs. Johnson at the Family and Child agency where I consult. When Mrs. Johnson first told me about them, they sounded as though an interview with them would illustrate issues of projective identification—that process first described by Melanie Klein (1946) and J. Scharff (1992) in which each member of a couple seeks to find split off and buried aspects of themselves in their partner. Henry Dicks (1967) first applied Klein's concept to couple therapy, describing also the way each marital partner tries to find his or her own missing parts in the other, and then treats the partner the way he or she feels about the part of his- or herself found in the other—spoiling and cherishing parts they treasure, denigrating and treating with contempt parts they disdain. Thus a husband who fears tenderness may treasure his wife for her sensitivity but berate her for her weakness. That same wife, fearing her own strength, might locate it in her husband and brag about his firm manner but complain about the bossy way he pushes her around.

When I first heard about this couple, I thought they sounded like a couple whose system of projective identifications included unconscious effects on their sexual life as they attempted to maintain their overall intimacy. It was with that expectation that I met them in the television studio where they had agreed to be interviewed. Thanks to their openness in agreeing to be interviewed in this setting, I have the record to draw on.

William and Janis, a young black couple, greet me as I enter the studio where they are already sitting. They are both engaging, but are also oddly discordant. Janis is slightly taller than William and sits up much straighter with one leg folded under the other; she is dressed in an elegant matching white silk sweater and skirt. William slumps in his chair, emphasizing the childish look of his sport shirt, shorts and sneakers. Nevertheless, they sit close to each other and their arms touch during most of the interview.

Dr. Scharff: Thanks for coming today. What brought you to ask for therapy in the first place?

William: We're engaged to get married, so we wanted to get counseling on certain things before making that step.

Dr. Scharff: A little difficulty...

Janis: Yeah. I wanted to go to counseling before we get married. We're having intimacy problems. Really sexual problems rather than intimacy problems. It took me a month to tactfully tell him what the actual problem was—that I wasn't attracted to him sexually. Once we got into sex, everything was fine, but getting me to want to participate was the problem.

Dr. Scharff: You could enjoy sex once you started, but getting interested was a problem?

Janis: And William actually didn't know that, and we had been together for a year and a half or so before I actually told him.

Dr. Scharff: What kept you from telling him for so long.

Janis: Because I didn't want to hurt him with something like that, you know. It can really damage the male's perspective on himself, and I didn't want him to feel bad. I didn't want to hurt him. I thought that I could make everything better on my own without having to tell him what the problem was, and then when it came to the point where it was getting closer to the time for us to get married—because we had a date set—I was just getting more frightened after a year or so had passed and it hadn't gotten any better. In fact we were having sex less than when we had first gotten together, so I decided to tell him.

Dr. Scharff: How did you take it, William?

William: I was surprised. I kind of felt as if she had deceived me by not telling me how she felt in the beginning. I was kind of upset at her. I thought we could get through it if she had told me.

Dr. Scharff: Is sex the only area that it has really bothered the two of you?

William: Communication, as well.

Dr. Scharff: What happens with communication?

Janis: Well, certain things upset us. We keep things aside from each other and get mad and talk to our close friends about them. It's hard to start talking to each other.

Dr. Scharff: You both do that?

Janis: Uh. Uh. I do it because I feel like he doesn't understand me. No one understands me in different situations and different mood swings that I go through. And so I won't talk to him and sometimes... Like I was telling him recently, I have a lot of emotional baggage from my family life, and I know that he does as well. I don't want to burden him when I go through these different mood swings.

William: I feel that she should talk to me and not protect me.

[Janis continues with the theme of what comes between them.]

Janis: And sometimes when I know he is mad at me... Oh, like . . . We have a new car. We turned in our Chevrolet. A nice car, but I didn't want it from the beginning. We turned in that Chevrolet for a sportier car. He didn't think we should do it, but I wanted it.

William: As with almost anything she really wants, once she wants it, she goes right after it.

Dr. Scharff: [To William.] Is there anything you have been able to say *no* to her about?

William: [Pauses for a moment, does not come up with an answer, then turns toward Janis.] I'm sure she can think of something. [He smiles mischievously.]

Janis: If he's doing one of those "teach me a lesson" type things. Like if... See, I shop a lot, and since I spend nearly all my money where I can't to get to work on the Metro, and he'll do something like, if... I don't like to ask people for anything, so if I spend all my money, well I'll just be hungry or whatever. But he'd never let me go hungry, so he'll go to the grocery store, and he'll let me get a couple of things. I mean, I won't volunteer that I want anything. He'll just get things anyway. So this one time we went to the store after I had spent all my money shopping, and I did ask, "Can I have some soda?" Soda that didn't even cost a dollar! And he said, "No!" I was so ... "He denied me food! He said, 'No!'" I was very upset. I was managing for a long time... [She is smiling as if to indicate that she also sees the humor and absurdity in the story but felt deprived just the same.]

Dr. Scharff: This was one of the times you had spent all of your money, so he was having to fund you.

Janis: [Smiling and nodding.] Uh-huh. Because, basically, I spent part of the grocery money, too, when I went shopping. So I had settled on not being able to eat. And he said "No!" And I hadn't asked for anything. And when I did ask for a soda, he's like "No!" And I was mad! Because now I wasn't going to ask him for anything else anymore, ever!

Dr. Scharff: Were you trying to teach her a lesson?

William: No. I was just saying *no.* I don't think it was so much teaching her a lesson...

Janis: That's how I felt.

William: I knew she had to have something to eat, but to me soda was like a luxury, you know. And she'd already had the luxury of the clothes.

Dr. Scharff: Okay, I see this area in which you have difficulty when Janis wants things and, William, you feel you won't be allowed to set a limit. Let's come back to your current situation. You said that you had a date to get married, and you postponed it. Why was that?

William: I wanted to work through our problems. [Janis nods in agreement.]

Dr. Scharff: So it's specifically with this task of understanding the problems in your relationship that you postponed the wedding?

William and Janis in unison: Yeah.

What we have seen so far is the first few minutes of the interview and the couple's statement that their reason for coming for help is, in the first instance, their sexual problem. It is, in a general sense, a problem of uneven desire. William desires Janis sexually, while she does not desire sex with him, although she is quite clear that, when they do get involved sexually, it goes well. The details of this discrepancy have not been clearly defined in this first few minutes of the interview. Instead of asking at first about the sexual difficulty, I tried to see if they could broaden the picture of their relationship. They responded by telling me about what they call "communication problems," which can mean almost anything to us as therapists. What they meant is that they have difficulty about whether Janis can get what she wants, and, from William's point of view, about whether he can ever say *no*.

While I did not yet understand the relationship of these two issues—sexuality and saying *no*—I begin to see that the couple has a problem which is shared by being divided into different spheres of their life together. It is a question of whether he can get what he wants sexually and whether she can get what she wants in just about every other way. In an odd way of accounting, things are even. Sex is on one side of the scale and everything else on is the other. The question about sex is really the same question put the other way round: Whether Janis can say *no* in the sex is balanced with whether William can say *no* when he feels her requests are excessive.

I found Janis and William intriguing and quite charming. They had established an atmosphere of intimacy with me in the first few minutes of our interview by their attitude of openness and humorous honesty in telling their story. While their manner was quite appealing, it was more important to me that it conveyed an attitude of trust toward me, that they assumed, without having to be told, that I intended to be helpful to them, and that in my presence—and despite the exposure of the television studio—they could expose their vulnerabilities in an undefended way. I took my feeling about them as a positive countertransference, a response to their positive transference to me in my therapeutic role. In object relations therapy, we term this area the "contextual transference and countertransference" because it occurs in the area of the affect which characterizes the entire context of the therapy (D. Scharff & J. Scharff, 1987, 1991; J. Scharff & D. Scharff, 1998). We use the metaphor of the way the mother does all the work to provide psychological holding for her infant in order to prepare and support the context in which the child will grow and develop, and compare this to the "focused relationship" between them when the mother is the focused object of the infant's interest, love and hate. Then we look later in therapy for the way individuals form focused transferences to their therapists when the therapists come to stand in for old internal objects and a patient treats them the way the patient feels towards those original family members. For now, however, I used my counter-transference as a guide to the contextual transference, and felt it was positive.

The difficulty which Janis and William outline poses a fundamental problem about intimacy for all couples: Can both partners get what they need from their relationship, and can they at the same time maintain reasonable personal boundaries, their separateness and their right to say "no"? Couples need both the connectedness of intimacy—including sexual connectedness—and the ability to remain separate, to decide when and how to relate. When Janis says, "You can't say 'no' to me. How can he say 'no'? It costs only less than a dollar!" she defines William's setting of limits and boundaries as rejection. When he says, "How can she want that when she had already spent all the grocery money on luxuries?" he says that he is willing to support her needs, but not her excesses. That is his limit; it remains unclear whether she can respect it. So far I have seen some sense of humor about her insistence, but no sign that she can see his limits in other that rejecting terms.

I can now see this problem as one which mounts a fundamental attack on their capacity for intimacy—that is their shared capacity for empathy, mutual support, and reciprocal give and take. But I do not yet see how it is so, nor do I understand the dynamic origins of their difficulty. In order to try to understand the origins of this attack on intimacy, I asked each of them about their families of origin. In object relations terms, we would say this is their object relations history. We do this not by collecting information for a genogram, but by following the affect in a session, and asking for "living family history," that is the history of a moment of impasse or problem either in their external lives or in the here-and-now of the therapy (D. Scharff & J. Scharff, 1987, 1991; J. Scharff & D. Scharff, 1992, 1997.) We had now reached a point in the interview where the external impasse—the inability to say "no" and not having needs satisfied—had entered the therapy because the couple agreed only that they could not solve the problem they had posed. So I asked each of them their family stories, which are also stories about the origins of intimacy in the first relationships. In doing so, I hoped to find information that would illuminate the impasse this couple brought to their consultation, and which would also lead to an understanding of the sexual impasse that I planned to ask about later in the interview.

Dr. Scharff: What was it like for you growing up, Janis?

Janis: My mother had three kids. I'm the middle child, the only female. My oldest brother passed five years ago, a month before I entered college. I went away to college and my youngest brother passed just a year and a half ago, when I had almost finished school. And I still finished school in four years and one semester. The only reason I was a little late was that I changed my major. I kept a lot inside, just trying to make it through.

Dr. Scharff: What did your brothers die from, Janis?

Janis: They were killed. Murd...

[She has mouthed the first part of the word "murdered," but it trails off as she sinks into herself. Then she rouses herself and continues.]

Janis: Basically, I'm not dealing with that. John, the older one, was killed while I was in college and all. All those pressures and no real support.

Dr. Scharff: How much older was John?

Janis: We were all three years apart. John was the only positive male figure I ever had in my life. Ever!

[I can see Janis is still occupied with the deaths by the change in the way she talked about them. She has become suddenly sad and preoccupied. So I follow her affect by focusing on these losses (D. Scharff & J. Scharff, 1991). I also have in mind that unmourned losses usually lie at the heart of later difficulty, including difficulties in establishing and maintaining intimacy.]

Dr. Scharff: How was John killed?

Janis: He was murdered. He went to live back with my grandmother, because she was ill. She had a stroke or something. He was very close to her. He was outside late one evening, and somebody shot him about some silly argument.

Dr. Scharff: It just came out of the blue?

Janis: Yeah. We had never dealt with any sort of a death. No one had ever died, and for it to happen so sudden! It was like a dream, and I dealt with it like a dream. There would be long periods when I wouldn't see him before he died, and so, after he died, I found I was just pretending that I hadn't seen him, because he was at Grandma's house.

Dr. Scharff: Then what happened to your younger brother?

Janis: He was killed, too. About year and a half ago. It was sudden too. He was starting to try to do the right thing, get back on track in terms of school and everything.

Dr. Scharff: Had he been kind of off the track?

Janis: Because of my oldest brother's death. John was like the world to us. He was the only male role model we had. All the rest, uncles and stuff, were drunkards and just no good. And our father was never around. He always made promises and never lived up to them.

Dr. Scharff: He didn't live with your family?

Janis: Right. So then when my oldest brother was killed, my youngest brother just did a 180 degree turn! He was always really quiet, you know. But he just did a 180. I didn't have the time to sit and mourn, because I felt like I might not stop...you know, I might...

Dr. Scharff: ...Never stop crying?

Janis: [Nodding, now crying] I know I'm going to mourn forever.

Dr. Scharff: There is a lot of sadness. Is it more than you have let William know about?

Janis: I think he knows, but I don't talk about it. He wouldn't know anything from what I say, because I don't really say what I feel.

Dr. Scharff: Has he had an idea of how important and special John was to you?

[Janis is crying deeply. She nudges William's arm with her elbow. He knows instinctively she needs a tissue and hands it to her from the table nearer him. I take it as a sign of his understanding her grief.]

Janis: I don't know if he does. John protected me. He used to walk us to school and all that kind of stuff. I always felt safe. When someone would pick on me, and I would be crying after school, all I would have to do was tell him, and he would take care of it. I never had a problem with anyone bullying me, never. I miss him! But then a few months ago I had a dream. He came to me in the dream and said to me that he was all right, that I didn't need to worry about him. I woke William up. Do you remember?

[She turns to William and touches his arm. He nods softly.]

Janis: So that helped me feel he would be okay.

[I could tell John was an idealized figure, and I thought the dream, for which she had awakened William, meant that having William had helped her recover from the loss and begin to set her inner world right. The deep extent of feeling I had as she was talking made me feel that the couple had continued to trust in the therapeutic situation, and that this trust also reflected their shared capacity for intimacy. Now I wondered about Janis's father. Was he the denigrated figure, the bad object, whom John earlier and now William were supposed to make up for?]

Dr. Scharff: I can see how much John meant to you. How about your father? Did he live with you? Was he was unreliable?

Janis: Yeah. He was an alcoholic.

Dr. Scharff: Had he ever lived with you and your mom?

Janis: Yeah. I told my mom that one of my earliest memories was when she left him. I wasn't even in school. I must have been in prekindergarten or something like that. I remember standing at the door of the apartment with her holding my hand and then leaving him in the dark apartment. The apartment was always really dark, and him asleep on the floor or the couch or something. If he had been the man that he was supposed to be or the father that we needed, then a lot of the stuff I feel, the stuff that happened after that could have been avoided.

[She stops crying as she gets angry at the image of her father she is painting. She laughs self consciously and continues.]

Janis: I know I'm placing blame on everyone. But all those promises he made! When John passed, and my mom called my father, when my youngest brother started to change for the worse and started to be real rebellious or whatever, my father said, "OK, I'm going to come over and talk to him, spend more time with him." He never showed up! Do you know how disappointing that is? And then I remember when my brother came home, my youngest brother came back home. My oldest brother had already passed, and my father called out of the blue. He came by to see us. And he was drunk! My youngest brother said, "I wish he had never even come over here." I felt the same way. I wished he had never even come over. Like I didn't even see anything good. I wouldn't have to have that last memory of him. Still drunk after all these years. Still irresponsible. I just felt he was choosing alcohol over me and my youngest brother. Knowing all the crap that we had gone through in our young lives, to still choose that!

[She is furious at the image of her father before her.]

Janis: Like take it away from me! I have not called him, talked to him, and I won't ever see him again. I'm not going to bother myself and hurt myself up for that kind of disappointment ever. It's so funny because, she grew up in the same kind of a home, you know, alcohol all the time, people drunk all over the place.

Dr. Scharff: Do you mean your mother grew up in that kind of home?

Janis: Uh. Huh. And actually we did too, because my grandmother raised us because Mom worked a lot. So we were raised by my alcoholic grandmother and experienced the same sort of things Mom did. People lying all over the place, drunk all the time, drinking and laughing, you know, always loud and always card games, alcohol and all that kind of stuff.

Dr. Scharff: Was there much violence?

Janis: My grandmother used to spank us, but that was all. Alcohol meant there is arguing and fighting amongst the grownups, but no one ever hit us except for discipline.

[Janis's history begins to make sense of her need to get unlimited things from William, and perhaps of her inhibition of sexual desire which has not yet been fully spelled out. She grew up in an alcoholic setting, and her most vivid memories concern leaving her father at the age of about five because of his drinking. In consequence, she split fathers into two—the bad, negligent object personified in her father, and the idealized one personified in her older brother. Now, we can see that she keeps trying to test William to prove he can be the idealized father, but at the same time keeps daring him to be a strong father who could tame her insatiable and self-destructive neediness. In her terms, she hopes William can be the man who will not let her down. The lack of desire must, in part, be in consequence ot her feeling that William should take the place of her older brother with whom sex would be taboo, but at this point in the interview I speculated that it also stemmed from an association of sex with the destructive people who were drunk and "lying all over the place" in her grandmother's house—a reference, I thought, to displays of sexual behavior she would have found stimulating and terrifying. These speculations formed my hypotheses about the inhibition of sexual desire and intimacy. I now turned to William to ask about his object relations history.]

Dr. Scharff: William, what was it like for you growing up?

William: My parents divorced when I was around seven or eight. So up till that time, from the kids perspective, things were pretty stable. I can never remember when they started turning bad, when it was that my father began to be violent with my mother. I remember us leaving and going back a couple of times, and I don't remember sleeping so good after that.

Dr. Scharff: Was he drinking?

William: No. Well, his father was an alcoholic, and I think his whole obsession with life was to not be like his father. So he wasn't an alcoholic but he was like completely opposite, a real perfectionist.

Dr. Scharff: A kind of perfectionistic tyrant?

William: Yeah. That's pretty much it.

Dr. Scharff: And did he beat your mother much?

William: Yeah, but it didn't last too long. And then we moved, so she got her own place. He still used to come around some times, and they would get to fighting. Then she began to drink, and the whole structure of family life just ceased to be anymore. I have two younger brothers, so I can understand how Janis felt about her brothers because I was the older brother. I was the one that took care of everybody. I always said my brothers were my kids and my mother was as well, because I took care of everybody.

Dr. Scharff: Did you take care of your mother when she was drinking.

William: I took care of everybody. I made sure everything was OK. For instance, I made sure everybody had something to eat.

Dr. Scharff: Did you support your family?

William: For a while. When I got old enough.

Dr. Scharff: So when you have to buy food for Janis, you feel you've been there before.

William: Yeah.

Dr. Scharff: Did your family run out of food often?

William: Yeah. I'd call my grandmother to help us out. Sometimes I'd call my father, but like her father, he would say, "I'll be over later," and never show up.

Dr. Scharff: Do you think that the two of you have something going where you, Janis, are another one of William's kids because you're looking for an older brother? And William, you're looking to take care of her as one of the kids?

William: Yeah, because I want somebody to take care of, and she wants to be taken care of. We fulfill those needs for each other.

Dr. Scharff: So then, it's hard when she won't let you say *no*. Do you feel pretty guilty?

William: I get mad at myself for not saying no. Because I know when I say *no* it's only because it needs to be said, not because I want to, or because I want to deny her.

Dr. Scharff: You both are trying to make up for missing people. It's really fathers you both miss.

William / Janis: Yeah.

Dr. Scharff: Although Janis, you miss your brother most.

William: [Answering for her.] But he played the father role.

Dr. Scharff: Yes, he was filling in already for there not being a father. You also spent your life after six or seven being the father.

[Like Janis, William came from a broken home with a missing, negligent and violent father. His attempt to be the missing father and to take care of his brothers and mother gives him a wish to fill a complementary role for Janis—the role vacated by the idealized lost brother. For William, Janis is the needy sibling and mother he can take care of, love and cherish, making up for his punishing and negligent father by being the caretaker he longs for himself. By this point in the interview, I speculated that William equated sex with the violence of the relationship between his parents, and that he might be willing to forego sex in a loving relationship in order to ensure a more loving and care-taking overall emotional relationship. That is to say that I guessed he equated sex partly with violence and damage, and that this was the reason that he partly accepted Janis's inhibition of sexual desire as protective of both of them. This would have to be tested out by asking directly about their sexual histories and sexual relationship, as we will see in a moment.]

Intimacy originates in the earliest relationship between parent and child where emotional intimacy is closely linked to physical intimacy—what Winnicott called a psychosomatic partnership (Winnicott, 1971; Scharff, 1982). The mother starts by providing an arms-around envelope to her child. She holds the baby in her arms and positions the baby for relating to her, for the safety that the child needs. She also offers what Winnicott called physical care and an attitude of emotional "holding" (1963). We explain this by saying that in the physical experience of mother holding the baby, the baby has an emotional experience of being held in the mother's mind. This offers safety and the conditions in which the baby can begin to develop as a person. Once the mother holds the baby safely in the arms-around attitude, she offers a more focused kind of relating, an eye-to-eye relationship. They look into each other, they talk to each other intimately. Their bodies move in an exquisite dance, with a rhythm led by the baby. They have an emotionally intimate experience. This is the beginning of the I-to-I relationship, in which they offer to become each other's subject. What every person wants, and what each wants from the beginning, are these two elements of relating. The first is trust and security—to be held in the mind and held physically by somebody who cares about the baby. Infants and children have the right to take their parent's provision of safety and loving care for granted. It is supposed to be there, and parents generally expect to offer it without specifically being thanked. Within that holding context there is an experience of penetration, by which I mean most significantly the interpenetration of two minds, the experience of being entered and understood and of being able to enter the other person's psyche. This experience of infants and growing children is the psychological precursor of physical sexual interpenetration. It is the experience of wanting to be known. Interpenetration goes on as mother and baby gaze into each other's eyes and into each other's inner worlds, where they come to know each other, and, as they know each other, they put things of central importance of themselves into each other. Being mutually held and gazing into each other, mother and child develop an intense psychosomatic partnership, that is, a partnership which in the beginning is both entirely physical and entirely psychological, which organizes the infant and the parent-infant pair. The early psycho-somatic partnership is also the infantile precursor of later sexual relationships which in adolescence and adulthood are also extremely physical and extremely psychological at the same time. As the child grows, and especially in adolescence, it becomes linked to sexual interests and bodily capacity. In later life, it is only in adolescent and adult sexual relating that there is a replication of intense physical and psychological relating at the same time.

For a child and parent to have full pleasure in their intimate relationship, the pleasure has to be mutual. The pleasure is in living with, and in, and through another person. When the child looks into the mother's eyes, the child sees himself reflected in her gaze, and when the mother looks into her child's eyes, she sees herself lovingly reflected. Each of them is being borne in the other's mind.

By analogy, adult emotional and physical intimacy has to occur in the context in which each partner has the other in mind, so that, regardless of the mechanics of sex, each is fully involved in taking the other in psychologically.

The early exchange between an infant and each of its parents involves a give and take which is not sex, but the mutual pleasure they experience is the precursor of all later pleasures, sex included. With development, intimacy occurs across a larger and larger gap as the parents have to give the child more and more room for autonomy and yet be able to exchange the same kind of psychological interpenetration, while also recognizing each other's individuality. So when adults come together and penetrate each other's psychological worlds in an intimate way, they do so across the gap that represents their capacity for individuality. Indeed, adult intimacy has no meaning unless it crosses the normal gap which exists between any two people. The story of development from childhood is, in part, the story of how children learn to enlarge the gap between themselves and others, and the establishing of intimacy is the recreation of the bond which spans the gap.

Then there is the story of each person's inevitable disappointments. In optimal development these disappointments are mild. But we have been hearing about the terrible disappointments William and Janis have experienced. Limitations on their ability to trust and to risk intimacy follow inevitably. Hearing their early histories, we can make sense of the problems they have, and would no longer be surprised to hear of inhibition in sexual trust. But we also get a sense of their shared longing for trusting and caring relationships, of a strength of commitment, which I felt during the interview so far, despite the trauma each of them had lived with. Intimacy can go a long way toward restoring trust and a sense of mutual safety if it can overcome the assault the couple carries within concerning those qualities.

William and Janis both had childhoods which were full of threat and loss. Issues concerning safety took precedence over needs for intimacy. There has been lack of trust in their capacity to believe in somebody who can provide caring and safety, and therefore in a relationship which would be emotionally satisfactory. They divide fear and hope between themselves in interesting ways. Janis speaks for fear through her sexual loss of interest, and for hope through her efforts to get William to give to her. William speaks for hope through his commitment to take care of Janis, and for fear in his inability to say *no* when it should be said, lest he deny her as he felt denied by his father.

In the last part of the interview, we deal with their sexual problem to understand how it represents an attempt to solve their issues concerning intimacy. Feeling I had begun to understand something about their development, I now returned to the problem which brought them to treatment.

Dr. Scharff: What about sex, Janis? You said you have not felt attracted to William for most of the time you have been together.

Janis: I recognized from the start what kind of a person he was. He is really gentle and warm and giving, very unselfish. I always felt safe in his presence. He's an attractive personality to me. I just wasn't sexually attracted to him.

Dr. Scharff: Right from the beginning?

Janis: Yeah, but I thought it would get better.

Dr. Scharff: You thought it would get better, you cared about him and you felt he cared about you?

Janis: I knew that he did. I could feel it, because we always hold hands and cuddle and kiss, and I like that kind of stuff more...

Dr. Scharff: More than...?

Janis: More than sex.

Dr. Scharff: Do you feel that you just don't like sex at all, or is that different with other people?

Janis: It was worse with other people. All of my relationships before him have been horribly abusive in one way or the other. Really violent towards me. I was physically restrained or controlled in different ways.

Dr. Scharff: Meaning tied up or...?

Janis: Grabbed. Pinned down. Forced to do things I didn't want to.

Dr. Scharff: Sexual things?

Janis: Like forced to have sex when I didn't want to. It took me a while to really realize that's what happened to me. One of my boy friends used to force himself on me. He tried to convince me that isn't what really happened. I said,

"You forced yourself on me. You raped me." He was like, "No. It didn't happen like that." Like I didn't know what I was talking about. It took me a while. I kept thinking about it, and realized, "I'm not crazy!" And I said, "No, you did make me have sex." And then he got mad at me because I wasn't responsive to him. The next boyfriend, who was the last one before William, he did a Dr. Jeckyl and Mr. Hyde on me. At first he was really sweet and wanted to listen to all my problems and all, and then, soon after, he was really controlling and violent. He was the one who used to grab me and force me to sit still or stay in one place, or whatever. Physically restraining me and then forcing himself on me.

Dr. Scharff: It sounds like it took you a while to break up with them, even though you felt this was happening. [She winces and nods.] But now the two of you have a similar problem in reverse. Not about sex, but about spending. When you, William, try to say *no* to Janis, she has trouble respecting that.

William: [Nodding and smiling a bit grimly.] Yeah.

Dr. Scharff: I wonder if there is some relationship between these two areas—sex and spending? If William says *no* to you Janis, does that feel to you like a rejection.

Janis (nods): Uh huh.

Dr. Scharff: It turns the situation around. There was this boyfriend who wouldn't let you say *no* when you wanted to say *no*, and now it's hard for you to take *no*.

Janis: I feel like when he says *no* to me, I feel like saying, "See! I knew I couldn't count on anyone." I always feel like I don't have anyone to count on. And so, I don't ask him for anything. I never do! And then I felt like, when I finally asked William for something, or I finally wanted him to do something for me, he didn't want to do it.

Dr. Scharff: That's what happened in the soda episode?

Janis: [Laughing at herself as though she knows the ludicrous quality of her logic.] Uh huh.

Dr. Scharff: You don't ask him for anything, but he seems to know what you want without your asking.

Janis: [Nodding vigorously.] Uh huh.

[I felt we had been able to establish the connection between the "communication" problem they had introduced at the beginning of the consultation, and the sexual difficulty. Both represented a relationship in which one person forced things on the other. The only difference was that Janis was the victim in the sexual forcing, and the perpetrator in the financial forcing. Both of these situations invaded the couple's intimacy, for in each case one person felt coerced while the other felt guilty. And each case could be understood to represent an attempt to deal with feelings of deprivation and threat. I returned to the current sexual situation, and to William's sexual history.]

Dr. Scharff: William, what's your reaction been to Janis saying that she hasn't been interested in sex?

William: I was upset for her not saying it to me directly. I would like her to be honest with me, and if that's how she felt, just tell me. I would hope we can deal with it, but if we can't by ourselves, we'll do whatever, like come for help. But it's like she'd almost prefer this suffering in silence thing. I didn't want that. I was more upset about that.

Dr. Scharff: More upset that she hadn't spoken about it?

William: I always tell her, "Tell me how you feel."

Dr. Scharff: Janis, you weren't telling him to protect him from feeling bad?

Janis: Uh huh.

William: She doesn't have to protect me. I can deal with it. I honestly think she cares about me, but I don't want her to protect me. She should take care of herself.

Dr. Scharff: William, how about your previous sexual experience?

William: Even if I didn't like the person, I would sleep with them.

Dr. Scharff: Just for sex?

William: Yeah. It wasn't an act of love. I didn't take most of my relationships seriously. I didn't see any long term thing like marriage in the relationships. I just considered them as seasonal or a matter of time before this person would move on and I would move on. Except the woman just before Janis. She didn't believe in sex before marriage, so I went along with that. But even there, I could respect her, but I didn't expect to marry her.

Dr. Scharff: What made the difference when you met Janis?

William: She was different. I perceived her as someone sincere as opposed to most of the other people. She's kind of unselfish. [He pauses and thinks for a moment.] She seemed like someone who could love.

Dr. Scharff: I can see you feel differently about her, and that you have been willing to work at this relationship despite the sexual difficulty. But what we are trying to understand at the moment is the difference between the very fond, loving feelings you have for each other and what's happening with sex—in which Janis has been pretty guarded. Yet you both say that once you get going sexually, it's OK.

Janis: [Nods again vigorously.] Uh huh.

Dr. Scharff: He does things well. He's a good lover?

Janis: Uh huh. He's really gentle.

Dr. Scharff: Do you have orgasms? Or is that a problem?

Janis: I have orgasms. That's no problem.

Dr. Scharff: You don't think there are any sort of technical problems about how you make love?

Janis: No. Once we get into it, it goes fine.

Dr. Scharff: Do you feel the same way, William? Has she been a good lover?

William: Yeah.

Dr. Scharff: So this was a surprise to you?

William: Quite!

[I could tell from the way William's answers had become ever so cryptic that this was difficult territory for him.]

Dr. Scharff: You had no idea that she was really...

William: Of course!

Dr. Scharff: ...wishing it didn't happen? Is that the right way to put it? [He nods.] Janis, tell me about your feeling about not being interested.

Janis: I don't know much about it. But I do know that sometimes when, like earlier in our relationship, if, you know, we were going to get in the mix, and I said *no*, or whatever, and he kept pushing. Automatically I would think, "He's just like those other guys."

Dr. Scharff: Just like the other guys who were controlling and wouldn't stop?

Janis: Uh huh. And it would make so me so sad—all of a sudden I got really sad. I'd think, "He's just like that too. I guess I'm going to have to go through this all over again." That's what I used to think. Or if he kept pressing, then I'd feel like I needed to go ahead and give in, even though I don't want to.

Dr. Scharff: And you felt it was just like the situation you had been in before?

Janis: Uh huh. Every time.

Dr. Scharff: Now with the other guys, I gather there was much more pressure. And sometimes you were feeling really abused. So, with William it wasn't...

Janis: It wasn't that extreme, but I would connect it to those times anyway.

Dr. Scharff: And then you would get sad, like when you felt that, you were loosing the good brother, the good father, the good guy? So when you would make love then...

Janis: It made the situation totally different...

Dr. Scharff: ...Not just that you had given in, but that you had lost what you had. So how often were you having sex?

Janis: It got down to once a month.

Dr. Scharff: Which was still feeling like too much to you, Janis? [She nods.] And it was feeling like too little to you, William? [He nods slowly.] Had sex been more frequent earlier on?

Janis: Every day or every other day, in the beginning. [She looks at him to check, and he agrees.]

Dr. Scharff: So then it fell off to once a month. And has it pretty much stayed there?

Janis: [Smiles and looks again at William, who smiles back knowingly.] No. Mrs. Johnson, our therapist, suggested that we just alleviate the whole pressure, and just not have sex. She said we should work more so on learning about each other. And ever since she told us to do that a few weeks ago, we've been having sex more often.

Dr. Scharff: And what has your feeling been about it been since then?

Janis: Oh, I've been enjoying myself. [William looks at her and agrees.] And also at the same time we've been talking about it more. About the way we really feel. We've been opening up outside of our counseling sessions.

Dr. Scharff: [Surprised at the ease with which the therapy has restored sexual intimacy.] Really?

Janis: And I think that along with that, we've begun to spend a lot of quality time together. It's a new closeness that I feel with him.

Dr. Scharff: Do you feel the same, William?

William: Yeah. It's been like a new thing with us again.

Janis: I don't feel all the tension. And mostly, I don't feel obligated or like I have to do what I don't want to.

Dr. Scharff: You don't? So then if he's interested, it's OK with you, and that's a very different attitude?

Janis: Yeah. I can relax and just let it go.

Dr. Scharff: Has it felt different to you, too, William?

William: Yeah. It's like it is more relaxed. When we got to the one month thing, it was very tense. I don't think I was enjoying it by then any more than she was. But this is different, and I can feel the relief, too.

Dr. Scharff: Now you've met with Mrs. Johnson about how many times?

William: About six times, once a week for about that long.

Dr. Scharff: And what has that been like?

Janis: She's been repeating things back to me, things that I said. I'm like, "Did I just say that? Oh, my God." You know, she really got me to see things in a different way. It really helps.

Dr. Scharff: Are there any things that have particularly been helpful to you about what she replayed to you?

William: Yeah. About commitment. And how it ties to what we grew up with.

Janis: I have been telling her about my mom. She said to me how I tend to want a committed relationship, but when I do have one, I tend to push it away. And then she asked me about my mom. She said, "Did I ever learn or see an example of a committed relationship, or whatever?" My mother, on the other hand, actually told me not to get committed. She vehemently told me throughout my high school and college career, "You're too young to get into a social relationship. You should date, do this and do that, you're too serious." Constantly.

Dr. Scharff: Did you feel your mom didn't trust men?

Janis: [Nods vigorously.] Definitely She would tell me, "Don't ever rely on a man for anything." That's why I have such a hard time with him. In trusting him with my shelter and food and things like that. It's like I can't trust him even when he's so good to me.

Dr. Scharff: On the other hand, you want to trust him.

Janis: I want to! But it's hard.

Dr. Scharff: Do you think sometimes you sort of spend yourself down to the ground so you can see if he'll be there for you?

Janis: [Thinking about that, and then elaborating on it.] Um. Maybe, because I do know he will be there. It's like I do trust him, even though I've been conditioned by my mom not to ever do anything like that. I do trust him. I know that he cares.

Dr. Scharff: It does sound like you have to keep testing him. That can wear people down, when you don't need to. Because basically you think you can really trust him. He is there, but the real test comes for you when he says *no*. And then you want to see if he will take care of you, even when he doesn't seem to want to.

Janis: That makes sense.

Dr. Scharff: I think your feeling, William, is that taking care of her would include saying *no* when it's a good idea to say *no*.

William: Yeah. When *no* needs to be said.

Dr. Scharff: And that's hard for you to do.

William: She's always told me she doesn't like *no*. That's why she doesn't ask, because she doesn't like to hear *no*. It's hard for me to say, because I really want to take care of her. I don't want to be like my dad, who left it to me to take care of every one.

Dr. Scharff: You're afraid you'll be depriving her, or at least that you'll leave her feeling that way, even if what you say *no* about isn't really necessary. And you just can't bring yourself to do that because then you'd be like your dad?

William: Yeah. I don't want to be like that.

Dr. Scharff: Janis, you don't like hearing *no*, and also you're frightened to say it yourself.

Janis: That's true.

Dr. Scharff: Because you're afraid somebody won't care about you either if you are the one saying *no*?

Janis: Yeah, That happened with my mom. She helped me get in credit card debt. It took me a long time to tell her *no*. She's the only person who I had left to love me, so I just couldn't turn her down when she wanted things from me. Anything she'd ask for, I couldn't say *no*.

Dr. Scharff: Did you buy a lot of things for her?

Janis: I would let her use my credit card. Just take it. It took me a long time to...I was, like buried by how much she spent. Finally it got to be so much, I said to her, "Mom, you just can't do that anymore."

Dr. Scharff: Is some of that debt you're still carrying?

Janis: Yeah. It's about $3,000. It's the whole amount I'm in debt for.

Dr. Scharff: So you couldn't say *no* to her either. And you couldn't say *no* to the men, because they wouldn't care about you. And then you felt you couldn't say *no* to William.

William: She needs to protect herself. She needs to take care of herself.

Dr. Scharff: [Nodding in agreement with William, and then turning to Janis.] Do you think you spend yourself down so he'll have to take care of you? Are you afraid that if you look like you can take care of yourself, he wouldn't want to bother with you?

Janis: No. Sometimes I feel like...All my life I've always been really serious, had to do this, do this, do this. And with him, I feel so safe, I can just relax and just let it go. I know he'll take care of me.

Dr. Scharff: But as you've let go with him, you've found some new parts of yourself, some of which feel real good, some of which give you a little trouble. Like pushing some things beyond the limit of what is really useful for you. It sounds like you're in a position now to be able to work on that—both for yourself, Janis, and together. Because that's the stuff that will get you in trouble. And William, what gets you in trouble is letting yourself be pushed further than you want to go for fear of hurting her. I hope the two of you can do work on that with Mrs. Johnson.

[They nod at the same time.]

Janis: I think we can. She's real good with us.

Dr. Scharff: Thank you for coming in to talk. I hope everything goes well for you.

Janis: Thank you.

William: Thanks a lot.

We can now see that Janis has used sex in an unconscious manner to guard herself against the unconscious certainty that others—especially men—will let her down. I did not think she had a feeling of being tortured in the beginning of the sexual relationship when the pull towards William was strong enough to overcome the unconscious fear, but once the bond was established, she expected that she would be controlled and abused. However the unconscious processes do not stop there: It is not enough for William to behave in a kind, caring fashion. William and Janis share an internal object relations set—that is, an internal model—which says that relationships are always threatened following the pattern of the kind of abuse and neglect they lived with earlier in their lives. So, when William does not fit that pattern, she pushes him in an effort to see if she can reassert the pattern of abuse with herself in either role—victim or perpetrator. What is reasserted over and over is the perpetrator-victim role, which itself establishes the kind of familiarity that carries a rough angry caricature of intimacy which substitutes for loving closeness.

Janis fears that an interpenetrating relationship will expose her to abuse. As soon as a relationship becomes more committed, it brings the threat of penetration, which she unconsciously fears will release the perpetrator-victim relationship and destroy the loving one she has just formed. Her lack of desire gives her safety by establishing physical distance. In this defense, she uncon-sciously locates danger as being expressly contained in genital interaction. She acts as though a relationship constellation, with commitment but without sex, will protect her from invasion and exploitation.

William has also split sex from intimacy. In all his previous relationships save one, there was sex without intimacy or commitment. The women did not mean much to him. He was in it for sex. In the relationship just before Janis, he endured the opposite split—valuing the woman's integrity and tolerating the lack of sex. In either case, sex and intimacy were kept apart. With Janis, he had both at the beginning, but soon the same split surfaced so that he experienced intimacy with diminishing sex. However, their bond was strong enough that they sought help, and the therapist's provision of holding and understanding enabled them to refind each other, and in doing so, to find an integration of sex and emotional intimacy neither had experienced before.

There are couples who have a milder split between sex and intimacy, who are able to build trust gradually over time and overcome this situation without therapy. Not all couples with this constellation will require our help. Neverthe-less, one of the surprising things about William and Janis, given the amount of trauma both of them had sustained, was how quickly they were able to move towards an integrated relationship. Their therapist had not addressed their sexual problem specifically, although she had offered her understanding of the childhood origins of their difficulty. In a sense she gave what family therapists would call a paradoxical interpretation: "Don't have sex. Relax and learn about each other." However, the therapist did not intend her intervention as a paradoxical injunction. She was simply setting the frame for therapeutic relationship by offering initial support, and then providing comfort and safety and the beginnings of understanding. She offered an arms-around attitude toward them, and the beginnings of understanding. That allowed healing of their splits in an unusually rapid way. While they can still benefit from additional therapy for the ways they are still likely to undermine their relation-ship, they are off to a good start.

Through the attitude we convey towards patients, we enable therapy to shore up couples' safety and trust for each other. Therapeutic reassurance, the interpretation of fears and defenses, and the focus on factors which invade trust are all factors which lead to the reemergence of sexual desire and to a new integration of physical, sexual, and emotional partnership. This adult version of the psychosomatic partnership is the basis of marital intimacy, the place where two bodies and the desires of two psyches blend for moments of intense communication, understanding and pleasure, only to separate in order to allow for repeated reunion. For this to be possible, the couple must have a feeling of safely holding each other, and then of overcoming the obstacles to emotional and physical interpenetration. When any couple can accomplish this, they have established an intimacy which is among the highest of human achievements and pleasures.

REFERENCES

Dicks, H. V. (1967). *Marital Tensions: Clinical Studies Towards a Psychoanalytic Theory of Interaction.* London: Routledge & Kegan Paul.

Klein, M. (1946). Notes on some schizoid mechanisms. *International Journal of Psychoanalysis 27,* 99–110.

Scharff, D. E. (1976). Sex is a family affair: Sources of discord and harmony. *Journal of Sex & Marital Therapy 2*(1), 17–31.

Scharff, D. E. (1978). Truth and consequences in sex and marital therapy: the revelation of secrets in the therapeutic setting. *Journal of Sex & Marital Therapy.* 4(1), 35–49.

Scharff, D. E. (1982). *The Sexual Relationship: An Object Relations View of Sex and the Family.* London: Routledge. Reprinted: Northvale, NJ: Jason Aronson, 1998.

Scharff, D. E. (1988). An Object Relations approach to inhibited sexual desire. In S.R. Lieblum & R. C. Rosen (Eds.), *Sexual Desire Disorders.* (pp. 45–74). New York: Guilford.

Scharff, D. E. (1989a). An object relations approach to sexuality in family life. In J. S. Scharff (Ed.), *Foundations of Object Relations Family Therapy.* (pp. 399–417) Northvale NJ: Jason Aronson.

Scharff, D. E. (1989b). Family Therapy and Sexual Development: An object relations approach. In D. Kantor & B. F. Okun (Eds.), *Intimate Environments: Sex, Imtimacy, and Gender in Families* (pp. 1–27). New York: Guilford.

Scharff, D. E. (1990). Sexual Development and Sexual Psychopahology: An Object Relations Point of View. in M. Lewis & S. M. Miller (Eds.), *Handbook of Developmental Psychopathology.* (pp. 441–451) New York: Plenum.

Scharff, D. E. (1992). The early phase of treatment: The Object Relations approach. *Psychiatric Medicine 10*(2), 295–315.

Scharff, D. E. & Scharff, J. S. (1987). *Object Relations Family Therapy.* Northvale NJ: Jason Aronson.

Scharff, D. E. & Scharff, J. S. (1991). *Object Relations Couple Therapy.* Northvale, NJ: Jason Aronson.

Scharff, J. S. (1992). *Projective and Introjective Identification and the Use of the Therapist's Self.* Northvale NJ: Jason Aronson.

Scharff, J. S. & Scharff, D. E. (1992). *The Primer of Object Relations Therapy.* Northvale NJ: Jason Aronson.

Scharff, J. S. & Scharff, D. E. (1994). *Object Relations Therapy of Physical and Sexual Trauma.* Northvale NJ: Jason Aronson.

Scharff, J. S. & Scharff, D. E. (1998). *Object Relations Individual Therapy.* Northvale NJ: Jason Aronson.

Winnicott, D. W. (1963). Communicating and not communicating leading to a study of certain oppposites. In *The Maturational Processes and the Facilitating Environment* (pp. 179–192). London: Hogarth. 1965.

Winnicott, D. W. (1971). *Playing and Reality.* London: Tavistock.

CHAPTER 11

A Postmodern Perspective on Relational Intimacy: A Collaborative Conversation and Relationship with a Couple

Harlene Anderson, Ph.D.
Diana Carleton, Ed.D.
Susan Swim, M.A.

> *I interviewed people on the phone to find somebody that would be suitable for him, that he'd be receptive to.... she [referring to the therapist she selected] was real equal from the beginning to the end.*
>
> Jane

In our experience most people desire and seek intimacy. And, most agree with the common dictionary definitions of intimacy and intimate:

Intimate...associated in close personal relations...characterized by or involving warm friendship or a familiar association or feeling...private; closely personal...pertaining to, or characteristic of the inmost or essential nature...a close friend.

Intimacy...the state of being intimate...a close association with or deep understanding (Random House Webster's College Dictionary, 1997).

From our postmodern perspective, definitions of intimacy and intimate are socially constructed within larger discourses, including cultural, societal, religious, political, and professional ones. The local constructions that clients and therapists bring to and develop within the therapy context are embedded in these discourses. For each of us, intimate and intimacy have highly personalized meanings. Being in an intimate relationship and encountering intimacy, therefore, are uniquely individualized in experience and expression. Intimate and intimacy, however, are often therapists' words, not clients'. Clients seldom introduce these words into therapy conversations, but they do talk about them in other ways as did Jane: "We want to communicate." "We're not close." "I want to be his friend." "I want peace and caring." In this chapter you will meet Jane who wanted a therapist she could be intimate with and who would allow her boyfriend Jim to be comfortable. Jane and Jim's story offers one illustration of how a couple[1] talk and think about intimacy in their relationship and in therapy.

From our perspective, though meanings, experiences, and expressions are individualized, intimacy and being intimate are not characteristics of the individuals involved in a relationship. Instead they are characteristics of the relationship itself. Although we do not often use the words intimate and intimacy with clients or in talking about our therapy, we do believe that these words portray an essential characteristic of the kind of *collaborative conversations and relationships* that we value, and in our experience, increase the possibilities for successful therapy outcomes.

In this chapter we discuss and demonstrate how intimacy is defined and created through collaborative therapy conversations and relationships.[2] We present our postmodern collaborative approach to therapy (a) summarizing our theoretical biases, (b) identifying factors that, in our experience, contribute to intimacy in couple relationships and in therapy relationships, and (c) illustrating an intimate conversation about intimacy with excerpts from a transcript[3] of Susan's interview with Jane and Jim and their therapist Diana, about their therapy experiences. We intertwine our comments throughout the excerpts.

---

[1] When we use the word couple, we refer to each member of the couple. Each has his or her own thoughts and actions. We choose to use "couple" throughout the chapter because repeating "each member of the couple system" or "the view of each member of the couple" would be awkward for the reader.

[2] We acknowledge that looking at our theory and clinical practice through intimacy lenses influences our descriptions and explanations. Another request, for instance, to write about impasses in couples therapy would have beckoned us to produce slightly different descriptions and explanations.

[3] We would like to thank Lisa Cook, a student at Our Lady of the Lake University, Houston for transcribing the videotape.

The chapter represents our combined voices and our narrative of their story and the interview.[4]

OUR PHILOSOPHY OF THERAPY

The metaphorical framework for our experiences in therapy reflects a post-modern philosophy based on a conceptual collage of social construction, contemporary hermeneutic, and narrative[5] theories (Freeman, 1995; Gergen, 1985, 1994; McNamee & Gergen, 1992, 1998; Shotter, 1993; Wacherhauser, 1986; Wittgenstein, 1953). This chapter does not permit the space to elucidate each theory and its umbrella assemblage of concepts. Some of the common threads, however, that weave through these theories, include:

• the meanings and understandings that we attribute to the events and experiences in our lives are communally, culturally, and historically embedded;
• meanings and understandings, including knowledge, are socially created and shaped through language;
• what is created is multiauthored among a community of persons and relationships rather than individually authored;
• what is created is only one of multiple perspectives and possibilities;
• language and knowledge are relational and generative;
• transformation is inherent in the inventive and creative aspects of language, dialogue, and narrative; and therefore,
• the potential for transformation and change[6] are as infinite in variety and expression as the individuals who realize them (Anderson, 1995, 1997).

Combined, these common threads have several implications for the nature of therapy, including how a therapist conceptualizes and acts regarding a therapy

---

[4] We prefer to have the people we talk about join in the narration through either coauthoring with us or including their reflections on what we have written. In this instance, we were unable to locate Jane and Jim. They had, however, previously given their permission to use the videotaped interview in whatever manner we choose for teaching purposes. We have changed their names and identifying data to assure confidentiality.

[5] We make a distinction between social constructionism and constructivism. Both reject the notion of knowledge as reflecting an objective reality and argue that knowledge is a construction. Constructivism emphasizes the individual constructing mind. Social constructionism, however, emphasizes the interactional and communal constructing nature. See Anderson (1997) pp. 43–44, and Gergen (1994) pp. 68–69.

We also make a distinction between the way narrative is conceptualized in a postmodern and a modern therapy perspective. Narrative is the substance of all therapy and not the distinction. The distinction is in the biases/intentions a therapist brings to the therapy, including how a therapist positions his or her narrative vis-a-vis another person's narrative. See Anderson (1997), pp. 212–215.

[6] We hesitate to use the word "change" because in therapy discourses it has acquired the connotation of a therapist as a change agent.

system, its process, and its relationships. These implications are:

- therapy systems are language, meaning-generating systems that are a product of social communication;
- therapy systems form and are organized around a particular relevance;
- all members of the therapy system participate in determining its membership and focus;
- the membership is fluid, can change as the conversation changes, and is determined on a session-by-session basis;
- the essence of the therapy process is dialogic conversation in which a client and therapist are conversational partners;
- the conversation is characterized by shared inquiry, a joint exploration between people with different perspectives and expertise;
- a client is the expert on his or her life;
- a therapist is an expert in, and responsible for, creating a space for dialogic conversation and facilitating its process;
- opportunities for change come from within the conversation, are generated by the combined membership, and are inherent in the creative aspects of language, dialogue, and narrative;
- responsibility and accountability are shared; and
- both client and therapist experience transformation within.

These implications influence a therapy that is characterized by a collaborative conversational process and relationship. They also influence a therapy that naturally becomes less hierarchical and more egalitarian; and in our experience, and similar to Weingarten's (1991), becomes more intimate.

Given these implications, important questions emerge for us. How can we participate as therapists, trusting and allowing intimacy to occur? What makes one conversation or relationship or both intimate and another one not? How do we understand shifts from tense, blaming, defending, and isolating exchanges filled with pain, misery and hopelessness—lacking intimacy—to ones filled with hope, peace, care, and closeness—having intimacy? How can a therapist create a space for and facilitate a relationship and conversation where possibilities emerge, or at least a sense that possibilities exist? (Anderson, 1997).

INVITING, DEVELOPING, AND SUSTAINING INTIMACY OVER TIME THROUGH CONVERSATION AND RELATIONSHIPS

There are many kinds of conversations and situations that characterize these conversations. By conversation we refer to the numerous ways in which people communicate with themselves and with each other—spoken words, gestures, symbols, and silent thoughts. As therapists, we are concerned with a particular kind of conversation that we call *dialogic conversation*. By dialogic conversation we mean talking that is generative and transformative. It is talking where participants are engaged in speaking with each other rather than to each other, talking that is characterized by back and forth exchanges, and crisscrossing utterances, and joint actions (Shotter 1993). As therapists, we are interested in, and our expertise is in, creating a space for and facilitating this kind of social exchange, a *conversational partnership*.

This partnership is invited and sustained through what we call the therapist's philosophical stance. Philosophical stance refers to a way of being in relationship with others—thinking about, talking with, and behaving with them (Anderson, 1995, 1997). It is a stance that embodies our postmodern principles, that flows naturally from them, and that enables a therapy with the characteristics described above. Central to this philosophical stance is a belief about client-therapist expertise. The client is the expert on his or her life and lived experiences and the therapist is an expert on creating a space for and facilitating dialogic conversation. The therapist is not an expert on how other people should live their lives, is not an expert with predetermined theories and explanations of human behavior. Rather, the therapist is a learner whose attitudes, words, and actions embody an authentic commitment to continually being informed by the client and understanding the client's life. Toward these aims the therapist expresses a genuine and spontaneous interest in and desire to learn about the client's story as he or she chooses to tell it.

The therapist's stance acts as a natural invitation to the client to join with the therapist in a shared inquiry—a mutual exploration toward understanding the familiar (e.g., problems, dilemmas, concerns) and developing the new (e.g., meanings, behaviors, attitudes). Embedded in this is that both client and therapist venture into the known (the certain and predictable) before inviting the unknown (the uncertain and unpredictable). Shared inquiry is invited by a therapist's attitude and action that the client is the expert on his or her life. This means that a therapist allows clients to be center stage, allows clients to talk about what they deem important, in the manner they want to express it, and at their own pace. The therapist's nonexpert position is partly accomplished through asking questions, making comments, and wondering. The intent of all utterances and actions is to invite and encourage a collaborative conversation and relationship. Everything a therapist does, therefore, must be effected in a tentative and unassuming manner.

Through this philosophical stance, a collaborative environment that is psychologically safe is established. Safe refers to a space and process where each member of a couple feels his or her story is worthy of telling and feels that it will be valued and not judged. It is an environment conducive to open expression in which participants are freed from repercussions by others. It is an environment where people feel they can contribute to the conversation and influence its direction and outcome. John Shotter (1993) describes such a conversation as one "in which people feel they belong." Or, as in the spirit of this chapter, an intimate conversation.

The therapist is responsible for setting the tone for a conversation in which people feel they belong. This tone is promoted through the therapist's engagement in carefully and actively listening with interest and enthusiasm to each person's description and explanation of the dilemma as it unfolds. In our experience, when people feel they are part of a conversation in which they can contribute and be heard, they listen and interact differently. The difference is a newfound interest in intense issues, previous misunderstandings, and conflicting opinions. This new attitude and behavior are in contrast to previous ones that interfered with or prevented dialogue; for instance, defensiveness, interruption of others, or rigorous promotion of views. Instead, with this newfound interest people become more able or willing to listen to each other's ideas, appreciate the other's point of view, and respect differences. In turn, dueling descriptions and explanations begin to dissolve. In other words, the therapist's inquisitiveness becomes contagious, resulting in each member's listening in ways that he or she has not listened before and "hearing the unheard" (Levin, 1992). Couples often comment, for instance, that talking in therapy is "different from the usual way we talk at home."

Although dialogic conversation and the philosophical stance have identifiable characteristics and expressions, they are unique to each human system, its circumstances, and what that system and its circumstances require. Each couple, for instance, is new to us. Each couple is one we have not met before, one we do not know ahead of time, and one we have to learn about. Each couple demands from us responses, questions, and understandings that are unique and uncommon. Each couple, therefore, demands that we take a not-knowing position (Anderson, 1995, 1997; Anderson & Goolishian 1988, 1992).

Not-knowing is an important element of the philosophical stance. It has to do with how a therapist thinks about and locates oneself in a conversation and a relationship vis-a-vis the preunderstandings he or she brings to it. In other words, the emphasis is on how therapists position themselves with what they know, or think they know. Not-knowing refers to being open to the other person, being curious about what they are saying and not saying. It refers to taking people seriously and signaling that what they have to say is worthy of hearing. It refers to respecting the other person's logic and trying to understand it as they do. In essence, not-knowing means that a therapist is always in the process of learning from, and about, the other. Their meanings and understandings take precedence over a therapist's. Not-knowing is expressed through maintaining coherence with the client's narrative, listening respectfully, staying in sync with their pace, trusting and believing in their reality and understanding, and honoring their beliefs (Anderson, 1995, 1997). All expressions involve being immersed in what the client has to say and being close to it.

As one student expressed this closeness,

> I have to allow myself to get near my clients, to put down the wall that I feel will protect me from their problems and their pain. If I do not get too close, I do not have to touch them or feel responsible for them. The problem is that in not getting too close to them I feel I do nothing. (Swim, Helms, Plotkin, & Bettye, in press)

In our experience intimacy demands a not-knowing posture. Allowing oneself to be intimate with another requires that we do not know about them ahead of time. We do not know how or what they think; we do not know what is best for them. Instead, we are always in the process of learning. Not-knowing does not refer to therapist ignorance, naivete, or denial of previous knowledge and experience. It does not refer to a therapist being a blank screen; that would be impossible, because we bring all of our past learning and experiences with us into the therapy room. To reiterate, the emphasis is on how therapists position themselves with what they know, or think they know.

In a collaborative environment, and in this new kind of conversation, couples, as you will see with Jane and Jim, begin to think about, experience, and relate to each other and themselves differently. As this happens, they also become eager to participate in the therapy. And in this participation they connect, collaborate, and construct with each other—producing shifts in thoughts, feelings, emotions, or actions (Anderson, 1992, 1995, 1997). Importantly, relationships are transformed through conversation. These shifts epitomize the transformative nature of dialogue. Put differently, if "the kinds of conversations we have *are* [our emphasis] the kinds of relationships we have" (Boyd, 1996, p. 3), then inherent in new forms of conversation are new forms of relationships. This includes the relationship between the couple members and between the couple and the therapist.[7]

It is important to note that because each person is an integral part of the conversational process and its dynamic complex web of interchanges, no one person can be identified as the source of the newness—or the outcome. The process enhances self-agency, therefore, each person has a sense of competency for the dilemma at hand and a sense of authorship for the outcome. Because each participant's circumstance is distinct and each course of therapy is novel, how the in-the-room therapy transfers outside of therapy is unique. And, because a conversation's consequences cannot be predetermined, it may often lead participants to surprisingly unanticipated ends.

The social construction notion that language and knowledge are generative and that meaning and understanding are mutually constructed imply that conversation is always in-motion, always changing. Therapy conversations are local conversations. That is, what is generated and constructed comes from

---

[7]Couples have commented that working in a collaborative manner with the therapist models for them new ways in which they may interact with each other, although modeling is not our intent.

those immediate conversations, and is indicative of the language, interpretations, and understandings, of the people involved in them. The intimate sense is a product of the local conversation (Anderson & Goolishian, 1992, p. 33).

A conversation, however, is not a singular, encapsulated event with a discrete beginning and ending. Nor is a conversation ever complete. Each is part of, will be influenced by, and will influence past, present, and future conversations. Equally important, client and therapist conversations are embedded within larger discourses. We want to maintain an awareness of these discourses and their influence, but we do not have an agenda to either promote or dispel them. That is not to say that we do not have our own biases.

We do not want to confuse intimacy as a critical element of therapy with intimacy as a goal for our clients. Our intent is not to lead another toward intimacy. That is, we would not have a bias (a preunderstanding) on the level of intimacy a couple should have, or predetermine that a couple should achieve intimacy with each other, or make an assessment that intimacy is wanted. Instead, we want to learn from each person what is important to him or her, what each wants to achieve in the relationship and for him- or herself and whether that is defined in terms of intimacy or not. We want to work with a couple to achieve their goals not ours. Some couples, for instance, may not be ready for intimacy in their relationship or, may be beyond the point of desiring intimacy with each other. For instance, one or both may feel some need for psychological or physical distance to heal or contemplate. Or, one or both may want separation, divorce, or another relationship. Paradoxically, in our experience, a conversation about not wanting intimacy in a relationship often is a new, more open conversation that may itself be a form of intimacy or create a possibility for intimacy. Joining in a conversation and relationship that feels personal and safe invites an immersion into intimacy. In our experience, the intimacy is inherent in collaborative conversation and relationship.

We think of intimacy and nonintimacy as a continuum not an either-or. Some conversations and relationships are more intimate than others. Any can have more or less intimate moments. What matters is that intimacy is invited, developed, possible, and sustained over time. Each participant may experience intimacy differently. What matters is the overall quality of the affiliation and the interaction.

"SO IT'S KIND OF A HAPPY
FAIRY TALE"

We now turn to Susan's interview with Diana and Jane and Jim, a couple Diana was currently seeing in therapy. Diana invited Susan to interview the couple and her. The purpose of the interview was to learn Jim and Jane's views of therapy, including what was helpful and what was not helpful. Diana and Susan also wanted to videotape the interview and use it in a conference workshop on couples. Diana explained the agendas to Jim and Jane who readily agreed to both, being especially eager to "help other therapists understand what has been helpful for us."

This interview is consistent with an aspect of our collaborative approach, including the client's voice in the evaluation of therapy, learning from their experiences and feedback, and doing this on an ongoing basis (Anderson, 1997). Such continuous reflection can also be thought of as research as a part of everyday practice (Andersen, 1996; Anderson 1997; Schon, 1988). Toward this aim we continually seek a client's reflections during a course of therapy and afterwards. We want to know their experiences of us and therapy and its usefulness, and their suggestions about what, if anything, could be or could have been more helpful.[8] We do this because we think the people participating in a conversation need to be involved in its analysis and evaluation. Norwegian psychiatrist Tom Andersen (1996) refers to this as "insider research." Only the people involved can say whether it was intimate. For this reason, we are sharing this couple's own description and evaluation of their therapy process and intimacy.

At the time of this interview Diana had seen Jim and Jane for six months. Jane initially called Diana in crisis when she was interviewing therapists for herself and Jim. She had been to a local mental health clinic for anxiety and suicidal ideation brought on by a recent discovery that Jim, her married boyfriend of three years, was also dating another woman. The intake worker at the clinic gave her several therapists names to call. Jane called Diana to interview her to see if she was the right person to work with her.

Susan: Okay. So how is it that you, that both of you found out about Diana or sought her services.

Jane: I interviewed people on the phone to find somebody that would be suitable for him, that he'd be receptive to.

Susan: So what were you doing in the interview at that point in time?

Jane: What was I doing? Just asking questions. What they had dealt with in the past. Issues on sexual addiction or, you know, the fact that he was married at the time and we'd been seeing each other for three years and that he was going to soon be divorced and how did she feel about that? Did she have any bad feelings about him? And she kind of fit the bill so we went to see her.

Susan: So I'm curious, what kind of answers did you get to your questions when you were doing your search?

---

[8] We believe that research should be part of a therapist's everyday practice. For an expanded discussion see Anderson (1997) pp. 101–102.

Jane: From other therapists? Well some of them were aggressive on the phone, some of them were introverted. A lot of them were real hasty until they found out I was possibly a new patient. You know, money. Then they'd change their attitude, and I thought, "No, I wouldn't do that." Or they thought I was soliciting something, until they found out, and then they were much nicer. And, of course, I threw all of those away. So . . .

Susan: So Diana was sort of the same from the beginning to the end of the conversation?

Jane: Sure, she was real equal from the beginning to the end.

[Jane is looking for a therapist she can be intimate with. She especially wants someone who will allow her boyfriend to be comfortable or safe. Jim was married and was dating Jane and also a multitude of other people. Previously married for seven years, five years into the marriage he discovered that his wife was having an affair with his best friend and others. After that discovery, he "ran around on her" for years. When they divorced Jim got custody of their three children ages six, four, and three, and later married his current wife. He described the lack of intimacy in his life in the following terms.]

Jim: Probably at one time, one given time, I was dating 20 people. Um, none of them I loved or cared about. Don't know if it's a revenge cycle or what, but I just dated anybody and whoever. Didn't care if I hurt them or didn't hurt them. And then my wife, my ex-wife, moved to New York. Came back. As soon as I knew she was coming back, I met someone. Maybe just a pretty face or something, just someone. And when she got back into town, notified her that I was getting married. I think more to hurt her. And it ended up being my worst nightmare. I married someone that didn't like my kids, wasn't nice to me, wasn't nice to anyone that she met.

Susan: Not a nice person to be around.

Jim: No. Everyone at my office hated her. All my kinfolk. Anyone that she got around. She thought that she was better than the rest of the world. And just because we had money, she threw it up in everyone's face. That, uh, you know, I bought her a Mercedes. She was like, you couldn't talk to her for five minutes without her talking about her Mercedes, her diamond rings, and so she was bad for me and my kids. She didn't like my kids. She wanted me to let my ex-wife have my children so we could be together and enjoy life, and so I could raise her daughter. Anyway, so I didn't go back to an extreme of dating everyone else, but I started dating Jane.

Jane: Mind you, I knew nothing about anything, other than the fact that he was married, soon to be divorced. I had no intentions about anything else at all.

[Jim describes the antithesis of intimacy with his ex-wife and present wife. Jane offers a possibility of creating some closeness and intimacy in his life. At this point Jane, sees the intimacy between them as one thing (openness), when it is another thing (dishonesty and secrets) to Jim. He continues to describe the developing intimacy between Jane and him over time.]

Jim: And when I told her that I was planning on getting a divorce, I was. Getting a divorce ended up taking two and one-half years, you know. And in those two and one-half years she was just always my friend, and my therapist. She was my therapist half the damn time. And I went over a lot of things with her, my feelings, my fears, and I guess she learned a lot about me that most people didn't know. It took three years for her to really know me. One day I would tell her a little bit more about me, the next time I would tell that plus a little more. It actually took three years for me to tell, I mean, for her to really find out everything about me. And then even when she found out everything about me, she didn't know everything about me, you know. Um, after me and Jane dated, we'd see each other every Tuesday night just like therapy.

Diana: Now they come to me on Tuesday night.

Jim: We're still in therapy together. But we have a professional therapist now.

[Jim has described in his own words some factors in his developing intimacy with Jane. Gradually, in small steps over time, he self-disclosed bits and pieces of his life to Jane. The consistency and predictability of the routine Tuesday nights seemed to help the process. He even described their meetings like "therapy" and Jane as his "therapist." However, even then, Jane did not have the whole picture. Then he skips ahead in his story to tell about bringing a professional therapist (Diana) into the picture, conversing about their lives. Jane comments on her concerns about Jim entering therapy and her effort to be sure the therapist did not blame or label him as others had.]

Jane: And of course he wasn't convinced that the therapy together, you know, wasn't putting the horse before the cart, because the divorce wasn't final. And so, what I did was try to be extremely supportive, because a lot of it was caused from lots of past things that I had known about over the last three years, of course, talking to him. And realized that a lot of the actions were happening. And then, um, we went to talk to a man, I think, who gave us Diana's name, too, before I started interviewing over at [the agency that referred her]. And he was like "I really don't want to go." I remember when he went, he was really condemned. You know, "I'm the bad party here, it's all my fault."

Susan: What do you think he was perceiving?

Jane: I think that he felt that way about himself because he was guilty. And I think that everyone perceived him as being bad. But it's almost like that's the image he had made for himself, so that was acceptable. Coming from all sides. Now people were baiting him constantly. You know, you live this way and you're the excitement of this office, and why don't you do this, and we've got a woman we can fix you up with.

[They talk about Jim's fear of the first appointment, how he felt "just literally sick to his stomach" because, Jane thought, the "reality finally hit home."]

Jim: And I didn't know if I would like going to that. Uh, I was really hesitant at first because, you know, I've been to therapists, but never with someone else. I went to marriage counseling by myself.

Jane: And lied.

Jim: Yeah. And uh, no. I went and talked about the marriage while I was there, but I didn't talk about the reasons.

Jane: [The reasons] Why.

Jim: The reasons I act the way I do. So, um, anyway we went and talked to Diana. She was real patient. She'd let me talk about things on my own pace, and if I didn't want to talk, then we would move on. As good as she is, I could always out maneuver her on a subject. Cause she would ask me a question. I would answer part of the question and then change the subject before it was all over with. And she knew that I was doing that, but then she would circle right back and ask me the same question in a different way, cause I didn't want to answer the questions. Anyway, she was patient. She knew, with time, that I would change over. And then it just kind of caught on, I started feeling okay about talking to her about things. I didn't feel challenged, I didn't feel threatened and just with patience, after a couple of weeks of talking to her and stuff like that, I started feeling good about...

Jane: The changes that were being made.

[Jim describes his experience of the therapy process. His experience includes feeling Diana's patience, letting him go at his own pace, persistence in wanting to understand, confidence in his ability to change, and nonthreatening position. These appear to be the ingredients that both Jim and Jane found helpful in including a third person in their intimate relationship. Jim continues by describing how he was determined to change his life by getting a divorce and arranging his finances so that he could be with Jane. He introduced her to his kids who really liked her, bought a house on the lake and moved all of them into the house. His statement, "So it's kind of a happy fairy tale," sums up his perceived progress.]

Susan: Yes, a happy love story.

Jim: Yeah, we made all the moves. I'm divorced now. I'm in therapy every Tuesday night.

Diana: Still.

Jim: Yeah. Yeah. Cause I mean, when you are as bad as I am for as long as I am, I think you need reinforcement every week. I kind of feel better, like I made it another week, and that wasn't as hard as it was the week before, you know.

[Susan raises an important consideration while reflecting on the therapy.]

Susan: And I was just...I couldn't help during listening...I know this is the only conversation that we've all had, of course, on what if they had, maybe, went and saw someone else that came from a different theoretical position than you [Diana] do. Or someone, uh, someone that you were consulting with, um, had some different ideas on this. And I was just thinking what a different story that might have made out of this.

Jim: ...I could have had the house, everybody has new vehicles, us living together, and still be doing the same thing that caused the divorce of my first and second basically. But what she solved is why I did it. And what motivated me, and why I thought sex and love were the same thing. And she kind of divided them, and I thought I had a sex addiction and she basically...

Jane: She never labeled him.

Jim: When I came here I thought I had a sex addiction. And she said "I don't think it's a sex addiction, I think there's more to it." So what she did...we dissected each section of it. She always asked me, "Why do you think it's a sex addiction?" And, well, that's the only title I know for it, I mean.

[Jane had a friend who is a therapist in New York. This therapist had told her that Jim had a sexual addiction and told her to read *Recovery from Sexual Addiction*. As Jane goes on to explain, this label was definitely not conducive to intimacy between Jane and Jim or their desired relationship between them and a therapist.]

Jane: Yeah, because the only feedback that I had was talking to a friend in New York that was a therapist, and I said, this is an example, "What type of therapist do I need to?" Cause I've know him for years. He said, "You need to get someone who is real well developed in working with people who have sexual addictions. You know they are con artists, they'll tell you anything you want to hear." And so, I began to read, and it was a nightmare. It was a total nightmare. I was ready to just give up and leave the relationship and go, "God, I'm not gonna stay with this person? He's crazy." But I decided that somebody's got to believe in Jim, cause he had a hard time believing in himself. And, he believed in me. And I finally had somebody that I could believe in. And we kind of supported each other, and it worked out.

[Jim and Jane shift from talking about factors that influenced intimacy in their relationship to intimacy in the therapy relationship. Throughout the interview Jim identifies several of these variables.]

Jim: ...I'd always went to men therapists before, and if they were too aggressive, then I got more aggressive, and maybe I lied to the therapists, told them whatever they wanted to hear...She [Diana] would ask a question and then give me until I just quit talking. And the other therapists I often went to, they would ask me the question and, while I stumbled around, they answered it for me. And I always thought "I don't know why I am in therapy with you, because you are answering your own damn questions, you know.... Cause every time I would talk, I would just get deeper and deeper in a hole. She brought out things in me that I never told anybody. Whys and why nots. ...I think she could verbally push me in a corner and the only way I could get out of that corner is to go in a different avenue. In other words, nick the edge of something I had never talked about before. And so, I think that was it because, you know, and then if I made a statement, instead of just letting me get away with making a statement, she goes, "Why do you feel that way?" And then I have to back up, and when I get to a point she goes, "Why do you feel that way?" And she just kept hammering at me straight down into something deeper, I don't know. But she already kind of knew where, I think. I mean, on sex addictions or people that usually have problems, there's something other than that.

[Intimacy in relationships, especially the therapy relationship, opens up space for new meanings or ideas to be created. New possibilities evolve in the conversation. Jim describes above how this happened for him. In continuing to talk about the current therapy and the therapist, he described Diana as "not very aggressive ... poised ... aggressive in a circular motion ... no intimidation...being patient...letting me do the talking." He said that he experienced Diana's "curiosity" and "not accepting an answer at face value," as probing in a direction that she already knew. Diana, however, did not have a direction in mind, except to keep opening up the conversation for new meaning to be created or considered. He felt that there could be other, not-yet-explored explanations for his behavior other than sexual addiction. He further described this process for him as, Diana "let me come up for air...didn't label...took us for who we were...did not make judgements...worked with us just right where we were and walked with our desires...didn't make either one of us feel threatened."]

Jane and Jim brought up another variable that can be important to the maintenance of intimacy—history. History appears to be a continuing link in the evolution of intimacy in the relationship as described below.

Jim: And probably it would have been so much easier to meet someone that knew nothing about me. But, then again, it's probably best that it worked the way it did, because she [Jane] understands. Someone else wouldn't have understood what the dos and don'ts of me are.

Susan: You don't have to hide your history.

Jim: Yeah.

Jane: And history always comes up, I think, and it's important. It's taught me too, I mean, I've learned some really valuable lessons with him. Grow-up lessons.

A goal of collaborative conversation is to open up space for the kind of talking we referred to earlier to occur. Inherent in this kind of talking is the generation and evolution of new meanings. These meanings occur in thinking about future actions as well as different explanations for past behavior. Often significant meanings are attached to a specific word that a couple uses in communication. We do not look at this new meaning as a reframe, which implies a static state, but as a meaning that is important only in a particular conversation. This implies that the meaning changes as it is used in conversation, often to the point of just fading away or losing its usefulness to the conversation. This can be thought of as problem-dissolving process (Anderson & Goolishian 1988; Anderson, 1997).

[With Jim and Jane the word "probation" evolved in their conversations with Diana to refer to talk about Jim gaining back Jane's trust. This word by its very nature implies something temporary that will end at some time, that the record will be cleared at some point to continue, change courses, or stop. Jim is in a line of work where he deals with people accused of some crime, so the term "probation" was already in their language. It was not a word introduced by Diana. At some point in the therapy, probation quit being talked about. It just seemed to dissolve without actually being acknowledged as other issues and meanings began to take up more of the conversation and came to the forefront. As problem conversation dissolves, space for intimacy in the conversation and possibilities open up as demonstrated in the following excerpts.]

Diana: Well, one of the things I remember being talked about that isn't talked about now, which is interesting, is we talked about probation. And, um, that was sort of the period when all these other things kept coming up. And "Could you (Jane) trust him?" I'm not sure whose idea that was? But somehow...

Jim: I kept, I mean, that's my line of work. I kept calling it "being on probation." Maybe you (Jane), alright, you kept calling it that.

Susan: But it came up in a lot of conversation?

Diana: Yeah. And it somehow made it, I don't know if it made it easier, but it gave it something to hang onto. Like, "Well, he's on probation, so..."

Jane: It was a name.

Diana: Wait for him to screw up, and if he doesn't screw up, he'll get off probation, eventually.

Jane: And she would confirm it every time we went in. "Are you doing okay?" or...

Diana: How's the probation going?

Jane: Yeah. Yeah. And so, we just left that as a term. It was comfortable, and it wasn't negative really. You know, it didn't condemn him.

[Susan summed up the interview following a comment that Diana made in agreement with Jim's assessment that their situation was quite complicated. He said that when he came in he knew he wanted to get from A to B, but did not know how and relied on Diana to help him.]

Susan: [To Diana] That therapy was able to develop in a way that this couple was able to come up with their own solutions and their own self-agency. [To Jim and Jane] Self-agency is a term... having the competency to solve your own problems. And I think what happens sometimes with traditional therapy is that the self-agency is taken away, so that people don't go in feeling confident with their own problems. Not that they're problem-free, but that they have some competency that they can solve them. To have some sense of normalcy, that they are not so broken that they are beyond repair. And, I think just from the nature of calling things addiction, you don't have cures to addiction.

Jane: Sure.

Susan: And, so those aren't really terms that help lead to self-competency or self-agency. But I think it's just been delightful for me to have sat here and listened to the ways that you were able to, with the help of Diana of course, to solve the problems. I don't think that anyone could have come in and given you a list of things to do and that it would have been as helpful as when you were able to do it among yourselves.

[The session ends with Jim's once more recounting what he had hoped would happen in therapy—that he would "spook Jane and she would run like hell," his fear of what might happen—the dissolution of their relationship, and his current relief—that his dream, and their dreams and plans, were materializing. Diana continued to meet with Jane and Jim after this session, at first weekly and then intermittently, until they decided that Diana no longer needed to participate in their conversations with each other. They married and, in a telephone follow-up conversation one year later, reported that things were "going very well," and that they had moved to a "new *home* (as opposed to house)."]

Jane and Jim had moved from creating intimacy in their own relationship over time, and through many obstacles, to including Diana as part of the evolving intimate relationship. They felt comfortable now to include an outsider (Susan) in this conversation and also wished to share their struggle and accomplishments with other therapists. They hoped that, by sharing their story and their ideas about why talking with Diana had been so helpful, other therapists would have more understanding of how intimacy is created in couples and in client-therapist relationships.

SOME REFLECTIONS ON
COLLABORATIVE THERAPY,
INTIMACY, AND JANE AND JIM

To help establish this kind of relationship and conversation, a therapist must relate to each person, showing interest, respect, and sensitivity to what each voices. She must engage actively, inviting each story fragment, listening with interest, checking to determine if she has heard what each person intended her to hear, and valuing each perspective. Importantly, all utterances must come from and develop within the conversation. That is, each contribution, whether question or comment is formed by the conversation at the moment and in the experiences that the therapist and couple are having with each other. All combine to elicit, elucidate, and expand the clients' telling of his and her stories and the therapist's understandings of them. Essential to this therapist position is being a learner, permitting each person to be a teacher. This learning-teaching therapist-client relationship and process soon naturally shifts to a more mutual relationship and process as each client joins with the therapist in shared inquiry.

Each voice adds ingredients to the conversation that extend, modify, or support other voices, and influence its direction. In turn, in our experience, as with Jane and Jim, people begin to listen and hear each other differently, becoming less defensive, feeling safer and more open. An observer commented on this experience: "talking [to the therapist rather than to each other] seemed to help get them [the clients] out of the old conversations and seemed to shift something, or at least contain or limit the finger pointing."

Our experiences resonate with a quote attributed to Gregory Bateson, that "in order to entertain the new and the novel there must be room for the familiar." We have found that therapist agendas, for example, choosing what is important to talk about or statements of fact made with authority, can stifle conversation. Jim described this when he talked about his previous treatment and how the therapist knew the answer to the question before it was asked.[9] Jane's mention of her therapist friend who suggested that Jim confront his "sexual addiction" in therapy is another example. We might be curious about her friend's suggestion and about Jane's not wanting to pursue it. And, if we had an opinion about it, we would express it without judging and without trying to maintain the conversation within that parameter or channel it in a direction that Jim and Jane did not want to go.

Equally important to what creates and encourages an intimate environment is what hinders or erodes it. When a therapist is unfamiliar—out of sync—with a client, she risks being out of dialogic conversation. Some examples include, letting therapist prejudgments and interpretations leap to the forefront of the

---

[9]We have heard other clients talk about therapist questions in this same manner. See the example of Tom in Anderson (1997) and Bill in Anderson & Goolishian (1992).

conversation; choosing sides or favoring one narrative over another; trying to discover, uncover, or lead toward any content; and keeping the conversation within any parameter or guiding it in one direction or away from another. We have also found, as reported by our students, that being curious and respectful must be natural and genuine. To force oneself to have curiosity and respect becomes a cookbook technique that hinders intimacy.

In summary, intimacy is in the relationship and is a process. That is, intimacy influences, and is influenced, by the way we are in relationship with each other, and it is active. It involves humanness—being human. Our primary aim in therapy is to create an opportunity for collaborative conversations and relationships. Such cultural expectations of "other-expertise" begin to diminish from the very first contact between couple and therapist as the therapist acts to acknowledge and invite the couple's expertise and wisdom regarding their life situation. Therapy becomes a partnership, something couple and therapist do together rather than something a therapist does to or for a couple. In our experience as couples engage in the kind of conversational process that we are talking about, familiar expectations that the therapist will have the answer or "tell us what to do" fade away as the couple creates their own solutions, whether in behaviors, attitudes, thoughts, meanings, or feelings. Collaborative conversations offer a couple an innovative way to discuss their dilemmas and arrive at solutions of their own design and challenges rather than foster an expectation that the therapist will provide the answers.

Being intimate does not necessarily suggest agreement or lack of differences. Intimacy suggests that there is a secure climate in which to express, entertain, and challenge differences. It suggests a way for each couple partner to have a voice, speak, and be heard by the other. As they experience each other differently, intimate ingredients begin to enter into the way they describe each other, themselves, and the relationship. With Jane and Jim, unexplored avenues to discuss a multitude of present and potential dilemmas emerged out of a new dialogue process. That is, new voices embedded in a new relationship could still process complaints, but now they did so with an attitude of intimacy. This is not to imply that a couple is taught to talk differently, or is told to be gentle or intimate. Instead intimacy evolves, and, once the "instances" occur more frequently, there appears to be a quest to be drawn to these types of dialogues.

Both Jim and Jane found their relationship with Diana as intimate. They described her as respectful of, and familiar with, their personal and private thoughts. Commenting on her participation with them, they described her as not categorizing, not acting impatient[10], not intimidating, not asking questions from an informed position, and not judging. In their words

She did not label us. She took us for who we were. She knew we loved each other,

[10] We do not think of our stance as patience, because patience often connotes waiting for the other to finish so that you can say or do what you desire without interest in the other.

and she worked with us just right where we were and just walked us through everything, our desires. ...She walked with us through our desires.

For us, this approach is energizing, dynamic, engaging, and intimate. And most important, it eliminates elements of frustration and stagnation often encountered in therapy with difficult couples whose life circumstances challenge therapist values and biases.

REFERENCES

Andersen, T. (1996), Research on the therapeutic practice: What might such research be—viewpoints for debate. *Fokus Familie, 1*: 3–15.

Anderson, H. (1992), *C* therapy and the *F* word. *American Family Therapy Association Newsletter 50* (Winter), 19–22.

Anderson, H. (1995), Collaborative language systems: Toward a postmodern therapy. In R. Mikesell, D. D. Lusterman, & S. McDaniel (Eds.). *Integrating Family Therapy: Family Psychology and Systems Theory*. Washington, DC: American Psychological Association.

Anderson, H. (1997), *Conversation, language, and possibilities: A postmodern approach to therapy*. New York: Basic Books.

Anderson, H. & Goolishian, H. A. (1988), Human systems as language systems: Evolving ideas about the implications for theory and practice. *Family Process 27*: 371–393.

Anderson, H. & Goolishian, H. A. (1992), The client is the expert: A not-knowing approach to therapy. In S. McNamee & K. J. Gergen (Eds.), *Social Construction and the Therapeutic Process*. Newbury Park, CA: Sage.

Boyd, G. T. (1996), *The A.R.T. of agape-listening: The miracle of mutuality*. Sugarland, TX: The Agape Press.

Freeman, M. (1995). Groping in the light. *Theory & Psychology, 5,* 353–360.

Gergen, K. J. (1985). The social construction movement in modern psychology. *American Psychologist 40*: 255–275.

Gergen, K. J. (1994). *Realities and Relationships: Soundings in Social Construction*. Cambridge, MA: Harvard University Press.

Levin, S. B. (1992). Hearing the unheard: Stories of women who have been battered. Dissertation, Union Institute. Cincinnati, OH. Union Institute.

McNamee, S. & Gergen, K. J. (1992). *Therapy as Social Construction*. Newbury Park, CA: Sage Publications.

McNamee, S. & Gergen, K. (in press). *Relational responsibility*. Newbury Park, CA: Sage Publications.

Schon, D. A. (1988). *The reflective practioner: How professionals think in action*. New York: Basic Books.

Shotter, J. (1993). *Conversational Realities*. Newbury Park, CA: Sage Publications.

Swim, S., Helms, S., Plotkin, S. & Bettye. (in press). Multiple voices: Stories of rebirth, heroines, new opportunities and identities. *Journal of Systemic Therapies*.

Wacherhauser, B. R. (Ed.). (1986). *Hermeneutics and Modern Philosophy*. Albany: State University Press.

Weingarten, K. (1991). The discourses of intimacy: Adding a social constructionist and feminist view. *Family Process 30* (3) 285–306.

Wittgenstein, L. (1953). *Philosophical Investigations*. Trans. G. Anscombe. New York: Macmillan.

CHAPTER 12

Creating Intimacy
Through Reality Therapy

Robert E. Wubbolding

Intimacy in the context of this chapter is the fulfillment of the deepest longing of both men and women, that of human closeness, the desire to be one with another human being. Some of the world's greatest literature tells the story of the human struggle to achieve this goal along with the conflict which often accompanies it. The pursuit of this elusive, fragile, and immaterial quality has resulted in wars fought, murders committed, and fortunes gained and lost. Such literature endures because of the universality of this desire. The failure to need intimacy as in the case of the psychopathic personality is regarded as an aberration (Meloy, 1988). On the other hand, some human beings seek a higher form of intimacy with God and are willing to forego the human closeness. But many such individuals seek to live a community life. The dwindling numbers of persons choosing this lifestyle can be partially attributed to the inability of people to find the desired intensity of human intimacy in these traditional institutions.

This chapter focuses on the intimacy of couples from the point of view of choice theory and reality therapy.

ORIGINS

Reality therapy was developed by William Glasser (1965) in a mental institution and a correctional setting. It was then applied to schools (Glasser, 1968, 1990, 1992), management (Wubbolding, 1996) and recently to relationships (Ford, 1981); (Glasser 1995); (Wubbolding, 1993). Choice theory provides the rationale, the psychological justification for the practical or "how to" aspect of the delivery system. It is a derivation of control system theory (Powers, 1973) which describes the human brain as analogous to a thermostat (i.e., the furnace or air conditioning unit) which attempts to control its own behavior, so as to control or impact the external world in some way. Glasser (1985) has further developed this theory by making it an educational and clinical model and by significantly adding to it (1998).

This chapter integrates choice theory and reality therapy by applying them to human relationships. Couples using these ideas can add to the quality of their relationships as they journey toward the elusive relational goal of intimacy.

NEEDS

Intimacy between couples is the result of overlap and common ground in need fulfillment. While this phrase is widely used in a popular sense, it has a technical meaning when seen from choice theory and reality therapy points of view. The human brain like the thermostat controls its behavior for a purpose: to impact the external world around it to gaining something from the external world.

Like the thermostat, the human control system is purposeful, but unlike the mechanical system, the human control system is a thinking and feeling system which is free to choose among many options (Glasser, 1998). Moreover, the human brain is motivated by five universal, general, and often conflictual needs. They are universal in that they are truly multicultural, all people have them. They are general rather than specific. And they can conflict with each other as well as with the needs of other people. These needs are: survival; belonging or love; power or achievement; freedom or independence; and fun or enjoyment.

From the point of view of the reality therapist, couples have an intimate relationship if there is overlap in their specific desires, wants, and goals related to the sources of human motivation. These sources are the human needs. They are the engines of human behavior. They provide the fuel and the energy which motivates people to move toward each other, thus achieving intimacy or move away from each other, resulting in alienation or estrangement.

Furthermore, couples need to talk about their respective levels of need intensity. Only then can they make an informed decision about whether to maintain the relationship.

Survival   The basic source of motivation is the need to survive, to maintain health, to belong. The sexual drive is related to this need. Casual sex is also said to be more connected with this need than with the other needs.

Belonging or Love   People seek to be affiliated with one another in a variety of ways: clubs, church groups, teams, and especially family relations. When these ties are strained or broken, feelings of rejection, alienation, isolation, and loneliness are often the result which leads to guilt, shame, hurt, resentment, anger, rage and even revenge.

Each person has an innate need for belonging and love. This need expresses itself in the desire to receive love from a specific person as well as a desire to give love. This need to give and receive love is the basic motivator in the search for intimacy (Glasser, 1998). In the case of Lucy and Harry described later, Harry fulfills his need to give love at a time when Lucy needs to receive love. This complimentary behavior related to belonging and love leads to enhanced intimacy.

Couples seeking a happy relationship are well advised to talk about their level of need intensity related to love and belonging. Deciding and expressing what they want from each other before a crisis develops can be a very useful tool. This can be done during quality time described later.

Power or Achievement   People want to be in control or, at least, feel a sense of accomplishment in their activities. When individuals first enter a relationship they feel a strong satisfaction in belonging. They tend to be altruistic and generous with each other. They wish to please. As the lustre of infatuation cools, conflict often surfaces over the fulfillment of power. Many times couples see the fulfillment of power as a zero sum game, a win-lose arrangement. This perception results in lessening the intimacy or even fracturing the relationship. Couples argue over such issues as:

- Who will control the money,
- How money will be spent,
- How will leisure time be spent, (e.g., at whose family will they spend the holidays),
- Who will discipline the children and how, and
- Who will help the children deal with their problems and what kind of advice will be given to them.

If they have learned choice theory and reality therapy, they will argue about how it will be applied to the children. However, the arguments will be friendly, less intense, short term, and resolved without hurt to each party. Moreover, they will be seen as opportunities for growth and more intense intimacy.

Freedom or Independence   Another source of human motivation which the couple can discuss is that of freedom or independence. Some individuals have a high need for freedom. Others prefer structure and a clear set of expectations from their environment. But all human beings are born with the propensity to make choices and to stand on their own two feet. If a person in a relationship feels trapped by the other person's domineering behaviors, intimacy cannot result.

Fun or Enjoyment   Innate to human beings is the urge to have fun or at least to enjoy life. When couples seek an added sense of intimacy they sometimes find it effective to start with more effective ways to fulfill this need. Often, but not always, they can agree on performing enjoyable activities. As with such choices related to the other needs, they then build a storehouse of pleasant memories and perceptions toward each other.

These needs are continually present in our lives. They cannot be denied. In Glasser's choice theory they are seen to be universal, that is, common to all people and general or nonspecific. They can also be used as a kind of diagnostic schema for couples to begin to examine areas of commonalities, areas for conflict, and plans for future growth.

If the needs are general and universal, the wants growing out of them are specific and unique within each human being. As people grow, from infancy on they build inside of them a collection of specific desires which are satisfying to the five needs. Part of human development is the clarifying of a want or picture of someone who will help to satisfy the need for belonging. If such a picture is clarified, the person will be capable of intimacy. There are individuals, about 5% of men and 1% of women, who are incapable of intimacy and who relentlessly and remorselessly exploit, maim and even murder others. These psychopathic individuals can fulfill their need for belonging only in a shallow and temporary manner. They are not the subject of this chapter. The allusion is made only to point out the importance of both the need and specific related wants, as well as the possible disasters that can result from the inability to nurture and be nurtured.

The collection of wants serves as motivators of human behavior. At a given moment a specific want prompts a specific behavior. The behavior system is the interconnection of four inseparable components: actions, thinking, feelings, and physiology. All four components are present in all behavior and so the technical term is "total behavior." The importance of this idea will be evident in the discussion of quality time.

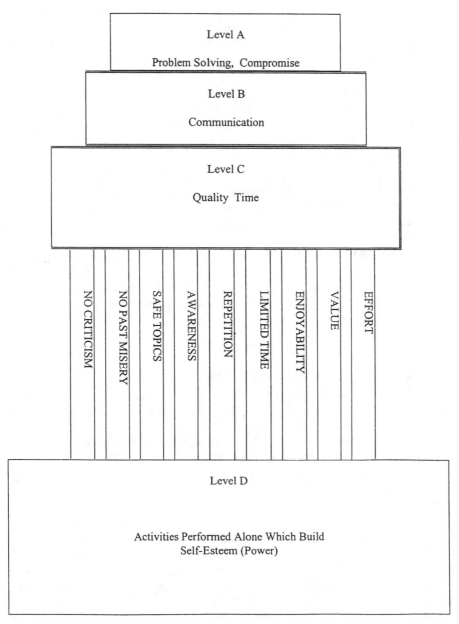

Figure 1

Most behavior is chosen (Glasser, 1998), and all behavior is directed to the external world so as to mold it like a sculptor molding clay in such a way that the world matches his or her internal want. Paradoxically, the only thing we can control is our own behavior. In achieving intimacy, the couple members focus on their respective behaviors rather than trying to coerce the other person to change.

The goal of all behavior is to gain input from the world around them. This input or information is filtered through two levels of perception: low and high. In the low level of perception the information is labelled and recognized, but no judgment is made. The high level of perception includes a judgment on the incoming information. Experiences, ideas, behaviors, and all input data are given a value—positive, negative, or neutral.

Commonalities If intimacy is part of a couple's relationship, there is overlap in their quality worlds (wants), in their four components of behavior and in the values they put on the information they receive from their external worlds.

The following four levels of behavior provide a way for couples to view their interactions in a developmental manner. If there is to be intimacy in the relationship, all four levels need to be functional. The progression is from the least demanding (Level D) to the most difficult (Level A). (see Figure 1.)

LEVEL D
ACTIVITIES PERFORMED ALONE

Samuel Johnson once remarked that, if people are to bring something home from their travels, they must take something with them. The same is true in relationships. When relationships are need satisfying to both people beyond the acquaintanceship level, both people bring a degree of autonomy, independence, ego-strength, or self-worth based on what they do independently of the other person.

From the point of view of the reality therapist the individual brings some ability to satisfy his or her needs. The person has at least some behaviors in the suitcase of behavior that are separate from those used in the relationship. Having a job, a hobby, friends, social involvements, even a set of opinions or beliefs that individuals can claim as their own is very helpful in maintaining healthy intimacy. Such autonomy prevents the intimacy-destroying behaviors seen in overdependence. Codependent spouses allow their lives to be dominated and ruled by the behaviors of the addicted person. In a way, they derive their identity from the addict. Their choices are reactions to the all consuming, inconsistent, and even threatening behavioral patterns they see around them. In their embarrassment and shame, they abandon their outside interests which leads to more loneliness, depression, and anger. Through self-help groups such as Alanon, they can regain a sense of purpose, a sense of the universality of their plight, and intimacy. After gaining a sense of identity and a feeling of strength, they can change their role in the relationship from codependence to more, though not complete, independence. They are ready to choose behaviors which, at least, render them capable of intimacy. Whether such closeness can be found in the marriage depends on levels B and A.

Not every relationship is characterized by such conditions. Still, a certain amount of autonomy enhances the relationship and precludes a less than healthy enmeshment. The following dialogue illustrates a conversation between a therapist and a client. Background: Lucy, 43, wished to deal with her husband, Harry whom she discovered had an ongoing affair with a woman in another city.

(TH = Therapist, L = Lucy)

TH: How can I help you?

L: My husband has had an ongoing affair with someone in Mexico where he frequently travels. [Describes in detail how she learned about it. She talks about what he did.]

TH: Tell me how this has impacted on you.

L: Well, he wants to stay together. He says it's over between them. They've seen each other for years. I don't know how he can give her up. I've seen the letters and the pictures of them together. They seemed happy. He looked happier with her than he does with me.

TH: Tell me a little bit about how you have handled the situation.

L: He just refuses to talk to me about it except to say that it's over and we don't need to get into the details. He's very quiet around the house...Just doesn't seem happy. He needs to be cheered up. He just mopes around when he's not working. Sometimes he brings work home and does some paper work. He's got a good job with the steel company and works a lot with the plants in Mexico. I'm not sure what he does at work....

TH: You said, "I'm not sure what he does" That's the first time I heard you say "I."

L: He's very secret about things. Always been that way. Even when he married me, he didn't talk much about work.

TH: Here is another question. Do you want to stay together?

L: I'm not sure what he really wants to do. He says he wants to stay together, but he's only said that once or twice. He just doesn't say much.

TH: Let's try again. Do *you* want to stay together?

L: Well... That's what marriage is about... staying together.

TH: I want to say something which I believe is important. Would you be willing to think about it?

L: Well, I guess so.

TH: Is that a "Yes?"

L: Yes.

TH: A firm "Yes?"

L: A firm yes.

TH: I notice that when I ask you about yourself, you switch to a discussion about him.

L: He's my husband, after all.

TH: Yes. But could you express your own viewpoint? I have other questions. But I'm asking you to express your own beliefs, etcetera.

L: That's not easy.

TH: But would it hurt you to do so?

L: That's hard to answer... I might have to ask...

TH: (Interrupting) No. I want you to say unequivocally whether you think saying what you want, what you believe or, how you feel will hurt you. Keep in mind you're saying them only to me.

L: Well, I... a... a... a...

TH: Yes or No?

L: No. It won't hurt me.

TH: Now, I'm asking you about your want. Do you want to stay with your husband?

L: [Pause] Yes.

TH: Congratulations. Was it easy or hard to say that?

L: Very hard.

TH: I wonder why.

L: I'm not used to saying what I want.

TH: I understand that. I'd like to help you develop such a skill.

L: I think we need marriage counseling.

TH: That's terrific. You expressed your opinion and I agree.

L: You do?

TH: You seemed surprised that I agree.

L: I'm not used to anyone agreeing with me.

TH: I believe I can help you with some of these things, including marriage counseling. First, I think I should see you alone about ten times.

L: I guess it would be all right with him.

TH: Is it all right with you?

L: Yes.

TH: I would like to help you first, so that when we do the marriage counseling it won't take as long.

L: That would be OK.

TH: You sounded firm when you said that.

L: I did?

TH: Yes. And I'd like to help you express how you feel, what you think, what you want, etcetera. Would that be something you'd like?

L: Yes. You know, he does say that I have low self-esteem.

TH: You can give any name to it. But I believe that after we work on a few of these things. you'll feel better and stronger... maybe more self-confident. Then the marriage counseling will work better.

L: Sounds good.

[In this situation Lucy was unable to fulfill any of her needs satisfactorily. Deficits were evident in belonging, power or achievement [self-esteem], fun and freedom or independence. The therapist chose to help her with self-esteem and independence. The strategy of seeing her alone for a while was based on the judgement that marriage counseling might be less effective until she was able to make at least some choices on her own which would be designed to help her feel better about herself. Then she would be more suitable for marriage counseling. In other words, she would have something to bring to the therapy. If she is to gain anything from the journey of therapy and the journey of the relationship with her husband, she will need to bring something, at least a modicum of accomplishment and independence.]

From a different perspective, increasing intimacy can serve to be an effective antidote to domestic violence. Jennings (1991) found that three approaches can be helpful. The unilateral emphasis that full responsibility be taken by the male and that he make the major number of changes. The bilateral approach expects both spouses to change, but treatment is conducted separately. The dyadic approach focuses on the couple's interaction and on their work toward a common goal. Each of these, from a reality therapy standpoint, implies that the parties involved decide that they want a better relationship, examine the effectiveness of their behavior and make more effective plans. This could involve examining the strength of their needs as well as their commitment to regular quality time.

LEVEL C
ACTIVITIES PERFORMED TOGETHER

As has been stated, in formulating the principles of choice theory and reality therapy, a conscious effort has been made to use words which are easily understood by most people. There is some, but not much, esoteric language. The words "quality time" have become in some ways a worn out phrase overused in the media. Still it can be a useful idea as understood by couples wishing to achieve more intimacy in their relationships.

As shown in Figure 1, Level C summarizes quality time which is one of the foundations upon which is built better communication and skill in resolving conflict. Quality time implies more than being together. Many people can be in the same place, do the same thing and even feel the same way about something. Thousands of people attend sporting events and have virtually no relationship with each other before, during, or after the event. And so, for an activity to qualify as quality time and thus be a building block for intimacy, several characteristics must be present.

Takes Effort   Passive activities such as watching television, sleeping in the same bed do not qualify. Even eating or driving together are less helpful than playing a game together, having a hobby or an interest that is satisfying to both parties.

The average television set is turned on more than seven hours a day in the United States. It is not surprising that people can live under the same roof and feel alienated, lonely, anxious and even panicky. During this time there is little strength, much less intimacy, built into the relationship. In fact, behaviors antagonistic to intimacy are often inserted into the mind of the viewer. It is sufficient to state here that a high school graduate in America has seen 18,000 murders, 350,000 commercials, not to mention having spent 22,000 hours in front of the TV and only 11,000 hours in school. The lessons learned include:

violence is glamorous, promiscuity is to be valued, problems are solved by anger, and rage, and finally, people best interact by demeaning and belittling each other. The popularity of educational and uplifting programs have yet to equal, much less exceed, that of the aforementioned kind.

Has Value for Each Person   The activity is seen as mutually positive. Going to a political fund raiser might be a lifetime high point for one person but a total bore for another. If grocery shopping is enjoyable to both, it can be used to build the relationship. But if one person is annoyed and sees it, at most, as a necessary and burdensome task, the togetherness is diminished. On the other hand, if it is fun for both people, intimacy is enhanced. If the activity is agonizing, irritating, uncomfortable or even performed exclusively as a painfully altruistic behavior, it will not build intimacy into the relationship.

The exact nature of the activity is thus negotiated. The grocery shopping trip is a relationship building activity for some people. For others it provides more than an ample supply of tension and aggravation.

Includes Enjoyability or Fun   This component is the reverse of discussing past misery or criticism. The activity is something which builds a storehouse of positive perceptions or memories. Picnics, exercise, even housecleaning are enjoyable to some. But if the activity is repulsive, it will diminish the relationship. When the necessary unpleasant activities are performed, they need to be balanced by enjoyable discussions, joke telling, hobbies, or some agreed upon fun. Victor Borge once remarked that the shortest distance between two people is a laugh.

Is Done for Limited Time   The activity is carried out for short periods. It is not recommended that it be for long periods, especially if there is tension in the relationship. Ten or 15 minutes per day, or even less, can suffice. The actual time depends on the inclinations of the couple. The decision is based on the amount of already existing intimacy. But 10 to 15 minutes per day is often realistic and attainable; it does not require a major revolution in scheduling. The outcome of this time together provides a solid basis for intimacy. It would be a mistake to minimize the value of these few moments spent together. The more connectedness existing between the two people the longer the time can be. If the couple has a high degree of overlap in their wants, behavior, and perceptions, the time can be longer.

Requires Repetition   For the time to be useful in enhancing intimacy, the activity needs to be repeated regularly. Just as one 30-minute period of running or jogging does not produce an accomplished athlete, so too, one brief period of quality time, or an occasional effort, does not result in a solution to the problem. This tool is not a quick fix. A solid basis for intimacy is built on activities performed over and over. The results are often seen after weeks and even months of repeated decisions, planning and follow-through on this joint effort.

Involves Mutual Awareness   The activity is such that both people are cognizant of the other's presence. Thus, watching television is again disqualified or at least rendered less effective than a tennis game or a brisk walk. Driving and riding in a car is barely within the rubric of quality time. Even sleeping together is questionable. For at such times of unconscious proximity the partners are oblivious to each other's presence.

Discussion Of "Safe" Topics   Strengthening and deepening intimacy occurs when couples spend time together talking, not only about intense subjects but also about topics which correspond to the lower level of perception. It is evident that difficult topics and painful issues need to be dealt with. Still, it is useful to have some time set aside when light conversation is the focus. Wubbolding [1993] describes a couple whose son was hit by a car. The family talked about the pain, the regrets, and the if onlys. He asked them if the continuous repetition of such discussions helped them feel better. They agreed that their feelings of depression and guilt were worsening. He assisted them to conduct a self-evaluation about the value of such endless speculations and self-blame. They agreed it was accomplishing nothing. They agreed to put the pain on hold for one hour a day. During that time, they would do something together which incorporated effort, light conversation and at least an effort to laugh for a few minutes.

Has No Discussion Of Past Misery   Every human body has its tender spots. And when one part hurts, the effectiveness of the person is lessened. Every relationship is a system. When communication focuses on what went wrong, how things reached their current but less than pleasant state, further talk about past failures and long standing misery adds to the pain and suffering. Intimacy is not built on the shifting sands of tribulation. Developing the attitude that "things are the way they are because they got to be that way" helps couples find other topics for discussion.

Has No Criticism   When there is stress in a relationship, it is often characterized by criticism. "You always..." "Why didn't you...?" "That really gripes me..." These and dozens of other stingingly critical statements regarding specific situations are uttered with unwelcome, uncomfortable, and even tormenting results.

When the relationship is strained, constructive criticism is an oxymoron. The urge to speak one's mind can accelerate the downward spiral of the relationship. These last three characteristics of time spent together are, for some, the most difficult to implement. Yet, there must be a rule rigidly adhered to that neither party will criticize the other, that they will not engage in disputes. Rather, they will discuss "safe", non-controversial topics. Thus, when a couple takes a brisk walk together, there is no criticism, no lectures, no admonitions, no discussion of what is good for the other person.

This is not an avoidance of serious discussion of problems. Rather, it is recommended merely because continual, one-way, worn-out lectures and criticism rarely help, and often turn off the listener. Nevertheless, it is difficult for some couples to abandon such conversation, especially if they have felt alienated. Meaningful communication, compromise, and problem solving will occur and lead to intimacy if there is a solid foundation of creating and committing to need satisfying time that builds a storehouse of mutually positive perceptions and memories.

The following is an example of how a couple examines their own behavior and makes helpful plans.

(TH = Therapist, H = Harry, L = Lucy)

Th: Well, I've seen you both separately for a few times, and you've mutually decided to talk together about how to proceed from this point.

H & L: Yes, we're ready to move on now.

Th: Just to clarify something: You've talked at length about the problems and about conflicts and about past hurts, affairs, and misery?

L & H: Yes, we've rehashed those things a thousand times.

Th: Is it going to help if you continue to talk about them?

H & L: No. [They go into detail about why.]

Th: Then, I think we need to take a new road. OK?

L & H: Yes.

Th: I want to ask you about how you spend your time.

L & H: [They talk at length about how they are getting along better but spend time separately working on their own projects, etc.]

Th: Tell me about the last time you did something enjoyable—a fun activity together without anyone else being involved.

H & L: [They agree it has been a long time.]

Th: I want you to talk to each other now, without arguing, about something you could do together which would fulfill the following conditions. [Explains the components of quality time.]

L: I would like to get some exercise. There is a park near by, and we used to go there and walk for about half an hour every day.

H: I would like that, too.

L: You would?

H: Yes, it would be good. I would sleep more soundly too.

Th: Will you do it every day for a week?

L & H: Yes.

Th: What will you avoid talking about?

H & L: [They enumerate the items that are "out of bounds."]

Th: What will you discuss.

H: How our day went.

L: How I'm different than I used to be.

Th: That's a good start. Now let's make a list of what's in bounds and what's out of bounds.

They make the following list:

In Bounds	Out of Bounds
the neighbors	the affair
the day's work	problems to face in the future
television shows	what they dislike
the children	what they get angry about
politics (they agree on this topic)	past mistakes
church (they agree on this topic)	anything blameful
jokes	complaints about other people

[The session ends with specific plans for time spent together.]

It is important to note that the transcript is abbreviated and a therapist is included. But couples do not necessarily need a third person to accomplish this. They can follow this format by discussing the ideas, evaluating their current behaviors, and making plans which are specific, realistic, and executed immediately or soon.

In the last analysis, the amount of time, the activity, the topic for discussion are determined by the couple. This self-assessment can be enhanced with the help of a counselor or therapist. The couples themselves decide how much overlap they have in their quality worlds, behaviors, and perceptions. They then decide how much they wish to accomplish. This is followed by strategies designed to reach their agreed upon goal.

LEVEL B
COMMUNICATION

It is impossible for couples to fail to communicate. Total silence and shunning each other's company is a strong form of communication. The message delivered in this way might even be effective in communicating displeasure, dislike, anger, resentment, rage and a host of other signals. But while the effort might be effective, the goal of intimacy is defeated.

Helpful communication in reality therapy is not radically different from that commonly accepted by therapists such as using "I messages." Still there are some additions based on the formulation summarized by the letters **W D E P**.

Each component of this system provides helpful ideas for communicating in a practical, direct, responsible manner while maintaining sensitivity to the other person.

W Couples using this system describe what they Want. They talk about what they want in such areas as professional/career, familial, personal, financial, intellectual, recreational, and spiritual.

D Couples can discuss many aspects of their current behavior, that is, what they are Doing. The action component of the behavioral system is but one aspect of conversation, however. Others include what each person thinks, how they feel, and even their physiology. The last component seems to assume more prominence as the years take their toll. But it is the action component which is useful to emphasize in building intimacy. In building relationships, emphasis is put on discussing common interests, areas of agreement, and activities which are pleasant. This, in no way, implies that avoidant behavior, or the defense mechanisms of minimizing, denying, or shunning controversy are encouraged. It means that intimacy begins and is founded on common ground, similar quality worlds, and a common behavioral direction.

Feelings are, of course, the topic of conversation in many communication workshops. Couples are encouraged to be frank and open, to "share your feelings." "Don't suppress or deny how you feel," is the admonition. In this system, however, couples are encouraged to talk about feelings in connection with actions. These are not separated as definitively as in some methods. The reason is that feelings are seen as behaviors. They are not the cause of actions. Rather they accompany actions. The causes of behavior are rooted in the quality world, that is, the wants of the person. Also, the feelings can be used to bring people together when the communication is related to what each person does with the anger, impatience, irritation, depression, etc. Further, plans for current or future resolution of upsetting feelings can be made when discussing actions. Conversely, joy, excitement, friendliness, tolerance, and empathy can be prolonged and used to facilitate the intimacy if they are linked to what each person is doing within the relationship. Two people become a system when they interACT with each other. Also when they translate the feelings into wants, efforts can be made to resolve differences, lessen the intensity of negative feelings and increase the positive ones.

Below is a dialogue between a two-career couple which illustrates the above principles. Sam is a 35-year-old junior executive for a computer information company. Nan is a sales representative for a dental equipment company. Nan comes home after a very difficult day attempting to sell equipment and supplies to dentists in her area. Sam is already at home and is watching TV. Nan enters the house, walks in with a heavy foot and drops her purse and briefcase on the floor in the living room.

(N = Nan, S = Sam)

S: Not a good day, huh?

N: I don't want to talk about it.

S: That bad?

N: Worse. I'm fed up with Shelby [Shelby is the manager]. And some **!♯@* almost hit me on the expressway.

S: Do you need some time to settle down? [Turns off his favorite TV show.]

N: I'll tell you later. You don't need to turn off *Crossfire*.

S: It's OK. I don't need to watch it. Besides, I'd rather be with you for a few minutes.

N: Sometimes you don't even want me to talk when that show's on. You don't even know I'm in the room sometimes. That's another thing.

S: I think I've been a little remote lately and put you on hold during this show.

N: Don't give me that "I'm guilty crap."

S: OK, but I really do want to hear what happened today.

N: I've been selling like crazy lately as I've told you. But I don't want to dump the other stuff on you.

S: Maybe you need a little time to come down. I can see you're upset. You have that steely look on your face that tells me you are really upset.

N: [Smiles slightly.] Give me a half hour to change clothes, wash up and get my briefcase in order. Why don't you watch your show?

S: I don't need to. Do you need any help?

N: You could rub my back.

S: Of course.

[In the above segment, Sam reads Nan's nonverbal behavior and reflects on it. He is aware that doing something alone might help even more than ventilating her feelings. He does not attempt to impose this on her, but he asks her about her own quality world at the moment. Does *she* think she needs some time to settle down, time to be alone but not completely alone. He is there in close proximity and is available. He even gives up a high priority want, watching his favorite TV show as a selfless gesture in order to be available to Nan if she decides to talk. Clearly upset about what happened today, she links her unpleasant anger-inducing experience with her previously unexpressed annoyance, even anger, at him for putting his TV show before her.

Harry accepts the criticism, refuses to be defensive, and declines to attack back. From much experience, he knows that it is easy to make the situation worse by trying to win. Still angry, Nan jabs him again with the remark about his guilty feelings. Harry does not add fuel to the fire by justifying his statement which, in fact, might have been based on guilt. Rather he says, "OK, but I really do want to hear what happened today." Instead of elaborating on his own behavior, he shares his quality world, using "I messages" rather than attacking.]

Note: This is a major principle in using the **W D E P** system of reality therapy effectively. Instead of justifying one's own action, it is often useful to share one's quality world, especially if the picture in the quality world (want) at that moment includes the best interest of the other person.

[From past experience, Sam knows that the quality world of Nan at the time of upsetness includes support but not encouragement, and physical nearness but not hovering over her. Because he is willing to be there for her she asks for physical contact to help her relax. She also appreciates his willingness to be there for her 100% and not turn on the television. She recognizes that he is able to read her deeper quality world picture (want) for him to attend to her rather than the more surface but also genuine want for him to meet his own needs by watching the TV show. The dialogue continues.]

S: What do you want me to do now? I would like to do something that would really help.

N: Just rub my back and listen.

S: That's fine. What do you want to get off your chest?

N: [Goes into detail about her hurt and anger at the supervisor who wants her to break in a new sales rep who is overly flirtatious with her and who will be awarded some of the territory which she has developed. To make matters worse the supervisor is a decent and fair-minded person who is honest and has the welfare of the company at heart. Nan further states the issue would be less troublesome if he were a jerk. To top it all off she almost had a wreck on the expressway, which would have been her fault. "But the guy should have seen me," she adds.]

At this point Sam could take either of two directions in his communication. He could help her develop a plan to talk to the supervisor about the territory. She could also discuss the behavior of the new sales rep, which is not too threatening but which is rather annoying. He could help her deal directly with the sales rep in order to solve this vexing problem. But Sam is aware of her quality world, having made many mistakes by trying to impose his "get to a solution" mentality on her. Instead, he listens carefully and empathically not only to her feelings, but also to her self-talk and what she has done regarding these aggravations. He hears her annoyance, connects it with the fact that she is expecting too much from the company as well as expecting reasonable behavior from the sales rep. He reflects on what she's done by reminding her gently that she is a high flyer for the company and they are really quite proud to have her in their employ. He knows that at all costs he needs to avoid the "How are you going to work it out?" "What's your plan?" "We need to develop a strategy," approach. That is for later.

Nan at this moment seems to be behaving with choices related to belonging. If Sam can connect on that level, intimacy is increased, maintained, or at least not damaged. But if Sam were to take the problem-solving approach, he would be misreading her need, at the moment, for power and for control or for freedom from the stress and strain of the situation. Her real need is belonging. The signs and cues are not easy to read, and Sam might take a long time learning them. But if he uses his two ears and one mouth in a two to one proportion he has made a major step.

A SPECIFIC SUGGESTION

One of the areas couples can discuss is the role of television and the Internet in the lives of their young children. While this discussion does not, by itself, create intense intimacy, it is nevertheless an area for interaction. They can study the issue, gain information from many sources, and come to agreement about the place of television and the Internet in their own lives and that of their families. They should, of course, involve the family in the discussion, but they can come to an agreement between themselves first about priorities around the use of television set(s). This discussion is never a merely intellectual conversation even though it begins on a rather cerebral level. Liebermann (1996) has pointed out that part of being a parent is monitoring what young children are exposed to. When parents discuss such issues on a foundation of quality time, they can become more intimate.

The benefits of a couple who have intimacy-building skills can hardly be overemphasized. Couples who are able to stay closely connected with each other, help each other fulfill the innate need of belonging. It is very painful for people who want a close relationship but experience distance, aloofness, rejection, and especially violence. The disappointment is deep, the resentment intense, and the bursts of anger more frequent. Couples not experiencing closeness in their relationships are forced to lead unfulfilled lives resulting in bitterness, affairs, withdrawal to excessive television watching or worse, to chemical abuse, workaholism, or other ineffective behaviors. Quality time and communication built around the W D E P system lead to closeness and intimacy.

But the benefits to each other are not the only ones derived from closeness and cohesion. Stephenson, Henry and Robinson (1996) found that the least amount of adolescent substance abuse was found in families where there was cohesion as demonstrated by a nurturing environment, celebration of family rituals and other signs of family intimacy. Though these results are not emphasized here, they provide an additional motive for couples.

LEVEL A
DECISION MAKING,
PROBLEM SOLVING,
AND COMPROMISE

When the lower levels of quality time and individual need fulfillment are taken care of adequately, the level of decision making, problem solving, and compromise is more easily addressed. When intimacy breaks down, it surfaces at level A. The temptation is to address this most obvious problem at this most obvious level. Yet, if there is not a groundwork to build on, the superstructure of problem-solving skills is shaky and could even collapse, that is, be ineffectual in times of stress when most needed.

On the other hand, when a storehouse of pleasant memories and mutually positive perceptions exist, decision making is easier. In this process, it is important that solutions include the use of the E and P of the WDEP system; Self-Evaluation and Planning. Both people must feel that they have fulfilled their quality worlds in some way. Only then is an individual willing to insure that the other person's quality world is met.

Inability to compromise is best addressed by asking whether levels C and D are firm. Experience has shown that attempts to deal only with level A results in frustration. There is no foundation to build on.

A higher level of intimacy exists when altruism becomes need satisfying. Negotiation can become a cold and lifeless mindset; "I give in, if you give in." Intimacy is not like buying an automobile.

Coleman McCarthy, not a reality therapist, has formulated a process which is compatible with the principles described in this chapter. He says it is crucial to develop the mindset that "it is not me against you. It's you and I against the problem." This is followed by a discussion of areas of agreement. Only then should differences be the focus. Each party must come away with at least part of what he or she wants.

If the basic three levels are emphasized in the relationship, the level of compromise and problem solving present little challenge. But when there is little connection between the parties, efforts to enter the couple's interaction at the level of problem solving often exacerbates the tension. Intimacy is enhanced if built on the foundation of individual self-esteem, quality time and nondefensive communication using the W D E P system.

REFERENCES

Ford, E. (1981). *Permanent love*. Minnesota: Winston.

Glasser, W. (1965). *Reality therapy*. NY: Harper Collins.

Glasser, W. (1968). *Schools without failure*. NY: Harper Collins.

Glasser, W. (1985). *Control theory*. NY: Harper Collins.

Glasser, W. (1990). *Quality school*. NY: Harper Collins.

Glasser, W. (1992). *Quality school teacher*. NY: Harper Collins.

Glasser, W. (1995). *Staying together*. NY: Harper Collins.

Glasser, W. (1998). *Choice theory: A new psychology for a new century*. NY: Harper Collins.

Jennings, J. (1991). Multiple approaches to the treatment of violent couples. *American Journal of Family Therapy. 19*, (4), 351–361.

Liebermann, J. (1996). Why parents hate TV. *Policy Review, 77*, 18–19.

McCarthy, C. (1995). Unpublished material on negotiation.

Meloy, R. (1988). *The psychopathic mind: Origins, dynamics, and treatment*. Northvale, NJ: Jason Aronson.

Powers, W. (1973). *Behavior, the control of perception*. NY: Aldine.

Stephenson, A., Henry, C., Robinson, L. (1996). Family characteristics and adolescent substance abuse. *Adolescence. 31*, (121), 59–63.

Wubbolding, R. (1993). Reality therapy. In A. Horne (Ed.), *Family counseling and therapy* (pp. 435–462). Itasca: Peacock.

Wubbolding, R. (1996). *Employee Motivation*. Knoxville: SPC Press, Inc.

CHAPTER 13

Love is a Noun (Except When It's a Verb): A Solution-Oriented Approach to Intimacy

Steffanie O'Hanlon, M.S.W.
Bill O'Hanlon, M.S.

The idea of sustaining intimacy past the wooing and spooning phase of courtship through the course of a long-term relationship is relatively new. Ozzie and Harriet, and even June and Ward, didn't seem to expect passion and intimacy in their relationships. They were about raising children, affiliation, and economic security. Couples in the past few decades are pioneering new territory in our relationships and don't know how to sustain or maintain what we have come to expect, enduring intimacy. We're in a period of trial and error experimentation, and there are some successes and many failures. Certainly no one has uncovered the guaranteed formula for success. In that spirit, we have some ideas and observations to share but no definitive answers.

In our view, there are two components of intimacy. The first is the ineffable chemistry of love and attraction or liking for a person, and the second is the constellation of actions that support or dissipate love and connection. If the first component isn't there, all the actions in the world that the therapist suggests won't be sufficient to create it. But the second area is the one in which we therapists can make an impact. We can coach couples to start doing, or to increase the actions that enhance or create intimacy. And we can coach couples to stop doing, or change the actions that have been diminishing or dissipating intimacy.

Until 1994, Bill believed that love was a verb. He thought that if he did the behaviors one does when one is in love, the feeling would follow. What in fact followed was a divorce. While Bill's head was willing for love to be a verb, his soul wasn't, and he was broadsided when the two collided. This chapter is a revision of Bill's previously published ideas on couple therapy (Hudson and O'Hanlon, 1992; O'Hanlon and Hudson, 1996). The premise of those publications was that love is a verb and that one can "rewrite" love stories merely with different actions. In our view, that is part of the story, but it is incomplete. Here we will combine the noun and verb parts of love and intimacy in a solution-oriented context.

THE ATTIC

A man and a woman separately enter a house that is for sale and having an open house. They eye each other warily as they wander about, because each is very interested in buying the house, to which they are strangely attracted. They continue to wander around until by separate stairways, they find themselves face to face in the attic. As their eyes meet, they remember in a flash that they have known and deeply loved each other in a previous life. And they have found each other again in this life. They embrace and soon make plans for marriage and jointly owning this house that has brought them together again. They walk down the attic stairs arm in arm, but as they step off the last step, they develop an instant amnesia and forget their connection. They quickly let go of each other. But each remains in the house, feeling some disturbing sense that something significant has happened that they can't remember. After wandering around the house for some time, they find themselves in the attic, where they rediscover each other as long lost lovers. But they realize that they will develop amnesia if they come down from the attic. They also realize that they cannot stay up in the attic. Someone else is sure to buy the house, and they need food. But they are not willing to lose the love they have so recently refound. They finally decide that they will sign an agreement while in the attic to jointly purchase the house and then they will remember, as they live there, to revisit the attic as often as possible, because there is something very important that they forgot there.

For us, this story illustrates the relationship between the noun and verb parts of love. One can't just stay in the attic; life's duties and responsibilities call. But one can do things that bring one back to the attic. In many relationships, the stairs to the attic no longer bear weight and require repair.

But people don't ever seem to find the time to repair them, and couples just stop going to the attic. Time goes by. And, while the intimacy of the attic is wistfully remembered on occasion, somehow the time and effort is never made to regain access to the attic. So, we will start by examining the "attic" or noun parts of intimacy and then detail the steps to regaining them when they have dissipated or been lost.

While we believe love is a noun, it is mysterious and its chemistry hard to explain and often difficult for therapists to create directly. Couples can identify its absence or presence but pinpointing its mercurial mechanics can be like asking for a description of air—elusive. While therapists can't create chemistry, compatibility, or acceptance, we can help couples reclaim the intimacy that has been lost or help them see that it just isn't there. This chapter is about how to revive and support the noun aspects (feeling, attraction, compatibility) of love with various actions.

The first noun thing to help couples settle is whether they have compatibility in even their preferences for ways of connecting.

PREFERRED VALUES OF CONNECTION AND INTIMACY

Intimate connections can take many forms: friendship, sex, companionship, money, politics, or business. There is no ideal form; one is not better than another, and successful relationships have been based on all of them. What is important is that both partners have similar or complementary preferences about types of connective intimacy. For example, if one partner is primarily interested in friendship and the other is interested in an intense soul and sexual connection, there may be difficulty. Sometimes these preferences are clear from the beginning, and for others they don't emerge until the initial, often intense and passionate phase of the relationship has ended and the more enduring connective styles become apparent. Most of us don't enter a relationship thinking about connective style. We enter with all the excitement and fanfare that new relationships bring.

Steffanie worked with a couple for whom from the beginning sex had been less than ideal. The wife wanted frequent, passionate, and creative lovemaking and the husband preferred less frequent sex in a predictable style, usually right before they went to sleep at night. The wife admitted she was concerned about the differences in their lovemaking styles but thought that the infrequency was because she was inexperienced and that, as she got more comfortable initiating, things would improve. What she found out was that their sexual relationship didn't improve and that her husband really valued the friendship and companionship aspect of their relationship. She valued these as well but wanted passion also. They made some efforts to alter their sex life, but the husband acknowledged he just wasn't interested in making changes. At one point she told her husband she didn't love him in the passionate way she thought she should, and he said this was okay. The love that she expressed was enough for him. Unfortunately, it wasn't okay with her. He could live happily in a relationship based on friendship. While she tried for many years, she was unable to. She said, "I just kept trying to make it okay in my mind that I could live without a passionate sexual life." Ultimately, they broke up. Each expressed relief, recognizing that incompatibility allowed them to salvage their friendship. The wife stated, "I was frantically trying to change him or myself and it was becoming ugly."

So we may need to help couples identify if their connective values are compatible. We can either help them realize when the noun aspect is missing or incompatible or help the couple remove barriers to intimacy. One member of the couple may assume the other intentionally withholds intimacy or is incapable of intimacy, when in fact the partner merely prefers a different form of being connected. As Steffanie's client alluded to by saying it was becoming quite ugly, these impasses often become quite personalized, and couples generate stories about what is wrong with each other or with themselves. Therapists can defuse this type of conflict by pointing out the shared desire for intimacy and the different views of what it may look like. The therapist can then negotiate a mutually accepted form of intimacy, using action steps. On the other hand, as with Steffanie's clients mentioned above, if the couple is not able to find a mutually compatible connective style, the therapist can help the couple end the relationship without blame or rancor.

The next thing we think supports intimacy is radical acceptance.

RADICAL ACCEPTANCE:
A CORNERSTONE
OF INTIMACY

Radical acceptance is voting for the other person, flaws and foibles included. How many times do people think, "He (or she) would be perfect if only..." and a fissure opens in the relationship? At first it is quite small, barely perceptible. But once you notice it, your eye returns to the imperfection over and over, until that is all you see. "If only he would manage money differently," or "...she didn't have to be the center of attention."

Many of us have a sense of acceptance in the beginning of our relationships, but with the growing awareness of imperfections and imperfect fits, the acceptance fades. With the realization of imperfections, many of us want to either fix the other person or dispose of him or her. We want user-friendly (easy to operate) VCRs with lots of features. Couples sometimes decide that, if acceptance requires too much work, something is wrong and there has to be something better and easier out there.

We consider radical acceptance a noun because, if it isn't there at base, all the actions in the world won't create it. As a noun, if it is there or once was there, it can be enhanced or revived.

Steffanie worked with a woman, Ann, who admitted to "having a mind that fixates on flaws" (in herself and her relationships). Ann had been in several relationships with men she referred to as "basically very nice" and observed in herself a pattern of focusing on the flaws of her partner and of ultimately leaving the relationship. Now, she was in a relationship that she valued, saw the old pattern repeating, and didn't want the focus on flaws to end the relationship this time. First, Ann came to view her critical thoughts as stories and not facts. She and Steffanie then discussed viewing her thoughts as the climate versus the weather. The weather is what is happening in the immediate moment but the climate is the overall perspective. Yes, there are colds snaps, storms, heat waves, and hail, but how do you feel about the overall climate? For Ann this was very helpful. It allowed for her to put her critical thoughts in perspective but not to ignore them all together. If the climate wasn't right, then she would rework or reevaluate the relationship. But if it was just the weather, she didn't need to question her partner's basic acceptability.

Steffanie grew up in a very small town in New England, and Steffanie's family was friendly with another family, the Greys, who lived down the street. At one time, Mrs. Grey became very sexually flirtatious and carried on a series of very public affairs with some of the town's most prominent men. As is typical of small towns, gossip was rampant. Mr. Grey, while aware of the affairs, stayed with his wife. He explained to Steffanie's parents that he and his wife were going to therapy and that she had a "sexual problem." She stopped the affairs and sexualized behaviors and the Greys remained happily married until Mrs. Grey's death several years ago. Mr. Grey not only demonstrated radical acceptance but relational integrity as well. He kept the overall view of who his wife was in mind, while they jointly dealt with her troubling behavior.

RELATIONAL INTEGRITY

Relational integrity is a commitment to the larger well-being of your partner or relationship that transcends the feelings or considerations of the moment. We say commitment to your partner or relationship, because sometimes, in a heated moment, you can't locate the part that cares about your partner. In those moments, it may be easier to act in a selfish, destructive manner, but a commitment to the maintenance and survival of the relationship can overcome the spat of the moment. It's like a parent's love for a child, even in the midst of some challenging behavior like a temper tantrum.

Simone Weil has said, "What we love in other people is the hoped for satisfaction of our desires. We do not love them for *their* desires. If we loved them for their desires we should love them as ourselves" (quoted in Whyte, 1989–1996). David Whyte adds, "And isn't that the great road of relationship, that the hardest thing in the world is to love the other person's desires and that would be the thing you would come back to all the time and it would be greatest giving away because in doing that those very desires could lead them away from you and yet you have no choice. What is the center of a person but their desires in the world?" (Whyte, 1989–1996). We readily accept those aspects of our partners that fit our needs and preferences and often try to fix or eradicate the parts that conflict with our desires.

In the movie *Jerry Maguire*, Jerry's wife embodies relational integrity. She realizes he married her out of guilt and obligation and perhaps out of some fear on his part of being alone. When she comes to terms with this, she lets him go, taking her share of the responsibility for the marriage. "I pretended to take your proposal seriously," she tells him. "I wanted it to be true. I created this mess." She easily could have portrayed herself the victim. Instead she took responsibility for her part in their troubled relationship. Ultimately, they stay together, but only after she lets Jerry leave, and he discovers for himself that he loves her and wants to be with her. Bill and Steffanie call this type of relational integrity, trusting your partner's process. It's what Simone Weil refers to as loving your partner for their desires. Even though she loved him dearly, Jerry's wife knew she had to let him follow his soul. If he discovered his love for her and came back, that would be right; and if he left, that too, would be the right answer.

Many relationships degenerate into an "everyone for themselves" and a "watch your own back" philosophy, particularly when things get tough and blame and fault emerge. John Taylor (1997) describes this phenomenon in his poignant article about the dissolution of his marriage. He says, "We sought to invalidate each other's grievances by establishing prior grievances of our own, as if all subsequent wrongs could be traced to some mythic first wrong, and whoever committed it could be held responsible for everything that had transpired."

A couple consulted Bill over the phone. Bill had seen the man before for individual work and for previous couples work with another partner. The couple was engaged to be married, but the man kept getting frightened and backing off on a wedding date. When he would express his doubts, his fiancée would react and then they would be off to the races. Bill had seen this pattern in the previous relationship, so after ascertaining that in his clearest moments, the man truly did want to get married and that he loved his fiancée, Bill asked to speak alone to the woman. Bill told her that her partner was uncertain, so she could really help the situation if she just maintained a confidence and calm in the face of his doubts and fears. She said that if she knew he wasn't really seriously intending to leave the relationship, she would find it easy to do her part to keep things on an even keel. After this brief consultation, she was able to keep the bigger picture in mind, even when her partner wasn't and to transcend her initial reaction for the good of the relationship. After a few more incidents of the man getting scared and the woman just remaining clear and connected, his fears diminished and they were able to set a wedding date. They remain happily married now six years later.

Two methods to elicit and acknowledge relational integrity are inclusive anger and including the other person's reality and perspective.

Inclusive anger Inclusive anger is an aspect of relational integrity and radical acceptance. Inclusive anger happens when one or both of the partners simultaneously honors and includes the "bigger picture" that the couple loves one another *and* is going to stay in the relationship *and* that one or both of them is upset.

Bill was working with a couple who, during several recent arguments, had reached an impasse. At that time, one of the partners, Debbie, would leave the house, because the argument was going nowhere and was producing a level of conflict and tension that she found destructive and intolerable. Sarah, the other partner, found herself being really frightened by these incidents, which led to further conflicts, either before Debbie left or after she returned. As we talked, Sarah realized that at some level, she thought Debbie was leaving the relationship when she left the house. After some discussion, we mutually decided that if Debbie would just reach over and touch Sarah during an argument, that would give her a message of connection that would diminish Sarah's fear and defensiveness. If the conflict escalated to the point where Debbie felt she had to leave, it would help immensely if she told Sarah that she only needed to get some distance to get a different perspective and that she didn't intend to end the relationship. Debbie agreed to this rather simple means to include both her anger and her partner's concern.

The key here seems to lie in the word "and." "I love you *and* I'm upset by what you did." "I'm mad at you *and* I'm not going to leave you." "I don't like what's going on in our relationship *and* I'm committed to resolving it." The inclusion of the two perspectives, truths, or realities at the same time seems crucial.

Beyond "I" messages: Including the other person's reality and perspective Another type of inclusion involves giving weight or credence to the other person's perspective or feelings during times of disagreement or conflict. "I" messages and acknowledgment can sometimes be helpful ways to structure communication, but, in our experience, they don't always go far enough. The content may be correctly phrased but still not communicate the necessary level of understanding.

Bill and Steffanie worked with a couple who were having conflict over some blended family issues. They had conflicting family demands over a holiday weekend that would result in them spending the weekend apart. The husband's daughter was graduating from college and the wife had an annual family reunion. They both acknowledged that it wasn't the most earth-shattering problem, but they were at an impasse. The husband felt badly that his wife was unable to attend the graduation with him. They were both therapists and adept at the use of "I messages." The husband said, "She says the right words, and I know she regrets not being able to come, but something is missing for me." Steffanie asked, "But does it have the weight and consideration you need?" The husband eagerly nodded his head and said, "Yes, I need to feel like she is getting it on a deeper level and giving it real consideration. It's like she says the right words, but doesn't really stop to listen." We went on to discuss what it would look like when she gave what he was upset about the kind of weight and consideration that was right for him. She might take a bit longer to respond, speak more slowly, and ask more questions about what he meant, rather than quickly responding with something like, "I see what you mean," or, immediately after he speaks, telling him her feelings and perspective.

Since we have discussed some of the noun aspects of intimacy, now we are going to talk about actions that can erode or enhance intimacy.

WHAT DESTROYS OR DISSIPATES CONNECTION AND INTIMACY

There are obvious behaviors that can destroy or disrupt intimacy, like violence, dishonesty, and affairs. We are going to look at some of the common but less overt diminishers of intimacy.

We live in Santa Fe and one of our favorite local bumper stickers reads, "Don't believe everything you think." We call "everything you think," *stories*. The mind comes up with stories about the way things are, and then we believe the stories. Each of us has our own set of typical stories. You have yours, and your partner has his or hers. We filter information through our stories, and that information often, in turn, supports the stories we already have. Stories aren't bad in and of themselves. Stories that lead to solutions and understanding can be quite useful. On the other hand, stories that create impasses and misperceptions aren't helpful.

We have identified four typical problematic stories that can interfere with intimacy.

Impossibility Stories

The first type of problematic story is the impossibility story. Couples often believe that change is impossible in their partners or in their relationships. For example, "He'll never change. He just can't express his feelings." Or "She is just like my mother." These impossibility stories involve conclusions we make about ourselves, the other person or the situation.

Blaming Stories

Secondly, stories of blame assume or view oneself or others as having bad intentions or bad traits. "He's a controller," and "She just wants to get attention," are examples of these blaming stories. These stories involve deciding that your partner has unchangeable characteristics.

Invalidating Stories

Thirdly, ideas of invalidation lead to clients' personal experience or knowledge being undermined by others. For example, a person might say to her partner, "You aren't really upset with me, you just haven't dealt with your father's death and are taking it out on me." If one partner doesn't agree with that idea, and the other partner insists it is true, that becomes an invalidating story. One partner might accuse another of being "too sensitive" or "too emotional," thereby invalidating in another way. These stories involve one person claiming to be able to see into someone else's experience and telling them that what they experience isn't right or valid.

Deterministic Stories

Finally, stories of nonaccountability or deterministic stories suggest that someone has no choices about what he or she does with his or her body (voluntary actions) or no ability to make a difference in what happens in his or her life. For example, one partner might say, "I was raised in a home where silence was the way to express anger. So when I get angry, I stop talking and go my own way." The underlying message is that the person is determined by his or her past and, therefore, has no choice about what he or she does in the present. Another common idea of nonaccountability is the attribution of the cause of one's behavior to another person, as in, "If she didn't nag me, I wouldn't hit her."

ACTION COMPLAINTS AND REQUESTS

If people have the sense that they are being criticized at core, or that someone is telling them that they have to change who they are, they naturally react defensively. First, they have the sense that they cannot change who they are. Second, they often feel a sense of shame when given the message that there is something not right about who they are.

"You're not going to change me!" Bill was doing the second session of a difficult couples therapy. The husband was a bit obnoxious, but Bill had made a nice connection with him despite the fact that he was a reluctant participant in the therapy. At one point, Bill and the wife had been talking for several minutes about what she wanted her husband to do differently. The husband unexpectedly exploded in anger, exclaiming, "You two are trying to change me, but I tell you I'm not going to change!" Bill turned to him and said, "I think you misunderstand. I have no interest in changing you or helping your wife change you. I find you obnoxiously charming. (This got a laugh out of the husband, since he was well aware of his ability to be obnoxious and was somewhat proud of it.) All we're trying to do is to get you to speak and act a bit differently with your wife in some circumstances. There's no need to change your personality or any essential quality." With that reassurance, he quickly relaxed and the session continued.

One way to engage cooperation and avoid a sense of invalidation, then, is to use what we call videotalk, or action talk. This keeps the focus on what people *do* rather than who they are. Changing what one does is more workable and less threatening. We focus on changing behaviors rather than character or personal deficits. With video or action talk we help couples get specific. We call it videotalk, because we try to get people to describe what we, or anyone else, would see or hear if what they were referring to were being shown on a videotape. We sometimes find it helpful to get them to focus on specific incidents and describe the actions that occurred without adding stories or attributions about the behavior. When vague, easily misunderstood words like "communication," "love," and "respect" are used, we help clients translate those terms into specific action words. For example: "What does your partner do that makes you feel he (or she) has poor communication skills?" "What do good communication skills look like for you?"

Action complaints are the first way to translate the couple's concerns into videotalk. We get people to tell each other what they don't like about each other's behavior very specifically. Action complaints deal with the past and what people haven't liked about their partner's behavior.

The next step is to get the couple to specify what actions they would like each other to do in the future and by what time they would like it to happen. "I would like you to...by..." These are **action requests**. These have more to do with the future.

Stop snorting, start "respecting" A couple came to see Bill for marriage counseling. The wife's main complaint was that her husband "didn't respect her." He disagreed. He believed he respected her. Using the action complaints—action requests idea, Bill asked her to detail a recent time when her husband had shown her lack of respect. The wife told about a party they had jointly attended a few weeks before at which he had snorted after she gave her political opinion while they were standing around in a circle of people. Obviously, she wanted him not to snort when she gave her opinion. But what else could he do to actively to show her respect in a similar situation in the future? (This is the action request.) She said that he could walk over and stand next to her after she made the comment, hold her hand, put his arm around her, and, perhaps, introduce her to other people she didn't know at the party who had heard the remark. All these would indicate to her that he respected her, even if he disagreed with her opinion, by letting others know that she was his wife.

WHAT ENHANCES OR CREATES CONNECTION AND INTIMACY

We have several methods for creating connection and intimacy. We help couples use action praise, tell each other action hopes and dreams for the relationship, start doing actions that could create feelings of intimacy, and use radical honesty, vulnerability and authenticity to invite intimacy.

INTIMACY MOMENTS/ACTIONS FROM THE PAST: ACTION PRAISE

One thing that we do is ask for couples to recall intimate moments from the past or to describe past behaviors of their partner that enhanced intimacy in the relationship. We mine experiences from the past for clues as to how to build intimacy in the present and future. We call this **action praise**.

As we wrote earlier, it's easy to slip into the habit of focusing on the things you wish you could change about your partner, the negatives. Action praise helps shift the focus to what is good about one's partner and what is working about the relationship. It also reinforces these behaviors, and, in the process, is likely to build more intimacy and communication. As the old saying goes, you attract a lot more flies with honey than with vinegar.

Action praise involves getting people to describe current or past actions their partners did that they liked. We suggest that they use videotalk and be as specific and detailed as possible. For example, "I like it when you call me on my lunch break. It makes me feel loved that you are spontaneously thinking about me like that." This detail provides two pieces of information on which to build intimacy in this relationship. One would be calling during lunch break. The second would be hints about other ways to demonstrate spontaneous thoughtfulness.

Ben Furman and Tapi Ahola (1992) also describe using a similar technique to evoke a desired behavior when the behavior you want to see isn't happening yet. One of them was coaching a losing soccer team and found himself on the sidelines yelling at the kids like the rest of the losing coaches typically do. However, at the next half-time, he changed strategies. (It wasn't making the kids play better just telling them what they were doing wrong and asking them to change it.) Instead, he started to compliment the kids on how he wanted them to play. "Great, you're looking to make those passes and hustling down the field!" Lo and behold, the kids actually started doing those behaviors and playing the way the coach hoped. So, we encourage couples to catch their partners doing something right and compliment them on it or, if all else fails, find some behavior that is remotely like what they want to have happen and compliment their partner on this. For example, for someone who is chronically late, "I really appreciate that you made an attempt to get home earlier tonight (or to get ready to go on time)."

INTIMACY FANTASIES/ACTIONS FOR THE FUTURE: ACTION HOPES AND WISHES

The past is one source of information about intimacy in relationships, but sometimes previous ways of connecting no longer fit or have grown stale, and the couple needs to develop new forms of intimacy. We ask couples to look ahead to a time in the future when they are being intimate and connected in the way they would like and get them to tell us what they are doing, what their partner is doing, and what is happening differently in the relationship. Again, it is important to be specific. Statements like, "We will be more loving toward each other," or "We will be more romantic," don't provide enough information about how to operationalize these things. We need to know what behaviors will be happening. If I were going to *do* romantic in your relationship what would I do? Make a candlelight dinner? Go for a camping and hiking trip together? Stay in bed late in the morning to snuggle? Or something else altogether?

Remember that we are in verb-land here, helping couples communicate about action or take actions to either enhance or stop destroying intimacy. In the next example, we show that the verb part of the equation can, at times, create the noun of intimacy.

BEGIN DOING INTIMACY: ACTION CAN CREATE FEELINGS

Bill saw a couple whose passion had gone out of their 30-year relationship. They reported that, during the early years of the relationship, they had had quite a wonderful and varied sexual relationship, but that it had dissipated over the years, to the point where it had been some years since they had had any sexual contact at all. The wife attributed the loss of intimacy to the fact that her husband had some years ago gone out and bought her a "dream vacation," a backpacking trip through Nepal, as a surprise. The wife was surprised, indeed, and told him that the vacation he arranged was not the kind she wanted to take. The husband canceled the reservations. The wife felt he was resentful of this and that this had brought about a subtle estrangement, which they had never discussed because the incident had been so painful for them both. She had assumed that this was the reason they had not had sex much since that time. The husband, hearing his wife's explanation this many years later, said that in fact that wasn't why he hadn't been initiating sex. When asked why, he sheepishly admitted that the fact that she had gained a lot of weight was the main reason. He hadn't wanted to hurt her feelings by mentioning it and also was keenly aware of the fact that he had gained quite a bit of weight as well. So, it wasn't really fair to criticize her. Nevertheless, this had diminished his sexual interest. Both of them had recently begun active exercise and diet programs to begin losing weight. It would take some time, however, for the effects of these programs to be seen. Bill, therefore, focused the couple on immediate actions they could take to improve their sexual intimacy. Bill asked the couple to describe what they did when they had a more "hot" (their word) sexual relationship. They described themselves as sexual adventurers who liked to vary their lovemaking locations and practices. Bill suggested they try to act as they did when they were passionate lovers. When the couple returned for their next session, they reported that they had gone home the evening following the session and immediately had sex, and they had had lots of "hot" sex since. They were pleasantly surprised to find that actions had created feelings.

Another point to the above story is that radical honesty, as painful or uncomfortable as it may be, can lead to new levels of intimacy.

The next set of methods might be thought of as Advanced Intimacy Methods or Intimacy 601.

RADICAL HONESTY

We think radical honesty is the wellspring of deeply intimate relationships. It's an acquired taste and not for the faint of heart. It demands a willingness to hear things one might rather not know and to say things that leave you vulnerable. Many people, particularly those who are in relationships that are based on companionship and friendship, don't necessarily want to know all the gory details, painful truths, and paradoxical feelings. They aren't looking for that type of connection.

Radical Honesty Creates Wall-Socket Sex.   David Schnarch, a well-known sex and marital therapist, told Bill the story of how he developed his approach to sexual intimacy. He was treating an "empty nest" couple who found themselves feeling a distance and lack of intimacy with one another. Their sex life was either nonexistent or unexciting. David discovered during their initial discussions that they really didn't know one another anymore, after all these years being busy with family and work. He persuaded them that the only way back to true intimacy was to begin telling each other the truth about everything, which could sometimes be quite surprising and painful, but would in the end bring them much closer. As they began to both discover and speak their unspoken feelings, thoughts, fantasies and desires to one another, it was very stormy, but they made it through the crisis much stronger, with a renewed sense of life and intimacy. They told David that they were having "wall-socket sex," which came out of both their newfound closeness and their enhanced communication. David congratulated them, but something began to bother him. He realized that he and his wife were not having wall-socket sex and that they weren't as close as this couple had become. He went home with a commitment to change that. David's wife didn't know what hit her at first, as David began his course of radical honesty with her. But after the initial shock wore off, she joined in, telling him things she had held back for years. They began to be much closer and have a better sex life. David's contention is that we overemphasize sexual techniques, when what we should really be focusing on is intimacy, to enhance our sexual relationships.

Radical honesty, while an easy concept to which to give lip service, is often hard to actualize in relationships. It often pushes us up against all those fears that we have in relationships, like being abandoned or thought of as selfish or a bad guy. Steffanie worked with a woman who was going through a divorce and who said that, while she spoke in small ways about her unhappiness in her relationship, she never really went "pedal to the metal" with her soon to be ex-husband about what dissatisfied her. She was afraid he would leave and that she wasn't being fair. "In point of fact," she said, "I think I was afraid it would make it clear that we couldn't work things out, and then I would have to leave, or he would leave, and I just wasn't ready for that."

As David Schnarch indicates in his story, radical honesty can cause great storms in a marriage. On the other hand, it can keep things alive and vital, and there aren't all those cobwebs silently building up that create distance and a deadening barrier to intimacy.

AUTHENTICITY AND VULNERABILITY CREATE A CONTEXT FOR INTIMACY

Bill had a colleague, Rick, with whom he worked many years ago at a hospital. Bill was very critical of Rick's approach to the patients. Rick treated them as if they were all sick and fragile and would likely be sick the rest of their lives. Bill had a very different philosophy. Plus, Rick was very slow, with little sense of humor, in contrast to Bill's rather quick pace and constant, irreverent humor. Rick, however, had taken a liking to Bill and routinely made attempts to spend time with him, which Bill fastidiously avoided. Near the end of Bill's tenure at the hospital, Rick came in and sat down on one of the chairs in Bill's office. He began to tell Bill how sorry he was going to be to see him go. He had always wanted to get some of the energy, confidence and enthusiasm he saw Bill had when working with patients. Rick said that he often felt inadequate and incompetent and felt that he was really an impostor, even though he had a lot of training and advanced degrees. As he continued to speak about his heartfelt vulnerability and sadness, Bill began, despite his previous dislike, to like Rick and feel a warmth he had never felt. That incident stuck with Bill and showed him the profound power of vulnerability to create intimacy.

In our view, couples need nouns, verbs, adjectives, and anything else they can get their hands on to maintain intimacy across the course of a relationship. Sometimes actions can recreate the noun aspect of intimacy, and sometimes they can't. We have tried to provide an integrated model that includes both the noun and verb aspects of intimacy, showing the contributions of both to the sometimes daunting challenge of sustaining intimacy in relationships.

REFERENCES

Furman, B. & Ahola, T. (1992). *Solution Talk*: *Hosting Therapeutic Conversations*. New York: Norton.
Hudson, P. O. & O'Hanlon, W. H. (1992). *Rewriting Love Stories*: *Brief Marital Therapy*. New York: Norton.
O'Hanlon, B. & Hudson, P. (1996). *Stop Blaming, Start Loving*. New York: Norton.
Taylor, J. (1997). Divorce Is Good For You, *Esquire*, May, 52–59.
Whyte, David (1989–1996). *Belonging To The World* (Audiotape). Langley, Washington: Many Rivers Company.

CHAPTER 14

The Self-to-Self Connection: Intimacy and the Internal Family Systems Model

Richard C. Schwartz, Ph.D.

Like pornography, people have trouble defining intimacy, but they know it when they feel it. People also know intimacy by its absence, by the times when they don't feel it. It's as if we all have relationship thermometers that make us feel warm with some people and chilled with others, or feel hot and cold with the same person at different times.

While most people want as much intimacy in their close relationships as possible, they don't often know how, or are afraid, to turn up the heat. There are two reasons for this. First, because intimacy is so ephemeral, people often don't know how to get more. If our house becomes too cold we can turn up the thermostat. The thermostats in our relationships can be hard to find, however, and sometimes searching for ways to turn them up can backfire, and we wind up colder than ever. Second, intimacy can be dangerous. It involves being open and unprotected—giving another person the power to inflict more pain than if we remained distant and protected.

In this chapter, I will use the internal family systems (IFS) model to address these two problems of achieving intimacy and making it safe. The IFS model provides a definition of intimacy that offers clear steps to turning up the heat and doing so safely.

THE INTERNAL FAMILY
SYSTEMS MODEL

The IFS model (Schwartz, 1987; 1988; 1992; 1995; 1997; Goulding & Schwartz, 1995; Nichols & Schwartz, 1997; Breunlin, Schwartz, & Mac Kune-Karrer, 1992) represents a new synthesis of two already existing paradigms: systems thinking and the multiplicity of the mind. It brings concepts and methods from the structural, strategic, narrative, and Bowen schools of family therapy to the world of subpersonalities. This synthesis was the natural outcome when I, as a young, fervent, family therapist, began hearing from clients about their inner lives. After I was able to set aside my preconceived notions about therapy and the mind, I began to listen to what my clients were saying. What I heard over and over were descriptions of what they often called their parts—the conflicted voices or subpersonalities residing within them. This was not a new discovery. Many other theorists have described a similar inner phenomenon, beginning with Freud's id, ego, and superego, and more recently the object relations conceptions of internal objects. This phenomenon is also at the core of less mainstream approaches like transactional analysis (ego states), psychosynthesis (subpersonalities), and is now manifested in cognitive-behavioral approaches under the term schemata. Prior to IFS, however, little attention has been given to how these inner entities function together.

Since my family therapy background left me steeped in systems thinking, it was second nature to begin tracking sequences of internal interaction in the same way I had tracked interactions among family members. I learned that, across people, parts take on common roles and common inner relationships. I also learned that these inner roles and relationships were not static and could be changed by intervening carefully and respectfully. I began conceiving of the mind as an inner family and experimenting with techniques I had used as a family therapist.

The IFS, then, sees a person as containing an ecology of relatively discrete subminds, each one intrinsically valuable and seeking a positive role within. Life experiences force these subminds or parts out of their valuable roles, however, which can reorganize the internal system in unhealthy ways. This process is similar to the way, in an alcoholic family, children are forced into protective and stereotypic roles by the extreme dynamics of their family. While a common pattern of sibling roles is evident across alcoholic families (e.g., the scapegoat, mascot, lost child, etc.), those roles don't represent the essence of those children. Instead, each child is unique and, once released from his or her role by intervention, can find interests and talents separate from the demands of their chaotic family. The same process holds for internal families—parts are forced into extreme roles by external circumstances, and, once it seems safe, they gladly transform into valuable members.

What circumstances force these parts into extreme and sometimes destructive roles? Trauma is one factor and the effects of childhood sexual abuse on internal families has been discussed elsewhere (Goulding & Schwartz, 1995). But more often, the values and interaction patterns of a person's family create internal polarizations which escalate over time and are played out in other relationships. This also is not a novel observation; indeed it is a central tenet of object relations and self psychology. What is novel to IFS is the attempt to understand all levels of human organization—intrapsychic, family and culture—with the same systemic principles, and to intervene at each level with the same ecological techniques.

Are there common roles for parts across people? After I worked with a large number of clients, some patterns began to appear. Most clients had parts focused on keeping them functional and safe. These parts tried to maintain control of their inner and outer environments by, for example, keeping them from getting too close or dependent on others, criticizing their appearance or performance to make them look or act better, and focusing on taking care of others rather than on their own needs to ensure acceptance. These parts seemed to be in protective, managerial roles so they are called the managers.

Where a person has been hurt, humiliated, frightened or shamed in the past, they will have young parts that carry the emotions, memories and sensations from those experiences. We've all experienced at times child-like fears of aloneness, shame, vulnerability or pain. Managers often want to keep those feelings out of consciousness and, consequently, try to keep these vulnerable and needy parts locked in inner closets. Those incarcerated parts are known as the exiles.

The third and final group includes those parts that go into action whenever a young exiled part floods the person with extreme feelings or makes the person vulnerable to being hurt again. When that is the case, this third group tries to put out the inner flames of feeling as quickly as possible, so they are called the firefighters. They tend to be highly impulsive and seek stimulation that will override or dissociate the person from the exile's feelings. Bingeing on drugs, alcohol, food, sex, or work, are common firefighter activities.

The most crucial aspect of the IFS model that also differentiates it from other models is the belief that, in addition to these parts, everyone has at their core a Self that contains many valuable leadership qualities like perspective, confidence, compassion and acceptance. After working with hundreds of clients over the past decade, some of whom were severely abused and suffered severe symptoms, I've been convinced that everyone has this Self, despite the fact that many people have little access to it initially. When working with an individual, the goal of IFS is to differentiate this Self from the parts, thereby releasing its resources, and then, in the state of Self, to help parts realize that it's safe to leave their extreme roles.

DISCOURSES ON INTIMACY

Kathy Weingarten (1991) noted that although the marital and family therapy literature contains remarkably little on intimacy for a field concerned with intimate relationships, what is written corresponds to the two most common discourses on intimacy in our culture, discourses that she believes are problematic. The first, she calls the individual capacity discourse which focuses on a person's ability to be in touch with his or her own feelings and then to be able to disclose those feelings to another. The implication of this view is that, to be capable of intimacy, people have to work on themSelves. The second, she calls the quality of relatedness discourse which sees intimacy as the sense of belonging and connectedness that often takes years to achieve and is found exclusively in committed, long-term relationships. This suggests that interactions in casual or brief relationships that haven't undergone the requisite epigenetic stages cannot be truly intimate and are instead superficial.

Weingarten (1991) criticizes those two discourses because they take the focus away from single episodes of interaction and instead either point to individuals or to global assessments of relationships. She argues that each interactional sequence in any relationship, no matter how casual, can be classified as intimate or nonintimate depending on whether or not the interactants are involved in a process of mutual sharing or cocreating of meaning. By this she means whether or not they are interacting harmoniously—without imposing, rejecting, misunderstanding, or nonengaging with each other. She believes that this single episode definition of intimacy gives people more responsibility for creating intimacy in their everyday lives and in all their interactions.

The IFS perspective on intimacy doesn't take an either/or position regarding these three discourses—the individual capacity, the quality of relatedness, and Weingarten's single episode. Instead, the model offers a way to understand each of them as an important aspect of intimacy.

THE IFS MODEL'S DEFINITION
OF INTIMACY

From the IFS perspective, intimacy exists in any relationship when the interactants' Selves are involved to some degree in their interactions. This definition fits with each of the three discourses on intimacy. Relative to the individual capacity discourse, this definition suggests that in order to lead with his or her Self, a person has to convince parts that it is safe to do so. Relative to the quality of relatedness discourse, Self-to-Self connections can increase over time as parts gradually trust that they don't have to protect each person from the parts of the other. In the single interaction view, as people become increasingly Self-led, all their interactions become more harmonious and involve mutual exchanges, no matter how brief the encounter. Indeed, Self leadership is a major goal of the IFS model.

THE SELF

This IFS definition of intimacy cannot be grasped fully without a clear understanding of what is meant by the Self in the IFS model. The Self has been described in some detail elsewhere (Schwartz, 1995; Goulding & Schwartz, 1995), but here I will focus on the spiritual aspects of the Self.

In the IFS model, the Self is not analogous to the ego, as it has been traditionally defined, but rather the Self is more like the soul as described in many religious and spiritual practices. When people are able to convince their parts that it is safe to separate from their core, they gradually sense their defenses dropping and their hearts opening. They report feeling increasing equanimity, compassion and perspective. They sense a warm energy glowing through their bodies and their awareness is increasingly present-oriented—uncluttered by the usual stream of thoughts or fantasies. This is what I am calling their true, or core Selves.

I agree with Deepak Chopra's (1997) recent thoughts:

> Self and spirit are the same. Asking "What is spirit?" is just a way of asking "Who am I?" There isn't spirit outside you; you are it.... The "I" that is truly you is made of pure awareness, pure creativity, pure spirit ....(p. 33). What is important here is that the Self is a real experience. It is not an ideal far removed from reality—which is how most of us think of the soul—but is as close to you as breath. The Self is love's source, and therefore, it is more real than the things that block love—anger, fear, egotism, insecurity and mistrust (p. 14).

Peoples' protective parts are the ones that carry extreme emotions and beliefs—anger, fear, egotism, insecurity and mistrust and many others—that keep them from leading their lives with their Selves. These parts don't trust that it is safe to allow the Self to lead a person's life because of how much he or she has been hurt, rejected, humiliated, or abused in the past. These parts try to protect this inner core of love and compassion by burying it under extreme emotions or obscuring it behind the inner voices that shout "danger" or fantasize revenge. These parts will not release their grip on the Self until they are certain that it won't result in further damage.

Thus, many people have little or no awareness of their Selves. They might have vague inklings of the love that exists within them, but they spend their lives trying to get love from Mr. or Ms. Right, or give up the search and withdraw within the safe, lonely fortress their parts provide, keeping away from anyone who might stir the love within them. I believe that the desire for connection with another's Self is innate and very strong, but it can be overridden by fear that creates walls of separation.

A person who is leading with the Self is easy to identify. Others describe such a Self-led person as open, confident, and accepting. They feel immediately at ease in a Self-led person's presence, as their parts sense that it is safe to relax and release their own Selves. They sense in the person's eyes, voice, body-language, and energy that they are with a person who is "real," solid and unpretentious.

THE SELF-TO-SELF CONNECTION

The Self of one person can sense the presence of Self in another, no matter how minor the encounter or how nonintimate the context (e.g., a bank-teller and customer). On the other hand, people can be married or working on themSelves for years without ever experiencing Self-to-Self intimacy. Thus, the degree to which people sense that their interactions are intimate is related to the degree to which they release their Selves in each others' presence, not to the length or type of their relationship.

This position is similar to Weingarten's (1991) in that each interaction can be classified as intimate or not, based on how much Self connection is experienced between the interactants. With this definition, the content of the interaction is irrelevant. When Selves connect, people can be talking about sports, the weather, cooking, or not talking at all, and they will feel intimate. On the other hand, where the Self-to-Self connection is missing, people can be revealing their innermost secrets to each other and feel nonintimate or distant. We all know someone, for example, who might be called "pathologically Self-disclosive," baring his or her soul to anyone who'll listen in an effort to create a pseudo-intimate exchange. How can you tell it's false? You can sense the absence of Self.

When two people taste the Self-to-Self connection they reach, at least temporarily, across the walls separating them and experience, perhaps unconsciously, the awareness that all human beings are the same at some level. This awareness comforts and nourishes both people. They sense the love and compassion that exists in each other's hearts, and they have a glimpse of who they really are behind their protective masks. The tone of their interactions reflects that awareness, and they desire each other's company.

BREAKING THE SELF-TO-SELF CONNECTION

I believe that Self-to-Self relating is the natural state of human beings. If two people had been raised in ideally nurturing environments, they wouldn't have to work at being intimate in this sense. It would just happen effortlessly. Few of us have been so fortunate, however. Each hurtful interaction we had as a child convinced some parts of us that Self leadership is dangerous. Like parental children, those parts arrogated from the Self responsibility for dealing with the world and increasingly boxed in the Self's exuberance and openness. Even when those inner managers allow some of our Self's energy to flow in a relationship, they can rapidly whisk us back within walls of anger or fear at the first sign of danger. It's as if they have formed a castle within which they keep our Self and our other vulnerable parts (the exiles). Like sentries they constantly scan the environment for threats, particularly when they have allowed us to become vulnerable by dropping the drawbridge and releasing our Self. When the alarm sounds, they reel in our love and compassion, bolt the door and ready our inner army for battle.

Some of these protective managers are so effective that our internal experience shifts dramatically. Even with people I love a great deal, at times, I can immediately lose that love and feel nothing but disdain or anger toward them when they hurt me. The Self-to-Self connection is broken, as each of us retreats behind the walls of our respective castles.

RESILIENT INTIMACY

These sudden and radical emotional climate shifts can be extremely distressing to people, particularly if they don't trust that the Self-to-Self connection will return. When the clouds (parts) roll in and it gets cold, dark, and stormy, they don't believe that the sun (love) is still there behind the clouds. Instead, they panic and either try to coerce the other person into shining his or her love on them again, or conclude that the love is gone forever, so they should leave the relationship.

If, on the other hand, each partner trusts that the break in Self-to-Self connection is temporary—knows that their own and their partner's Selves are still there, even if they don't feel them—then, they weather the storm. Indeed, either of them can be an "I" of the storm—can remain relatively calm and centered, despite the turmoil within and around them. When this is the case, relationships attain a resilient intimacy, an underlying connection that cannot be broken by events or by parts of either person. People in such relationships tell each other, overtly or covertly, "I will always love you no matter what happens."

For Self-led people, this is true from the outset with most of their close relationships, because they tend to be drawn to other Self-led people, and because they trust the abiding nature of the connection, even when things get cold and dark. For others, resilient intimacy takes time to achieve, and some never achieve it. It takes many episodes with the same partner in which the connection feels broken and then comes back before they finally conclude that, at least with this one person, they can trust that the connection perseveres.

EXPOSING PARTS

Intimacy deepens when one person exposes to another parts that he or she feels ashamed of or embarrassed by (exiled or extreme firefighter parts), especially when the other person is Self-led. If the witness accepts and offers love to the revealer, their intimate connection is strengthened. The revealer feels tremendous relief and delight at having something shameful accepted and feels grateful to the witness, and the witness feels greater empathy for the revealer and feels privileged to be allowed into the revealer's inner sanctum. For example, if John has a part that gives him sexual fantasies about men, and he tells his wife Jenny about it, if she can stay her Self and react in a loving way, then John feels far more trusting of and intimately connected to her than before.

Whenever any previously hidden part is accepted this bonding increases, but this is particularly true for those parts we feel most ashamed of or think the other person disdains the most. In every relationship, there are parts of each person that feel happy with the relationship and others that feel they don't belong. When he married, the writer Michael Ventura (1988, p. 19) said this about his parts:

Some of them are gladly and enthusiastically married, with, as the wonderful old phrase goes, "abiding faith." Some are married but frightened, nervously married, hesitant as to their capacities, their endurance. Some are hostile to the marriage. The frightened and hostile ones may be in the minority, yet they exist, they speak with our mouths sometimes.

When any member of that frightened or hostile minority is revealed and feels understood or loved by the witness, the part feels jubilant and less inclined to find ways to break the Self-to-Self connection between the revealer and witness. The intimacy between them deepens.

Parts can be revealed in a number of ways, each of which involves more risk. The least risky is to simply disclose the part's existence, to tell one's partner about it. For example, "There's a part of me that has always feared you would discover that I'm really not smart and will leave me." The most risky is to let the part take over and interact directly with the witness. For example (said in a child-like voice), "I'm so scared that you won't like me because I'm stupid and worthless and you'll leave me." Of course, the latter can produce more intimate connection than the former, so the risk may be worth it. In general, however, bringing a part in any way into the stream of love created by a Self-to-Self connection heals the part's pain and fear and deepens the relationship. This is the most healing aspect of any kind of psychotherapy.

THE INNER CRITICS

There are good reasons, however, why we hesitate to expose our secret exiles and firefighters to one another. Certainly, we fear triggering the other's judgmental or angry parts that, at best, might add to our already sizable burden of shame and, at worst, lead the other to abandon us.

In addition, however, we worry about further triggering the judgmental parts that exist in us, parts that can be much harder on us than any outside person can be. We all have inner critics that attack our exiles and firefighters, fueled by perceived disapproval of others. Many people misunderstand the nature of these inner critics and judges and consequently both fear and hate them. From years of helping people get to know these parts, I have learned that, usually, they are trying to get us to behave in ways that key people value.

Because human beings depend on their caretakers for so long, they need, for their survival, to be valued by those on whom they depend. If a child isn't valued, it may not be fed, sheltered or protected. As a result, people are born with parts whose primary job is to find out what their parents value and get them to behave in that way. To do this, these parts often take on the image and voice of one or both parents, a process called internalization in other models of psychotherapy. Out of the desperate need to be pleasing, these parental replicas often express a parent's most shaming attitudes. They hate and try to eliminate the parts of us that our parents or other caretakers didn't like.

THE BURDEN OF WORTHLESSNESS

When a caretaker gives a child the message that he or she is worthless, shameful, bad, or defective, it not only bolsters the child's inner critics, it also injects the child with the belief that he or she is worthless and with the emotional shame and humiliation accompanying that belief. This message is sometimes delivered overtly (e.g., raging at a child and calling him "good for nothing"), but often covertly (e.g., treating the child like an object, as with sexual, emotional or physical abuse, or neglecting the child, giving the message that he or she is not important).

In the IFS model, these extreme beliefs and feelings are called burdens which become attached to parts that ultimately become the exiles. These child-like exiles steadfastly believe they are worthless, the worst possible feeling for a child-part who believes that survival depends on being valued. Consequently, exiles become desperate for the love or approval of the person who gave them the idea they were worthless, or of people who look, sound or act like that person. This is a special kind of redemption transference that plays a large role in intimacy.

THE DRIVE FOR REDEMPTION

The desire for acceptance consumes these exiles who feel so worthless; as a result they steer you toward the caretakers who originally hurt you, or toward someone who resembles those people. These parts will feel elated when they get some approval, acceptance, protection or love from your designated redeemer, because they are suddenly released from the dreadful burden of worthlessness. Unfortunately, the redemption is usually temporary, and the burden returns with a vengeance the second that the chosen redeemer shows disapproval, contempt, or acts in ways similar to the original burdening. Because the burden is so oppressive, and the temporary release of it is so exhilarating, people can become addicted to redeemer relationships and mistake the relief from worthlessness for the joy of Self-to-Self love.

Thus, the burden of worthlessness and drive for redemption interfere with Self-to-Self connections. Such relationships are often quite volatile, vacillating between elation and despair. The burdened person alternates between idolizing the designated redeemer and having an enraged, suicidal, or vengeful reaction when the redeemer hurts him or her again. The parts involved in all these reactions obscure the person's Self and keep the repetitive dance going. The redeemer, in his or her need to be adored, also has extreme parts interfering.

THE DANGER OF INTIMACY

I explored the dance of redemption in some detail because it helps illustrate the perils of trying to be intimate with another person. If you have severe inner critics, or have exiles that carry dreadful burdens, then when you try to become intimate with someone, you are inviting them to enter, and possibly live permanently in, your delicate and polarized inner world. With that entree, you are giving them two ways to hurt you.

Inviting Internal Tormentors   First, if the person rejects you, they can become another image in your inner pantheon of redeemers who turned into critics. That is, in addition to the parental replicas, critical parts will take on the voice, image and behaviors of people you opened up to later in your life. When such a relationship goes sour, that person can become the latest internal tormentor, as the part imitating that person attacks you with imagined or actual versions of the person's negative opinions.

In this sense then, when you try to be intimate with another person, you invite him or her to live, possibly permanently, inside your mind. You give that person the opportunity to become an internal tormentor for the rest of your life. This is a quite an invitation. Given what's at stake, it's understandable that many people fear intimacy and offer few, if any, such invitations.

Adding to the Burden   The second way you are inviting people to hurt you when you try to become intimate is by enabling them to add to your burden of worthlessness. This is particularly true if the person you are inviting in is a designated redeemer. If that person rejects or scorns you, then the swamp of worthlessness expands, and your exiles sink deeper into it. Yet another terrific person saw how vile you were, once you dropped your guard, and was repulsed. That pain can trigger dangerous firefighters who might resort to bingeing on various stimulating or sedating substances or activities, or to enraged or suicidal thoughts or behaviors.

The additional burdening can also intensify the dance of redemption, increasing your exiles' desperation for approval. Often, the more abusive a redeemer is, the more your parts crave his or her redemption. Many abusers instinctively recognize and exploit this pattern.

The odds of being scorned or rejected by a designated redeemer generally are high because that person, by virtue of being similar to the originally hurtful person, usually has parts that can hurt you in the same ways. In addition, people who accept the invitation to be a redeemer often have parts that need to be adored but don't respect those who adore them.

UNBURDENING

People remain trapped in the dance of redemption until their exiles have been able to unload permanently the worthlessness they carry. Until that time, your exiles will blindly seek redemption, and their protectors will anticipate and create rejection or abandonment, even when it's not really there. Sometimes you get lucky. You hook up with a perceived redeemer who has some Self-leadership and, by exposing your exiles to the love and acceptance of that person's Self, they unburden. That process can be slow and explosive, however, because it takes repeatedly breaking the Self-to-Self connection and finding that it bounces back before enough trust is built up in the constancy of that person's love to believe that you can't be that worthless if he or she loves you.

Fortunately, there is an alternative. By showing your exiles that you, as your Self, love them, they can show you where they picked up the burdens originally. That is, they can show you scenes from your past where you were hurt, humiliated, abandoned and rejected. Once those exiles believe that you understand where they got hurt and appreciate how bad it was, they can permanently remove the burdens and, with them, the drive for redemption. This process is described in detail elsewhere (Schwartz, 1995, 1997; Goulding & Schwartz, 1995).

Once these parts have been unburdened, they transform. They change in ways that cannot be predicted in advance, but always in positive ways. They are no longer exiles, because the need to keep them isolated no longer exists. No longer are they hypersensitive, desperately needy, clingy, or overly trusting and idolizing. Instead they become creative, lively, and fun. They want to be close to others, but they don't desperately need to be. They realize that they never needed redemption because they never were worthless. They can trust the leadership of their Self and, consequently, no longer are the prime movers in mate selection.

When the exiles are unburdened, your inner critics can also relax and find new roles. This is because there is no longer the intense need to get you to behave in ways that please redeemers.

INTIMACY BECOMES SAFE AND POSSIBLE

When this has taken place, Self-to-Self intimacy becomes possible. Intimacy no longer is so scary because you aren't inviting people into your mind or giving them the opportunity to add to your burden. Instead, you are inviting them to bask with you in the Self-to-Self connection. If they reject you at some point, you can care for, rather than exile and shame, the parts that get hurt. You quickly unload whatever burdening was involved and move toward people who can hold the Self-to-Self connection with you. As a Self-led person, you will attract others who are also Self-led, rather than redeemers.

In this chapter, I have presented a new definition of intimacy and some ideas about how it can be dangerous and yet made safe. Through my own personal experience and the experience of countless clients, I have concluded that achieving and maintaining Self-to-Self intimacy is the hardest work we'll ever do, but it is why we are here.

REFERENCES

Breulin, D. C., Schwartz, R. C., and Mac Kune-Karrer, B. (1992). *Metaframeworks: Transcending the Models of Family Therapy*. San Francisco: Jossey-Bass.

Chopra, D. (1997). *The Path to Love*. New York: Harmony Books.

Goulding, R. & Schwartz, R. (1995). *Mosaic Mind: Empowering the Tormented Selves of Childhood Sexual Abuse Survivors*. New York: Norton.

Nichols, M. & Schwartz, R. (1997). *Family Therapy Concepts and Methods*. (4th Ed.). Cambridge MA: Allyn and Bacon.

Schwartz, R. (1987). Our multiple Selves. *Family Therapy Networker*, *11*, 24–31.

Schwartz, R. (1988). Know thy Selves. *Family Therapy Networker*, *12*, 21–29.

Schwartz, R. (1992). Rescuing the exiles. *Family Therapy Networker*, May–June, 22–28.

Schwartz, R. (1995). *Internal Family Systems Therapy*. New York: Guilford.

Schwartz, R. (1997). Don't look back. *Family Therapy Networker*. March/April, 40–45.

Ventura, M. (1988). In the marriage zone. *Family Therapy Networker*, *12*, 10–20.

Weingarten, K. (1991). The discourses of intimacy: Adding a social constructionist and feminist view. *Family Process*, *30*, 285–305.

CHAPTER 15

The Issue of Intimacy in Marriage

Dorothy E. Peven, M.S.W.
Bernard H. Shulman, M.D.

INTIMACY, COOPERATION AND EQUALITY

Many people believe they are missing something if they do not have what is called intimacy in their marriages. This concept has apparently developed within the last century. For thousands of years, and still today in some parts of the world, married couples were not and are not expected to be intimate. If intimacy developed, it was considered a bonus.

Marriages were contracts drawn up by parents in exchange for goods and services. Many marriages were arranged to join families and fortunes as well as land. A community often had a marriage broker such as Yentl in the musical *Fiddler on the Roof*. When Tevye, the protagonist, asks his wife, "Do you love me?" she answers, "For 25 years I kept his house and he asks if I love him." Little consideration was given to romantic love.

It has always been acknowledged, however, that there must be a warm, secure place in which to raise children. But not all societies raise children in the setting of a nuclear family with two parents. Yet all societies have developed an institution of marriage—a type of social, sexual, and economic unit whose most important function has been to rear the young. In the past, when life expectancy was much lower than now, people did not expect to be married for 50 or 60 years even though the sexual behavior of humans tends to bond the mates together beyond child rearing.

One of the consequences of this increased life expectancy is that we ask much more of our marriages than we did in the past. Previously, we reached physical maturity, found a mate, raised children and died. Today, we expect our mates to be companions, friends, lovers—to provide everything we want and like about other people combined in one person for 50 years! And we are disappointed if the excited tingle of romantic love does not last for half a century. Yet, for centuries, the consideration of intimacy and romantic love was not thought of as a prerequisite for marriage by many philosophers and psychologists.

For example, Alfred Adler believed that the primary requisite for a successful marriage was cooperation. He says:

> Love, with its fulfillment, marriage, is the most intimate devotion toward a partner of the other sex, expressed in physical attraction, in comradeship, and in the decision to have children. It can easily be shown that love and marriage are one side of co-operation—not a co-operation for the welfare of two persons only, but a co-operation also for the welfare of humanity. (Ansbacher & Ansbacher, 1978, p. 122.)

This passage reflects Adler's views of the laws of human nature. We are a species designed to reproduce "for the welfare of humanity." And in order to do so, we must be able to "put aside personal pride and private striving," to understand that "...we are living in two sexes...on the crust of this earth...with the future of our race dependent on the relations of these two sexes." (p. 123). Adler does not suggest that the married couple have to share every thought and feeling. Rather, he believes that the basis for marriage has more to do with consideration, respect and trust. He says:

> The fundamental guarantee of marriage [is] the feeling that you are worthwhile, that you cannot be replaced, that your partner needs you, that you are acting well, that you are a fellow man and a true friend. [But] comrades must be equal, [for] when people are equal, they will always find a way to settle their difficulties." (1978, p. 125)

Adler traces many difficulties in social relationships, including marriage, to the issue of equality. He asks for an increase in equality between men and women, for he sees the consequence of inequality as resentment and hostility. Dreikurs (1946) defined social equality as a relationship of mutual respect and task cooperation. In marriage, with its division of labors, this respect and cooperation results in the smooth functioning of the marriage itself. However, personal expectations, demands, idealized images and private motives can impair the relationship. When one spouse feels the other is disrespectful, mutual accusations and hurt feelings result. Once couples are in conflict over dominance or anything else for that matter, there will be no intimacy.

Rubin (1983, p. 90) defines intimacy as "...some kind of reciprocal expression of feeling and thought...out of a wish to know another's inner life and to be able to share one's own." She believes that problems in intimacy have to do with the differences between men and women...how they are raised (antithetically), and how they resolve their Oedipal and Electra complexes. Woman do not have to break ties with mother, while men, on the other hand, are forced to repress the bonding with mother which leads to the inability to express feeling and be intimate (Rubin, pp. 38–46).

SEX AND INTIMACY

Usually, young couples in the first throes of romantic, erotic love will wish to know everything about the other person and want to share everything about themselves. In fact, in the earlier stages of a marriage an erotic attraction is almost required. Sexual passion usually includes a desire for intimacy. In fact, that is how we choose to define intimacy, as a desire, the feeling of curiosity, wanting to know everything about the loved one, the feeling of wanting to share everything, the longing to be as close, physically and emotionally, as possible. Each wants the other to be a best friend. Each wants to be able to tell the other anything and to feel assured that whatever is said will be received with tolerance, sympathy and empathic understanding.

In the beginning, couples overlook many things. They may forgive or not notice foibles. As time goes by and they start to deal with the realities of living, the feelings of closeness may diminish. Children, instead of drawing them closer, often interfere and disrupt the harmony that has been established. He sees her as tied to the baby. She sees him as another baby, crying for attention. He snores, she hangs her stockings in the bathroom. The other has become predictable. The absence of novelty reduces the curiosity, and the need to know recedes. They get busy as family and careers develop, and partners often start to feel deprived.

For some, intimacy means sexual intimacy. But sexual intimacy itself is influenced by the state of the relationship and the couple's willingness to cooperate. In fact, the couple's sexual behavior is not usually the source of trouble in a marriage. Behavior in bed is most likely a reflection of the partner's willingness to cooperate, and, if they know how to cooperate with each other, they will find an accomodation in bed. For example:

Joe and Mim were married for over 20 years when laissez-faire sexual attitudes of the late sixties and seventies came along. They discussed their sex life and decided that they had not been very adventurous. So they bought a sex manual and tried the exercises one chapter at a time. What they both enjoyed, they kept...the rest they just let go.

Joe and Mim demonstrate how cooperation is working together for the common good, promoting and enforcing the relationship bond. This requires trust, loyalty, appreciation, recognition, goodwill and respect.

CONFLICT

It is unreasonable, but not uncommon, for naifs to expect no conflict. It happens. Yet the response to conflict will depend on the coping method that has been developed. Some people respond to conflict with passivity or remove themselves. Others respond with aggressive attacks, and still others seek revenge. Many partners harbor unspoken hostility, while others feel critical whether they express it or not. Still another coping method is distance-keeping. And, strangely, some marriages work out well this way.

> Susan and George were married for 20 years when she came to the office complaining about the behavior of her 16-year-old son. The boy was fresh, disrespectful, paid no attention to her rules, was cruel to his younger brother, and listened only to father, and only when father came down hard. Eventually she started to talk about her marriage and how lonely and neglected she felt. Her husband, George, worked 10 hours a day and often on weekends. When he came home at night, he made business calls. Susan was a rather passive person, and, when she complained about feeling neglected, she was not very forceful. George ignored her and continued doing as he pleased (as did his son). They talked about nothing but the behavior of the children. They shared nothing but the house, and conversation was limited to the comings and goings of the household.
> Susan was close to her parents and her in-laws and found therapy a great relief. She spoke of all her feelings, longings and emotions but continued to complain about George's lack of interest in her. But she never, not for a moment, thought of leaving him or taking any action. She was even reluctant to invite him to join her in therapy.
> Over time, Susan became so accustomed to her situation she no longer invited intimacy. In fact, they continue to share very little other than the household and children affairs. Both partners feel they have a livable arrangement and express no interest in moving closer together.

By keeping himself, and all information about himself, from Susan, George successfully disengaged himself. He feels no responsibility for Susan's emotional life. He shows Susan little attention and treats her as if her needs are unimportant. And she, who feels inadequate to influence George, has accommodated by finding friends with whom she can share intimate thoughts and feelings. She cannot confront, nor does she feel able to influence George's behavior.

Perhaps a good, solid shouting match would have helped. After all, fighting is a very forceful way of being involved with another person, and people who fight can also be intimate with one another. Anger is a strong bond that keeps some people attached to each other.

> Jan and Bob were married for 10 years before they had children, and the two of them were completely wrapped up in each other. When their oldest son became an adolescent, he started using drugs, driving recklessly, sneaking out at night, and mouthing off at his mother and father. Jan and Bob fiercely disagreed about how to deal with their son. And one night, Bob got so angry he punched the boy who then proceeded to call the police and have his father arrested for child abuse.
>
> Mother wanted to defend her baby against his wicked, violent father, and father was raging incoherently against mother and her "ignorance" about raising children. In the office, the couple screamed at each other, and, when the boy came in with them, there was nothing but chaos.
>
> Yet, through it all, the therapist was aware that mother and father continued to feel very close to each other, that they shared each other's lives, and that they had a very satisfactory sex life. In fact, they both believed that, if it weren't for the children, they would have continued a relatively trouble-free marriage. In spite of their violent behavior toward each other (sometimes their fights became physical), they continued to feel close to each other and to share each others lives. They are passionately involved, and, in spite of their differences, they trust one another.

TRUST

Trust is the willingness to put yourself in the other's hands. When people feel betrayed they are no longer willing to share themselves with another. No longer will they disclose information since they feel the other will use the information against them, insult them, betray them or shame them. When trust dies, so does intimacy.

> Jamie and John came to our office about six months after they were married. They had used the money from their wedding gifts and money borrowed from parents for John to open a business. A few days earlier Jamie had gone over all the books and learned that John had lost all of the money invested in the business in a pyramid scheme and had been lying to her for six months about what happened to the money. She was prepared to leave him, but coming for counseling seemed to signal the possibility that she was looking for an alternative to divorce.

John got on his knees and begged her to forgive him. He swore he would never ever again do anything to betray her trust in him. After a few months, Jamie's anger dissipated, they thanked us and went on their way.

Five years later Jamie called. John had started his own business, again, and this time, she was keeping the books. She found an unpaid bill, and, when asked, John said he had taken care of it. Three months later the bill was still coming in. Jamie discovered the bill had not been paid and accused John of lying and doing what he had done five years before. Although she had forgiven, she had not forgotten and says she will never again trust her husband.

A reopened wound becomes harder to heal.

Marge and Hank had been married for 11 years and had built a rather stable marriage. They were of the same ethnic background, had come from the same neighborhood and the families knew each other and were very glad to be related to each other. There was one daughter, eight years old, and both parents worked and lived relatively comfortable lives in a middle-class suburb.

The secretary at Hank's place of work was an attractive woman and she made it known to Hank that she was available. Hank succumbed to the temptation, and they started an extramarital affair that lasted almost one year.

Marge knew something was wrong with the marriage and asked Hank to join her in marriage counseling. Since they were both Catholic, she suggested the Parish priest. He agreed. The priest saw them together and then asked to speak to each separately. Alone with the priest, Hank confessed his indiscretion. The priest then called Marge back into the room and told her that Hank was having an affair.

That was the end of the marriage.

The importance of confidentiality would restrict a therapist from acting as this priest did. But there is some reason to question whether it is helpful for a partner to share information about sexual misbehavior with the spouse. Betraying a mate and then informing the mate of the betrayal is not usually helpful to a marriage. The injured person feels humiliated, hurt. He or she may forgive, but, like Jamie, never forget. Bitterness, outrage and obsessive rumination about the details of the affair last for months. In effect, the act of confessing to the injured party may do more damage than the betrayal itself.

Straying partners will often say that they feel so guilty that they want to make things right. However, the confession is for the benefit of the one who feels the guilt, not for the benefit of the one who receives the news. The innocent spouse feels humiliated, and the straying one feels shame.

Intimacy, as commonly defined, means that each spouse can be free to tell the other everything that ever happened in the past and what they think or feel at any given moment, ignoring the need for tact, courtesy, and compassion and oblivious to the effect which the information will have on the spouse. Sharing information is not desirable when it risks severe damage to the mate. There is a difference between keeping secrets and maintaining privacy. For the therapist, the issue is not, "should there be a confession?" Rather, it is "Why did this happen?" "Why did this person put the marriage in jeopardy?"

RESPECT

One of the vital components of a satisfying relationship is respect.

> Lois and Bernie had been married for less than a year. He was a successful business man, and she was a recently graduated lawyer 15 years younger than he. It was the first marriage for both. They came with vague complaints about not being able to get along. They had fallen in love and married within three months and felt quite passionate about each other. Their fights were passionate, their sex was passionate, but they were dissatisfied with their marriage.
>
> It was difficult to discern what they were squabbling about, until Lois told a story about how a legal question had come up in Bernie's business, and he immediately called his lawyer. She was outraged. She had struggled through law school, been on law review, passed her boards on the first try, and was being courted by several big law firms. Yet her husband had not even asked her opinion about the legal matter before calling his old friend. Lois believed she deserved more respect than Bernie was giving her. On the one hand he saw her as a young, inexperienced woman and on the other hand, he truly loved her and wanted her as his wife. When it was pointed out to him that he was not demonstrating respect for his wife's intelligence and professionalism, he understood immediately, apologized to her, and asked her to please put up with him until he got used to being married.
>
> Unable to articulate what had so riled her, Lois was pleased and satisfied. The great goodwill between them survived. The marriage proceeded apace and five years later there were four children. (One set of twins.)

Past Influences

One of the psychological givens is that behavioral responses learned in childhood are used in the present. In order to discover these behaviors, the Adlerian therapist examines certain aspects of the past such as early family influences (Family Constellation) and the earliest childhood recollections. This information elicits the lifestyle which is the observations, interpretations and conclusions about life made as children and which are carried throughout life. The couple's interaction will be a demonstration of their lifestyle beliefs.

Jack and Mary came in because Mary noticed that Jack didn't seem to be happy and Mary insisted on marriage counseling. Jack was coming home later and later and expressing dissatisfaction with the marriage, with Mary, and with the behavior of their four children. Mary wanted to know why Jack was so unhappy, and Jack kept saying, "It's not your fault. It's something inside of me."

The therapist's first reaction was that Jack was having an affair. Alone, Jack denied an affair but talked about the lovely woman at the office with whom he could share his thoughts and feelings. With some probing, Jack admitted how very angry he was at Mary. His biggest complaint was that she tried to settle all problems and conflicts at the top of her voice. But what he actually hated about her was that she screamed and hollered at the children. He had not, however, ever discussed his feelings with Mary.

An examination of Jack's lifestyle revealed several pertinent issues. Jack was the middle of five children and he did not like nor appreciate his mother. He said she screamed and hollered at the children "constantly" and showed no tolerance, kindness nor understanding of how much her loud and public criticism hurt the children's feelings. Some of the children yelled back at mother, but Jack's response was to turn away. He had learned to avoid open conflict believing it was useless. And so, he never confronted Mary. The behavior he had developed as a child was carried over into the marriage relationship.

Comprehension of Jack's lifestyle helped to determine the source of conflict in their marriage. This type of examination helps to reveal what is important to each partner. Is one seeking attention? The other, power? Is there a battle for dominance going on? Does one insist things always go his or her way? Is one displaying inadequacy and the other resentful of carrying the burden of responsibility? Do they secretly enjoy the fighting and the wrestling and not really want to stop? Are they cooperating with each other in order to fight and create commotion, and can they learn to cooperate within the vicissitudes of daily living? Most important, what were the expectations each had of the other when they first married? For as Dreikurs (1946) says:

> Behind a concrete problem and overt frictions are general attitudes and erroneous conceptions. Many disappointments derive from comparing past expectations with present circumstances. Unfortunately, both are often misinterpreted. We rarely are aware of what we expected, and we frequently misjudge what we have (p. 185).

ANGER AND WARFARE

Anger is, by far, the most common emotion demonstrated by the couples we see. It can be understood in many ways, usually as an attempt to overpower. Often, angry feelings are not openly expressed, and people don't recognize how angry they feel and how it influences their behavior. Couples who are angry are fighting a war, and the various complaints they have reflect the battles that ensue between them as they fight. Once in a while, a cease-fire erupts, but a peace treaty has not been negotiated. It becomes the therapist's responsibility to work toward a peaceful solution to the war. Therefore, we try to understand exactly why these people are angry at each other and look for information that will be helpful.

Adlerian therapists most often see themselves as teachers. It is in this sense that we try to explain the couple to each other and, thus, demonstrate areas of possible conflict—what is important to one is not important to the other, demonstrations of affection, saving money, etc. As teachers we inform and define the conflict between couples as war. This allows both parties to be more honest about what they are doing to each other and helps them recognize their anger and discuss their fights as battles in the war. We believe that it isn't the lack of intimacy that makes the trouble between the couple, but the lack of intimacy is a consequence of the fight and the anger generated.

When couples complain about lack of intimacy, we understand them to be angry at each other, finding fault with each other, and going in different directions rather than cooperating. Therefore, we do not try to promote intimacy, but we do try to find out what the fight is about and stop it. Hopefully, when the couple become friendlier toward each other they will become more intimate. Yet, we understand that people can like each other and want to be with each other and, yes, even cooperate with each other, but may not want to share their secrets, thoughts, ideas and beliefs—the common currency of intimacy. How much intimacy is desired is a reflection of the individual lifestyle. Some people find it very important, but for others it is undesirable.

Revealing oneself completely to somebody else is something very few people do with very few other people. Married couples can cooperate, treat each other with mutual respect, and be affectionate with each other without knowing all the secret details of the other. What is required for a fulfilling marriage is information sufficient to permit cooperative interaction and loving interest.

REFERENCES

Adler, A. (1978). *Cooperation between the sexes: writings on women, love and marriage, sexuality and its disorders*. (H. Ansbacher & R. Ansbacher Ed. and Trans.) Garden City, New York: Anchor Books.
Dreikurs, R. (1946). *The challenge of marriage*. New York: Hawthorn Books.
Rubin, L. (1983). *Intimate strangers; men and women together*. New York: Harper and Row.

CHAPTER 16

Intimacy as a Goal and Tool in Adlerian Couples Therapy

Steven Slavik

Jon Carlson

Len Sperry

The value of clarifying feelings and opinions regarding oneself and one's partner in couples therapy seems understated in many current therapies. In *The Handbook of Family Therapy*, Volume I and II (Gurman & Kniskern, 1981, 1991), only Contextual Family Therapy and Integrative Family Therapy consider improved intimacy as either a primary goal or tool of therapy with couples. Such undervaluation of intimacy is supported by family therapy theories which cast family structure as adversarial and power based (Foley, 1984; Minuchin, 1974; Wile, 1981) and which do not contain a concept isomorphic with intimacy as used here.

The purpose of this chapter is to formulate a working concept of intimate transactions in relationships, and show how intimacy may be used in couples therapy as a goal and tool. The purpose is to develop a concept to facilitate working with couples, rather than to extend theorizing about intimacy. This chapter briefly describes how therapists might encourage couples to become more intimate and offers several techniques which both use and increase the intimacy in a relationship. An Adlerian formulation of relationships is used in this presentation (Sherman & Dinkmeyer, 1987).

UNDERSTANDING AND DEFINITION
OF INTIMACY

Intimacy is a condition in which persons know or are familiar with one another. It is facilitated through the intentional and accepting disclosure of feelings and thought by oneself or others (Wong & McKeen, 1992). Specifically, through the disclosure of one's long-term body sense, self-image, images of the world and of others, preferences, and current or momentary opinions, beliefs, judgments and feelings relevant to a given situation, one locates oneself and others in a common world (Shulman, 1973; Wong & McKeen, 1992). The idea of locating oneself is a generalization of the idea of taking an "I" position, as described by many authors (Dinkmeyer & Dinkmeyer, 1981; Freeman, 1991; Sherman & Dinkmeyer, 1987), with the difference that, here, an "I" position explicitly locates oneself in the social field. Locating oneself and others implies two abilities: the ability to reflect and comment on one's own and another's style of communication; and the ability to consider changes in how one communicates and relates (Perlmutter & Hatfield, 1980). For example, blaming is not an intimate form of communication, whereas saying, "I like to blame," may be.

AGREEMENTS

Partners in relationship function with one another as if they have agreements defining how they will interact (Dreikurs, 1968; Sperry, 1978). Their agreements both state and regulate what they habitually do under certain circumstances: who does what to whom, when, where, and with what consequence (Minuchin, 1974). When bad or undesirable events occur, agreements have particular importance. Agreements define, or punctuate, bad events and allocate who gets to be, on the one hand, angry or blaming, and, on the other, withdrawing or guilty. The particular style of anger and withdrawal is also defined. For example, if a couple habitually discuss differences of opinion and come to a decision, but one party does not carry out his or her end, and the other party wonders why and feels sad and helpless, they have an agreement. Agreements also define good events concomitant with who is allowed to feel loving, kind, secure, or happy. "When you buy me flowers, I feel respected," is an example.

Couples make both vertical and horizontal agreements (Allred, 1976; Mozdzierz & Lottman, 1973). Vertical agreements are strategies for short-term self-enhancement (Allred, 1976). They are characterized by communication in which a literal message is communicated and command aspects of the message, which connote who is superior and who inferior, are covert (Perlmutter & Hatfield, 1980). Intimacy, or location of one another, is neither overtly communicated nor desired. Horizontal agreements are strategies for common, long-term goals (Allred, 1976). Command aspects in horizontal agreements are less covert; location of one another is clearer, either from previous or current discussion. Horizontal agreements can be intimate or nonintimate.

An agreement is always cooperative. Whether horizontal or vertical, whether in desirable or undesirable events, whether overtly or covertly negotiated, partners always cooperate in agreements in which they participate (Dreikurs, 1967, 1968; Mozdzierz & Friedman, 1978). Even those agreements in which partners complain the most and in which they blame the most are cooperative; part of the agreement is to designate who blames and complains. There are only nominal victims and masters in agreements; in fact, no one dominates and no one submits (Mozdzierz & Friedman, 1978). The assumption that one can control others or be controlled by others is merely justification for blame. People are equal and enter into agreements for their own purposes, primarily in order to belong in a fashion to which they are historically accustomed (Dreikurs, 1946, 1971).

THE VERTICAL AGREEMENT

Participants in a *vertical agreement* are concerned with establishing and preserving arrangements of authority, prestige, or control, or all three (Allred, 1976; Wong & McKeen, 1992). A vertical agreement is embodied and embedded in arrangements undertaken to gain prestige in the eyes of others, to initiate and manage impressions, to preserve preferred status through fictions of domination and submission, to maintain roles, privileges, and obligations, and, simply, to control self and others (Wong & McKeen, 1992). The command level of language use communicates the intent to control (Allred, 1976; Perlmutter & Hatfield, 1980). It is usually through subtle, covert, hinting cues or messages that an individual who seeks to relate vertically attempts to control the responses of others. In a vertical agreement, one locates oneself and others through roles, duties, and obligations, rather than through inquiry, observation, curiosity, and choice. Intimacy between parties is discouraged; reflection on vertical agreements is not welcomed.

Vertical arrangements in relationships are readily established and accepted by discouraged and pessimistic partners. Agreements between such partners are seldom overtly negotiated because neither expects to be dealt with fairly, to be listened to, or to be respected. Further, they act on beliefs that they are not efficacious in life. They expect to be defeated, and they expect to have to continue to safeguard themselves as they always have. Accordingly, partners attempt to force one another into roles or maintain one another in roles where each feels secure or safe. In so doing, they encourage, arrange, or pull behaviors from one another that enable them to confirm, justify, and maintain usual responses toward one another. As they respond, each continually obtains proof that his or her opinion of the other is correct and that he or she is justified in responding in the usual way. In sum, vertical agreements verify, justify, and maintain partners' guiding lines, resulting in a system of repeated, habitual interactions.

Through these tactics, partners maintain self-esteem and the sense that "I'm right," or righteousness, at the expense of the other. This self-esteem is based on payoffs or results of tactics rather than on valuing oneself and others more-or-less unconditionally (O'Connell, 1975). A fragile self-esteem based on results might be contrasted with a gentle self-compassion or appreciation for oneself (Wong & McKeen, 1992).

In summary, vertical agreements are made to produce guaranteed results. They avoid intimacy; the greater one's discouragement and pessimism, the more expedient and the less intimate one is.

Examples

Covert vertical agreements in relationships frequently seen in marriage counselors' offices include the following.

1   We never express anger to one another.

2   We never have or discuss differences of opinion with one another. But it's OK to complain to others.

3   When we discuss differences, I get to be angry and you get to give in, feel resentful, and have physical problems.

4   If I initiate sex, you refuse and I/you feel...; if you initiate sex, I accept and I/you get to feel... We don't discuss it.

5   I get to withdraw when you are excited or angry and want to discuss a problem you experience with me.

6   I get to be cold and haughty regarding issues, and you get to be hot and demanding.

7   I get to be angry and fearful whenever you drink alcohol; you get to be furtive, guilty, and resentful.

8   You get to hit me and I get to complain and be resentful. I won't do anything effective about it. I get to blame you. You get to blame me for blaming you.

9   I get to be ambiguous about any issue or task and you get to be frustrated, angry, and critical.

10   I get to worry and you get to try to talk me out of my worries.

Mozdzierz and Lottman (1973) describe other, more general and stereotyped agreements. The examples presented here are specific and their operation depends on specific sensitivities of individuals in relationships.

MECHANICS OF VERTICAL AGREEMENTS: PAMPERING AND ABUSE

Two typical ways of establishing vertical agreements involve: pampering, doing for others what they can do for themselves; or abuse and neglect, expecting and/or trying to force others to do what they are not capable of doing (Adler, 1956).

In order to initiate and/or maintain either a pampering or an abusive and neglectful relationship requires two positions: the one up and the one down position (Mozdzierz & Friedman, 1978). The one down must take a stance that "I can't manage without help in life." "I can't manage" is shown through arranged helplessness or symptomology (both representing pessimism and discouragement, or extreme sensitivity [Adler, 1956; Wile, 1981]). It is a tactic designed to produce a certain result. The one up must act as if "I can help you manage" (pampering) or "I'll make you manage" (abuse or neglect), that is, must act either actively to accept or to reject the helpless position. It also is a tactic. Agreements and arrangements originate with the pessimism, discouragement, and extreme sensitivity of the person(s) responding to the original stance. Neither represents interest in the other person.

Any combination of adult-adult or adult-child interaction can be pampering or neglectful and abusive. Children can neglect and abuse or pamper their parents as well as vice versa. Parents and children train one another (Howing, Wodarski, Kurtz, Gaudin, & Herbst, 1990). In couples, each partner establishes and maintains the relationship in the fashion which he or she understands, and as a way to retain a lifestyle. Pampering or abusive and neglectful agreements are established in which both partners consent and cooperate, and they are used to justify or excuse one's own style.

THE HORIZONTAL AGREEMENT

Partners make many overt and covert agreements that are directed toward a mutual goal, and that can be called horizontal. For example, agreements regarding housework, sexual relations, and parenting may be agreements in which both partners cooperate to accomplish a goal. One must frequently, but not always, disclose wants, preferences, and feelings in order to negotiate a horizontal agreement. In the operation of a nonintimate, horizontal agreement, just as in a vertical agreement, no communication about the agreement occurs and no possibility for change exists unless the agreement is readdressed. However, close collaboration in daily living requires extended disclosure of one's judgments and feelings regarding one another and regarding tasks.

THE ANTIDOTE TO VERTICAL AGREEMENTS: INTIMACY

An intimate agreement is a horizontal agreement in which one is concerned with location of oneself and another, knowing and revealing self and being interested in one's partner. It is not a tactic intended to pull a certain response from another (Wong & McKeen, 1992). Being intimate is a mutually negotiated transactional pattern in which the openness in feelings and judgments of one partner is met with similar openness and curiosity from the other.

Rather than arranging situations where one continuously feels good, justified, or righteous, in an intimate agreement the pretense of control of one's partner or by one's partner is (at least eventually) revealed openly, discussed, negotiated, and, perhaps, discarded. In an intimate agreement, it is possible to recognize and acknowledge one's intent to control and one's usual methods of control. One can also recognize one's ongoing competence in life and discard blaming others for one's difficulties and opportunities.

As partners gain confidence, vertical agreements in a relationship can be modified and discarded. When partners modify vertical agreements and become more intimate with one another, each becomes self-accepting and compassionate. Partners then grow into further courage and self-encouragement. When one has courage, one lives with fewer vertical or expedient arrangements with others. As one becomes more intimate with oneself, one is likely to become more intimate with others. Many vertical agreements can be discarded when one lives and shares one's opinions and feelings about one's partner without trying to change him or her (Sherman, Oresky, & Rountree, 1991). Wile (1981) states a similar assumption: "Problems occur between partners when they act on feelings rather than acknowledge them" (p. 197).

GENERAL THERAPEUTIC CONSEQUENCES

An advantage this conceptual schematic offers for therapy with couples is a clear-cut analysis of difficulties. All difficulties in relationships are construed as covert, vertical agreements where both partners are stating, "I'll have my own way," or "I won't be defeated." This is a hostile stance in regard to one another. The position may be disguised with guilt or shame, resulting in further reduced intimacy. This schematic also offers a resultant simplified idea of doing therapy: to promote intimacy, directness, and egalitarian agreements in a relationship.

In promoting intimacy, the therapist neither opposes partners nor sides with either one. To oppose or take sides pampers or abuses or both (Mozdzierz & Friedman, 1978). The therapist joins in a horizontal fashion to explore alternatives without pampering and to disagree without abusing or closing down possibilities (Hudson & O'Hanlon, 1991). If, through warm curiosity, the therapist helps the couple formulate intimate solutions to difficulties—if solutions is the correct word at all—he or she helps to create lasting and flexible relationships. Duhl and Duhl (1981) believe that for many couples those approaches that cool off the power games and demonstrate processes of curiosity and intimacy are appropriate. Likewise, from a Bowenian perspective, Freeman (1991) states that it is effective to take "I" positions to prevent being triangled and to take a research stance to help family members learn about themselves and solve their own problems.

Curiosity signifies the therapist's willingness to be interested in others and to respond to vertical agreements in such a way as to open opportunities for partners' intimacy. Curiosity is the essence of social interest in the therapeutic situation (O'Connell, 1975; Sherman, Oresky, & Rountree, 1991). The curious therapist "must stop, look and listen, paraphrase and guess gently at... feelings, assume attentive postures, and be willing to be open about his own mistakes and feelings in a nonsuperior, nondemanding way." "Spitting in the soup" is often required: One must anticipate, verbalize, but *not reinforce* [another's] useless goals or ways of influencing others (O'Connell, 1975, p. 49).

The curious therapist does not work on or trick the client to change since the client is not an adversary. He or she does not try to fix a client who is not broken. He or she does not assume that paradox is essential in working with a couple who can be responsible for themselves and who can understand themselves in direct ways.

In being curious there is no guaranteed result, only mutual exploration, recognition, and, perhaps, appreciation. Curiosity may work, but it is not a tactic and its motive is not to obtain results. The therapist understands and encourages each partner to make decisions without guilt or shame. The curious therapist helps each partner quit excusing himself or herself. The aim is for the therapist "to come to see and appreciate the world through the client's eyes,... not try to manipulate their clients' lives from arm's length... or passively listen and understand;... instead, they become *involved* in their clients' experiences, mutually sharing thoughts, interpretations, and feelings as a way of facilitating clients' awareness of themselves in relationship" (Wong & McKeen, 1992, p. 137). In the process, therapist and partners recognize, enjoy, and explore diversity and difference, rather than approve movement in certain directions (Kiesler, 1983; O'Connell, 1975).

Such recognition may look confrontative; it may even be confrontative for clients who are not used to and do not want intimate relationships. But it is not adversarial, since the therapist's motive has changed. He or she tries to know and to understand partners, not change them. Technique is not needed as an armamentarium to change (Carlson & Slavik, 1997). One needs heart and understanding. One needs to know how to make a common goal with someone. One needs to know how to give up distance. As the therapist gains more courage, he or she can abdicate vertical arrangements in therapy and treat the members of a couple and himself or herself as individuals who can be involved (Duhl & Duhl, 1981; Wile, 1981).

SPECIFIC THERAPEUTIC CONSEQUENCES AND TECHNIQUES

Specific therapeutic consequences follow from this position. Specific therapist qualities and the goals of therapy in working with couples become important aspects of treatment. A number of techniques seem appropriate expressions of curiosity and useful means to help clients increase intimacy.

THERAPIST QUALITIES

A therapist who has goals for a couple that are not mutually negotiated is trying to arrange a vertical agreement and to impose goals on the client. The therapist is, then, either pampering or abusive or both. A therapist who needs control or prestige through work will be involved in a vertical struggle in which he or she assumes the client is wrong and needs fixing, or helpless and needs aid. A therapist who tries to force certain results by creating clients' goals may become frustrated, may become angry and aligned with some partners against others, may meet resistance, may need to find tactics to overcome it, and may burn out. Such attitudes do not create and maintain a cooperative therapeutic climate. The therapist may have unexamined assumptions regarding how couples should operate and regarding his or her own position in life (Slavik, Carlson, & Sperry, 1993). In sum, the therapist must not be more ambitious than the client (Adler, 1956).

The therapist neither pampers nor abuses the individual. The therapist neither accepts a burden of helplessness from another nor tries to force another away from this position. He or she recognizes the position. The therapist may point out inclinations of a partner to create helplessness or may point out other arrangements that either partner seeks to maintain (Kiesler, 1983; O'Connell, 1975). The therapist may recognize how partners use one another as obstacles in justifying blame. But if the therapist helps to establish vertical arrangements in relationships, he or she is, in the long run, helping people to retreat from the task of intimacy and, likely, helping to formulate arrangements with little lasting value.

THE GOALS OF THERAPY

The only goal that is not vertical is using simple curiosity in a mutually agreed upon goal. Accordingly, marital therapy may address two primary points. The first is to help in making specific covert, vertical agreements overt, and to aid in negotiating new, horizontal agreements. The second is to teach those who are interested to be intimate: to clarify expectations, assumptions, and sensitivities about oneself and one's partner, to clarify how each tries to force assumptions and expectations into covertly negotiated agreements, and finally to clarify styles in general.

Couples can be helped to work toward overtly negotiated, horizontal agreements. The covert can be made overt, and the overt can be renegotiated. Over specific issues, the therapist may help each partner to dissolve guilt (Dreikurs, 1989), to take an "I" position in expressing oneself, to ask clearly for arrangements he or she may like, and to accept consequent ease or difficulty and positive or negative feelings in the relationship. In so doing, partners might give up fear of self and others (Dreikurs, 1989). One can accept that one is not defective for wanting what one wants. One takes courage to be ordinary, one begins to have ordinary things on one's mind and to enjoy it.

The second primary point which marital therapy addresses is to understand partners' general ways of avoiding intimacy through justification of behaviors, and to communicate those ways to one another. Each can understand and admit what he or she wants and how he or she insists that the world accommodate one. Each can understand his or her ambitions and methods to have control over, and to use, the other partner, and each can gain the courage to communicate those ambitions and methods. Each partner can understand his or her pattern of trying to force results in the relationship and then be willing to discuss that pattern. To do so, one must understand one's sensitivities, judgments, feelings and intents. Allred (1976), Perlmutter and Hatfield (1980), and Wile (1981) refer to this as metacommunication. Change may happen as people begin to overtly negotiate agreements and to become intimate (Beisser, 1970). Dreikurs (1968) calls this a change in attitude from antagonistic and adversarial to courageous and collaborative.

What drives this process are the many real benefits in telling the truth about oneself and in creating an environment of curiosity. These benefits include: creation of arrangements one likes and for which one feels pride; appreciation of oneself and another; feeling more trusting and trustworthy, more secure, less worried, less obsessed; and having more real accomplishments, more mutual respect and actual cooperation with another person. These social and intimate benefits eventually blend into self-respect, inner freedom, and social interest.

TECHNIQUES

Many techniques aid this process (Carlson & Slavik, 1997). Two are mentioned here that, although designed for problem-solving therapy, can be effectively used in promoting intimacy: the use of early memories in eliciting couples complementarity (Slavik, 1997) and the contract of expectations (Hawes, 1997). Neither is presented here in detail. Interested readers should consult the original sources.

Using Early Memories

The use of early memories in couple counseling helps partners understand how they have cooperated to create vertical agreements and how they can learn to encourage one another. It also increases one's understanding of how the partner understands himself or herself, others, and the world.

The technique is straightforward but may take several sessions to complete. In step one, the therapist encourages each partner to present the difficulty he or she experiences in the relationship in his or her usual way. In step two the therapist asks one partner for his or her earliest memory and, in the usual Adlerian manner, writes it down verbatim. In step three the therapist interprets the memory, using the individual's presented problem and the early memory as two points on a line. In step four the therapist discusses the meaning of the memory with the individual until an agreement is reached about an interpretation and its relevance to the individual's current behavior. In step five the other partner is asked for an opinion. He or she may be asked, "Do you recognize this in your partner? How do you see it happening?"

Agreement is not required if the therapist has agreement with the first partner. Step six focuses on how the model which has been developed for the first partner's behavior helps them both to understand how and why the first partner behaves as he or she does. The therapist may focus on how this model both aids and makes trouble for one in life, particularly in an intimate relationship. Subsequently the same process is undertaken with the other partner. At the end, if it has not already become apparent, the cycle in which the partners cooperate can be clarified.

The Contract of Expectations

The contract of expectations (Hawes, 1997) is the covert contract which partners make when they first meet that each will live up to specific expectations. Explication of this contract in counseling enables the couple to clarify why they have problems and to break the impasse of blaming. It also allows the couple greater understanding of one another and enables intimacy to occur. In "acknowledging the contract, assuming responsibility for it and becoming sensitive to its destructive features" (Hawes, 1997, p. 91), a couple can address vertical agreements and become more intimate with one another.

The technique is a set of questions. First the therapist asks one partner, "What do you remember about the time you first set eyes on your partner?" After that story is told, the therapist then asks, "At that time, what did you notice about the other that made you realize this person was special in some way?" Descriptive words are noted. Then the therapist requests the story of their first date or time together by agreement. The therapist follows this story with the question, "What did you notice that made you want to be with this person?" and again the descriptive words are noted. Two further, more specific questions follow. "When you first knew that this person was the one you might want to marry, what was it that made him or her special?" Descriptive words are noted. Finally, the wedding day is focussed on: "On the day of your wedding, what was the highlight, the clearest detail?" This is recorded.

This process can then be gone through with the other partner. The recorded descriptive words make up the contract of expectations which partners expect others to satisfy.

Finally, since Adlerians believe generally that "the very element that is most distressing in a relationship is a variation of the positive factors which most attracted one to the other initially" (Hawes, 1997), the partners are asked, "These days, what is it that most distresses you about your partner?" Most partners are surprised, or dismayed, to find that their partner has changed little over the years, but their attitude toward him or her is less positive than before. This insight allows partners to see one another's strengths anew and fresh and to renew their affection for one another.

CONCLUSION

Intimacy is undervalued in couples therapy, either as a tool or as a result. However, it can be used to clarify and resolve dilemmas in which couples find themselves. To do so, a therapist must be clear about his or her own "I" position. Results of promoting intimacy can be an increased ability of couples to solve problems without becoming locked into other short-lived bargains which, in turn, become problematic.

REFERENCES

Adler, A. (1956). *The Individual Psychology of Alfred Adler: A systematic presentation in selections from his writings* (H. L. Ansbacher & R. R. Ansbacher Eds. and Trans.). New York: Basic Books.

Allred, G. G. (1976). *How to strengthen your marriage and family*. Provo, UT: Brigham Young University.

Beisser, A. R. (1970). The paradoxical theory of change. In J. Fagan & I. L. Shepherd (Eds.), *Gestalt therapy now: Theory techniques applications* (pp. 77–80). Palo Alto, CA: Science & Behavior.

Carlson, J., & Slavik, S. (Eds.). (1997). *Techniques in Adlerian psychology*. Muncie, IN: Accelerated Development.

Dinkmeyer, D., & Dinkmeyer, D. (1981). Adlerian family therapy. *The American Journal of Family Therapy, 9*(1), 45–52.

Dreikurs, R. (1946). *The challenge of marriage*. New York: Hawthorn.

Dreikurs, R. (1967). *Psychodynamics, psychotherapy, and counseling*. Chicago: Alfred Adler Institute.

Dreikurs, R. (1968). Determinants of changing attitudes of marital partners toward each other. In S. Rosenbaum & I. Alger (Eds.), *The marriage relationship: Psychoanalytic perspectives* (pp. 83–102). New York: Basic Books.

Dreikurs, R. (1971). *Social equality: The challenge of today*. Chicago: Regnery.

Dreikurs, R. (1989). *Dreikursian theory* (J. R. Fowler & J. W. Croake Eds.). Seattle, WA: Seattle Institute for Adlerian Studies.

Duhl, B. S., & Duhl, F. J. (1981). Integrative family therapy. In A. S. Gurman & D. P. Kniskern (Eds.), *Handbook of family therapy*, (Vol. I) (pp. 483–513). New York: Brunner/Mazel.

Foley, V. D. (1984). Family therapy. In R. J. Corsini & D. Wedding (Eds.), *Current psychotherapies* (pp. 447–490). Itasca, IL: Peacock.

Freeman, D. S. (1991). *Techniques of family therapy*. Northvale, NJ: Aronson.

Gurman, A. S., & Kniskern, D. P. (Eds.). (1981, 1991). *Handbook of family therapy*, (Vols. I & II) New York: Brunner/Mazel.

Hawes, C. (1997). Brief couple therapy: The contract of expectations. In P. Prina, C. Shelley, & C. Thompson (Eds.), *Adlerian Society (of the United Kingdom) and the Institute for Individual Psychology Year Book 1997* (pp. 88–99). London: Adlerian Society (of the United Kingdom) and the Institute for Individual Psychology.

Howing, P. T., Wodarski, J. S., Kurtz, P. D., Gaudin, J. M., & Herbst, E. N. (1990). Child abuse and delinquency: The empirical and theoretical limits. *Social Work, 35*(3), 244–249.

Hudson, P. O., & O'Hanlon, W. H. (1991). *Rewriting love stories: Brief marital therapy*. New York: Norton.

Kiesler, D. J. (1983). The 1982 interpersonal circle: A taxonomy for complementarity in human transactions. *Psychological Review, 90*(3), 185–213.

Minuchin, S. (1974). *Families & family therapy*. Cambridge, MA: Harvard University Press.

Mozdzierz, G. J., & Friedman, K. (1978). The superiority-inferiority spouses syndrome: Diagnostic and therapeutic considerations. *Journal of Individual Psychology, 34*(2), 232–243.

Mozdzierz, G. J., & Lottman, T. J. (1973). Games married couples play: Adlerian view. *Journal of Individual Psychology, 29*, 182–194.

O'Connell, W. E. (1975). *Action therapy and Adlerian theory*. Chicago: Alfred Adler Institute.

Perlmutter, M. S., & Hatfield, E. (1980). Intimacy, intentional metacommunication and second order change. *The American Journal of Family Therapy, 8*(1), 17–23.

Sherman, R., & Dinkmeyer, D. (1987). *Systems of family therapy: An Adlerian integration*. New York: Brunner/Mazel.

Sherman, R., Oresky, P., & Rountree, Y. (1991). *Solving problems in couples and family therapy: Techniques and tactics*. New York: Brunner/Mazel.

Shulman, B. H. (1973). *Contributions to Individual Psychology*. Chicago: Alfred Adler Institute.

Slavik, S. (1997). Early memories in eliciting couples complementarity. In H. Rosenthal (Ed.), *Favorite counseling and therapy techniques*. Muncie, IN: Accelerated Development.

Slavik, S., Carlson, J., & Sperry, L. (1993). An Adlerian treatment of adults with a history of childhood sexual abuse. *Individual Psychology, 49*(2), 111–131.

Sperry, L. (1978). *The together experience: Getting, growing and staying together in marriage*. San Diego, CA: Beta.

Wile, D. B. (1981). *Couples therapy: A nontraditional approach*. New York: Wiley.

Wong, B., & McKeen, J. (1992). *A manual for life*. Gabriola Island, BC: PD Seminars.

CHAPTER 17

Experiential Approaches to Creating the Intimate Marriage

Augustus Y. Napier, Ph.D.

Writing about intimacy in marriage is something of a luxury. After all, our grandparents would hardly have considered intimacy a desirable goal; they were worried about survival, and about enduring life's hardships. Many of our clients also approach therapy with less than idealized goals: they want to function better, to enjoy life a little more; often, they simply want the pain of unremitting conflict to stop. The conscious goal of creating an intimate marriage is likely to come later in treatment, after a number of other changes have occurred. While the couple's intention of achieving marital intimacy is a first step, there are often formidable unconscious barriers standing in the way, barriers which were built as psychological protection during the vicissitudes of childhood.

And what is intimacy? We tend to think of candlelight dinners and of romantic evenings by the fire; and, of course, we associate intimacy with sexuality. Yet it is difficult to think of a more intimate moment than a colleague recently described to me. She and her husband had married in their forties, and for five years they were extremely happy together. Then he developed cancer; and after the two of them fought the illness long and heroically, it claimed his life. As he was about to become comatose, they sensed that this would be their final conversation. With weak smile, he said, "I say tomāto,'" and, as was their fond fashion, she said, "I say tomäto." And he drifted away. More than a year later, she could not relate this moment without crying.

This exchange contains many of the essentials of the intimate experience: it is caring; it incorporates awareness of their separateness, even of their conflicts and differences; and it momentarily bridges the distance between them. The intimate moment creates a world of safety and caring within which both partners feel protected, safe, and deeply valued. It is as if for a moment they are simultaneously swaddled in the tenderness that is created between the infant and its mother.

In this volume, there will probably be as many definitions of intimacy as there are writers; yet there will also be common elements. The intimate moment is not a steady state; it is a peak experience that occurs from time to time. It is not readily programmable, as though the couple could decide, "Now we will be intimate." On special occasions like wedding anniversaries when there is the expectation of caring and intimacy in marriage, the couple's inability to will themselves into emotional closeness can produce truly miserable days.

Couples cannot be maturely intimate if they are psychologically fused. While they may feel close in the enmeshed relationship, they may also feel suffocated, limited, and compromised by the omnipresent demands of dependent togetherness. Intimate experience demands that the partners be psychologically individuated. Intimacy is, then, a bridge between two people who don't feel forced to be together but who make a choice of reaching out to each other. Having reconciled themselves to the realities and terrors of biological isolation that are every organism's fate, the partners who live on opposite sides of this canyon of separateness can, from time to time, venture out on the delicately connected bridge between them, feeling the danger and the exhilaration of holding hands above the abyss.

There is of course a well-developed literature and a firm tradition of valuing individuation within the family context. All the work of Murray Bowen (1978) is relevant here, and the recent writings of David Schnarch (1991, 1997) are good examples of the adaptation of this theory and practice in treating sexual dilemmas.

Just as the partners must be psychologically individuated, they must also be willing to relinquish this separateness in forming a connection that is vulnerable and unprotected. What is contained in this handclasp above the abyss that allows both to feel safe, joined, not alone, and deeply valued? How do they learn about this place in the relationship? What is the model for this experience in childhood? How is this early experience modified in marriage?

The most profound intimacy in our lives may have occurred when we were infants being held in the arms of our mothers. If we were fortunate, we felt profoundly surrounded by love and caring, and we gradually learned the delicious and anxious border between self and other. If we were frequently plunged into terrifying pain and frustration, we learned that there was an other outside ourselves who promised relief. Our needs were met by our mother's tender voice, by her comforting and enveloping flesh, and by the bounties of her breast. And as the mothers of infants report, the mother is also a participant in and a beneficiary of this primal connection. If she dares, she moves toward, and joins in this deliciously shared experience; she may also experience sexual stimulation in nursing. Many mothers report this intimacy with their infants as among the most pleasurable of their lives; but some mothers become fearful and withdraw in the face of the infant's powerful neediness (Bolby, 1969, 1988).

In marital intimacy, both partners seem to enter into an altered state (translate: hypnotic state) in which they join in a partial recapitulation of the infant-mother experience. An important difference in marriage, of course, is that each partner is simultaneously parent and child with the other. That is, each partner holds the other in a protective and cradling embrace and is at the same time held in this way by the other. The deeper levels of adult intimacy may also contain elements of play, sensory pleasuring, and simple flesh sharing that were first learned in infancy. In all these fusion experiences, however, the partners do not lose the awareness of self and other; in fact, the joys of physical touch all occur at the border of self and other, the surface of the skin.

Entering into the shared vulnerability of intimacy involves emotional risk; part of the joy of the experience is that the abyss is always there. If one partner becomes vulnerable, the other may tease, make fun, become critical, or withdraw. This experience of hurt and disappointment is likely to reactivate childhood trauma in which we experienced similar disappointments at the hands of our parents.

The emotional scars from disrupted or disappointed bonding experiences during childhood are among the primary impediments to adult intimacy. Since many couples unconsciously approach marriage as a pseudo-parenting experience (Whitaker and Ryan, 1989), they may initially invest heavily in a sense of emotional fusion that taps deep needs from childhood. Also unconsciously, they are likely to predict a recapitulation of the traumas of their childhoods; and when they inevitably disappoint each other, the defenses they learned as children are called into play. Rather than risk reinjury, both partners retreat from emotional exposure and remain safely protected by emotional distance, wariness, defensiveness, and in some instances, critical attack. Overcoming these deeply scripted and often bilateral negative predictions is one of the central challenges of the therapy process. If as an adult either partner has experienced a traumatic negative recapitulation of a childhood injury, such as being rejected by a lover or spouse, the emotional scar tissue is more difficult to overcome. These layers of emotional injury are often the greatest impediments to marital intimacy, and dealing with them successfully is the real work of therapy.

As in many other approaches, experiential family therapists work actively on helping both partners be healthily individuated, and on helping them risk emotional bonding or connection, and we see these capacities as developing synchronously (Whitaker and Ryan, 1989). The adult who feels securely separate and independent will not be as vulnerable to fearing loss of self in partnered intimacy; and the individual with the ability to bond intimately with the partner will feel more secure in being alone and separate.

Mature intimacy involves dealing with more than hypnotic images of the other. It requires that we see, clearly and accurately, the present, idiosyncratic, flawed person of our mate; and, at least in the intimate moment, it invites us to cherish the other. We must also be willing to reveal that flawed and unique aspect of ourselves, hoping to find ourselves cherished. This degree of self-openness is disarming; it allows both to feel safe in the presence of the other. While intimacy may be expressed in the tender buds at the end of the tree's branches, it has beneath it the heft of the entire tree, the years of investment and accumulated meaning of two juxtaposed lives. While young couples may find intimacy mainly in passionate sexual encounters, older partners may need only cradle each other in a fond word or two, or in a knowing gaze, to find an intimate moment.

It is relatively easy to say what intimacy is not. Couples cannot be intimate unless they are honest and truthful; fake sentiment or affection is always transparent. While intimacy can occur between strangers who find themselves in extraordinary circumstances (often involving physical danger or close encounter), it usually demands a history of acquired meaning between two participants; over time, they develop significance to each other. Intimacy cannot exist if either party is trying to exert power or control over the other, or if they are attacking or blaming. The natural corollary to coercion or attack, defensiveness, is equally inimical to intimate exchange. Adult intimacy demands relative equality; it depends on a democratic mutuality of risk and vulnerability. Intimacy extends to the recognition of the other's humanity, and it is fundamentally loving. While it is a link of knowing another, it finds its true power in the background awareness of the painful solitude of the individual.

THE SYMBOLIC-EXPERIENTIAL APPROACH

The symbolic-experiential approach is almost as difficult to describe as the experience of intimacy. The fact that this therapeutic universe is so identified with the dynamic and often quixotic personality of Carl Whitaker makes it tempting to use his style of working with families as a definition of the approach. Although I studied for a number of years with Whitaker, in recent years I have worked closely with my wife, family therapist Margaret Napier.

The two of us have developed a style of working that is very different from Whitaker's, and we place different emphases on what we find important in therapy. In this chapter, I will attempt to present some general principles derived from the symbolic-experiential approach, and I will describe our own variations on this way of working.

The experiential therapist sees the primary focus in therapy as the encounter between individuals in the therapy session. This meeting is seen as a symbolic event, highly charged with meaning and often with strong affect. In Symbolic-Experiential Family Therapy (S-EFT), (Neill & Kniskern, 1982; Roberto, 1991; Whitaker & Keith, 1981) we presume that the couple or family brings an emotionally laden and often unconscious set of needs to the therapist, needs that they had originally focused on each other. The S-EFT therapist believes that most couples approach marriage with the unconscious hope that the other will help reparent them, making them whole in ways that they feel inadequate or deficient. When this self-help project fails, it replicates for the partners the sense that they have symbolically reentered their families of origin, and they feel consigned to the same position of dependent, isolated defensiveness that they experienced as children. Typically, both partners find ample evidence in their partner's behavior that the relationship is disappointing or unsafe, and, in the face of these triggering words or actions, they quickly retreat to deeply learned modes of self-protection.

Like most other practitioners of S-EFT, we believe that the best therapist for couples and families is a cotherapy team; if possible, it should be a male-female pair (Napier, 1988). Cotherapy reactivates for the patient couple the symbolism of the two-parent family; it also provides them with a visible model for intimacy, fairness, openness, and peer negotiation. While there are some dangers that both therapists will develop subtly shared countertransference stereotypes of their patients, aware teams bring the protective complexity of bilateral perceptions. They also offer the buffering effects of their being from separate families of origin. If one therapist overpersonalizes a client's dilemma, for example, the cotherapist can often provide a more reasoned view.

Since gender sensitivity is a prerequisite for competent family treatment, having female and male points of view represented on the therapy team is especially important. Male-dominated gender bias is so prevalent in our society that it is essential that the female cotherapist be an active advocate for women's perspectives. But in some instances, the male cotherapist must serve the same function for a male client. While the two of us also work alone and with other cotherapists, we find working together not only effective but highly enjoyable. The practiced teaming that comes from years of marriage is incorporated into the treatment process; but this mixture of the professional and the personal also necessitates constant work on our marriage. If one partner dominates several sessions, for example, or is constantly late for sessions, these dynamics demand discussion. Conflicts regarding different perceptions of a couple's dilemmas must be resolved before treatment can continue. It is also essential that both cotherapists be able to identify empathetically with all members of the family, a challenge that presents a constant demand for growth on the part of the therapists.

While the costs of cotherapy sometimes make it prohibitively expensive, we find it so valuable, especially with very disturbed couples and families, that we are often willing to cut our fees in order to be able to work together. And while all cotherapy arrangements demand constant work on the relationship, cotherapists who care about and respect each other bring these aspects of intimate partnership to the client couple. This is perhaps the best argument for the use of cotherapy in couples and family therapy: the caring of the therapists for each other is an implicit gift to their clients.

ASSESSMENT PHASE

The assessment of couples is an extended conversation, often scheduled for two hours, about their complaints, their histories, and their hopes for the future. Sometimes this phase lasts for several shorter sessions, and it is a beginning intervention as well as an evaluation. Like other S-EFT therapists, we are firm about therapeutic structure: even if the couple sees the problems as contained within their relationship, we are usually reluctant to begin without a commitment from them to involve their children at whatever time we deem appropriate. We know that important aspects of their intimacy as a couple are organized around their children, and that therapeutic involvement of the whole nuclear family not only protects the children from being scape-goated, but also offers many resources to the couple. Since we want to begin fairly and with a balanced perspective, we rarely see one individual first; our commitment for an indefinite period of time is to see the couple together. We make it clear that if only one member comes to the session, the session will be cancelled and the couple charged for it.

While Whitaker would be very tough in his insistence on a certain structure at the beginning of therapy (Napier & Whitaker, 1978), the two of us are a bit more flexible in the way that we set these parameters. We will explain the rationale for our structural decisions, and, though we remain firm in witholding treatment until our minimum conditions are met, we will sometimes negotiate with the couple, as in agreeing to postpone their bringing their children in until the third session. What is usually not negotiable is the requirement that neither spouse be in therapy with someone else, and that both partners agree to be in therapy together.

We are clear from the start that our inquiry involves understanding patterns that extend across three generations: the couple, their parents, and their children. While we know that we will eventually want to involve the couple's parents in treatment, we do not push this issue in the beginning, unless the parents support the couple financially, are paying for the therapy, or are massively intrusive into the couple's lives.

As we ask about problems, we listen hard for a number of themes, often thinking aloud with the partners about what we hear. As always, clinical judgement dictates what we share with our clients, but we want them to see the ways in which we think about their conflict. We seek to shift focus away from individuals into the social context: concurrent situational pressures, such as job stress or someone's physical illness; family of origin pressures from the past and the present; and traumas or situational dilemmas in the couple's history, including deaths in the family, affairs, past divorces, miscarriages, house fires, or multiple moves. As we intuitively add up the stresses on the couple, we listen for defense mechanisms. How well or poorly are they coping with their current dilemmas? Where possible, we attempt to point out ways in which their strengths are evident.

Without asking these questions directly, we ask ourselves how individuated the partners are? Do they seem to have distorted, highly projective images of each other? Can they claim responsibility for self or are they in entrenched blaming stances? As we offer ideas about their system, do they seem open or closed regarding information from others? Do they want us to fix them or do they see themselves as active agents in their therapy? Underlying these concerns is the question of whether the partners are basically adults with the capacity to use insight to alter their behavior, or whether they are more primitively dependent with little sense of being two separate individuals.

We are also attempting to assess the pair's basic connectedness, or the quality and strength of their bond (Napier, 1988). Are they deeply estranged, with little conversation or energy between them? Are they enmeshed in perpetual conflict and confrontation? Do they cycle between intense engagement and traumatic disconnection? How long does it take them to recover from a break in their relationship? What seems to trigger a disruption in their communication? Is it perceived rejection, or direct criticism or implied condescension? When they separate emotionally, where does each partner go psychologically: into rage, or depression, or quiet withdrawal? We listen intently to the couple's ability to handle conflict. We know that unresolved conflict is a common denominator in the failure to achieve intimacy, and that this failure is always tied to unresolved family of origin issues.

As we listen for the depth and quality of the partners' emotional engagement with each other, we wonder if there was deep emotional commitment in the beginning of their relationship. If so, what happened in their histories to disrupt it? When did the change occur? If we have questions about the couple's basic caring for each other, we ask what led them to get married? What keeps them married? While we attempt to be hopeful about every relationship, an accurate assessment of the couple's bondedness not only allows us to be realistic about the degree of progress we can expect to occur, but it also enables us to protect the couple from unnecessary risk. One supervisee encouraged a separated couple to be close and intimate; and when the wife discovered that her husband had not given up a prior affair, she felt betrayed, not only by her husband but also by the course of the therapy.

As we explore the couple's issues, we need to evaluate whether they are both telling us the truth about themselves and their relationship. Nonverbal cues may signal us that one partner is being dishonest about his or her attempt to work on the relationship. He or she may have entered the therapy with the conscious intention of dumping the other partner on the therapist. And, of course, we need to assess quickly whether anyone in the family is endangered, either from violence or suicidal impulses.

Assessing the couple's connectedness involves evaluating where their loyalties lie. Often, neither partner has separated psychologically from the family of origin. They may have transferred a family struggle to the spouse, as in the daughter who was intimidated by her father's judgment and has now refocused her struggle with a dominant male on her husband, who of course plays his part by being critical and judgmental. The involvement with the family of origin may be occurring in the present, with the husband, for example, caring for his divorced mother while attempting to be available to his wife and children. Of course either spouse's overinvolvement with one of their children creates the same kind of abandonment of the loyalty which the intimate marriage requires. We S-EFT practitioners share many of the concerns of structural therapists regarding the desirability of within-generation coalitions, and of firm between-generation boundaries. When couples find it difficult to make their primary investment in their own marriage, we work intensively on current family of origin issues that are often blocking this commitment. We also target historical issues in the family of origin, such as a childhood disruption in bonding that may have produced fearfulness about intimacy.

We look carefully at obvious and pronounced differences between the partners, especially when the two individuals seem polarized around different personality styles, values, or other relationship stances. Distinct differences between the partners can be a sign of the strength of the relationship, in that both can appreciate the other's point of view or personality style. But frequently, couples are polarized and blaming regarding their differences, at the same time that they unconsciously depend on each other's contrasting way of dealing with the world. Here are some of the areas we listen for.

Dominance/Submission   Relationships in which one person is 'in charge' are rarely intimate. The dominant partner has hidden vulnerability that he or she does not divulge, and this person often disparages the more vulnerable partner as an extension of the lack of self-acceptance. The one-down partner has hidden power that is not acknowledged; he or she expresses power in covert or passive-aggressive ways. Some partnerships are organized around bilateral dominance and submission patterns, with each partner feeling talked down to or directed in one area of the relationship, while doing the same to the other in another aspect of life. In the latter instance, each may complain of being dominated by the other.

Unlocking these hierarchical stances is often a difficult job, particularly when both partners gain covert security from their unequal positions. They may complain but be unwilling to make changes. As we work with these positions, we must understand the depth of the spouses' scripting in their respective families of origin. As an initial opening, we attempt to fish for the vulnerability of the dominant partner, often around that individual's overfunctioning in the relationship. "Isn't it lonely or stressful feeling responsible for so much?" we ask. Not until we have established a relationship with the dominant partner do we confront him or her forcefully, though we may do so to a limited degree early on: "When you talk to her like that, she will feel put down and not appreciated, and (turning to the other partner) you may get him back subtly in some way." Since we want to avoid stigmatizing one partner, bilateral growth-assignments are the order of the day. But, if we must, we are not shy about confronting an intimidating partner.

Pursuit/Distance   When one partner is in charge of the principle of verbal and emotional togetherness (usually the wife), and the other seems to specialize in maintaining boundaries and emotional distance (typically the husband), one suspects that both are anxious about true intimacy, but they specialize in avoiding it. The pursuing partner may make a negative prediction about men's emotional responsiveness which is based on her experience with her father, and she may pursue her husband in a way that is unconsciously designed to make him withdraw. He may be so ready to see women as needing too much and as being invasive that he responds defensively at the slightest hint of his wife's emotional approach. We might ask the wife to examine the overdetermined nature of her needs for closeness, and we counsel her to try to stop pursuing her husband. At the same time, we may ask the husband to examine his fears of not being able to meet his wife's requests, and we often suggest that he begin by becoming a better listener, and that he try to **believe** that he can be a more satisfying partner. At the same time that we suggest these common sense moves, we look for evidence that both partners are served in some unconscious way by their pattern. The husband may be protected from the possibility of rejection by his wife's pursuit, hence he may complain about but, subtly invite, her pursuit of him. Similarly, the pursuing wife in the couple may have unconscious fears of intrusion or invasion that had their origins in childhood. Her husband's distancing protects her from this deeper level of anxiety.

In the sexual arena, the pursuit distance dance is often reversed, with the husband in the pursuing role. As in most areas where couples are polarized, the secret to working with these issues is in dealing with largely unconscious anxieties (often about intimacy) that are shared by both partners and that dictate their uncomfortable, but collusively maintained, stances. Not until the childhood vulnerabilities that set up these conditions in both individuals are exposed and healed can the couple be genuinely ready for intimate exchange.

Self/Other Focus   In the intimate couple, both partners must be able to be self-aware and self-advocating while they are simultaneously aware of and sensitive to the needs of the other. Disturbances in what might be called interpersonal balance are common in marriage, and they may be subtle or glaringly obvious. One partner may be blatantly narcissistic while the other is self-denying in the extreme. These situations can of course be abusive. In some marriages, both partners are narcissistically needy and are in constant conflict about not getting their needs met. In other couples, self-denial is the order of the day for both, and failure to advocate for self results in a deep backlog of unresolved anger.

Narcissism can of course have a variety of causes, as can self-denial. The narcissistic individual can be the proverbial spoiled child who was taught to expect constant praise and attention, and the rough and tumble negotiations of marriage can feel to this individual like a profound betrayal. Often, however, narcissism bespeaks significant unmet needs from childhood. Similarly, the self-denying partner may be the product of a nonreinforcing family, or he or she may be the victim of abuse who learned to hide emotionally.

As in other problem areas in marriage, work proceeds on different levels according to the severity of the issues. The back and forth of dialog in the therapy hour can be good behavioral practice for the partners, as each learns to cultivate new habits in listening sensitively and in speaking accurately about themselves. They may be given homework to learn to track the other's experience over time; they may be asked to make requests for themselves regularly. Often, however, the deeper problems of emotional deprivation and trauma that underlie these failures to balance self and other require symbolic reparenting, in which childhood issues are raised in relation to the therapists.

Fairness/Responsibility   Often, one partner overfunctions in relation to the other, and this process, in which responsibilites are unequally shared, results in the accumulation of resentment and anger in the overfunctioner. While these inequalities may be related to patterns of narcissism and self-denial, they are often culturally determined, with women finding themselves in the role of giving to and thinking of others. As some popular writers have noted (Hochschild, 1989), this pattern is particularly likely when women are employed outside the home and their husbands are not carrying their share of the household responsibilities. Often men are unaware of their wives' anger about these inequalities until later in the marriage, when this resentment is suddenly expressed.

While it may seem like a nonintimate task, sorting out both partners' hidden resentments about unfairness or perceived unfairness in the relationship is basic to establishing a climate of trust and mutuality that is a fundamental precursor to more intimate exchange.

During the Assessment and Early Intervention Stage, we are active and highly visible to our clients. As we explore their world, we want them to see who we are and how we think. Can we understand their problems? Are we fair to both partners? Are we caring? Are we optimistic about life? How confident are we in our approach? Can we lead and be in charge of the therapy? Are we genuinely curious about their lives? We know that both we and they are being assessed, and we want our clients to be somewhat surprised and reassured by what we bring to them. We also want to be assured that we are not wasting our time with couples who are not really interested in change.

PROCESS PHASE

Symbolic-experiential therapy is strongly process-focused. Communication regulates the emotional temperature of the relationship. Communication allows one partner to dominate or intimidate the other. And communication makes up the intimate experience itself. We assume that real communication is impossible to avoid in marriage, and that while partners may badly misunderstand and misinterpret each other, it is often the underlying emotional state which is the problem rather than communication itself. Over time, hostility will confess itself, as will indifference, arrogance, and cowardice. Similarly, courage, love, and tenderness are revealed in time, even if indirectly. We are convinced that most partners share certain core dilemmas, like fear of strong affect, or prudishness, or profound neediness, and, while they may present themselves very differently and communicate in very different styles, we seek to find the inner realities that bind the partners to each other. If they can begin to acknowledge the underlying emotional structure in their marriage (such as, "We don't love each other but are afraid to divorce," or, "We are both frustrated that the other won't give in and do things our way"), they can decide whether these issues can be tackled.

The couple's communication is the royal road into this inner reality. Often we listen for subtle cues of emerging or half-conscious thoughts or feelings much in the way that the analyst does; only our patient is a relationship which is groping for a better way of living. The couple may present complex metaphors of mutually created conflict which point to deeper issues (Napier, 1988). For example, a couple came to the third interview fighting about the wife's having picked up a spot of tar from the floormat of the car during their drive to therapy, when the husband had commanded her to throw it out the window, she refused, and he became enraged. Not only did this incident reveal the wife's resentment of her husband's heavy-handed domination, but it also brought to their awareness (with the therapists' help) the fact that the wife had not resolved her feelings about a former lover (the dark spot). This revelation eventually led to their beginning to explore their strong ties to other competing loyalties, especially to their respective opposite-sex parents.

As this phase begins, we direct the couple or family to begin working on, and talking to each other about, a problem that concerns them. We are attempting to shift the intiative and responsibility for the content of the session to our clients; and from this point forward, we will begin each session waiting for the couple to set the agenda for the session. While many couples initially resist revealing to us the ways they communicate with each other, we reassure them that they need not be embarrassed; we have seen many times any style they are likely to have. And then we wait. Gradually, the pair begins to play out their frustrating ways of dealing with each other.

As we explain to the couple, our intent in this phase is to help them develop a productive process for problem solving. At what point in the exchange do they begin to get impatient with each other? What do they misunderstand in each other? What happens when they hit familiar obstacles? Do they disconnect and retreat silently? Do they escalate into mutual blaming? Do they give up in despair? We hope that the therapy hour can become a safe and creative place in their lives, and eventually we want them to transpose to their everyday lives what they learn here.

Their communication patterns reveal the structure of the relationship. Is this a traditional, husband-dominated system, or is the wife the dominant figure? Is dominance or leadership bilateral? Is control constantly being contested by the partners? Does he direct her with regard to certain issues, while she directs him in other areas? As the partners talk to each other, we let the interactions develop naturally to the point that they become nonproductive, then we intervene. Our interventions invariably disrupt familiar but toxic sequences. We may block the husband's talking down to his wife, or the wife's analysis of the husband's relationship with his mother. We may challenge the husband's sly smile as he subtly baits his wife's mounting anger. We may point out logical inconsistencies: she wants him to participate actively in household duties but insists on controlling his actions; he attempts to be sympathetic with her struggles to discipline the children but is subtly critical of her failures.

In these interventions, we have common sense goals: we discourage any form of one-upmanship, but the one-down person is also responsible for having abdicated self-responsibility. We are actively promoting: respectful and fair treatment of each other, teaming and cooperation, clear requests and responses, and above all, peer relatedness. As we try to discourage and to actively interfere with the pseudo-therapeutic pattern in the marriage, we hope that we can detoxify the hierarchical communications that trigger transferential associations to childhood. The explicit message is: "Try to move into the same generation with each other. Be friends and lovers. Try not to help each other in ways that imply parent or child roles. If you need things that you didn't get from your parents, elect us (the therapists) as your temporary foster parents."

The partners' overreactions are plainly visible to us. We want them to see the out-of-proportion nature of their responses to each other. He is bitterly scornful of her creative, "messy" style, and, of course, he grew up in a profoundly disordered and "messy" household. She is hyperreactive to his criticism, and, of course, she had an attacking, abusive stepfather. While we are trying to get the partners to move into a more here-and-now peer relatedness, we take insight-garnering forays into the origins of their reactivity. The purpose of these explorations is not to do major uncovering, but to help the partners to gain cognitive control of their overreactions. We help them see themselves as they were as children, help them to have empathy for their situations and to use that self-understanding to reassure themselves that they are not back in childhood, that the partner is not either of their parents. "Things are not nearly as impossible now as they seemed then. You have the power to change your own part in this marriage. You can also ask your partner for change."

As we are counseling self-knowledge and self-control, we also ask each partner to be less willing to volunteer as a transference figure. "If you would stop critizing her for being messy and talk about how her style makes you anxious, maybe she would listen to you more." And to her: "You let him put you down. Tell him when he is doing it, and ask him forcefully to change the way he is talking to you."

As the couple's habitual patterns are challenged, they feel threatened; and the tension between them usually escalates. The dominant husband may threaten to withdraw from treatment when he is confronted, but he may also break down and admit the way he learned to be so controlling. He saw his abusive father lose control and beat his mother, and he vowed to always be in control of himself. He has not realized the sub-text of his resolution. In order to control himself, he feels that he must control those around him who might provoke him, his wife, his two sons, and all of his three hundred employees. His wife takes heart when we begin to confront him, and, instead of enlisting the defiant younger son as her ally, she begins to challenge her husband herself. Then, as she feels more empowered, she recalls the reason she needed her husband to be so strong. Her father committed suicide when she was a teenager, and she was willing to subjugate herself to her husband because she needed a stable male figure in her life. Along with her self-assertion comes the repressed grief from the tragic loss of her father.

Our blocking the couple's habitual responses leads to their uncovering historical affect, and the surfacing of this painful material creates new empathy within the marriage; it also "frees up" energy to enable contemporary problem solving.

As we are deconstructing the couple's usual way of communicating, they become confused and frustrated. "I feel like I can't say anything right," is a common complaint. Indeed, we are often micro-managing many of their interactions, refusing to let blaming or description of the other take place, insisting that each person reveal themselves. Sometimes we are helping them analyze a transaction which occurred at home ("Let's see what went wrong there"), but often we are literally rebuilding their present dialog. We know that intimate exchange between the partners is an anxious process, and we adopt a variety of strategies in promoting it. Sometimes we confront; sometimes we cajole or suggest or provide support and empathy; at times we simply push, saying, "Try it. Try it right now." [For a more thorough example of emotionally connecting process work, see Johnson, 1996.]

CASE EXAMPLE

Shela and Heath are a dual-career couple in their mid-thirties with two children, Jeffrey, 7, and Wade, 3. Heath is an accountant; Shela is head of recruitment for a division of a large company. They came at Shela's insistence because of severe marital distress, and they were not happy at our requirement that they be willing to involve their children in the therapy process. The session cited here was their fifth.

Shela: The reason I got mad last night is that I felt that you were avoiding getting Alan ready for bed the way you had promised.

Heath: I'm sorry [sounding irritated], but I was on my way to do it when you spoke to me in that way you have. Like I'm a kid who has screwed up.

Margaret N.: Shela, do you really think you are telling him anything about your feelings? You are speaking about his behavior. Go back now, talk directly to Heath, and try again.

Shela: Well, you make me mad. You had committed to helping me with his bedtime. You promised; then you didn't do it.

[Shela avoids looking at Heath. She wants to talk to Margaret.]

Margaret N.: Keep looking at him. Tell him about feelings, not about him. You felt angry, and...[Margaret is leading Shela toward vulnerability beneath the anger.]

Shela: Angry, frustrated...let down. I felt like he let me down, again.

Heath: Well I was going to...

Gus N.: Stop rescuing her, Heath. Keep looking at her; but let her talk, and try to listen to her feelings, not to the part that is about you.

[Intuitively aware that Shela is moving toward her own hurt and vulnerability, Heath becomes anxious. By becoming self-referential and defensive, he offers to be the target of her anger. They know that beneath her strong and controlling exterior, Shela is very wounded, and they often conspire to avoid her vulnerability. It seems easier for both of them if Heath is the one who "screws up," so that Shela can be angry at him.]

Margaret N.: Go on Shela. You felt let down.

[Margaret ignores Shela's anger, which is quickly triggered by Heath and is a constant presence in their relationship. Margaret is going for more vulnerable affect.]

Margaret N.: Say more about the feeling. Let down and...

Shela: Again. I had gotten my hopes up that something could change. Maybe I could get some help from him.

Margaret N.: So... hopes, expectations, then...

Shela: Disappointed. [after a pause.] Again.

Margaret N.: Look at Heath now, and talk about the disappointment.

[This is territory that Margaret knows personally, and she knows where it is leading. Shela avoids looking at Heath, then glances furtively at him.]

Shela: I was disappointed in you.

Margaret N.: Can you leave out the you? Just the feeling.

Shelia: I was disappointed.

[Her voice is softer; she seems at the edge of tears. Leaving out the reference to Heath is difficult for her, and pushes her toward feelings she fears.]

Margaret N.: And I think hurt, maybe.

[Margaret's voice is warm, caring.]

Margaret N.: You had gotten your hopes up for more support, and felt hurt and disappointed when it didn't happen.

[Margaret, too, is dropping reference to Heath. She is aware that a family of origin wound lurks just beneath the surface. Heath seems disarmed by Shela's near-tears.]

Heath: But I said... [he introjects, now more apologetically.]

Gus N.: [to Heath] Seeing her hurt, instead of her anger, touches you, doesn't it?

Heath: Yes. Usually, she's just angry.

Gus N.: Maybe you could look at her now, try to acknowledge just that you see her hurt. And, by the way, don't think this is all about you. You're OK. You haven't done anything terrible. For now, try to focus on **her**, her disappointment, hurt.

[I am thinking here of issues in Heath's family of origin: his younger brother's death when Heath was nine; and Heath's mother's long depression following that death; then, later, her anger at Heath, instead of her husband, who had distanced into work; and finally, Heath's conclusion that somehow it was all his fault.]

Heath: I see that you were, are, disappointed, let down.

Gus N.: [with empathy] And hurt.

[With the softness in my voice, Shela tears up, and Heath's face flushes. He is looking at Shela's sturdy, grieving face, and he can't stand the tension. I offer him a suggestion.]

Gus N.: What could you say to her now, an apology, or understanding?

Heath: I'm sorry. I know I build you up and then let you down.

Gus N.: Can you keep looking at her? You see how hurt she feels sometimes when she is disappointed?

Heath: I do see that.

[Shela is looking away, again at the edge of tears.]

Margaret N.: [softly] Would you try looking at him, Shela? He does see you.

[Shela glances furtively at Heath, exposing her now tear-streaked face. He reaches his hand out to her, and awkwardly, she lets him take her hand. Shela's body is tightened against his groping attempt; she dares not accept his offer of tenderness.]

Margaret N.: [to Shela] Try to take it in, Shela. He's trying to apologize, to support you. It seems foreign.

[Shela does soften a little to Heath's touch. The room is quiet, respectful, as though something important has happened.]

Margaret N.: [warmly, to Shela] There was so much loneliness in your life as a child. So much responsibility. [She pauses, resumes.] And disappointment when your dad would come and then leave you, again. With your mother and her problems.

[Margaret has picked up on Shela's word "again," joining with her in understanding of the disappointment she experienced as a child. Shela looks up as if from a trance at Margaret, as if to ask, "What is this about? My family? I thought this was about Heath and me?" It is material we have been over: Shela's alcoholic, profoundly narcissistic mother; Shela often left with responsibility for her two younger brothers; and Shela's father—charming, energetic, who would bring hope and stability when he came home. For a while, things would be fine, the world worked; she could be a normal teenager. Then, there would be the inevitable fight and her father would leave, again, for his job as a traveling salesman. And there Shela would be, stuck with it all, the way it seemed now with Heath and his needs, his job, and their two demanding kids. Shela is startled, because Margaret has been eavesdropping on these unconscious themes that keep emerging in Shela's complaints about Heath.]

Margaret N.: You know, your expectations for when your father would come home, and then your disappointment when he would leave you with it all.

[The affective exchange between the partners seems to be concluded for this session. We are working at redefining their struggle as complicated by family-of-origin issues.]

Shela: Oh, so Heath reminds me of that when he makes promises.

Margaret N.: And you feel let down. Only Heath thinks your anger is all about him. [turns to Heath] Can you see that? It's not just you she is disappointed in. It's all those times as a kid when her father would raise her hopes, and then leave?

Heath: Yeah, but why turn on me? I was trying to help more with the kids. No matter how hard I try, she is angry at me. It really pisses me off that she constantly acts like I am the problem in her life!

[Having been empathic and understanding as long as Shela was vulnerable, Heath now sounds angry and combative. Margaret and I glance at each other. Our work for this session is clearly not over yet.]

Gus N.: And this is your work, Heath. Can you hear the underlying assumption about Shela that you are making? "No matter what I do, I can't please her; she will always be angry at me?"

Heath: But she **is** always angry at me.

[Now Heath becomes blaming. Both partners are probably anxious about the shift in their relationship. If we allow him to, he will undo what they have accomplished.]

Shela: See, he was understanding for a minute. Now he is furious at me!

[She is moving back toward her conclusion that she cannot be vulnerable.]

Gus N.: [ignoring Shela] Heath, wait a second. Look what is happening. You were great. You listened carefully to Shela, and you didn't get defensive. Now you are beginning to feel some anger at all the times you have felt blamed by Shela. We need to make time and space for you to talk about that anger, and to get some of it out. But right now, both of you are preparing to spoil what you just accomplished, a moment of empathy and understanding. I would hate to see you lose that connection, even though it may have scared you both. [turning to Shela] Can you see that, Shela? He got scared by the intimacy, and maybe you did too. It is so tempting to return to your old convictions. You know: you can't let down, can't be undertood and nurtured. And, Heath, you are convinced that you will always be blamed. Those convictions are like bedrock in both of you; they are so deeply scripted into your lives. Then you have a breakthrough, and Heath discovers that he can be pleasing and nurturing to you, Shela—the woman in his life might actually be pleased with him. And you discover that you might be able to be nurtured and understood, and it scares both of you.

Margaret N.: [speaking warmly to Heath] Heath, take a deep breath. Try looking at Shela, again.

[Margaret is capitalizing on the word "again," this time pairing it with the promise of **support** for Shela—instead of disappointment. As she invites Heath to reconnect with Shela, Margaret is also reaching out warmly to him. She sees his bewilderment and frustration, and agrees with the need to make space for him to deal with the unexpressed anger about being blamed.]

Margaret N.: We will help you with how blamed you feel, not just by Shela but by your own mother. But right now, I think it's important for you both to realize, and come back to, what you had here for a moment.

[Heath returns Margaret's warm gaze. He seems grateful for the connection with her, and, as Margaret talks softly to him, he calms.]

Margaret N.: Do you think you could take her hand again? [Heath looks reluctant.] OK. [Margaret concedes.] If you could just look at her. [turns to Shela:] And would you look at him as well?

[This is not a calm moment. Shela looks wary, and Heath's lean, somber face is still clouded with anger. Nevertheless, they keep the exchange between them for a moment. The session has run overtime. As Heath and Shela rise to leave, Margaret gets up with them, looking worried.]

Margaret N.: Would you both try to keep this tension in check until the next appointment? Especially you, Heath? [reiterates] We will give you more time to work on your side of this more next time.

Following this session, Shela and Heath had a rough week, as we had sensed they would. While we hoped they would bring the tumult of their relationship back to the session, Heath's anger erupted at home. He wound up yelling at Shela, and she felt very hurt. In the next session, as we worked with the after effects of this intense fight, we tried to help Heath examine the depth of his anger at being blamed so unfairly by his mother. And we reminded him that when his father distanced from the family's inner life, he had set Heath up to be the target of his mother's frustration.

As the couple moved deeper into the depth of feeling between them, it became clear that Heath felt as though he deserved the anger that had been directed at him, as if he really were responsible for his brother's death. This profound sense of guilt became the focus of several sessions, and, in those sessions Margaret worked with him carefully and lovingly. The image of an eight-year-old kid feeling responsible for his sibling's death, and then being abandoned by his father and attacked angrily by his mother, pulled on Margaret's heart. As she moved to help Heath, he seemed deeply grateful for Margaret's attention and concern.

We also discovered one of the reasons that Shela had been so vocally angry, and why Heath's anger had been blocked. When Shela's father was away and she was left with her mother and younger siblings, her mother would start drinking, then become maudlinly sentimental and, finally, rageful. Shela was frightened by her mother's abusiveness, particularly when it was directed at her younger siblings. She had apparently made an intuitive decision to volunteer as the target of her mother's anger by challenging her. Identifying Shela as being in coalition with Shela's father, and yet dependent on her daughter's support, Shela's mother often dumped both rage and responsibility on her daughter. Though most of the time Shela looked, to Heath, as if she were very strong and tough, she was in fact vulnerable to being the target of anyone's anger, especially his. Heath had, of course, discovered that Shela couldn't take his expressing anger, and so he reached the same conclusion he had as a child: "You can't get angry; the best strategy is to withdraw." Of course, when he withdrew, he provoked Shela's anger about her father's constant leaving, so Heath felt in a terrible bind. Unable to protect himself by withdrawing, and realizing that Shela was terribly wounded when he got angry, he was seriously depressed when we began therapy.

As we continued to work on the couple's process, we moved deeper toward their family of origin issues. Here we helped them see that though their interpersonal strategies were different (mobilized, efficient, directive, and highly stressed, Shela was focused outside of herself; passive, moody, and often depressed, Heath was inward-turned), they had strikingly similar life dilemmas. They both had mothers who dumped anger on them and for whose unhappiness they felt responsible. And they had much more rational fathers who repeatedly abandoned them. They both had younger siblings who triggered their guilt and an excessive sense of responsibility—Shela for the care of her siblings, Heath for the death of his younger brother.

Gradually, the couple began to gain insight into and control over the processes that separated them, and they began to build a sense of common cause, which they had enjoyed in the beginning of their marriage. Rather than locating the source of their problems in the other person, they began to see the origins of their difficulties in their families of origin. All of our clients have certain family of origin dilemmas in common, and their shared awareness of these issues can allow them to develop a new level of intimacy. Instead of being alienated by their histories, they learn a kind of empathic consensus about their life-dilemmas.

BEHAVIORAL PHASE

The reader will note that in the above couple's process work, the couple made reference to Heath's promise to be more active in their children's care. Since Shela had been left as the only adult to care for her two brothers, and since the couple now had two school-age children, this issue was intensely symbolic; and we had worked on it in the previous session. Heath, convinced that he could not please Shela, readily quit trying when his halting efforts were criticized. Shela's rage at the unfairness of her situation (she also worked full time) made contracting for change difficult, but it was an important part of their work.

As many other therapists might do, we had asked Shela to make several clear requests of Heath, and to back off and allow him, with our assistance, to address her needs. She wanted more help with their house, but her most urgent need was for his involvement in the care of their sons. We coached him on doing these tasks, and we cautioned Shela not to attempt to direct or control Heath. And, of course as we see, Heath "forgot," and, with a sigh of disgust, Shela stepped in.

After the first few sessions, which are intensely focused on process, the meetings tend to alternate between behavioral contracting and review of those contracts, and process work. This rhythm is not dictated by the therapists but seems to be a naturally occurring sequence. Perhaps the relative calm of talking about life at home is a welcome relief from dealing directly with each other. It is also necessary that change begins to invade the couple's home life. It is particularly important that women see that men, instead of just making promises of change, can actually deliver what they promise. We hope that the couple will save their more volatile exchanges for the therapy hour, where we can help them be more constructive, and that they will work on being cooperative with each other at home. When the partners have greater control of their communications processes, we will encourage them to use these skills at home. But in the beginning of therapy, talking about problems at home often results in more disappointment and injury.

Behavioral change assignments, including their going on dates and making time for themselves as a couple, may allow them to build newly positive associations to being with each other, but they also raise anxieties about intimacy. Just as we push the couple to take risks in communication, we also strongly encourage behavioral experiments. We help the spouses verbalize their fears about fighting or about confronting sexual disappointments, and we offer to help them through these difficulties. Often, the partners have intuitively, and accurately, sensed increased emotional turbulence in being together intimately, and they may need a good deal of support to risk trying new possibilities. When the partners see a behavioral expriment as a failure, we reassure them that the failure is useful information about the work to be done before they reach their goals.

As both process issues and behavioral follow-through unfold, the family of origin underpinning that has impeded change comes into focus. It was very difficult for Shela to allow Heath to be in charge of their sons without struggling with an sense of impending disaster: "He always forgets, or gets dreamy. I can see Wade wandering out in the street if Heath doesn't pay attention." These fears were of course related to what might have happened in her family if she had not been "in control." In this dilemma, Margaret was able to offer Shela a good deal of identification and support: "I came out of my childhood with the same problem, and I responded in the same way you did. As a child, I knew that, if I wasn't constantly vigilent and watchful, and trying very hard to please my parents, they would have disasterous fights." Then she added: "Learning to let down your vigilance and to accept support will be hard for you. It was for me. But you can do it!"

I also found a way to identify strongly with Shela. My alcoholic father's maudlin sentimentality was distasteful to me, and I, too, learned to associate it with impending rage. Like Shela, I was very suspicious of affection, often confusing it with what I saw in my father, and associating it with my mother's overinvolvement. Shela seemed encouraged to hear about my experience, but the important issue was my ability to have empathy for her situation. I was also able to encourage her to attend Alanon meetings, as I had done.

Both of us were also able to feel empathy for Heath's family of origin dilemmas. While neither of us had lost siblings, we struggled with guilt about several issues in our families. Margaret had a keen sense of the injustice of Heath's childhood, and she responded with a kind of maternal warmth which Heath hungered for. In sometimes being his advocate in learning to confront Shela's criticism, I also tried to make up for some of the male advocacy which his father did not provide.

CRISIS RESOLUTION

The complex transactions of the initial push in therapy often result in the resolution of the couple's sense of crisis, ushering in a period of stability and good will. The therapists are, at different times, serving as communication coaches, as referees (blocking toxic exchanges), as teachers (providing insight into historical issues), and as support figures (increasing their hopefulness and morale). We are also modeling a level of marital teaming and cooperation which the client couple did not see in their parents. They get to view, at close range, a deeply committed and satisfying marriage. Not that Margaret and I have resolved all our marital problems. But we have had a lot of marital and family therapy, as well as some individual work, and we are able to share the gains from that work with our clients. When we discover a conflict between us in the therapy hour, we feel fairly confident in our ability to address it in the presence of our clients and to resolve it quickly.

As therapists, we are also participating in a complex emotional exchange in which we identify empathically with aspects of the couple's struggle. Even when we are confronting the couple, we are often functioning as symbolic parent surrogates. That is, we are providing some of the emotional resources that their parents did not offer them. We see this function as a basic requirement of the therapist: to be a partial substitute for the original parents. We do not supply the depth of resource which our clients need; it is a symbolic slice of the needed quality; but it gives them a taste of what is possible for them, and often these experiences can be transposed into new models for intimacy within the marriage.

The era of good feelings which accompanies crisis resolution usually results in the couple's reevaluating the therapy process. "Are we ready to stop, at least for now?" is a common consideration, and we help them talk about this possibility. Often, we encourage their taking a break from therapy. Some couples are finished with therapy, and, if they are not, they need to think about whether to go further. They know intuitively that the deeper course of further work will lead them into painful territory. They have examined these issues intellectually, but often have not committed to dealing with them directly.

THE INDIVIDUAL CRISIS

The typical introduction to deeper work on individual issues is the couple's appearing again in therapy, or coming to a scheduled session, and complaining that "things have gotten worse." There may be an attack on the prior therapeutic effort, or simply renewed attack on each other. Our retort is usually simple and direct: "You are worse because you haven't really dealt with these historical issues that we all talked about, and that you found too painful to tackle. Your coming back to therapy is the result of your willingness to allow the pain of those problems to surface. It takes courage to let things get worse like this; let's get to work and solve these conflicts." While the couple may still see the source of their problems as being that handy scape-goat, the other partner, they intuitively know what has to be faced. Often, fear of disloyalty to the family of origin is part of what blocks direct work on historical issues. We encourage the couple to have the courage to put their own lives first, and to be willing to face the problems in their families of origin: "We aren't blaming your families, but you need to look at what happened to you there."

The newly surfacing pain in the marriage usually emerges more powerfully in one partner, who complains, "I've had it with your...(passiveness, criticism, depression, drinking, anger, and so forth). But the underlying translation is, "I'm fed up with this marriage." This rebellion against the status quo in the marriage represents a courageous stand that comes out of being thoroughly unhappy with a certain stance in life. This willingness to give up on the marriage has its roots in the availability of the therapists. That is, the invididual has seen certain possibilities in reaching out to the therapists. While the implication may be, "I'm sick of your promises (the spouse's failure as a social therapist); I'm going to get me a real therapist," there is also reassurance in the therapists' commitment to the marriage's possibilities. So this passionate, distressed rebellion is a striking out, but it is in the implicit context that the therapist will bring the individual back to self-examination and, eventually, to attempting to work on the marriage. It is trust in the therapists as a safety net that allows this escalation.

We term this individual crisis the Individuation Regression, in that it is a symbolic leaving of the marital homeostasis that allows a deeper linking up with one or both therapists. In response to this affective distress, we do what an individual therapist might do. We listen empathically; we support the expression of affect; and, as the storm moves through, we gently bring the individuals back to themselves, and to their histories. "It makes sense that this would be so painful to you, given what you experienced as a kid." We are functioning here like understanding parents: we nurture, comfort, and we attempt to educate.

What makes this approach crucially different from the individual therapist's is that the work takes place in the presence of the partner. While the spouse of the "patient" may be dismayed by the affect directed against him or her, the therapists' turning the course of discovery toward the distressed individual is informative and reassuring. The other spouse may realize, "This isn't all about me! Now I see what I walk into." Not only can the "nonindividuating" partner develop a new level of empathy by watching the therapists work with his or her partner, but this spouse may conclude, "I want some of that kind of attention and support."

While the function of earlier work with the couple is to restore stability, this portion of the therapy is often inherantly destabilizing, whether we wish it that way or not. If the encounter goes well, the partner who became distressed and reached out to the therapists begins to feel better. He or she has a new ally. Sensing these new possibilities, the individuating partner may confront or challenge the other spouse, or take dramatic new actions, such as returning to school or quitting a boring job. He or she may work on being more assertive in a number of relationships, including coworkers, friends, and even parents. The extent of this individual work can vary a great deal. There may only be two or three sessions devoted to this partner's crisis, but, if a major depressive episode occurs for example, the need for a more extensive intervention is clearly evident.

Change in the individuating partner is likely to threaten the other spouse. He or she may attempt to get the faster-growing spouse to undo these changes. If the individuating partner holds firm, the nonindividuating partner is thrown into crisis. He or she may threaten to leave the marriage, to start drinking again, to have an affair. This often acute distress is what we call the Individuation Accommodation. That is, it is an attempt to recapture the other spouse or, if that fails, to accommodate to the changed relationship. If the individuating partner holds firm, the nonindividuating spouse is thrown into his or her own individual issues from which the marital pseudotherapy has protected them. In fact, the origin of this phase of therapy is related to the diminished function of the marriage conflicts as refuges from facing the self. The success of the earlier work, then, opens the the individuals to the chasm of their unhappiness with themselves.

We, of course, reach out to this second, also acutely unhappy, spouse. We have been tracking his or her response to the first partner's work, and we have kept in contact with this nonindividuating partner's emotional reactions. As before, we follow the affect and bring it back to the individual's own issues and own history. In this way, we attempt to empower this person as well to be less dependent on the spouse and to be aware of more options for self-determination.

When both partners experience firm alliances with the therapeutic team, the stage is set for them to challenge the status quo in the marriage in new and exciting ways. If they have modulated their feelings out of fear of loss of the relationship, they may have intense conflicts, surfacing feelings which they have hidden for many years. The safety of the therapeutic relationship allows them to plunge into issues which they alluded to in the earlier therapy but did not address directly. They may move toward examining their reasons for being together. If a couple divorces during therapy, it is likely to occur during this phase. These forceful encounters between the partners may also create an existential shift, in that the rules and parameters that held previously are rewritten. The partners may become more honest, more openly caring, and more successfully separate. This phase of powerful encounters between the partners is carefully guided by the therapists, and this work often resembles the earlier process work. Only, in this instance, the affect is more open and direct, and the therapists have deeper levels of connection with both partners.

FAMILY OF ORIGIN WORK

Inherant in facing individual issues is dealing with family history. While insight into these problems is helpful, successful resolution often demands an ameliorative emotional encounter with these generative figures. The most powerful alternative is to bring the family of origin into the couple's therapy. This process is too complex to deal with extensively in this chapter, but some general guidelines follow.

While the families of origin may be invited in for get acquainted sessions early in therapy (and these two branches of the family are dealt with separately), more focused work usually occurs later in treatment. It is crucial that the individual spouse whose family comes for sessions is motivated to make changes in his or her family. The partner must be willing to feel, instead of merely have insight into, the connection between the marital issues and dynamics in the family of origin. Heath, for example, said, "I get angry when I think about the way my mother treated me, and I am angry with my father, too, for withdrawing from all of us after Samuel died." He had gotten past his loyalty conflicts, and, though he was anxious about the prospect of doing it, he wanted to talk to his family about his brother's death and how it had affected them all. Like many of our clients, he needed encouragement and support in getting the courage to ask them to come to therapy.

The goals of the sessions must be thought out in advance with both partners. The spouse whose family is attending will be the active participant; the in-law connection is explored only if it is a major issue. It is too easy for nonproductive fights to occur between in-laws; we try to focus on the deeper connections between family of origin members.

The family of origin must not be scapegoated, neither should we allow them to discredit or blame our client. The therapists need to be able to identify with all members of the extended clan. Therapists who are near the age of their clients may over-identify with them and blame the older parents. It is important, as well, that we not attempt to make the extended family our clients; they are there to help the younger couple. If painful issues arise in the older parents, however, we must be prepared to shift our focus and refer them to therapists in their home community.

Extended family sessions may have a variety of foci. Our client may need to address critical events in the past. We need to help everyone in the family share their experiences about these times. We need to work hard to make sure the discussions are safe emotionally. We may help the family uncover conflict that has led to cut-offs. If possible, these alienated relationships may be reconnected. We may encourage people who don't know each other well to become closer. Family myths, secrets, and taboos may be explored.

In our efforts to facilitate marital intimacy, we may help the extended family examine the hidden codes and rules that govern the level of emotional expression in the family. If our client's family of origin can make changes in the degree of their intimacy with each other, these shifts can be tremendously freeing and permission-granting for our client.

In all our work with couples, we rarely experience changes that are more powerful and more significant than those that take place in extended family sessions. So passionate and long-constrained are the issues in these relationships, and so grateful is the family for this opportunity, finally, to address each other, that it is the rare extended family session that does not produce important change in our clients.

RENEGOTIATING THE MARRIAGE

The last push in couple's work occurs after the issues and problems related to the extended family are at least partially resolved. At any rate, these conflicts have been addressed and are in perspective. The latter couple sessions are more here-and-now focused, and both partners are aware of each other, not as symbolic figures but as real people. These sessions may include confrontation and hard bargaining: "I am sick of your forgetting to do what you promised. I know you can do better, and I expect you to." Here is where we call on our clients' goodwill, intentionality, and determination. Here is where character, courage, honesty, and the willingness to try come fully to the fore. This is the stage of growth when the therapists may say: "We can't do this for you. You understand the issues. You know what you need to do. Just do it!"

These sessions may also be playful and enjoyable, with more peer status between us and our clients. Margaret and I may joke, "Well, that's not a problem we've ever had!" The clients laugh, knowing full well that Margaret and I do have that problem. We may also kid, "You are going to have to fire us as your therapists; otherwise, we will keep you around forever because we enjoy you so much." Often we acknowledge, directly to them, caring about our clients, these people whom we could barely stand to be in the room with when therapy began. Over time, we have become like family to each other.

As their marriage, and their relationship with us as well, seems more like the real world, that is, a mixture of blessings and curses, something like the Serenity Prayer that is so meaningful to Alcoholics Anonymous creeps into our discourse. We have tried for changing the things that we can change, and we must also accept the things that we cannot. Acceptance of self and other, warts and all, may be the final sigh of relief.

EPILOGUE

The middle phase of Heath and Shela's therapy seemed interminable. The first phase was about a year of work. Then, they took a break of about three months, and came back, as we might have predicted, complaining that the earlier therapy had been helpful but hadn't worked. Shela was more critical than ever. Rather than being depressed, Heath was retaliating more. And the tensions between them had escalated. They had talked about divorce; their eldest, Jeffery, who was now eight, was doing poorly in school.

We confronted them forcefully. Rather than really dealing with their own issues, they were back into blaming each other. And now, they were scapegoating their child as well. We forced them to bring their kids for a number of sessions and to include them periodically for the remainder of the therapy. Very quickly, it became apparent that Heath was spending a lot of cozy time with Jeffrey, and subtly recruiting him as an ally against Shela. Shela had become very critical of Jeffrey, who seemed depressed and sullen. They were both enfantilizing Wade, who had turned four. And neither of them saw his immaturity as a problem.

As we interferred with their using their kids (both were surprised upon realizing what they were doing), the conflict between them escalated sharply, with Shela becoming verbally abusive toward Heath about his narcissism, his passivity, his irresponsibility toward their children. Margaret was quite confrontive with Shela, challenging her to let herself feel the injustice of her own childhood. "It is your **mother** who was really irresponsible, your mother who was locked in her narcissism. And, Shela, you don't want to become verbally abusive in the way that she was." This confrontation shook Shela, and she became very depressed. Memories of seeing her mother drunk, and of sheparding her brothers away flooded her. The loneliness, the panic about their being "nobody home" during her childhood came back.

I, too, was able to connect with Shela during her depression. "Shela, there are many families like yours. There are many who will understand what you went through." I encouraged her to attend some Alanon meetings, and I accompanied her to her first meeting. These meetings too brought back memories and brought up further pain. As Shela became more depressed, we increased the frequency of the sessions, and for about six months, Shela took one of the newer anti-depressants. As she began to feel better, we referred

Shela to a women's codependency group led by a therapist whom we trusted and knew we could work well with.

Heath expressed his panic about Shela's depression by trying to get her to focus on him. Without her mobilized, efficient codependency, he felt adrift. He fell and broke an ankle and had to be driven to work. He had a fight with his boss, and there was worry about the stability of his job. This self-punitiveness not only served to distract Shela temporarily from her work on herself, but it also expressed Heath's lifelong struggle with guilt about his brother's death. I intervened forcefully with Heath, challenging him to develop other resources, to need Shela less. I had just started a men's therapy group, and to help Heath learn that he could derive support from men, I brought him into that group. Heath made an immediate and lasting connection with this group, and he remained in it for several years.

As both partners were thrown back on their own individual issues, our sessions focused increasingly on family of origin concerns. When they began to work productively on these problems, the conflict between them lessened dramatically. Instead of two angry partners, we had two depressed and sad individuals who realized what their childhoods had done to them. In the family sessions, Jeffrey and Wade began to speak up about their concerns. At four, Wade had been worried about his parents, and his strategy to help them had been to be cute and cuddly. Jeffrey felt that his mother was unfair to his father, and his verbalizing this worry allowed him to be more age-appropriate. Though we kept bringing the kids in periodically, they were essentially asymptomatic through the rest of our involvement with the family.

There were four family of origin sessions, and they were highly productive. By the time we worked with the family, Shela's mother had died and her father had remarried a somewhat younger woman. Shela's father, Samuel, was as she described him, charming, active, and emotionally elusive. We knew that Shela loved her father but was very angry with him. So, we asked him to bring his wife to the session. I met separately with Samuel and Ann to sound out Samuel's willingness to hear out Shela's feelings about the family's past, and he agreed to try to listen as well as he could.

Shela did what she needed to do. She affirmed her love for her father, but told him what it had been like to be left with her alcoholic mother and younger siblings. She expressed a lot of anger about her father's failure to protect her, and asked why he had never insisted that Shela's mother get treatment. Samuel then described his attempts to get Shela's mother to a psychiatrist, and the failure of that effort. He also related details about Shela's mother's childhood that were informative, particularly her loss of her own mother when she was five. But he also made a tearful, genuine apology to Shela. He knew that he had left her with too much responsibility, and that his excuse—"Somebody had to earn the living"—sounded feeble. In a shift that was especially important to Shela, he promised to be more actively involved with her younger siblings, and to try to get treatment for Shela's brother Adam, who was alcoholic, and about whom Shela worried a lot. These two three-hour sessions were the turning point for Shela. After they were concluded, her relationship with her father improved, and she felt more charitable toward Heath.

The two sessions with Heath's family were painful and difficult, and we entered into them cautiously. Heath's parents, Alice and Timothy, were in their early sixties, and they seemed symbiotically attached and rather fragile. But the obvious issue had to be tackled, and Heath tentatively and courageously raised it: could they talk about his brother's death and what happened to the family afterward? The parents agreed, and Heath began to ask questions. Heath thought that his brother had died of pneumonia, and that his taking Timmy out to play in a puddle the day before his death may have made him sick. It turned out that Timmy died of an asthma attack, and the parents were surprised that Heath had blamed himself. Timmy had severe asthma and had had several dangerous attacks before the one that killed him.

The crucial revelation in the sessions was Heath's mother's confession of her own guilt about Timmy's death, and her frustration that her husband had been unavailable to talk about the sadness of those days. Timothy was surprised that Alice felt that way. She had never mentioned wanting him to talk about the boy's death. With a good bit of trepidation, Margaret and I helped the family talk about the loss of Timmy, and how it affected all of them. At one point in the discussion, Alice broke down and wept, and both Heath and Timothy cried quietly with her. Late in the session, Heath was able to talk about how unfair his mother's anger was, and how it made him blame himself more. Like Shela's father, Heath's mother made a belated apology.

After this session, Heath reported that an "enormous weight" had been removed from his shoulders. With the lifting of that weight, his depression improved substantially.

Toward the end of our contacts with the couple, Margaret saw both partners individually. They both had such negative experiences with their mothers, and both seemed grateful for Margaret's caring and perceptive involvement with them. I continued to see Heath in the men's group, and, with this group's support, he became much more assertive and more emotionally available to Shela and to his kids.

Our work with the couple spanned four years, though we were not always meeting weekly. It has been approximately two years since they ended therapy, and they report that, while they still struggle with some of the same issues, they are doing well.

Are they an intimate couple? Toward the end of therapy, Heath seemed to address that issue: "One of the things we discovered, is that feeling close isn't always about being romantic (though they reported a rejuvenated sexual relationship); sometimes it's about sharing and getting through pain."

REFERENCES

Bowlby, J. (1969). *Attachment and loss*, (Vol. 1). *Attachment*. New York: Basic Books.

Bowlby, J. (1988). *A secure base*. New York: Basic Books.

Bowen, M. (1978). *Family therapy in clinical practice*. New York: Jason Aronson.

Hochschild, A. (1989). *The second shift*. New York: Avon Books.

Johnson, S. (1996). *Creating connection: The practice of emotionally focused marital therapy*. New York: Brunner/Mazel.

Napier, A. (1988). *The fragile bond*. New York: Harper/Collins.

Napier, A. & Whitaker, C. (1978). *The family crucible*. New York: Harper/Collins.

Neill, J. R., & Kniskern, D. P. (Eds.). (1982). *From psyche to system: the evolving therapy of Carl Whitaker*. New York: Guilford Press.

Roberto, L. G. (1991). Symbolic-experiential family therapy. In A. S. Gurman & D. P. Kniskern (Eds.), *Handbook of family therapy* (pp. 444–476). New York: Brunner/Mazel.

Schnarch, D. (1991). *Constructing the sexual crucible*. New York: Norton.

Schnarch, D. (1997). *Passionate marriage*. New York: Norton.

Whitaker, C. A. & Keith, D. V. (1981). Symbolic-experiential family therapy. In A.S. Gurman & D.P. Kniskern (Eds.), *Handbook of family therapy* (pp. 187–224). New York: Brunner/Mazel.

Whitaker, C. A., & Ryan, M. C. (1989). *Midnight musings of a family therapist*. New York: Norton.

CHAPTER 18

Increasing Intimacy in Couples through Distance Writing and Face-to-Face Approaches

Luciano L'Abate

A specific and concrete definition of intimacy can lead to structured, long-distance, as well as less structured face-to-face couple interventions. Intimacy grows in close, committed, and prolonged relationships. It does not grow in short-lived, superficial, and uncommitted ones. Once intimacy is defined as the sharing of joys as well as the sharing of hurts and fears of being hurt, then specific and concrete methods can be designed to improve intimacy in those couples who find it difficult to become intimate (Cusinato & L'Abate, 1994; L'Abate, 1994, L'Abate & Baggett, 1997b). Hurts are defined as the accumulation of traumas, abuses, losses, stresses, strains, rejections, put-downs, and offenses that are inevitably received throughout the course of life. Admittedly, some receive more hurts than others. Some may be more sensitive to certain hurts than others. Some hurts may be more intense and long-lasting than others. Nonetheless, being alive means receiving some hurts, no matter how small. We are all vulnerable to hurts from others, and we all fail by hurting others intentionally or unintentionally. We are more vulnerable to being hurt by loved ones than by strangers. Strangers do not have the power to hurt us emotionally the way intimate others do. To protect ourselves from being hurt, we develop defenses that keep us distant from the very people we love and who love us, where intimacy is the necessary ingredient for an evolving and deepening relationship.

INTIMACY, SHARING JOYS, HURTS, AND FEARS OF BEING HURT

The foregoing definition of intimacy leads to several implications and derivations in clinical practice. We cannot share joys unless we share hurts and fears of being hurt with our loved ones. This statement derives from three seemingly paradoxical conclusions.

1   We hurt those we love the most because it is they who are more vulnerable to what we say and what we do than are strangers. A stranger can physically hurt us, but, if someone we do not know is rude or discourteous to us, we will eventually forget it. We do not forget when a loved one is rude to us. Loving someone means giving that person, more often than not, our partner, the power to hurt. By the same token, our partners are vulnerable to whatever we do that may be hurtful to them. This is why loving and hurting are intrinsically intertwined (L'Abate & Baggett, 1997b). There is really nothing paradoxical about this conclusion. Think of the child who is spanked or punished for a misdeed and who needs to seek comfort from the very parent who punished him or her. We may forgive or be forgiven for an error. However, the painfulness of that error may be still remembered, especially if the same error is repeated.

2   We need to be separate as individuals in order to be close and together as a couple. Being separate as an individual means (a) being in charge and in control of oneself, (b) avoiding reactions to provocation's or distractions from loved ones, (c) keeping focused on substantive issues rather than on tangential ones, (d) being able to empathize about a loved one's plight, and (e) being emotionally available when the partner hurts. It is important for this process of being and keeping separate to take place because it provides reciprocity. When we hurt, we want that very same intimate to be emotionally available to us. Whenever there is a loss of a family member, for instance, death of the parent of one partner, grieving that loss may be much more intense for the partner who is the child of that parent. Hence, the partner who might not be as effected by the loss as the other, needs to be available to the one who is grieving more. One day in the future, the loss of a parent may occur to the partner who is grieving less now but who will grieve more later.

3   Support, comfort, and forgiveness need to be present in ourselves as well as in those whom we have hurt or who have hurt us. This presence is the outcome of a process whereby trust and reciprocity are paramount. We need support and forgiveness from the very one we have hurt. The ultimate act of intimacy is demonstrated in crying together. Inflicted hurts need to be shared

and forgiven and then used to improve and deepen the relationship to avoid further and future hurts.

These three conclusions also suggest that the ultimate nature of our existence is comprised of:

1   Our *fallibility* in hurting those we love, in spite of our best intentions not to hurt them. Whether intentionally or unintentionally, there is always room for error, even in the very best relationships: a stupid forgetting of an important anniversary; a thoughtless remark, meant as a compliment, that turns sour; a criticism; a misintended word that sounds offensive; etc. We may mean well, but what ultimately counts is how what we say or do is received by our partner. Even the best intentions may not be enough, as demonstrated by the proverb, "The road to hell is paved by good intentions."

2   Our *vulnerability* in being hurt by the very one we love. We are not hurt, at least emotionally, by mere strangers who mean nothing to us. We are much more vulnerable to the words and deeds of those we love, because they are the most important persons to us. They are important for our survival and for our enjoyment of life (L'Abate & Baggett, 1997b). Therefore, whatever loved ones say or do becomes important. How else will they know that we love them? Once a sense of importance is attributed and imparted to the partner, anything that is said and done that detracts from that sense of importance will become hurtful. For instance, a man could tell his partner that he loves her immensely. However, if he comes home late at night drunk, this behavior would indicate that alcohol is more important to him than is his partner, especially if this behavior repeats itself.

3   Our *neediness* in wanting and in giving or exchanging love from the very people we might have hurt or who might have hurt us. We need to love and to be loved. Very few of us deny the need to be dependent on someone who is reciprocally needy of us. Once dependence is accepted as a necessary and indispensable ingredient of intimate relationships, there are at least three possibilities: (a) both partners are extremely needy of each other, but are unable to express and exchange their needs, and, contradictorily and inconsistently, deny their needs for dependency; (b) one partner is extremely needy, while the other partner denies any dependency; and (c) both partners acknowledge, accept, and express congruently their reciprocal need for dependency. This need also leaves room for personal autonomy, producing autonomous interdependence. The first possibility is extremely dysfunctional. The second possibility is semifunctional. The third possibility is functional.

By this process of reciprocal admission of our frailties, faults, and failures—the full admission of our humanness rather than its denial—we obtain autonomous interdependence, that is, reciprocal and mutual understanding that our partner is as fallible, needy, and vulnerable as we are. Unless we are able to admit reciprocally to being fallible, vulnerable, and needy, it is difficult to become intimate with another human being. Only strong people can admit to being weak. Weak people find it very difficult to admit to any weakness, lest someone take advantage of them or crucifies them for their perceived or admitted shortcomings. Adequate people have no trouble admitting to inadequacies. It is much more difficult for inadequate ones to admit any inadequacy.

Hence, intimacy, because of its complexity and its paradoxical nature, can be found in well functioning couples because they are able to express, acknowledge, and share their vulnerability, fallibility, and neediness while still loving each other unconditionally. The expression of intimacy is sporadic and occasional in semifunctional or semidysfunctional couples because one partner is either too dependent or too adamant in denying dependency. Intimacy is absent in very dysfunctional couples, who are not able to admit to any inadequacy lest these inadequacies be used against them. These couples cannot tolerate stresses of any kind, especially the admission of possible inadequacies in either partner. The denial of dependency and its extremes is found in everyday news media. Stereotypically, many men ignore and neglect their partners emotionally. Neglect is the other side of the coin of emotional abuse. This is another way to deny their own dependency on them. Dependency is a dirty word for many men. However, when women want to leave or do leave them, denying that they wish to be dependent on their men any longer, men will typically push limits, harassing, stalking, and even killing these women at times, because they "can no longer live without them." Under these conditions, dependency and denial of dependency become confused. Extremes are found in the murder-suicide of couples where one partner, usually the woman, can no longer put up with the emotional abuse and neglect from the man. These couples cannot be emotionally available to each other.

Being emotionally available means sharing both hurts and joys. The sine qua non of intimacy is reciprocity in sharing feelings, especially hurt ones. It is relatively easy to share superficial victories and triumphs. Any bar will do, if you are willing to celebrate a victory in that kind of setting. It is much more difficult to share deep and lasting hurts with a loved one, because this process makes us more vulnerable to the whims and will of the other. This inequality upsets the balance of power established in the couple, and presents the possibility of losing the partner. Admitting to hurts may be tantamount to being perceived as weak, wanting, inadequate, and incomplete. This is why many men have may greater difficulty in crying and admitting to their hurts than women. Many men are raised in the image of John Wayne, the strong, silent, and surly stereotype of the macho man. We can celebrate victories in a bar, but we cannot share our defeats with our partners, because, in doing so, we may feel diminished and "less than a man."

Consequently, joys cannot be shared fully unless hurts are shared just as fully, as in crying together. Unfortunately, many men see their partner's tears as manipulation. Hence, they prefer to withdraw rather than remain feeling manipulated. Without reciprocity in sharing feelings, however, there cannot be intimacy, because a one-way-street in sharing feelings cannot work. Reciprocity in functional couples assumes such a sharing, In semifunctional couples, where reactivity rather than reciprocity is the norm, it is much more difficult to achieve such a sharing. It is virtually impossible to achieve it in dysfunctional couples, where abuse and neglect are the norm. Most of us want to be close. On the other hand, many of us are afraid of being close, especially if we have never experienced intimacy while growing up in our families of origin. Most clinical couples, for instance, do not remember seeing their parents crying together. If one parent, usually the mother, did cry, the other parent, usually the father, would get mad or drunk or leave the house.

Diagnostically, the relevant questions to ask couples in the process of facilitating their intimacy are: (1) "Did you ever see your parents cry together?"; (2) "What happened when one of your parents cried?"; (3) "What did the other parent do?" Both partners also need to be asked: (1) "What do you do when one of you cries?" For men, it is usually relevant to ask: "When was the last time you cried?" However, one should be careful not to fall victim to gender stereotypes, making sure to avoid precipitous conclusions about which partner is able to cry.

What is relevant here is to find whether there is a polarization in the expression of feelings. For instance, one partner gets mad and walks out whenever the other partner cries. A discussion of the various meanings of crying might include exploding the myth, "Strong men don't cry," and then explore what it means to be strong or weak. Strong people admit to being needy, vulnerable, and fallible. It takes a great deal of strength to ask for help, especially professional help. Weak people are those who deny being human, by denying their neediness, vulnerability, and fallibility. It follows, then, that asking for professional help means being strong because weak people deny the need for help. Hospitals, jails, and cemeteries are full of them. Consequently, the rationale for asking for help is love and strength, to the point of contradicting the couple's negative reasons for referral: "You should be congratulated for asking for professional help. It takes guts to ask for help. It takes a lot of care and strength to ask for help. Those who do not care for themselves and each other prefer to spend good money to pay a lawyer. It is much easier to destroy a marriage than to build one up."

DISTANCE APPROACHES

From the foregoing introductive definition and its implications, it was relatively easy to develop structured and less structured ways of helping couples become more intimate.

Homework Assignments

To help couples become more intimate, the author wrote a workbook consisting of six homework assignments to be completed by couples through writing (L'Abate, 1986; L'Abate, 1997). Theoretically, this workbook was based isomorphically on an early model of intimacy that made love and caring (assignment 1), seeing the good in self and partner (assignment 2), and forgiveness (assignment 3), prerequisites to the sharing of hurts (assignments 4, 5, and 6). Practicably, this workbook was part of a whole range of workbooks to be used as written homework assignments for individuals, couples, and families (L'Abate, 1990, 1991, 1992; L'Abate & Baggett, 1997a, L'Abate & Baggett, 1997b). Preliminary results from a study evaluating the usefulness of two negotiation and intimacy programs are found in L'Abate (1992). A review of research to evaluate these programs is found in L'Abate and Baggett (1997a). Esterling, L'Abate, Murray, and Pennebaker (1998) reviewed the research that supports the use of distance writing (away from the presence of a professional) in prevention and psychotherapy.

On the basis of Pennebaker's work and research (1997), the author routinely asks all clients, whether individuals, couples, or families, from the very outset of therapy, to write about their hurts for 20 minutes a day for four consecutive days. In couples and families, they have to make an appointment with each other to share, compare, and discuss what they have written about their hurts. Variations on this assignment consist of listing hurts given and hurt received, including also targets of given hurts and sources of received hurts. On the basis of these homework assignments with clinical couples, it can be readily seen that the process of intellectualization is still present. Often, even though they may be cognizant of the inflicted hurts, partners are not ready to share them in an affective fashion. When couples bring their lists of hurts to the therapist, this homework assignment is very informative. However, most couples are not ready to share their mutually inflicted hurts in a cathartic fashion, at least not in front of the therapist and not at the beginning of therapy. This area of sharing hurts through writing is completely open to clinical and preventive applications (Esterling et al., 1998; L'Abate, 1997; L'Abate & Baggett, 1997a; Riordan, 1996).

Structured Enrichment Programs

This approach consists of written exercises to be administered by semiprofessional trainers under the supervision of a professional (L'Abate & Weinstein, 1987; L'Abate & Young, 1987). These exercises are administered verbatim from the text to couples and families (L'Abate, 1990; L'Abate, in press). An early version of an Intimacy Enrichment program was published *verbatim* in L'Abate and McHenry (1983, pp. 357–362). In another collection with hundreds of exercises on a variety of topics (L'Abate & Weinstein, 1987), one exercise (p. 162) addresses avoidance of intimacy and a complete program on helpfulness (pp. 300–309) contains lessons on (a) establishing levels of caring, hurts, and strengths, (b) seeing the good, (c) caring, (d) sharing of hurt feelings, (e) forgiveness, (f) protectiveness, (g) responsibility, and (h) enjoyment. Two case studies (L'Abate & Young, 1987), illustrate specific applications of this program to issues of parentification (pp. 134–153) and to a psychosomatic family (pp. 163–179) and describe how this program was applied with pre- and post-enrichment test batteries. This author is in the process of transforming these exercises for computer administration.

FACE-TO-FACE APPROACHES: SOME EXEMPLARY PATTERNS

The Hurt Exercise (L'Abate, 1986, p. 235) was developed for use in therapy sessions with couples and families. It has been reproduced more recently within the same context of intimacy as the sharing of joys, hurts, and fears of being hurt (L'Abate & Baggett, 1997b, pp. 320–321). This exercise requires partners to face each other on a sofa or two chairs, to close their eyes, and to hold each other's hands. They are asked to concentrate on their physical sensations first, those elicited and expressed by holding each other's hands, before concentrating on their hurts. Once the request to concentrate on their hurt is given, the professional is to wait for the outcome. One may repeat the request for a second time, but no more than twice altogether. Once they are in touch with the hurts that are dwelling inside their bodies, partners are asked to acknowledge and, if possible, share them ("I hurt, I am hurting").

CASE EXAMPLE[1]

A couple, in their middle 30s, married for 12 years, with two children, came in because of their frequent fighting and bickering that ended up with both not speaking with each other for days. Their major concern in asking for professional help, was not only the painfulness of their poor relationship but also how their fighting was affecting their children. Both children, a boy, 11 and a girl, 9, were beginning to fight with each other and becoming very reactive and competitive with each other, expressing sibling rivalry, as they saw their parents fighting.

　　From the first to the second evaluation session, they were told to write down all the hurts they had received in their lives including those prior to the marriage. At the end of this initial evaluation session ("You evaluate us to see

---

[1] This is a composite of many cases, rather than a specific case sample.

whether you think we can help you."), they were given an informed consent form agree asking that they agree to complete written homework assignments discussed with them from the very first session. ("This is the way we practice. However, you should know that this practice may be unique for us. Many other therapists do not have this requirement. We want you to be free to choose what is best for you.") They were asked to read this informed consent form and think about it before signing it during the third evaluation session. They were also asked to complete two short rating sheets, a Self-Other Profile Chart (SOPC) and the Beck Depression Inventory (L'Abate, 1992; L'Abate & Baggett, 1997a, L'Abate & Baggett, 1997b). During the second session there was a discussion of their lists of hurts. The wife listed 55 hurts versus 12 hurts for the husband. Their SOPCs showed that the husband valued his importance more than the importance of others, including his wife, while the wife valued the importance of the husband and children more than she valued herself. Predictably from this discrepancy, the husband showed a very low score on depression while the wife showed a middle to high depression score. We interpreted these discrepancies as indications of mixed and confused priorities that would be destructive in the long run since, successful marriages are based on equality of importance. As homework from the second to the third session, they were asked to discuss the informed consent form before signing it. No therapeutic contract, without their signed informed consent about completing regular (one hour of written homework for each hour of couple therapy) written homework assignments, would take place. They came back for the third session with the signed contract.

Since fighting was their referral reason and since it had not abated during the first three sessions of evaluation, they were given the first assignment of a matching fighting workbook (L'Abate, 1992). This workbook requires respondents in the first assignment to rate intensity, frequency, duration, outcome, and content of their fights. After completing each assignment individually, they were to make an appointment with each other to compare and contrast their answers, keeping notes of their discussion to bring to the next therapy session. A predictable pattern was present in their answers. The wife exaggerated rate, duration, frequency, and intensity of their fights, while the husband tended to perceive these characteristics in much milder terms. At the end of this session, they were given the second assignment of the fighting workbook that requires individual rankings of 10 explanations for fighting, all framed positively. If they did not like these explanations, they could come up with ones of their own. Again, they had to keep a preset appointment to compare and contrast their individually completed assignments. Their notes about this last appointment indicated a gradual lowering of intensity in their discussion. After a confrontation of how feelings were expressed in their families of origin, with a conclusion that intimacy was not present in either family, their fighting was explained as a fear and inability to be intimate. They loved each other dearly, they wanted for their marriage to succeed, but they did not know how to be intimate because they had never experienced it in their families of origin ("If you do not know what it is, how can you obtain it?") Once, intimacy was explained in concrete terms, as the sharing of joys as well as of hurts and fears of being hurt, they agreed that that was the goal they wanted to achieve.

At the end of this session, they were given the third assignment of the fighting workbook. This assignments requires in detail that the couple has to set up an appointment beforehand and have a fight following seven specific "suicidal" patterns (suicidal in the sense that they kill selves and marriages). The patterns are: (1) blaming; (2) bringing up the past; (3) threats and ultimatums; (4) excuses for self but not for the other; (5) mind-reading of the partner's intentions and behavior; (6) bribery and blackmail, usually emotional; and (7) distracting, bringing up topics that are tangential or extraneous to the issue at hand. In their detailed instructions on how to fight, they were also told to tape-record their fight. They came back for the next session confessing that they had been unable to have a fight because they discussed issues without fighting, instead of indulging in most of the suicidal patterns described in the homework assignments. Now that they recognized these patterns, they felt sure that they would not repeat them. The therapists expressed surprise and chagrin at this unexpected course of events. They doubted very seriously and expressed great reservetions about whether the couple would be able to carry out their stated agreement to discuss issues rather than to fight. They would not only not be able to give up the seven suicidal patterns but would regress back to their guerrilla tactics of sudden and unexpected attacks. Therefore, they were urged to have another fight by appointment during the forthcoming week. ("Be sure to tape-record it.")

As a proof of their newly found awareness, the tape presented during the fourth session contained a dispassionate discussion of how painful their past fights had been and how painfully aware they were of how they used to fight "dirty." They had learned to speak for themselves and not for the other. Their major concern, still lingering in their minds, consisted of their children's rivalry. Resolving this problem together would be a proof of whether they really had learned to cooperate rather than to fight together. Consequently, they were given the first assignment of the sibling rivalry workbook (L'Abate, 1992). The same three-assignment workbook asked them individually to describe the rate, frequency, duration, and intensity of sibling rivalry episodes in the first appointment with each other. This time, their answers were in general agreement about the characteristics of this behavior. Following the same format of many other symptom-related programs (L'Abate, 1992), the second assignment asked the couple to rank order the explanations (all framed positively) about the sibling rivalry. They both disagreed with these explanations and chose instead to assume responsibility for their being, in the past, poor models to their children for the sibling rivalry. Essentially, they undertook responsibility without, however, blaming themselves or each other for how they fought in the past. The third assignment of this workbook consisted of their prescribing the sibling rivalry at preset times for a given length of time, usually 15 minutes. ("Fight all you want but you cannot touch each other.") Through this prescription, there is the possibility that the children would be reassured that the parents were in control. Furthermore, they were both cooperating in reassuring them that the sibling rivalry was unacceptable to them by taking control of it, rather than just reacting to it. One of the principles behind this approach is "Start it, if you want to stop it." Again, when the parents reported that the children refused to fight when asked to do so by the parents, the therapists expressed surprise and chagrin at such an unexpected outcome. They were asked to follow the prescription of sibling rivalry for at least two more weeks ("To make sure.") and then report for a possible termination session. They reported that the children had given up fighting and were cooperating with each other much better, and that the whole family atmosphere was a happy one. Just to make sure, they were asked to face each other, hold each other's hands, keep their eyes closed, and concentrate on all the hurts that they has experienced in the past and present, as individuals as well as a couple. Both were able to express these hurts and cry together, hugging each other closely, kissing each other warmly, agreeing to let the past go, and concentrating on the present. Posttreatment testing of the SOPC and depression scale showed a much greater balance in attribution of importance to self and intimate other, with no depression in the wife.

REACTIONS TO THE SHARING OF HURTS EXERCISE

A good outcome to this exercise may consist of both partners starting to cry and holding each other tightly. A mediocre outcome may consist of one partner crying but the other partner reassuring him or her verbally but not physically. A poor outcome may consist of the noncrying or seemingly nonhurting partner saying nothing and showing no outward reaction to the partner's crying. A very poor outcome may consist of the noncrying, seemingly nonhurting partner getting up and leaving the room. These four patterns illustrate the range of reactions obtained from couples over the years that this exercise has been administered as a diagnostic approach to evaluate (1) the level of intimacy at the beginning of therapy, (2) possible polarizations in the expression and sharing of hurt feelings before starting therapy, (3) the potential to become intimate, as well as (4) a way of assessing at the end of therapy the outcome of intimacy homework administered to the couple. One way to classify these patterns is to consider them according to a human arithmetic, where a victory is a + and a loss is a − (L'Abate & Baggett, 1997b). Whenever both partners win with each other (+, +) their victories represent a multiplication and growth (X) in the relationship. Whenever one partner wins (+) at the expense of the other (−) or vice versa, the relationship remains stagnant (0). Whenever both partners lose with each (−, −) a breakdown in the relationship, a division, might occur (/). The patterns given below are composites drawn from a very large number of couples who have been administered this exercise.

Pattern 1 (+, +)   In this pattern, both partners are able to cry together, to express and share their hurts reciprocally, by coming together with hugs, kisses, and promises of definite changes in their behavior. Here, one partner cries and the other does as well, ending with each hugging and comforting the other. A variation on this theme has the woman weeping and the man wanting to comfort her but not knowing how to do it. In this case, the noncrying partner is encouraged to embrace the crying partner and reassure her of his love and devotion. Partners who start with this pattern are good candidates for the intimacy workbook described above (L'Abate, 1986). This workbook is administered if, however, there is no depression shown and both partners are able to negotiate. Otherwise, if there is depression in either partner, the dyadic depression workbook is administered first and the negotiation program is administered afterwards (L'Abate, 1986). If the couple's referral symptom is too much arguing and fighting, the appropriate program for arguing and fighting is administered first (L'Abate, 1992). The intimacy program is administered last because, at this point in the therapeutic process, the couple is strong enough to admit to being weak. This pattern is rare, but it does occur in relatively well functioning couples who come to therapy for a specific and circumscribed problem that can be usually treated in a few sessions, as in the case example given above.

Patterns 2 and 3 (+, − or −, +)   In these patterns, one partner is ready to throw in the towel and to walk out of the relationship, either because of years of abuse and neglect, which have turned one into a nag, or because of a hidden agenda, like an affair that is unknown to the other partner but which comes to life after the partner has left the relationship. One partner, most often a woman, cries out and shares her hurts openly and directly. Unable or unwilling to respond to her tears and hurts, the male partner walks out of the session, increasing the intensity of the woman's crying. Eventually, the wife will call to inform the therapist that the husband has moved out and has started divorce proceedings.

Pattern 4 (−, −)   In this pattern neither partner is able to share hurts and both are unable to cry together at the beginning of therapy. They might be able to achieve the criterion of crying together if therapy proceeds on two tracks: (1) face-to-face confrontation with the therapist and (2) parallel and isomorphic written homework assignments. If therapy has progressed through predictable stages, like (1) depression or a referral symptom in one partner, or fighting in both partners, (2) learning to negotiate, and (3) intimacy, then this sharing of hurts exercise would test whether the couple has become intimate. They are intimate if they can share their hurts at the end of therapy. In one couple, the husband, a divinity student, admitted to physical abuse toward his wife over a period of years, much to his shame and sorrow. His abuse was explained, but not condoned, as a sign of helplessness, an explanation to which he heartily agreed. They left the penultimate therapy session where they did share their hurts, crying together. After leaving the session, they phoned their teenage children to inform them they would be late for supper, and checked in to a hotel to consummate properly their honeymoon of twelve years earlier that had culminated in abuse.

CONCLUSION

A specific and concrete definition of intimacy as sharing of joys, hurts, and fears of being hurt has been productive, if not successful, in creating distance and face-to-face approaches to improve intimacy in couples. The next step will consist of determining the validity of the present formulation.

REFERENCES

Cusinato, M., & L'Abate, L. (1994). A spiral model of intimacy. In S. M. Johnson & L. S. Greenberg, (Eds.), *The heart of the matter: Perspectives on emotion in marital therapy* (pp. 108–123). New York: Brunner/Mazel.

Esterling, B. A., L'Abate, L., Murray, E., & Pennebaker, J. W. (1998). Empirical foundations for writing in prevention and psychotherapy: Mental and physical outcomes, *Clinical Psychology Review*.

L'Abate, L. (1986). *Systematic family therapy*. New York: Brunner/Mazel.

L'Abate, L. (1990). *Building family competence: Primary and secondary prevention strategies*. Newbury Park, CA: Sage.

L'Abate, L. (1991). The use of writing in psychotherapy. *American Journal of Psychotherapy, 45*, 87–98.

L'Abate, L. (1992). *Programmed writing: A self-administered approach for interventions with individuals, couples and families*. Pacific Grove, CA: Brooks/Cole.

L'Abate, L. (1994). *A theory of personality development*. New York: Wiley.

L'Abate, L. (1997). Distance writing and computer-assisted training. In R. S. Sauber (Ed.), *Managed mental health care: Major diagnostic and treatment approaches*, (pp. 133–163). Philadelphia, PA: Brunner/Mazel.

L'Abate, L. (in press). Structured enrichment and distance writing programs for couples. In R. Berger and M. T. Hannah (Eds.), *Handbook of preventative approaches in couple therapy.* Washington, DC: Brunner/Mazel.

L'Abate, L., & Baggett, M. S. (1997a). *Distance writing and computer assisted interventions in mental health.* Atlanta, GA: Institute for Life Enpowerment.

L'Abate, L., & Baggett, M.S. (1997b). *The self in the family: A classification of personality, criminality, and psychopathology.* New York: Wiley.

L'Abate, L., & McHenry, S. (1983). *Handbook of marital interventions.* New York: Grune & Stratton.

L'Abate, L., & Weinstein, S. E. (1987). *Structured enrichment programs for couples and families.* New York: Brunner/Mazel.

L'Abate, L., & Young, L. (1987). *Casebook of structured enrichment programs for couples and families.* pp. 1–387. New York: Brunner/Mazel.

Pennebaker, J. W. (1997). *Opening up: The healing power of confiding in others.* New York: Guilford.

Riordan, R. J. (1996). Scriptotherapy: Therapeutic writing as a counseling adjunct. *Journal of Counseling & Development, 74,* 263–269.

CHAPTER 19

Integrated
Psychoeducational
Approach

Carlos Durana

INTRODUCTION

Rapid socioeconomic, technological and cultural changes during the last few decades have enabled people to base their relationships more on feelings of love and intimacy and less on tending to the necessities of life. For many, intimacy in marriage is becoming a path for developing inner possibilities (Welwood, 1990). As a critical dimension of close relationships, intimacy impacts on the health and life span of a couple (Kiecolt-Glaser & Glaser, 1991; Lowenthal & Haven, 1968; Waring, McElrath, Mitchell & Derry, 1981). It is a broad, multilevel and multidimensional concept not widely studied, unlike concepts such as marital satisfaction and adjustment. More importantly, although enhancing intimacy through psychoeducational means has received some attention from some clinicians (Frey, Holley & L'Abate, 1979; Gordon, 1993; Hatfield & Rapson, 1990), it has not been widely emphasized nor have these processes been widely evaluated (Durana, 1997a). Thus, the study of intimacy, in particular its development and what enhances and sustains it through psychoeducational means, is a vital area for clinicians and researchers alike.

A psychoeducational program for the enhancement of intimacy, PAIRS, (Practical Application of Intimate Relationship Skills)[1] developed by Gordon (1984), is a four-to-five-month, 120-hour psychoeducational program serving as a bridge between enrichment and therapy. In addition to providing participants with skills for developing successful relationships, the program teaches deeper self-exploration to enhance intimacy. The program integrates a variety of cognitive, affective, and behavioral approaches in an experiential couple and group format and draws from a wide range of theories and methods.

UNDERSTANDING AND DEFINING INTIMACY

Intimacy may refer to a process as well as to a state or an experience. As a process, intimacy deals with the self-revelation and self-confrontation which reveal a personal theme in the presence of one's partner; it is an intrapersonal as well as an interpersonal process. It emerges out of a desire to know oneself and be known at a deeper level, and it is determined by one's capacity for attachment and level of self-differentiation.

Intimacy resides both in an individual and in a relationship, in interactions. In the process of self-revelation, whether a behavior is intimate or not depends on subjective appraisals of revealed information. It also depends on whether the self-revelation influences an ongoing quality of relatedness which can be characterized by trust, commitment, mutuality, and caring. Across stages of the life cycle of a relationship, intimacy develops as a function of the capacity and motives of the individuals involved. Yet, because the experience of connectedness requires awareness of our separateness, intimacy is a source of both strength and stress. By its very nature, it is paradoxical (Durana, 1997b).

As a multifaceted concept, intimacy can be seen to be composed of several facets. These may include: sharing, closeness and affection, understanding and acceptance, support and caring, trust and commitment, conflict resolution, positive feelings such as self-confidence and love, and, to a lesser degree, sexual satisfaction. Of these, sharing and closeness are the most important aspects of intimacy (Durana, 1997a); however, sharing (or self-disclosure of thoughts, beliefs and feelings) alone accounts for more than half of the

---

[1] The PAIRS program includes weekly or bi-weekly 3-hour classes and four or five weekend workshops lasting about 21 hours. Participants vary widely ranging from healthy functioning to highly distressed relationships. The program costs, on the average, about $1,200 per person. Leaders for the PAIRS program are licensed mental health professionals, and classes are often led by one or two leaders.

variance of intimate couples (Waring & Chelune, 1983). A multifaceted and broad definition of intimacy has clinical implications, as will be seen later.

PRINCIPLES FOR CONNECTING AND CREATING INTIMACY

A useful way of conceptualizing intimacy, with therapeutic implications for creating intimacy and removing blocks to intimacy, involves a framework that may include (a) determinants and context, (b) process, and (c) outcomes and consequences of intimacy. Determinants and context refers to the attributes of each individual and the conditions in which intimacy blooms. This first part of the framework includes individual capacities and preferences (gender-role preferences, self-esteem, history of communication and conflict resolution, capacity for attachment, barriers to intimacy, and degree of self-differentiation) as well as family of origin history and modeling, and the couple's experience with and expectations about intimacy. It encompasses the situational and the generalized long-term context of the intimacy experience.

Second, the process segment of the concept of intimacy describes the interactional attributes: for example, how intimacy arises, develops, and is sustained; the patterns, frequency and quality of interactions; the influence of other processes (such as power and conflict resolution); and the level of intimate interaction at which conflict and anxiety begin to appear.

Third, outcomes and consequences involve qualities of relatedness such as satisfaction, trust, connectedness, adjustment, cognitive views, etc. Outcomes and consequences involve, as well, an integration of the relationship of intimacy to other interpersonal concepts. It is those qualities of relatedness which enhance the relationship and serve, in a circular fashion, to impact the determinants as well as the frequency and quality of future intimate interactions. Thus, an integrative view of intimacy encompasses the views of intimacy as a property of individuals, as a result of their interactions, and as a quality of relatedness.

An integrative psychoeducational approach for the enhancement of intimacy must consider the intrapsychic, interactional, and affective components. Such a program is PAIRS. The PAIRS program consists of five segments involving communication and conflict resolution, self-exploration, bonding and emotional literacy, pleasuring and sexuality, and changing expectations and goals (Gordon, 1996b).[2] Work on self-differentiation (Schnarch, 1991), training in listening and conflict resolutions (Bach & Wyden, 1968; Rubenstein & Shaver, 1982), self-disclosure (Waring, 1988), expression of hurt feelings (Frey, Holley & L'Abate, 1979), bonding (Gordon, 1993), and resolving distorted

---

[2] The author appreciates the contributions of Lori Gordon to this chapter.

perceptions (Reis, 1990) are all important in the enhancement of intimacy. Together the work of these clinicians and researchers validates the importance of a multifaceted approach to enhancing intimacy.

There are several principles connecting and creating intimacy. First is the notion that affect in interpersonal interaction is a biologically based signaling system which is therapeutic and growth producing (Casriel, 1972; Greenberg & Johnson, 1988; Satir, 1967). Although PAIRS attempts to affect cognitions, emotions, and behaviors, for instance, by uncovering hidden assumptions and negotiating requests for change, the use of evocative techniques not only encourages new affective experience but can also lead to corrective emotional experiences, enhanced self-disclosure, and attachment bonds. It can, as well, transform intrapsychic patterns, which have acted as determinants of intimacy, and thus lead to an enhancement of intimacy (Durana, 1996a, 1996b, 1996c; Gordon, 1993; Greenberg & Johnson, 1988; Nichols & Zax, 1977; Satir, 1972). The emotional aspect of sharing or self-disclosing—the major dimension of intimacy—is the emotional aspect most related to marital communication and satisfaction (Fitzpatrick, 1987; Tolstedt & Stokes, 1983). It is the biological adaptivity of primary emotions (Greenberg & Johnson, 1988) which can lead to therapeutic change. When conducted in the context of a dialogical process of I-Thou mutuality (Buber, 1970), this sharing of emotions can dissolve barriers to intimacy and have positive consequences by increasing connectedness and trust.

Another important principle for creating intimacy is the notion of bonding or the ability to be physically close and emotionally open (Casriel, 1972; Gordon, 1993). The biological need for bonding lies at the core of what it means to be intimate, for closeness is a fundamental dimension of intimacy (Durana, 1997a). Bonding can not only act as a solvent for resistance, but it can also facilitate attachment behaviors (Bowlby, 1958, 1977). It can provide symbolic parenting, can differentiate the need for sex from the need for love, and can enhance commitment as well as increasing self-exploration and self-disclosure (Durana, 1994, 1996b, 1996c). Thus, as process elements of intimacy, bonding (closeness) and sharing help develop and sustain as well as enhance the overall quality of relatedness.

Two of the several determinants affecting the development of intimacy include the preferences and expectations of the individuals involved. An individual's capacity for intimacy is influenced by childhood developmental patterns, family of origin history and modeling, and the degree of individuation and self-differentiation from family of origin. It is also influenced by the history of communication and conflict resolution from previous relationships and by societal influences. Partners bring into a relationship certain dysfunctional beliefs, expectations, and non-adaptive patterns based on unmet needs and fears from childhood (Gordon, 1993, 1996a). These unresolved patterns (conflicts) are projected onto the partner who is then expected to make up for the early wounds (Paolino & McGrady, 1978). If partners do not see each other for who they are, they then misperceive one another, causing further suffering. Alongside this misperception is the human motive to develop satisfactory object relationships (Fairbairn, 1952) and to heal the unresolved conflicts and wounding. A key principle for creating intimacy, then, is the utilization of an intimate committed relationship as a crucible for transforming maladaptive determinants by clarifying the projection process, by satisfying early unmet needs through symbolic parenting, and by developing higher capacities such as compassion, courage, forgiveness, and interdependence.

Finally, establishing the context or the conditions under which intimacy can bloom is a foundational principle. A context of safety consisting of caring, trust, and understanding, all important dimensions of intimacy, must be created so that the healing potential of the relationship can unfold (Durana, 1997a). Honest self-revelation, acknowledgment of differences in the presence of one's partner, and conflict resolution are facilitated through respect, empathic understanding, and valuing the other person.

TACTICS AND PROCEDURES USED TO CREATE INTIMACY

Underlying the framework of the PAIRS course are two general goals: first, to help participants gain knowledge of themselves and their partners; and second, to make a relationship a continuing source of pleasure. These goals are articulated through the concept of the Relationship Road Map or the Logic of Emotion, a conceptual structure that unifies the goals with a process of self-actualizing and of developing a nurturing intimate relationship.

The concept of the Logic of Emotion suggests that human beings are drawn to what enhances well-being or pleasure and that they tend to avoid what gives pain. Central to this notion is the idea that bonding (emotional openness and physical closeness) constitutes a biological need that when left unfulfilled creates pain and gives rise to symptoms. The Relationship Road Map also describes the underlying beliefs, emotions, and behaviors that cause pain and shows how to transform these beliefs, emotions, and behaviors in order to develop a greater sense of well-being and intimacy.

The procedures used for creating intimacy enhance the capacity for intimacy by teaching new skills, by increasing knowledge of self and others, by providing a context of safety for developing new experiences of intimacy, and by increasing and improving the quality of intimacy interactions, thereby enhancing the quality of relatedness between partners.

Sharing or self-disclosing of thoughts and feelings is essential for intimacy and well-being, but only when this is done in a manner that is nondestructive. Such an approach is encouraged in PAIRS through the technique called leveling or congruent communication style (Satir, 1967, 1972). This type of sharing helps participants learn to speak honestly on their own behalf (using "I" statements) without blaming, with empathy for their partners, with logic and feeling, and with a balance of purposefulness and pleasure.

The Dialogue Guide (Gordon, 1993) is a technique that utilizes the congruent style with a series of sentence stems for helping clarify thoughts, feelings, and requests. The technique encourages participants to be very specific in content and to talk while maintaining physical touch and eye contact. A few of the starter sentence stems include: I assume, I believe, I am hurt, I am frustrated, I want, I appreciate, and so forth.

The Daily Temperature Reading (DTR) is a technique for self-disclosing. Satir (1972), originator of this technique, described it as a way of keeping each other up-to-date and allowing the relationship to be a source of pleasure. The DTR has five steps: (1) sharing appreciations about partners as well as learning to receive appreciations; (2) sharing new information, the trivial as well as the important; (3) sharing puzzles or asking about things not understood in order to avoid making assumptions (mind reading); (4) making complaints with requests for change while being specific and congruent in style; and (5) sharing wishes, hopes, and dreams since these are vital parts of who we are and what we want from ourselves and our relationships.

An important dimension of intimacy is understanding. In sharing we hope to be understood and heard, with empathy. Empathic or active listening requires attending to "how things are for our partner" rather than "picking up only on those things that have some direct bearing on us" (Gordon, 1993, p. 89). The technique called Shared Meaning is used as a foundational block in the PAIRS program. It teaches partners to understand and feel what is being said—without judgment, advice, or interruptions—from the perspective of the speaker (Guerney, 1977). The second part of the technique involves sharing the meaning of what was heard and then checking to see if that was what the partner meant. As the course progresses and participants explore issues from their family of origin through exercises (such as the three-generation family map, the Parts of Self, and the Parts of the Couple), the empathic listening skills that have been developed allow for a deeper understanding of the other than was previously possible.

The encouragement of pleasure and positive feelings is essential to intimacy because it helps to strengthen the commitment to the relationship. It is not enough to focus on what blocks intimacy; many people can learn to stop dysfunctional behaviors and yet find that the level of pleasure in the relationship does not increase perceptibly. Feeling good requires cultivation, it requires learning to feel joy with one another, and it is an active pursuit where time for fun and pleasure are an integral part of the relationship. The Caring Behaviors (Stuart, 1980) exercise encourages this active pursuit of pleasure and well-being in a couple. Participants are asked to make lists of things their partners do, or could do, that would give them pleasure and make them feel cared about or special. These lists are exchanged and talked about. Participants are encouraged to post these lists in a visible place and to perform at least three caring behaviors from their partner's list each day.

The sensuality and sexuality segment of the course also focuses on pleasuring by learning about affection, comfort, bonding, sensuality, and sexuality. Learning to feel as a source of well-being and pleasure for one's partner, in the sense of feeling lovable and good enough, goes hand in hand with the ability to give pleasure. An example from this segment is the technique of bonding used in PAIRS to enhance pleasure and facilitate closeness, probably the second most important dimension of intimacy (Durana, 1997a). When fulfilled, the biological need for bonding facilitates attachment behaviors, increases self-exploration, provides symbolic parenting, enhances commitment and pleasure as well as enlarging the capacity for intimacy (Durana, 1994, 1996b & c). Bonding as a technique entails the use of various nurturing positions where one partner holds the other. In these relaxed positions, participants can express painful emotions from the recent to the distant past in a safe and supportive manner and can express pleasurable feelings, thereby allowing bonding to become a source of pleasure in the relationship.

Basic to the course is the development of conflict resolutions skills that allow the couple to resolve problems. An adaptation of Bach and Wyden's (1968) Fair Fight for Change model takes participants through a series of steps that incorporate sharing empathic listening, giving feedback and reward, and other skills that are essential for attaining a mutually agreeable solution within a win/win context. In addition, the role of coaches (another couple) in providing feedback and support to the couple engaged in the fair fight is essential in facilitating change. Peer coaching and group support add to the impact of the program by creating a context in which growth and intimacy flourish. This conflict resolution model, combined with group support, is particularly important in the contracting segment (Sager, 1976) at the end of the course where participants clarify expectations and goals in order to arrive at a mutually pleasurable couple contract.

An indispensable foundation for intimacy is a positive sense of self-worth (Gordon, 1993). At the center of this idea is a sense of believing and feeling that one is good enough and lovable. By drawing forth the competencies of the individual and his or her innate capacity for growth, intimacy can flourish. This growth is encouraged in PAIRS through exercises that emphasize appreciation for one's partner for developing more positive attitudes about oneself, for acknowledging needs, for taking risks, and so forth.

Finally, numerous lectures, meditation and journaling exercises are presented to help increase self-knowledge and facilitate the capacity for growth and the enhancement of intimacy. For example, in understanding the emotional stages of development, participants become aware of how adults can remain emotional infants (self-centered), emotional children (tell me what to do), or emotional adolescents (don't tell me what to do), rather than adults capable of mutual concern, interdependence, and self-respect. Humor is also used throughout the course in the form of stories, jokes, and role playing exercises that help illuminate faulty assumptions and relationship patterns.

TECHNIQUES USED TO REMOVE
BLOCKS TO INTIMACY

Procedures are used for transforming faulty determinants that block intimacy and personal growth. These determinants include individual attributes and style as well as the history of communication and conflict resolution, the family of origin history and modeling, individual expectations, grudges and other emotional blocks, as well as power struggles, blocks to pleasuring, and the degree of self-differentiation.

Often the style of communication does little to enhance intimacy or solve problems. Style can become the problem. Under stress, people use defensive communication styles that alienate their partners. Satir's (1967, 1972) four stress communication styles are presented in PAIRS in the form of lectures, humorous slides, and role playing. These styles include Placating, Blaming, Computing or Super-Reasonable, and Distracting or Irrelevant. Stress styles are the result of low self-esteem and fear. For example, the Placater doesn't want to rock the boat: he or she feels apologetic and worthless and derives a sense of value mostly from other's approval; he or she is afraid to express anger and entitlement and is often prone to depression. Yet, in its positive aspect, the Placater becomes our capacity for empathy, caring, and the desire for our partner to be happy.

Misunderstandings in communication also arise from faulty assumptions and mind reading our partner's thoughts. Unconscious assumptions and expectations about love, feelings, etc., act as land mines that erode relationship (Gordon, 1996a). Gordon calls these love knots: for example, "If you really love me, you would know what I want and you would do it. Since you don't, you obviously don't care. So why should I care for you or what you think, feel, say, want, or do? When you tell me what you want, I won't be very interested. I will be withholding" Gordon, 1996a, p. 8). In PAIRS a lecture and an exercise are introduced for untangling these knots so that they can be rewritten. In the above love knot, one cannot assume what the other knows; instead, one needs to ask for what is wanted and convey the necessary information so that the partner knows one's needs.

Emotional blocks can hamper the development of intimacy. Bottling up feelings or expressing them in destructive ways reduces our ability to solve problems. In the first segment of PAIRS, participants are introduced to the concept of the Triune Brain (McLean, 1973), and the Emotional Jug to highlight the importance of being able to experience and express a wide range of emotions with the purpose of reducing stress, of uncovering unconscious feelings and attitudes, and of enhancing communication and intimacy. Introduced at this point of the course are exercises for releasing anger and pain (Bach & Wyden, 1967), such as the Haircut, the Museum Tour of Past Hurts, and the Letting Go of Grudges Letter. The latter, although most often not sent, includes a series of sentence stems that, when completed, help reveal unfelt and unexpressed feelings thus making way for forgiveness and understanding. These exercises help clear the air before attempting to resolve conflicts. During the Fair Fights, participants receive feedback from coaches (often another couple) about fighting styles, in particular focusing on areas such as facial expression, specificity, communication, authenticity of information, injury, responsibility, and openness to change. Participants also receive feedback about dysfunctional habits that come into play in resolving conflicts: bullying, name calling, sarcasm, playing the victim, and stonewalling, to name a few.

The second part of the course focuses on the self. Tracing their history through the three-generation family map helps participants discover the beliefs, decisions, and models that sabotage intimacy in their relationships. Concepts such as the invisible scripts, loyalties, the revolving ledger, emotional allergies, early decisions about love, and early parental negative injunctions are presented in the form of lectures, meditations, guided imagery, journaling, and sharing exercises. For example, the revolving ledger introduces the concept of transference in a language that is simple and free of psychological jargon. This idea describes how a partner receives an emotional bill or invoice from his or her partner for what has occurred in past situations with others, hoping to get even with the partner for what others did to him or her and to make the partner make up for what was missing in early significant relationships or both. These ideas and processes are then followed by the Parts of Self and Parts of the Couple psychodrama exercises developed by Satir (1967, 1972) which help allow for the recognition of the different roles and masks partners use. Evaluating what works and what doesn't work encourages new possibilities to emerge for enhancing understanding and intimacy.

During the next section, Bonding and Emotional Literacy, participants explore in greater depth how early experiences and repressed emotions from the recent past and from childhood affect their relationships. This is an emotionally intense segment that uncovers early determinants of intimacy. Participants learn about bonding as a crucial biologically based need for sustaining intimacy. They learn how to differentiate the need for bonding from the need for sex and how to provide symbolic parenting for early unmet needs. In this section, work is also done on restructuring deeply held negative decisions and attitudes with positive beliefs, thereby enhancing self-esteem and the capacity for intimacy. Introduced are concepts such as the Triune Brian, Emotional Allergy, Acceptor (a person who will do anything to be loved) and

Rejector (a person who will not accept love because the price connected with it is too high), and Joyless, Mindless, Loveless life scripts.

The section culminates with the Healing the Ledger exercise developed by Durana and Gordon. This exercise is preceded by the Negative Emotional Allergy Infinity Loop, a concept that describes how early wounds activate defenses and highly charged responses that are mutually generated between partners in a closed loop which can be exited in several ways. The Revolving Ledger exercise, then, is used as an avenue for exiting these destructive cycles. The exercise begins in a bonding position with one partner (sender) describing an emotional reaction to a partner's behavior. This description includes feelings and thoughts and is followed by how it is related to his or her personal history. The sender describes the price that this reaction incurs in the relationship and the unmet need from the distant past that fuels this reaction. The sender requests words from the past that he or she wished had been said. The receiver then speaks those words with empathy and sensitivity, and the sender allows them in. At this point, the sender reacts with whatever emotions surface as he or she is being held. This process can often result in a strong outpouring of feelings from childhood. The sender is guided to recognize that the receiver is not that person from the past who has caused the initial hurt. Then, the sender is encouraged to think about ways of helping himself or herself when this emotional allergy might occur in a later situation, and to think about ways to request help from the receiver. Partners then hold each other for a few minutes and share appreciations. Next, the sender and receiver roles are reversed.

In segment five, Sensuality and Sexuality, exercises used for removing blocks to pleasuring involve affection, bonding, and various forms of touch. More importantly, learning to feel like a source of pleasure (not just sexual) is fundamental for enhancing self-esteem and the quality of connectedness in relationships. Concepts about jealousy, self-differentiation and early messages about pleasuring are introduced along with films, meditations, readings, conflict resolution, and massage. For example, the sexual pleasure inventory (72 items) is used to assess the relationship and remove blocks in this area. This is followed by a problem-solving sequence for helping negotiate solutions on what would make sex more pleasurable.

The course concludes with the Clarifying Expectations or Contracting section, an exploration in developing a new joint contract of conscious vision for what is wanted in the relationship by making use of all the knowledge and skills learned during the course as well as the support from coaches. Lectures included in this final segment provide guidelines for mapping issues, avoiding power struggles, and developing a healthier relationship. The Fair Fight for Change model is the key structure used in this section for resolving differences and developing a new contract.

CASE EXAMPLE

Consider this case example of a couple in their early fifties. They have been married for 22 years and have three children who are now in college. Both are attractive, upper middle class, successful professionals. A few months earlier, the husband (Paul) moved out to live with a woman with whom he had been having an affair, on and off, for over a year. Over the course of the marriage, Paul had had numerous brief affairs prior to this one. The wife (Mary) came to a PAIRS preview and then invited Paul to come to a preview. After he had left her, Mary was depressed and was hospitalized once. They both had tried marital therapy for several years, and both experienced that it had not been very helpful. In fact, they said it may have been harmful to their marriage. Their last therapist, a psychiatrist, had recommended that they separate. They had also tried a marriage encounter weekend but felt it hadn't worked. They decided to do the PAIRS course, expecting only to learn about what had happened but not expecting that the marriage was salvageable.

During the PAIRS's training, they met with the therapist leading the course (Durana) for a few couple-therapy sessions. They both showed a great deal of pain and mistrust. Paul's (pre-PAIRS) Dyadic Adjustment Scale (DAS) score was 98; Mary's was 76. After participation in PAIRS their respective scores were 139 and 134. The DAS yields an overall measure of marital adjustment defined as a process over time, rather than an unchanging state (Spanier, 1976). Scores below 100 are indicative of distress. The higher the score, the better is the person's adjustment to the marriage. Scores can range from 0 to 151 (Corcoran & Fischer, 1987).

At the onset of their relationship, Mary was fond of Paul's expressions of love, the cards he sent, the nice trips they took, the values they shared about family and career and lifestyle. Paul also felt loved, happy, and not criticized; he liked Mary's looks, her "spunk," intelligence, and high energy.

When they came to the course, Paul expressed a desire to "find out what it is that makes me do what I do." He felt he had hurt his wife and his family with his affairs. For Paul, the marriage relationship lacked warmth; he felt unloved by Mary and resented being "scoffed at or treated as a child." He seemed distant, ashamed, and remorseful. Mary, on the other hand, was baffled by his extramarital behavior and by being shut out by his leaving. She felt that he had not put her at the center of his life but rather "at the fringes, unimportant." She said that he was right in that she "hadn't loved him enough for a while, for there were no rewards in it" for her, yet she was "not prepared to leave the marriage" (except early on in the relationship when she decided not to leave Paul after her parents encouraged her to stay). Subsequently, as a way of tolerating the marriage, she decided to pursue her interests and get her "strokes" elsewhere. She seemed hurt, angry, critical, and suspicious. They both, however, felt proud of their children, their professional successes, and financial accomplishments.

For Paul, the problems began early in their marriage when they went back to England, his birthplace, to see if they could make it work there. They lived with his parents and his five siblings for a while, but he felt that Mary was put into an impossible situation. Mary experienced Paul's mother as cold and unaccepting, and, a few months later, she decided to return to the United States whether he came back or not. Subsequently, Paul felt Mary didn't care for him. These earlier years of marriage were very difficult, as Paul worked long hours up the management ladder in an isolated part of Iowa. Mary was not happy there either, and Paul felt that, no matter what he did, he couldn't please her. In arguments, he felt sure she was more articulate and very sharp tongued.

Mary also thought that their problems had started at the beginning of the marriage. She saw Paul as locked into marriage with problems he felt hopeless about solving. This she attributed to a defeatist attitude arising from his cultural background. She felt that, early on when she tried to talk and solve their problems, he would shut down and wouldn't talk, giving her the feeling that she didn't have the right to have differences. She couldn't understand nor resolve the situation since, "I didn't have the skills to reach him." They both complained that one of their biggest problems was talking about feelings and personal issues, since such talk always degenerated into arguments, making it difficult to deal with important issues.

After participation in PAIRS, Paul found that the communication and conflict resolution part of the course helped him to have direct contact with his partner over an expanded period of time and to talk about things that "we have danced around." Although he didn't think that they had resolved anything, he thought the skills were very valuable. Particularly useful was an exercise for expressing anger (prior to conflict resolution), since he has great difficulty expressing feelings and being honest with his feelings. Not wanting to hurt someone else, he often avoids being direct and is fearful of having his words thrown back at him. During the course, however, he looked forward to expressing more feelings that "are pretty buried. Helping get them out would clear the air...not the slate...but would improve things a lot." In this part of the class, Paul valued listening and being appreciated when he expressed what he felt. Both Paul and Mary appreciated the support from others in the group and found it comforting to know that others have similar struggles.

From her point of view, Mary found the anger-releasing exercises to be "tremendously helpful" as they were done within the safety and structure of the class under coaching by another participating couple. Expressing "some of the anger and hurt I feel about the affairs and his leaving, feelings which had been unexpressed and which I hadn't shared,...felt good to get it off my chest." For Mary, it was an eye-opener to hear Paul saying during one of the sharing and listening exercises: "Listen to me, I am not sure I can get through to you." She felt he meant it, and she saw he came to the class because maybe he wanted to come back, rather than just to make a half-hearted attempt to save his image with the children before he ended the relationship.

Mary also liked the structure for communicating and resolving conflict since it seemed like a good approach for addressing many of their issues. They received feedback from the trainer and their coaches during the fair fights, receiving it well after several tries. Paul accepted his withdrawing and his impatience with Mary's hurt and anger, and Mary recognized she was expressing her anger in indirect ways through sarcastic put-downs and psychoanalyzing. Both Paul and Mary bonded well to the rest of the group. For Mary bonding with the group was very important, given the isolation she felt during her marriage and her childhood—an issue that she had recognized before but began to experience in a more profound way during the next segment of the course (work on the self) as she tracked her life history through the genogram and discovered family models, decisions, unmet needs, and fears. She uncovered hidden expectations and beliefs developed in childhood that were influencing her intimate relationship with Paul.

Mary did not feel valued or given enough attention as a child, and she vowed not to have that as an adult. In her marriage, however, she felt left out as she had in childhood. She grew up in a country setting, as an only child to older parents who didn't want children. Her father was home only on weekends because he worked in the city, and her mother was often busy with community activities. There were few children near their home. Mary's main companion was her grandmother who died when Mary began to turn to school work. So, she spent her "time studying and reading, very lonely." When she met Paul, she hoped to become part of a larger family; instead, she felt rejected by his mother. Mary also felt isolated within her own family, claiming that at times Paul excluded her from the conversations at the dinner table with the children, for instance, when talking about sports.

While away on business, Paul missed a large part of the second segment of classes, although he managed to read much of the class material and was particularly interested in how patterns are transferred from one's family of origin onto one's spouse. During the third segment, the Bonding and Emotional Literacy weekend, Paul made some important discoveries. He was able to "uncover and express several deeply held emotions: shame hurt, rage, sadness, joy and tender feelings." He became aware of the anger and resentment he carried towards his father and himself. He realized that over the years of marriage he was really angry at himself and not Mary. "It really surprised me. I was always on a slow burn and full of suppressed anger.... I was ashamed of my father for letting me down, and I turned around and did the same sorts of things he did.... In the workshop, I felt shame about how I emulated him and felt anger at not doing what I should have done.... I acted out and drank in shameful ways.... I discovered much of this during the one day group with the men in one of the imagery exercises. I didn't have to feel guarded about what I said.... Having a better understanding of the dynamics helped with the commitment to not walk away.... I feel that I am growing out of adolescence. On Sunday of the workshop, I discovered that Mary was a friend and ally, and not an enemy.... How could I have been so blind to all those things?"

Mary was astounded at hearing Paul assume blame for his own behavior and not blame her. "I was shocked. I thought all his negative traits came from his mother, not his father. I blamed his mother and liked his father.... In the group with the women, I didn't work on anything about my parents, but I raged at this woman Paul was seeing. It was helpful.... I also became more aware of how abandonment is a trigger for me.... Seeing him in pain made me want to comfort him.... I didn't feel alone then."

Paul and Mary were interviewed two weeks after the Sensuality and Sexuality workshop, which also deals with issues of jealousy. Mary thought she hadn't made much progress on the jealousy issue and acknowledged it would be there for a while. She said, "Now I understand that Paul didn't get much love as a child from his mother, so he didn't learn to give love in his marriage, and so he looked elsewhere,...but it was all short-lived, Band-Aids,...and he is here with me not her. Now I feel OK..., and it also helps when Paul talks so often about how terrible his girlfriend was and how much better I am...and that he is not with me out of guilt."

For Paul, it was very painful to go over certain events with Mary about what happened. "I have regrets and to rehash it is hard.... I worry this will be a problem for her for a long time...the jealousy.... Something small can turn into a huge thing..., so I get nervous.... I would like to move on.... I realized that, from those other women, I was looking for love but got quick fixes, and I spiraled down...destructively.... I was in a haze. I didn't believe Mary could love me...like my mother. I get impatient and have to tell myself I am going to work through this and not give up.... I have caused pain.... I love her. We still get stuck, but it's wonderful when we get out of it.... A lot of it is recognizing false perceptions and not running away.... All the techniques and bad habits that were pointed out in the first weekend are the key for me. I wish she didn't feel bad, nor I."

The last interview took place two weeks after the final segment of the course, Clarifying Expectations. The couple talked about what they had gained from the course. Paul said, "I gained a lot of understanding and consciousness...about what I had been doing..., about the past and transferring things to other people.... I learned about techniques for discussing problems, and where Mary is coming from, and not just understanding a book by its cover...being so literal.... We can deal with things directly rather than ducking them.... I learned about commitment, hanging in there.... Having things in the open with people who didn't run away was very positive. We led separate lives. I have now changed certain things in my schedule so we can focus on each other.... The support from the group and learning from others was invaluable."

Mary valued dealing with childhood fears that were suppressed. "We weren't nurturing each other.... I channeled my needs for strokes into decorating the house.... I am amazed now at how good it can feel just to spend a lot of time with each other.... I learned about what was driving his behavior. It was mystifying before.... I didn't see him as vulnerable or uncertain.... I had married him because I knew he would be a success. To see that we were both deprived in similar ways was really helpful."

Finally, the couple was asked about their definition of intimacy, what it meant to them, and if, during the program, it had changed at all. Paul said that it had changed: "I wasn't intimate before. I grew up in a family that wasn't. Part of intimacy is just being friends, the biggest part for me—just feeling you are really together in this world, and with that feeling you feel nice and very close.... The course helped us get closer.... Things got in the way, but we kept coming back.... Feeling that and how good it felt increased my resolve to hang in there.... It was deep, not superficial like the life I had been living and detested."

Mary didn't think that her definition of intimacy had changed but did think that the course had helped them "open up the door to allow each other in.... We were never intimate enough.... We were very close initially, but in marriage things happened that precluded our being intimate.... I think he respects me for what I do and for the job I did with the kids.... I am now more acceptable to him." After the PAIRS course, Paul and Mary continued in couples therapy because work still needed to be done to maintain and enhance the gains they had made.

This couple exemplifies what is common to so many marriages. The early feelings for love and intimacy soon turn into unresolved disappointments, hurts, and power struggles because the couple lacks adequate skills and knowledge. These blocks to intimacy accumulate, leaving scars and distance between the partners. For Mary and Paul, the internalized conflicts from their pasts were recapitulated in their relationship. The unconscious "ledgers" (Boszormenyi-Nagy & Spark, 1973) of what was given and was owed in the past, which they presented to each other soon after marriage, could not be fulfilled. Such unconscious expectations are impossible to meet and have to be resolved in the light of awareness, understanding, acceptance, and open communications. Through a conscious and experiential return to their past and the roots of their maladaptive patterns, Mary and Paul could begin the transformation process of their relationship. As they brought down barriers to intimacy, such as lack of trust and understanding, and tackled the inadequate determinants of intimacy within a context of safety and support, their relationship began to transform.

This couple exemplifies the interrelated and reciprocal nature of the various facets and the process of intimacy. For example, as Paul shared honestly about the origin of his problem and his pain, that vulnerability opened a new window through which Mary could see him. The closeness that they experienced was instrumental in enhancing his commitment. That commitment engendered trust in Mary; she felt accepted by Paul. New interactions and experiences of intimacy created a different quality of relatedness which Paul described as that feeling of being really together and close, a connectedness which then made it possible for him to work harder on himself and the relationship. None of this would have been possible without developing the new skills of communication and conflict resolution which helped cement their new learnings.

SUMMARY

Intimacy is a skill which can be learned through gaining self-awareness, experiencing insight, and by making changes in behavior, attitudes, and feelings. Today, being in a long-term intimate and satisfying peer relationship requires both partners to be self-referential, that is, to speak on their own behalf about their needs and feelings, to have a healthy amount of self-differentiation, to be good listeners, and to be capable of resolving conflicts in a positive way. These skills are not something that can be accomplished in a month or two; comprehensive psychoeducational programs, such as PAIRS, run counter to the growing demands of managed care with its thrust for quick solutions and fixes. Psychoeducational approaches can be valuable for facilitating individual and relationship maturational processes, for treating distressed couples (Durana, 1996a), for enhancing interpersonal exploration, and for marital enrichment, as well as for use as an adjunct to therapy. Clinicians may enrich their therapeutic interventions by emphasizing emotionally focused interventions and bonding techniques while taking into account gender differences that produce distress in relationships and, at the same time, enhancing the equality, not the sameness, of the sexes.

There are important clinical and conceptual ramifications to a program based on a broad conceptual framework. Relying on the utilization and interpretation of concepts and techniques from experiential, object relations, communication, behavioral, and family systems approaches, the PAIRS psychoeducational approach makes an important contribution to learning and transformation. By emphasizing the value of experiential and analytic traditions that make use of affect, depth knowledge of self, and the importance of how experiences from the past can be transferred into marital interactions, the course encourages both self-understanding and growth of intimacy.

REFERENCES

Bach, G. R., & Wyden, P. (1968). *The intimate enemy.* New York: Avon Books.

Boszormenyi-Nagy, I., & Spark, G. M. (1973). *Invisible loyalties: Reciprocity in intergenerational family therapy.* New York: Harper & Row.

Bowlby, J. (1958). The nature of the child's tie to his mother. *International Journal of Psychoanalysis, 39,* 350–373.

Bowlby, J. (1977). The making and breaking of affectional bonds. *British Journal of Psychiatry, 130,* 291–210.

Buber, M. (1970). *I and thou.* New York: Scriber's.

Casriel, D. (1972). *A scream away from happiness.* New York: Grosset & Dunlop.

Corcoran, R., & Fischer, J. (1987). *Measures for clinical practice.* New York: Free Press.

Durana, C. (1994). The use of bonding and emotional expressiveness in the PAIRS training: A psychoeducational approach for couples. *Journal of Family Psychotherapy, 5* (2), 65–81.

Durana, C. (1996a). A longitudinal evaluation of the effectiveness of the PAIRS psychoeducational program for couples. *Family Therapy, 2,* 11–36.

Durana, C. (1996b). Bonding and emotional re-education for couples in the PAIRS training: Part I. *The American Journal of Family Therapy, 24* (3), 269–28.

Durana, C. (1996c). Bonding and emotional re-education for couples in the PAIRS training: Part II. *The American Journal of Family Therapy, 24* (4), 315–328.

Durana, C. (1997a). Enhancing marital intimacy through psychoeducation: The PAIRS program. *The Family Journal, 5,* 3, 204–215.

Durana, C. (1997b). *Marital intimacy: A review of the literature.* Manuscript in preparation.

Fairbairn, W. R. D. (1952). *An object-relations theory of the personality.* New York: Basic Books.

Frey, J., Holley, J., & L'Abate, L. (1979). Intimacy in sharing hurt feeling: A comparison of three conflict resolution models. *Journal of Marriage and Family Therapy, 5,* 35–41.

Fitzpatrick, M. A. (1987). Marriage and verbal intimacy. In V. G. Derlega & J. Berg (Eds.), *Self-disclosure: Theory, research and therapy.* New York: Plenum.

Gordon. L. (1984). *PAIRS.* Unpublished manuscript.

Gordon. L. (1993). *Passage to intimacy.* New York: A Fireside Book.

Gordon. L. (1996a). *If you really loved me.* Palo Alto, CA: Science and Behavior Books.

Gordon, L. (1996b). *Training Manual and Curriculum Guide.* Pembroke Pines, FL: PAIRS Int'l.

Greenberg, L. S., & Johnson, S. M. (1988). *Emotionally focused therapy for couples.* New York: Guilford Press.

Guerney, B. (1977). *Relationship enhancement.* San Frrancisco, CA: Jossey-Boss Publishers.

Hatfield E., & Rapson, R. (1990). Emotions: A trinity. In E.A. Blechman (Ed.), *Emotions and the family* (pp. 11–33). New Jersey: Hillsdale.

Kiecolt-Glaser, J. K., & Glaser, R. (1991). Stress and immune function in humans. In R. Ader, D. I. Felten & N. Cohen (Eds.), *Psychoneuro-immunology* (2nd ed., pp. 849–864). San Diego: Academic Press.

Lowenthal, M. F., & Haven, C. (1968). Interaction and adaptation: Intimacy as critical variable. *American Sociological Review, 33* (1), 20–30.

McLean, P. (1973). *A triune concept of the brain and behavior.* Toronto: University of Toronto Press.

Nichols, M. P., and Zax, M. (1977). *Catharsis in psychotherapy.* New York: Garner Press.

Paolino, T. J., & McGrady, B. S. (1978). *Marriage and marital therapy.* New York: Brunner/Mazel.

Reis, H. T. (1990). The role of intimacy in interpersonal relations. *Journal of Social and Clinical Psychology, 9* (1), 15–30.

Rubenstein, L., & Shaver, P. (1982). *In search of intimacy* (pp. 169–207). New York: Delacorte Press.

Sager, C (1976). *Marriage contract and couple therapy.* New York: Brunner/Mazel.

Satir, V. (1967). *Conjoint family therapy.* Palo Alto, CA: Science and Behavior Books.

Satir, V. (1972). *Peoplemaking.* Palo Alto, CA: Science and Behavior Books.

Schnarch, D. (1991). *Constructing the sexual crucible.* New York: Norton.

Spanier, G. B. (1976). Measuring dyadic adjustment: New scales for assessing the quality of marriage and similar dyads. *Journal of Marriage and Family, 38,* 15–28.

Stuart, R. B. (1980). *Helping couples change.* New York: Guilford Press.

Tolstedt, B. E., & Stokes, J. P. (1983). Relation of verbal, affective, and physical intimacy to marital satisfaction. *Journal of Consulting Psychology, 30* (4), 573–580.

Waring, E. M. (1988). *Enhancing marital intimacy through cognitive self-disclosure.* New York: Brunner/Mazel.

Waring, E. M., & Chelune, G. J. (1983). Marital intimacy and self-disclosure. *Journal of Clinical Psychology, 39* (2), 183–190.

Waring, E. M., McElrath, D., Mitchell, P., & Derry, M. E. (1981). Intimacy and emotional illness in the general population. *Canadian Journal of Psychiatry, 26,* 167–172.

Welwood, J. (1990). Intimate relationships or path. *The Journal of Transpersonal Psychology, 22* (1), 51–58.

CHAPTER 20

The Power of Shared Subjectivity: Revitalizing Intimacy through Relationship Enhancement® Couples Therapy

Maryhelen Snyder, Ph.D.
Bernard G. Guerney, Jr., Ph.D.

The root of "intimate," the Latin word "intimus," is the superlative of "intus," meaning "within." To be intimate is to go within, to know deeply. Thus, the knowledge of self and other are inextricably connected.

AN UNDERSTANDING OF HOW INTIMACY DEVELOPS

Our ability to know our own experiencing of experience, (i.e., our subjectivity), originates in the responses we receive from primary caretakers. Through their reactions to our wants and needs, we learn to give language and meaning to our feelings and ideas. As we learn about our own subjectivity, we are discovering the separate subjectivity of others.

Needless to say, much can go wrong in this developmental journey of being known by others, knowing our own subjectivity, and knowing the separate subjectivity of other people. Much of what goes wrong could be described as a failure of empathy in the caretakers. When human beings do not receive adequate empathy, their emotional needs are not sufficiently met, and their natural instincts to defend and assert themselves lead to self-protective behaviors of withdrawal or aggression or both.

The clients who come to see us for therapy fall on a continuum of defendedness. Where they fall on this continuum depends in large measure on such factors as how much, when they were growing up, their needs were met by their caregivers, and how much empathy they received from them. The latter can often make the difference between whether as children they experienced trauma or neglect versus open communication and responsiveness to their physical and emotional needs. Caregiver empathy determines guardedness not only indirectly, but directly by affording a model for open and responsive communication.

Relationship Enhancement® (RE) couples therapy (Guerney, 1977) empowers clients with the knowledge and skills that provide a context for knowing one's own experiencing and becoming conscious of the experiencing of others. Some clients have described RE therapy as a civilizing method, meaning that it requires and permits us to suspend our animal instincts to fight, flee, or yield when we feel threatened, while we listen openly and speak vulnerably. Martin Buber has observed that to truly enter the life world of another human being, to listen at the deep level that allows the subjectivity of another human being into our consciousness, requires the "deepest stirring of one's being" (Buber, 1957, 1988).

To allow another person to experience our authentic subjectivity requires a similar level of courage. Although we all fall in different places on the continuum of defendedness, we have all been hurt, we have all experienced inadequate empathy, we are all born with the critical instincts to defend and assert ourselves, and we are all relatively new to this evolutionary journey toward the greatly enhanced possibility, in language, of creating and communicating meaning.

RE has been shown in comparative outcome studies to be very powerful and reliable (Giblin, Sprenkle, & Sheehan, 1985; Ross, Baker, & Guerney, 1985). It has three modes, often chosen on the basis of time available: Crisis Resolution (1 to 5 hours), Experiential (5 to 10 hours), and Time Designated (indefinite, but usually 10 to 20 hours). The RE techniques used in each differ in emphasis. As one would expect, all other things being equal, the longer the therapy, the more one can expect to achieve. Nevertheless, the points made in this chapter could apply in one degree or another, for one reason or another, to all three modes.

Our goal in this chapter is to describe how RE therapy can provide, for couples, both a structure and a method for deepening understanding both of self and other. This mutual understanding permits a dynamic process of cocreative intelligence. When couples are able to use the method competently after careful coaching and sufficient practice, the willingness to change tends to flow naturally out of the heightened awareness that comes from speaking authentically and being deeply understood. The method has been used successfully with couples in which there is spouse battering (Guerney, Waldo, & Firestone, 1987; Waldo, 1986, 1987, 1988), in which one or both members have been diagnosed with alcohol abuse (N. Armenti, personal communication, March 18, 1980; Waldo & Guerney, 1983; Matter & McAllister, 1984), and borderline (Waldo & Harman, 1993) or narcissistic (Snyder, 1994) personality disorders, as well as with the more typical outpatient couples, such as the couple in the case example to be presented later. There are also forms of RE therapy applicable to: family units with adolescents or families of origin with adults (Ginsberg, 1977; 1997); families with young children down to preschoolers (Guerney & Guerney 1985), and individuals wanting either family oriented therapy (see "unilateral therapy" in Guerney, 1977) or intrapsychically oriented therapy (Guerney & Snyder, 1997). In addition to therapy, there also are RE enrichment/problem-prevention programs designed for couples and for families that are based on the skills that had been developed for RE therapy (Guerney, 1988). RE programs also are applicable to nonfamily groups for purposes of organizational development (Guerney & Yoder, 1990; Rathmell, 1991; Accordino & Guerney, 1993).

RE PRINCIPLES FOR CREATING INTIMACY

The concept of subjectivity is central to the methodology of RE Therapy. A foundational assumption is that the meaning-infused consciousness of each human being—what the phenomenologists called the lifeworld—is unique to that human being. This makes each of us, generally speaking, the best expert on ourselves. In a field that often pathologizes people and assumes expert knowledge to be the province of the therapist only, this concept is itself quite radical. Shared subjectivity requires two relational capacities, the capacity to listen for the subjectivity of the other person, and the capacity to be aware of and express our own subjectivity. Although these capacities develop naturally during a normal childhood, most of us, as mentioned above, have suffered some impairment of them, perhaps largely because so much of society's current socialization processes are shame-based and increase the already existing instinct to protect ourselves. It also can be said that, historically speaking, the concept of each person being worthy of "unconditional positive regard," to use Carl Rogers' term, is relatively new. Furthermore, it is only in recent years that there has been widespread attention by couple/family therapists to the distinction between language as a meaning-making phenomenon and "reality" as known only through each person's separate consciousness.

PROCEDURES USED IN RE THERAPY
TO CREATE INTIMACY

The focus of this chapter will be on the first two skills of RE Therapy. The full nine-skill method is described elsewhere (Guerney, 1987). Each skill comprises a set of highly specific guidelines, like the rules of a game. When the guidelines are followed, skilled behavior is the result. Included are skills for (a) protecting the space in which each person can speak and be heard; (b) problem/conflict resolution to assist couples in applying changes in attitude to their concrete life situations; (c) helping others, including family members, to be willing and able to treat one in ways that are growth-enhancing rather than emotionally destructive; (d) changing one's own behaviors in desired directions; (e) helping others to reshape their personal and interpersonal behaviors in ways they desire; including, (f) the mastery of the RE skills themselves; and (g) incorporating these skills as a permanent part of one's personality. In addition, there are the two skills on which we will concentrate here. They are key components of the foundation on which the RE rests: the *Expressive* and *Empathic* skills. Both are of central importance to fostering subjectivity and an intimacy that is optimally balanced for the particular couple with their coexisting needs for independence.

From the moment the couple enters the therapist's office, the session is structured in a way to optimize empathy and allow each person to experience his or her own subjectivity without interruption. The therapist introduces the session by saying something like this: "Today, since I have just met you, I am very eager to understand as much as I can about each person's perspective. For this reason, I'm going to ask each of you to speak directly to me instead of to each other, and to not interrupt each other. I'll be sure to hear from you both as fully as possible in the time we have. I may spend quite a while listening to each of you, one at a time, so that I can be sure I understand." The distinction between empathy and agreement is one that clients often do not have when they first come to therapy. So the therapist also makes it clear that she takes it for granted that each person probably has a very different perspective of the difficulties in the relationship. As each client speaks, the therapist empathizes.

The model for empathy used in this method has its historical roots in Carl Rogers' Client Centered therapy (Rogers, 1951, 1957). The empathizer's goal is to experience as much as possible what it is to be the other person, and to show that he and his thoughts and feelings are deeply comprehended, appreciated, and cared about. As viewed and used in RE, empathy is most powerful when the empathizer reveals those things by sharing-back the things which the original speaker has experienced, but not said. The empathic response is not diluted with phrases such as, "I hear you saying," or "As I understand you," but the therapist makes it very clear that if the understanding is inaccurate, it should be corrected or clarified. Each client's perceptions or goals for positives in the relationship also are elicited.

It can be extremely useful toward the end of this first session, or at least before the completion of the initial phase of couple therapy, to use the unique RE method of Becoming each of the two members of the couple (Snyder, 1995). This usually is introduced as early as the intake interview in the following manner: "Before you leave today, I'd like to be sure that I've fully understood everything that each of you has told me so far. I find that there is something that helps me do this, if it's all right with you. I'd like to speak 'as' each of you to the other. This can accomplish three goals: The first is to take your experience 'inside' me as much as possible, to really 'get' it as much as I can; the second is to give you another opportunity to see whether I do understand accurately. So, I'd like you to interrupt me if I get anything wrong, and when I'm finished speaking, I'll ask you for any corrections or clarifications. And the third goal is to demonstrate for you this way of speaking to each other, because I can teach it to you if you like. In this way of speaking, if I do it right, the speaker can be completely truthful about perceptions and feelings, and the listener's feelings of being blamed or attacked will be minimized. So, I'll also be asking the person I'm speaking to to tell me if you felt defensive at all. And, if you did, it may well have to do not with what I said but with how I said it, and perhaps I can correct that." This latter statement introduces the idea that a speaker who is openly and honestly experiencing her own thoughts and feelings, can also take responsibility for attempting to free their partner from defensiveness.

When this goes well, and it almost invariable does, the clients immediately become interested in learning the RE skills, because they have had direct experience of the two critical aspects: being heard compassionately and being spoken to with a conscious subjectivity that sharply reduces psychological threat to the other. The next step in the therapeutic process is to teach the Empathic and Expressive skills that were demonstrated through the Becoming. However, how soon to impart the skills to clients requires judgment. It is sometimes necessary, (e.g., in resolving a pressing crisis), for the therapist to continue for a while to use this technique of Becoming and another technique unique to RE therapy which will be described later, called Laundering. In applying these methods, the therapist uses the RE skills instead of, and on behalf of a client, as if she were the client.

Teaching the Empathic Skill

Usually, the first skill taught in the RE approach is empathy. It is taught by what is called the Identification Method or the I Mode. Similar to Becoming, the person who is learning to empathize speaks in the first person, as if she were the person who has just expressed something. The rationale for this order and method of learning is that it vividly illustrates the meaning of empathy as the act of putting oneself in the other person's shoes. The topic suggested to clients for practicing empathy by the Identification Method includes experiences that have some significance for them but are not related to the couple relationship, preferably events from childhood or adolescence. This allows each member of the couple to listen without being distracted by the defenses that are likely to be evoked by relationship topics. We have found that taking some time to introduce the range of experiences that might be appropriate to describe is useful in evoking memories that are important to each person and that these memories, when deepened and elaborated by the empathic response, evoke an intensification of awareness.

The memories can have a variety of emotions connected with them, negative or positive. Many therapists using this method have commented that, although these experiences are not about the relationship, they almost always demonstrate something about each person that is core to how they relate to others. First, each client tells a memory to the therapist who demonstrates the I Mode by speaking as them. The therapist explains that this process of incorporating another person's experience intellectually and emotionally into one's self involves experiencing while undergoing and looking back at that experience—as if experiencing it oneself. These thoughts and feelings not stated by the speaker, may have been experienced by the speaker, just as you, the therapist, experienced them now. Thus, as the other, people often discover the emotions deepening in their own consciousness. When they speak, the words that go with this deepening or expanding of the emotional or meaning dimension of the experience are expressed. The feelings that were expressed by the original speaker are expressed quite differently after they became the empathizer's experience. The words and metaphors are more likely to be fresh and new than would have been the case if the empathizer had not so fully identified with the original speaker.

Of course, the person receiving the empathy can correct and modify what the empathizer has experienced while identifying. The empathizer then reidentifies and makes appropriate changes. Thus, when it is not accurate, there is no damage done, because it can be corrected. And often, the correction further clarifies the experience for the original speaker. When the empathy feels complete, the empathizer still asks if there are any corrections or additions, and empathizes with these. Time constraints might require limiting the additions, but never the corrections and clarifications. After the therapist has demonstrated empathy via the Identification Method, the clients practice the method with each other using different memories. The therapist coaches, trying, among other things, to elicit from the empathizer feelings, wishes, or conflicts experienced by the empathizer as the original speaker, but not expressed by the original speaker.

While learning empathy, the clients may practice responding empathically to their partner using the Identification Method until they are able to absorb the thoughts and feelings of their partner with consistency. Also they can return to using it in any future dialogue should their empathy lapse into merely mirroring or paraphrasing what their partner has said. It usually is very helpful in enabling empathizers to make their partners' experiences their own, thereby helping them to recognize their partners' deeper unstated feelings, wishes, and conflicts. To avoid confusion about whose thoughts and feelings are being conveyed the empathizer can use an introductory phrase such as "As I identify with you, it's like this..."

After the Identification Method of teaching empathy is completed, the You Method or You Mode of conveying empathy is then demonstrated by the therapist and practiced by the clients ("You are angry because," "You wish," "On the one hand you want," etc.). That is, the empathizer is instructed to continue to identify—to pretend, while listening, to be the client—but now, when speaking, to use the second person pronoun, saying "you" instead of "I." The feelings, wishes, and conflicts the empathizer experiences while identifying with his partner, continue to serve as a preliminary guide to what is probably going on within the partner. And the therapist encourages the client to take the risk of making use of those internalized thoughts and feelings when giving the empathic response. Inaccurate, mechanical or formulaic empathy can be experienced as pointless or hurtful. The corrective feedback for the person receiving the empathy, and the therapist's word by word coaching, attention to non-verbal behavior, and other procedures, such as Troubleshooting, to be explained later, assure that deep empathy, satisfying to the listener, is always provided. The first session in which empathy is taught is often moving for both the giver and the receiver of the empathy. When people experience this quality of empathy, they are more ready to go on with the journey of learning and practicing the skills with increasingly difficult topics and issues.

It might seem excessive, in a brief chapter, to devote such attention to the beginning process of teaching empathy as something quite different from reflective or active listening, as those are usually taught to therapists and to clients. (In RE, the appropriate metaphor for empathy would be X-raying rather than mirroring.) We have taken the time to detail it to this extent because we believe the quality of the empathy provided by the clients to one another is one of the keys to the extraordinary effectiveness of RE as shown in rigorous comparative studies and meta-analyses (e.g., Giblin, Sprenkle, & Sheehan, 1985; Ross, Baker, & Guerney, 1985).

Recently, in professional training workshops and in couple or group sessions with clients, the senior author has asked for people's preferences as recipients of empathy between I Mode versus the You Mode. The great majority have expressed preference for the I Mode, particularly when emotions are complex. The giver of empathy also reports that, although it may seem awkward at first, the "I" form seems to allow a deeper engagement with the experience of the other and an increase in the ability to suspend one's own reality temporarily. At present we use the I Mode for teaching empathy and whenever clients are mirroring rather than deeply empathizing. One outstanding example of the aid provided by using the I Mode was experienced by the senior author with a man who was prone to intense anger. In a therapy session, his face had become flushed and his neck muscles had visibly tightened as he listened to his partner's expression of her perspective regarding a conflict between them. When he was asked if he thought he could empathize with her, he said, "I don't know. I don't feel empathic; I just feel angry." And then he added spontaneously, "Maybe, if I Became her, I could do it." During the time in which he spoke as her, his face and body became calm. She told him how surprised she was by how fully he had understood her, expressing it "even better than I did." He also was surprised by how well he understood, and he said, "I understood what she's been saying for the first time." He reported that both the anger and the problem had disappeared.

Teaching the Expressive Skill

Receiving empathy from others greatly enhances our ability to be accurately subjective about our own experience. For this reason Empathic and Expresser skills, work interactively to create the enhancement of intimacy that occurs with shared subjectivity.

Subjectivity in no way negates the concept of reality, nor is it meant to dilute the necessity of allowing to surface the outrage and passion that human beings naturally and healthfully feel when they are hurt physically or emotionally by other human beings. But, among other things, subjectivity does highlight that all experiencing is through the vehicle of consciousness. It is consciousness of consciousness that allows human beings freedom from conditioned meanings. And it is consciousness of consciousness that allows for intimacy in dialogue. However civilized and structured the RE approach may be, it is not tame, unemotional, or dispassionate. On the contrary, it is designed precisely to help clients focus on their deepest emotions rather than on others or the outside world, and to express their emotions fully and freely with the assurance that within the RE context they need not fear that they will be ignored or rejected, and can count on their being appreciatively acknowledged (Guerney, 1994).

Although the Expressive skill has five distinct elements, each one of them can be thought of as an aspect of attunement with one's own subjective experience. Stated most briefly, the five aspects of the Expressive skill are: (a) speak subjectively, and only subjectively, thereby laying no exclusive claim to knowledge or wisdom; (b) speak authentically about feelings, risking expression of the deeper, more vulnerable feelings; (c) speak specifically and concretely about experience and avoid generalizing, especially about the character of others; (d) speak about the whole picture, including one's subjective experience of the positive parts, especially the positives that underlie negatives (that which is valued in the other person or in the relationship and is relevant to the issue at hand, [e.g., caring deeply about the other's opinion of one that so often underlies the hurt that, in turn, underlies the anger when one feels criticized or ignored]) and; (e) speak fully, openly, specifically and only subjectively about one's wants, and the positive feelings and benefits both parties would derive from the satisfaction of those wants.

The last two elements of effective expression are those that clients are most likely to leave out if there is not adequate coaching from the therapist. One viable hypothesis about these omissions is that they involve more risk-taking on the part of the person speaking subjectively (called the Expresser in RE). In our experience, the positive feelings toward another human being often are the most vulnerable feelings. For example, when a person feels hurt by someone who is significant to them, the least vulnerable emotion might be hatred or cold anger. Warm anger is more vulnerable because it is engaged. Fear and sorrow are even more vulnerable because one is allowing oneself to feel the importance of the connection with that other person. If one directly expresses the importance of that connection (a common underlying positive in the fourth aspect of effective expression), one is likely to feel extremely vulnerable. In practice, people often cry when coached to allow this feeling into awareness and into expression. Yet, the person being addressed, typically, is most likely to listen with the most interest and compassion when this vulnerability is expressed. The fifth aspect of effective expression seems very risky. First of all, society condemns selfishness and this appears, to many, to be selfish or at least self-centered, therefore, it invites condemnation and criticism, not only from others, but also from one's own superego. Secondly, asking the other to give us what we want, simply on the basis that it would please or be helpful to us, is like handing power to them on a silver platter. It tells the other, and makes us admit to ourselves, that he or she have the power to give or withhold a significant measure of our happiness. If we don't ask at all, or don't ask on the basis of our own wants only, we don't have to admit that. Admitting it seems very dangerous. If we don't admit that, we can't be denied, we only can be deprived, and deprived when we simply asked for something clearly deserved on moral, or other socially approved grounds. To be deprived under these circumstances allows us to feel martyred and righteously angry. But to ask for ourselves, simply because it would make our lives easier or happier, means we can be denied. And to be denied means we will feel unloved, unwanted, and rejected. These are feelings much more feared by most than martyrdom and righteous anger.

Ironically, taking this risk—as is also the case of risking the expression of underlying positive feelings along with negative feelings—enormously increases your chances of getting what you want. With someone who loves you, asking for what you want, quite simply because it would ease your pain or make you happy or both, is far, far more likely to yield positive results than asking for it because it is correct, because it is mature, because it would be sensitive, because most other husbands or wives get it from their spouses, because it is moral, because it is just, because it is the norm, and so on. What the latter reasons almost invariably lead to is getting not what you want, but a long argument about what is correct, mature, sensitive, moral, just, or the norm. Such an argument ends in feelings of frustration, anger, hopelessness, and resentment. Since these reasons, and all of their kin, are ruled out when you must be subjective, as that is defined in RE, the Expressive Skill guideline of subjectivity automatically places one on the former, more promising, path.

Additionally, clients sometimes report finding it difficult to know what they want; this is the missing attunement to self that exists at times in almost everyone. Again, as will be described in more detail below, the therapist's attunement to a client's probable subjective world through the therapist's identification-empathy with the client can be employed, through Coaching the Expresser and Becoming, to very quickly and easily promote and deepen awareness of wants.

As with the Empathic skill, the Expressive skill is taught with demonstration, coaching, and practice. When time constraints or the wishes of the clients make it necessary to resolve emotionally heavy issues before the clients can be sufficiently trained to take on the major responsibility of doing so (even with heavy coaching) themselves, then the Crisis Intervention or Experiential modes of RE Therapy are used. These include most notably, Becoming, and Laundering. Otherwise, it is desirable to begin skill practice with those positive feelings and perceptions the couples still have toward one another and then to proceed to finding a way to enhance the relationship that seems desirable to both partners. After two or three therapy hours, the conflicts and problems are worked on. Front-loading (two to four hours in the first week or two) or minimarathon sessions (three or four hours at once) can sometimes accomplish enough skill training to give the clients sufficient skill to tackle (with coaching) any problem, especially if they have done reading and tape listening assignments at home.

TECHNIQUES USED TO REMOVE
BLOCKS TO INTIMACY

A flexible level of intimacy, balanced to meet the changing needs of the couple, but always including commitment, openness, empathy, and expressed caring at the very highest levels, is so central to the goals of RE couple therapy, that we are unable to think of anything the RE couple therapist does that is not designed to remove blocks to its achievement. This would be true whether the obstacle was as straightforward as a lack of appropriate skills or as complex as the need to overcome, say, the effects of sexual abuse in childhood through catharsis and the attainment of psychological insight into its effects on a wife's self-concept and repressed feelings about men. We cannot go into every RE technique used to overcome these obstacles in the space available here. But we can describe a fair portion of those that are central to that goal.

In understanding the methods to be described it would be helpful for the reader to know that the guidelines for the Discussion/Negotiation skill of RE are such that once the Expresser and Empathic Responder skills have been taught to clients, they never speak to one another in the therapy sessions except in one or the other of those modes, and that they must remain in that mode until they have exchanged modes with their partner. Such an exchange follows additional guidelines of the Discussion/Negotiation Skill. These allow the switch to take place in a coordinated way that promotes open, honest, and on-topic dialogue. An example of these guidelines is: an empathic response—one that your partner finds satisfying both in content and tone—must be made to your partner before you can express your own ideas and feelings. Another example is: whomever you consider the most stressed at the moment should take on, or remain in, the Expresser mode.

Modeling for the Expresser. In this type of coaching, the therapist, rephrases anything that the client has said that did not meet the requirements laid out in the Expresser guidelines, and asks her to repeat it, or say something like it, to her partner. Parenthetically, we'll note, in the problem discussions that clients typically schedule one or more times weekly at home, they use a Phrase Finder (Guerney, 1991) to help them—since they have no therapist there to coach them—to make translations of commonly used "incite-full" statements into insightful statements. Modeling for the Expresser is also used in another circumstance. That is when the therapist, who always empathically identifies with the Expresser as the Expresser speaks, experiences as the client, conflicts, wishes, or emotions that seem very important to the issue the client is talking about, yet have not been stated by the client and seem unlikely to be stated by him in the foreseeable future. In such a circumstance, the therapist states those feelings to the client, phrased in the manner the client would say them to his partner, and asks the client to add something like that to his statement if it is true. Modeling for the Expresser is just one of a variety of ways of coaching the Expresser. All of them however, serve to deepen the Expresser's attunement to his own subjective world.

Modeling for the Empathizer. Again, this is one form of coaching the empathizer to provide a good empathic response to his partner. The client is free to use his own words, but a modeling type of therapist-coaching response, by definition, is one in which the client would not need to change a single word, not a pronoun or anything else, to make a good empathic response to his partner. The advantage of modeling over the therapist simply empathizing directly to the client's partner are many: (a) assuming the empathy is of good quality, experiencing the empathy within oneself, or coming from one's partner, is almost invariably far more transforming than when it is provided by an outsider such as the therapist; (b) modeling is a fast and reliable way of teaching good, potent empathy, and having clients quickly learn that empathy at its highest levels speeds up effective therapy; (c) having the clients learn empathy quickly enables them to make use of it sooner in problem-solving sessions at home and speeds up therapy, making therapeutic effectiveness more certain; (d) in addition to having a truth serum effect on the receiver, deep empathy has a strong bonding effect and, after strong bonding with the therapist has occurred, which in RE therapy takes only a session or two, it is far more desirable that the bonds between the partners be strengthened than that the bonds between therapist and client be strengthened.

Becoming. As already indicated, in this method the therapist speaks as if she were the client. The method is used when a client seems unable now, and unlikely in the near future to be able to convey his thoughts and feelings as openly, fully, deeply, insightfully or with sufficient emotion as seems to be required, and when such expression would be too lengthy or complex to allow for modeling to do the job. The therapist therefore Becomes the client's partner as if she were the client. (The partner makes her empathic response to the client, not to the therapist.) The therapist may continue in the Expresser role as the client until such time as she feels the client can speak adequately without requiring a level of coaching that would interfere with genuine dialogue. While engaged in Becoming, the therapist is careful to check out with the client anything that the therapist is saying which has not been said or strongly implied by the client earlier in the therapy. The clients also understand that they may interrupt the therapist anytime the therapist's statement did not reflect the client's thoughts and feelings. Space prohibits further explication of Becoming here, and the interested reader is referred to a videotaped demonstration (Snyder, 1996).

Laundering. This method is central to the Crisis Intervention mode of RE couple/family therapy and, on occasion, plays a critical role in the other two modes of RE couple/family therapy as well. Laundering was developed by the junior author in the earliest years of the development of divorce mediation to test the application of general RE principles and methods to that field. For that reason, he did mediation work with divorcing clients who had no knowledge of RE skills, no interest in acquiring them, and intense general hostility and many specific conflicts that needed to be resolved quickly from a starting point of complete unwillingness to yield any ground. Having worked well in that context, Laundering then came to be used in RE therapies. It is used when an extensive couple dialogue is required to resolve a problem and it is predictable that the emotions of both clients would simultaneously become too intense or complex for them to skillfully conduct such a dialogue, even with a lot of coaching.

In RE therapy, clients seldom talk to the therapist; they talk to each other with the therapist coaching their dialogue. This remains true in Laundering, in that dialogue between the client or couple occupies center stage at all times. The difference is that, in Laundering, the therapist, with continuing input from the clients, Becomes, not just one client, but both.

Some instructions to clients and seating arrangements are similar to those used during an RE intake session. Then, the purposes were primarily to prevent anger-escalation and to facilitate communication from client to therapist. In Laundering those instructions, and other important ones, are being used to facilitate communication between the couple and to resolve a problem or conflict. Clients are asked not to speak to each other at all, and not to speak to the therapist until the therapist addresses them. If feasible, the partners are prevented from seeing each other's faces by having the clients sit facing the therapist straight-on, sitting side-by-side except that one of them is moved back a few feet behind the other. The therapist is not addressed by her own name. Rather, each client addresses her by the name of his or her partner. If one partner is Susan and the other is Bill, whenever the therapist speaks to Susan she "is," and is called, "Bill." Whenever she speaks to Bill she "is," and is called, "Susan." When Susan is talking to the therapist about Bill always criticizing her, she does not say, "Bill criticizes me all the time." She says, "You criticize me all the time." When it comes time for Bill to speak, the therapist as Bill does not say, "Bill has been trying hard in recent months not to be so critical. He says, "I have been trying hard in recent months..." Once agreed-to by each party, all of these interlocutory guidelines are enforced with extreme compassion and great consistency. Following not only those guidelines, but all the guidelines of RE skills, the therapist-as-partner goes back and forth between the clients, listening to them, absorbing their feelings, empathizing with them, bringing out the pain and the longings that underlie the frustrations, anger and resentments, and introducing as many strong underlying positives as early as emotional-reality permits.

When the clients speak to the therapist as if she were the partner, their statements are not required to be skilled, and so the therapist does not coach. Hence, the statements of the clients are unskilled. Generally speaking, in the situations where Laundering is used, the clients' statements present only the negatives, contain many generalizations, and in many other ways are psychologically threatening and would tend to evoke much defensiveness, anger and withdrawal (i.e., the statements are "dirty"). Catharsis is recognized as beneficial and sometimes as essential in RE therapy, and sometimes some of the usual guidelines are suspended to facilitate it (Guerney, 1994), and so, there is some benefit being derived from the clients' "dirty" expressions, although they also do much damage to the problem-solving process, damage which needs to be undone as much as possible by the Laundering process. As has been said, when the therapist speaks for each of them she expresses their point of view skillfully. Thus, she cleans or launders, the clients' statements. All laundered statements are made subjective, the generalizations are replaced with specifics, etc. Although laundered, the sentiments of the clients are not watered down or bleached-out. Anger, for example, is expressed fully, but always subjectively, and the hurt, sorrow and pain behind the anger are now also included. Also, insofar as is feasible, the caring, the vulnerable feelings, the longings and, most importantly, the love are included and, as quickly as is feasible, are taken to their deepest levels. Having these parts of the picture fully included, and preceding their expression with empathy makes all the difference in the world. It allows the statement to be received with some compassion instead of only defensively. It can elicit some caring and love in return. Eventually, these factors very frequently turn the dialog from obstinate disagreement to agreement.

This is achieved by the direct use of the standard RE skills in the hands of the RE-skilled therapist in the Laundering context. Among many other things, the Laundering-specific interlocutory guidelines serve the purpose of allowing the therapist to become a lightning rod. The partners must say what they say, not to their all-too-familiar partner, but to a dignified professional and one who is extremely empathic and always expresses "his" (i.e., the partner's) thoughts and feeling skillfully and who includes "his" (i.e., the partner's) underlying positive feelings whenever feasible. Thus, despite the fact that the therapist "is" the partner, ingrained, intense, negative emotions are not so automatically or frequently triggered as they would be if the clients were speaking to their true partners. In this sense, and also because the immediate, direct target of the client's own unlaundered statement is the therapist-as-partner not the partner himself, Laundering grounds, harmlessly absorbs to some extent, the lightning inherent in such a statement. The hostility more often just heats-up partners, instead of severely burning them. Similarly, but on the nonverbal dimension, the seating arrangement described earlier provides what is termed in RE as visual shielding. It further reduces the chances of burning by partially insulating the clients from withering, anger-provoking nonverbal cues that clients may wittingly or unwittingly express while they are talking or while their partner is talking.

As with Becoming, which is a large part of what the therapist is doing in Laundering, the clients are given to understand that the therapist's role is to edit what they say to facilitate the resolution of their problem. That means they understand that the therapist will omit things she deems counterproductive to resolving the problem whenever such things are not essential to expressing the client's feelings strongly and completely. The clients also understand that the therapist will be adding things that they did not say, things that the therapist believes would be helpful to resolving the problem (these are usually the underlying positive feelings), providing, of course that she believes those things are true to the client's thoughts and feelings. The client, say Bill, whom she has Become, is further told that the therapist will frequently, as she is speaking, check with Bill to make sure that the things she has added are accurate. Bill is also assured that before she asks his partner to tell her views, the therapist will check with Bill to make sure nothing that Bill thinks should be said now has been left out.

When Laundering, the therapist is free, as "Susan" or as "Bill," to negotiate solutions to problems and conflicts from both sides in a way that would not otherwise be possible. Skilled Laundering usually makes it possible to negotiate solutions to intensely emotional problems or crises (such as, whether to continue the relationship after the discovery of an affair) to the mutual satisfaction of both parties within one to three hours. A demonstration of the use of Laundering may be seen in a videotape (Snyder, 1996).

Trouble Shooting. This term applies to what the therapist does in any touchy or difficult situation that calls for temporarily abandoning the usual mode of RE therapy. Unlike most couple therapies, in the usual RE therapy, the clients are engaged in dialogue with each other (with whatever level of role-taking this requires of the therapist) almost all the time; talk between the client and the therapist-as-therapist is almost nil. That kind of unusual situation may arise for a variety of reasons. One example would be that the client has become emotionally overwhelmed and needs a level of empathy that the partner is not yet able to provide or that she is herself too upset to provide a high level of empathy at the moment. Another example would be that the client shows "resistance" to using the skills.[1] A third example would be that the

---

[1] "Resistance" is placed in quotes because in RE we do not view objections to what the therapist requests as residing within the client, and certainly not as an element of pathology. Rather, we view it systemically, as a conflict between the therapist and the client about what should be done. The therapist resolves it in exactly the same way as she is teaching the couple to handle their conflicts: by Troubleshooting. That is, by using the RE skills to resolve a difficult situation.

therapist has feelings that are interfering with an optimal relationship. These might arise if a client has repeatedly failed to live up to some commitment, such as not doing what he or she had agreed to do as a home assignment or failing to show up for appointments without canceling in advance. Another reason would be that the therapist wants to convey information, hypotheses, or ideas that she thinks would be of significant import to the couple. In all such situations, the therapist does the same thing: Troubleshooting. The category encompasses any significant dialogue between the therapist and one or more clients. It is a dialogue in which the therapist uses any or all RE skills and says nothing outside of the RE guidelines. When clients have sufficient skill, and it is not deemed inappropriate for some other reason, they likewise make use of the RE skills in the dialogue. At other times (e.g., when there is resistance in both), the therapist and the client(s) would be using RE skills, and the structure of the dialogue would be the same as when the couple uses them to resolve their own conflicts. Such a dialogue would continue until the conflict was resolved to the complete satisfaction of all parties concerned.

REIT (Relationship Enhancement® Individual Therapy). With the RE approach, it is not unusual for a therapist to do some individual therapy within the context of the couple therapy. This can be done either with each client alone (if that is preferred temporarily) or in the context of a couple session. When there is enough support available, a partner's witnessing of another partner's individual work makes a significant contribution to the empathy. It also graphically illustrates how the meanings that have emerged in the couple relationship have an historical context. In REIT, the basic principles of the RE approach are used. Among other things, this means the therapist is conducting the individual work within the framework of the Empathic and Expressive skills. An article on this approach by the authors is in manuscript form (Guerney & Snyder, 1997).

Exploration of Cultural Context. It is not unusual for a block to intimacy to exist because of largely invisible cultural meanings in which both members of the couple have been submerged. Most of these invisible cultural meanings have to do with the historical existence of dominant/subordinate relationships. Perhaps the major damage of these hierarchical relationships is that they become internalized. The last few decades have brought an increase in our awareness of the effects of internalized oppression, in which members of the culturally subordinate group (e.g., children, women, poor people, oppressed racial and ethnic groups) have internalized the attitudes of the dominant group toward them. The attitudes of members of both the dominant group and the subordinate group may be invisible to them because of the prevalence of these cultural assumptions. It can easily happen, for example, that a couple coming for therapy is demonstrating cultural assumptions regarding gender roles and gender relationships, without having examined these assumptions. Both members of the couple may be experiencing frustration and confusion about being upset with each other's feelings that can be clarified when the cultural meanings are deconstructed.

But this process of deconstructing meanings requires assistance from the therapist, as Berg indicates in her chapter in this book. The Troubleshooting technique described earlier can be used to explore with the clients the less visible meanings that underlie their attitudes toward self and other. They can also be coached to explore these meanings with each other. Powerful sessions can result from these exploratory dialogues. Culturally embedded meanings that have hardly been articulated and have been inadequately understood by both members of the pair can be clarified in the open dialogue created by the structure and skills of RE.

When a man "becomes" a woman, and a woman "becomes" a man, empathy and understanding replace being judgmental and confused, and meanings are separated from the human being who holds them, to be examined in their own right. Most significantly, shifts in meaning, attitude, and behavior tend to occur, simply as a result of this process of deconstruction. The couple then is freed to coconstruct alternative meanings. Maryhelen Snyder and Susan Snyder (1997) have produced an audiotape in which some of the deconstructive methods of narrative therapy are integrated with the RE approach.

The case example below illustrates the way in which an exploratory dialogue using the two essential skills of RE therapy allows for shared subjectivity. This shared subjectivity is intimacy and is immediately experienced as such. Problems tend to dissolve or cocreative solutions to them tend to unfold more readily.

CASE EXAMPLE

When the couple and the therapist remain focused on the process of discovering meanings and desires, the interactions that occur are experienced as intimate in themselves and cocreative intelligence occurs naturally. Such change is, as Harry Goolishian explained, "the evolution of meaning in dialogue" (Anderson & Goolishian, 1988), and Kathy Weingarten (1991) described it in her definition of intimacy as the "co-creation of shared meaning." In this case, the therapist, the senior author, focused on what she calls the exploratory dialogue, seeing it in this way.

Mark and Audrey (names and identifying characteristics have been changed to protect anonymity) came for therapy because they hadn't had intercourse, with only two or three exceptions, for several years. They reported that they loved each other and felt committed to their marriage, but that the sexual part of their relationship had always been something of a problem. Audrey had decided not to make love any more unless she wanted to, and she had discovered that she hardly ever wanted to. Prior to her decision, she had succumbed to Mark's strong desire for sexual closeness and his feeling that this closeness was very effective in counteracting the effects of depression. His bouts with depression had existed most of his adult life, and, when they came for therapy, he had been using a low dose of an anti-depressant for close to a year. This combined with his greater awareness of the causes and effects of his depression was enabling him to live with considerably greater freedom from depression than he had had earlier in their 20-year marriage. Mark expressed support for Audrey's decision to respect her own feelings in this way, but he described how hard it was for him that there was not only an absence of intercourse, but a considerable absence of touching and physical closeness in their relationship.

Although their communication abilities were good relative to most couples, Mark and Audrey had not been able to resolve this problem. They were very interested in learning the tools of RE couple therapy as a way to deepen their understanding of themselves and each other. They were particularly interested in the Identification method, since they had felt confused and critical of each other's perspectives on this issue, each pathologizing the other to some degree.

As is the case with RE therapy, with the clients, the therapist avoided analyzing dynamics and giving strategic interventions. Practices that fit within the model are: teaching the RE skills, which, in addition to other things, also protect the space in which each person can speak and be heard; coaching; seeking information; sharing her own subjective perspective through Troubleshooting when that seemed useful; Becoming, and applying the various methods described above for assisting clients in understanding and breaking through blocks to their optimal capacity for relating and functioning as they desire, and so forth.

The therapist used the structure of the intake interview for our initial session. Becoming each of them speaking to the other heightened her own deep respect for what each of them was wanting and a sense of the offering that each was making to the other in their resistances to the status quo. In subsequent sessions and, necessarily in their home, the primary work was done by Audrey and Mark. Each would speak to the other following the Expressive Skill guidelines, and the other would empathize using the I Mode, (i.e., speaking as if he or she were the partner). Once the partners were taught the skills, the therapist continued to coach them, as described above. Secondly, she occasionally Became one or the other of them speaking to their partner, especially when what they had said was complex and they were struggling hard to understand themselves, or when their partner was having difficulty understanding them, or both. In this Becoming process, the therapist joins in the experiencing of the client's experience. As clients listen more fully to "themselves" speaking, their self-awareness is often enhanced and they are able to enter more fully into their own feelings. (This works also, of course, with more traditional forms of empathy, but the Becoming method can be particularly effective in the regard. The possible reasons for this are described in more detail in a recent article on that subject by Snyder, (1995).

And of course, the partner, the one to whom the therapist is expressing for the client, gets to hear the deepest levels of the client's feelings, including all of the underlying positive feelings; all expressed at the highest level of skill. Remember that everything that the therapist says while Becoming is fully endorsed by the client. Thus, the partner's ability to deeply and compassionately comprehend the client is generally maximized. (Had the therapist not expected such a maximizing effect on the partner as a result of taking over for the client, the therapist probably would not have done so.)

The therapist also used Troubleshooting to engage in a deconstructive dialogue with the pair about prevailing cultural meanings regarding sexuality. In doing this, the therapist spoke of her own experiences and what she had learned from other clients, and determined the clients' experiences and conditioning, empathizing with them, of course, as they revealed them. They devised plans for deepening their exploration of what each of them wanted at home. Some of the elements of the Problem/Conflict Resolution skill were applied, particularly making their plans specific and concrete, and establishing procedures for monitoring and following through on their plans.

For example, Audrey and Mark discovered through these exploratory dialogues how much Audrey was holding back from touching Mark out of fear of arousing him, and also holding back from exposing her body to him. Furthermore, they discovered that Mark was now very willing to take responsibility for his own arousal, and did not want Audrey to hold back touch or the visual pleasure of her body for the sake of protecting him from that arousal. They also learned more about how much Audrey had been taught by parental messages and modeling not to cherish her own sexuality and sensuality, and how much Mark had been taught by cultural messages to closely associate sensual, affectionate, and sexual needs and desires. As a result of these discoveries, Audrey was interested in hugging Mark more, and in setting aside time to give and receive massages. Mark had already been interested in these possibilities. Audrey began to keep records of her activities in these areas, and to observe any cyclical or other factors affecting her sexual desire. Mark became interested in experiencing desire as a satisfying experience in itself and separating it from the impulse toward satisfaction. He observed that when his needs to give and receive physical affection felt satisfied, the sexual needs became relatively minor. Audrey noticed how deeply satisfied she was by physical closeness and also by the pleasure of being a body when she was free of fear that there would be an implicit or explicit demand for her to respond sexually. She noted how hard it had been for her that, for many years she made it into her problem that she did not want to respond sexually and forced herself to do it against her own desires. Each of them reported great pleasure in the dialogues themselves, speaking of the intimacy created by this way of knowing each other.

SUMMARY

Subjectivity is the experience of experience. Experience itself is organismic, dynamic, preverbal, concrete, and only in the precise moment. The process of experiencing experience, of being conscious of consciousness, involves the mediating function of language or other symbolization forms. These symbols are embedded in cultural meanings that we are, to a large extent, born into. In the experience of formulating these meanings, however, to another person who is listening without judgment, with interest and with openness, we hear our own meanings even as we are heard. We begin to know ourselves and what we know is dynamic and flowing in nature. As The Stone Center therapists have put it: "Self is movement-in-relation" (Miller, 1986). At the same time, listening to another consciousness of consciousness revealing itself to us heightens our awareness further of possible ways of seeing and organizing reality. As though we were blind people touching parts of an awesomely large, unknowable, and to some degree modifiable elephant, we begin to share consciousness with each other to our mutual benefit. In this process of conversation, we turn together and experience the intimacy of shared subjectivity and cocreative enterprise.

The RE therapy model gives the therapist and the couple a structure and skills for this kind of intersubjective dialogue. The RE Empathic and Expresser skills described and illustrated above, when taken together, reveal the subjectivity of self and other. We have described them as relationship skills rather than communication skills, because the latter term does not encompass the intimacy inherent in this particular method. The method enhances autonomy (awareness of each person as the agent of his or her own existence) simultaneously with intimacy. It places high value on each person's separate experience of experience, and it supplies the essential structures and tools for mutual respect of that separate experiencing.

The result stems not only from what has happened but from what will happen in the years ahead because of the couple's desire and capacity to continue to use the skills from which they derive so much. And that result is a strong and enduring intimacy. It is strong and enduring because it is based on skills which enable a continual and synergistic balancing of each partner's dynamic, fluctuating, needs for joining and giving on the one hand and for independence and self-fulfillment on the other hand.

REFERENCES

Accordino, M. P., & Guerney, B. G., Jr. (1993). Effects of the Relationship Enhancement program on community residential rehabilitation. *Psychosocial Rehabilitation Journal, 17*(2), 131–144.

Anderson, H., & Goolishian, H. A. (1988). Human systems as linguistic systems: Preliminary and evolving ideas about the implications for clinical theory. *Family Process, 27*(4), 371–395.

Armenti, Nicholas (March 18, 1980). Personal communication. *5*(2), 31–50.

Buber, M. (1957). *Pointing the way: selected essays.* (M. S. Friedman, Trans. and Ed.). New York: Harper & Row. (Original work published.)

Buber, M. (1988). *The knowledge of man: selected essays.* (M. S. Friedman & R. G. Smith, Trans.). Atlantic Highlands, NJ: Humanities Press.

Giblin, P., Sprenkle, D. H., & Sheehan, R. (1985). Enrichment outcome research: A meta-analysis of premarital, marital, and family interventions. *Journal of Marital and Family Therapy, 11*(3), 257–271.

Ginsberg, B. G. (1977). Parent-adolescent relationship development program. In B. G. Guerney, Jr., *Relationship Enhancement: skill-training programs for therapy, problem prevention, and enrichment.* San Francisco: Jossey-Bass.

Ginsberg, B. G. (1997). *Relationship Enhancement family therapy.* New York: John Wiley & Sons.

Guerney, B. G., Jr. (1977). *Relationship Enhancement: skill-training programs for therapy, problem prevention and enrichment.* San Francisco: Jossey-Bass.

Guerney, B. G., Jr., (1987). *Relationship Enhancement® therapist's manual.* Rockville, MD: IDEALS.

Guerney, B. G., Jr. (1988). Family Relationship Enhancement: a skill training approach. In L. A. Bond & B. M. Wagner (Eds.), *Families in transition: primary prevention programs that work* (pp. 99–134). Beverly Hills, CA: Sage Publications, Inc.

Guerney, B. G., Jr. (1991). *Relationship Enhancement® program manual.* Rockville, MD: IDEALS.

Guerney, B. G., Jr. (1994). The role of emotion in Relationship Enhancement® marital/family therapy. In S. M. Johnson & L. S. Greenberg (Eds.), *Emotion in marriage and marital therapy* (pp. 124–147). New York: Brunner/Mazel.

Guerney, B. G., Jr., & Snyder, M. H. (1997). Relationship Enhancement individual therapy. Manuscript in preparation.

Guerney, B. G., Jr., Waldo, M., & Firestone, L. (1987). Wife-battering: a theoretical construct and case report. *The American Journal of Family Therapy, 15*(1), 34–43.

Guerney, B. G., Jr. & Yoder, P. A. (1990) The strategies and skills needed to resolve family firm conflicts. *Proceedings of the Annual Conference of the Family Firm Institute* (pp. 128–129). Johnstown, NY: Family Firm Institute.

Guerney, L., & Guerney, B. G., Jr. (1985). The Relationship Enhancement family of family therapies. In L. L'Abate & M. Milan (Eds.), *Handbook of social skills training and research* (pp. 506–524). New York: John Wiley and Sons.

Matter, M. & McAllister, W. (1984). Relationship Enhancement® for the recovering couple: Working with the intangible. *Focus on Family and Chemical Dependency, 7*(5), 21–23 & 40.

Miller, J. B. (1986). What do we mean by relationships? *Work in progress #22,* Wellesley, MA: Stone Center Working Paper Series.

Rathmell, C. G. (1991). *The effects of the Relationship Enhancement program with industrial work teams.* Unpublished doctoral dissertation, The Pennsylvania State University.

Rogers, C. R. (1951). *Client Centered Therapy.* Boston, MA: Houghton Mifflin.

Rogers, C. R. (1957). The necessary and sufficient conditions of therapeutic personality change. *Journal of Consulting Psychology, 21,* 95–103.

Ross, E. R., Baker, S. B., & Guerney, B. G., Jr. (1985). Effectiveness of Relationship Enhancement therapy versus therapist's preferred therapy. *American Journal of Family Therapy, 13*(1), 11–21.

Snyder, M. (1994). Couple therapy with narcissistically vulnerable clients: Using the Relationship Enhancement® model. *The Family Journal*, *2*(1), 27–35.

Snyder, M. (1995). "Becoming": a method for expanding systemic thinking and deepening empathic accuracy. *Family Process*, *34*(2) 241–253.

Snyder, M. (1996). *Demonstrations of becoming and laundering in Relationship Enhancement® couple therapy*. [videotapes]. Rockville, MD: IDEALS.

Snyder, M. & Snyder, S. (1997). *Co-constructive family therapy*. (Audiotape). Albuquerque, N.M.: M. Snyder.

Waldo, M. (1986). Group counseling for military personnel who battered their wives. *Journal for Specialists in Group Work*, *2*(3), 132–138.

Waldo, M. (1987). Also victims: Understanding and treating men arrested for spouse abuse. *Journal of Counseling and Development*, (*65*), 385–388.

Waldo, M. (1988). Relationship Enhancement counseling groups for wife abusers. *Journal of Mental Health Counseling*, *10*(1), 37–45.

Waldo, M., & Guerney, B. G., Jr. (1983). Marital Relationship Enhancement® therapy in the treatment of alcoholism. *Journal of Marital and Family Therapy*, *9*(3), 321–323.

Waldo, M., & Harman, M. J. (1993). Relationship Enhancement® therapy with borderline personality. *The Family Journal*, *1*(1), 25–30.

Weingarten, K. (1991). The discourses of intimacy: adding a social constructionist and feminist view. *Family Process*, *30*: 285–305.

CHAPTER 21

Searching for the Mythical Mate: A Developmental Approach to Intimacy

Ellyn Bader, Ph.D.
Peter T. Pearson, Ph.D.

Ellyn recently asked a couple what intimacy meant to each of them. The wife said, "It is long romantic candlelit dinners." The husband replied, "It is the elegant teamwork of a well honed basketball team." Just how far apart are they? Bridging these imposing gulfs is the recurring challenge often presented to us when doing couples therapy.

DEVELOPMENT OF SELF: CRUCIAL TO GREATER INTIMACY AND SATISFACTION UNDERSTANDING AND DEFINITION OF INTIMACY

The problem of defining intimacy is that most couples at least have some notion of what it is. Ask them and you get some variation of feeling close, feeling good about each other, being accepted, cherished for who you are, and so forth. What is the problem with couples having their own definition of intimacy? Not much, except that it generally runs contrary to what we believe and teach. This creates a three-way challenge for each person in the couple and the therapist. The result is an ongoing series of negotiations, overt and covert, about whose definition will predominate. The stakes are high because the dominant definition sets the trajectory for the therapy and the next chapter of the relationship. Most couples intuitively know that if they accept a nonenmeshed definition of intimacy, somebody is going to part with some cherished wishes.

However, most couples will not even admit it takes work to maintain intimacy. When pushed for details, they say something about the importance of compromise. Tell couples that compromise too often sets the stage for big, really big, problems down the road, and a very quizzical look shows up on their faces. Actually, you can compromise a portion of your desires and smooth some relationship speed bumps. But start compromising your core values, principles, and ethics and you now have an intimacy path strewn with boulders, deep potholes, and a host of other obstacles. The intimacy journey has taken a grim turn for the worse. And if you don't compromise yourself? Ugly choice number two now emerges. You still get boulders, potholes and slippery slopes.

It gets worse. You cannot create sustained intimacy with your partner without changing yourself. Many couples prefer not to hear that. Then comes the final indignity. You can't create enduring intimacy with one grand burst of awareness, or one elegant solution, or even a very determined effort to change your partner for the better. No wonder people would rather believe in Hallmark cards, romantic movies, books, music or advertisements.

"What is Intimacy?" We believe this is a necessary, complex, and even occasionally, counterproductive question for therapists to ponder. Why counterproductive? After generating a satisfactory definition, there is a strong temptation to impose our newfound definition on our clients.

So how do we define intimacy? We believe it comes in two basic flavors. Intimacy with yourself and intimacy with another. Intimacy equals the emotional result of a series of complex processes of knowing and being known, understanding and being understood, accepting and being accepted, tolerating and being tolerated. Getting to the feeling of intimacy may be excruciating, exhilarating, or somewhere in between.

As you mature, you expand your greeting card notions of intimacy. You appreciate the complexity and contradictions within yourself and your partner. You take into consideration life's shifting and changing circumstances. Your demands lessen and your perspectives widen. As you progress through the developmental challenges of being in a committed relationship, your beliefs about and experiences of intimacy change. Thus, intimacy will never have a static definition for any individual. So, while our definition of intimacy is an evolving one, it does not excuse us from taking the time to explore the meaning for each client at the time they arrive for therapy.

The feeling of closeness or connection that so many humans desire seems too often impermanent or illusive. Why is this so? At the beginning of a relationship, the intimacy may come very easily. As the relationship progresses the intimacy seems to disappear. Why?

In the beginning, one partner may feel exhilarated because "I can talk about anything with you!" Discovering each other is new and exciting and feels intimate. There is a high level of mutual trust leading to emotional disclosures. Self-revelation generally means this person trusts me enough to let me know something about themselves or their past. Early in the relationship, close feelings are attained almost effortlessly. However, as time goes on and the interdependency in a relationship increases, it takes more and more self-disclosure to recreate this same feeling of knowing or being known at deeper levels. When it stops being so easy, the culprit is easy to identify—my partner! There can only be one reason—it's my partner's fault. Rarely does one partner think their peewee efforts are insufficient to the task of sustaining intimacy.

It's common to hear a couple say they want a more intimate relationship. It's uncommon to understand that you can't develop a more intimate relationship. A "relationship" cannot be intimate. Only individuals can increase their capacity to be self-revealing and to invite or recognize intimate revelations from their partners. In fact, the foundation for supporting ongoing intimacy is counterintuitive. It is not necessary to have your partner participate or cooperate to increase your capacity for intimacy.

We believe through self-development couples are better able to define their inner feelings. With ongoing practice they can more clearly identify and express their intimate desires. Increased self-development also results in clearer separation between self and partner. As the boundaries become sharper, clients are able to know and understand their partners more. Unexpectedly, they often also develop a broader range in what is experienced as intimacy. In this way intimacy is dynamic. What is experienced as intimacy expands markedly as couples progress through the different developmental stages of their relationship.

Our observation is that most couples in our culture are socialized to view the wonderful initial idealized period of romance as the ultimate intimacy experience. Anything less and you are wrenchingly cheated out of life's grand relationship prize.

This initial period of symbiosis is a normal stage. It is part of falling in love and it does indeed feel glorious! The grass is greener. The sky is bluer. The birds are singing. And everything is wonderful! These exhilarating feelings from merging boundaries lead partners to feel deliciously close and special. Gone is the existential anxiety of being psychologically alone in the world. Intimacy is effortlessly attained. It is euphoric, like a chocolate or other chemical high. Unfortunately this is the model that most couples hold themselves and each other to as the relationship progresses. This model of intimacy is vigorously and invasively reinforced culturally and portrayed daily in songs, movies, romance novels and television shows. Few people in our culture are immune to this siren call of intimacy. It is the type of intimacy that gets a relationship started and helps to form the foundation for caring, for connecting, and for selecting a lifelong partner. However, it is not a foundation for the hard work of sustained intimacy or a foundation for individual growth.

Yet, are there only cultural factors that primarily drive our quest for intimacy? We think not. There are many elements in this beginning stage that are parallel to early childhood. Primitive desires and fantasies are evoked by the intensity and by the promise of returning to unconditional love. Because these feelings are so intensely positive, many individuals try to perpetuate this stage. They hold the fantasy of romantic intimacy making up for all the unmet hopes from childhood. It isn't long before couples get mugged by the realities of daily life. Then comes the inevitable disillusionment. The partners don't conform to each other's fantasies, and their flaws become more visible. This disillusionment phase is ripe for wrenching growth and movement into the stage of differentiation. Instead of growing in ways that are required to manage this painful disillusionment, many partners never progress past the original symbiotic lure. They meet the disillusionment with a demand for continuing symbiosis. They turn expectantly or hopefully to their partners with the often heard lament, "you aren't meeting my needs." Then they chase these symbiotic beliefs that are pervasive in our culture:

Common Symbiotic Beliefs

1   If you really loved me, you would know what I want without me telling you.
2   If you really loved me, you would have the same needs for intimacy and closeness as I do.
3   If you really loved me, you would change your personality to please me.
4   If you really loved me, you would give me what I want in an ongoing way and it should be easy, effortless and enjoyable for you.
5   If you really loved me, you would give me what I hope for, long for, and expect. And will you please do it on my time schedule?
6   P.S. By the way, please do not expect me to seriously inconvenience myself in responding to you.

It is not recognized that to even approximate responding to these demands requires a complex awareness of yourself and who your partner is. It is hard to accept that this knowledge is arrived at only after years of being together and multiple intimate conversations.

Individuals who don't transition beyond symbiosis get entrenched in circular nonproductive patterns. The symbiotic pull is first hinted at, then suggested, and finally demanded. The partners stagnate in either a primarily conflict-avoidant or conflict-dominated relationship. Individuals in these relationships end up sacrificing their own development for the maintenance of the partnership.

In order to build the foundation to sustain intimacy, someone must take the lead to move beyond symbiosis into differentiation. Differentiation is built on a foundation of clear separation between self and other. It includes the ability to manage differences while remaining open and curious about each other and yourself. To do this requires managing complex feelings of grief, disillusionment, envy, anger, disappointment, jealousy and competition and ironically, even many positive emotions. Is there anyone who wouldn't be challenged by these daunting tasks?

We believe there are different and predictable developmental stages of relationships. By understanding these stages, couples can direct their own evolution. The predictable stages of couples relationships are: Symbiosis, Differentiation, Practicing, Rapprochement, Mutual Interdependence and Synergy.

Our work is based on viewing couples relationships as paralleling the stages described by Margaret Mahler in *The Psychological Birth of the Human Infant* (Mahler, Pine & Bergman, 1975). We have described these stages extensively in *In Quest of the Mythical Mate*, (Bader & Pearson, 1988) (see Appendix A.) We will not repeat the description here, but have reproduced a summary chart for those readers who are not familiar with our work.

These stages are predictable and essential. In going through these stages, partners develop different self capacities that enable them to keep the relationship intimate, vital and alive. The most difficult transition for most couples to make is between symbiosis and differentiation. The symbiotic stage is strongly maintained by cultural and individual beliefs and by the normal, intuitive ways humans try to reduce anxiety. The two most common ways people try to minimize anxiety are:

1 I'm anxious (when I see our differences), so I'll give up myself and agree with you, or
2 I'm anxious (when I see who you are), so I'll try to control you so you will be how I want you to be.

The capacity to sustain intimacy requires increasing capacities to manage differences and to use the discomfort of anxiety for emotional growth. However, there is a major problem. Differentiation is a conflictual time. Who likes to willingly engage in conflict with their beloved? Who likes to risk losing what they care about the most? Who will lightly risk being shunned or left? Yet going through the hell of differentiation enables partners to strengthen themselves.

Differentiation is the active, ongoing process of defining self, activating self, establishing and maintaining one's own boundaries and managing the anxiety that comes from risking loss (separation) and greater closeness (intimacy). The more you can manage the anxiety that comes from risking separation or loss and merging, the more differentiated you become. The following chart, taken from our book *In Quest of the Mythical Mate* (Bader & Pearson, 1988) describes some of the different aspects of differentiation.

DIFFERENTIATING OF THE SELF

- Knowing one's own thoughts, feelings, and desires
- Expressing one's thoughts, feelings, and desires
- Diminishing emotional contagion, not getting pulled into having to feel the same feelings as the partner at the same time
- Developing awareness of what works for oneself in solving conflicts
- Handling alone time, including private thoughts and private physical spaces
- Developing individual goals

DIFFERENTIATING FROM OTHERS

- Developing more balanced perceptions of the partner and being able to give empathic responses even at times of disagreement
- Handling discrepancies in desires for closeness
- Developing mechanisms for resolving conflicts with the partner
- Developing mechanisms for "how we do things as a couple"
- Recognizing and handling different value systems

ESTABLISHING BOUNDARIES

- Developing separate friendships
- Delineating separate areas of family and household responsibilities
- Planning for separate activities
- Delineating separate areas of financial responsibility
- Developing the capacity to handle privacy within the relationship

Differentiation is not the same as the autonomy or individuation which occurs in the practicing stage. It is easy for a therapist to make an assumption that, when one partner is taking more independence in a relationship and the other is searching for closeness, the autonomous one is the healthier partner. The autonomy seeking partner may have skipped the differentiation stage and, as a result, be equally lacking in the capacities that will build intimacy over the course of a lifetime.

PRINCIPLES FOR CONNECTING AND CREATING INTIMACY

In the following list, we have highlighted some of the principles that we believe are helpful in creating and sustaining intimacy.

1 The foundation for ongoing sustained intimacy comes from partners being able to explore, appreciate and persevere in managing differences with and from their partners and contradictions within themselves.

Almost everything is predicated on this first principle. After the initial bond is formed, the intimacy potential in a relationship will always remain low when couples avoid exploring their differences and contradictions. Without this exploration, differences and contradictions become walls and barriers instead of bridges. Differences are the pathways to strengthen the individuals and the partnership. For most couples, the significant growth and evolution that occurs over time started out as conflict, disagreement, or abrasiveness. Those couples who are able to tolerate and use the conflict are able to deepen their intimacy.

Other couples use the differences to try to change or exert power and control over the partner. Couples who learn to welcome their differences are invigorated instead of feeling finessed and bullied by one another. When partners adopt the attitude that a difference is something to be explored, they create an open system and become genuinely curious about themselves and each other.

It is not just managing differences from our partner, it is crucial to come to terms with our own contradictions that create binds for all parties. We believe it is natural for people to have contradictory desires. However, it is not natural to want to explore and grow from a reconciliation of these contradictions. It is reconciling our own contradictions and welcoming, accepting, and tolerating differences that forms the foundation for differentiation.

2 Progressive levels of self-definition and self-disclosure will stimulate increasing levels of fear and anxiety.

It is a rare person who deeply knows and actively reveals him- or herself in an ongoing way to his or her partner. It is especially rare to do this knowing he or she will face disapproval, disagreement or anxiety from the partner. Also, as time progresses, some of the personal revelations are feelings of inadequacy, bad habits, or critical thoughts about the partner. These expressions have implications for the partner and carry all types of loaded meanings. As a result, when a partner makes a personal revelation, they may feel very uncomfortable.

Then it may be compounded by the partner not hearing it or sidestepping it. Neither partner may want to discover what they find displeasing in themselves or unattractive in the other. The greater the self-disclosure the more likely they learn what they don't like about each other, or themselves! The more of these that are uncovered, the more it creates anxiety about how to stay married to someone you don't like or don't respect. It is even more unusual to find a partner who can pursue intimacy while feeling threatened by aspects of the partner that are emerging. To do this in an ongoing way requires a mature ability to leave personal concerns, interests, opinions and defensiveness out of some very tension filled discussions.

In the transcript that follows, Ned initiated a discussion with his partner, Julie. They had been together for four years, and he had not been able to decide whether or not to get married.

N: This is hard for me. This week I knew I was upset. I kept thinking, "What am I so upset about?" Last night, I finally realized it's about money. You can't make a living totally on your own. Then I realized I've thought you were only in the relationship for my money. [long pause] Are you a gold digger?

[His partner Julie replied in a way you might expect:]

J: A gold digger? Only for money! How could you think such an awful thing? [incredulous and a little angry]

N: I've never said that before.

[Sitting in the room with them, I (Ellyn) could feel the tension building. I knew this conversation had the potential to be very volatile, and I also knew it could promote more intimacy between them.]

E: What do you feel when you say that?

N: Very anxious. She's going to go into a rage and storm out. I was afraid to bring it up. I'm afraid she will leave.

E: I think you two could move ahead if you weren't afraid to ask and answer tough questions. You really just raised your fear that she is a gold digger? That's hard to surface and talk about when there's a big money imbalance like you two have. This is the kind of tough issue that will help you move ahead through this limbo of not separating and not committing.

E: So, Ned. It's been hard for you to risk and initiate this issue. So let's stay with you a little longer. Julie may surprise you and sit still and listen and ask you questions. She has wanted you to talk more to her for a long time.

E: Julie, is there anything you want to find out about Ned?

J: Do you think I'm a gold digger?

N: I've thought so. You were always angry when I was out having my good times—parties, windsurfing trips. I work hard and play hard, and you were always angry when I wouldn't spring for the money to take you along.

J: You thought my anger was about you not spending money on me?

N: Yes. We exist in two different worlds. I sometimes think you just want to party and have me spend money on you.

J: This is getting very hard to hear.

E: Try to remember this is about Ned, not about you. If you can keep asking hard questions, you might find out what this has to do with him.

J: In the past I would have screamed and yelled or left the room, and that would have been the end of this discussion. I have felt constant pressure and fear that the bottom will fall out financially, but that hasn't been why I've stayed with you.

[Here I notice that Julie is containing her own emotions better than ever in the past, but she is still having difficulty exploring Ned's internal life.]

E: Julie, ask him more about how you being a gold digger is a problem for him.

J: What reaction do you have to me being a gold digger?

N: I have felt angry and put down by you. I believed our issues were unresolvable, and I got bad advice from friends. I've told myself, the only reason you stayed, if I was so awful, is that you wanted my money.

J: And how do you feel about that?

N: Angry, lonely, empty.

J: I'd feel empty too if I thought you were just in it for the money.

N: Let me tell you what I realized. I asked myself who is anxious, and I realized you've been under real financial pressure. What I put together is that being with me has increased your financial problems. I used to say it was hormonal, but now I realize it has to do with me.

J: Did you think I wouldn't stay with you if you didn't have money?

N: Of course. What else would keep you hanging in for so long?

J: Wow. That's lonely, sad. You never realized that I enjoy you, I care about you? I wanted to go on the trips to be with you, not for the money.

N: No one ever felt that way about me before .... I thought my money would help me get a good mate. When I was in high school, I decided to work hard and be rich. Then girls would like me. I thought that was how all the popular guys got dates. I thought that's what most women care about.

J: What do you think now?

N: I realize we are a couple with two very different financial situations. I realize it's not windsurfing or parties. It's me not being sure anyone can love me. And it's you trying to keep up with my lifestyle. It's me not being committed that scares you. Suddenly, I feel more generous than I can ever remember.

J: I can't believe this. When I heard comments about being a gold digger, I thought, "Here we go again." And when Ellyn said, ask questions, I couldn't believe I didn't get angry and blame, didn't get defensive. Then I could see, you were scared and you'd been thinking about it for a long time and couldn't talk about it before. It's been influencing a lot.

E: Think how different the outcome of this conversation would be if you started trying to prove you weren't a gold digger.

3 Moments of greatest defensiveness are not to be avoided. They provide some of the best opportunities for intimacy with self and intimacy with the partner.

Ironically, tension filled moments of defensiveness offer some of the best opportunities for increased closeness to develop. However, due to the law of unintended consequences, one partner's defenses elicit defenses in the other. Then the other reacts to these defenses. The most common defenses are blame, withdrawal, confusion, resentful compliance and feeling like a victim. These defenses lead each person to create a pinhole perspective. From this pinhole perspective, they each get locked into one way of viewing the problem. This tyranny of the partial perspective becomes oppressive for both. The tyranny will persevere until one or both become more open minded. What do couples want from us? It's obvious, to help their partners enlarge their pinhole perspectives and become more open-minded.

But relinquishing the defenses is not the goal. The defenses are natural reactions designed to reduce and minimize threat. They are developed in the family of origin and supported by the personality and temperamental style that each person inherited.

However, in order to facilitate the development of intimacy, these defenses must be managed, put aside and converted to an open curiosity. They must be converted to an ability to ask questions during situations of high tension. Partners must be able to develop the ability to explore what we call their own webs and the webs of their partners. The web consists of values, goals, fantasies, concerns, interests and core beliefs about self and other. Doing this requires certain predictable self-capacities: capacity to self-soothe, capacity to delay gratification, capacity to be empathic, capacity to tolerate frustration, capacity to internally self-reflect and externally express (congruently) one's thoughts, feelings, and desires.

In the preceding transcript, Julie's ability to get out of herself and ask questions about Ned enabled them to see Ned's belief that he could only be loved for his money.

4 In the absence of differentiation, a core orientation may develop. Each person often makes entrenched decisions about the other. Each may also solidify negative beliefs about her- or himself. These core beliefs may inhibit their ability to recognize intimate communication or to pursue conversations that are anxiety laden yet rich in intimacy potential. Some examples are as follows:

Core Beliefs About Self

I'm unlovable
I don't deserve to be loved

Core Beliefs About Other

He's selfish and never interested in what I feel
She's so self-absorbed. All she cares about is herself

Core Decisions About the Relationship

All I ever get is crumbs
I give and give and sacrifice myself and there's still nothing there for me
I made a mistake when I married you

Core Beliefs that Inhibit the Ability to Pursue Intimate Communication

I'm too invasive
I'm too needy
I can't handle my partner's anger

Core Beliefs that Inhibit the Ability to Recognize Intimate Communication when it is present

My desires don't matter
I don't deserve to be loved
You'll never ever give to me

5 **The foundation for progressing through the later developmental stages and arriving at ongoing more sustained intimacy is achieved by countering our natural instincts for self protection and self preservation.** It is the process of countering these natural instincts and natural defenses that leads to the individual strengthening the following capacities.

Self Capacities that are Developed and Strengthened in the Differentiation stage

An increased ability to internally self-reflect and externally self-define
The ability to initiate more openly and congruently who one is
An increased ability to tolerate anxiety and to manage emotions with more self-responsibility and less reactivity to one another
The establishment of clearer self boundaries
An increased capacity to experience and communicate empathy
An increased capacity to delay gratification

By strengthening these parts of the self, partners are able to deepen the emotional intimacy within themselves and between them. Until this occurs the moments of defensiveness will be experienced as problematic and traumatic instead of welcomed as illuminating.

Cindy and Jack arrived for a session with Jack very angry at Cindy. He believed she was hoarding some of their mutual friends to herself. He said, "How dare you plan to go to the Renaissance Faire with Sue and Stan. You made the plans and didn't even give me a chance to say no for myself." As the discussion evolved, it became clear that Cindy had made the plans to give Jack a day alone at home, as he had been requesting. Furthermore, he had been helping to cook dinner for their friends when the plans were made. He recognized his belief, "People won't like me just for me, unless I'm doing something for them (cooking)." When the plans were being made, he couldn't include himself because he felt unwanted. Secondarily, in his marriage, he was angry at Cindy, rather than appreciating that she actually wanted to give him the free day he had been requesting. He recognized this would counter a core decision, "No one will give me exactly what I want." Being angry at Cindy was actually more comfortably familiar than feeling tender and appreciative to her for giving to him.

PROCEDURES USED TO FACILITATE INTIMACY

The following section is how we begin to translate theory into practice.

1   Together the therapist and client identify "Who owns what problem." By identifying what issues belong to each partner, the therapist knows where to focus attention and what developmental capacities to build in each partner. This is not always obvious at the beginning of therapy. In the transcript that follows, Nick was blaming his wife, Adriane, for the lack of intimacy in their marriage and for the affair he had. As you read you will find an example of how Ellyn uncovered Nick's contribution to the problem.

N: I can't trust you with the precious part of me, my hopes, my dreams, my sexual fantasies.

A: Why not?

N: Because when I do, you don't respond in a helpful or inviting way.

A: How do you want me to respond?

N: I want you to change how you respond, be more tender, more supportive. I want to trust you to support me more.

[At this point, it was tempting for me to ask Nick what type of support he wants from her and then to ask her if she was willing to give it. When the therapist responds in this way, it bypasses Nick's developmental collapse. Instead, I decided to explore what created discomfort for Nick.]

E: How is her response a problem for you?

N: I keep my dreams to myself, and I'm lonely.

E: How else is this a problem for you?

N: I take it to other women and continue to hold on to my fantasy of finding an ideal partner.

E: If Adriane doesn't change, what will happen to you?

N: I'll get divorced or keep having affairs.

E: What is the worst thing that can happen if you tell Adriane your dreams and fantasies anyway?

N: I can't risk being hurt again.

E: Because then what?

N: I'm too fragile.

E: Too fragile for what?

N: I'll fall apart.

E: What is falling apart?

N: When I was 21, my first girlfriend dumped me suddenly. I was very much in love. That hurt too much.

E: You were filled with grief.

N: Yes and I didn't know if I'd graduate from college, I was so upset.

E: And yet you did go on. Only you feel fragile because you have never involved yourself that much again.

N: That's right.

E: And you've never tested yourself again, not since you lost your first love.

[What was initially presented as an intimacy problem due to Adriane being deficient in tenderness and lacking in a supportive response, soon evolved into Nick's fear of persisting in initiating heartfelt, intimate parts of himself. Further exploration revealed that he believed his girlfriend had suddenly dumped him because he had shared a sexual fantasy with her. Instead of asking if she had left him for another guy, he decided that she had been threatened by seeing his sexuality. Now as Nick risks and stops waiting for Adriane to change, he will begin initiating his sexual desires and persist in sharing his sexual fantasies. In doing so, he will experience anxiety. Managing his fear and then using it as a springboard for growth will strengthen him and lead to more intimacy.]

2   As individual issues are identified, it's important for the therapist to keep the anxiety/issue located with that partner. Often this means an individual focus in some sessions, even when the goal may be more intimacy for the couple. Frequently clients will try to avoid the spotlight because they feel such high tension. They may try to externalize the problem and focus attention back on their partners' contributions. The therapist's task is to keep the client working on what creates tension for him or her.

In the following session, Steve and Sadie came in during an explosive fight. They had a long standing symbiotic relationship. Sadie had begun to challenge the symbiosis, but felt quite guilty about her own movement. Here, she wants to blame her feelings on her husband. Ellyn has to persist in keeping her working and focused on the part that belongs to her.

Steve: We're hot today. No shortage of topics. We're in a Rashomon situation. We both view the same wreck differently. It's about the visit of Janet, Sadie's friend. She's here for six weeks. Janet said she was sensitive to the issue of disrupting our lives. But, the fact is, she's looking for mothering and wants to spend all her time with Sadie. She's in a bad way and likes Sadie's caretaking. There's all kinds of confusion about our schedule now. Who is eating with whom and where. I'm finding it difficult to adjust to the chaos. But I told Sadie I would adjust to the chaos. Then she said she felt guilty and torn, caught between Janet and me. I said there was no reason for her to feel guilty as long as she understands that her first loyalty is to her husband. In a marriage, when there is any conflict, your first loyalty is to your mate, and then you work out all other problems around that. But I told her anyway I'd adjust, and she should take care of her friend. But she said she felt guilty and it was my fault she felt guilty. It's unrealistic not to expect it will create upheaval in our house, especially since Sadie is an A-to-Z person and does everything wholeheartedly. Last night we had a fight, and I was stunned to hear her say it's all my fault, when I've been trying my best to accommodate.

Sadie: I'm so tired of fighting about these things. He doesn't hear me. He says I don't hear him. So what's the point.

E: What are you saying, that he's not hearing?

Sadie: Just like it always happens—when I'm looking forward to something, it's always a big disappointment because of someone else. I want him to leave me alone and understand that, for this visit, I'll spend more time with her and less with him, and I can't make exact plans—breakfast at 9 each day. I don't want a rigid schedule, and he can't relax. I've tried to give you your freedom and as much time alone in the house as I can, but you should understand for six weeks it won't be just peace and quiet, you and me time. You're like a parent putting restrictions on me. Just let go a little bit and don't be such a complainer.

E: What are the restrictions?

Sadie: Do this, don't do that. Come over and eat, or I'll starve to death. I hear the upset in your voice. That things aren't regular, that dinner's not at 6:30 every night. So, what's the big deal? You don't seem to understand that I'm at the point of walking out. Leave me alone! [said angrily]

Steve: I think you're exaggerating. I proposed you do whatever you want for the six weeks.

Sadie: You shouldn't have to propose it. It should be obvious.

Steve: I don't agree with that. I'm your spouse.

[To the reader. Here, will you pause a moment and think about what is happening? Think about what your goals might be and how you might intervene?]

E: Can I be blunt with you both? I can see how you are each making this tougher on yourselves than it needs to be. Steve, I think there's a problem with your assumption that Sadie's loyalty should be to you rather than herself.

Sadie: That's right. You want me there all the time, and, this time, I'm saying take care of yourself for six weeks.

Steve: It's okay with me. Go act like a single person.

Sadie: Didn't you say, "I don't know if I'm coming or going?" And that you couldn't go on like this?

Steve: Yes, and I'd like some indication of how you see the six weeks unfolding.

Sadie: You want a rigid, day-by-day plan.

E: Sadie, here is where your problem starts. Steve tells you what he wants to handle the situation, and you believe you have to take care of his distress in a big way, and you set up your own disappointment.

Sadie: How?

E: Steve tells you his distress—you have a filter that says you have to respond to his distress and then you feel pulled between them. What you want to develop is a thicker, more permeable skin, an easy way to take in his distress and say, I will do this and I won't do that, without feeling responsible for making all his discomfort go away.

Sadie: [Big sigh]

E: What are you thinking, and what's happening in your gut?

Sadie: I'm just too tired to explain again to Steve what he's doing.

E: Sadie, I'm going to be tough on you today. I think a big part of your tiredness comes from what you do to yourself when you see his upset. I think you might want a thicker skin.

Sadie: But he sure makes it clear he's upset. When he says, "In a marriage your first loyalty is to me," I get confused. Maybe he's right, maybe he's wrong. Then I start wondering. I'm so tired of fighting, and I don't have the strength to stand up to him.

E: It's not about standing up to him.

Sadie: What is it?

E: This is about what happens inside your head.

Sadie: What happens in my head is I'm always thinking how everyone else is feeling. Are they in pain? No one ever thinks about me, and I'm tired of it. I'm just sick of it. I want to do it differently.

E: Sadie, can you imagine a scenario like this? "Steve, I want to spend the next six weeks functioning like a single person, coming and going as I please and no meals on a schedule. And he says, "Okay." Can you imagine enjoying that?

Sadie: Yes.

E: Now can you imagine yourself saying the same thing, and he says, "Okay, but I want to complain about the disruption a few times in the six weeks." Could you imagine doing it and you enjoying yourself?

Sadie: I could do it, but I'd walk away with guilt.

E: Right there is the central way you set up your own disappointment and end up with bad feelings so often in your marriage. Do you understand what I'm saying?

Sadie: I think I do.

Steve: That's what I want. You put words to it. I want her to do it without guilt.

E: When you talk to her about loyalty and you convey your expectations of marriage, you sound guilt-inducing, and Sadie already struggles with defining what she desires actively without rebelling.

Sadie: Yes, If you truly saw me as an independent person, you wouldn't say my loyalty should be to you. You'd know I was your wife and I'd be back when she was gone.

E: And Sadie, when you feel okay about your own wants and desire's, Steve's uneasiness will not be a problem for you. He'll be able to be grumpy, and you'll be able to enjoy yourself.

Sadie and Steve were able to go forward and spend the six weeks differently than they had done in the past. Sadie had ongoing revelations about how she created her own hell by not staying separate from Steve's grumbling.

In this session Ellyn did not focus on helping them understand each other better. Instead she stayed on the track of Sadie's core difficulty with setting up her own disappointment and anger with Steve. At first, she encountered some predictable resistance from Sadie. When the therapist focuses attention on the impasse, it is not unusual for a partner to resist doing something that will help her or him feel better. The client may deny, diminish, or attempt to defuse the confrontation. Being compassionate while being persistent helps the client hold the tension.

TACTICS USED TO STRENGTHEN
DIFFERENTIATED INTIMACY

Beyond Active Listening

We frequently use a process called the Initiator/Inquirer with couples (or I-I). This is designed to identify individual stuck points and then build intimacy by holding the partners to going through that which creates fear for them. The letter "I" suggests and underscores our emphasis on the importance of developing a differentiated self.

The Initiator is asked to:

- Bring up one issue, and only one issue
- Do this without blame or externalization
- Say "Here is what I feel about the issue" (i.e., sad, scared, happy, angry)
- Be open to more self exploration, learn more about yourself by the end than you knew when you started

The Inquirer is asked to:

- Listen
- Ask Questions of the Initiator about the Initiator
- Respond with Empathy
- Continue with Empathy until a soothing moment is reached

The "I" to "I" process is rich and multidimensional. It illuminates a clear direction for each person's growth no matter where each is on the continuum of differentiation. It encourages the development of different self capacities in each partner while providing a framework to manage defensiveness and explore the partner's more private and sensitive feelings.

The structure is designed to interrupt the back and forth restimulation of the couple's typical traumatic interactions. The process is effective in many ways:

1   It prevents partners from using predictable defenses such as accusing, blaming or withdrawing when symbiotic demands are expressed.

2   Because one emphasis is on the Initiator exploring, revealing and managing self, the process provides an avenue for this partner to become more intimately aware of him- or herself. Being an initiator is more than just a means of calming-down an acute interpersonal crisis. It points the way towards developing self capacities that promote differentiation and deepen intimacy. Persisting in working in the initiator role increases internal self-reflection, promotes self and other differentiation and interrupts the blame cycle. Also

because the Initiator is helped to claim their own issues nondefensively, he or she is able to attain greater self-acceptance and to dismantle familiar defenses.

Being understood by your partner feels great. But too often being understood only will not increase the necessary self capacities for continued differentiation. That is why we do not place the focus on the Initiator being understood as the primary goal of this process.

3 In this process the Inquirer is asked to stretch him- or herself. There is an interplay between asking questions and empathy. The purpose of inquiring is twofold. It helps the Initiator, and it strengthens the Inquirer. The Inquirer helps the Initiator explore her or his own world, the web of passions or desires, feelings, thoughts, concerns and core beliefs.

However, to do this role successfully, the Inquirer must develop greater separation between self and other. Effective Inquirers can get out of their own skins and understand how reality is viewed from their partners' perspectives.

The Inquirer is encouraged to develop an attitude of increasing curiosity. By continuing to ask questions, the Inquirers will successfully sidestep projections of Initiators, while helping Initiators to take their concerns to a deeper level. By dealing with only the partner's side of an issue at this time, the Inquirer can stay very intimately involved while not compromising parts of his or her self held near and dear (core values, desires, etc.).

4 Inquirers learn to delay gratification of their own issues. Until couples learn to stop competing over who will be heard and understood, a low limit will always exist on their intimacy potential. Holding one partner to being successful in the Inquirer role is particularly helpful in strengthening that partner's ability to regulate anxiety, control impulses, and maintain clear boundaries.

5 Asking the Inquirer to be empathic is also a powerful way to promote differentiation in the Inquirer. The primary purpose of the empathy is to serve not the Initiator's desire for merging, but the more relevant goal of increasing the developmental capacities of the Inquirer. Developing empathy decreases self-absorption, increases the ability to give when it is inconvenient, and helps solidify the intrapsychic and interpersonal boundary between self and other. All of these capacities are necessary for intimacy to be recognized and sustained.

It is often difficult for either or both parties to accept that their partner's have current limitations in their abilities to be responsive. Peter once asked a very angry, demanding woman if she thought her husband was deliberately withholding the multitude of requirements she was expecting. "Frankly, that's what I prefer to believe," she stated barely pausing. She wanted to believe it, because to think he couldn't respond to her was just too depressing an alternative. Thus, her solution had to be just tell him often enough, loudly enough and angrily enough, and he would finally get the message: stop withholding, and become the great gratifier. To really understand and empathize with partners will often mean accepting current limits to their responsiveness. Ironically, if you ask each partner if he or she is limited in their responsiveness, they readily agree. Each often wishes his or her partner would recognize this reality.

The irony does not always reside in the couple. Often we do not feel very good about urging the inquirer to extend him- or herself when there has been a wrenching history of neglect, abuse, or having to cope far beyond their abilities. Yet without this stretch, they are more likely to stay churning in agonizing patterns.

When a couple discusses a hot issue using these roles, they inevitably arrive at either more intimacy or break down in one or both roles. Where they repetitively break down enables them to identify the needed area for growth. Each partner can set goals to focus on the self capacities that will ultimately result in more intimacy.

Common Breakdowns in Roles when doing the I-I Process

Initiator:

- Blaming. Focusing on other rather than exploration of self
- Bringing up too many issues
- Underdeveloped ability to identify or articulate feelings
- Demanding a merged response
- Not connecting the event or situation at hand with a deeper understanding of themselves or the couple's dynamics

Inquirer:

- Start problem solving or fixing
- Getting defensive, self-referencing and not holding the role
- Asking questions that have more to do with the Inquirer than with the Initiator
- Projecting and operating from the projection
- Low ability to access empathy
- Asking leading questions (Did it ever occur to you that I had good intentions?) Underdeveloped ability to self-evaluate, validate or soothe.

In the following transcript, the Initiator-Inquirer process is used with a lesbian couple to help them recognize intimate communication instead of fighting.

Ann and Jill are in their early 40s, have never been married and have no children. Ann comes from a middle class family with a father who was alcoholic. Jill comes from a large family with a very low income, ghetto background.

This couple had been dating and fighting continuously for five years. After three months in therapy, they had made a decision to live together and are now in the early phases of the differentiation stage. They arrived for this session fighting about their living together arrangement. This transcript begins part way into the session with Ann as the Initiator and Jill as the Inquirer. (T = Therapist.)

A: This is such a big step. I've wanted it for so long, but I don't know if we can sustain it.

J: What do you mean sustain it?

A: Can we really afford such a nice home? I look ahead for a year and I wonder, will we still be here?

J: When you say that, it cuts to the quick. It feels like you're taking away my stability.

T: Do you know what Ann is feeling?

J: No, but I'm not sure I want to know.

T: If you know, then what?

J: I'll find out how unsure she is about me.

T: Will you risk finding out if you are correct by asking more questions?

J: OK. What are you feeling?

A: Scared. It's almost too good to be true. I've wanted this for so long, but can it last?

J: When I hear that, I think you don't believe I'll hold up my end of the bargain. Like you don't recognize that I've been paying my bills conscientiously for the last 20 years.

T: It seems like you're hearing Ann through your lens of growing up poor. [the projection] See if you can stay in the Inquirer role and ask about Ann. Do you know what her issue is? Are you sure she's talking about money?

J: Is this mainly about money?

A: It's both money and our relationship. My career is shifting. I'm completely dependent on my paycheck, and the electronics field is unstable right now. People are getting laid off right and left, and I gave up my consulting where I made some extra money. I want to devote myself to my job and our relationship, but it's scary to have all my eggs in one basket.

J: Are you afraid of being fired?

[Here Jill assumes that all the eggs in one basket refers to Ann's job. It does not occur to her that it might have anything to do with Ann's feelings about their relationship.]

A: Yes. That is a possibility and it might take awhile to find another job.

J: If you got fired, how would that effect us?

T: Instead, will you ask Ann what she means by having all her eggs in one basket?

J: OK, what do you mean?

A: It's like, suddenly, I'm relying too much on externals for my life to work out. You and my job staying stable . . .

T: [to Jill] Now see if you can ask two or three questions that only have to do with Ann's feelings.

J: What are the externals?

A: My job and you.

J: This is hard for me, but what is it about me?

A: I've wanted something like this my whole life. To have a partner, to dream with someone! I can't believe it's really happening to me.

T: [to Ann] Will you tell Jill more about your fear of moving forward with her.

A: Yes. I'm terrified right now that something will happen to you. When you walk out the door in the morning, I have a flash that you'll be killed on the freeway, or, when you go to the doctor next week, that you'll come home with terminal cancer. I tell myself these thoughts are crazy, but I'm frightened.

J: Is there anything else?

A: Yes. I love you, and I want this to last so I can really enjoy something positive in my life.

[Jill is looking uncomfortable]

T: [to Jill] What are you experiencing?

J: I really don't want to hear Ann's anxiety.

T: Why?

J: I believe she doesn't want me. It can't mean anything positive about me.

T: So, if Ann is fearful, it's a signal to you to become vigilant?

J: Yes. If I see that she's anxious, I think that I've done something wrong.

T: What do you do next?

J: I prepare to defend myself. I can't imagine that Ann's anxiety could mean anything positive about me.

T: What did you hear today?

J: That loving me and what we are doing is at the root of her anxiety. It's not that I'm flaky about paying my bills.

T: Anything else?

J: No.

T: Think about Ann and what she told you about herself. What did you learn about her?

J: That she's frightened.

T: About?

J: Losing me.

T: And that, in her most private self, she never believed she'd have something this good in her life.

J: Is that right?

A: When I was little, I always felt like I was looking through a window at other people who got to be normal, and that I'd never be lucky or normal myself. When we came to therapy and we were fighting so much, I thought we'd just break up and, again, I'd feel like I couldn't have what other people have. I feel more exposed and dependent loving you than I've ever felt in my life.

As this session began, Ann was unable to voice her increasing anxiety as the intimacy and her commitment to the relationship were deepening. When she started trying to describe her fear, Jill quickly reacted from her own life position: "I must be the cause of her anxiety." Jill had a great deal of difficulty staying separate enough from Ann to recognize the intimate feelings being cautiously expressed.

With careful therapeutic intervention, Jill began to ask more questions. As the session evolved, she got more out of her own skin and understood more about Ann's reality. She helped Ann voice more about her fear, desire, feelings, and core beliefs. By the end, both partners understood much more than they knew when they started. Actually, it was the strong feelings of love and fearing loss that triggered the initial fight.

COUPLES GROUPS AND WORKSHOPS

While we enjoy and value working with couples in ongoing psychotherapy, we have found couples groups and workshops to be particularly valuable. These groups help couples get beyond the isolation that is so endemic in our culture. We have developed workshops that are one to three or five days long. These are designed both to teach concepts of differentiation and to give couples the opportunity to apply the Initiator-Inquirer principles to their own relationship. In the presence of their partners and other couples they learn skills and develop a variety of other competencies that enable them to investigate the sensitive, private aspects of themselves and their partners.

Sharing the experience with other couples makes it especially rich. In small groups of two couples they learn how to coach each other. Being a coach for another couple greatly accelerates their own learning. Also, hearing other couples struggling with similar issues helps partners who have been closed off for years begin to open themselves. The amount of giving, sharing, supporting, and challenging done by other couples saves enormous time, energy and money for the participants. Universally we hear participants say that, ironically, being in the couples group provided an avenue for them to feel safer and be more authentic. We will always remember a former member of the elite Navy Seals who attended a five-day couples workshop. At the end he said, "I now know what true courage is. I thought I knew in the Navy, but going into dangerous frigid water was nothing compared to showing myself here."

Personal and communication evolution is difficult and very often involves learning from experiences. Repetitive arguments or repeated withdrawals generally imply very little is learned from those painful interactions. Partners get trapped in their partial perspectives. These lacerating traps may be preferable to having a hole ripped through cherished beliefs and hopeful dreams. Increasing personal power is often a demanding and lonely pursuit.

In a culture that seems to seek rapid relief and absolute answers, it is easy to underestimate what it really takes to sustain intimacy. Truly, it is an extraordinary gift we bring to our partners when we can be present, open and curious about what they offer us!

REFERENCES

Bader, E. & Pearson, P. (1988). *In Quest of the Mythical Mate.* New York: Brunner/Mazel.
Mahler, M., Pine, F., & Bergman, A. (1975). *The Psychological Birth of the Human Infant: Symbiosis and Individuation.* New York: Basic Books.

SUGGESTED READINGS ON DEVELOPMENTAL THEORY

Bowlby, J. (1988). *A Secure Base*. New York: Basic Books.

Horner, A. (1979). *Object Relations and The Developing Ego in Therapy*. New York: Jason Aronson.

Kaplan, L. (1978). *Oneness and Separateness: From Infant to Individual*. New York: Simon and Schuster.

Pine, F. (1985). *Developmental Theory and Clinical Process*. New Haven: Yale University Press.

SUGGESTED READINGS ON DIFFERENTIATION

Bader, E., Pearson, P., & Krohn, P. (1997). *From Symbiosis to Synergy: Stepping stones to intimacy for couples*. Menlo Park: The Couples Institute.

Bowen, M. (1976). *Theory in the practice of psychotherapy*. In P. Guerin (ed.), Family therapy. New York: Gardner.

Kadis, L. B. (Ed.) (1985). *Redecidion Therapy: Expanded Perspectives*. Watsonville: Western Institute for Group and Family Therapy.

Kerr, M. E. & Bowen, M. (1988). *Family Evaluation*. New York: W. W. Norton.

Schnarch, D. (1991). *Constructing the Sexual Crucible: An Integration of Sexual and Marital Therapy*. New York: W. W. Norton.

CHAPTER 22

The Conscious Heart: A Body-Centered Approach to Creating Intimacy

Gay Hendricks, Ph.D.
Kathlyn Hendricks, Ph.D.

Our approach to relationship transformation had its roots in a series of observations we made in the early 1980s. These observations led to a paradigm for relationship dynamics and therapy that was substantially different from anything we had learned in our professional training. We verified these observations in our work with approximately one thousand couples prior to the publication of our book on the new approach, *Conscious Loving* (Hendricks & Hendricks, 1990). Our 1997 book, *The Conscious Heart*, carries the work further and is based on research with approximately three thousand couples and clients in other relationship arenas such as business and sports.

THE EMERGENCE OF A
BODY-CENTERED APPROACH

The body-centered approach we use came from observing that the major phenomena of which therapists need to be aware are nonverbal and psychophysical, not verbal and mental. For example, a man describing his marriage as "fine" on the verbal level is at the same time twisting his wedding ring unconsciously. The nonverbal behavior of twisting the wedding ring usually has more significance for the therapist than any verbal communication. This conclusion has broad implications both for the practice of relationship therapy and the training of relationship therapists.

An example, drawn from a first session with a couple, may illustrate what we mean in more depth. Jim and Barb, a couple in their early 50s and married 29 years, are seeking help at Barb's instigation. Jim has reluctantly agreed to come, although he has stated, "There is no real need; we're doing okay." Barb's complaint is that Jim has been acting "strange" over the past six to eight months. According to her, Jim works late, is gone for unexplained periods, and has spent unusually large amounts of money that he has difficulty accounting for. She thinks he is having a sexual relationship with another woman. He rigorously denies this in a tone of indignation. His complaint is that she has become hypercritical lately, and he suggests that this issue is related to menopause. She becomes angry at his interpretation, and it is clear to us that they have been down this path before.

To navigate this impasse, we make two body-centered interventions. We observe to Barb that she breathes shallowly and hesitantly. She says she has noticed this and asks what it means. We tell her that there are three major feelings that get people into difficulties when ignored. These are anger, fear, and sadness. We suggest she take a few deep breaths and ask herself which of these feelings occur most prominently in her body experience. After a few breaths, she whispers that she's afraid. We ask her to wonder about what frightens her most. She does so and begins to cry. She says that she is afraid of being betrayed, then goes further to say that her deeper fear is of being alone.

At the moment she takes her first deep breaths, Jim shifts in his chair, and as she talks about her fear of being betrayed he folds his arms across his chest. When she talks of the fear of being alone, he uncrosses his arms and looks downward toward the floor.

Gay turns to Jim and makes an intervention we refer to as a "flag move." He says, "Jim, I notice that as Barb talks about her feelings, you shift in your chair and cross your arms. Tune in to that for a moment." Jim sits upright in his chair and snaps a defensive remark: "These damn chairs...can't seem to get comfortable." There is an angry edge to his voice. Gay continues, "I notice when I asked you to tune into your body language, you sounded angry, and shifted the attention to the chair." Jim blinks rapidly and seems to be confused. Gay asks: "Jim, being absolutely honest, are you having an affair?" A flurry of nonverbal behaviors precede his verbal reply. He coughs, crosses his legs, shifts body posture in the chair, and twists his wedding ring—almost as one movement. Verbally he says, "Of course not!" Gay persists, "Jim, I notice when I asked you if you were having an affair, you coughed, crossed your legs and twisted your wedding ring."

This is a key moment. There are only two kinds of therapists: those who overlook the essential information that the body is broadcasting to them, and those who have the courage not only to see the information but also to bring it to the clients' attention. This moment, though subtle, holds a key to the practice and history of psychotherapy. According to legend, Wilhelm Reich, the pioneering body-centered therapist, split with Freud over this issue. Reich thought that the therapist had a sacred duty to observe body language as a key to repressed feelings. Freud disagreed completely, saying that the therapist must remain at a distance and not call attention to such volatile material. The point that Freud was probably making is that there is a trade-off. Clients may improve more quickly through a nonintellectual approach, but they also may sometimes drop out when the therapist brings more to their attention than they can comfortably integrate at the time.

Jim interrupts to say, "These are just uncomfortable chairs." He stands up suddenly and says he has to use the bathroom. When he returns he slumps into his chair and sighs. A long silence ensues. Suddenly, he leans forward and says, "Okay. Yeah. I've been seeing someone else." Barb explodes in a flash of rage that lasts about five seconds, then sighs in apparent relief. She begins to cry softly. She asks, "Do you love her?" He shakes his head "no."

We often say that healing a relationship begins in a 10-second window of clear communication. Although their healing process was a long and arduous one, taking over six months of weekly and bi-weekly sessions, the moment which started it occurred in this 10-second window. The body-centered interventions broke them out of the trance of denial and familiar patterns, facilitating a moment of authentic communication.

THE REASON FOR A
BODY-CENTERED APPROACH

A key question emerges: Would this amount of progress have been made using traditional verbal approaches? Possibly, but the reason we shifted to a body-centered approach was because of its efficiency. We found that the nine major body-centered strategies we use move the process of healing relationships at a much more rapid rate. In addition, since these strategies all use natural body-processes, such as breath, movement, and consciousness, our clients find that they can make immediate use of the skills in their lives outside of the therapy office.

In our own relationship of nearly 20 years and from our clinical experience with several thousand couples we have seen repeatedly that people are most interested in creating relationships where they can see and be seen clearly. The central question clients brought was, "Can I be in a relationship and be myself?" We began to call this longing the urge to reveal essence, to experience the core of ourselves and others. We began to orient all of our techniques toward the purpose of revealing the essence underneath social roles, learned patterns, and old wounds. The body-centered strategies we practiced allowed clients and students to have direct, rapid, and powerful experiences of essence.

We also made a key discovery that has shaped much of our relationship theory. Intimacy is not just being close; it also involves being autonomous. In other words, embedded in intimacy are two distinct urges: merger and individuation. Most clients had not been aware of or responded to the their pull toward both these natural relationship pulsations. In fact, many people had learned to doubt their relationships if one partner wanted to have separate time, interests, or friends. We found that body-centered strategies allowed clients to discover their unique relationship dance and to make their relationships big enough to encompass the different unity-individuation cycles that occur between partners and over time.

After the publication of *Conscious Loving* (Hendricks & Hendricks, 1990) our readers told us that four principles had the most impact in creating harmonious relationships: the six cocommitments, telling the microscopic truth, taking one hundred percent responsibility and the Upper Limits Problem.

The six cocommitments seemed to provide a solid, safe foundation for change. People told us that only after making the cocommitments did their unconscious barriers emerge. These were the countercommitments that prevented them from living consistently in what they said they wanted. Then, these barriers could be faced and dealt with rather than continuing to sabotage their efforts at intimacy. They also used the commitments to recommit when they ran into familiar patterns, rather than giving in to resignation or power struggles. We have continued to simplify the wording of the commitments since we published *Conscious Loving* (Hendricks & Hendricks, 1990, 55, 80–90). Here is our current version of the cocommitments:

- I commit to being close, and I commit to clearing up anything in the way of doing so.
- I commit to my own complete development as an individual.
- I commit to the full empowerment of people around me.
- I commit to taking full, healthy responsibility in my close relationships.
- I commit to revealing rather than concealing.
- I commit to having a good time in my close relationships.

Telling the microscopic or no-blame truth has embroiled us in more controversy than any other aspect of *Conscious Loving*. People tend to drop their jaws in disbelief or explode with rage when invited to tell the simple truth about everything. We recommend saying things that can't be argued about to people with whom you want to become more intimate. The most unarguable areas we've discovered are: body sensations, such as tension; core feelings, such as anger and sadness; facts, such as broken agreements; interpretations and fantasies, such as imagining a past flame during sex; and familiar patterns, such as noticing a way of interrupting that is reminiscent of family gatherings. We have been encouraged by the number of people who have told us that the truth really has set them free from complaints, competition, and despair. We have heard hundreds of stories that support our assertion that creativity and renewed intimacy flourish in relationships where partners practice speaking authentically.

Most people assume that responsibility in close relationships means assigning the fault or assuming the burden. We learned from our students and clients that power struggles start the moment either partner steps out of one hundred percent responsibility. For example, the most common complaint we have heard is: "I'm tired of doing more than my share, and I can't seem to get my partner to take more responsibility (or interest)." These strategies end only when each person chooses to take full, healthy responsibility for creating the issue or conflict. The heart of responsibility is genuine wondering, which is a whole-body experience, not just a cognitive task. If our complainer stepped into one hundred percent responsibility, he or she might say, "I wonder how I keep repeating struggle in our relationship? I wonder how I could create genuine celebration in the daily household chores?" As people wonder, organic body wisdom has a chance to emerge and shift issues into creative solutions.

We think of the Upper Limits Problem as the only problem that really needs attention, as we move more and more into revealing essence. In brief, we each have a thermostat setting for how much love and intimacy our nervous systems can handle. When we surpass that setting, we have a stock of unconscious patterns and behaviors to activate that bring us back to a more familiar, safe level. Clients, students, and colleagues have told us hundreds of hilarious and heartbreaking Upper Limits stories. Some people create the Friday Night Fights at the start of an open weekend. Others organize minutia, buy a fixer-upper home that always needs something, or wreck their new cars. Whole families often participate in these unconscious conspiracies to avoid the possibility of more (but scary) joy. For example, in one family, mom got a long-sought promotion. Shortly thereafter, one child developed a severe allergy to the local spring acacias, another started fighting after school with the football hero, and dad kept locking his keys in his car and calling his wife during her staff meetings.

We began to see that the Upper Limits Problem is actually about expanding our capacity to experience and express essence. Primal questions came up as clients wondered about what was really going on when they slid off enjoying and appreciating their relationships. They asked: "Will some catastrophe occur if I feel too good?" "How can I be happy if, my partner isn't, we have money problems, other people are suffering?" "Is it actually possible to become more expanded than I am now? How?" "What if my partner isn't interested?" "Can

I express my essence fully and also be in a relationship?" "Is there some way that a close relationship can enhance the capacity to be more of who I really am?" Rather than interpreting these questions, we began to use the following body-centering strategies to facilitate wondering and client-generated solutions.

THE CORE STRATEGIES

We would like to describe briefly the core strategies that our particular body-centered approach utilizes. These strategies are detailed in our book for professionals, *At the Speed of Life* (Hendricks & Hendricks, 1992). A central purpose of these strategies is to shift from the content or story to the larger context in which issues occur. These practices allow relationship partners to release blame and discover appreciation and the spontaneous flow of vitality that opens as people let go of their attempts to control and improve each other. The body-centered strategies quickly penetrate the verbal walls that most people hide behind in close relationships. They also make direct use of the incredible storehouse of wisdom that the body carries.

When facilitators utilize body-centered practices, the core patterns that repeat in stuck relationships become readily apparent. By not relying on one sensory avenue, facilitators can often bring another realm into focus. We notice this most easily in other countries, such as Germany, where we don't speak the language. As couples talk about their conflicts in seminars and sessions, ignorance of the language frees us to see and hear the tones and expressions that eloquently sketch the fundamental issue. Couples' verbal stories alone skate across the thin ice that covers a vast pool of feelings, memories, and subtle nonverbal interplay. One effective method to break the ice and dive more deeply is to notice and explore psychophysical patterns. These core patterns often involve polarized attitudes or defensive styles. These patterns can easily be recognized with some training. Familiar patterns we have noticed in the United States and in Europe include: the logical one vs. the emotional one, the pursuer and the withdrawer, super responsible and easy-going (which we sometimes call the sharp pencil and the happy idiot); and the one who is too fast paired with the one who is too slow.

We frequently utilize flag interventions with the core strategies to explore these core issues. A flag intervention quickly brings clients' attention to unconscious behaviors that signal an opening for deeper inquiry. Examples of flags: twisting a wedding ring; coughing as your partner begins to speak; holding your breath as your partner starts to cry; entering the therapy room and slamming the door. Flag interventions are especially useful in relationship therapy as they quickly reveal both partner's participation in a conflict. For example, in an argument where one person leans forward and speaks more loudly while the other person cringes and clamps their jaw, flag interventions can assist them to see that both are creating the pattern.

1   **Presencing** Presencing is the action of placing nonjudgmental attention on some aspect of yourself or another. Example: You shift attention from blaming your partner to being sensitively aware of the rolly sensations in your stomach area.

2   **Magnification** Magnification is the action of consciously making something bigger. Example: Instead of trying to control your anxiety when your partner starts talking about the monthly budget, you shift your intention to making the sensations more pronounced.

When couples are locked in a struggle, we use a magnification invitation to open the possibility to play with the gestures and expressions they have taken so seriously. Power struggles often melt away with playful exaggeration.

3   **Breathwork** This is a large subject (see *Conscious Breathing*, Hendricks, 1995), but for purposes of illustration, we will define it as the conscious use of breathing to produce a desired result. Example: Instead of restricting your breath to minimize the sensations of sadness over your recent divorce, you breathe deeply and fully into the sensations with the intention of experiencing the emotion and expressing it.

4   **Movement** Movement therapy has a long and rich tradition. Kathlyn has been a practicing movement therapist since 1971 and has developed a number of specific movement activities that facilitate relationship healing by illuminating and freeing relationship routines. Example: Instead of verbally discussing a couple's pattern of intimacy and autonomy, they are invited to move physically in the room exploring their unique relationship dance of getting close and separate.

5   **Authentic communication** In this context, authentic communication grows from the practice of reporting specific body-experiences. Example: When a couple is arguing about who flirted more outrageously at the office Christmas party, each is invited to describe in detail the body sensations they notice as they consider this event.

6   **Responsibility** In the relationship context, responsibility refers to a shift, perceptible in one's body awareness, to claiming personal ownership of the issue under discussion, as distinct from disowning it. Example: You feel angry at your mate and think he or she made you mad by not picking up the cleaning. Suddenly you shift to taking responsibility for being the source of the anger, realizing that it was one response among many that you might have had to this event. You begin to wonder about how you keep creating broken agreements and suddenly realize that there are several agreements you have not completed.

7   **Love/Acceptance** In relationship work, love and acceptance refers to the body-felt shift of moving from resisting, avoiding, or denying something to the feeling of loving acceptance toward it. Example: You are trying to pretend you don't feel disappointed that it's raining on the first day of your family's

yearly vacation. Suddenly you shift to letting yourself feel and lovingly accept your disappointment and the rain.

8 Manifestation Manifestation in relationships involves the shift from complaining about what's wrong, or not enough, to focusing on what you want to create in your close partnerships. Example: Couples often begin their manifestation exploration by listing the things they don't want or want to experience less, such as conflict, problems, distance, nagging, and so forth. A question we often ask is, "If this issue were resolved, what would you be doing with all that creative energy?"

9 Grounding Grounding refers to two things: the body-felt experience of integration and readiness to end a given session; and the clarity of a plan to transfer specific learnings into life outside the session. Example: We ask you to tune in to your body and sense if you are feeling integrated and in a balanced place to stop. Then we ask you to put the work of the session into practice by a specific task, such as making a phone call you've been avoiding, taking one of your children on an outing, telling your mate several appreciations, and so forth.

USING QUANTUM QUESTIONS WITH BODY-CENTERED STRATEGIES

In *At the Speed of Life* (Hendricks & Hendricks, 1992), we outline a simple progession that we have noticed in working with couples of different backgrounds, learning styles, and length of relationship. People start life in essence, a body-felt sense of unity with life that is free of conditioning. For each of us, something happens along the way to interrupt the experience of essence. This can happen through slow learning, those repeated experiences at home, at school, and in society that lead people to think, "That's just the way life is." Essence interruption can also occur through rapid learning at any age; those rapid learning experiences are sometimes called traumas.

When something interrupts essence, that jangle leaves people in an integrity dilemma if they cannot feel and express their authentic emotions, talk about their thoughts and inner experiences, and make new agreements that allow them to return to essence. Most people have not had a consistent presence in their lives to support their unfolding essence and to listen and encourage the return to essence when it's interrupted. When essence, or being, doesn't work, people develop personas or roles to protect them and to get some contact, even if it's for what they do rather than who they are.

People develop the personas that work in their unique families and living structures. Most of us have developed a stack of roles by the time we enter into adulthood relationships. These roles often obscure from each other who partners really are, unless they can loosen the grip of personas. The worst news about personas is that, while in their grip, people actually think that their perceptions are real. For example, while operating from a supercompetent persona your partner tends to look incompetent. While in the grip of a rebel persona, your partner really seems pushy and controlling.

We developed a series of questions that allow people in close relationships to shift quickly from interlocking projections and persona power struggles to the underlying feelings and integrity issues that conceal essence. We call these Quantum Questions because the shifts they produce allow people to shift states of consciousness quickly and unreasonably.

We ask one or more question in each area to facilitate these quantum shifts. Here are a few examples of the questions we've found effective.

The Projection Question

- What are your complaints?
- What issues seem to recycle in your relationship?

The Persona Question

- How is this situation familiar?
- When did you learn to see the world this way?
- If this issue were a play, what roles would other actors need to act to allow the play to work?

The Feeling Question

- What feelings does this persona cover?
- What were you feeling when you learned to see the world this way?

The Essence Question

- What would be the completely positive, healed outcome of this issue?
- Who was the you that existed before you learned to see the world this way?

The Quantum Questions themselves are powerful, and, when combined with body-centered strategies, they shift couples quickly to the experience of seeing and supporting each other's essence again.

For example, in a recent seminar in Germany, Karin and Michael started whispering heatedly in the middle of a discussion about how to resolve power struggles by taking healthy responsibility. Kathlyn was conducting the training, and summarizes the intervention. (Note: Karin and Michael's verbal exchanges were translated, which was often redundant.)

Kath: So, Karin and Michael, what's your main complaint about each other?

Mich: Well, she's too controlling.

Kar: And he's too wimpy and never seems to finish a job.

Kath: Karin, I notice that your head and shoulders lean more and more forward as you're talking to Michael.

Kar: Yes, he's not hearing me, like usual.

Kath: And Michael, I notice that the more Karin leans forward, the more your chin tucks into your chest. Go ahead and tuck more. What persona sees the world that way?

[Michael wonders for a moment and then mumbles, dutiful son.]

Kath: Karin, what persona of yours would require a wimp? In other words, in this play you enact over and over, when Michael's the wimp, what role are you playing?

Kar: I never thought about it, but it seems like a very competent person. I feel like, if I don't do things, they'll never get done.

Mich: Yeah, and I can never seem to do enough.

Kath: Michael, I notice you held your breath while Karin was speaking and then sighed heavily as you replied. What feeling is that connected to?

Mich: I feel nervous, no, scared.

Kath: Go ahead and breathe into that feeling and see what you notice.

[Michael takes a few deeper breaths and touches his chest.]

Mich: It feels like a heavy weight here.

Kath: Karin, I notice moisture behind your eyes. What feeling is that connected to?

Kar: I feel sad seeing Michael so collapsed.

Kath: Is this sad feeling familiar? What was going on when you first felt this sadness?

Kar: Uhmm, I remember standing in the dining room and giving my father my best grade report ever. He took a quick look at them and mumbled something about how soon he might expect consistent high marks, snorted, and dropped the paper on the wet counter. I could just never be good enough, there was always something more, something better.

[She begins to cry softly, and Michael tentatively reaches out to touch her shoulder.]

Kath: Michael, what happened in your life that you see in Karin right now?

Mich: Well, I just feel so helpless when I see Karin unhappy. I don't know what it reminds me of.

Kath: I notice when you said, "I don't know," your eyes darted toward Karin and then down at the floor. Let your nonjudgmental attention rest on those sensations in your face. Just notice and be with your experience.

[Michael closes his eyes for a moment, begins to cry himself.]

Mich: I could never reach my mother. She was always so busy, so organized. If I touched her, she would brush off her dress right away. I felt so lonely most of the time.

Kath: Take a moment now and turn and face each other. Karin, you can love Michael's sadness, can't you? [Karin nods.] And Michael, you love Karin even when she feels this kind of despair, don't you? [Michael smiles briefly as he touches Karin's cheek.] Take a moment and love each other. Then give yourselves that same love for everything you're feeling and remembering. [Karin and Michael fold into each other's arms.]

[After a few minutes Kathlyn speaks.]

Kath: What qualities do you see in each other that you most celebrate, that represent the core of what you love and appreciate?

Mich: I see Karin's love of beauty and aesthetics. She really does want to create a world of harmony for me and our kids.

[Karin takes a big breath as a flush of color ripens her cheeks.]

Kar: Michael, I love so much your gentleness and the way you make little poems for the children when they're upset.

Kath: Would you be willing to be allies in healing the sadness you both know?

[Both Michael and Karin nod vigorously and lean their foreheads against each other.]

Rather than continue to try to heal the past in a present relationship, couples can learn to create a new future while lovingly accepting the underlying feelings that are very often similar.

A NEW FORMAT FOR TREATMENT

In the mid-1980s we began using a new format for sessions which has replaced the traditional one-hour weekly or bi-weekly sessions which we had been trained to use. Dissatisfied with the inefficiency of the old format, we began inviting people to come in for what we called "intensives" of one to three days. During the intensive, we only work with one couple (or individual) at a time. Typically, we work approximately six hours per day (based primarily on client energy level), but sessions have been known to extend well into the evening.

Comparing our experience before and after the adoption of the intensive format, we have found that the new format is much more efficient (a two to three intensive being roughly equivalent to six months of weekly sessions). Part of the intensive includes two followup sessions of one hour, which are often done over the phone (approximately 75 percent of our clients come from other states or countries).

We have found that videotaping the intensive provides deeper exploration, as clients watch specific sections that we suggest in off-hours. Reviewing the videotape at home also provides more integration, as clients continue to apply learning to issues that emerge in daily life. The video is theirs to keep, and many people have told us that the video is one of the most powerful learning experiences of their lives. Being able to see and hear their own dynamics, defensive patterns, and other elements is often at first sobering, then enlightening.

SUMMARY

Intimate relationships can generate healing and reveal essence as powerfully as any spiritual path. Couples can learn to rekindle romance and become allies in creating their heartfelt goals by practicing simple skills such as speaking authentically and taking healthy responsibility. Professional facilitators who use body-centered strategies as part of their practice learn to follow the lead of clients rather than trying to maintain the role of expert or fixer. We have heard body-centered practitioners describe their experience as a cross between being an explorer, detective, and a scuba diver. We can evaluate the effectiveness of each day's work by noticing if we feel more vitality and well-being at the end of the day than when we started in the morning. Body-centered strategies contribute to both couple's and facilitator's renewal.

One of our primary life purposes is to help generate a world of relationships based on equality, authenticity and appreciation. We have been deeply touched to witness the courageous choices thousands of people have made to let go of power struggles and to focus on creating a heart connection. Beyond healing, couples can generate a new future based on continuing to discover each other's essence and appreciating the learning opportunities that each moment of interaction provides. When couples make the crucial shift from preferring to be right to preferring to create essence relationships, unlimited creativity flows out to support family, community and global harmony.

REFERENCES

Hendricks, G. (1995). *Conscious Breathing*. New York: Bantam.

Hendricks, G. & Hendricks, K. (1990). *Conscious Loving: The Journey to Co-Commitment*. New York: Bantam.

Hendricks, G., & Hendridicks, K. (1992). *At The Speed of Life*. New York: Bantam.

Hendricks, K., & Hendricks, G. (1997). *The Conscious Heart: Seven Soul-Choices That Create Your Relationship Destiny*. New York: Bantam.

SECTION THREE

Intimate Challenges

CHAPTER 23

Spiritual Intimacy:
A Christian Perspective

Michael L. Dimitroff, Ph.D.*

INTRODUCTION

In this book, the various authors have discussed aspects of intimacy that would help an individual to balance an intimate relationship with another person, and, at the same time, allow that other person to remain him- or herself and be what we would call an individual. In this chapter, spiritual intimacy from a Christian viewpoint will be defined as well as compared and contrasted with other various views of spiritual intimacy. Principles, as well as methods and techniques to connect, create, and remove blocks to spiritual intimacy will be given and a case sample will also be presented.

DIFFERENT VIEWS OF
SPIRITUAL INTIMACY

Spiritual intimacy, as a topic in a psychology book, can be quite controversial, because there are many types of religions, faiths, and views of God. In a chapter entitled "The Spiritually Disordered Couple" (Dimitroff & Hoekstra,

*I would like to extend a special thanks to Ron Johnson, pastor of Living Stones Fellowship, for several of the ideas presented in this chapter.

1997) in the book *The Disordered Couple*, the authors discussed aspects of spiritual disorderedness and related its importance as an area of evaluation and treatment in considering defects in interpersonal relationships. The case was also made for direct therapeutic intervention in treating spiritual conditions as related to the Diagnostic and Statistical Manual IV (DSM IV). When discussing intimacy, again, some of these same issues emerge. In this particular chapter, I will take a very obvious Christian orientation because it is my opinion that this value base is the best and most systematic way of understanding, developing, and solving spiritual intimacy problems with Christians as they emerge within the therapy session. It would be helpful at this point to briefly discuss and contrast some of the other views of God and intimacy that are taken from a non-Christian viewpoint.

When looking, for instance at Islam, it is helpful for the reader to understand, based on the Koran, some of the characteristics of Allah. Allah is not viewed by a Muslim as a deity with which one can have a personal relationship. The Koran teaches "...every soul shall be paid in full what it has earned" (Arberry, 1976). In other words, a relationship is implied on the basis of being obedient to Allah to obtain merit. Allah in the Koran is proclaimed by "There is no God but he, the living, the everlasting" (Arberry, 1976). The idea of a Muslim addressing God as father would be far from possible. Therefore, it follows that spiritual intimacy between an Islamic couple would be inculcated through roles, mutual respect, high moral values, and would be obtained by pleasing God and each other through a system of good works. In fact, in fundamental Islam such a system is tied very closely to a seventh century Arab culture. One can look at Islam with admiration and respect in its regulation of society, marriage, and the family.

Shifting to Orthodox Judaism, one is struck by the fact that in the Hasidic tradition, which is orthodox in its views, the relationship between the rebbe (teacher) and the yehidot (student) is important in understanding intimacy with God. Zalman Schachter-Shalomi (1991) states "Hasidim (followers) came to the rebbe to learn how to generate religious feelings to God," He also notes, "The spiritual life was a Jew's main occupation in this world. In order to justify his existence in the service of God, a Jew needed to know which acts are pleasing to God and which acts are not. He could not discover the answers in books." Such a view is not that far away from Islamic teaching, whereby an individual in authority, always a male, makes decisions on what is correct and incorrect. To please God would in essence improve the marriage relationship. In fact, a rebbe could even function in some instances as a psychotherapist within the Hasidic community. In fact, many Gentiles, as well as Jews would come to a rebbe in helping settle conflicts.

In Orthodox Judaism, laws of marriage, such as Leviret were strictly enforced and used in solving marriage difficulties. Again, there seems to be a reliance on laws, rules, and roles to enhance the spiritual intimacy between a man and a woman. The relationship between God and humans does not appear to be emphasized. One can look at Islam and Judaism collectively and note that many successful marriages, one might even say intimate marriages, exist within the framework of those values and traditions. But the point is that a personal or intimate relation with God from these two value systems is generally based on merit. Spiritual intimacy with couples would be based on roles and works. Intimacy with God would be more impersonal. Spiritual intimacy would be generated through shared traditions, values, works, and rituals. The couple's relationship would not necessarily focus on God as a person, and spiritual intimacy would be expected to grow as a result of works.

Another set of values emerging in society would be the New Age religious teachings that focus significantly upon spiritual intimacy. New Age is based on Eastern religious precepts extracted from Hinduism and Buddhism. Such interest is probably fueled by a desire to have a spiritual experience that could be viewed as intimacy with God. John Selby (1992) in his book *Peak Sexual Experience* presents "the spiritual intimacy questionnaire." Interestingly, this particular questionnaire is oriented towards sexual satisfaction and pleasure. He notes, "Sometimes, however, sexual love suddenly becomes transformed into a remarkable spiritual encounter with the divine as we discover the deeper mystic realms of sexual relating."

He goes on to discuss Kundalini (Serpent Power) lovemaking techniques. Kundalini meditation involves deep inner meditation that is related to the so-called seven different energy centers of the body. According to Selby, if one awakens the Kundalini power, even higher realms of consciousness can be realized. It is his view that this model is an advanced conceptual framework that attempts to describe the whole sexual peak experience as being one beyond understanding or even conceptualization. In fact, he states, "This is the true spiritual path of using orgasm energy for obtaining temporary enlightenment while making love." Thus, orgasm itself is the door to experiencing God and sharing in a spiritual manner.

In this way, Selby clears the air, so to speak, as to how some New Age believers conceptualize and even obtain spiritual intimacy. From his discussions, as well as from others that come from an Eastern religion mystical standpoint, the orgasm and sexual act itself is considered spiritual and therefore one becomes intimate spiritually through sexual contact. This is not to say that other experiences such as contacting your inner self or divinity are not important to a New Ager, but spiritual intimacy with another is generally highly orgasmic. Such an approach is quite at odds with a traditional Christian framework.

THE CHRISTIAN VIEWPOINT OF SPIRITUAL INTIMACY

An intimate relationship is modeled by very close association, contact, or familiarity. Such a relationship would include love, closeness, transparency, vulnerability, strength, and most importantly, commitment (Mayhue, 1990). The Holy Scriptures state that the uniting of humans' personality, namely their spirit, soul, and body can be brought about in various ways without a necessary relationship with God himself. Chambers (1962) states that the Bible reveals that sensuality will do it (Eph. 5:5), that drunkenness will do it (Eph. 5:18), and that the devil will do it (Luke 11:21). This reveals conflicts that exist between Christianity and the New Age views when understanding personal and spiritual intimacy. In Christianity, God is separated from man by sin. But God desires an intimate relationship with his creation and sent a part of Him in flesh (Jesus) to remove, through his blood sacrifice, the sin barrier. An opportunity exists for intimacy between God and man by the indwelling of the Holy Spirit at conversion. In New Age beliefs, man is automatically God, and godliness must be discovered through meditation, yoga, or even different kinds of therapy. To be spiritually intimate from the Christian value stance requires a couple to gain, grow and develop the mind of Christ, and to enjoy an ever increasing deeper relationship with themselves and God.

So, in treating problems with spiritual intimacy as a facet or focus from a Christian viewpoint, a relationship with God is quite important. As noted in the chapter on spiritual disorder in the *Disordered Couple* (Dimitroff & Hoekstra, 1997), a triangular relationship exists between marriage partners, with God being at the top and the two married individuals at the bottom. In order to have a spiritually intimate relationship with each other, married couples first have to have an intimate relationship with God. God is viewed as Father, but triune, with Son and Spirit aspects which can be experienced directly and relationally. The closer the couple grows to Christ, the more diminished is the distance between the partners. Eventually as couples become one with Christ, they become one with each other (Parrott & Parrott, 1995), and hence intimate. Both members of the relationship continue to grow in developing the mind of Christ. In fact, the goal of a Christian is to obtain such a mind.

The Apostle Paul writes (Phil. 2:2–8):

"Fulfill my joy by being like-minded, having the same love, being of one accord, of one mind. Let nothing be done through self-ambition or conceit, but lowliness of mind. Let each esteem others better than himself. Let each of you look out not only for his own interests, but also for the interests of others. Let this mind be in you which was also in Christ Jesus, who being in the form of God, did not consider it robbery to be equal to God, but made Himself of no reputation, taking the form of a servant, and coming in the likeness of man, and being found in appearance as man, He humbled Himself and became obedient to the point of death, even the death on a cross."

Thus, becoming spiritually intimate means becoming more Christ-like and like-minded. Being spiritually intimate translates into something that is inter-actional, as well as something that involves feelings and actions. Sharing your spiritual self, finding this reciprocated by your spouse, and having the mind of Jesus results in a sense of union (Harvey, 1991).

As mentioned earlier, intimate relationships are marked by very close associations, friendships, contacts, and familiarities. It can be concluded that within a marriage there would be evidence of warmth, transparency, and security. We would also expect individuals to be loving and kind to one another. There should be considerable security involved with the relationship, as well as willingness of an individual to allow vulnerability to be exposed (Mayhue, 1990). In fact, the Bible is replete, according to Mayhue, with illustrations about God's desire to actually have intimacy with us! He is viewed as being a shepherd with His sheep. He was described as the "Good Shepherd" to His flock, a person who is willing to die for their well being. In the New Testament (John 10:11), Jesus the Messiah serves as the Bridegroom for the Church. So the idea of marriage and intimacy with God relationally is a Biblical cornerstone. Also, there is the intimacy revealed as typified between a parent and child. God is our Heavenly Father, as we are His redeemed children. In fact, Jesus referred to God the Father as "Abba" which is the equivalent for "daddy." Thus, God is revealed as a relational being desiring fellowship with those made in His image but blocked by sin.

Finally, the relationship between man and wife is ordered by God Himself throughout the scriptures and clarified when we examine concepts written by the Apostle Paul. Paul gives an in depth prescription of what is required within a Christian marriage that will be discussed later. In fact, some Christians in the past, and even presently, have formed Christian communities, so that intimacy is an experience of what it is like to be loved and accepted and also of loving and accepting others (English, 1992).

Thus, an understanding of man, woman, and God is necessary in understanding the Christian view. When looking at the scriptures in a literal sense, we are struck by the fact that Adam himself was created out of the earth. He was not living yet, but God breathed life into him through the nostrils. He then became a living being. This act of creation was to produce a creature in the image of God and for a relationship with God. Eve also was created in the image of God and for a relationship with Adam and God. She was produced literally from the side of the man, coequal, and certainly loved as much by God as Adam himself, but with a different role and personality. Adam was created immediately by the hand of God, but Eve was created "mediately." Oswald Chambers (1962) notes that Eve stands for the soul side and the psychic side of the human creation, and that all of her sympathies and infinities were with the other creations of God around. She did not come directly from the earth. Adam stands for the spiritual side, the kingly Godward side, yet they both were made together in the likeness of God. The revelation that we see here is not that woman stands as inferior to man, but that she stands in a quite different relationship to all things, and that man and woman are required as a complete creation of God so that male and female would fall under the term humankind. This is an important concept basic to understanding how to connect and create intimacy.

It is helpful to understand the differences between men and women, especially when discussing their various different needs, personalities, and undertakings. It is also important that one realize that a mystical union had to occur between man and woman because they are both spiritual and physical. Jesus, in quoting the Old Scriptures (Mark 10:7–9), states "For this reason, a man will leave his mother and be united to his wife and the two will become one flesh, so they are no longer two but one. Therefore, what God has joined together let man not separate." Once this bonding takes place, there is a total commitment of body, soul, and spirit to each other. Commitment from a Biblical statement is, in fact, love, or love is commitment.

So, to have spiritual intimacy, one has to learn about God, relate to God, and understand what God wants within a marriage. Knowledge and understanding about God's own being (the mind of Christ) and how it is reflected in his creation is also important. Once attained, the triangular relationship becomes active and interactive, and grows over time. Les & Leslie Parrott (1995) quote a couple of real-life soul mates they had met: "We are at the two lesser points of the triangle and God is at the top. The closer we grow to Christ, the more diminished is the distance between us. As we become one with Christ, so do we become one with each other."

HOW TO CONNECT AND CREATE INTIMACY

Some of the most familiar scripture about Christian marriage is revealed, as noted earlier, in the book of Ephesians written by the Apostle Paul. Realizing that sin separated God from his two created beings, one can see that sin also had severe impact within Adam and Eve's relationship as well. Certainly, anything that could reestablish such a broken relationship would be important. This is exactly why the Christian view of the Messiah as the ultimate sacrifice and atonement of sin (administration of grace) is all important. This grace must pervade the relationship between couples for true spiritual intimacy to be instituted. Forgiveness is paramount in order that a couple can have a strong spiritual intimacy. Methods and techniques applied without a permeation or undercoating of grace will quickly lead to chipping, cracking, and eventually peeling. Grace needs to be applied liberally daily within a marriage.

The apostle goes on to discuss the roles and views of relationships between men and women and recommends that individuals within a marriage relationship must be able to share themselves spiritually, discover that this is reciprocated by the other, and have some sense of union. There is nothing in the Bible nor in Paul's writings that indicates that being spiritually intimate means that an individual be smothered. In Eph. 5:21, Paul states "Submitting to one another in the fear of God." Note that for a marriage to work, and certainly for there to be spiritual intimacy, each individual has to submit first to God, otherwise submission to each other can be disordered and lead to codependence as well. This idea of both being submissive to one another is initially overlooked but is important in realizing spiritual intimacy.

Paul goes on to note (Eph. 5:22–24):

Wives submit to your own husbands as to the Lord for the husband is head of the wife as also Christ is the head of the church and He is the savior of the body. Therefore, just as the church is subject to Christ, so let the wives be to their own husbands in everything.

The Apostle Peter (1 Pet. 3:1) gives similar advice:

Likewise you wives be submissive to your own husbands so that if some do not obey the word, they, without a word, may be won by the conduct of their wives, when they observe your chaste conduct accompanied by fear.

It is interesting that both Paul and Peter place the wife's role first in order before moving on to the husband's duties. As we will see later in the case study, this can be distorted and misused. Also, realize that women do not come by this view naturally. In fact, older women are commanded "to teach the younger women how to love their husbands..."! (Titus 2:4) But what of the husband's responsibility and role?

Paul goes on to say (Eph. 5:25–30):

Husbands love your wives as Christ also loved the church and gave Himself for it, that He might sanctify and cleanse it by the washing of water by the Word so that He might present it to Himself a glorious church not having spot or wrinkle, or any such thing, but that should be holy and without blemish. So husbands ought to love their own wives as their own bodies. He who loves his wife loves himself, for no one ever hated his own flesh, but nourishes and cherishes it just as the Lord does the Church. For we are members of His body, of His flesh, and of His bones.

This is a very weighty responsibility that is placed on husbands. This means that they are commanded to love their wives so much that they are actually willing to give up their life for her. Again, such characteristics and desires do not come naturally and need to be taught, practiced, and nurtured. This certainly relates to the principal of man being the spiritual leader of his home. He needs to create such a secure, loving, and selfless atmosphere that he could win over his woman from the standpoint of intimacy, love, and affection. It appears that both man and wife must satisfy the main role requirements to achieve a balance relationally, but where did these roles come from?

Again, there is this mystery in the scriptures whereby Adam was made from clay, but Eve was actually created from his side. This means that she actually came out of Adam physically and not directly from the earth and the dust. God told Adam "It is not good for the man to be alone; I will make a helpmate for him" (Gen. 2:18). The translation of the word for helpmate or helper actually relates to wholeness or even oneness. Eve was taken literally from his entire side in equality and both having a distinct power when united together (Rainey, 1989). It seems, since the Fall, that women often are set in crisis due to divorce and abuse (physical and spiritual) if they are left without a relationship with God. They can be fooled and tricked by many unscrupulous men, cults, and so forth. This is not to say that a man's intimacy also cannot be destroyed, but there is a greater danger here within a marriage whereby, if the man does not provide spiritual leadership, his wife would fall quick prey to feelings of insecurity and, ultimately, to some spiritual crisis. Yet, if a man does not receive love and affection from his wife, then he could fall into a spiral of addictions or even depression. Of course, so could the wife, but the point here is that selflessness, leadership, and security can provide prophylaxis to serious relational pathology. The woman desires leadership and security from the man, and the man literally tries to infuse that "missing part" that the woman represents within himself.

Thus, to connect and create intimacy within a Christian marriage, certain principles have to be carried out. As noted previously, for couples to connect and create intimacy, they must submit to God and one another, be familiar with the Scriptures, understand what is taught about their relationship to a God who has created them for specific intimate relationships, and obtain the mind of Christ in this process. They also need to know what God has planned within the marriage. The main point is that marriage itself is a model of a relationship between God and His created beings. If a man does not provide security for his wife, and likewise if a woman does not offer affection, spiritual disintimacy and marital discord will ensue. Therefore, it is within the broad context of Paul's teachings of Ephesians, as well as other passages as this chapter unfolds, that we will be focusing our attention on how to connect and nurture a spiritual relationship.

NURTURING INTIMACY

Researchers have investigated spiritual intimacy and marital satisfaction (Hatch, James and Schumm, 1986). It was found, while studying emotional intimacy as a possible intervening variable between spiritual intimacy and marriage satisfaction, that wives' perceptions of their emotional intimacy with their husbands was interactive with their spouse's perception of their marriages' spiritual intimacy. Yet, the differences in those perceptions seem to be more related to emotional distance, while similarities related to greater closeness. This study indicated that just getting people to be more religious or to pray together may not have an immediate, or necessarily direct impact on marital satisfaction. But it also indicated that increasing degrees of perceived spiritual intimacy were possibly associated with emotional intimacy. This is important to hold in mind because tactics to help create spiritual intimacy will be given later. Growth of emotional intimacy could be used to measure spiritual intimacy. Focusing on method, as opposed to applying grace, forgiveness, and a desire for a relationship with God does not appear to lead to spiritual intimacy. Religiosity itself can sometimes have a very undesirable backfiring effect. If method, and not acquiring the mind of Christ, is the goal, then one can slip into a rut of works and rituals at the cost of relationship.

The husband or wife who gets hyperreligious, but who does not, at least somewhere along the line, start "walking the walk" as opposed to just "talking the talk" will get into trouble. Quite often a counselor needs to assure the spouse that the religiosity in and of itself may not be false, but a process of growth and transformation is taking place, whereby that individual is becoming more related to Christ. To attain marital intimacy from a Christian standpoint, obviously Christ needs to be the Lord of both individuals' lives. They must be Spirit filled to be spiritually intimate. They have to understand how God works and how the Holy Spirit can fill marriages. Couples must believe that the Holy Spirit is imparted at conversion, and that He will reveal imperfections in the self as well as solutions and healing within the relationship. Through the study of scripture the Holy Spirit can reveal truth and build Christ-likeness.

Earlier the idea of submitting to one another was noted to mean that both individuals must have a submissive spirit. Men and women are to submit to each other and to serve each other's needs. Submission means voluntarily yielding our rights to one another in love (Anderson & Mylander, 1996). There has to be a mutual submission where a man denies himself in order to love his wife as Christ loves the church. Any husband who is living out these instructions, written by Paul and inspired by the Holy Spirit, can never treat his wife in a chauvinistic way. This means that husbands have been given a position of authority and headship, but this particular responsibility does not mean being a chauvinistic dictator. A man should be very concerned about how he functions to be the spiritual head of the household. This is the concept of "Servant-Leader" (Rainey, 1989).

Men must uplift their wives and create a hunger within them that demands that they find value as persons, especially if they are to understand the love that God has for them within the family context. A husband must lead within the family, and he must love his wife unconditionally, a rather tall order in this day and age. He must be a true servant to his wife, as Jesus was to this creation. It is interesting to note that Jesus lowered himself and washed his disciples feet (John 13:1–17), providing a vivid example of such humility. Also, women must give affection to their husbands. This does not mean blind obedience and doing everything that the husband says to do. An ungodly man demanding ungodly acts is not to be obeyed. In no way does submission mean to be a nonassertive coward, but actually being loyal, flexible, adaptable, agreeable, deferring to, faithful, and obliging. Loyalty and allegiance are important when being submissive.

To have true spiritual intimacy within a marriage, a wife must give respect to her husband, and this means preferring him, esteeming him highly, paying attention to him, valuing his strength, intellect and character. This would not mean being a critical, insulting, non-supportive person. One can look at all of this and say, "Fine, this is all well and good, but what does one do when the other violates these principles?"

Sin, or not doing what God has told us to do, leads to committing harm within a relationship and prevents a couple moving into an intimate situation. If either party sins, there must be repentance and, certainly, forgiveness. Without such action, a Christian marriage will falter and lead to destruction, as noted earlier several times. Lack of forgiveness, bitterness, and unrepentantness are sure fire ways to disrupt any type of relationship, as sin disrupted our relationship with God. This is exactly why God offered an animal skin covering to Adam and Eve (in Hebrew "Kepah"), and why Jesus' sacrificial death on the cross is so important within the Christian framework. Christians plead the Blood and ask the Father for forgiveness when a sin is committed. When a marriage situation is harmed by sin such as adultery or abuse, first God's mercy and forgiveness, and then the individual's mercy and forgiveness must come into play to bring back the relationship. Again, the couple is asked to imitate, or gain the mind of Christ.

The Scripture also says "Love covers over a multitude of sins" (1 Pet. 4:8–10). Here we mean willingness to our own desires second and the other's first as an important concept to apply in any marriage. The Apostle Paul writes:

> Love suffers long and is kind; love does not envy; love does not parade itself, is not puffed up; does not behave rudely, does not seek its own, is not proud; thinks no evil; does not rejoice in iniquity, but rejoices in the truth; bears all things, believes all things, hopes all things, endures all things; love never fails (1 Corinthians 13:4–8).

One cannot be spiritually intimate unless there is an absolute identification of the concept of being selfless as opposed to selfish. Another attitude that will severely block any intimate relationship is a spirit of selfishness. Jesus himself stated "Deny yourself, take up your cross and follow me" (Mark 8:34). When asked what was the greatest commandment, he gave the great Shema "Hear Ye O Israel, the Lord your God is one," and then added, "You must love God with all your heart, with all your soul and with all your mind, then you are to love your neighbor as yourself." (Matthew 22:37–40). Any remnant of self love was the last thing that was mentioned. What is clearly indicated here is a selflessness and a lack of selfishness that is needed for healthy relationships. If one wants to distort an intimate relationship very quickly, especially from a Christian standpoint, all one has to say within the therapy session is: "You need to take care of your own needs, be yourself, do what is right for you." From a Christian standpoint, this is in most instances a dangerous recommendation and works at odds with creating spiritual intimacy. It is spiritual poison.

REMOVING BLOCKS TO SPIRITUAL INTIMACY

In establishing spiritual intimacy, and with a desire of applying Scriptural teachings within marriage, the following needs of women and men are recommended to be used within a counseling session. If these needs are not being met or are distorted, blocks will ensue. These needs were applied in the case study discussed later and are important in establishing a spiritually intimate relationship, or repairing one that has been damaged due to unforgiven sin or sin in general within a marriage situation.

The following seven basic needs of a husband are described to help establish what a man needs from a woman to achieve a spiritually intimate relationship with her. They are adapted from Stafford's 1985 *Biblical Counseling*.

1   A husband needs a wife who respects him as a man.
2   A husband needs a wife who accepts him as a leader and believes in his God-given responsibilities.
3   A husband needs a wife who will continue to develop inward and outward beauty.
4   A husband needs a wife who can lovingly appeal to him when he is going beyond his limitations and wisely respond to those who question his ideas, goals, or motives.
5   A husband needs quality time to be alone with himself and with the Lord.
6   A husband needs a wife who is grateful for all he has done and is doing for her.
7   A husband needs a wife who will be praised by other people for her character and her good works.

Looking at these seven basic needs of a husband, one is struck by the fact that in order to get these sorts of needs met, a husband obviously has to fulfill the role that was expressed earlier. That means being a Christian husband. In order for this to work, the husband, as well as the wife, must be focused on a Godly life and God himself. A man needs to be respected and lifted up. He needs not to have a woman nagging him, and not forgetting the virtues of good humor. Men love to be fussed over and coddled, and love a clean and well dressed woman. A woman also needs to be grateful for all that a husband provides for her and not compare her husband with her father, especially if that father has been in a position to be able to provide more in the way of luxuries.

Certainly these seven basic needs of a husband, if they can be met, are especially important in developing a strong spiritually intimate relationship. Much of this comes down to a wife who respects her husband, and one whom he can trust that when she questions some of his goals (and, in some instances, some of his ideas that might lead to disaster), she expresses that question in a loving way. Men respond very negatively to any type of shame and humiliation that comes from their wives. This "uncovering" of their sins that was covered in the Garden of Eden by the animal skin (Kepah) quite often can lead to devastating consequences. Yet such an uncovering of a man's sinful behavior, if he is willing to come and discuss this in a counseling session, can have great benefits. For instance, the man who has been a chronic alcoholic, physical abuser, or adulterer, when found out, can be helped through a counseling situation if the wife still focuses on grace and on God's provisions.

But more importantly, since the man is the spiritual leader of the home, he must strongly strive to meet the needs of the wife. Stafford outlines also the wife's seven basic needs as follows:

1   The wife needs the stability and direction of a spiritual leader.
2   She needs to know that she is meeting vital needs in her husband's life and has worth that no other woman (or situation) can meet.
3   She needs to see and hear that the husband cherishes her and that he delights in her as a person.
4   She needs to know that she is understood and in need of protection, especially in her areas of limitations.
5   She needs to know that her husband enjoys setting aside quality time for intimate conversation with her.
6   She needs to know that a husband is aware of her presence, even if the husband's mind is on other matters.
7   She also needs to see that a husband is making investments in her life that will expand and fulfill her world.

So, as in the seven basic needs of a husband that really focused more upon affection and respect, the wife's needs seemed to revolve more about a strong need for a sense of security. Recall that, in the relationship established between Adam and Eve, that was first given by God, that Eve was formed out of Adam. She needed to go through Adam within their marriage to understand and to relate to God. Adam did not protect her from the adversary. The sin of

Adam is Adam's. Sin came through Adam not Eve! This does not mean that she could not have access and relationship to God, but what is being stated here is a necessity to go through that husband and to have him provide the direction and leadership within the home. This provides for spiritual intimacy between husband and wife by God himself. If the father is a spiritual leader, and mother and children go through him for spiritual leadership, a relationship is necessary. Such order binds the family together and establishes relationships.

The reader may have experienced the Adam and Eve dysfunctional scenario themselves that is so typical within the counseling session. It is similar to what Adam said to God about Eve when he was caught naked or "uncovered" in his sin of eating of the tree of knowledge. Adam said to God, "The woman whom you have to be with me, she gave me of the tree and I ate" (Gen. 3:12). He tried to blame it all on God saying that He was the one who gave the woman to him and that it was His fault. A marriage situation, even a spiritually intimate one, would be greatly shaken by a man who takes the position of throwing blame on the wife when the strong need of his wife is that he provide the spiritual leadership. As we will see later, this is what can happen within a counseling session.

So, women need to be lifted up and honored. They have to be seen as the most important part of their husband's life. This means even above children! That is correct. In a solid spiritually intimate relationship and within the context of the family, children do not rate as high on the husband's priorities as his wife. This does not mean that parents are not supposed to love children and care about them, but the wife must come first. Quite often women take on too much responsibility that they simply cannot handle. They need to realize that their husbands understand their areas of limitations, and that they are protected in these areas.

Men readers should not be shocked in finding out that women just simply love to talk. Men, quite often, are off in "la-la land" in relationships and are preoccupied. Anderson and Mylander (1996) note that "Men fight for the freedom to be alone; women care intensely about their feelings." It is imperative that men put aside quality time for intimate conversation with their wives. As we will see later in the case study, certain methods and applications have to be provided to reestablish a broken spiritual intimacy that involves intimate conversation.

Along these lines, men have to understand that a woman is a partner and not property. When considering intimate conversations and relationships, it is deadly to think that your business is none of your wife's business. In the spirit of trying to protect a wife, no husband, if he expects to reach spiritual intimacy, should ever let anyone criticize his wife to his face and let them get away with it. This includes relatives, even parents. Also, men should always cooperate in establishing family discipline, something that has been well established by psychologists over the years. This consistency is important.

Finally, it should be said that it is difficult for a woman to be a wife and wage earner at the same time. This is not meant to be a severe criticism, but it certainly is a concern at the writing of this chapter in the late 1900s, close to the millennium. Many women are working now, and husbands simply do not have a realistic view of what a woman can handle within the home. This author has seen many mental breakdowns due to the preoccupation and selfishness of the husband who does not help within the home. This is the type of husband who does not make secure building of a home his first business, and is not a giver of spiritual leadership, or leadership at all, but merely a taker.

Thus, these particular principals and methods are necessary to remove blocks to any type of spiritual intimacy. In fact, we can go one step further and take Ephesians 5, in an even more literal sense. For a husband to be a spiritual leader within the home, he must literally pray with her and read scripture to her to present her, spotless, like the Messiah will do to the church. Remember, earlier, the Apostle Paul was quoted (Eph. 5:26) as saying that "He might sanctify and cleanse it with the washing of water by the word," but that it should be holy and without blemish. Jesus cleanses the church (His bride) by His word and the husband should do so to his bride. It seems as though a husband who loves his wife and desires spiritual intimacy must literally cleanse her "by the washing with water through the word." This is a daily necessity but it is quite often the most difficult one for men to apply and continue. Also individual spiritual growth must be maintained as well by prayer, meditation, and Bible study (Caldwell, 1992). Caldwell notes "...much of the weakness of the modern-day church can be attributed to the lack of a strong, personal devotional life among most Christians in general and many Christian leaders in particular." Thus, the man must guide, guard and govern (Cole, 1982).

CASE STUDY

This particular case study was chosen because it did not start out as a spiritual intimacy problem much less a marriage problem. This couple had been together for about ten years. The wife was 31 and was originally referred for evaluation due to the fact that she was having muscle contraction headaches. The referring neurologist wanted to know whether a behavioral component could be contributing to her headaches, and wondered what type of treatment our clinic could offer. The neurologist was thinking that possibly biofeedback treatment would be helpful. As a result of this initial referral, the patient was assessed by a thorough psychological examination, including the Minnesota Multiphasic Personality Inventory—2 (MMPI-2), the Millon Clinical Multiaxial Inventory—III (MCMI-III), the Millon Behavioral Health Inventory (MBHI), and the Pain Patient Profile (P—3). A clinical interview also occurred.

She was married 10 years to her 32-year-old Pastor husband, and they had two children, ages 4 and 8. She described the 4-year-old as being somewhat active and difficult to discipline, and noted that her husband sometimes became "very physical" with him. She got along well with her parents. Also, this young lady's father was a minister from a conservative church, and she was raised in a conservative Christian home. Both grew up in rural Pennsylvania.

Her medical history was essentially negative, except that she had headaches for over seven years, but these headaches ceased during her pregnancy. All medical laboratory tests relative to the neurological examination were normal, and she reported having anxiety attacks as well. She had some counseling in the past, but denied any other psychiatric or psychological history or treatment. Initially it seemed as though her muscle contraction headaches were stress related, probably due to stress at home with her children.

However, she was holding something back and, when pressed further during the interview, she revealed that she and her husband had sought marital counseling in the past because he had a problem with pornography. The previous therapist was a Christian. According to her, this pornography issue had greatly impacted their closeness. She and her husband attended a conservative Christian church where he was a pastor. Her husband came from a Christian background as well. She seemed to be very upset with his pornography involvement, and viewed it as almost an "adulterous" violation of the marriage. She stated when her husband would approach her for sex, her mind went into all types of scenarios involving the pornography and herself, which caused her to tense up even more and present with a psychophysiological reaction, including headaches. She felt dirty and ashamed.

When this couple had been seen previously in marriage counseling, the therapist identified the husband as being selfish and self-centered, and living the role of a "teenager." The wife was viewed as histrionic, and an attempt was made to deal with them at that level. The pornography issue was viewed as a reflection of some unresolved latency, as well as genital stage problem. This insight in and of itself, although probably fairly accurate, was not enough to resolve the conflict and reestablish intimacy.

As part of her workup for headaches, as noted earlier, psychological testing was dispensed. Her personality tests revealed an irritable, driven individual with periods of unconstrained energy. In fact, she endorsed enough questions to indicate a possible manic or bipolar condition. This was not true on all tests. She seemed to fit best the description of a histrionic personality disorder with narcissistic traits.

As a result of interview and testing, the couple was advised to come for conjoint therapy. Her husband was amenable to coming for treatment, and indeed he readily admitted to having a pornography problem. He stated that it was under control. His wife, because of his candor with me, was then very easily able to forgive him quickly for this. However, she was fearful that he was going to somehow relapse. She was concerned that not only was their sexual intimacy poor, but she also noticed that their spiritual intimacy was quite impaired. She thought, as did he, that they were pulling apart spiritually. There were some realistic fears on his part, that somehow he would be exposed or his problem found out. Evidently, if found out, he could lose his pastorate. Although he claimed his church was Bible based and grace oriented, he was still uneasy. Not surprisingly, he noted this as a source of anxiety for him as well.

As noted earlier, the husband came from a conservative religious background, seemed to be above average in intelligence, and did very well in school. He and his wife were married fairly young, and she was described as his high school sweetheart. They continued to date in college and their families seemed to get along fairly well together. There had been no major upsets within their marriage, although there had been some financial stress. On the surface what seemed to be impacting the relationship the most were the headaches. Also of clinical significance was the fact that the husband essentially blamed his wife, initially, for the pornography problem. He claimed he was also having "anxieties," and that, if she would not have sex with him when he wanted, he would turn to pornography for pleasure. This was quite high handed, and compounded difficulties.

She complained, not surprisingly, of his continually pawing at her, treating her like an object, and then she immediately began identifying herself within the context of a pornographic magazine or drawing. Notice that this scenario was not that much different from Adam and Eve in the garden. He was blaming his wife for the sad state of affairs. This is not to say that he was not unwilling to give up the pornography. But he perpetuated a state of misbalance by being manipulative in trying to get her to be intimate with him and in utilizing a negative reinforcement or threat of his possibly returning to the pornography for sexual satisfaction. Obviously, such a situation was unacceptable to her, and caused her more dysfunction and an increase in chronic headaches. Clearly, this couple was not able to reach the goals that they wished within their relationship, and their spiritual intimacy had been seriously damaged by the husband's utilization of pornographic material. Insight was not good, and, initially, he attempted to deal superficially with the "headaches."

After a few sessions, the husband was willing to take the MMPI–2 and Millon's MCMI–III. His personality tests indicated some defensiveness and an over-cautious approach to answering the questions. It seemed as though he was evasive and unwilling to admit quite a few personal problems, which seemed to be true during the interview, excepting he was very willing to fess up to the pornography problem. His profile was fairly "normal," although it revealed a tendency on his part to develop physical symptoms under stress, meaning that there was a submerged psychosomatic "V" similar to his wife's. It also indicated that he might be somewhat dependent and even passive in relationships, and he could utilize indirect means of making demands on others, and might even be afraid to assert himself because he feared disapproval. He did seem to be an outgoing and sociable person. Given the state of affairs, he could be described as having little insight into psychological issues, and probably was passive aggressive as well. So there was the distinct tendency towards avoidance of self-disclosure in his overall style and evidence of narcissistic personality features. Again his defensive posture would be important in treatment considerations.

Although both these individuals came from fairly religious backgrounds, and in fact were quite similar in their values, it was quite unexpected that they had little or no prayer life together whatsoever. He was quite astonished when the needs of husbands and wives were presented to him, and when he noted that it included the idea of praying and reading the Bible. He was very familiar with Scriptures and knew them as well as the therapist, but seemed not to focus specifically and in detail on these two particular duties.

Both were willing to entertain the possibility that spiritual dysfunction might be the root of their problems. A series of sessions were designed around studying, and then carrying into action the seven basic needs of husbands and wives described earlier. All sessions were commenced with prayer for wisdom and discernment. The basic needs of a wife were provided to both and then discussed one point at a time. Biblical references were provided. Then, the basic needs of the husband were furnished and again discussed. Both were advised to put into action each point and subsequent sessions monitored growth and accomplishment of the needs. Through sessions and homework assignments, a greater knowledge of the mind of Christ was realized. To the husband's surprise, once they started getting involved in daily prayer, and especially daily Scripture reading, he found that his wife's headaches disappeared. She was also much more willing to accept his needs for physical affection. Some of the needs they had met, others only partially, and some not at all. So, homework as well as discussion within sessions were applied to increase understanding and enactment of therapy goals based on these needs. Sessions were ended once both partners were knowledgeable and committed to fulfilling each other's basic needs.

She has been pain free and their marriage has improved since they have abided by meeting these goals, and also since he has applied the recommendations made in therapy, specifically prayer and Scripture reading.

SUMMARY

Thus, one can see in the Christian value system, spiritual intimacy issues can be very important, in fact, paramount to understanding the root cause of all sorts of dysfunction including even headaches. In this case study, we saw that a woman's headaches were eradicated simply by the husband taking a more loving, kind, and protective view of his wife. Then his wife reacted with more affection towards him. They were asked also to be gracious and forgiving. At least in this particular case, grace and forgiveness were not stumbling blocks to any great extent, but what seemed to be an issue here in causing the so-called disconnection was the fact that the husband was basically treating his wife high-handedly, blaming her for his pornography problem, and then not meeting his responsibilities as her spiritual head within the family. She desperately wanted this, and, once that role was reestablished, this marriage turned out to be much more functional. Interestingly, they were also able to cooperate better in disciplining their younger son and, one hopes, were better able not only to be more Christ minded, but also to put their knowledge into action.

It is hoped that the reader, whether agreeing or not with the Christian based values and methods presented, will be more knowledgeable about the system of therapy utilized here that is so value laden.

BIBLIOGRAPHY

Anderson, N. & Mylander, C. (1996). *The Christ centered marriage*. Ventura, CA: Regal Books.

Arberry, A. J. (1976). *The Koran interpreted*. New York: MacMillan.

Caldwell, J. (1992). *Intimacy with God: Christian disciplines for spiritual growth*. Joplin, MO: College Press.

Chambers, O. (1962). *Biblical psychology*. Basingstoke, UK: Pickering.

Cole, E. (1982). *Maximized Manhood*. Tulsa: Whitaker House.

Dimitroff, M. & Hoekstra, S. (1997). The spiritually disordered couple. In J. Carlson & L. Sperry (Eds.), *The disordered couple*. New York: Brunner/Mazel.

English, J. (1992). *Spiritual intimacy in community: An Ignatian view of the small faith community*. New York: Paulist Press.

Hagee, John C. (1997). *Prophecy Study Bible: New King James Version*. Nashville: Thomas Nelson.

Harvey, D. (1991). *The spiritually intimate marriage*. New York: Revell Company.

Hatch, R., James, D. & Schumm, W. (1986). Spiritual intimacy and marital satisfaction. *Family Relations, 35*, 539–545.

Mayhue, R. (1990). *Spiritual intimacy*. Wheaton, IL: Victor Books.

Parrott, L. & Parrott, L. (1995). *Becoming soul mates*. Grand Rapids: Zondervan.

Rainey, D. (1989). *Staying close*. Dallas: Word Publishing.

Schachter-Shalomi, Z. (1991). *Spiritual intimacy: A study of counseling in Hasidism*. Northvale, NJ: Aronson.

Selby, J. (1992). *Peak sexual experience*. New York: Warner Books.

Stafford, T. (1985). *Biblical Counseling*. Minneapolis, MN: Bethany House.

CHAPTER 24

Intimate
Bisexual Couples

David R. Matteson

Relatedness means staying in life, even when it becomes complicated and when meaning and clarity are elusive. It means living with the particular individuals who come into our lives, and not only with our ideals and images of the perfect mate or the perfect family. (Moore, 1994, p. 5)

UNDERSTANDING AND DEFINITION
OF INTIMACY

This book has focused on the paradoxical longing for both relatedness and individuation or separation. We sometimes seek acceptance by being false to ourselves—by pretending to be the person we think will please the other. But the acceptance we receive turns out to be dissatisfying, since it is not our real selves who are accepted. We do not enter into true relationship unless we are authentic.

It is a mistake to assume that authentic identity must precede intimacy. Identity and intimacy are mutually enhancing. Intimacy often provides the ground from which authentic identity can emerge. In the context of an accepting, caring relationship, we discover ourselves. It is in relationships that who we are unfolds. (See discussion of Hendrix on differentiation, in Bailey, 1996). In deeply intimate relationships, the paradoxical longing for both relatedness and individuation are not contradictory. (See review of research, Matteson, 1993).

For purposes of this chapter, I define intimacy as a holding close of another person without attempting to control or shape the other to fit one's own needs.

439

It is nonpossessively respecting and honoring the other for who she or he is. There is an unconditional quality to the intimate relationship.

If, when an intimate relationship develops, one partner gradually recognizes that he or she is bisexual, intimacy can be maintained only if both members can stay in life, "even when it becomes complicated" and give up living with "ideals and images of the perfect mate," choosing instead to commit to "the particular individuals who come into our lives" (Moore, 1994, p. 5).

My own research and clinical experience have focused on mixed-orientation marriages in which a bisexual and a heterosexual partner form the primary relationship. It appears that mixed-orientation marriages in which the husband is bisexual and the wife is straight are far more prevalent than those in which the wife is lesbian or bisexual and the husband is straight (see Matteson 1990, pp. 131–133). The couple described below are such a couple. In this case, they chose to stay married after the discovery of his bisexuality. But the decision to stay in an intimate relationship does not always mean a decision to marry or to stay in a marriage.

I do not claim the objectivity of a clinical or research perspective for this case study. My hope is to describe a couple who have achieved a very high level of intimacy, and to provide a sense of the development of the relationship over decades, which I could not base solely on my knowledge of clients or research respondents, since it is rare for such relationships to last decades. Therefore I have chosen a couple with whom I am close personal friends. However, I have also used some concrete incidents from other couples (whom I've known as a researcher, counselor, or friend) to illustrate particular issues. This makes it harder to identify the model couple, yet results in a rich composite case study which more concretely illustrates the development of intimacy.

CASE EXAMPLE

It was September, and orientation week of her freshman year at a small coed university. Marge was returning from her first meeting of the Outing Club, thinking about Ken, the outgoing president of the club. She was quite sure that he had been attracted to her. Ken was a senior liberal arts student. He was planning, after graduation, to spend a few years in the Peace Corps before going on to graduate school.

Less than two hours passed, and Ken called Marge to set up a date for later that week. Less than two months passed and Ken changed his mind about the Peace Corps; he decided that being overseas wasn't as important as pursuing a lifelong relationship with Marge. Instead he chose a graduate school within a hundred miles of where she would be continuing her undergraduate work. By the end of that second year of dating, they were engaged. A year later they were happily married, very much in love. Two years later they chose graduate programs at a large east coast university, and moved to begin a new phase of their lives together. Neither one had a clue that Ken was bisexual.

When Marge was completing her master's program and Ken was well into a doctoral program, Ken entered counseling to deal with competition issues and anxiety around other men in his supervision group. Much of Marge and Ken's time together was spent relating their studies to their own lives, sharing their backgrounds, their motivations, their hopes, and trying to understand and deeply accept one another. The first clue came in a dream. Ken recognized the dream as a transference dream about his therapist, an attractive man less than 10 years older than Ken. The dream was pleasant, and explicitly sexual. Both Ken and Marge viewed this dream as one more aspect of Ken's complex personality. To both it seemed interesting but not very important, certainly not threatening. When Ken dutifully shared the dream with his therapist, however, the only response he got was nonverbal—the psychiatrist moved his chair back several inches. This only reinforced what Ken and Marge felt as a couple—their own trust and communication was good, and each was more able to accept the other's uniqueness and differences than were most of the people around them. They both placed a high value on understanding and respecting differences.

In his usual academic style, Ken's first explorations into homosexuality were readings—but he soon discovered, in this pre-Stonewall period, that almost everything he could find pathologized homosexuality. Yet he knew, in his own experience, that there was nothing "sick" about the close, warm feelings he had in his dream. So he treated the psychiatric literature in the same way he treated his psychiatrist's reactions—a sign of the authors' limitations and prejudices. Ken had already been exploring more closeness with men as friends, sharing more emotionally with men who seemed sensitive, hugging men when they seemed receptive—though all of these men friends, as far as he knew, were heterosexual. A few years later, the Stonewall rebellion brought gay liberation to the public's awareness, and news of the gay liberation movement became more and more important to Ken. He began reading the gay political press, and subscribed to a gay activist newspaper. Some years later Ken and Marge spent a vacation near the city where that activist paper was published, and Ken interviewed some of the journalists. Social activism had been important to Ken's identity as early as high school, and Martin Luther King was one of his heroes. As his commitment to justice now melded with his own identity search, he became more and more passionate about the sexual liberation movements. The phrase "I have a dream" echoed in Marge's ears with threatening contrapuntal bass tones that distorted it into a nightmare. She became anxious that Ken would abandon her to become the Martin Luther King of the gay movement. It wasn't homosexuality, or even sharing Ken, which provoked the major trauma for her—it was the fear of losing Ken and the close supportive relationship they had. But Ken had been an explorer even before she met him in Outing Club, and by now Marge knew well that trying to control his strong needs to explore could never work.

Instead, she needed to concentrate on her own needs, and to get clear what she needed to do for herself to become a strong, independent person. What limits or boundaries were essential to her staying in the relationship? What information about his activities did she want to know, and what did she want him to deal with on his own, or with his friends? Fortunately, they knew each other's friends, and there were many that they both trusted deeply. For several years, much of the time Marge and Ken spent in serious conversation centered on working out contracts or agreements between them that respected each of their needs. An important early contract was that Ken agreed not to make any major decisions regarding involvement in gay activism without talking it through with two of his close friends whom Marge trusted.

They were 10 years into the marriage, with two children, when Ken had his first sexual relationship with a man. Ken philosophized about his dream of love without boundaries. Marge felt deeply hurt, and fearful that their marriage must end, though Ken continued to claim to love her. They knew of no one living a bisexual marriage, though popular writings were beginning to emerge advocating "open marriage" (O'Neil & O'Neil, 1968). Their close friends knew their deep love and honest communication, and supported them in trying to hold their marriage together.

Marge found counseling a crucial place to work through the anger and fear she felt around the possibility of abandonment and the reality of Ken's lack of emotional presence in the midst of his new identity crisis. The counseling provided a safe place to deal with extremely angry fantasies toward Ken, and toward herself. The long term outcome of the counseling was an increased confidence that she could make it independently. Only the assurance she could live without Ken made it possible to choose to live with him. A piece of Marge's growth was individuating, especially in learning that her way was not Ken's way and did not need to be. After some brief exploration, she decided that her own values and desires were for monogamy, and that she did not need to mirror Ken's involvements in order to provide balance. She needed to choose her own type of outside support. It was hard to get Ken to hear that Marge was not going to mirror his way. She had to find her unique style, just as he did.

It seemed there were endless talks about their future, about how to better manage their differences and conflicts of needs. But they also spent time just being together, engaging in common interests, and sharing their love. Marge developed the concept of "moratorium days," days when either of them could declare off limits all serious discussions of fears, doubts and problems, times they could just be close. This sharing of quality time, when their relationship was absolutely primary and conflicts were suspended, was very important to their maintaining their commitment to each other.

When they resumed negotiations on how to handle their marriage in the context of Ken's bisexuality, Marge's need to limit communication was clearer. There was no question that Ken would be honest with her; he placed a high value on openness and communicating everything. It took enormous perseverance on Marge's part to convince him that most of the time she did not want to know anything about what he was doing in the gay/bisexual part of his life, whether it was political, educational, intimately sexual, or other. For Marge, when the going was rough, it was important to focus on Ken when Ken was with her, and not focus on the Ken who was absent or with someone else.

Ken's ability to hear Marge's pain was extremely important. And when Marge was in a secure enough space to hear the details of Ken's exploration and identity development, this was very healing for him.

Fortunately, their history of good communication had helped them develop the skills to hear and understand each other's point of view even when they didn't share it or agree with it. Each tried to respect what was important and meaningful to the other. This allowed them to work out practical compromises, to make changes in patterns, to reach concrete agreements about behaviors they would and would not do in respect for each of their needs (contracting), and to develop ways of meeting their needs that were sensitive to the other.

Also important was the quality of support from friends. A supportive relationship with another man, even though it was a man who lived many miles away, was extremely important in reassuring Marge that she was an OK person who had a lot to offer. Though she and Ken worked hard to design ways to mesh their two lives, at times Marge still felt emotionally abandoned by Ken, which she experienced internally as rejection. At one point, Marge decided she needed to try living away from Ken for a period of a month or so, to be clear whether she really wanted to live with him. A friend they both trusted allowed Marge to live in his home with him, close enough to the family home so Marge could still help with child care. This period away resulted in a new commitment on both their parts to make this unique marriage work.

About seven years after Ken had become actively involved in the gay scene, both Ken and Marge reached a point that they wanted to confirm their new style of marriage, and recommit themselves in the presence of about 10 of their closest and most supportive friends. Two of these friends were ministers, who officiated at an informal remarriage ceremony which Marge and Ken wrote together. This ritual of remarriage was very important for Ken, and in his mind, recemented their commitment and the primacy of their relationship. To Marge, it was legitimate as an important practical recommitment, and preparing the ceremony helped them clarify how their love differed from Ken's other involvements. However, in Marge's view the emotional ties were not really resolidified until six to eight years later.

A more important event from her perspective was a decision they made five years later to enter a part-time postgraduate program together. This built in a block of time each week doing something together they both enjoyed, and encouraged a lot of communication around safe, nonconflictual subjects. Interestingly, it took them back to being students together again.

Similarly, a year later, searching for a new home together provided a nonconflictual project that encouraged togetherness and symbolized commitment. By then, the gay identity issue no longer consumed the major portion of Ken's psychic energy, and Ken became more and more able to allow Marge back into his life. Meanwhile, Marge had become very successful in her line of work, and much more sure of her professional and financial independence. Her work required a high degree of involvement, and continued to provide fulfillment. This made it much easier for her to tolerate Ken's involvement in the gay world.

However, even 15 years after Ken's actively entering the gay world, the crises were not over. Ken continued to long for *two* primary relationships, one with Marge and one with a man. After a number of limited steady gay relationships, eventually Ken fell madly in love with an younger man, José, who fit his adolescent dream. This relationship would have destroyed the marriage if Marge and Ken's communication, problem solving skills, negotiating ability, and contracts about how to deal with his gay life had not been so well developed, and their love for each other had not been so deep. It was as if Ken were living an adolescent gay life, intermingled with a mature marriage. Though this adolescent relationship met some deep needs in Ken, it was anything but realistic, although Ken could barely see this through his rose-colored glasses. At Ken's insistence, he and José began couple therapy together with a gay therapist. When José stopped coming, Ken entered some very intensive psychotherapy himself, seeing a therapist whom Marge knew and trusted around the issues and personal projections involved with ending that relationship. Ken deeply grieved both the abortion of this love affair and having missed the gay part of his adolescence. When that therapy was complete, the unfulfilled adolescent longings seemed to lose much of their power in motivating Ken's search for male partners. From Marge's perspective, the ending of this affair clarified for Ken the difference between limerance ("falling in love") and long-term love. Marge had never appreciated Ken's frequent statement that one reason he treasured Marge in his life was that she knew his history—the continuity of his personality through many developmental stages. But during the end of the affair with José, Marge began to trust the emotional depth of Ken's words. What Ken was expressing was that he felt connected to Marge in terms of every stage of his life development; whereas with José, the connection was mainly an idealized projection from the part of Ken that had missed a healthy adolescence.

The two years following were deeply healing in Marge and Ken's relationship. The threats of new lovers, and new potential abandonments, had been largely defused. Ken's adolescent romantic needs were no longer projected onto others.

Presently, there is little doubt in either partner's mind that the two of them will live out their lives together. Marge and Ken are preparing to celebrate their fortieth wedding anniversary. They are looking forward to retirement in the not too distant future. They realize there will be new adjustments to make when Marge no longer has her career to balance Ken's outside relationships. But their continued love for one another, a pleasing sex life together, the many interests they share, and the skills they have integrated into handling their relationship, leave them confident that they can remain intimate in this next phase of their lives together.

GENERALIZATIONS ABOUT BISEXUAL RELATIONSHIPS

The case above is not presented as typical of bisexuals, or even of mixed-orientation marriages. Information on the differences when the bisexual is female with a straight husband, or with a lesbian primary partner, and other constellations are discussed in Matteson (1996).

Mixed-orientation marriages are only one of many possible lifestyles among bisexuals. Information about lifestyles when bisexuality is recognized before marriage, and personal examples of other bisexual lifestyles, can be found in Hutchins and Kaahumanu (1991). For a social-psychological and political analysis of bisexuality and its lifestyles, see Firestein (1996).

Though there is no one lifestyle which characterizes bisexuals, the case of Marge and Ken does illustrate some issues which are common in committed relationships in which one partner is bisexual:

1 These couples must deal with societal taboos against same-sex relationships, and against multiple partners.
2 They must cope with the identity struggle in the bisexual partner precipitated by the recognition of his bisexual orientation.
3 The heterosexual partner must develop enough sense of individuality and equality to cope with the social implications of a mixed orientation partnership, and to make decisions about meeting her or his own needs.
4 As a couple, they must develop strategies for managing their unique lifestyle that take into account her or his emerging sexual identity.
5 And they must face the potential hazards of triangling which are built into an actively bisexual lifestyle.

For convenience, in what follows I shall refer to the bisexual partner as "he" or "husband", and the heterosexual partner as "she" or "wife."

PRINCIPLES FOR CONNECTING AND
CREATING INTIMACY IN
MIXED-ORIENTATION COUPLES

The experience of facing the fact that one's spouse is bisexual has the benefit of encouraging a stance of noncontrol:

> I've learned...that I have no control over anyone but myself.... I can't change him. I no longer want to.... What he wants, it's something I really can't give him, and so it's no reflection on our own relationship (Latham and White, 1978, p. 205).

Control Over One's Own Life

The ability to surrender trying to control one's partner's life seems to depend largely on the belief that one has a fair degree of control over one's own life, as discussed in the section on individuality and equality, above. Financial independence is also important—both for the sense that one could survive the loss of the partner, and so that the straight partner has the freedom to go out and in other ways take care of herself, rather than sitting home resenting that her husband is out spending money and enjoying his life in the "gay world."

Respectful Communication

What are often labeled communication skills involve far more than the ability to articulate, and to understand the other's messages. In an emotionally loaded issue, a key factor is each of the partner's ability to hear their spouse's perspective and to respond with understanding, even if they do not agree. A firm basis of respect for the other and a willingness to empathically hear the other's needs can form the ground for negotiating the particulars of the new marriage, or the revised relationship. This requires developing the skills in negotiating, tolerating, changing, compromising, and acquiescing that are necessary on both sides. If the arrangements are to work, they must meet needs on both sides.

Since rethinking the expectations and rules of these relationships is crucial, and since not all wishes can be met, an open expression of feelings, and the willingness to hear the other's feelings becomes essential. Again, this requires more than skill; it demands a deep trust that one's sharing will not be used as ammunition. Where feelings are heard, even if it is not possible to meet the wishes of the other, and where the respect is mutually felt, the bond can continue despite disappointments and unmet desires.

Communication of the positive bond, as well as communication in conflict areas, is crucial. Marge & Ken had a note posted where they would each see it daily, which read:

> We will both try to express our love for the other, congruent with our feelings at the time, to be sure the other knows (s)he is not taken for granted.

Boundaries

Boundary issues are faced concerning what information is to be shared, and what is private. First, the bisexual partner is faced with the question of sharing with the spouse the wish to have outside partners. If the husband's homosexual desires are disclosed to his wife, she is faced with the likelihood of having to share her spouse. This usually leads to the issue of justice (and guilt), and decisions about whether the straight partner will also have extra-marital sexual relationships. Does a bisexual man who prefers to be open have the right to tell his wife's parents or friends? Or does a wife, who is hurting, and considering a separation, have the right to explain to her friends the sexual orientation of her husband when he is not yet open? There are no clear "right answers" to these ethical dilemmas, but a couple counselor may help each partner to develop greater sensitivity to the spouse's feelings, and a commitment to discuss these issues before acting on them.

Primacy

There is some evidence from a longitudinal study (Matteson, 1985, p. 165) that a sexually open relationship is more likely to work if the couple have spent a number of years in which each felt sure she or he was primary for the other. In most cases, even then, the straight partner has needed to experience herself as primary in order to allow the outside relationships to go on without feeling threatened and being overly reactive. Since it is harder for the nonprimary partner to feel commitment to the relationship, those partnerships tend to be shorter-lived.

As an interesting exception, occasionally one sees a mutually satisfying open arrangement in which three persons live together in a stable relationship. The ideal of nonhierarchical relationships, even in couples, is too new historically (Broderick, 1988, pp. 2–14, 30–35) to know whether triads with equal power and commitment could work if culturally supported. These are wonderful, if precarious, experiments in equality and caring.

Growth Together

As the couple share in forming their own unique relationship, it becomes a project in which they both experience new truths and understanding. The joy and excitement of new romances can be recognized for what it is, rather than as a threat to the richness and depth of long term love.

TACTICS AND PROCEDURES USED TO CREATE INTIMACY

A number of tactics and communication practices, present in the case of Ken and Marge, played a part in the level of intimacy they were able to develop. These are listed here as suggested directions counselors might encourage in mixed-orientation couples.

- Sharing changes in sexual and interpersonal interests as they emerge, rather then letting the differences build and then surprise the partner.
- Respecting the limits of what the partner wants to hear, but avoiding deceit around basic issues which affect the partner.

[Agreeing on the rules concerning what and when to communicate (and not communicate) was an important step in this couple's new marriage. Marge's recognition that limits on communication were very difficult for Ken, and her patience in reviewing and reexplaining these, were helpful.]

- Contracting (developing clear agreements) about specific behaviors they will and will not do in respect for each of their needs.
- Reaching outside the relationship for support, from friends of each partner, friends of the couple, and counselors.
- Clarifying how much sharing of information is helpful to each of them.

- Overcoming the expectation that what one desires (e.g., extramarital sex) the other should also desire.
- Developing a special time and space for the primary relationship of the couple.
- Working out agreements between them that respect each of their needs.
- Doing individual work with counselors, but making sure that the counselors do not forget the couple relationship.

[There is a danger that individual counseling will undermine rather than strengthen the communication between partners. The fact that both Ken and Marge chose individual therapists whom the other already knew and trusted, and both were willing to come to the other's therapy for occasional joint sessions, prevented this undermining from occurring. (Garfield & Bergen, 1978).]

- Designing rituals which affirm the specialness of the relationship even though it does not fit conventional views of marriage.

[Gay and lesbian commitment ceremonies are increasingly common in mainstream Protestant churches, and offer models for unconventional vows of commitment. In one triad I know, the heterosexual couple had a remarriage ceremony; separately, the two men also had a ceremony expressing the nature of their commitment and acknowledging the heterosexual marriage. One mixed-orientation couple I know had a creative silversmith make special rings symbolizing their new marriage, which they exchanged in the presence of close friends. Rituals need not be limited to celebrations of commitment. They may be used to encourage developing a trust in the specialness of the relationship. A couple who moved to a sexually open marriage felt the need for some activity that only they shared with each other. They both loved modern dance, and found watching beautiful choreography an ecstatic experience. They agreed to never go to dance performances with other partners. Though monogamous dance attendance may sound amusing, it became a very special sharing for this couple. Suggestions concerning incorporating rituals into therapy can be found in Combs & Freedman (1990).]

- Investment in a common project, as a way of symbolizing a willingness to work together. The concreteness of projects (such as a search for a specific vacation spot that combines their interests, or a course of training in which they do homework together) gives a needed sense of groundedness to the relationship, counteracting the uncertainties.

Though all of these issues have implications for therapy, the issue of respecting the limits of what each partner wants to share, and to hear, is of particular importance. Often this means respecting the fact that the bisexual partner is not ready to be open about this with some of the people in his intimate network. Allowing the client to decide with whom and when to disclose is crucial to work with sexual minorities.

Often the nonbisexual spouse who is struggling to live with the loss of monogamy does not want to be exposed to some of the explorations and struggles in which the bisexual partner is engaged. One couple in a couples group with me had an agreement that the bisexual husband would give advance warning to his wife if he wished to discuss topics that might trigger her vulnerability; the group understood her choice to leave the group for that portion of the meeting.

BLOCKS TO INTIMACY, AND TECHNIQUES TO REMOVE THEM

Deception and Deceit

One very important block is the wound that develops if there has been a period of deception and deceit. (See Buxton, 1991, pp. 175–216). The context and nature of the period of disclosure need to be understood in order to understand the treatment needs of the couple. Typically, disclosure to a spouse is not a single event, but a series. If the straight spouse has been misled and, for example, has internalized blame during a period of sexual dysfunction, there may be considerable damage to her self-image and her perception of sexual interactions, which may necessitate longer therapeutic intervention once the crisis period is over. "The profound effect that the deception has on straight spouses isn't readily understood by others, especially their partners." (Buxton, 1991, p. 175). Gochros' sensitive description of the continuum of disclosures and their implications is very helpful in assessment and treatment planning with the straight spouse (1989, pp. 53–74). It is important to realize that secrecy is not always a simple issue of one person hiding information from the other. I have discussed elsewhere the pattern of a conspiracy of silence that can emerge in couples who don't have the strengths to handle disclosure of and communication around threatening issues (Matteson, 1990, p. 128). Often the bisexual's failure to risk disclosure is, in part, a response to earlier communications which showed that communication would destroy the relationship. Continued secrecy may be viewed by the bisexual as "protecting my spouse from the hurt," though it may also be self-servingly designed to protect himself from risking the loss of the relationship. Since most of the mixed-orientation marriages that continue involve a male bisexual with a straight wife, the power differential in our male-dominated society makes it likely that the issue of deceit will be compounded with the issues of power and control of "dominating men" over "dependent" women. The lines between deceit, a mutual conspiracy of silence, and implicit decisions to respect the other's limits and boundaries, are very difficult to judge.

The effects of deceit and the loss of trust are similar to those in couples where one has had a hidden heterosexual affair, except that they are compounded by the confusion about whether the homosexual needs can be suppressed. Rebuilding trust is aided by developing a profile of trust—that is, clarifying the areas in which the offended wife does still trust her husband. (Do you still believe he will bring home the paycheck? Will he tell you the truth about his spending?) The attempt is to keep mistrust from becoming too generalized, so that the areas of competence and genuineness will still be recognized.

Homophobia, and Internalized Homophobia

After several years of an apparently good marriage, a husband begins to recognize his feelings of sexual attraction toward persons of the same sex. After some minor excursions into gay settings, he feels guilty and wishes he could share with his wife, who is his most intimate friend, what he is feeling. He tests the waters by asking her about her opinions about the gay marriage laws that are being discussed (or some similar news event), and she responds saying "I can't understand why people would act that way, instead of behaving normally!" Her negative response, combined with his own insecurity about communicating feelings, inhibit him from sharing the next steps he takes in exploring his desires. It is not just a question of wanting to avoid his wife's homophobic responses. It also reflects his own internalizing of oppression concerning homosexual desires. It is nearly impossible to have grown up in a culture that views homosexuality as "sinful" or "abnormal" and not to have incorporated some of those feelings. Even those who have overcome such views intellectually may still retain the "gut responses" that homosexual acts are disgusting or revolting.

Dealing with internalized homophobia in an individual counseling session is well illustrated in the video "Psychotherapy with Gay & Lesbian Clients: Coming Out" (A.P.A., 1995). In my experience, the most successful couple work with homophobia is done using cocounselors, one straight and one openly bisexual or gay. The straight therapist's relationship with the bisexual therapist becomes a model of a straight person's acceptance of bisexuality; the bisexual counselor's listening to the needs of the straight spouse becomes a model for the husband to hear and respect his wife's needs and feelings without feeling guilty about his own. Mutual respect between cotherapists of different orientations is the key to this modeling, and is far more important that the orientations themselves. For further clarification of systems issues in this therapeutic work, see Matteson (1996), pp. 197, 205–206.

The opportunity to participate in a counseling group for men who are dealing with coming out issues can be very helpful for the partner dealing with identity issues. This is an especially helpful supplement to individual or couple counseling for clients who are working with therapists who are not really knowledgeable about the gay subculture.

The Bisexual's Identity Search

The amount of time and energy that the bisexual partner invests in the identity search may become a bone of contention for the straight partner. Contracts around the management of time can be helpful—specifically around responsibilities when the bisexual partner reenters the marital home after an evening of adventure, or exploration. An example is a request Marge made, in a note to Ken:

> Remind yourself that you are responsible to the children and to your work when you come home from your outside involvements. If you are tired and need rest, it should not be taken from the time you've committed to the children, or to me, especially at these times when I'm most vulnerable.

When a person is in an identity crisis, they are likely to function somewhat like a narcissist, constantly interested in and talking about themselves. Reviewing the details for each exploration into the gay world can be affirming for the bisexual. But this can be very trying to the partner, not only because she feels abandoned, but because the details of his identity exploration are often painful for her to hear. This difference in reactions to discussing these details needs to be recognized, and agreements need to be worked out to reduce the negative impact of these different needs. Often it is helpful to encourage him to share these with a friend who is not so directly impacted.

The intensity of the crisis and the excitement around new involvements in the gay world may make it seem that the "gay side" of the person is far more prominent than the "straight side." Often this shifts when the newness of the experience simmers down, and a more balanced bisexuality emerges. The couple should be forewarned against early assumptions that the husband is really totally gay, though, of course, only time will tell. Many men, once they have overcome the internalized homophobia, become more sexually alive, and sex within the marriage actually improves with the self-acceptance of their bisexuality.

Isolation

Mixed-orientation couples most typically seek counseling when the bisexual or gay spouse has disclosed his orientation to his wife, often after he has accepted his orientation enough to begin exploring sex with men. The husband's identity search, or coming out of closet, is a liberating experience for him. For her it may feel anything but liberating. Typically it has taken him years to get to a level of self-acceptance to initiate this. His becoming acquainted with other men like himself feels like the end of a long isolation. The spouse may be unprepared for this; her reactions may include self-blame and embarrassment. She now has a huge secret to deal with, which could potentially stigmatize her. She may feel that his coming out of the closet puts her into the closet, afraid to tell her closest friends or relatives what she is dealing with, and unaware of anyone else who has been through this. Though there is an identifiable community of gay men as a potential support group for him, support groups for the spouses are not as visible. She often knows no one like herself, and feels very isolated. Especially in the early stages of coping with this revelation, if a support group can be found, it can be extremely valuable for her. Groups for the wives of gay/bi-men exist in the larger cities, and can be located by calling the gay switchboard or hotline. Even if such a group is not available, the nearest chapter of Parents and Friends of Lesbians and Gays (P-FLAG) can provide support and possibly link her with at least one other wife who has gone through this. There are two cautions: persons who have lived through a family member coming out as gay may not be aware of the differences for bisexuals; and individuals sharing their life experiences have a tendency to over generalize and not notice how another couple may differ.

For specific recommendations for coping with the coming out stage, see both Gochros (1989) and Buxton (1991). It can be very useful for the couple to read books like these and discuss them together.

In areas that involve intense fear or extreme value differences, it is helpful to avoid polarization. One way to do this is by involving persons trusted by both partners. Ken's commitment to social activism and Marge's fear of abandonment had the potential of escalating one another. Marge's request that Ken pledge not to take any risks in the way of social activism without first talking it through with two of his friends, whom she trusted, and Ken's willingness to honor this request, greatly reduced this threat. Their communication around these emotional subjects, moving to contracts, resembled, unknowingly to them, the sequence of mirroring, validation, and empathy used in Hendrix' Couples' Dialogue—leading to behavioral requests (Hendrix, 1988).

Grief of Lost Dreams

The expectations that surround a committed love relationship are very often influenced by the portrayal of romance in films and TV. As a husband and wife face the fact that one of them is not strictly heterosexual, the dream is punctured. Often there is an assumption that the marriage (or relationship) must be abandoned altogether. In fact, the typical marriage is unlikely to work. And grieving of each of their hopes and expectations is a necessary part of rethinking what kind of relationship is right for them. The hard work of designing a new and unique relationship, rather than a precut or prefabricated one, cannot progress healthily without acknowledging the pain and loss.

In those cases in which a gay male couple, or lesbian couple, discover that one of them is bisexual, there is not only grief and loss, but also a revisiting of a previously painful identity search.

> If a person has come to identify as lesbian or gay, and become a part of lesbian or gay communities, she/he has probably undergone a grieving of heterosexual models, and quite possibly has experienced the loss of support from some friends and relatives in the heterosexual community. Should he or she then recognize heterosexual attractions, coming out as bisexual to gay or lesbian friends may involve new rejections and new grief. (Matteson, 1996, p. 190. See this work for further information about bisexuality emerging after a lesbian or gay identity).

Regardless of sexual orientation, the grieving of unmet hopes and expectations is often a counterpoint to the excitement of the new discovery of oneself and the creation of a unique partnership.

Unresolved Earlier Grief

I believe that one common block to intimacy among sexual minorities is related to the trauma of the adolescent period, when the person has not been able to openly date and develop sexual relationships with persons of his or her own gender, and when feelings of failing to fit the norm were internalized. Persons who have not sufficiently mourned their lost adolescence may develop an intense sexual attraction to someone who has adolescent-like characteristics that trigger their unmet longings. Such was the case when Ken, in his early 50's, fell "madly in love" with an adolescent-like man. Fortunately, through "cast of characters" work, Ken was able to access the adolescent aspects of his personality which were triggered in this affair, and learned to nurture these subpersonalities and complete the grieving of this portion of his life (Watanabe-Hammond, 1987; Schwartz, 1995).

Jealousy

The emphasis on romantic love in the mainstream American media, and our myopic view of the history of marriage, feed into the perception that jealousy is natural and monogamous marriage is the only ethical sexual lifestyle. We fail to notice that jealousy confuses love with possessiveness and control. The equating of outside sexual relationships with "being unfaithful" feeds into this confusion. Fidelity has to do with honesty and integrity in a relationship, and with the "intention to permanence," and may not "require . . . sexual exclusivity." (United Church of Canada, 1980).

The root of jealousy is usually the fear of losing love. The recognition that "love casts out fear" (1 John 4:18) suggests that restoring trust and overcoming jealousy come from strengthening the expression of love within the marriage, not from focusing on the third party and the outside relationship. The bisexual partner must be challenged if he uses open marriage or multiple relationships as a way to maintain unhealthy triangles, or as an abstract, idealized view of love that avoids concrete commitments and fails to face squarely the limits of time and energy. Concrete pledges concerning what each partner will do *in this relationship* can help the other feel special, and are more healing than attempts to control what is done outside the relationship. This involves learning to hear the other deeply, including hearing the pain, without rushing to fix it. It also may involve concrete agreements, such as those that Marge and Ken reached around reentry (See "The Bisexual's Identity Search" above). The point is that the quality of interaction when the partners are together defines the relationship much more than what happens when they are apart. The discipline is to learn, when together, to be as fully and concretely present as possible in the relationship.

Fear of Loss of Primacy or Specialness

Another block to intimacy is the fear of being taken for granted in the marriage, with the bisexual partner giving greater attention to the new and exciting love affair(s) outside the marriage. This commonly arises in mixed-orientation marriages when routine events in the marriage are interrupted by spontaneous opportunities for contact with an extramarital partner. This problem tends to be most acute in the period of identity exploration of the bisexual, particularly if there has been a long period of repressing gay desires. Ken and Marge made a contract that went something like this:

> If we have set aside time for ourselves, it is not to be violated without a discussion which includes hearing the other's needs and feelings and weighing these carefully before making a decision to do something with someone else.

Each couple must work out their own unique agreements. What can be accepted as a loving affirmation of the primacy of the marriage by one bisexual man, could be experienced by another bisexual husband as an attempt to control.

A Tendency to Stay Focused on Conflict

A recognition of this tendency led Marge and Ken to institute what they called "moratorium days"—conflict-free periods of relaxed, joyful experiences. It is important that the couple experience times of just being together in the present, not trying to solve problems or plan the future. When that focus is lost, they lose sight of what makes it worthwhile to stay together, and their life becomes one big worry.

Remaining Stuck in Stereotypes

A final block to intimacy is the failure to develop a new, personalized understanding of marriage. The beliefs and dreams of a traditional, monogamous romantic marriage have been shattered, and, if the partners make a decision to continue the marriage, it must be based on a revision of their views of marriage and the creation of a new shared dream (See Buxton, 1991, p. 257–271). In many cases, the husband's facing that his desires (and often his personality and interests) do not fit the traditional male stereotype, leads the couple into greater acceptance of their individual styles of being male and female. Her need for greater independence than is usually encouraged in women also encourages them to reassess stereotypes of masculinity, femininity, and of "gay" and "straight." The new marriage is likely to involve freeing themselves and their relationship from conformity to these roles, growing into much more personalized styles as individuals, and taking risks to find their unique style of marriage. However, these steps are not easy. It "takes enormous personal development to sustain counter-cultural behavior" (Silverstein, 1996).

The bisexual experience, like so many of life's difficult experiences, may have unique spiritual potentials. Bisexuals are perceived, in many cultures, to have a special relationship to the spiritual. The Lakota tribe (Native American) choose as their shamans (spiritual leaders) persons who are "two-spirited", that is, have both the male and female spirits. Many of these shamans have both a male and female sexual partner. In short, persons we would call bisexual are considered ideal teachers, counselors, and spiritual leaders, because they are presumed to contain aspects of and understanding of both genders (See Conner, 1993 for a review of anthropological evidence of this connection.)

To relate this to our own culture, and place it in psychological language: If the bisexual man overcomes not only the taboo against sex with other men, but the taboo in some homosexual subcultures against genuine emotional intimacy with another man—in short, if a man allows himself to experience really loving both genders, his view of love may change, as well as the depth of his love of himself. The process of facing one's identifications as they are projected onto both male and female lovers provides a remarkable opportunity to know one's self and one's "shadow" (Jung, 1966) that may allow a unique self/other knowledge in bisexuals, since only they have the chance to include both genders in the alchemy of the "sexual crucible" (Schnarch, 1991). Bisexuality provides some unique challenges that may lead to greater self-acceptance and a more unconditional love.

Perhaps, when a couple face the bisexual experience, as each member of the couple becomes more authentic and individuated, and the levels of intimacy deepen between them, they may sense a connectedness that transcends their own relationship, transcends gender issues, and spills over into the rest of their lives. Love becomes a spiritual dimension.

CONCLUSION

The emergence of bisexuality in a couple's relationship may seem like a curse. As with other challenges, if the couple are capable of "staying in life, even when it becomes complicated and when meaning and clarity are elusive" (Moore, 1994, p. 5), dealing with bisexuality can provide growth-producing experiences which deepen the couple's understanding of love. The "curse" may be transformed into a blessing.

RECOMMENDED READINGS FOR COUNSELORS

Gochros, J. S. (1989). *When Husbands Come Out of the Closet*. New York: Haworth.
Matteson, D. R. (1996). Counseling & psychotherapy with bisexual and exploring clients. In B. Firestein (Ed.). *Bisexuality: The Psychology and Politics of an Invisible Minority* (pp. 185–213). Thousand Oaks, CA: Sage Press.

REFERENCES

American Psychological Association (1995). *Psychotherapy with gay & lesbian clients: Coming out* [videotape]. Santa Anna, CA: Buendía Productions.
Bailey, D. (1996). Bader, Schnarch, and Hendrix. *Journal of Imago Relationship Therapy, 1*(2), 35–51.
Broderick, C. B. (1988). *The therapeutic triangle*. Beverly Hills, CA: Sage.
Buxton, A. (1991). *The other side of the closet: The coming-out crisis for straight spouses*. Santa Monica, CA: IBS Press.
Combs, G. & Freedman, J. (1990). *Symbol, story and ceremony: Using metaphor in individual and family therapy*. New York: Norton.
Conner, R. P. (1993). *Blossom of bone: Reclaiming the connections between homoeroticism and the sacred*. San Francisco: Harper.
Firestein, B. A. (Ed.). (1996). *Bisexuality: The psychology and politics of an invisible minority*. Thousand Oaks, CA: Sage.
Garfield, S. & Bergen, A., (Eds.). (1978). *Handbook of psychotherapy and behavior change: An empirical analysis*. (2nd ed.). (pp. 823, 832, 835). New York: John Wiley.
Gochros, J. (1989). *When husbands come out of the closet*. New York: Haworth.
Hendrix, H. (1988). *Getting the love you want: A guide for couples*. New York: Henry Holt.
Hutchins, L. & Kaahumanu, L. (1991). *Bi any other name: Bisexual people speak out*. Boston: Alyson.
Jung, C. (1966). On the psychology of the unconscious In *Two Essays on Analytical Psychology* (2nd ed.) (pp. 30–33). Princeton, NJ: Princeton University Press.
Kohn, B. & Matusow, A. (1980). *Barry and Alice: Portrait of a bisexual marriage*. New York: Prentice-Hall.
Latham, J. D. & White, G. D. (1978). Coping with homosexual expression within heterosexual marriages: Five case studies. *Journal of Sex and Marital Therapy, 4*, 198–212.
Litwoman, J. (Winter, 1990). Some thoughts on bisexuality. *Lesbian Contradictions 29*, 4–5.
Marcia, J., Waterman, A., Matteson, D., Archer, S., Orlofsky, J. (1993). *Ego identity: A handbook for psychosocial research*. New York: Springer-Verlag.
Matteson, D. (1985). Bisexual men in marriages: Is a positive homosexual identity and stable marriage possible? *Journal of Homosexuality, 11*, 149–172.
Matteson, D. (1987a). Counseling bisexual men. In M. Scher, M. Stevens, G. Good & G. Eichenfield (Eds.), *Handbook of counseling & psychotherapy with men*. Newbury Park: Sage.
Matteson, D. (1987b). The heterosexually married gay and lesbian parent. In F. W. Bozett (Ed.), *Gay & lesbian parents*. (pp. 128–161). New York: Praeger.
Matteson, D. (1990). Gays and lesbians in mixed-orientation marriages. In R. J. Kus, *Keys to Caring*. Boston: Alyson.

Matteson, D. (1993). Differences within and between genders: A Challenge to the theory. In J. E. Marcia, A. Waterman, D. Matteson, S. Archer, & J. Orlofsky (Eds.), *Ego identity: A handbook for psychosocial research.* (pp. 69–110). New York: Springer-Verlag.

Matteson, D. (1996). Counseling & psychotherapy with bisexual and exploring clients. In B. Firestein (Ed.), *Bisexuality: The psychology and politics of an invisible minority.* (pp. 185–213). Thousand Oaks, CA: Sage Press.

Matteson, D. (February, 1997). Bisexual and homosexual behavior and HIV risk among Chinese-, Filipino-, and Korean-American men. *Journal of Sex Research, 34,* 1, 93–104.

Moore, T. (1994). *Soul Mates: Honoring the mysteries of love and relationship.* New York: Harper Collins.

O'Neil, N., & O'Neil, G. (1968). *Open Marriage.* New York: Avon Books.

Scarf, M. (1987). *Intimate partners: Patterns in love and marriage.* New York: Ballantine Books.

Schnarch, D. (1991). *Constructing the sexual crucible: An integration of sexual and marital therapy.* New York: W. W. Norton.

Schwartz, R. (1995). *Internal Family Systems Therapy.* New York: The Guilford Press.

Silverstein, O. (1996, December). Enhancing intimacy. Paper presented at the Evolution of Psychotherapy Conference, Las Vegas.

Tessina, T. (1989). *Gay relationships for men and women.* Los Angeles, CA: Jeremy P. Tarcher.

United Church of Canada (1980). *In God's image...male and female: A study on human sexuality.* (p. 66). Toronto: Division of Mission in Canada for the General Counseling of the United Church of Canada.

Watanabe-Hammond, S. (March-April, 1987). The many faces of Paul and Dora. *The Family Networker,* 54–55, 87–91.

CHAPTER 25

The Psychopathological Couple

Michael P. Maniacci, Psy.D.

Couples in need of psychotherapy vary in their needs, issues, dynamics, and presentations. In this chapter, the focus is rather specific: These couples have at least one person who has a clear cut DSM diagnosis, and quite frequently, more than one member has more than one diagnosis (American Psychiatric Association, 1994). The term "psychopathological" has many potential meanings, but for the purposes of this chapter, it will mean "diagnostic disorder," whatever the particular diagnosis may be.

UNDERSTANDING AND DEFINITION OF INTIMACY

Intimacy can have manifold meanings as well, as no doubt the reader of this text is by now aware. In the context of this chapter, I want to offer a definition. For reasons that will become apparent below, intimacy can be defined as the willingness of partners to expose their vulnerabilities to each other and still feel accepted, acknowledged, and valued (Sherman, 1993). For such a working definition to make sense, a detour into the world of psychopathology is called for.

I utilize a biopsychosocial approach to understanding and working with individuals (Adler, 1956; Maniacci, in press; Sperry, 1989). Biologically, these individuals may have compromised organs or organ systems which make them particularly vulnerable to the effects of stress. In particular, central nervous system irregularities, neurotransmitter abnormalities, or genetic weaknesses may predispose these people to dysfunction. Psychosocially, they have typically been raised in an environment which was not conducive to their particular needs, expectations, and temperaments. The concept of "goodness of fit" is crucial in understanding their psychosocial and neurodevelopmental histories.

For example, Jimmy was born with a slow to warm up temperament. He was his mother's last pregnancy, delivered while she was in her early 40s, after she had six other children. His father was already entering midstage alcoholism, and mother had a history of periodic drinking in-between recurrent bouts of major depression. He was raised by his older siblings, who did a reasonably good job. But they were not old enough nor mature enough to handle his squirmy, "difficult" temperament, and their frustrations with his "fussiness" increased tensions in the already tense home. Jimmy was five years younger than his next sibling, and he spent a lot of time alone, keeping to himself and watching others interact. He longed to be involved, but was fearful of the contact and typical "bumpiness" of the common transactions he witnessed and experienced in his family of origin. He was described as an odd child, nice, but hesitant, with a timid style but a good imagination, and, given enough distance, he could be reasonably social.

Jimmy developed the following convictions about life, himself, and other people. "Life is hard, especially when I'm confronted with other people. I want to be a part of them, but I don't know how to fit in. Women make me nervous, and men intimidate me. People give 'report cards,' and I can't seem to be able to get a 'good grade' even though I try." In diagnostic language, Jimmy has an avoidant personality disorder (Sperry & Mosak, 1996). He is tense, ill at ease with himself, and unsure about how to belong. The farther away he keeps people, the "safer" he is, for they are less likely to see his "mistakes," or so he hopes. He had some good interpersonal experiences in childhood, so he didn't develop a schizoid style, but such experiences were few and far between. More care, sensitivity, and patience on the part of his caregivers would have done a great deal to modify his temperament, and a cycle of dissatisfying transactions and early learning might have been headed off. His siblings were not mature enough and his parents were relatively unavailable to the extent they needed to be, so Jimmy's hesitant style solidified, and he began operating in such a way which nonconsciously elicited the types of responses he feared. Jimmy became cautious, on edge, and too self-focused, therefore inhibiting his performance, increasing his already low level anxiety to more obvious proportions, and looking "weird" to his peers. He seldom was outright shunned, but he was seemingly always on the periphery, as if he had one foot in and one foot out of the social world.

Intimacy, for people like Jimmy, is painful. From their skewed perspective, too much exposure results in disapproval, rejection, and discomfort. Yet, they do develop relationships. Jimmy's partners would have some severe tests ahead of them, and their abilities to successfully navigate such challenges and still negotiate their own issues would be a barometer of their potential success, or failure.

More generally, psychopathological individuals are rigid in their styles, defensive in their transactions, pessimistic in their outlooks, and typically unaware of the self-defeating and self-perpetuating nature of their dynamics (Millon & Davis, 1996). Successful adaptation requires a balance between the person and the situation (Adler, 1956), as symbolized in the following equation:

$$\text{Person} \times \text{Situation} = \text{Degree of Adaptation}$$

If either the person or situation element is dysfunctional, the degree of adaptation suffers. Yet, if either the person or the situation element is particularly strong, the degree of dysfunction is likely to be minimal, if present at all. In other words, if a very strong, resilient woman is put in a difficult situation, she will probably be all right. Similarly, if a maladaptive woman is placed in an ideal situation, she may show the same degree of adaptability as the aforementioned resilient woman. Psychopathology is the result of the person/situation interaction, or, more precisely, is a result of the degree of goodness of fit between the person and the situation.

The range of potential situations psychopathological individuals can successfully deal with is relatively small. They have such rigidity in their styles that they limit the number of types of situations they can successfully negotiate. Their defensiveness and pessimism leads them to expect the worst, and given their difficult developmental experiences, probably justifiably so.

Intimacy, for them, requires placing themselves into a situation in which their defensiveness and pessimism is challenged. Instead of characteristically avoiding such situations, they need to meet them in a relatively open, mutually satisfying manner. What does that mean? In theory, this: In situations which would normally elicit characteristic security operations in order to protect the potentially vulnerable self-esteem, the psychopathological individuals would drop those operations and take a chance that their insecurities, inferiorities, and weaknesses would not be exploited, and therefore, their worst fears not confirmed. For such people, intimacy is a growth experience, and such growth experiences are typically avoided (Sullivan, 1956).

The focus needs to shift. Till now, I was discussing psychopathological individuals. Psychopathological couples present a more complex picture. The above symbolic equation takes on this presentation:

$$[\text{Person 1} \times \text{Situation}] \times [\text{Person 2} \times \text{Situation}] \times \text{Couple's Situation}$$

$$= \text{Degree of Adaptability}$$

In this model, we have two people, each with his or her own biopsychosocial developmental history, expectations, and style, interacting with his or her own current situation, which then interacts with the situation the couple finds themselves in, to produce the particular degree of adaptability. There are two individuals and three situations which need to be taken into account. Each individual has a unique situation she or he is currently experiencing; in addition, the couple also has a situation they find themselves in, and that may or may not overlap with each individual's situation.

For instance, John and Joan are the pathological couple we are discussing. John has his biopsychosocial history and current functioning, which open him up to certain types of situations and exclude him from others. Similarly with Joan. They also have the situations they find themselves in as a couple, with each having expectations of how the other is perceiving and processing the same situation. Let me elaborate.

John is narcissistic in his style and Joan is dependent in her style. John will typically only involve himself in situations in which he can be number one, superior. Joan overvalues togetherness, and she tends to only seek out situations which increase bonding. Joan becomes pregnant at the same time John is offered a major promotion which involves a major increase in his hours at work and the couple having to move across the country. While John sees the situation as an opportunity to further his superiority, he sees Joan's pregnancy as a potential hindrance. Joan sees her pregnancy as a chance to increase the bonding, especially with her family of origin, but she is afraid of the move with her husband out of fear of being less connected to her family and her husband. The same situation is perceived differently by each person and could be diagrammed this way:

[John's goal of superiority × opportunity for advancement]

× [Joan's goal of bonding × the pregnancy]

× Major life change of pregnancy and possible move for career

= Challenge to the Couple's Adaptability

If each individual is rigid and defensive, the couple will not be able to negotiate successfully a way around such major life changes. If either one gives in to the other, the consequent resentment could go a long way to disrupting the future happiness of this relationship.

PRINCIPLES FOR CONNECTING AND CREATING INTIMACY

In order to create intimacy in psychopathological couples, clinicians need to do a thorough assessment. An integrative, comprehensive assessment and diagnostic work up would entail focus upon a crucial issue. In technical language, clinicians need to assess what needs to be reconstructed and modified or both versus what needs to be adapted to and supported or both. In plain language, what has to change versus what can be worked around. This is not a text on psychotherapy, but by definition, these couples require psychotherapeutic interventions. Without them, there is little opportunity to create intimacy. The work typically shifts between individual and couple dynamics, sometimes during conjoint sessions with the couple, sometimes during individual sessions. I tend to follow a step-down model that works this way (Maniacci, in press; Pinsof, 1995):

1   Behavioral focus emphasizing transactions and overt skill building
2   Cognitive focus emphasizing perceptions, meaning, and interpretation of events
3   Motivational focus emphasizing early learning, nonconscious processes, and purposes.

By and large, it is efficient and practical to start the work with a clear, behavioral focus on level 1. Emphasis is placed upon what the couple needs to *do* to foster intimacy. If and when the clinician's attempt to increase intimacy is blocked along this dimension, then the shift is to level 2, a cognitive focus, which explores what the couple *believes* is the meaning of intimacy and how each couple has characteristically defined such behaviors. Should that not clear the block to behavioral skill acquisition, the focus is shifted to a more analytic emphasis along level 3, with early learning in and around the issue of intimacy being the focus, along with the possible motivation and purpose behind the hesitancy to be intimate being explored. Along any level, one or both partners may be present. While Joan is working on level 1, skill acquisition, John could be working on level 2, cognitive processes, at the same time in the same session. For example, while she could be practicing assertiveness exercises with John in order to more directly ask for what she wants, he could be exploring what such assertiveness means to him, such as a threat to his superiority. Such a focus may frighten Joan away from her practice, and her hesitancy to continue with her skill building may have to be explored via her early learning in passivity in her family of origin, where she learned that by being passive, she could win her father's approval over her competitive older sister.

As a rule, the ability to create intimacy is directly related to the willingness to address the issues of psychopathology. In some cases, the psychopathological issues do not need to change; teaching each person about the other's "hot spots" or "red flags" is enough to relax the tensions to the point where intimacy is fostered (Westen, 1991). Teaching Joan how to handle John's prestige issues and approach him sensitively may be enough to keep things running smoothly. Similarly, working with John to be more attentive to Joan and understanding of her issues may be therapy enough to have them receive more satisfaction out of their relationship. The focus is upon dealing with situation specific issues, and teaching them to deal more effectively with specific transactions (Gottman & Silver, 1994).

In many cases, however, the emphasis of working upon situations leads to two types of therapeutic blocks. In the first type of block, there are too many situations. The learning does not seem to generalize across situations, and the couple seems to need constant coaching and intervention. The second type of block involves stonewalling. Couples, or more precisely, individuals, refuse to handle the situation in the prescribed manner. The refusal is seldom blatant; more frequently, it is passive and displayed in the form of forgetting, quibbling about details, and so forth, which make the work upon the situation extremely tedious. In either type of block, the bottom up approach to addressing the issue is not efficient.

When such an approach is not working, the couple probably needs to address the underlying issues, typically more cognitive and motivational in nature. This top down approach doesn't address specific behaviors per se, but classes of behaviors, and addresses molar concepts, not microtransactions and skills. In this case, we wouldn't focus upon John's tone of voice with Joan, but probably his attitude in general.

Creating intimacy entails teaching clients how to relate differently to each other. Whereas with nonpsychopathological couples, the behavioral emphasis and situation specific focus may be all that is needed, with psychopathological couples, much more emphasis upon the context of the interfering symptoms needs to be made. As an example, with Kate and Tom, whose overall functioning (both as a couple and as individuals) is good, teaching active listening and mirroring may be all that is needed. With our couple from above, John and Joan, while such skills may be needed, the emphasis upon nonconscious dynamics and goals inherent in each's style may have to be addressed in order to increase the opportunity for them to utilize the skills they have acquired.

This brings a crucial point into relief. Initially, the psychopathological couple's willingness to learn and use the standards techniques nonpathological couples use to foster intimacy may be the same. The generalization and maintenance of those techniques, and therefore skills, will decline however, and therefore, it is quite common to find these couples having serial contacts with numerous therapists or multiple cycles of therapy with the same therapist over the course of time. They can't seem to maintain what they gain. Their course of therapy will typically mirror their marriage: many good starts with typically bad endings.

Clinicians who become aware of such repeated courses of therapy over the life span of the couple, especially for issues which seem to be repetitive, need to be aware that until the more personality-based, long-standing dynamics are addressed, the issues are likely to be only marginally repaired. Working around such issues only works for so long, and, quite often, while such a process produces rapid results, the long term efficacy of such a therapeutic approach can be questionable.

TACTICS AND PROCEDURES TO
CREATE INTIMACY

There are two categories of tactics used to create intimacy with psychopathological couples. First, there are general procedures utilized to foster intimacy with any rigid, defensive individual. Second, there are client specific tactics which are tailored to particular diagnostic presentations and particular psychodynamic and systemic challenges. I will address each in turn.

In general, there are a number of tactics which I have found helpful in working with such couples (see Gottman & Silver, 1994; Sherman, 1993). The first is a modification upon Corsini's First Aid Kit for Marriage (Corsini, 1967) that I call the "back to back" technique. It works this way.

1 I ask couples to set aside two 20-minute time periods during the week when they will not be interrupted, for example, Tuesday and Friday. During those 20 minute periods, there are to be no distractions, such as eating, smoking, television, or phone calls. They are to sit on the floor, bed, or couch, back to back, leaning against each other for support. A clock is to be in clear sight of both of them. For 10 minutes, one person speaks without interruption. Nancy, for instance, can use the 10 minutes to talk about whatever she wants, without fear of being cut off. She can use any or all of the time allotted, but her partner, Bill, cannot speak until the ten minutes are up. Should Nancy not use her full amount of time, the couple will have to sit, in silence until the time is up. If she is in midsentence at the 10 minute mark, she will have to stop and allow her partner to begin. Bill now has 10 minutes to respond to Nancy should he choose, or to discuss another topic if he likes. Nancy cannot cut in, interrupt or interfere in any way. Bill is free to use as much, or as little time as he would like. At exactly 10 minutes, he must stop, and should he not use all of his time, they must sit quietly for the rest of the allotted time. Whoever goes first the first night will go second the second night. Whatever they talk about during the back to back cannot be discussed again until the next back to back. Finally, they are instructed to do something nice, together, afterwards. These rules are to be strictly followed for a number of reasons, none of which should be explained in advance to the couple. The purpose of this technique is to build communication skills along with clear boundaries. What frequently causes psychopathological couples problems is their inability (or unwillingness) to "fight fairly." They interrupt each other, read body language too easily, and classically spill the contents of their conversations into other transactions too often. Therefore, their conversations never seem to be focused and never seem to be resolved. What they start talking about one evening bleeds into the next day, and they become hesitant to raise new issues for fear of going around and around, and "never hearing the end of it." This technique is designed to break such patterns. They must lean on each other, for support, and back each other up. They know their discussion will have a clear ending and not have to be raised again and again, and neither of them will be interrupted. I have found this increases communication during the week, in between sessions, about other topics and that, as this happens, I can begin to take away the rules, one at a time, and have them maintain some limits and boundaries.

2   I assign strategic tasks which are used to foster intimacy (Shoham, Rohrbaugh, & Patterson, 1995). One of my favorites is to have the couple go home and feed each other once during the week. They are to go home, and during a private dinner, they are to literally feed each other. I have even had couples bring in food to my office and do this during a session. It can be quite revealing and a wonderful exercise in learning to meet each other's needs, especially in couples whose cultures value food and eating. Another, more extreme task I sometimes assign is more fun for certain couples, but they need a streak of adventure and excitement-seeking in them, and just a bit of a sense of humor. I ask one of the members to act as if he or she is blind. I have them wrap a bandage around the partner's eyes and have the other lead that partner not only around my office, but, also, if they are willing (and a surprisingly large number of them are), one evening go on a "date" like this. All sorts of issues of trust, leadership, and support can be raised and worked on if they try this task.

3   I ask couples to engage in what I call a critical incident review, a form of mutual storytelling (Wachtel, 1994). In my office, and at their home, I ask them to relate childhood tales which typically mirror the issues they have presented for therapy. For example, if Chris and Matt come in because of their intense fighting, I may ask Matt to talk about childhood conflicts he got into with people and how he handled them and felt about them. I would ask him to tell stories about how he successfully avoided some scrapes and how he didn't avoid others. As they talk about these childhood incidents in a warm, support-ive manner, they frequently discover solutions to their current conflicts. Even when they don't directly find solutions, their ability to empathize and commu-nicate improves, especially around what were one's "hot topics." A similar technique asks them to relate childhood stories about their parents displaying similar behaviors. For example, I would ask Matt to discuss how his father and mother handled conflict when he was a child, and elicit how he felt and what he thought. Having him tell these stories to Chris in a sensitive, gentle tone often does a great deal to increase sharing and communication, particularly if I can get Chris to share some similar stories as well.

4   Another technique I have found helpful is sculpting (Satir, 1983). I ask the couple to act as if each were clay. If Matt goes first, I ask him to sculpt how he would see the relationship if he could create it anyway he wanted. He is instructed to put Chris into any position he would like that would symbolize how he would like to see the relationship. He can pose her in any position he wants, in any place in the room. After he creates his sculpture, she creates one using him. This often presents for them a concrete, pictorial sense of how each would like to see the other. The discussion which follows is generally quite intimate. Similarly, I teach them to pause and sculpt the relationship as they are seeing it in the here and now, at this very moment. Particularly during arguments, I ask them to sculpt one another. Not only does this allow them the moment to pause and reflect for awhile, it graphically shows each of them how the other is perceiving the transactions.

5   I ask couples to create caring lists (Dinkmeyer & Carlson, 1989; Sherman, 1993). I give each of them a sheet of paper and ask them to put their own name on the top. They are then asked to list a minimum of 10 things that would help them feel loved. While the list starts out with 10 things in my office, they are asked to go home and add as many more to the list as they can think of. The items must be specific, such as "hold my hand," and not general, such as "be happy." After each person has generated a listed, I ask them to exchange lists and negotiate any potential problems. Once both agree with the other's list, I instruct them to do a minimum of three things from the other person's list per week. If they do, they will find that the tension in the home is less. If they fail to do three things from the other person's list per week, they will typically find that they will be in an argument by the end of the week. As we discuss each list, I try to explain that we all have different ways of feeling loved. As time goes on, we get lazy, and start to assume that how we feel loved is automatically how our partners must feel loved. In other words, I begin to assume that if I like Italian food, my partner will like it. Therefore, I take her to a nice restaurant that serves Italian food in order to show her I love her. In reality, that is how I would feel loved, if she took me to such a place. We begin to do for our partners what we would like done for ourselves. As they use the caring lists, they begin to learn to speak the other's language, and intimacy is fostered.

6   I use this exercise in session. I ask them to look around the room, and silently to make note of all of the green items in my office. I give them ten seconds. At the end of the ten seconds, I have them close their eyes and tell me how many blue things they spotted. Most of the time, they cannot. When I ask them why, they explain that they weren't looking for such things. I explain that that is exactly what they have been doing with each other. They have been looking for the negative, and that is what they tended to find. I ask them to try an experiment. I want them to go home and try and find only positive things for one week, and most importantly, share these with not only each other but also their friends and family. Bringing concerned others into the picture and telling them about such positives usually is not only refreshing, it elicits much support.

7   I have them buy a large calendar and bring it into session. Given the hectic schedule many of my couples have, I ask them to turn to a month in advance and mark out the following days. First, each is to take one day for him- or herself. After each has done that, I ask them to mark off one day for the couple. If they have kids, I ask them to then mark off one day for the family. Out of thirty or so days, they now have four days marked off in which they are to spend quality time doing positive things for themselves and each other. They are to repeat this every month, for what happens, especially in psychopathological couples, is that they have very little quality time with each other. They do all of their work first, and with the time left over, they spend quality time on themselves and with each other. Typically, they have very little quality time left over. By shifting priorities, I ask them to put each other and themselves first and to fill in the rest of the calendar with chores and work only after they have taken care of their relationships first (Dinkmeyer & Carlson, 1989). Frequently, this is novel to them. They have usually gotten all of their

business done first, and only later tried to spend time with each other. If they have kids, they frequently complain that the "kids need to come first," and I tell them that that is a noble, but typically a misplaced sentiment. The kids should not supersede the couple's relationship, for that is like building a pyramid from the point upward. A healthy family has a strong parental relationship at its base, and without it, there is little chance of the family being very solid.

8   One last technique I will discuss seems trivial, but I have found it to be crucial for developing intimacy. I ask them to distance themselves from other people who are badmouthing the couple's relationship. If the couple's in-laws are talking down about the daughter-in-law, they need to create a little distance from the in-laws. If Karl's friend Pete is talking badly about marriage and Karl's wife, Karl needs some distance from Pete. The reinforcing quality of the negative influences needs to be put in check, for they can do a great deal of harm to the couple's relationship. Removing this constant reminder of how bad things may be or may have been, generally increases the tone of the relationship. In addition, it signifies one key shift for the couple: They are willing to choose each other over these "bad (but, admittedly sometimes, well meaning) influences." This sense of us bonding against them can do a lot to foster a togetherness, if not done in a paranoid, hostile manner.

These are some generic techniques which apply to the typical kinds of problems psychopathological couples encounter. Some specific techniques which are tailored to specific diagnostic and case dynamics will be discussed next. These kinds of techniques are designed to counter the specific issues certain couples have which prevent them from developing or maintaining intimacy. Classically, they entail addressing psychopathological dynamics at both the individual and systemic level, and are characterized by their focus being one of removing blocks which inhibit intimacy, not necessarily fostering intimacy itself.

TECHNIQUES TO REMOVE BLOCKS TO INTIMACY

What blocks intimacy? As alluded to above, our safeguarding operations do (Sullivan, 1956). If we were to drop these operations, we would feel exposed, vulnerable, inferior, and open to assault. It is safer to be on guard then to risk being hurt. When these clients' family histories are examined, it is easy to see why they developed the strategies they did. Relatively nonpathological individuals attempt to compensate for such issues in constructive, useful ways. Pathological ones do not compensate; they hide, obscure, and evade dealing with these painful issues. By not looking at them, they never seem to learn to successfully negotiate them.

Alex was an abused child. He adopted an "I'll get them before they get me," attitude to such abuse. He became so attuned to any potential abuse that he set his radar too sharply; he spotted potential abuse in even the mildest rebuff. Because he never learned to deal with such issues, he never developed a repertoire of skills for handling rebuffs. Instead, he simply attacked, sometimes in his imagination, sometimes in his verbalizations, and occasionally in his behavior. He was not going to let anyone push him around anymore. For the most part, they didn't, but they didn't get too close either. Now, as a large, imposing adult, Alex still acts as if he were a child, at the mercy of whatever a big, mean person is going to do to him. His wife is clearly not a big, mean person, but he can nonconsciously treat her as if she were, and after a few years, she gives in, and starts to treat him that way. You see, in her childhood, Gail had a hard time saying, "No." She believed that to be what others expected was to make them happy. She never figured on the paradox called Alex.

The more Gail tried to please Alex by playing his game, the more dissatisfied he became. This was a losing game for each of them, but boy did they play it well. Teaching them to be intimate with each other in a constructive manner involved removing several blocks from their relationship.

1   Early recollections can be very useful (Adler, 1956). Asking each person to remember specific, directed, painful memories from childhood can provide an opportunity to process and analyze certain conclusions he or she came to about certain issues. For example, asking Alex to recall his most painful memory from childhood, and having him and Gail work on it in session to clarify what he learned from such an issue can do a great deal not only to foster communication, but also to point out what Alex is trying not to let happen now. Unlike the childhood storytelling technique involving critical incidents, these early memories are single, focused, and worked on in session, not between sessions, under therapeutic guidance and direction. The intensity of these memories, and the intensity of the feelings frequently associated with them, require professional supervision and support. With time, couples can begin to see how their expectations regarding life, other people, and the world have influenced their current relationships (Maniacci, 1996).

2   This technique is called the FECK, the First Encounter of the Close Kind (Belove, 1980). Couples are asked to recall the first time they saw each other. In a manner analogous to the early recollection procedure noted above, Gail can be asked, "What is the earliest memory you have of Alex?" She is asked to be specific and detailed, and to describe how she felt during it. Alex is then asked for his earliest memory of Gail. Three or four additional memories are then elicited from each about the other. Parallels are then pointed out between these memories and their childhood recollections. What each person in the couple chooses to remember about the other will be indicative of their expectations regarding the nonconscious contract they have with each other.

This contract will mirror their childhood expectations regarding intimacy and couple relationships. For instance, asking Alex to recall his earliest memory of his parents being together, and then for his earliest memory of his father and then his mother, will elicit his expectations regarding marriage, masculinity and femininity, respectively. Asking him to then provide his FECK of Gail plus three or four others will highlight a remarkable consistency: She somehow is trying to be fit into his model of male/female relationships. When the same procedure is done with Gail, the loop can be completed. It can be shown how each is attempting to fit the other into his or her own expectations.

3   The grand reversal can be pointed out to them (Beck, 1988). It has been said that should a couple break up, the very thing which brought them together will be the thing which pulls them apart (Dreikurs, 1946). The FECK can be used to clarify this, but there are other ways as well. One tactic I use is to ask one member of the couple what his or her favorite food is. For example, if I ask Quintin what his favorite food is, and he says steak, I ask him how he would feel if I gave him steak for dinner that evening? He generally says he'd love it. I then push the example to an extreme. How about for breakfast the next morning, and then lunch, dinner again, and so forth? For a week straight, a month, for a year? He typically says he would hate it. Has the steak changed at all, I ask? He smiles and says no, it hasn't. What has changed is his perception of the steak. What was once palatable has now become distasteful, if not repulsive. Much the same can be pointed out regarding Quintin and his relationship. Too much of a good thing has occurred. Both started out the relationship doing something for each other which worked, otherwise they usually would not have stayed together. Now, after some time, they have been doing the same type of transactions for so long, in such a rigid, inflexible manner, the niceness has worn off, and what was once palatable is now distasteful. Much more often than not, neither partner has changed, but the perceptions of the partners' behaviors has changed. Flexibility can be asked from each of them. Novelty can be introduced into the mix, with the hope that enough variation can be introduced so as to spice up the relationship again.

4   Reframing can be used as well. Not only is this a good generic technique, it can be used to build upon the insight gained from the grand reversal technique. It can be pointed out that the reason each partner has continued to do more of the same is because it is a misdirected attempt to keep the other involved. To return to the example cited above, Quintin was appealing to Jenny because he was strong, forceful, and secure. Now after eight years, she perceives him as rigid, controlling, and a bully. He has not significantly changed; rather, he has simply become too inflexible in his approach. He continues to be so even when she asks him not to be, because he feels her pull away and becomes insecure, and he resorts back to the very behaviors and attitudes that attracted her to begin with. That is, he becomes more controlling, forceful, and so forth. He does this in order to win her back, and from his perspective, it makes sense. After all, this is what won her over to begin with.

5   The superiority/inferiority dynamic can be explored with them (Mozdzierz & Friedman, 1978). I ask them to discuss what they think their biggest asset is as individuals. Very often, they discover that their greatest

superiority is exactly where they feel their most intense inferiority. Let me elaborate. Diane will most often feel most inferior just where her greatest strength is, because she is so used to being good, if not excellent at that, that she is used to exceptional performance. Anything less than that is a source of frustration and feeling inadequate. If she is particularly talented at organizing and leading others, she probably expects that anything less than stellar performance in that area is a let down for her. The rigidity with which couples approach each other regarding certain tasks and issues can be, at least partially, clarified using this tactic. Diane may feel particularly threatened when she fails to live up to her own standards in this area, and she may have a hard time letting her partner lead. She may have found her place in her family of origin by doing such things, and to challenge that now is not only not helpful, it leads to her becoming defensive.

6   If Diane feels superior yet oddly inferior in this type of task, her partner Carol may feel inhibited in approaching such tasks. In fact, I have often found that this is a crucial weakness in Carol's style. This leads to the next technique I call matching and complimentary. Couples tend to attract each other because they complement the scripts/styles of each other (Berne, 1972). Carol's lack of organizational skills allow Diane to shine. For Diane to expect Carol to excel in this area might prove threatening to Diane's sense of superiority and the way she finds her place. I elicit from the couple what they see as the biggest weakness in each other, and then attempt to show them how this is a weakness precisely in order to complement the other. I reframe it as a gift of love to the other person (Benjamin, 1996). It is as if Carol is saying to Diane, "I know you need to feel special in this area, therefore I will act clumsy in it in order to allow you to be special." Such insight frequently breaks through much of the tension and resentment about the other person's seeming inability to learn certain tasks. Main and Oliver (1988) have some interesting research about what the potential pitfall may be if a couple is too complementary, so this technique should be used judiciously.

7   The "what if...?" technique can be very helpful in removing blocks. I ask couples to explore this question with each other: What would happen if they got the intimacy they so much wanted yet somehow seem to evade? This is a variation on Adler's use of "The Question," a technique currently used a great deal by the solution focused group of practitioners (Adler, 1956; Shohan, Rohrbaugh, & Patterson, 1995) . The answer most often clarifies what they are afraid of and leads to some very interesting discussion.

8   I teach couples how to fight fairly and make their therapy contingent upon their fighting on a regular basis, but under my direction and by my rules. Using the standard communication and problem-solving techniques the literature has identified, I teach such skills as conflict resolution and reflective listening. Next, though many couples initially think I'm a bit crazy, I prescribe they fight, every two weeks, for ten minutes, but about nonsense, silly topics. Some of the more interesting topics we select include (but are not limited to) what color plastic forks should be used at picnics, or whether or not the 1969 Chicago Cubs could have beaten the New York Mets (which for some, I realize, is not a silly matter), or if the other person blinks enough. I ask them to remember when they began first learned to drive and ask them where they

learned to drive. They say in a parking lot or some such place. I ask them why they didn't learn to drive on the highway during rush hour, and they say because that would have been ridiculous, too difficult and particularly dangerous. I agree. That is why they need to learn how to fight in a safe way, with unimportant, noncrucial topics. They are in the process of skill acquisition, and they need to learn to do such tasks in a controlled manner before they try them in the real world, where it is much more dangerous and the consequences can be much more devastating. Generally I find that the more they get into this exercise, the less often they fight overall. In addition, they begin to learn how to fight.

9   A final technique is specifically symptom focused. Whatever the particular symptom or symptom complex being used by the couple or an individual within the couple, I ask them to first personify it, then distance themselves from it, and finally to debate it (White & Epston, 1992). George is drinking. Sharon cannot stand it, but for years she has been living with it. I ask them to try something. Would they be willing to act as if the drinking were an invited but no longer welcomed guest? Who invited him? Why? Initially, there was a good reason, I'm sure, but he overstayed his welcome. What purpose did having such a guest serve? When in the couple's particular developmental cycle did they need such a guest? When did it become clear that such a guest would no longer be needed? What was the guest's response? What changed to make the guest no longer welcomed? How has the guest come between them? How can they unite against such an intruder? Are they sure they want to? As the couples distance themselves from the symptom—be it drinking, fighting, depression, or whatever—they can begin to align with each other against a common enemy, and a potential block to intimacy can be removed (White & Epston, 1992).

These are some of the techniques I use with psychopathological couples. It is now time for me to come full circle and address in somewhat more detail some of the points with which I began this chapter.

Intimacy cannot be defined in advance for these couples (if it can be defined in advance for any). Given the vast array of backgrounds they have come from, what constitutes intimacy varies from person to person. Given their particular styles, especially whatever personality disorders may exist, they may forever and always be comfortable with only a certain type of intimacy in a certain manner. We can strive to increase that type of intimacy, but not necessarily change that type of intimacy. Personality reconstruction may not be probable, if it is possible, and more importantly, it may not be what the individual is asking for. Given limited time, resources, and motivation, grandiose plans by the clinician need to be kept in check unless the couple seems ready, willing and able to undertake such goals. If so, then maybe such reconstruction is possible.

Something else to consider is this. Given what I call the matching and complementary technique, too much change in one person may dissolve the bonds that hold the couple together (Main & Oliver, 1988). Unilateral changes in one may lead the other to feel betrayed, disoriented, and without a place. Frequently, these couples want changes, but not too much. Too much change is not considered good by them, and clinicians need to respect the functional as well as dysfunctional aspects of the case. Given the perspective advocated by the technique called the grand reversal, most, if not all, of the dysfunctional traits associated with individuals could have a useful component, if done in a gentler, softer, more mellow manner. In a certain time at a certain place, such a style is not only useful but appealing. Interventions which are too targeted in too intense a manner may produce justified anxiety and resistance on the part of not only individuals but also couples as well.

Defining intimacy as sharing in each other's weaknesses, inferiorities, and vulnerabilities without the need for defensiveness, safeguarding, and stonewalling implies that the feelings of vulnerability will probably always be present, but not necessarily problematic for the couple. It brings expectations for the couple into a reasonable focus, and highlights what I feel is an extremely important point: Having deficits, problems, or whatever you may call them, is not the crucial issue. How they are dealt with is. The benign acceptance of each other's faults may be one of the cornerstones of a successful couple. As a senior colleague has repeatedly emphasized to me in our multiple therapy with couples, successful relationships are based upon finding someone whose flaws you can live with. Yes, there are some flaws you cannot live with. No, there will never be a person without flaws. Working with each other's flaws becomes part and parcel of being together, not an excuse for coming apart.

Finally, as noted above, with certain people, it is so very difficult to separate the problems a couple has from the people having the problems. In nonpathological couples, such a distinction is easier to make. When working with these couples, I get the sense that (for example) Joseph is okay, but he never really learned some basic skills, and as noted above, if I teach him those skills, he'll use them and be fine. There are other times, however, when I get the sense that (for instance) Valerie is not okay. Even if I teach her skills, she will still implement them (if I can get her to want to continue trying, that is) in a manner which just doesn't quite cut it. It is not Valerie's communication skills which are at issue, it is Valerie herself. She brings her style to whatever she does, and somehow, some way, she either has to modify her style, or her partner has to learn to accept that style the way it is—or some combination of both.

This leads me to the most basic of all techniques I can show couples: acceptance. This is difficult terrain to navigate. I frequently find that it is hard to tell what should be tolerated and accepted versus what has to be modified and changed. Almost exclusively, I try to leave this to the couples themselves. Many times, they dump it right back in my lap. I don't know that I have ever found a satisfactory answer to this type of question. It is akin to asking "What's normal?" I generally feed it back to the couple and ask them, "What can you live with and still be able to feel intimate with? If he or she continues to do this or that, can you still be open with him or her? Can you still accept him or her?" The answer can take a long time to figure out, sometimes longer than the current situation the couple finds themselves in provides.

CASE EXAMPLE

Betty and Larry were in their early 30s when they came to see me almost two years after a successful course of brief family counseling to deal with their extremely intelligent but difficult to manage six-year-old son. I received a crisis call from Betty on a Friday. She had to see me immediately. Fortunately, I was able to see her within a couple of hours. She was devastated, furious, and on the verge of what she called a "nervous breakdown." Her husband of almost 10 years, Larry a prominent physician, had just summarily been fired from his administrative position at a hospital. As the story unfolded, I realized there was trouble.

Larry had been addicted to heroin. He had been smoking and dealing it for months, having numerous affairs with several women, and sexually harassing his female staff at work. Several complaints had been filed against him by women, two of which were brought to the senior administrative staff's attention via a lawsuit which had been served just three days before. Larry had been rerouting records and trying to keep everything under wraps. Now, his entire life was blowing up in his face. He was extremely suicidal, on the verge of running away, and going through mild physical withdrawal which he had been trying to manage on his own. He was at home under the supervision of a friend while Betty came to see me. He refused to leave the house, though he was threatening to disappear forever.

I quickly called Larry and negotiated for a psychiatric and medical evaluation and stressed to Larry that he probably needed immediate hospitalization. He talked with me over the phone, agreed to go to a nonarea hospital (where he was not known), and to wait until I had a chance to see him before he came to any conclusions. He agreed, went for the evaluation, was immediately placed inpatient, and detoxification began under medical supervision. During his stay, Betty and I contacted a lawyer, set in motion some immediate crisis stabilization procedures (which are not the focus of this chapter), and prepared for what had to happen upon Larry's eventual discharge.

Couples Counseling: Sessions 1-45

Eventually Larry stabilized, and his legal and financial issues were managed (he had spent considerably large amounts of money that he had been hiding from Betty). Couples counseling was determined to be the place to start. While he continued in a substance abuse program for impaired professionals on an outpatient basis and attended narcotics anonymous (NA) meetings, I worked with him and Betty two times a week for several weeks. Betty only came once a week; the other session was Larry's. While he looked at his issues (which will only be briefly summarized here), we worked to determine how the couple would handle the first few difficult months out of the hospital. Betty felt betrayed, angry, and vengeful. She wanted to leave him, wanted to stay married to him, and wanted him dead. At one time, just after his discharge, she physically attacked him, and he let her. We agreed that working together on the marriage was what both wanted in order to determine whether or not they would stay together, but in the interim, they could not live together. Betty was still furious and extremely distrustful, and Larry was too depressed, confused, and ashamed to offer much defense or active effort to improve his situation. He lived in a motel for weeks while they continued to meet with me.

During this initial phase, stabilization of their relationship was my primary goal for the couple. Because of their son, they knew they would have some kind of contact with each other for years to come, even if they divorced, and therefore, they needed to find some way to "tolerate each other" (Betty) and "work together" (Larry). At this point, the distancing and debating technique worked well. They were able to align themselves against his drug habit, see it as a common enemy, and team up to fight against it.

Another useful technique at this stage was to address Betty's anger and outright rage. They decided that they wanted to stay together, but only if Betty could let go of her resentment, and she didn't know that she could. We designed a series of therapeutic rituals that helped Betty deal with her anger. First, I recommended a letter writing exercise. Larry was given a list of 25 people Betty thought needed to know and was asked to write to them, informing them of what he had done, how badly he felt about it, and asking for their help and support in rebuilding his life. He personally hand wrote each letter, and showed them to me. Both Betty and I were impressed with his sincerity and diligence on this task. He mailed the letters to these people and, almost universally, received encouraging support. Next, Betty's anger was addressed. Over the course of these first several months, rituals were established that asked Larry to win back Betty's support. He agreed to try them, and she agreed to let him. I will highlight three of them.

First, he provided her with a detailed list of his drug abuse and sexual activities for the last two years. Instead of detailing such incidents in a repetitive, out of control manner, an agreed upon time was established during which she could ask any question she wanted, and Larry had to respond. Typically, this was done every Thursday evening, after his visit with his son (and symbolically, just before Friday mornings, the worst time of the week for Betty). It worked. Betty became less driven to question him all the time and more willing to exercise some control over her "need to know everything," as she called it.

Second, two strategic exercises were put in place, the feeding and blindfold ones. These helped win some trust back. In addition, the back to back exercises were put in place. These helped improve communication. Eventually, Larry moved back in, but for over a year, slept in another part of the house.

Couples Counseling: Sessions 46–88

The couple had little if any physical contact with each other. While Larry continued to see me individually on a weekly basis, and continued with his weekly NA meetings, it was agreed the couple sessions would be reduced to every other week. They were stable, but things were still too "hot" to work on in more than a cursory, educational manner. After some starts and stops in our couple counseling, they decided to give it a more serious try. They wanted intimacy, but they didn't know if they knew what that was. They thought that they did, but they weren't sure. Couple counseling became the primary focus, with Larry's individual sessions being reduced to every other week.

Betty was somewhat obsessive in her style. She was a secondborn who had an older brother who was described as a saint. In fact, he eventually joined the priesthood. Betty was rather detail oriented, responsible, and by her own admission, fairly controlling. She hadn't dated much before she met Larry, and despite his being Jewish, she fell in love. He had been divorced after a brief marriage to an artist who was too "flighty" for his taste, and he valued Betty's stability, consistency, and organization. He was an oldest born, the pride of his family, the boy wonder, who blew through college, medical school, and residency. He was top dog his whole life, knew it, and enjoyed it. He had a clear narcissistic personality disorder, which he managed well because he was almost always the best, brightest, and fastest moving in the area. He seldom was severely challenged. What was not so obvious was the subtle but strongly present paranoid streak that ran throughout his life. He was always on guard, watchful, and looking to see who was "coming up from behind." He was extremely charming, but beneath his charm, he could be extremely cold, calculating, and downright vindictive. Larry seldom had to use it, for his intelligence and charm got him by. But he could when he had to, and when he did, he could be surgical in his attacks. Betty had seen it only fleetingly, and thought that side of him was an aberration and product of overwork rather than part of his character. She soon began to realize how ill at ease he was with his success.

These 44 sessions of couple counseling had periods of great intensity. The couple's individual styles were the focus. Larry was filling the role of Betty's brother. He was the star she was supposed to support and provide a secure base for. Betty was Larry's adoring little sister, similar to his sister in childhood. Both came from intact marriages, and our explorations of their parents' marriages opened up new vistas for them.

Betty's parents had been the traditional Roman Catholic 1940s marriage. Father was in charge, and to displease him was akin to questioning authority. He was head of his household. Betty's earliest memories of Father were of a strong, silent man who came home to a clean house, sat down at the table, and ate, barely saying a word to anybody. Mother provided the food. Her earliest memories of her mother were of a hard working but quiet woman who nurtured the children.

Larry's earliest memories were similar, but different in a key ingredient. His parents were older, had fewer children, and were Jewish. Father was not a professional, and that was looked down upon by Mother. He ran a machine repair factory, fixing broken machines for industry. He was very successful, but in Mother's eyes, he wasn't successful enough. She wanted him to be a doctor. He thought to help other people through fixing their machines was enough. One of Larry's earliest memories involved seeing Mother bad mouthing Father to an aunt. He felt ashamed for Father, but he vowed to make Mother proud of him. He did.

Their respective FECKs were fascinating. Larry's memory of Betty went like this: He was walking on the campus of his medical school, into a room, and saw her sitting with friends. She saw him come in and stood up; he went over to her and asked some directions. She gave him some directions, and he left, thinking how helpful and attractive she was. Her memory of him revealed the following. She remembered him walking in, but didn't remember standing up. She said she was already standing. He seemed lost but attractive, and she went over and helped him.

We laid out their respective styles. He expected her to wait on him, open doors for him, and be there when he needed her. She expected to be his direction setter, to be the firm grounding he needed to continue his journey of helping others in life. The birth of their child, their only child, proved extremely stressful. He was brilliant but challenging, and most of Betty's time was spent dealing with him. Larry was jealous and dethroned. He wanted as much attention as his son got, and his son appeared every bit as smart, if not smarter, than Larry was at his son's age—a fact repeatedly pointed out by

Larry's parents. Betty, for her part, felt Larry no longer needed her. He was seemingly launched, independent, and successful. Her son needed her.

These sessions focused upon how such styles played out in their day-to-day functioning. Larry felt he could approach her only when he was successful. To talk about the times he was insecure, ineffectual, and having difficulty gave him the sense that he was being too much like his father, and potentially letting Betty down. He expected her to talk badly about him to others. Nonconsciously, he arranged for her to do just that.

Betty, for her part, felt she was being disloyal if she had too many needs or made too many demands. She had her place in life, and should be happy with that. She did not know how to shine on her own, and she frequently shunned the spotlight, all the while hoping that, by being a "good wife and mother," the spotlight would shine on her. Larry getting into trouble, like her son years earlier, only served to highlight just how "good and loyal" she was. Nonconsciously, this was just the type of opportunity she was waiting for, and while she did not ask for it, she embraced it when it arrived.

Larry always had affairs with women who looked up to him and made him the center. He turned to drugs because they provided him with a way to stop his competitiveness and shut down his "incessant thoughts" about work, moving faster and faster, and being number one. Without some help from the heroin he smoked, he couldn't shut off his driven style.

Couples Counseling: Sessions 89–104

After more than 18 months, the couple began to get closer, not only emotionally but physically. We began to reduce the frequency of sessions, and I met with Larry and Betty for individual sessions interspersed with their couples sessions. These final sessions were spent using many of the standard intimacy producing tactics. They were more receptive to them now that they were less defensive. Larry learned to be open and somewhat more revealing of his flaws, though only to some extent. Betty learned to keep Larry as the focus, though not the only focus, of her life. Betty, by her own admission, didn't want Larry to be less than a star for too long, for she then felt less comfortable with him. She liked his driveness. He learned to tone it down a bit. She accepted more of an equal relationship with him, went back to school (part-time), and started feeling better about herself. She became a special education teacher. At one- and two-year follow up, they were still together, relatively happy, and Larry was still clean and sober. They reported marital satisfaction and felt close to each other, though Betty still felt somewhat scarred and slightly cautious about her husband.

SUMMARY

Developing intimacy in psychopathological couples is a challenging task. Their defensiveness, inflexibility, and security operations often interfere with their ability to share, accept each other, and be open and vulnerable. Fostering intimacy entails helping them feel more at home in the world, helping them to find more peace with themselves and each other, and to let down their guard. It can be a difficult task, but a rewarding one nonetheless. The willingness to take a risk, to be close, and to accept the other, even with his or her flaws, can very often prove to be the first step in learning to accept themselves.

REFERENCES

Adler, A. (1956). *The Individual Psychology of Alfred Adler: A systematic presentation to his selected writings*. (H. L. Ansbacher & R. R. Ansbacher, Eds.). New York: Basic Books.

American Psychiatric Association. (1994). *Diagnostic and statistical manual of mental disorders*. (4th ed.). Washington, DC: Author.

Beck, A. T. (1988). *Love is never enough*. New York: Harper & Row.

Belove, L. (1980). First encounters of the close kind. *Journal of Individual Psychology, 36,* 191–208.

Benjamin, L. S. (1996). *Interpersonal diagnosis and treatment of personality disorders* (2nd ed.). New York: Guilford Press.

Berne, E. (1972). *What do you say after you say hello?* New York: Grove Press.

Corsini, R. J. (1967). Let's invent a first-aid kit for marriage problems. *Consultant, 7,* 40.

Dinkmeyer, D., & Carlson, J. (1989). *Taking time for love*. New York: Prentice Hall.

Dreikurs, R. (1946). *The challenge of marriage*. New York: Duell, Sloan & Pearce.

Gottman, J., & Silver, N. (1994). *Why marriages succeed or fail*. New York: Simon & Schuster.

Main, F., & Oliver, R. (1988). Complementary, symmetrical, and parallel personality priorities as indicators of marital adjustment. *Individual Psychology, 44,* 324–332.

Maniacci, M. P. (1996). An introduction to brief therapy of the personality disorders. *Individual Psychology, 52,* 158–168.

Maniacci, M. P. (in press). Clinical therapy. In R. E. Watts & J. Carlson (Eds.), *Strategies and interventions in counseling and psychotherapy*. Washington, DC: Accelerated Development/ Taylor & Francis.

Millon, T., & Davis, R. D. (1996). *Disorders of personality: DSM-IV and beyond*. New York: Wiley.

Mozdzierz, G. J., & Friedman, K. (1978). The superiority-inferiority spouses syndrome: Diagnostic and therapeutic considerations. *Journal of Individual Psychology, 34,* 232–243.

Pinsof, W. M. (1995). *Integrative problem-centered therapy: A synthesis of family, individual and biological therapies*. New York: Basic Books.

Satir, V. (1983). *Conjoint family therapy* (3rd ed., rev. & expanded). Palo Alto, CA: Science and Behavior Books.

Sherman, R. (1993). Marital issues of intimacy and techniques for change: An Adlerian systems perspective. *Individual Psychology, 49,* 318–329.

Shoham, V., Rohrbaugh, M., & Patterson, J. (1995). Problem- and solution-focused couples therapy: The MRI and Milwaukee models. In N. S. Jacobson & A. S. Gurman (Eds.), *Clinical handbook of couple therapy* (pp. 142–163). New York: Guilford Press.

Sperry, L. (1989). Assessment in marital therapy: A couples-centered biopsychosocial approach. *Individual Psychology*, *45*, 546–551.

Sperry, L., & Mosak, H. H. (1996). Personality disorders. In L. Sperry & J. Carlson (Eds.), *Psychopathology & psychotherapy: From DSM-IV diagnosis to treatment* (pp. 279–335). Washington, DC: Accelerated Development.

Sullivan, H. S. (1956). *Clinical studies in psychiatry*. New York: Norton.

Wachtel, E. F. (1994). *Treating troubled children and their families*. New York: Guilford Press.

Westen, D. (1991). Cognitive-behavioral interventions in the psychoanalytic psychotherapy of borderline personality disorders. *Clinical Psychology Review*, *11*, 211–230.

White, M., & Epston, D. (1992). *Experience, contradiction, narrative, and imagination: Selected papers of David Epston and Michael White 1989–1991*. Adelaide, South Australia: Dulwich Centre Publication.

APPENDIX A

AN OVERVIEW OF OUR DEVELOPMENTAL MODEL

Stage	DESCRIPTION OF STAGE		Diagnosis	Treatment
	Developmental Task	Developmental Stalemate		
Symbiotic-Symbiotic (Enmeshed) "We are one"	Bonding Falling in love Emphasis on similarities Nurturing Establishing "coupleness"	Consuming need to merge; inseparable Dependency Loss of trust Loss of individuality Fear of abandonment Behavior becomes passive and reactive rather than self-initiated Interactions focused on masking differences Ego-syntonic ways of relating	Nonverbal manipulative communication designed to mask or obscure differences Use of *we* and *us* rather than *I* in therapeutic sessions Severely symptomatic child, or severe symptoms in one partner who is the identified patient *Paper Exercise:* Swiftly evokes clear pattern of enmeshed interaction: marked lack of self-definition with excessive efforts to obscure conflict *Diagnostic Questionnaire:* Provides a historical over-view of the emergence of the enmeshment over time	Establish initial treatment contract focused on couple's view of the problem Establish "no-suicide" and "no-divorce" contracts when indicated Build an alliance with couple (family) and then facilitate personal responsi-bility taking in each partner When working with a family, use art or projective technique that elicits each member's perception of the family as a whole When appropriate, begin shifting from the family as a whole to the couple's relationship Use gestalt or TA techniques for working with each partner's family-of-origin Facilitate differentiation between partners

Symbiotic-Symbiotic (Hostile-Dependent) "I can't live with you, and I can't live without you"	Bonding Nurturing Establishing "coupleness"	Conflict and aggression used to maintain distance and emotional contact Poorly developed sense of self; little differentiation Emerges when symbiotic fantasy begins to crumble as reality sets in Common pattern in borderline and narcissistic personalities Open and ongoing expressions of anger, bitterness, and blame Competitive, escalating interactions often ending in violence Unable to negotiate Unable to perceive impact of their own behavior on partner Strong projection of feelings and assumptions onto partner *Paradoxical patterns of interaction:* Demand nurturance yet reject it when offered Simultaneous fear of abandonment and engulfment Pronounced separation anxiety that is adamantly denied Positive responses of one partner often interpreted as manipulative or rejected outright as given "too late"	In therapeutic sessions, extremely difficult for partners to identify and articulate what each wants, thinks, and feels Rapid escalation into regressive behavior *Paper Exercise:* Competitive, angry, escalating transactions without any negotiation or give-and-take *Question of Attunement:* Expect mind reading, so requests are vague, generalized demands for nurturance leading to failed responses; since there is very limited capacity for autonomous interaction, as soon as one errs the other will punish or withhold	Diffuse conflict as quickly as possible Establish limits and behavioral agreements about fights (see Limits Questionnaire in Appendix B) Keep both partners thinking when angry and channel their anger through yourself Teach them to complete transactions Signal a confrontation Predict future fights Provide support and positive reinforcement for partners during session Help partners learn how to apologize Facilitate direct, positive interactions Develop consistent, caring behaviors Encourage cooperation and joint activities Encourage partners to develop outside friendships and activities Use humor *Once conflict is contained:* Help partners develop and maintain a vision of a better future that each will work to create Help couple develop an empathic process

DESCRIPTION OF STAGE

Stage	Developmental Task	Developmental Stalemate	Diagnosis	Treatment
Symbiotic-Differentiating "Don't betray me"	*Symbiotic* (see above) *Differentiating* Learning to express self clearly and openly Shift toward internally defining sense of self with independent thoughts, feelings, and wants Reestablishment of boundaries Developing the capacity to tolerate differences Learning to risk expressing one's differences Defining clear areas of responsibility and authority	System becomes unbalanced for the first time *Symbiotic Partner:* Feels threatened and betrayed Attempts to tighten the symbiosis via "clinging" behavior May be characterologically passive Little empathy for partner's needs *Differentiating Partner:* Feelings of guilt Anger at denial of differences Increased efforts to define identity	Look for anger, grief, or despair at disillusionment of romantic fantasy *Diagnostic Interview:* Symbiotic partner will focus more on similarities and highlights of initial bonding, while differentiating partner will focus on differences and disillusionment *Personal History Exercise:* Use this exercise to diagnose origin of impasse in the symbiotic partner, such as "I'll never go out alone again" (see Chap. 2) *Paper Exercise:* Symbiotic partner does not define what the paper is and tends to relinquish it rapidly to the differentiating partner, who defines it	Help partners resolve the loss of the symbiotic stage Help partners identify and express thoughts, feelings, and desires Help partners tolerate the anxiety inherent in recognition of differences Encourage *differentiating* partner's movements toward self-expression while interrupting symbiotic partner's dependency patterns Help partners identify their individual contributions to current difficulties Establish clear lines of responsibility taking with regard to issues being discussed Break down issues into manageable homework assignments Generate motivation for change in passive symbiotic partner by stressing personal benefits Help partners learn to tolerate anger

| Differentiating-Differentiating "I'll change if you change" | (See above), actively working out how to manage the differences that do exist in personality styles, goals, and desires | Successful fight style not yet developed
Use of projection and manipulation to push partner toward change
Ongoing hassling | Discover how couple has managed conflict thus far in relationship
Discover if couple has developed a workable fight style
Discover if partners have begun to reestablish their boundaries via separate activities, friendships, etc.
Paper Exercise: Effort spent in examining the *process* of how partners are going to decide who gets the paper
Question of Attunement: The level of differentiation in each individual will determine how clearly the request is made and how accurately they assess their own capacity to respond | Pace of therapy is determined by degree of differentiation present in each partner
Use of nonstructured involvement to create therapeutic environment that provides autonomy in the unfolding of partners' differentiation
Use of questions to help partners identify, understand, and articulate feelings
Bring pertinent intrapsychic childhood issues into awareness
Facilitate conflict management via use of the "initiator/responder" format for interaction
Provide positive role model for partners, as therapist interacts with their demands and outbursts
Discriminate between problem-solving issues and issues involving more complex developmental factors
Provide a larger context for viewing of specific problems
Facilitate differentiation from family-of-origin
Identify familial, societal, cultural, or work-related factors that may be inhibiting the differentiation process |

DESCRIPTION OF STAGE

Stage	Developmental Task	Developmental Stalemate	Diagnosis	Treatment
Symbiotic-Practicing **"Don't leave me"/"Leave me alone"**	*Symbiotic* (see above) *Practicing* Attention directed to external world, independent activities and relationships Rediscovery of self as individual Consolidation of self-esteem and individual power Development of healthy fight style Blossoming of individuation process whereby the individual learns to express him/herself creatively in the world	*Symbiotic Partner:* Feelings of betrayal and abandonment Attempts to intensify enmeshment Fear of loss of relationship escalates into angry and demanding behavior *Practicing Partner:* Stance of stubbornness and self-centeredness Loss of empathy for partner's needs Lack of emotional connection to partner; withdrawal Feels betrayed by partner's engulfment	Previous history of mutually satisfying symbiosis Minimal differentiation An unexpected developmental shift in one partner resulting in increased demands for independence *Diagnostic Interview:* Reveals historical evolution from an intense symbiotic phase, to a phase in which active differentiation did not occur between the partners, to the stage in which one partner shifts to intense individual self-preoccupation *Personal History Exercise:* This exercise often reveals parallels between the current practicing behavior and how the individual separated from the family-of-origin	Help partners learn how to manage differentiation and support one another's independence Therapist must balance opposing therapeutic goals of partners: Symbiotic partner wants the spouse to "be like he/she used to be"; practicing partner wants to continue self-expansion unimpeded Initial establishment of discrepant goals is sometimes necessary Expose common grief that underlies partners' reactive anger Help partners structure time together Help practicing partner set self-selected limits that circumscribe the scope of activities Help symbiotic partner initiate activities that are self-directed and self-focused Use of the "Symbiotic-Practicing Questionnaire" to help partners identify what they want from one another (see Chapter 8) Identify and resolve pertinent intrapsychic conflicts from childhood

| Practicing-Practicing "I want to be me!" | (See above) | Energy overinvested in self-development and expression

Relationship viewed as secondary

Staunch defense of boundaries

Fear that greater intimacy will lead to loss of self

Power struggles characterized by "I-want" demands

Use of projection and transference under emotionally charged circumstances

Repetition of early script decisions

All of the above are greatly intensified when the couple does not have a foundation of positive bonding and active differentiation | Marked lack of emotional connectedness throughout session

Defensive presentation of each partner's side, and polarized views

Competitive dialogue leading to impasses in problem solving

Practicing-practicing couples who have differentiated together will still have power struggles, but with decreased intensity

Paper Exercise: Both partners are well defined about what the paper represents, but often are unable to give to the other or compromise; often the exercise is not completed in the five minutes allotted

Diagnostic Interview: Reveals no anxiety for either partner in having separate activities or friendships | Focus on process rather than content

Help partners learn ways of protecting separate individualities while resolving conflicts

Help partners relax boundaries

Help those couples who have not actively differentiated together to learn how to manage differentiation, while continuing their independence

Help partners identify and express feelings

Use of "The Thirty-Day Plan"

Help partners identify and resolve intrapsychic childhood issues

Help partners develop a decision-making process that involves giving without anxiety |

DESCRIPTION OF STAGE

Stage	Developmental Task	Developmental Stalemate	Diagnosis	Treatment
Practicing-Rapprochement **"One foot in, one foot out"**	*Practicing* (see above) *Rapprochement* Return shift toward relationship for intimacy and emotional sustenance Reemergence of vulnerability Greater ease in negotiating Balance between "I" and "us" becomes more firmly established Ongoing utilization of skills learned in previous stages Capacity to respond with consistency Capacity to give to partner even when inconvenient to do so Further resolution of remaining childhood impasses that interfere with successful coupling	*Practicing Partner:* Fearful of "putting myself second" Equating *intimacy* with *sacrifice* Overcompromising; reduction of options Conflict over empathizing with partner's intimacy needs versus responding to personal needs for growth and individuation *Rapprochement Partner:* Alternates between periods of intimacy and efforts to reestablish independence Conflict over supporting partner's growth and independence versus seeking to gratify personal needs for greater intimacy	*Diagnostic Interview:* Elicits the characteristics described under the developmental stalemate (see Appendix E for how this unfolds)	Identify temporary incompatibility of respective stages Explore each partner's needs with a view toward finding points of intersection and compromise Use a future focus to evoke a mutual image of the relationship that combines both sets of needs Learn to balance one's own wants and desires with partner's
Rapprochement-Rapprochement **"Homeward bound"**	(See above)	At this advanced stage of development, stressors to the relationship usually come from external sources such as a job promotion, a potential move, an ailing relative; intra- and interpersonal processes are generally highly developed and integrated	Diagnosis at this level occurs primarily through the elicitation and observation of what is *right* in the relationship: all the strengths and abilities that are present and operative in the relationship	Therapy at this level is primarily facilitative rather than treatment-oriented Ask partners what most deeply touches them when they are vulnerable Focus them on learning to give when it is not convenient Use a future focus via developing a relationship purpose, setting goals, or using "The Thirty-Day Plan"

Index